THE PAPERS OF JOHN MARSHALL

Sponsored by
The College of William and Mary
and
The Institute of Early American History and Culture
under the auspices of
The National Historical Publications and Records Commission

SEAL OF THE GENERAL COURT OF VIRGINIA

This seal is affixed to a deed in Marshall's hand dated 24 June 1796 conveying land in Kentucky. *Courtesy of Swem Library, College of William and Mary*

THE PAPERS OF JOHN MARSHALL

Volume V

Selected Law Cases, 1784–1800

CHARLES F. HOBSON, *Editor*

FREDRIKA J. TEUTE, *Associate Editor*

GEORGE H. HOEMANN, *Assistant Editor*

INGRID M. HILLINGER, *Consulting Editor*

The University of North Carolina Press, Chapel Hill
in association with the
Institute of Early American History and Culture
Williamsburg, Virginia

The Institute of Early American History and Culture is sponsored jointly by The College of William and Mary in Virginia and The Colonial Williamsburg Foundation

Manufactured in the United States of America
Set in Linotron Baskerville by the
University of North Carolina Press
ISBN 0-8078-1746-5
Library of Congress Catalog Card Number 74-9575

The ornament on the title page is based upon John Marshall's personal seal, as it appears on a gold watch fob that also bears the seal of his wife, Mary Willis Marshall. It was drawn by Richard J. Stinely of Williamsburg, Virginia, from the original, now owned by the Association for the Preservation of Virginia Antiquities, Richmond, Virginia, and is published with the owner's permission.

Library of Congress Cataloging-in-Publication Data
(Revised for Vol. 5)

Marshall, John, 1755–1835.
The papers of John Marshall.
"Sponsored by the College of William and Mary and the Institute of Early American History and Culture under the auspices of the National Historical Publications Commission."
Includes bibliographical references and indexes.

CONTENTS: v. 1. Correspondence and papers, November 10, 1775–June 23, 1788. Account book, September 1783–June 1788.—v. 2. Correspondence and papers, July 1788–December 1795. Account book, July 1788–December 1795.—[etc.]—v. 5. Selected law cases, 1784–1800.

1. Marshall, John, 1755–1835. 2. United States—Politics and government—Revolution, 1775–1783—Sources. 3. United States—Politics and government—1783–1865—Sources. 4. Statesmen—United States—Correspondence. 5. Judges—United States—Correspondence. I. Johnson, Herbert Alan, ed. II. Cullen, Charles T., 1940– ed. III. Institute of Early American History and Culture (Williamsburg, Va.). IV. Title.
E302.M365 347.73'2634 347.3073534 74-9575
ISBN 0-8078-1233-1 (v. 1)
ISBN 0-8078-1302-8 (v. 2)
ISBN 0-8078-1337-0 (v. 3)
ISBN 0-8078-1586-1 (v. 4)
ISBN 0-8078-1746-5 (v. 5)

To the memory of
LESTER J. CAPPON
1900–1981
Historian, editor,
friend, and adviser to
The Papers of John Marshall

The publication of this volume has been assisted by special grants from the Robert G. III & Maude Morgan Cabell Foundation, the Richard Gwathmey and Caroline T. Gwathmey Memorial Trust, and the William Nelson Cromwell Foundation.

CONTENTS

II. THE HIGH COURT OF CHANCERY

III. THE UNITED STATES CIRCUIT COURT OF VIRGINIA

IV. THE BRITISH DEBT CASES

V. REPORTS OF CASES IN THE GENERAL COURT

VI. SELECTED ARGUMENTS IN THE VIRGINIA COURT OF APPEALS

ILLUSTRATIONS

Preface

In the introduction to the first volume of *The Papers of John Marshall*, the editors announced their intention to publish a separate volume devoted solely to Marshall's law practice. Three more volumes of correspondence and papers subsequently appeared, taking Marshall to the eve of his appointment as chief justice of the U.S. Supreme Court. With the publication of Volume IV, the series had reached the logical point for the long-promised law volume to assume center stage. Volume V accordingly presents a selection of cases in the state and federal courts with a view to providing a more detailed and systematic reconstruction of Marshall's practice than is possible within the confines of a strict chronological format. It draws on a body of legal papers that were not published in the earlier volumes but were either calendared or listed at their respective dates. It serves at once as a conclusion to the documentary record of his early career and as an introduction to the volumes that will chronicle the Supreme Court years.

The plan of the volume and its relation to the preceding volumes (which also contain legal papers) are spelled out in the introduction that follows. The introduction also includes a description of the court system of Virginia and an extensive discussion of common law procedure that covers each step of a lawsuit from the initial writ through the execution of the judgment. This consolidated treatment is intended to acquaint the reader with eighteenth-century Virginia procedure and eliminates the need for repetitive footnotes throughout the text. Those unfamiliar with the legal and historical context of Marshall's practice should consult the introduction first, referring to it as necessary when reading the cases.

A preface is the appropriate place to give a brief account of the background of the law volume. The collecting of Marshall's legal papers was accomplished under the editorship of Herbert A. Johnson, now professor of law and history at the University of South Carolina. Mr. Johnson selected certain cases for publication, organized them by legal topic, and supervised the transcription of documents, though the editing phase had not begun before he left the project in 1977. After his departure, research associate George M. Curtis III continued the work under the direction of Charles T. Cullen. Curtis was soon joined by Ingrid M. Hillinger, a Williamsburg lawyer who was subsequently appointed to the faculty of the Marshall-Wythe School of Law. In 1979 Mr. Cullen moved to Princeton as editor of the

Papers of Thomas Jefferson. The following year Mr. Curtis departed to join the faculty of Hanover College.

This frequent turnover in personnel understandably retarded progress on the law volume. In time a measure of stability was achieved, so that a concentrated effort could be made to bring the volume to fruition. Though now a regular member of the law faculty, Professor Hillinger remained with the project as consulting editor. Her most active involvement was during the academic year 1980–81, when she was on half-time leave from teaching. (The editors wish to express their special thanks to Dean William B. Spong for arranging this leave.) Such was Professor Hillinger's dedication to the task of preparing this edition of Marshall's law cases that she continued to be closely involved long after resuming full-time teaching. Focusing her chief attention on procedure and on the Virginia Court of Appeals, she and her students (whose names appear below) produced voluminous research notes that were useful not only in providing background information but also in annotating particular documents. In the early stages of her work she was associated with Mr. Curtis, a specialist in Virginia legal history. Together they prepared digests of all the Court of Appeals cases, which have served as a valuable reference tool for analyzing and interpreting Marshall's role as an appellate lawyer.

While building upon work begun under their predecessors, the present editors bear entire responsibility for the selection of cases, the organization, the editorial method, and the annotation. In this endeavor they have enjoyed the full cooperation of Mr. Johnson, who graciously gave advice when called upon and shared his great knowledge of Marshall and eighteenth-century law.

The editors owe a large debt of gratitude to a host of individuals and institutions who aided them in various ways. The late William F. Swindler, John Marshall Professor, Emeritus, at the Marshall-Wythe School of Law and longtime member of the editorial advisory board, held a proprietary interest in this project from the beginning. His enthusiastic support and friendly counsel will be greatly missed in the years to come. At his death in May 1984 he had largely completed the manuscript of his three-volume "Studies on the Bicentennial of American Legal Education." Professor Swindler generously supplied the editors with drafts of this work in progress, greatly facilitating their entry into the forbidding terrain of Virginia's early legal history. It is to be hoped that this manuscript will eventually make its way into print.

One of the great advantages of a Williamsburg location is immediate access to the abundant resources for the study of Virginia history that exist in this former colonial capital. The Earl Gregg Swem Library at the College of William and Mary, the Colonial Williamsburg Foundation Library, and the Marshall-Wythe Law Library provided virtually all the research materials needed for annotating the volume. The staffs of these institutions gave prompt and courteous attention to the editors' numerous requests. Special thanks go to Edmund P. Edmonds, head librarian at Marshall-Wythe, for allowing the editors to roam freely through the vault in search of old treatises, reports, and other treasures of English law.

Many of the documents presented in this volume came from the Virginia State Library, Richmond, the depository for the records and papers of the federal circuit court in which Marshall practiced. That institution also maintains an outstanding collection of county court records on microfilm that were indispensable in researching his cases. Conley Edwards, of the state library staff, spared the editors several trips to Richmond by finding and sending important materials. The editors also acknowledge the cooperation of the Office of the Clerk of the Circuit Court, Fredericksburg, where the suit papers of Marshall's cases in the Fredericksburg District Court are deposited. An important set of papers relating to Marshall's British debt litigation is in the Public Record Office, London. Documents from that depository are held by crown copyright and are published by permission of Her Majesty's Stationery Office.

The following students at Marshall-Wythe assisted Professor Hillinger in executing various research tasks: Kevin Cooper, Kathryn Devoid, Jocelin Hackathorn, and Kendall Newman. Two graduate students in the history department at the College of William and Mary, J. Thomas Wren and William Maddox, also served as research assistants. Lisa Mullins, an editing apprentice at the Institute of Early American History and Culture, did exemplary work in compiling a secondary source bibliography and in checking footnotes, secondary citations, and quotations for accuracy. Trudi M. Heyer did double duty as secretary and editorial assistant. In addition to producing accurate transcriptions of difficult legal documents, she performed skillfully as a proofreader and checker of footnotes and quotations. Katie Miller joined the staff after Ms. Heyer resigned in the summer of 1985. Although she was involved with this volume only in its final stages, Ms. Miller nevertheless contributed significantly to the preparation of the manuscript for the publisher. Gilbert Kelly, managing editor at the Institute of Early American History and Culture, worked closely with the editors in copyediting the manuscript. His painstaking efforts to solve the special problems presented by this volume, along with his sound advice on points of style and usage, are much appreciated.

Among many others who supplied useful information on specific topics covered in this volume, special acknowledgment is due to James H. Kettner of the University of California, Berkeley; W. Hamilton Bryson of the University of Richmond; E. Lee Shepard of the Virginia Historical Society; James R. Perry of the Documentary History of the Supreme Court; John Catanzariti of the Papers of Robert Morris; and John M. Hemphill II of the Research Department, Colonial Williamsburg Foundation.

An editorial enterprise of this scope would not be possible without the continuing support of its two sponsoring institutions, the College of William and Mary and the Institute of Early American History and Culture. The college, through an appropriation from the General Assembly of Virginia, has provided major funding for the project, as has the National Historical Publications and Records Commission. Generous financial support has also come from the Robert G. III & Maude Morgan Cabell Foundation, the Richard Gwathmey and Caroline T. Gwathmey Memorial Trust, and the William Nelson Cromwell Foundation.

SELECTED LAW CASES
1784–1800

Introduction

1. The Sources of John Marshall's Law Practice

For nearly twenty years John Marshall practiced law in Richmond, his adopted home and the capital of the Commonwealth of Virginia. Beginning soon after the War of Independence, Marshall built up a highly successful practice in the superior state courts and after 1789 in the U.S. Circuit Court as well. It was an extensive and varied practice, embracing trial and appellate cases at common law and in equity. For most of this period Marshall concentrated on his profession, resisting the call to public life except for occasional service in the state legislature. After accepting a federal diplomatic commission in 1797, he never again resumed the full-time pursuit of his private career. The mission to France was followed in short order by his election to Congress and by his appointment as secretary of state. The temporary leaves of absence from his law practice became permanent with his accession to the chief justiceship of the Supreme Court early in 1801.

The editors began work on this volume knowing that they lacked the materials to reconstruct the law practice of John Marshall in anything like its fullness and variety. All that remains of what must have been a massive legal corpus accumulated during two decades at the bar are a few scattered pieces. The contents of the law office that once stood next to his Richmond house have largely vanished. Moreover, virtually all the records of the higher courts of Virginia that sat in the capital were destroyed by fire in April 1865. What survives from both private and public sources is an eclectic mix of correspondence, commonplace notes, accounts, opinions, petitions, court records, pleadings and other litigation papers, and reports of cases. Taken together they reveal much about Marshall as a practitioner of the common law, though at best they draw a picture that is fragmentary, with whole sections missing and others in varying degrees of completeness.

The want of documentation for Marshall the lawyer becomes readily apparent from the survival of a voluminous mass of papers generated by another famous lawyer-statesman, John Adams. Adams's legal papers repose today in the family archives, supplemented by a substantially complete set of records and file papers of the principal court in which he practiced. In the published volumes of Adams's legal papers, the primary documents are his minutes of the trial, along with his notes of arguments, authorities, and evidence. These were his "working papers as a trial lawyer," hastily jotted down during the trial or drawn up shortly before.[1] Except for stereotyped pleadings, no such working papers produced by Marshall have been found—no briefs, no notes of authorities or evidence, no appeal to a jury, not even an outline of an argument.[2] To document his trial cases (as opposed to his appellate cases), the editors have searched the case files that survive for two of the courts in which he practiced. Although the litigation papers shed light on the nature of the dispute, they reveal little of the lawyer's thought processes in preparing his case and in conducting the trial.

Users of this volume should bear in mind that many of Marshall's extant law papers have already been published in the preceding four volumes (particularly the first and second) of this series. These include (1) an extract from his commonplace notes compiled during the period he attended the law lectures of George Wythe at the College of William and Mary; (2) his account book between September 1783 and October 1795 (reproduced as an appendix to the first and second volumes), which is invaluable for identifying his cases and tracing the growth of his practice; (3) correspondence and other office practice documents such as legal opinions and petitions; (4) manuscript reports by St. George Tucker of cases argued by Marshall in the General Court; (5) Marshall's printed arguments in several notable cases: *Hite* v. *Fairfax* and *Bracken* v. *College of William and Mary* in the Virginia Court of Appeals, and *Ware* v. *Hylton* in the U.S. Supreme Court.

Documents arising from Marshall's law practice are thus presented throughout the first five volumes of *The Papers of John Marshall.* In Volumes I–IV legal materials are intermingled with other papers not legal in nature, which together are presented in chronological order beginning in November 1775 and ending in October 1800. Volume V covers approximately the same years but is devoted exclusively to the law practice and in particular to litigation. It consists of forty-three cases, which in turn are divided into six sections corresponding to the court in which they were heard. Within each case and section chronology prevails, though between one section and another there may be a considerable overlap in time.

In a broader sense the volume divides itself into two parts. The first (Case Numbers 1–18, Sections I–IV) embraces suits brought in a court of original jurisdiction and presents numerous documents drawn principally from the case files. The second (Case Numbers

1. L. Kinvin Wroth and Hiller B. Zobel, *Legal Papers of John Adams*, I (Cambridge, Mass., 1965), xx, xxxi–xxxv.

2. See Case No. 2, Doc. VIII, for what appears to be a brief outline of an argument.

19–43, Sections V–VI) is a selection of reported cases and appellate arguments in the General Court and the Court of Appeals. In three cases (Numbers 3, 5, and 7) Marshall also argued the appeal, and his reported argument has been included with the documents in the original action rather than presented separately in the Court of Appeals section.

Documentation has been supplied from a variety of sources, manuscript and printed, public and private. Mentioned briefly here, they are described in detail at the appropriate places in the volume. The largest group of manuscripts comes from the case files of two courts Marshall attended: the Fredericksburg District Court and the U.S. Circuit Court. The Marshall documents in these files consist mainly of pleadings. Only a few of these are printed in full in this volume; the rest have been calendared or listed in the four preceding volumes.

The file of a case at common law often consists of no more than the writ, pleadings, and jury verdict. The editors have therefore selected cases that contain additional documents, such as depositions, which make possible more than simply a skeletal reconstruction of the controversy. Common law pleadings, the reader must be forewarned, are largely boilerplate productions that give little indication of the lawyer's ability or of his legal strategy. Often, however, this is the only evidence we have of Marshall's participation. The most interesting documents of this type are the special defensive pleas Marshall submitted in the cases brought by British creditors for recovery of their pre-Revolutionary debts. A chancery suit file is more illuminating than a common law file because all the testimony had to be reduced to writing; the pleadings also offer a more detailed and straightforward narration of the circumstances of the dispute.

Case papers are the main source used in the first eighteen cases. The remaining twenty-five cases are based on manuscript and printed reports. Case Numbers 19–31 (Section V) are reports by St. George Tucker of General Court cases not published in preceding volumes, having only been recently discovered among Tucker's loose manuscripts. Case Numbers 32–43 (Section VI) are a selection of Marshall's arguments in the Court of Appeals, taken from the printed reports of Bushrod Washington and Daniel Call.

Supplementing the case papers and reports are miscellaneous groups of documents from the personal papers of litigants and complete transcripts of two cases deposited in the British Public Record Office. The editors have also made use of new material in the famous British debt case of *Ware* v. *Hylton* (Case Number 13). A notebook kept by Justice James Iredell summarizes arguments of counsel at the federal circuit court trial in 1793. In addition, recently identified notes taken by William Tilghman at the Supreme Court hearing in 1796 supplied Alexander Dallas with the source for his published report of the case. The Tilghman and Dallas texts of Marshall's argument are printed in parallel columns in this volume.

2. The Plan of the Volume and Editorial Policy

Although divided into six sections, the cases are numbered consecutively with arabic numerals (1 through 43) throughout the volume. Each section is introduced by an editorial note, as are most of the cases. Immediately below the title of the case are the inclusive dates—the years of the initial writ and final judgment. The documents of the case (if more than one) are then listed in order, each numbered with a roman numeral and supplied with a title and date. This eliminates the need in most instances of repeating the case name and document title in cross-references to other cases in the volume. Such references take the form of "Case No. 2"; "Case No. 7, Doc. IX." With court documents the date usually represents the day (or month) the paper was filed with the clerk or sworn before a magistrate rather than the time it was actually composed. Many documents either have dates or can be assigned an exact date from another source. Where the dating is conjectural, the editors have justified their choice.

An editorial note to the case follows the list of documents (or the case title where there is only one document). Editorial notes introduce each of the cases except those in Section V, which are brief reports of arguments. (For these, one general editorial note and footnotes to the individual reports are sufficient.) The documents are then presented with accompanying annotation in the form of footnotes.

Legal materials by their nature require denser annotation than general correspondence, which often annotates itself without editorial aid. In preparing this volume, the editors, without presuming any knowledge of law on the reader's part, have attempted to strike a balance between too little and too much commentary. The method and approach are historical, reflecting the tastes and training of the chief editor. The litigants in the disputes here chronicled are seen not as so many A's and B's but as flesh-and-blood persons rooted in place and time.

The editors have adopted the following policy of annotation: to supply enough information and explanation to make the documents intelligible, so that the reader can follow the course of a given case from its origins through its final disposition. The footnotes address matters—identifications of persons, places, technical words and phrases, authorities and cases cited, and the like—arising immediately from the documents. Every effort has been made to track down references to old legal treatises and abridgments of the law and to English cases. Supplementary court records, along with papers belonging to a particular case file that have not been published, are summarized or mentioned in the footnotes if they cast light on the controversy or provide a connecting thread to the narrative.

The content and form of the editorial notes preceding the cases vary with the particular circumstances and available materials. While summarizing the factual background of the dispute and covering broader issues of law and history that cannot be conveniently addressed in the footnotes, these longer notes develop the principal theme arising from the case and discuss related Marshall cases not included in the volume. Editorial notes also appear at the beginning of each of the six sections. They serve two purposes: (1) to describe the organization, jurisdiction, and surviving records and papers of the various courts Marshall attended and the general pattern of his practice in those courts; and (2) to give extended treatment to topics of special importance, such as the British debt litigation and the cases in the Virginia Court of Appeals.

Selecting cases proved less difficult than originally anticipated. The essential requirements were that the case had to contain at least one Marshall document and had to illuminate some area of his practice. This eliminated many routine cases and those for which the evidence of Marshall's participation was scanty. Further winnowing was achieved by applying other criteria: Was the case broadly representative of a particular type of legal action common in Marshall's Virginia? Was it significant from the perspective of social and economic history as well as that of legal history? If possessing only modest legal and historical significance, did it at least yield an interesting story?

Each of the cases presents one or more Marshall documents, here defined as any manuscript or printed item that he wrote or that derives from his written or spoken words. This definition embraces documents either in Marshall's hand or signed by him, those known to have been produced by him though not in his hand or signed, and those by others reporting Marshall's words spoken in court. Selection of other documents depended on their capacity to elucidate the dispute and their suitability for illustrating various stages of pleading and procedure. Stereotyped writs and pleadings have been restricted in most instances to one example of each kind. One declaration in debt on a bond or one in indebitatus assumpsit for goods sold and delivered can easily stand for all such declarations. The same is true of a writ for commencing a suit or for executing a judgment. The cumulative intent is to draw from the surviving records a composite picture of the kinds of legal documents and cases prepared by Marshall in the Virginia and federal courts.

3. The Court System of Post-Revolutionary Virginia

In terms of judicial organization, the law practice of John Marshall naturally divides itself into two periods of nearly equal length. His first nine years at the bar, from 1780 to 1789, roughly coincides with the existence of the first court system of the new commonwealth. In 1789 a second judicial establishment, along with a new system of federal courts, came into being and continued in operation until after Marshall quit the bar.

The Virginia Constitution of 1776 laid the foundation of the first state court system by providing for the appointment of "judges of the Supreme Court of Appeals, and General Court, Judges in Chancery, Judges of Admiralty," and other officers. The details of organization were left to the General Assembly, which by a series of enactments between 1776 and 1779 established a Court of Admiralty, a High Court of Chancery, a General Court, and a Court of Appeals.[3] These superior courts were engrafted upon an existing system of inferior county and corporation courts. In essence, the new courts (excepting the admiralty court) replaced the colonial General Court, which had exercised both original and appellate jurisdiction and united the functions of law and equity. This court, made up of the governor and his councillors, ceased to exist following the collapse of the royal government.

The impulse to remodel the courts antedated the Revolution, which merely provided the occasion and opportunity, and did not play itself out until more than a decade after Independence. To the goals of a more efficient administration of justice and of greater professionalism on the bench was added a new imperative in 1776: erecting a judicial structure appropriate to a republican commonwealth. Court reform was a perennial theme of politics during the early years of the new state, one that can only be touched upon incidentally in the course of this brief sketch. As both legislator and lawyer Marshall was a conspicuous participant in efforts to improve the judiciary system.[4]

Marshall's practice was almost wholly confined to the superior courts sitting at the capital in Richmond: the General Court, the

3. Hening, *Statutes*, IX, 117, 217, 389, 401; X, 98.
4. *PJM*, I, 124, 193–97, 248; II, 48–50.

VIEW OF THE CITY OF RICHMOND

This sketch was drawn by Benjamin Henry Latrobe on 24 May 1798. The view looks west from the banks of the James River, with the Capitol in the center. *Courtesy of the Papers of Benjamin Henry Latrobe, Maryland Historical Society*

High Court of Chancery, and the Court of Appeals. He never attended the Court of Admiralty, which continued to meet at Williamsburg after the seat of government was removed to Richmond in 1780.[5] The new General Court succeeded to the common law jurisdiction of the pre-Revolutionary General Court. Its jurisdiction was "general over all persons, and in all causes, matters, or things at common law" where the debt or claim was ten pounds or more. It was a court of oyer and terminer for the trial of treasons, murders, felonies, and other crimes and misdemeanors committed by a free person. The General Court also had appellate jurisdiction over judgments of the county and corporation courts. It held four terms a year, two for civil and two for criminal cases. The bench was composed of five judges, who were elected by joint ballot of both houses of the legislature and held office during good behavior. Of those originally elected to this court in its first incarnation, only Paul Carrington was still sitting when Marshall began to attend. Other General Court judges whose tenure coincided with Marshall's practice

5. This court ceased to exist after 1789, when admiralty jurisdiction was transferred to the federal courts.

were Bartholomew Dandridge, Peter Lyons, William Fleming, James Mercer, and Henry Tazewell.[6]

The equity jurisdiction of the colonial General Court was transferred to the High Court of Chancery. Like its common law counterpart, it had general jurisdiction "over all persons and in all causes in chancery" where the value was ten pounds or above, both in original cases and appeals from the chancery side of the county courts. (Law and equity continued to be united in the county courts.) The chancery court held two terms a year, later (in 1790) extended to three. A striking innovation in the act establishing this court was a provision for the trial of facts by a jury upon oral testimony in court, although this provision was later abolished.[7] There were three judges, or chancellors, of the High Court of Chancery, chosen by the General Assembly, who were to have precedence of rank over the judges of the other superior courts. Those originally elected were Edmund Pendleton, George Wythe, and Robert Carter Nicholas. Nicholas died in 1780 and was replaced by John Blair. Pendleton, Wythe, and Blair served as chancellors until the court was reconstituted in 1788.

The first Court of Appeals was not a separate court but was composed of all the superior court judges in this order of rank: the three chancellors, the five judges of the General Court, and the three admiralty judges. Given jurisdiction over cases brought by appeal or by writ of error, the appeals court reviewed decrees of the High Court of Chancery, judgments of the General Court, and sentences of the Court of Admiralty, where the amount was fifty pounds and above or the matter involved a freehold or franchise.[8] By staffing the appellate court in this manner (from motives of economy), the General Assembly unwittingly planted the seeds of a crisis that eventually brought about the collapse of the first judicial establishment of the state. The members of the appellate bench held their commissions as judges of their respective courts rather than as judges of the Court of Appeals. This anomaly furnished a pretext for the judges later to claim that they "contracted no new obligations by becoming judges of the court of appeals," that their services on that tribunal were "voluntary," performed "with a view to relieve the state from the necessity of sustaining additional burthens in times of difficulty."[9]

The crisis came to a head early in 1788 with the passage of the

6. Hening, *Statutes*, IX, 402, 412–13, 414, 460–61; Tucker, *Blackstone's Commentaries*, III, App., Note A, 11; "Brief Sketch of the Courts of this Commonwealth," 2 Va. Cas. x–xi.

7. Hening, *Statutes*, IX, 390, 394; XIII, 121, 411. Jury trial in chancery causes lasted until 1783. See Sec. II, editorial note.

8. Hening, *Statutes*, IX, 89–91.

9. "Cases of the Judges of the Court of Appeals," 4 Call 135, 138 n, 139–40.

district court act. Pressure had been building since before the Revolution to bring about a more efficient administration of justice at the local level. The county courts had long since proved unequal to the task, driving suitors (those who could afford the trip to the capital) into the General Court in increasing numbers. In 1787 "it was computed that the suits then depending therein could not be tried in less than five years, and they still continued to accumulate."[10] One remedial plan was assize, or circuit, courts, modeled on the English system of nisi prius courts.[11] Under this scheme circuit courts would try issues of fact made up in the General Court, to which the verdict would be returned and judgment entered. Legislation for such courts had been introduced in 1772, again in 1776, and finally enacted in 1784. The act never went into effect, however, owing to resistance from those who believed the plan too complicated and inconvenient and especially from the county court establishment. As Marshall observed: "Those Magistrates who are tenacious of authority will not assent to any thing which may diminish their ideal dignity & put into the hands of others a power which they will not exercise themselves. Such of the County Court lawyers too as are suspicious that they do not possess abilities or knowledge sufficient to enable them to stand before judges of law are opposd from motives of interest to any plan which may put the distribution of justice into the hands of judges."[12] The judges of the Court of Appeals were also opposed to the assize plan, for they would have to ride circuit; but since the act was suspended and ultimately repealed, the judges said nothing "officially . . . respecting it."[13]

The district court act of January 1788 appeared to offer a more eligible plan. Unlike the assize courts, the district courts were to decide both law and fact, indeed, were to be clothed with the full power of the General Court within their respective districts. Again, however, the judges of the Court of Appeals were required to attend the districts, reflecting the assembly's unwillingness to incur the expense of additional judges.[14] This time they registered their official objections by refusing to implement the act, explaining their reasons in a

10. Tucker, *Blackstone's Commentaries*, III, App., Note A, 11.

11. Technically, all cases before the king's courts were to be tried at Westminster, unless before (nisi prius) the designated time judges of assize came into the county in question to try it. Thus, assize courts were circuit subdivisions of the central court in London (Baker, *English Legal History*, 26–27; Blackstone, *Commentaries*, III, 58–61).

12. JM to Charles Simms, 16 June 1784 (*PJM*, I, 124). See also James Madison to Thomas Jefferson, 9 Jan. 1785 (Hutchinson, *Madison Papers*, VIII, 222–23); Tucker, *Blackstone's Commentaries*, III, App., Note A, 11–12.

13. "Cases of the Judges of the Court of Appeals," 4 Call 139.

14. Hening, *Statutes*, XII, 535.

"respectful remonstrance" drafted by Pendleton in May 1788. Their chief complaint was that the act assigned new duties (beyond their commissions as judges of chancery, admiralty, and common law) without a commensurate increase in pay, undermining the principle of the independence of the judiciary embedded in the constitution. Circuit duty, moreover, would compel resignations (the crippled Pendleton, for one), in effect depriving them of offices that by the constitution they were to hold during good behavior.[15]

The result of this protest by the bench of the superior courts was a complete overhaul of the judicial structure of the commonwealth, accomplished by three acts of 22 December 1788: a revised district court act establishing eighteen district courts, to be attended by judges of an enlarged General Court; an act constituting a separate Court of Appeals composed of five judges; an act reducing the High Court of Chancery to one judge.[16] Happily for the economy-minded assembly, this reorganization required only four additional judges. Although the General Court was increased from five to ten judges, three of these—Richard Cary, James Henry, and John Tyler—came from the now-defunct state admiralty court. Already serving on the court were Paul Carrington, Peter Lyons, William Fleming, James Mercer, and Edmund Winston. Carrington, Lyons, and Fleming were soon promoted to the new Court of Appeals, along with two of the chancellors, Edmund Pendleton and John Blair. The four new positions on the General Court were filled by Joseph Prentis, St. George Tucker, Richard Parker, and Cuthbert Bullitt. George Wythe remained as the single chancellor of the High Court of Chancery.

These reforms at length brought a large measure of stability to the judicial system of the state. The most important change was the decentralization of the General Court. For all practical purposes the district courts succeeded to the jurisdiction of the former General Court, though the minimum jurisdictional amount was raised to thirty pounds (one hundred dollars)—a concession, no doubt, to the sensibilities of the county court establishment. A General Court, consisting of the district judges collectively, continued to exist, but it was a remnant of its former self. Virginians could now boast of enjoying a relatively cheap and efficient administration of justice, one that stood (so pronounced St. George Tucker in 1803) "upon as respectable a footing . . . as in any state in the Union, and perhaps in any other country." Clogged dockets continued to be a problem, but these

15. David J. Mays, *Edmund Pendleton, 1721–1803: A Biography* (2 vols.; Cambridge, Mass., 1952), II, 273–75; "Cases of the Judges of the Court of Appeals," 4 Call 135–47.

16. Hening, *Statutes*, XII, 733, 764, 766.

actually reflected the virtues of the system: "In Virginia the cheapness of the law is perhaps one great cause of the multitude of suits, and the delays which attend their decision."[17]

4. Common Law Procedure in Virginia

I. THE FORMS OF ACTION

Unlike lawyers today, John Marshall thought about law more as a series of procedures or "forms of action" to enforce particular legal demands than as a body of abstract rules and principles. Instead of systematically studying broad topics of law such as torts or contracts, he directed his attention to the peculiar attributes of "trespass," "case," "assumpsit," and "debt." To be sure, Marshall learned a great deal of substantive law, though it had not yet transcended the procedural boundaries in which it had developed. He had already been practicing a decade when the first treatise on contracts was published, and a like work on torts did not appear until the nineteenth century.

Of ancient origin, the forms of action continued to flourish and to serve as the foundation of the common law system as Marshall understood it. In this highly formalized system, the essential task of the lawyer was to fit the facts of his client's case into one of the known formulas, which were embodied in the writs and pleadings. He had to decide whether this or that action would "lie," that is, could be sustained, on a given set of facts. The entire proceedings from the initial writ to the execution of the judgment were governed by the rules of the action in which the plaintiff sued. A lawyer had to be thoroughly familiar with these rules or risk having his case dismissed. Although choosing the appropriate action was in most instances routine and mechanical, there was room for creativity when two or more actions might lie on the same facts. Such cases might require a delicate judgment as to which action offered the easiest means of proof or held out the prospect of recovering the greatest damages. If the common law actions fell short of a complete remedy or failed to provide one at all, a party might seek relief in equity, a system of law that had grown up alongside the common law and supplemented it at many points.[18]

At one time there had been numerous forms of action. By Marshall's day all but a dozen or so had become obsolete. This was particularly true of the "real" actions, where a party claimed a freehold

17. Tucker, *Blackstone's Commentaries*, III, App., Note A, 5.
18. Equity procedure is discussed in Sec. II, editorial note.

title to land. Virtually all of Marshall's surviving common law cases were "personal" actions, brought for the recovery of a debt or for damages for some personal injury. What follows is a brief summary of the personal actions most commonly arising in Marshall's practice, which by no means includes all that were available and in use in late eighteenth-century Virginia. (For some of the actions a more extended discussion or additional details are supplied in the annotation of the cases.)

In the great mass of Marshall's cases the plaintiff sought to recover a debt owed by the defendant. For such cases there was a form of action appropriately named "debt," though it was not the only remedy. The action of debt lay where the demand was for a fixed sum of money due. In practice, debt was confined mainly to cases in which the sum was acknowledged to be due by a special contract under seal ("specialty"), such as a bond. Debt could also be brought on a "simple" (unsealed) contract, such as a bill of exchange or promissory note or an oral agreement to pay a certain price for a quantity of goods. At common law the defendant in debt on a simple contract could "wage his law": by swearing that he did not owe the debt and by then producing eleven neighbors who swore that they believed him, he could be discharged.[19] In simple contract cases, accordingly, the action of debt gave way to a newer remedy, "assumpsit," which did not permit wager of law. Debt, nevertheless, remained the only remedy for demands arising on sealed contracts, and for this reason it was far and away the most usual action in the courts of Virginia. Loans of money, sales of property, settlement of accounts, and other commercial transactions were routinely secured by executing a bond. Virginia law also made debt the preferred action to recover money due by unsealed writings such as bills of exchange and promissory notes.[20]

Another action that frequently appeared on the court dockets in Virginia was *assumpsit* ("he undertook"), which was applicable to the breach of undertakings or promises entered into without the formality of a seal. Usually the promise was to pay a debt, though assumpsit embraced a variety of other kinds of undertakings—for example, to build a house, to shoe a horse, to marry, and so on. Nearly all the assumpsit cases in Marshall's practice were for the recovery of a debt. Unlike the plaintiff in the action of debt, the plaintiff in assumpsit sued not on the debt itself but on the express or implied

19. Wager of law, if not abolished, was obsolete in Virginia (H. St. G. Tucker, *Commentaries on Va. Laws*, II, Bk. 3, 284).

20. On bonds, see Case No. 9, editorial note. For pleadings in debt on a bond, see Case Nos. 3, 9, and 12. On bills of exchange, see Case No. 10, editorial note.

(fictitious) promise to pay the debt. He recovered his debt as "damages" for the breach of the promise. Typical assumpsit cases in Virginia were those arising from "open," or unliquidated, accounts between merchants and planters or farmers.[21]

Assumpsit was an offshoot of the ubiquitous action of trespass "on the case"—indeed, these words rather than "assumpsit" were used to identify the action on the writ of capias. Actions on the case, or "case" for short, had emerged to cover a variety of wrongs or injuries that did not allege the use of force. Typical actions on the case besides assumpsit were slander and libel, negligence, nuisance, and conversion. The parent form of both case and assumpsit was trespass *vi et armis* ("with force and arms") or, simply, trespass. In the eighteenth century it was more or less settled that trespass was the appropriate remedy where the injury was the direct or immediate result of force applied by the defendant. Trespass against the person—assault and battery—was the most common action of trespass. Within these three important actions of trespass, case, and assumpsit, much of the substantive law of torts and contract developed. The boundaries between trespass and case and between case and assumpsit were by no means always clear, but the courts insisted on maintaining the distinctions to preserve the integrity of the forms of action. As a result, the ablest jurists expended much of their intellectual energy in formulating these distinctions with ever greater refinement.[22]

In Marshall's practice the only surviving trespass actions (other than ejectment) were cases of assault and battery, while the only actions on the case (as distinguished from assumpsit) were suits for slander.[23] Other actions known to have been used by Marshall were covenant, detinue, and ejectment. Covenant lay for the breach of a promise or agreement under seal. Because of the requirement of the seal, covenant had only a limited range and never developed into a general action for the breach of contract as did assumpsit. Unlike debt on a bond, covenant was brought for the recovery of unliquidated or uncertain damages. Actions of covenant typically arose over deeds executed in conveyances of property. It was not unusual to secure agreements to do something (or agreements to refrain from doing it) by a bond with a penalty. On such bonds, the plaintiff could either bring debt, in which he could recover no more than the pen-

21. For a more detailed discussion of this important action, see Case No. 2, editorial note.

22. Baker, *English Legal History*, 82–85; Sutton, *Personal Actions*, 56–66. The importance of keeping the distinctions in mind was well illustrated in a Virginia case of 1808, Rainbow v. Taylor, 2 H. & M. 423.

23. For assault and battery, see Case No. 1; for slander, see *PJM*, II, 56–57.

alty, or bring covenant, in which he might recover damages amounting to more or less than the penalty.[24]

Detinue was the remedy for the recovery of specific personal property and damages for its detention. It had fallen into disuse in England, having been superseded by an action on the case called "trover and conversion," which did not have the disadvantage (as did detinue) of permitting the defendant to wage his law. In trover, however, the plaintiff recovered the value of the property, not the thing itself. If the specific thing was desired, only detinue would lie. In Virginia, detinue was a common action for regaining possession of slaves.[25]

The last of the forms of action most frequently occurring in Marshall's practice was ejectment, usually described as a mixed proceeding, for it combined the attributes of both real and personal actions. Ejectment originated as a personal action, a form of trespass, brought by a lessee ousted from his land before his lease expired. In time, through an elaborate fiction, the remedy was extended to freeholders claiming title to land. In cases for the recovery of real estate, ejectment became the usual remedy, superseding most of the older real actions, which thereby became obsolete both in England and Virginia.[26]

II. PROCESS: THE WRIT OF *CAPIAS AD RESPONDENDUM*

The legal machinery was set in motion by "process," the means by which a court compelled a defendant to appear. If the court did not thus acquire personal jurisdiction over the defendant at the outset, a lawsuit could not proceed; no judgment could be rendered and no execution levied. In Virginia this was accomplished, for most personal actions, by suing out a writ of *capias ad respondendum* ("that you take to answer"). An aggrieved party or more likely his attorney would apply to the clerk of the court for one of these writs, supplying the necessary information to be filled in. The capias commanded the sheriff to take the defendant into custody and produce his body at the next meeting of the court to plead to the action brought—debt, trespass, case, or whatever.[27]

Arrest of the person by capias had once been an intermediate process, resorted to after original process of summons and attachment

24. Tucker, *Blackstone's Commentaries*, III, 156–57 and n. 10; H. St. G. Tucker, *Commentaries on Va. Laws*, II, Bk. 3, 122–23. For a discussion of debt and covenant, see Eppes v. Demoville, 2 Call 22 (1799), which JM argued in the Court of Appeals.

25. Tucker, *Blackstone's Commentaries*, III, 151–53 and n. 5; H. St. G. Tucker, *Commentaries on Va. Laws*, II, Bk. 3, 84–85; Case No. 23 and n. 1.

26. Ejectment is more fully described in Case No. 11, editorial note.

27. See Case No. 1, Doc. I, for a capias from the General Court; Case No. 12, Doc. I, for a capias from the federal circuit court.

of goods had failed to produce the defendant. It had also been restricted to actions involving a breach of the peace. By statutes (enacted between the thirteenth and sixteenth centuries) the capias was extended to nearly all personal actions and came to be used in the first instance under the fiction that the defendant had ignored the original summons to appear. Although the language of the writ suggests that the sheriff actually arrested the defendant and kept him in jail until the court met, by Marshall's day this was no longer true for ordinary cases. For these the capias was no more than a summons to appear; in certain cases, however, the sheriff could continue to take the defendant into custody unless he gave bail for his appearance.[28] If the first capias failed to make the defendant appear, a second and third writ (alias and pluries capias) issued. If these were ineffectual, the plaintiff had the option of suing out an attachment against the defendant's estate, a process that was infrequently employed in Virginia unless the defendant was "well known to be a man of considerable substance." The usual last resort was to have a proclamation issued warning the defendant to appear or suffer a default judgment.[29]

Process by capias, based on the practice of the English Court of Common Pleas, was also the practice in most other American states at this time except New England. There the initial process was by summons combined with attachment of property, the ancient mode of proceeding that was still used in the inferior courts of England. In New England, moreover, the plaintiff's "declaration," or statement of his claim, was embodied in the writ. In Virginia and other jurisdictions proceeding by capias the declaration was filed separately after the defendant's appearance.[30]

III. BAIL

In English procedure, which Virginia adopted, service of the capias was personal, the sheriff or his deputy traveling to the defendant's house and giving him a copy of the writ. At the time he served the writ, the sheriff took bail for the defendant's appearance if required (as noted by endorsement on the writ). By Virginia law the defendant

28. Blackstone, *Commentaries*, III, 279–83, 287–88; Robert W. Millar, *Civil Procedure of the Trial Court in Historical Perspective* (New York, 1952), 74–77. For a case discussing the laws and practice of Virginia concerning the capias and bail, see U.S. v. Mundel, 6 Call 245 (U.S. Cir. Ct., Va., 1795).

29. Tucker, *Blackstone's Commentaries*, III, App., Note C, 42.

30. Millar, *Civil Procedure*, 79–80; Wroth and Zobel, *Adams Legal Papers*, I, xlv; Julius Goebel, Jr., *Antecedents and Beginnings to 1801*, in *The Oliver Wendell Holmes Devise History of the Supreme Court of the United States*, ed. Paul A. Freund, I (New York, 1971), 511–12, 519.

had to give appearance bail in actions of debt on a bond, bill of exchange, or promissory note for the payment of money or tobacco, and in actions of covenant and detinue. In actions on the case and all other personal actions, a judge upon proper affidavit or affirmation could also order (by endorsement on the writ) appearance bail to be given. If the sheriff neglected to take appearance bail or to take the defendant into custody, he became liable for the action. The defendant gave bail by entering into a joint bond with one or more sureties (relatives, friends, or neighbors) to the sheriff, with the penalty usually double the amount of the debt and conditioned upon the defendant's appearance.[31]

Appearance bail, or "bail below" as it was known in England, was the first of two stages in the bail proceedings. In the next stage the defendant made his appearance by putting in bail "to the action," called "bail above" in England and "special bail" in Virginia. The person or persons serving as special bail (usually the same as the appearance bail) entered into a recognizance in court or before a judge or magistrate, undertaking that the defendant (if he lost) would pay the judgment and costs or render his body to prison, or that they would do it for him.[32] Bail procedure in Virginia was set forth in precise detail in statutes, with particular attention given to those cases where the plaintiff took action against a sheriff who neglected to take bail or took insufficient bail or against the bail when the defendant failed to appear.[33] Virginia allowed summary proceedings against the sheriff and bail by making them parties to the original suit against the defendant. This avoided the "circuity of action" that characterized the practice in England, where the plaintiff had to institute separate actions against the sheriff and bail. Yet even in Virginia the plaintiff often endured great delay by these proceedings, for the sheriff and bail enjoyed the same rights of defense as the original defendant had. By exploiting the bail mechanisms, the defendant could procrastinate the suit "in the same manner as if [he] had some solid defence to make."[34]

31. Hening, *Statutes*, IX, 404–5; XII, 740–41. For an example of an appearance bond, see Case No. 12, Doc. II.

32. Hening, *Statutes*, IX, 406; XII, 742; Tucker, *Blackstone's Commentaries*, III, 290–91 and n. 17. For an example of a recognizance of special bail, see Case No. 12, Doc. III; the form of the recognizance was embodied in a statute of 1792 (Shepherd, *Statutes*, I, 34).

33. Hening, *Statutes*, IX, 404–7; XII, 740–43.

34. Tucker, *Blackstone's Commentaries*, III, App., Note C, 43–47 (quotations at 45).

IV. PROCEEDINGS AT THE RULES

Lawsuits in the Virginia courts were placed first on the "rule docket" and then on the regular court docket for trial. Preliminary proceedings—appearance and pleading—took place "at the rules" in the clerk's office, which in the superior courts were held monthly. The General Assembly first created a rule docket for the General Court in 1727 to expedite proceedings that formerly took place in open court at twice-yearly sessions.[35]

Once the defendant made his appearance and entered bail (if required), the plaintiff had to file his declaration at the next rule day (one month later), or the defendant could then enter a rule for him to declare. Likewise, one month after filing his declaration, the plaintiff could enter a rule for the defendant to plead. Subsequent rules might then be given for the plaintiff to reply, the defendant to rejoin, and so on until issue was joined either upon law or fact. At this point the dispute was ready to be transferred to the court docket for trial.[36]

Numerous suits began and ended at the rules, particularly those in which the defendant did not intend to contest the action and therefore did not appear. Although in England there could be no judgment against a defendant in any personal action without his appearance, Virginia law provided for office judgments in such cases. If the defendant failed to appear, the plaintiff could enter a conditional judgment known as a "common order," which would be confirmed at the next rule day if there was no appearance.[37] An office judgment could also be entered if the defendant appeared but then failed to plead after being given a rule to that effect. Similarly, the plaintiff could be nonsuited for not filing his declaration (or any subsequent pleading) when ruled to do so.

Such office proceedings were provisional, however, and could be set aside at the next term of court. The defendant could set aside an office judgment by appearing in court, giving bail, and pleading an "issuable" plea, that is, one that went to the substance of the claim (as opposed to a "dilatory" plea grounded on some jurisdictional question or procedural irregularity). It was common practice in Virginia for defendants to allow judgment by default at the rules and then to set it aside in court. This was apparently a tactic to postpone the trial for a term. A plaintiff who was nonsuited at the rules could also reinstate his case at the next court. Office judgments not set aside at the next court became final at that term, except those in which a jury

35. Robinson, *Practice*, I, 39.

36. Hening, *Statutes*, IX, 408–9; XII, 745; Tucker, *Blackstone's Commentaries*, III, App., Note D, 54–55.

37. Robinson, *Practice*, I, 166.

had to be sworn on a writ of inquiry to assess damages. These cases were placed on the regular court docket along with those that had proceeded to issue at the rules.[38]

V. PLEADING

Before a case could be decided by the court or a jury, the dispute had to be narrowed down to its essence. This was accomplished by the parties themselves through pleading, a series of reciprocal allegations whose end result was one or more "issues" of law or fact. Issues of law were decided by the court, issues of fact by a jury. Ideally, the system of pleading was designed to produce the precise points in dispute, eliminating all extraneous and undisputed matters and separating issues of law and fact. In Virginia the pleadings phase of the suit took place either at the monthly rules in the clerk's office or at a regular term of the court where the defendant intended to set aside an office judgment. The pleadings were submitted in writing and copied by the clerk into the formal record.

The plaintiff took the first step by filing his declaration, a precise statement of the facts necessary to support his action and of the injury he had sustained. Drafting a declaration was in most cases a routine task, for sample pleadings were available in numerous books of "precedents" that were an essential part of every lawyer's library. For each of the forms of action and their subforms there was an appropriate declaration format, with its particular identifying stock phrases such as "owes and unjustly detains" (debt) or "being so indebted" (indebitatus assumpsit). Most of the declaration consisted of formulaic material that was used over and over again.

To the plaintiff's declaration the defendant had several ways of making his "defense," meaning in the strict sense his denial of the validity of the complaint. At the rules certain preliminary, or "dilatory," pleas that did not go to the merits of the cause were allowed, but these could not be used to set aside an office judgment. Dilatory pleas were to the jurisdiction of the court, to the plaintiff's disability to sue, and in abatement for some defect in the writ or declaration. If the defendant succeeded with one of these pleas, the suit was either dismissed or suspended. If he was overruled, he was required, unless he confessed the action, to plead to the merits.

Pleas denying the cause of action (pleas "in bar") were either the "general issue" or a "special" plea. The general issue was a complete denial of the allegations in the declaration, consisting in its unextended form of two or three words appropriate to the particular action. In trespass, for example, the general issue was "not guilty"; in

38. Tucker, *Blackstone's Commentaries*, III, App., Note C, 47–48; Note D, 54–55.

debt on a simple contract, "does not owe"; in debt on a bond, "not his deed"; in assumpsit, "did not assume." The effect of the general issue was to "tender" an issue of fact to be tried by a jury. When the defendant tendered issue, either immediately by means of the general issue or at some later stage, he concluded his pleading "and of this he puts himself upon the country."[39]

If the general issue alone was pleaded, which was not uncommon, the pleadings came quickly to a close, and the case was ready for trial. Special pleas took the proceedings through at least one more stage. Such pleas, instead of directly denying the allegation, admitted it, but added new facts that if true barred the plaintiff from maintaining his action. The classic example of a plea in "confession and avoidance" was the plea of self-defense in assault and battery. The statute of limitations was likewise a special plea.[40] In Virginia the usual plea in debt on a bond for money was a special plea of payment, in which the defendant admitted that the bond was "his deed" but alleged payment of the debt mentioned in the condition. A special plea was easily identifiable by its conclusion, "and this he is ready to verify."[41]

If the defendant pleaded specially to the declaration, the plaintiff was required to reply. In his "replication" the plaintiff could either totally deny ("traverse") the plea, tendering issue, or set forth new facts to contradict or to confess and avoid.[42] If no issue was tendered, the plaintiff's replication was followed by the defendant's "rejoinder," the plaintiff's "surrejoinder," and so on (the pleadings have no names after "rebutter" and "surrebutter") until issue was joined.[43] As noted, a party tendered an issue of fact by concluding his pleading "to the country." At any point during these proceedings, one could also "demur" to the opposite party's pleading. A "demurrer," identifiable by the phrase "not sufficient in law," tendered an issue of law. It admitted the facts pleaded but denied the legal consequences arising from those facts.[44]

At common law a defendant could answer a declaration only by one plea, though he might have had several possible defenses. The

39. For an example of an extended plea of the general issue and conclusion "to the country," see Case No. 12, Doc. V. The wording varied slightly when the plaintiff tendered issue (Case No. 1, Doc. IX and n. 2).

40. Case No. 1, Doc. VIII and n. 1; Case No. 14.

41. The Court of Appeals later held that the plea of payment amounted to a general issue in debt on a bond (Case No. 3, Doc. II and n. 2). Of particular note in Marshall's legal practice are the elaborate special pleas he entered on behalf of his clients in British debt cases (see Sec. IV, editorial note, and Case No. 12).

42. For examples of the plaintiff's replication tendering issue, see Case No. 1, Doc. IX; Case No. 9, Doc. IV.

43. For a rejoinder and surrejoinder, see Case No. 14, Docs. IV, V.

44. Case No. 12, Docs. VI, X.

rule against double pleading was relaxed by an English statute of 1705, which permitted the defendant with leave of the court to plead as many matters as necessary for his defense. Under this statute, however, the defendant could not plead and demur at the same time. This continued to be the rule in England, but Virginia in 1788 enacted a law permitting both defenses to the same declaration. Defendants in Virginia courts thus incurred no risk in demurring and in fact were advised to do so if they intended to defend the suit. The demurrer and plea were considered independent of each other, so that admitting the facts in the demurrer did not preclude denying the facts in a separate plea.[45]

The evidence supplied by Marshall's cases suggests that special pleading was not extensively practiced in the courts of Virginia. In the majority of cases the defendant pleaded the general issue; if he answered specially, the pleadings seldom advanced farther than the plaintiff's replication. This was also largely true of the practice in contemporary England, where, as Blackstone noted, a reaction had set in against the abuses of special pleading. Adroit pleaders under this system too often were able to prevail without an inquiry into the real merits of the cause. As a result, the courts and the legislature broadened the scope of the general issue, allowing in many instances special matter to be given in evidence at the trial under this issue instead of requiring it to be specially pleaded. The enlarged general issue proved to be an effective barrier to special pleading, for it brought the pleadings to a close at an early stage and left all matters of law and fact to be raised at the trial. In time, this simplified system of pleading disclosed its own peculiar defects and abuses—for example, uncertainty and surprise at the trial, the entangling of law and fact, and the additional expense incurred in proving matters not essentially in dispute or in having the case retried.[46]

Special pleading was rare in Virginia but not unknown. In one extraordinary class of cases, the British debt litigation, Marshall and his fellow practitioners demonstrated their proficiency in the science to arrive at an issue of law. These cases afford excellent examples of some of the finer points of special pleading. For example, where the defendant set up his payment into the state loan office as a discharge of his liability, the pleadings went as far as the defendant's rejoinder.

45. Hening, *Statutes*, XII, 745; Robinson, *Practice*, I, 217–18; H. St. G. Tucker, *Commentaries on Va. Laws*, II, Bk. 3, 269, 274; Beverley Tucker, *The Principles of Pleading* (Boston, 1846), 67–70.

46. Blackstone, *Commentaries*, III, 305–6. In the next century England restricted the application of the general issue, and special pleading enjoyed a great revival. In Virginia, however, pleading remained a backward science (Sutton, *Personal Actions*, 163–67; Baker, *English Legal History*, 96–97; B. Tucker, *Principles of Pleading*).

A particularly fine specimen was the plaintiff's replication to the loan office plea; it contained a *protestando* and was stated in the form of a special traverse with an inducement, an *absque hoc*, and a conclusion. And in one of Marshall's cases the pleadings were drawn out to the surrejoinder on the plea of the statute of limitations.[47]

VI. TRIAL

In England after issue was joined, the court awarded a writ of *venire facias* commanding the sheriff that "he cause to come" to court on a designated day "twelve good and lawful men" of the county as the jury who would decide the matters in dispute. Jurors were impaneled well in advance of the date of the trial, giving the parties ample notice of their identity so that they could be challenged if necessary. The English system was apparently too technical and expensive to reproduce in the colony of Virginia, which instead adopted the mode of impaneling juries from courthouse "bye standers" on the day of the trial. The laws concerning juries enacted during the colonial period remained essentially unchanged until well into the nineteenth century. In personal actions no writ of venire facias issued; the law directed the sheriff on each day the court sat to summon a sufficient number of qualified men to attend court on that day, from whom juries would be selected. The only legal qualifications for jurors in the superior courts were that they had to be freeholders possessed of a visible estate of one hundred pounds (later three hundred dollars) and to be twenty-one years of age. Although sheriffs were required to summon only qualified jurors, no exception on this account could be made after they were sworn.[48]

Before the trial began, the parties collected their evidence and had the clerk issue subpoenas for witnesses and for any necessary documents. Although testimony in a common law trial was to be given orally in open court, Virginia law allowed depositions to be taken and read in evidence in special circumstances. If a witness was about to leave the commonwealth or was unable to attend because of age, sickness, or some other reason, his deposition could be taken *de bene esse*, or provisionally. Provisional depositions could also be taken of a single witness to a material fact. Such depositions were permitted to be read at the trial only if the witness was unable to attend. The courts also awarded commissions to take the depositions of witnesses outside Virginia upon proper notice to the opposite party.[49]

47. Case No. 12, Doc. VI; Case No. 14.

48. Hening, *Statutes*, V, 525–26; Shepherd, *Statutes*, I, 19; Tucker, *Blackstone's Commentaries*, III, 352–53 and nn. 4, 5; App., Note F, 64–67.

49. For procedure concerning depositions taken de bene esse, see Case No. 1, Docs.

Since no transcripts were kept, little is known of the actual proceedings in Marshall's trials. The party maintaining the affirmative was allowed to present his evidence first. If, as frequently happened, the trial was upon the general issue, the plaintiff led off. The defendant could then refute the plaintiff's testimony—for example, by attacking the credibility of a witness—and also make his own case. The plaintiff then had a chance to rebut. The same order was followed in the argument before the jury after the evidence had been presented.[50] In presenting their cases, counsel had to observe strict rules of evidence, which differed according to the particular form of action employed or plea entered. For instance, a defendant in trespass for assault and battery who pleaded "not guilty" could not offer evidence under this plea that he had acted in self-defense. Such evidence was admissable only under a special plea of self-defense.[51]

After the presentation of evidence and the arguments, the court if necessary instructed the jury as to the law applicable to the facts in the case. Virginia courts strove to uphold the maxim that courts were to pronounce the law and juries were to decide the facts. Unlike their English counterparts, Virginia judges refrained from commenting on the weight, effect, or sufficiency of testimony or even from summing up the evidence—this was considered an invasion of the province of the jury.[52] The jury, after receiving its instructions, then retired (unless the case was absolutely clear) to determine their verdict. The usual course was to return a verdict in the form "We find for the plaintiff" or "We find for the defendant." This was known as a general verdict and was written down and signed by the foreman, usually on the verso of the plaintiff's declaration. The clerk later extended the verdict to make it conform to the specific issue or issues when recording it in the order book.[53]

In a general verdict the jury exercised power over both law and fact. The court by instructions aided the jury in applying the law to the facts, though how often and to what extent Virginia judges instructed juries is unclear. Juries not uncommonly relinquished their law-finding power to the court, particularly in complicated cases. The usual device for this purpose was a "special verdict." A special verdict

---

III and n. 1, IV, V. On foreign depositions, see Case No. 15, Docs. II and n. 1, III and n. 1, IV.

50. Blackstone, *Commentaries*, III, 366–67; Robinson, *Practice*, I, 353–54.

51. See Case No. 1, Doc. VIII and n. 1.

52. H. St. G. Tucker, *Commentaries on Va. Laws*, II, Bk. 3, 195, 199; Robinson, *Practice*, I, 338, 342.

53. For an unextended general verdict, see Case No. 12, Doc. XIII; for an extended verdict and the judgment upon it as recorded by the clerk in the order book, see Case No. 1, Doc. X.

stated all the facts necessary for the decision of the case but left that decision to the court. In practice special verdicts were drawn up by counsel, with the jury deciding any facts remaining in dispute. The jury could refuse to return a special verdict, but almost never did so in civil cases when so instructed. Similar in nature to a special verdict was a "case agreed," in which the parties agreed on all the facts without the intervention of the jury.[54] Another means of taking the case out of the hands of the jury was the "demurrer to evidence." Like a demurrer to a pleading, which admitted the allegations but denied their legal sufficiency, a demurrer to evidence admitted the truth of the facts presented by the other party while denying that the evidence was sufficient to maintain the issue. To demur to evidence was procedurally risky, however, and was probably resorted to only if for some reason a special verdict could not be brought in.[55]

In their Declaration of Rights of 1776, Virginians affirmed that "the ancient trial by jury is preferable to any other, and ought to be held sacred."[56] A generation later, however, St. George Tucker concluded that trial by jury in Virginia had serious defects and in no way merited the panegyric Blackstone wrote in favor of that system as it operated in England. Virginia juries, complained Tucker, were too often composed of unqualified and incompetent persons. The qualifications established by law for jurors were widely ignored in the haste to procure a sufficient number for a trial. In practice the bystanders from whom the jurors were drawn were not the "most respectable freeholders" (most of whom went home after the first day or two of court) but "idle loiterers about the court, who contrive to get themselves summoned as jurors, that they may have their expences borne." Moreover, because the jurors were summoned on the same day as the trial was to take place, counsel were unprepared to challenge them. Symptomatic of the flaws of the system of jury trial in Virginia, Tucker noted, were the increasing numbers of cases in which new trials were granted or in which the jury's role was entirely circumvented by means of special verdicts and demurrers to evidence.[57] Trial by jury continued to remain in bad repute in Virginia for many years thereafter, as Tucker's sons both attested. According

54. For a special verdict, see Case No. 3, editorial note, and Doc. III; for a case agreed, see Case No. 11, Doc. III and n. 1.

55. Tucker, *Blackstone's Commentaries*, III, 372–73 and n. 26; Robinson, *Practice*, I, 349–53; H. St. G. Tucker, *Commentaries on Va. Laws*, II, Bk. 3, 295–98. No demurrers to evidence have been found in JM's case files, though he did argue a case dealing with the nature of a demurrer to evidence in the Court of Appeals (Stephens v. White, 2 Wash. 203, 207–8 [1796]).

56. Hening, *Statutes*, IX, 111.

57. Tucker, *Blackstone's Commentaries*, III, App., Note F, 64–65.

to Beverley Tucker, writing in 1846, parties usually consented to dispense with a jury, "unless one or the other, conscious of the badness of his cause, refuses to surrender his chance of finding enough of ignorance and prejudice in the jury to confound right and wrong." Speaking of his own practice, he noted that he had "gone through whole terms without impanelling a jury except in criminal cases."[58]

VII. JUDGMENT, APPEAL, AND EXECUTION

After the jury returned a verdict, the court proceeded to pronounce judgment. Before judgment became final, the losing party could pursue several means of redress. He might move for a new trial or an arrest of judgment, addressing himself to the same court in which the trial took place. If these motions were denied, he could take an appeal to a superior court—in Virginia, this would be the Court of Appeals if the case had originally been tried in the General Court or (after 1788) in a district court. These were remedies available at law to correct a verdict or judgment at law. Under certain circumstances a party could apply to a court of chancery for an injunction to stay execution of a law judgment. Equitable relief could be granted only where redress could not be obtained at law.[59]

The most common mode of rectifying a judgment founded on a jury verdict was for the trial court to order a new trial. This order had the effect of suspending the original judgment pending the outcome of the second trial.[60] Motions for a new trial had to be grounded on errors or defects occurring at the trial that did not appear in the record—for example, the misbehavior of the prevailing party in attempting to influence the jury, the misconduct of the jury in returning a verdict contrary to the court's instruction upon the law, mistakes by the jury in returning a verdict contrary to evidence or in awarding excessive damages, and the misdirection of the judge to the jury.[61] If there were errors on the face of the record, such as in the pleadings, the proper course was to move in "arrest of judgment." These had to be of a substantial nature, however, for by the common law and by statute defects of form were cured by verdict.[62]

If no redress could be obtained from the trial court and there were no equitable grounds for an injunction, the aggrieved party could

58. B. Tucker, *Principles of Pleading*, 60–61; see also H. St. G. Tucker, *Commentaries on Va. Laws*, II, Bk. 3, 285.

59. For injunctions, see Case No. 10, editorial note, and Doc. V.

60. No more than two new trials could be granted (Hening, *Statutes*, XIII, 749).

61. Blackstone, *Commentaries*, III, 387–93; H. St. G. Tucker, *Commentaries on Va. Laws*, II, Bk. 3, 305–8; Case No. 9, Doc. VII, n. 2.

62. For a motion in arrest of judgment, see Case No. 9, Doc. VI and n. 3; see also JM to William Branch Giles, 22 Sept. 1786 (*PJM*, I, 169).

seek a reversal of the judgment in a superior court. The common law mechanism for this purpose was the writ of error. This writ issued only for the correction of errors of law arising upon the record proper, which consisted of the pleadings, verdict, and judgment. Trial proceedings ordinarily formed no part of the record and could not be reviewed on a writ of error. Judgments on special verdicts or agreed cases could be reviewed because they were entered on the record, but the only means of correcting a jury's general verdict was by a new trial in the same court. If this was refused, there was no other recourse at common law.

A general verdict, however, might be based on erroneous instructions or rulings by the court. For such cases there was a statutory remedy dating from 1285 that allowed a dissatisfied litigant to file a bill of exceptions. This device brought before a superior court on a writ of error matters of law occurring at the trial below. If, for example, the judge at the trial court gave erroneous instructions to the jury or improperly admitted or excluded evidence, a memorandum of the error or errors was drawn up, signed and sealed by the judge (as required by the statute), and made part of the record.[63]

The writ of error was rarely used in Virginia. To reverse a judgment of an inferior court, the practice was to issue a "supersedeas," commanding the sheriff to stop execution of the judgment below and to give notice of a rehearing in the superior court. Although in England supersedeas was an auxiliary process, in Virginia it was in most cases a substitute for the writ of error.[64] The party seeking a reversal petitioned the superior court for a supersedeas, assigned errors, and procured an attorney practicing in the court to certify that there was sufficient error to reverse the judgment. The attorney so certifying usually drew the petition as well. The court in session (or one of the judges during vacation) at discretion ordered the writ to issue or rejected the petition, which was signified by endorsement at the foot of the petition.[65]

A writ of error or supersedeas was essentially the commencement of a new suit to reverse a judgment, in which the reviewing court was confined to errors of law appearing in the record. This proceeding was distinct from an "appeal" of cases from a court of chancery or other court (admiralty, for example) where the testimony, instead of being given orally in open court, was reduced to writing and entered

63. For a bill of exceptions, see Case No. 1, Doc. XI and n. 1.

64. See Case No. 19, Argument, n. 1.

65. Hening, *Statutes*, XII, 753; XIII, 410. For a petition for a supersedeas, see *PJM*, I, 126. The federal courts used the writ of error. See the petition and writ in Case No. 11, Docs. V, VII.

on the record. An appeal, which was unknown at common law in civil cases, was a continuation of the suit below for the purpose of hearing it anew in a higher court. The whole case, law and fact, was brought before the court and was heard on the same testimony produced below. In hearing a case brought up from the High Court of Chancery, the judges of the Court of Appeals in effect acted as chancellors and tried the case in the same way that it had been tried in the first instance.

In addition to the writs of error and supersedeas, Virginia law also allowed a party "thinking himself aggrieved" to bring an appeal "as of right" from judgments of the common law courts. Although termed an "appeal," this remedy for ordinary common law cases was in substance no broader in scope than the writ of error or supersedeas. Whether such cases came up by appeal or by error, the reviewing tribunal was restricted to errors of law appearing in the record.[66] The differences between these two remedies were mainly procedural. Writs of error and supersedeas were granted only by petition to the superior court and at the discretion of that court. For most litigants, particularly in areas remote from the appellate court, the appeal was more convenient and less costly. The party simply "prayed" an appeal in the same court where judgment had been rendered, which was allowed as long as he gave bond with sufficient security to prosecute his appeal. No petition, assignment of errors, or certification by a superior court attorney was necessary, and thus the intermediate step required in writ of error proceedings was eliminated. An appeal had to be prayed at the same term in which judgment was given, however. If one lost his chance to appeal, one could still resort to the common law remedies, for which the time limit was five years after judgment.[67]

Arbitrary appeals (appeals of right) had been the practice in Virginia during the colonial period. From the beginning, as shown by the first General Court statute of 1705, the motive behind them was to expedite the appellate process and reduce the costs to the parties. After Independence similar provisions for appeals from county court judgments were embodied in the act of 1777 establishing the

66. For certain extraordinary cases within the cognizance of the common law courts, the reviewing power extended to the reexamination of facts. These were contests concerning mills, roads, probate of wills, and letters of administration. Until 1810 the Court of Appeals heard oral testimony in such cases. A law of that year eliminated this practice and provided that in future cases of this type the evidence below would be spread on the record (H. St. G. Tucker, *Commentaries on Va. Laws*, II, Bk. 3, 335–36; *The Revised Code of the Laws of Virginia* . . . [2 vols.; Richmond, 1819], I, 194).

67. Hening, *Statutes*, XII, 736–37, 753; H. St. G. Tucker, *Commentaries on Va. Laws*, II, Bk. 3, 335–36.

new General Court and in the district court act of 1788. During the existence of the first Court of Appeals (1779–89), there was no such provision with respect to judgments from the General Court. Presumably the common law remedies were deemed sufficient, since the General Court and the Court of Appeals sat in the same place. With the creation of district courts, however, the remedy by way of appeal was added. After 1789 nearly all the cases coming to the Court of Appeals from the district courts were by appeal rather than writ of error or supersedeas.[68]

Final judgment in a court of law gave the prevailing party the right to enforce that judgment by process of execution. Supposedly, execution was "the end and fruit of the law." But as St. George Tucker observed in reference to the immense volume of litigation arising from these proceedings, execution "instead of being the *end*, has been but the *beginning*, of the law."[69] In the vast majority of cases the plaintiff brought suit to recover a debt. Although the threat or actuality of a lawsuit might be sufficient to bring forth payment from a recalcitrant debtor, often enough the creditor had to go the full limit of having the debtor's property seized and sold to satisfy the debt. This frequently involved additional legal steps, for Virginia law allowed the debtor to postpone immediate execution.

Where the judgment was for money, either as a debt or damages, the creditor could choose from among three different writs of execution, depending upon whether he wished to levy it upon the goods, person, or lands of the debtor. The execution most frequently sued out in Virginia was the *fieri facias,* a common law writ commanding the sheriff "that out of the goods and chattels" of the debtor he "cause to be made" the sum recovered by the plaintiff. By this writ the debtor's personal property—and slaves if there were insufficient goods and chattels—could be seized and sold to satisfy the debt. The debtor, however, could keep his property until the day of sale if he gave bond and sufficient security to have the property "forthcoming" at that time. If the property was not then delivered, the forthcoming bond had the force of a judgment, and upon ten days' notice the court would award a new execution. No forthcoming bond was allowed upon this second execution. Forfeited forthcoming bonds formed one of several classes of common law cases that in Virginia could be dispatched more expeditiously by way of motion for summary judgment.[70]

68. Hening, *Statutes*, III, 299; IX, 412; XII, 736–37.

69. Tucker, *Blackstone's Commentaries*, III, 422 n.

70. Hening, *Statutes*, XIII, 357–66. For a forthcoming bond and a writ of fieri facias,

A second writ, the *capias ad satisfaciendum* ("that you take to satisfy"), commanded the sheriff to take the debtor into custody until he satisfied the debt. This writ was a creature of statute rather than the common law and could be sued out against all persons subject to arrest under the initial process of capias ad respondendum. A creditor might resort to this drastic remedy as a more effective means to compel payment or perhaps to punish a particularly obstinate debtor. The law, however, was liberal in regard to debtors taken under this execution. To avoid immediate imprisonment, the debtor could tender property as under a fieri facias and give a forthcoming bond for delivery.[71] If actually confined to jail, the debtor might have the benefit of coming and going within certain "prison bounds" (a large area adjoining the jail) by giving good security not to escape. An insolvent debtor, moreover, could be discharged from prison by taking an oath and delivering his property over to the sheriff for the benefit of creditors.[72]

The third writ used in Virginia was the *elegit,* which enabled the plaintiff to get at the debtor's lands. At common law he could satisfy his debt only out of the goods, chattels, and profits of the lands by suing out a fieri facias or a writ called a *levari facias.* The latter fell into disuse with the introduction of the elegit, created by statute in 1285, by which the plaintiff at his "election" could resort to the common law writs or have the sheriff deliver him all the goods and chattels and also one-half (a moiety) of the lands to hold until the debt was levied. Instead of being seized and sold by the sheriff as under a fieri facias, the goods and chattels under this writ were merely appraised and delivered to the plaintiff. If these were insufficient to cover the debt, then the plaintiff was given possession of one-half of the lands and was called "tenant by elegit." As such he was entitled to all the rents and profits of the lands until the debt was satisfied, at which time the lands were returned to the debtor.[73]

A distinctive feature of Virginia law was that lands were not liable to be sold under execution. At most, a judgment creditor could gain temporary possession of half the lands and then only if the personal estate was insufficient. The elegit system remained virtually intact in

---

see Case No. 14, Docs. IX, XI. On summary proceedings, see Tucker, *Blackstone's Commentaries*, III, App., Note E, 56–63.

71. See Case No. 14, Docs. VIII, IX.

72. Hening, *Statutes*, XIII, 359, 371, 373–75; Tucker, *Blackstone's Commentaries*, III, 414–15 and nn. 7, 9.

73. Hening, *Statutes*, XIII, 358–59; Tucker, *Blackstone's Commentaries*, III, 417–19 and nn. 19, 21; H. St. G. Tucker, *Commentaries on Va. Laws*, II, Bk. 3, 371–80. For another writ, known as an extent, which could be sued out against the lands of an heir or devisee on the bond debt of his ancestor, see Case No. 7, Doc. VI and n. 3.

the commonwealth until after the Civil War.[74] During the colonial period Virginia, like the other colonies, came under the notable parliamentary statute of 1732 "for the more easy Recovery of Debts in his Majesty's Plantations and Colonies in America." This act directed that real estate and slaves should be considered as assets in the same way as personal property and therefore liable to sale under a fieri facias. The statute met a favorable reception in most of the other colonies (some of which had enacted their own laws making lands liable), but encountered resistance in Virginia.[75] The General Court restricted the operation of the law by instructing the clerk to issue executions under it only if the judgment was obtained by a British resident.[76] In 1790, when British creditors began to sue for recovery of their prewar debts in the federal court, the question arose whether the 1732 statute should operate upon the judgments they obtained. "Some of the ablest men & soundest lawyers in America (I can instance Mr. Jefferson)," wrote Marshall, "think that act will still subject lands to the payment of those debts which were contracted while the force of the law was acknowledgd by us." He himself was inclined to doubt this opinion, and his view was confirmed when the court held that the British law was not obligatory in such cases.[77]

5. A General View of Marshall's Practice

Full of ambition and talent to match, John Marshall rapidly ascended the professional ladder after a relatively late start because of military service. The beginnings of his law practice constitute perhaps the largest gap in the spotty documentary record of his career. Lacking correspondence or other contemporary sources, we know few details of his rise and progress at the bar. Marshall's laconic autobiography provides little help in this regard. He mentions "attending a course of law lectures given by Mr. Wythe" at the College of William and Mary. This course lasted all of three months, from 1 May to 29 July 1780, and soon after he obtained his license and was admitted to

74. In 1787 the legislature passed an act subjecting the lands of defaulting public collectors to sale upon execution if there was a deficiency of personal estate (Hening, *Statutes*, XII, 558–63).

75. The 1732 statute was one of those singled out for denunciation by Jefferson in 1774 (Boyd, *Jefferson Papers*, I, 125). See the comprehensive discussion of the act in the report of the Maryland chancery case, Coombs v. Jordan, 3 Bland 302–7 (1831).

76. See the General Court rule of 1745 in H. R. McIlwaine, ed., *Minutes of the Council and General Court of Virginia* (2d ed.; Richmond, 1979), 606.

77. JM to Patrick Henry, 31 Aug. 1790 (*PJM*, II, 60–61). See the argument of counsel in Lewis v. Bacon, 3 H.& M. 89 (1808).

practice in the Fauquier County Court. It was presumably under Wythe's direction that the aspiring lawyer compiled his commonplace notes, the only surviving record of his legal education.[78]

The sojourn at the college was a pleasant interlude during a lull in the war, when Marshall gave as much attention to the pursuit of Polly Ambler (whose name he wrote twice in his commonplace entry under "Assumpsit") as he did to the pursuit of legal science. The brief tuition under Professor Wythe, valuable as it was, did not turn him into a full-fledged lawyer even though his license pronounced him to be professionally fit. As it happened, his commencement at the bar was delayed a year, owing to the British invasion of Virginia and the closing of the courts.

Not until after the British capitulation at Yorktown in October 1781 was Marshall able to begin acquiring practical experience in the law. He also entered politics at this time, which brought him to the capital in Richmond. Elected as a delegate to the General Assembly in the spring of 1782, he served in both sessions of the legislature that year; at the end of the second he was elected to the Council of State. Council duties required his residence in Richmond between December 1782 and April 1784. On resigning from the council, he was promptly returned to the House of Delegates. "Immediately after the election," Marshall recalled in his autobiography, "I established myself in Richmond for the purpose of practicing law in the superior courts of Virginia."[79]

The two years of legislative and executive service in Richmond between 1782 and 1784 were crucial to Marshall's budding career in law. Here he completed his practical training and made acquaintances with important people that served him well in building up a clientele. Among those with whom he established close ties at this time was Edmund Randolph. Only two years older than Marshall but much his senior in legal experience, Randolph was the son and grandson of attorneys general of the colony and had himself been appointed the first attorney general of the commonwealth at the age of twenty-two in 1776. Randolph had tutored young law students since 1779 and also served as an examiner of applicants for the bar. In the latter capacity he expected candidates to have "a distinct knowledge of the common law," of the important English statutes prior to 1607, of the acts of the Virginia assembly, "of the principles of equity, and of the outlines of practice."[80]

78. John Stokes Adams, ed., *An Autobiographical Sketch by John Marshall* (Ann Arbor, 1937), 6; *PJM*, I, 37–87.

79. Adams, ed., *Autobiographical Sketch*, 7.

80. John Brown to William Preston, 27 Oct. 1779 (*WMQ*, 1st ser., IX [1899], 21); *Virginia Gazette and Weekly Advertiser*, 24 Apr. 1784.

Marshall first attracted Randolph's notice while serving in the House of Delegates in June 1782. The attorney general, who maintained a busy private practice in addition to doing the commonwealth's legal business, may well have taken the novice practitioner from Fauquier into his office as a kind of junior attorney. In any event, during the next four years Randolph acquired an intimate knowledge of Marshall's abilities and had sufficient confidence in the younger man to leave him his unfinished business upon his election as governor in 1786.[81]

As he suggested in his autobiography, Marshall did not begin the full-time practice of law until after he left the executive council in April 1784. He prospered from the start, helped greatly by a ready-made clientele: "My extensive acquaintance in the army was of great service to me. My numerous military friends, who were dispersed over the state, took great interest in my favour, and I was more successful than I had reason to expect."[82] In other ways, too, the war created opportunities for advancement. Not only was there a great backlog of business upon the reopening of the courts, but the creation of a state court system opened up the bar by elevating its senior members to the bench. Rising lawyers did not have to worry about competing with the likes of Edmund Pendleton, George Wythe, John Blair, and others who had put on judicial robes. Marshall in short order gained admission to the small fraternity of lawyers who practiced in the superior courts of the commonwealth in Richmond. His participation in the notable case of *Hite* v. *Fairfax* in May 1786, scarcely a year after his admission to practice in the Court of Appeals, signified Marshall's emergence as a leader of this elite bar. A fellow practitioner, writing soon after Randolph left the bar to become governor, placed Marshall along with Jerman Baker and John Taylor "at the head of the practice."[83]

By the mid-1780s Marshall had established a thriving practice in the higher courts of Virginia. His surviving accounts, which run from September 1783 through December 1795, reflect a phenomenal growth in his income from law between 1784, when he earned five hundred pounds, and 1787, when he earned more than one thousand. In the latter year he declined accepting a militia commission because of "the immense load of professional business" in which he was engaged.[84] Marshall subsequently declined other ap-

81. Randolph to James Madison, 20 June, 29 Nov. 1782 (Hutchinson, *Madison Papers*, IV, 358–59; V, 339); *Virginia Independent Chronicle*, 15 Nov. 1786.

82. Adams, ed., *Autobiographical Sketch*, 7.

83. *PJM*, I, 126–27, 150–65; William Nelson to William Short, 11 Jan. 1787, William Short Papers, DLC.

84. JM to Beverley Randolph, 6 Aug. 1787 (*PJM*, I, 234).

pointments, including the offices of federal district attorney, attorney general of the United States, and associate justice of the Supreme Court, unwilling to give up his lucrative practice.

In his account book Marshall recorded more than two thousand fees for actual cases, in addition to those received for giving advice or drawing a document. Beginning in 1787 his average yearly earnings exceeded £1,000, reaching a peak of nearly £1,500 in 1790. He did a volume business, receiving a large number of small fees ranging from £1 to £5. By statute an attorney could demand no more than a set fee before the suit was determined or the service was performed. For superior court lawyers these fees were £1.1.6 for an opinion or advice, £2.10 for common law cases, and £5 for chancery suits and for suits involving land titles or boundaries. The law evidently did not preclude an additional payment after the suit was finished, though no contract or agreement for more than the statutory fee was enforceable in the courts. The Richmond lawyers, including Marshall, publicly announced in 1784 that they would not take a case without prepayment of the statutory fee and the cost of the writ.[85]

Although the great majority of his fees were small, Marshall recorded more than thirty fees of £20 and above. By far the largest payment received was £150 in May 1794 from Samuel B. Cunningham in his suit against the commonwealth for seizure of his ship during the Revolution.[86] Merchants were a particularly lucrative source of income: £70 from Pringle & Company, £56 from Glass & Wails, £77 from Oxley & Hancock of London (three fees), £53 from Samuel Beall of Williamsburg (two fees), and £50 from John Hatley Norton of Winchester.[87] Many of the higher fees were for complicated chancery suits and land causes that frequently also included an appeal. Some were retainers, and occasionally Marshall described them as such. Contingency fees were not unknown, as shown by a detinue action in which "If I faild I was to receive nothing, if I succeeded I was to have a negroe or £50."[88]

For Marshall the monetary rewards of the law were not the least of its attractions. On finishing one of his suits in the High Court of Chancery, he looked forward to receiving "a few guineas more" in the appeal. "A client is just come in—pray heaven he may have money," he hastily concluded a letter to a friend. In a suit between Messrs. Rankin and Donaghue, Marshall with regret refused to ap-

85. Hening, *Statutes*, VII, 400–401; Shepherd, *Statutes*, I, 15; *PJM*, I, 126–27.
86. *PJM*, II, 263, 476.
87. *PJM*, I, 357, 359; II, 376, 379, 406, 415, 445.
88. JM to John Breckinridge, ca. Mar. 1790 (*PJM*, II, 54).

pear for the wealthy Donaghue: "I do not decline his business from any objection to his *bank*: to that I shoud like very well to have free access & woud certainly discount *from* it as largely as he woud permit, but I am already fixd by Rankin & as those who are once in the bank do not I am told readily get out again I despair of being ever able to touch the guineas of Donaghoe."[89]

Throughout the 1780s Marshall's practice followed a regular pattern of attending the twice-yearly terms of the General Court, the High Court of Chancery, and the Court of Appeals. Term time was especially busy, but there was also much to be done during vacation: filing pleadings with the clerk, sending out subpoenas for witnesses, taking depositions, collecting documents and other proofs, and preparing arguments of cases to be heard the next term. Except perhaps to take a deposition, he did not have to venture beyond Richmond on business.

This pattern was altered somewhat in 1789 by the splitting up of the General Court's jurisdiction among numerous district courts. In that year he began attending the courts in nearby Fredericksburg and Petersburg and continued to do so for a few years, mainly to finish up old cases rather than take on new ones. After 1790 a flourishing chancery and appellate practice along with a host of clients in the new federal circuit court allowed Marshall to cut back on his common law cases in the state courts. The bulk of his litigation in both the state and federal courts arose from commercial transactions, the buying and selling of goods, wares, and merchandise. Merchants, planters, and farmers dominated his list of clients. Plaintiffs and defendants in his cases were most frequently in the relationship of creditor and debtor. The multitude of suits founded on bonds and unliquidated accounts was the natural concomitant of an agricultural economy fueled by credit rather than by circulating cash.

In Virginia there was no formal distinction between an "attorney," who brought suit and filed the pleadings, and "counsel," who advocated the cause in court.[90] Marshall, of course, made his reputation in the latter role. He excelled in the argument of cases and developed a special talent for appellate advocacy.[91] He was less temperamentally suited for the routine work of an attorney and was sometimes careless in attending to details, as when he erroneously drew some declarations in debt instead of in assumpsit. His suits in consequence were dismissed. "I feel myself extremely chagrind at the issue

89. JM to Archibald Stuart, ca. Dec. 1789, 27 Mar. 1794 (*PJM*, II, 47–48, 261).
90. See JM's argument in Stephens v. White, 2 Wash. 207–8 (1796).
91. On JM as an appellate lawyer, see Sec. VI, editorial note.

of this business because I feel that I have been extremely culpable in the manner of conducting it," he apologized to the lawyer who had just taken over the cases.[92]

Marshall generously gave advice and encouragement to novice practitioners, responding unreservedly to frequent queries about substantive law and points of practice and procedure. Two youthful lawyers who sought Marshall's counsel at the start of their careers were William Branch Giles and John Breckinridge, later to become prominent Republican politicians. In his first surviving exchange with Giles, who practiced in the Petersburg area, Marshall advised him how to plead in a suit for a gambling debt.[93] Breckinridge, then practicing in the central Piedmont region, applied to open a correspondence in the spring of 1787. Marshall warmly replied that he would "with very much pleasure make you any communications on legal or any other subjects whenever you chuse. I cannot promise you that they will be worth receiving but such as they are—take them." He then went on to explain habeas corpus procedure in the General Court, providing just the kind of practical information that a neophyte would want to have.[94]

Marshall's unselfish sharing of his professional knowledge with junior members of the guild did not go unreciprocated. Mutual assistance, indeed, was standard practice, as lawyers frequently called upon each other to enter appearances, file pleadings, forward commissions and subpoenas, and the like. The creation of district courts in 1789 stimulated the growth of informal business relationships among the bar. Marshall, for example, turned over his unfinished General Court cases to younger colleagues practicing in the outlying districts and thereafter consulted closely with them about the disposition of the pending suits. They in turn directed appeals of their district court cases and suits in the High Court of Chancery to him. Marshall in effect was the senior partner of a firm centered in Richmond, with branch offices headed by Giles (Petersburg), Breckinridge (Charlottesville and Prince Edward), and Archibald Stuart (Staunton).[95]

In the summer of 1797 Marshall sailed for France on his diplomatic mission. On his return after a year's absence he resumed his practice, "not a little delighted to find that my prospects at the bar had sustained no material injury." The call to public life became

92. JM to John Breckinridge, ca. 20 May, 10 June 1791 (*PJM*, II, 91–92, 94–95). For another instance of JM's carelessness, see Case No. 18, Doc. VII.

93. JM to Giles, 22 Sept. 1786 (*PJM*, I, 168–69).

94. JM to Breckinridge, 1 May 1787 (*PJM*, I, 232).

95. See JM's correspondence with these colleagues in *PJM*, II, passim.

increasingly insistent, however. Former President Washington prevailed upon him to stand for Congress, to which he was elected in the spring of 1799. This was followed a year later by his appointment as secretary of state, the office he was holding when President Adams nominated him to be chief justice of the United States in January 1801. Until that moment, Marshall apparently had every intention of returning fully to private business, though in truth he had been "given up as a lawyer, and considered generally as entirely a political man."[96]

The credentials that John Marshall brought to the Supreme Court were not just those of a professional lawyer. With his background as a soldier, legislator, diplomat, and executive officer, he was also a statesman broadly versed in public affairs. He knew the ways of politics and the workings of the state and federal governments. He understood as well as anyone the nature and boundaries of legislative, executive, and judicial power. His participation in public life outside the courtroom contributed importantly to the formation of his jurisprudence, most notably in those cases that required him to interpret the Constitution. The search for the sources of Marshall's judicial statecraft must nevertheless begin with the facts of his training and experience as a lawyer, his abiding preoccupation, if not exclusive pursuit, for twenty years.

As a practitioner in the courts of Edmund Pendleton and George Wythe, Marshall had the good fortune to be enrolled in the best of schools for judges. While Pendleton more clearly than Wythe was the future chief justice's model, the chancellor no less than the president personified those qualities of judicial dignity and independence that Marshall came to embody. These eminent jurists were largely responsible for the emergence of the judiciary as a sturdy and independent institution of government in post-Revolutionary Virginia. What they accomplished for the judicial branch in the state, Marshall set out to do for the federal judiciary immediately upon his elevation to the bench.

As early as 1782 Marshall heard Wythe eloquently set forth the duty of a judge to "point to the constitution" and say to an overreaching legislature, "Here is the limit of your authority; and, hither, shall you go, but no further." In 1788 he witnessed another bold assertion of judicial independence when the judges of the Court of Appeals remonstrated against the district court law, obliging them "to declare," in Pendleton's words, "*that the constitution and the act are in opposition and cannot exist together; and that the former must control the opera-*

96. Adams, ed., *Autobiographical Sketch*, 25, 28.

tion of the latter."[97] The remonstrance was later cited to justify the first actual exercise by a Virginia court of the power to declare a legislative act unconstitutional.[98] Marshall's direct exposure to this judicial tradition helps to explain why in 1803 he could assert the Supreme Court's power to void an act of Congress in a seemingly perfunctory way, almost as if it were a commonplace unworthy of extended commentary. The question, while admittedly "deeply interesting to the United States," he said, was "happily, not of an intricacy proportioned to its interest. It seems only necessary to recognize certain principles, supposed to have been long and well established, to decide it."[99]

Much the greater part of Marshall's time as chief justice was taken up not with the "great cases" of constitutional law but with mundane private disputes involving mercantile transactions and conflicting land titles. It was in deciding precisely these kinds of cases, however, that the knowledge and experience acquired as a practicing lawyer were most directly applicable to his work on the court. The common law actions of debt, assumpsit, and ejectment, and equity suits upon injunctions that continually engaged his attention on the bench had been the staples of his practice in Virginia. His business both as a lawyer and judge was predominantly commercial, as attested by the plethora of suits upon bonds, bills of exchange and promissory notes, and open account. Marshall's special familiarity with Virginia law and practice served him well, for a disproportionate number of cases that came up to the Supreme Court originated in his native state, many of them by way of the federal court of the District of Columbia.[100]

The method and style that Marshall employed so effectively on the Supreme Court were perfected over many years at the bar of Virginia's superior courts of common law and equity. His technique, whether arguing a case or delivering an opinion, was to state the law in terms of general principles, laying down one or more premises from which he deduced the consequences and conclusion that inevitably followed. To decide a case, he characteristically remarked, it was "only necessary to recognize certain principles." These words, or ones to like effect, which appear like a refrain throughout his judi-

97. Commonwealth v. Caton et al., 4 Call 8; "Cases of the Judges of the Court of Appeals," 4 Call 142.

98. Kamper v. Hawkins, 1 Va. Cas. 20 (1793).

99. Marbury v. Madison, 1 Cranch 176.

100. George Lee Haskins and Herbert A. Johnson, *Foundations of Power: John Marshall, 1801–1815*, in *The Oliver Wendell Holmes Devise History of the Supreme Court of the United States*, ed. Paul A. Freund, II (New York, 1981), 378, 618–21.

cial opinions, also regularly recur in his reported arguments as a lawyer. "The original bias, as well as choice, of his mind," an intimate colleague observed, "was to general principles, and comprehensive views, rather than to technical, or recondite learning."[101]

Marshall's preference for general principles over abstruse learning cannot be ascribed simply to unique traits of personality—to the "original bias" of his mind—but must also be understood as an acquired habit of one schooled in the legal culture of eighteenth-century Virginia. In this culture talent and sound sense, assisted by a modest store of learning, counted for more than mere knowledge. Technical learning, as exemplified by the science of special pleading, never took root in Virginia because it was not essential to success at the bar. During the century and a half of the colonial regime, the administration of justice was in the hands of gentlemen judges, few of whom possessed much knowledge of law. A lawyer had to state his case with clear and simple reasoning that could be comprehended by laymen who distrusted "every argument which could not be understood without an effort." The motives for studying law as a technical science were thus largely absent in Virginia, a situation that remained essentially unchanged when Marshall came to the bar after the Revolution. Although professional judges were appointed to the courts of the new commonwealth, they were drawn from the ranks of lawyers trained in the practices and traditions that had become entrenched during the colonial period.[102]

The appeal to principle to resolve legal questions, so characteristic of Marshall both at the bar and on the bench, also reflected a common assumption of eighteenth-century Anglo-American jurisprudence that there was a distinction between "law" and the decisions of particular cases. Law was conceived to be a body of principles that existed independently of cases, which served merely as illustrations and evidence of the law. It followed that piling precedents one upon another did not make law and might even obscure the true principle. If by modern standards, then, Marshall's arguments and opinions seem to contain relatively few citations to authorities, this sparseness was not owing to his supposed ignorance of legal literature but to his conviction that principles, not cases, mattered.[103]

The relation between Marshall's background as a Virginia lawyer and his jurisprudence as chief justice of the United States requires

101. Joseph Story, *A Discourse upon the Life, Character, and Services of The Honorable John Marshall* . . . (Boston, 1835), 70.

102. B. Tucker, *Principles of Pleading*, 54–56.

103. Julius Goebel, Jr., "The Common Law and the Constitution," in W. Melville Jones, ed., *Chief Justice John Marshall: A Reappraisal* (Ithaca, 1956), 108–11.

detailed treatment that is beyond the scope of this introduction.[104] A systematic inquiry into this important topic, indeed, cannot properly be undertaken until the publication of the volumes dealing with the court years. When completed, this documentary foundation will facilitate closer study of Marshall's legal and judicial careers, which in turn may bring to light many connections between them that at present are unknown or unsuspected.

104. For a preliminary effort along these lines, see William E. Nelson, "The Eighteenth-Century Background of John Marshall's Constitutional Jurisprudence," *Michigan Law Review,* LXXVI (1978), 893–960.

Editorial Apparatus

1. Editorial Method

The editors have applied modern historical editing standards to rendering the texts of documents. The transcriptions are as accurate as possible and reflect the format and usage as nearly as is feasible with the following exceptions. The first letter of a sentence is capitalized, and redundant or confusing punctuation has been eliminated. Superscript letters have been brought down to the line, and thorns ("ye," "yt," "yn") have been expanded. Words abbreviated by a tilde have not been expanded, but the tilde has been omitted and a period added. Layout and typography attempt to replicate the appearance of the originals. However, the location of the dateline in letters has been standardized, placed on the first line of the letter, flush to the right margin. The salutation has been set flush to the left margin. The complimentary closing has been run into the last paragraph of letters. Signatures, regardless of whether they are autograph, have been set in large and small capital letters and indented one space from the right margin. Other names at the foot of a document (for example, those of witnesses, sureties, and pledges) are rendered in the same distinctive type as signatures and are placed approximately where they appear in the originals.

Obvious slips of the pen, usually repeated words, have been silently corrected, as have typographical errors in printed sources. Words or parts of words illegible or missing because of mutilation and letters or punctuation added for clarity are set off by square brackets. If the editors are uncertain about their rendition, the words are enclosed within brackets followed by a question mark. If a portion of the manuscript is absent, this is shown by ellipsis points within square brackets. Undecipherable words or phrases are indicated by the word "illegible" set in italics within brackets. Blanks filled in on printed forms are surrounded by angle brackets. Official and corporate seals are designated by the word "seal" set in capital letters and enclosed within square brackets. Wafer, or signature, seals are denoted by the initials "L.S." (*Locus Sigilli* ["place of the seal"]) within brackets.

Some changes in format have been introduced in this volume. Notes to documents no longer appear at the bottom of the page but follow immediately after the text. Identification of the source of each document, formerly appearing on the line below the heading, now occurs in an unnumbered provenance note that precedes the first numbered footnote. This note also supplies information on other copies, endorsements, dating, description, or peculiarities of the original. The provenance contains a full citation for the source of each document, except that National Union Catalog Symbols for depositories are used throughout. Elsewhere the editors have employed abbreviated titles for the most frequently cited public collections of manuscripts and secondary sources. These appear in the following lists of symbols and short titles. For other publications, a full citation is given in the first footnote and a shortened reference used thereafter.

For books, periodicals, and articles, the editors follow the style of citation used in standard academic history. Reports of cases, however, are given in legal citation form. The name of the case is followed by the volume number and abbreviated title (usually the reporter's last name); the page number on which the case begins; and, if needed, the court and year within parentheses. For the old English cases, the volume number and page of the reprint of the case in *The English Reports* (abbreviated "Eng. Rep.") are also given. Full titles of all reports cited in this volume are provided in the short-title list. References to statutes also follow the historical style. In citing English statutes, the editors use the standard abbreviated form giving the regnal year, chapter and section (if appropriate), and year of enactment (if not otherwise indicated). For example, 13 Edw. I, c. 31 (1285); 4 and 5 Anne, c. 3, sec. 12 (1705).

The principles of selection and policy of annotation followed in this volume have been set forth in the introduction.

2. Descriptive Symbols

AD	Autograph Document
ADS	Autograph Document Signed
AL	Autograph Letter
ALS	Autograph Letter Signed
DS	Document Signed
JM	John Marshall
LS	Letter Signed
MS, MSS	Manuscript, Manuscripts

3. Location Symbols

DLC	Library of Congress, Washington, DC
DNA	National Archives, Washington, DC
KyLoF	Filson Club, Louisville, KY
MdAA	Hall of Records, Annapolis, MD
MHi	Massachusetts Historical Society, Boston, MA
MoSW	Washington University, St. Louis, MO
NN	New York Public Library, New York, NY
PHi	Historical Society of Pennsylvania, Philadelphia, PA
P.R.O.	Public Record Office, London, England
Vi	Virginia State Library, Richmond, VA
ViU	University of Virginia, Charlottesville, VA
ViW	College of William and Mary, Williamsburg, VA
ViWC	Colonial Williamsburg Foundation, Williamsburg, VA

4. Abbreviations for Court and Other Records

Frbg. Dis. Ct.	Fredericksburg District Court
Law Ord.	Law Orders
Rec.	Records
	Virginia State Library (microfilm)
RG 267	Records of the Supreme Court of the U.S., Record Group 267
	National Archives
T.	Treasury Group Papers
	Public Record Office
U.S. Cir. Ct., Va.	U.S. Circuit Court, Va.
Ord. Bk.	Order Books
Rec. Bk.	Record Books
Rule Bk.	Rule Books
	Virginia State Library
Va. Ct. Ap. Ord. Bk.	Virginia Court of Appeals Order Books
	Virginia State Library

After the first citation of legal papers in a case, the court reference is omitted, and the suit record is designated simply by the names of plaintiff v. defendant. The exception is the provenance note, where complete depository information will be given for the document printed.

5. Abbreviations for English Courts

Ch.	Chancery
C.P.	Common Pleas
Ex.	Exchequer
K.B.	King's Bench
N.P.	Nisi Prius

6. Short Titles

The expanded titles for the English reports are taken chiefly from W. Harold Maxwell and Leslie F. Maxwell, *A Legal Bibliography of the British Commonwealth of Nations: Volume I, English Law to 1800* (2d ed.; London, 1955).

Anst.
A. Anstruther, *Reports, Court of Exchequer* (3 vols.; London, 1796–97).

Bacon, *Abridgment* (5th ed.)
Matthew Bacon, *A New Abridgment of the Law* (5th ed.; 5 vols.; Dublin, 1786).

Bacon, *Abridgment* (1st Am. ed.)
Matthew Bacon, *A New Abridgment of the Law* (1st Am. ed. from 6th London ed.; 7 vols.; Philadelphia, 1811).

Baker, *English Legal History*
J. H. Baker, *An Introduction to English Legal History* (London, 1971).

Blackstone, *Commentaries*
William Blackstone, *Commentaries on the Laws of England* (4 vols.; 1765–69; London, 1966 reprint, from 1st ed.).

Black. W.
William Blackstone, *Reports, Courts of Westminster-Hall, 1746–1779* (2 vols.; London, 1780).

Bland
Theodorick Bland, *Reports of Cases Decided in the High Court of Chancery of Maryland* (3 vols.; Baltimore, 1836–41).

Boyd, *Jefferson Papers*
Julian P. Boyd et al., eds., *The Papers of Thomas Jefferson* (21 vols. to date; Princeton, 1950—).

Bro. C.C.
W. Brown, *Reports, Court of Chancery* (4 vols.; London, 1785–94).

Brock.
John W. Brockenbrough, *Reports of Cases Decided by the Honourable*

John Marshall . . . in the Circuit Court of the United States for the District of Virginia and North Carolina, from 1802 to 1833 [1836] Inclusive (2 vols.; Philadelphia, 1837).

Burr.

James Burrow, *Reports, King's Bench, 1756–1772* (5 vols.; London, 1766–80).

Call

Daniel Call, *Reports of Cases Argued and Adjudged in the Court of Appeals of Virginia* (6 vols.; Richmond, 1801–33).

Cas. t. Talbot

Cases in Equity, during the Time of Chancellor Talbot (London, 1741).

Chan. Cas.

Cases in Chancery (London, 1735).

Chitty, *Pleading*

Joseph Chitty, *A Treatise on the Parties to Actions, the Forms of Actions, and on Pleading . . .* (5th ed.; 3 vols.; Philadelphia, 1828, from 4th London ed.).

Co. Rep.

Edward Coke, *Reports* (7 vols.; London, 1727).

Cowp.

Henry Cowper, *Reports, King's Bench, 1774–1778* (London, 1783).

Cranch

William Cranch, *Reports of Cases Argued and Adjudged in the Supreme Court of the United States, 1801–1815* (9 vols.; New York and Washington, 1804–17).

Cro. Car.

George Croke, *Reports of Cases in King's Bench and Common Bench.* Part 3, Charles (London, 1657).

Cro. Eliz.

George Croke, *Reports of Cases in King's Bench and Common Bench.* Part 1, Elizabeth (London, 1661).

Cro. Jac.

George Croke, *Reports of Cases in King's Bench and Common Bench.* Part 2, James (London, 1657).

CVSP

William P. Palmer et al., eds., *Calendar of Virginia State Papers and other Manuscripts . . .* (11 vols.; Richmond, 1875–93).

Dall.

Alexander J. Dallas, *Reports of Cases Ruled and Adjudged in the Several Courts of the United States, and of Pennsylvania . . .* (4 vols.; Philadelphia, 1790–1807).

Doug.

Sylvester Douglas, *Reports, King's Bench* (London, 1782).

Dy.
: J. Dyer, *Ascuns Nouel Cases. Les Reports des divers select Matters and Resolutions* (London, 1585).

Eng. Rep.
: *The English Reports* (176 vols.; reprint of all the early English reporters).

Eq. Ca. Abr.
: *General Abridgment of Cases in Equity argued and adjudged in the High Court of Chancery* . . . (2 vols.; London, 1732–56).

Evans
: Charles Evans, ed., *American Bibliography . . . 1639 . . . 1820* (12 vols.; Chicago, 1903–34).

Fed. Cas.
: *Federal Cases [1789–1880]* (30 vols.; St. Paul, 1894–97).

2 Freem.
: R. Freeman, *Reports of Cases in Law and Equity from 1670–1706* (London, 1742).

Hardres
: T. Hardres, *Reports, Court of Exchequer* (London, 1693).

Hening, *Statutes*
: William Waller Hening, ed., *The Statutes at Large; Being a Collection of All the Laws of Virginia, from the First Session of the Legislature* (13 vols.; 1819–23; Charlottesville, 1969 reprint).

H. & M.
: William W. Hening and William Munford, *Reports of Cases Argued and Determined in the Supreme Court of Appeals of Virginia* . . . (4 vols.; Philadelphia, 1808–11).

Hob.
: H. Hobart, *Reports in the reign of James I with some few cases in the reign of Queen Elizabeth* (London, 1641).

Holt
: John Holt, *Report of Cases determined by Holt, 1688–1710* (London, 1738).

Hutchinson, *Madison Papers*
: William T. Hutchinson and William M. E. Rachal et al., eds., *The Papers of James Madison* (14 vols. to date; Chicago and Charlottesville, 1962—).

JCSV
: H. R. McIlwaine et al., eds., *Journals of the Council of the State of Virginia* (5 vols. to date; Richmond, 1931—).

Jeff.
: Thomas Jefferson, *Reports of Cases Determined in the General Court of Virginia. From 1730, to 1740; and from 1768, to 1772* (1829; Buffalo, N.Y., 1981 reprint).

Jenk.

David Jenkins, *Eight Centuries of Reports: or, Eight hundred cases, Exchequer-Chamber or upon Writs of Error* (London, 1734).

JHDV

Journal of the House of Delegates of the Commonwealth of Virginia. . . .

Leo.

William Leonard, *Reports and Cases of Law in the Courts at Westminster* (London, 1658–75).

Lev.

Creswell Levinz, *Reports of Cases in the Court of King's Bench and Common Pleas, during the time of Sir R. Foster, Sir R. Hyde and Sir J. Kelyng were Chief Justices: also cases in other Courts during that time* (2 vols.; London, 1722).

Lut.

E. Lutwyche, *Un Livre des Entries; contenant auxi un Report des Resolutions del Court sur diverse Exceptions prises as Pleadings et sur auters matters en ley, surdant (pur la plupart) en le Court de Common Bank* (2 vols.; London, 1704).

Munf.

William Munford, *Reports of Cases Argued and Determined in the Supreme Court of Appeals of Virginia* (6 vols.; New York, Philadelphia, Fredericksburg, Richmond, 1812–21).

Park.

T. Parker, *Reports of Cases concerning the Revenue, Court of Exchequer* (London, 1776).

Peters C.C.

Richard Peters, Jr., *Reports of Cases Argued and Determined in the Circuit Court of the United States, for the Third Circuit . . .* (Philadelphia, 1819).

PJM

Herbert A. Johnson et al., eds., *The Papers of John Marshall* (5 vols. to date; Chapel Hill, 1974—).

Prec. Ch.

Precedents in Chancery; Cases, Court of Chancery, 1689–1722 (London, 1733).

P. Wms.

W. Peere Williams, *Reports of Cases, Court of Chancery, and of some special cases, King's Bench* (3 vols.; London, 1740–49).

Raym. Ld.

Robert, Lord Raymond, *Reports, King's Bench and Common Pleas* (2 vols.; London, 1743).

Rep. Ch.

Reports in Chancery. Reports of cases in chancery, in the reign of Cha. I and II and James II being special cases . . . (2 vols.; London, 1693–94).

Rep. t. Finch
Heneage Finch, *Reports, Court of Chancery, during the time Finch was Lord Chancellor* (London, 1725).

Robinson, *Practice*
Conway Robinson, *The Practice in the Courts of Law and Equity in Virginia* (3 vols.; Richmond, 1832–39).

Rolle
H. Rolle, *Abridgment des plusieurs Cases et Resolutions del Common Ley* (2 vols.; London, 1668).

Salk.
William Salkeld, *Reports of Cases in the Court of King's Bench, with some special cases in the Courts of Chancery, Common Pleas and Exchequer . . .* (London, 1717–24).

Shepherd, *Statutes*
Samuel Shepherd, *The Statutes at Large of Virginia, from October Session 1792, to December Session 1806, Inclusive* (3 vols.; 1835; New York, 1970 reprint).

Sid.
T. Siderfin, *Les Reports des divers Special Cases, Bank le Roy, Co. Ba., & l'Exchequer* (London, 1683–84).

Str.
J. Strange, *Reports of Cases in the courts of Chancery, King's Bench, Common Pleas and Exchequer* (2 vols.; London, 1755).

Sutton, *Personal Actions*
Ralph Sutton, *Personal Actions at Common Law* (London, 1929).

T.R.
C. Durnford and E. H. East, *King's Bench Reports* (8 vols.; London, 1787–1800).

Tucker, *Blackstone's Commentaries*
St. George Tucker, *Blackstone's Commentaries: With Notes of Reference, to the Constitution and Laws, of the Federal Government of the United States; and of the Commonwealth of Virginia* (5 vols.; Philadelphia, 1803).

H. St. G. Tucker, *Commentaries on Va. Laws*
Henry St. George Tucker, *Commentaries on the Laws of Virginia . . .* (2 vols.; Winchester, Va., 1836–37).

Tyler's Quarterly
Tyler's Quarterly and Genealogical Journal.

U.S. Statutes at Large
The Public Statutes at Large of the United States of America, 1789–1873 (17 vols.; Boston, 1845–73).

Va. Cas.
William Brockenbrough, *A Collection of Cases Decided by the General Court of Virginia, Chiefly Relating to the Penal Laws of the Common-*

wealth (2 vols.; Philadelphia and Richmond, 1815–26).

Vent.
P. Ventris, *Reports in two parts* (London, 1696).

Vern.
Thomas Vernon, *Cases argued and adjudged in the High Court of Chancery* (2 vols.; London, 1726–28).

Ves. sen.
Francis Vesey, *Reports of Cases in Chancery, 1746–1755* (2 vols.; London, 1771).

VMHB
Virginia Magazine of History and Biography.

Wash.
Bushrod Washington, *Reports of Cases Argued and Determined in the Court of Appeals of Virginia* (2 vols.; Richmond, 1798–99).

Wheat.
Henry Wheaton, *Reports of Cases Argued and Adjudged in the Supreme Court, 1816–1827* (12 vols.; Philadelphia, 1816–27).

WMQ
William and Mary Quarterly.

Wils. K.B.
G. Wilson, *Reports, King's Courts at Westminster* (2 vols.; London, 1770–75).

Wythe
George Wythe, *Decisions of Cases in Virginia by the High Court of Chancery, with Remarks upon Decrees by the Court of Appeals Reversing some of those Decisions* (1852; Charlottesville, 1900 reprint).

I. The General Court and the Fredericksburg District Court

Editorial Note

John Marshall obtained his lawyer's license in August 1780, but the war and then a call to public service allowed him little time to devote to law during the next four years. In October 1780 he returned to the army for five months. Resigning his commission in February 1781, he had to delay his entrance into professional life because of the British invasion of Virginia. He finally commenced practice after the surrender at Yorktown, first in the county court of Fauquier and then in the superior courts of the commonwealth located in the capital city of Richmond. Election to the state executive council in November 1782, however, again diverted him from his law business. Marshall did not begin his career at the bar in earnest until after he resigned from the council in April 1784.[1]

From the outset Marshall intended to leave the petty practice of a county court lawyer for the more remunerative business in the superior courts. This ambition lay behind his decision in 1784 to move permanently to Richmond, where he had lived since entering the House of Delegates in the spring of 1782. At that time the superior courts consisted of the General Court, the High Court of Chancery, the Court of Admiralty, and the Court of Appeals.[2] The General Court, the principal common law court of the state, was the scene of his most frequent appearances at the bar until the reorganization of the courts in 1789. It had general jurisdiction of all civil cases above ten pounds and of all crimes and misdemeanors brought before it. Marshall's practice was almost exclusively civil, being "very limited in criminal cases," most of them occurring in his early years.[3]

The extent and details of Marshall's practice in the General Court cannot now be recovered because the official records and case papers of the courts that sat in Richmond were destroyed by fire during the evacuation of the capital in 1865.[4] By good fortune, however, the

1. Adams, ed., *Autobiographical Sketch*, 6–7; *PJM*, I, 41.

2. JM never practiced in the state admiralty court, which sat in Williamsburg throughout its existence from 1776 to 1789.

3. JM commented on his limited criminal practice in his testimony in the 1805 impeachment trial of Samuel Chase (*Trial of Samuel Chase* . . . [2 vols.; 1805; New York, 1970 reprint], I, 259). Between 1784 and 1786 JM recorded about a half-dozen fees from accused felons. He apparently accepted no more original criminal cases after this time, though he occasionally petitioned for mercy on behalf of persons convicted of capital crimes (*PJM*, I, 311, 332, 339, 340, 360; II, 100, 207–9, 427). In 1793 he prepared some notes of evidence in the notorious infanticide case involving the Randolph family (see *PJM*, II, 161–78).

4. The General Court also had appellate jurisdiction over the county courts. St. George Tucker began in 1786 to report appellate cases and original cases in which

papers of the District Court at Fredericksburg, which Marshall attended, have been preserved in the office of the clerk of the Circuit Court of Fredericksburg and in the state archives at Richmond. The eighteen district courts created in 1789 succeeded to the jurisdiction of the General Court, which continued to sit for specified purposes. Marshall also practiced in the district courts at Richmond and Petersburg. He gave his pending General Court cases intended for outlying districts to lawyers practicing in those courts. John Breckinridge, for example, received those destined for the Charlottesville and Prince Edward districts, and Archibald Stuart the cases directed to the court at Staunton.[5]

Although the Fredericksburg court is the only one of those attended by Marshall for which the suit papers and records have survived largely intact, the cases heard there were undoubtedly similar to those brought in the other district courts and in the former General Court as well. The Fredericksburg cases thus provide a kind of cross section of Marshall's trial practice as a whole. The jurisdiction of the District Court at Fredericksburg embraced the counties of Caroline, Culpeper, King George, Orange, Spotsylvania, and Stafford. The court met twice a year for about ten days; the terms commenced on the last day of April and of September. On the first day of the first session, 30 April 1789, Marshall and thirteen other attorneys were admitted to practice. In addition to the future chief justice, the highly distinguished Fredericksburg bar included such notables as James Monroe, Bushrod Washington, who was to serve with Marshall on the Supreme Court, and John Taylor of Caroline, who later achieved fame as a political philosopher. Marshall stopped taking on new cases in this court in 1791, but continued to attend until 1793, when he turned over his unfinished cases to Charles Lee, a future attorney general of the United States.[6]

The completed case files, or term papers, of the Fredericksburg court typically include the writ, pleadings, depositions, and exhibits entered in evidence—the bond, bill of exchange, promissory note, or account on which the plaintiff's claim was founded. Many of Marshall's cases have been identified by pleadings and other documents in his hand. Also extant are the order books, record books, and rule

---

points of law were raised. His reports are preserved in bound manuscript volumes. Those reports in which JM's argument was noted have been published in *PJM*, I, II, and III. Reports of thirteen additional cases, recently discovered in Tucker's papers, are presented in this volume (see Sec. V and editorial note).

5. JM to John Breckinridge, 22 June 1789; to Archibald Stuart, ca. Mar. 1790 (*PJM*, II, 25–26, 54–55).

6. Frbg. Dis. Ct. Law Ord. A, 1789–93, 6; JM to Charles Lee, ca. 15 Apr. 1793 (*PJM*, II, 160).

books kept by the clerk for various purposes. They are helpful in tracing the progress of the cases and in providing copies of documents not found in the suit papers. The order book was the clerk's daily summary of the proceedings in court; it recorded the official orders and motions pertaining to various cases as they moved toward trial. The record book contained copies of the pleadings and papers entered as evidence, along with the judgment. Although by law the clerk presumably was to make a record of all ended cases, the record books of the Fredericksburg court (and those of the U.S. Circuit Court of Virginia as well) contain only a small fraction of the cases. The practice apparently was to record a case only if one of the parties contemplated an appeal and was willing to pay the costs of copying. The rule book was a docket of actions taken at the monthly meeting of the rules in the clerk's office. It noted the return of the writ, the various rules to declare, plead, and reply, and the joining of issue.[7]

Most of Marshall's Fredericksburg cases actually began in the General Court. In a few instances pleadings or other documents drawn by Marshall while a case was in the General Court survive in the records of district courts he did not attend. If these cases are added to those at Fredericksburg, the number of Marshall cases for which at least some documentation exists is approximately sixty-five. More than 80 percent of this total were suits for the recovery of a debt. Within this category two-thirds of the cases were actions of debt, nearly all founded on bonds given by the debtor to the creditor. The others were brought in assumpsit, the form of action used to recover unliquidated debts such as those arising on an open account. The remaining handful of cases were actions of ejectment, assault and battery, slander, detinue, and covenant. Marshall represented the plaintiff in an overwhelming number of these cases. This apparent disproportion is largely explained by the fact that the declaration was signed by the plaintiff's attorney, making such cases more readily identifiable. Marshall quite likely appeared for the defendant on many more occasions than can be attributed to him.

To a large extent the courts functioned as a collection agency of the last resort for creditors. In the cases for the recovery of a debt, judgment was almost always for the plaintiff, with the defendant frequently confessing judgment. The purpose of bringing suit was to have execution levied against the debtor's property, which could not be done without a court judgment. Even if they did not seek immediate payment, prudent creditors obtained judgments as a greater security for their debts. The defendant in most instances did not dis-

7. Hening, *Statutes*, IX, 409–10; XII, 745, 751–52; XIII, 443, 445.

pute the justness of the plaintiff's claim. Like the creditor, he too used the courts to serve his own purposes. His object was to keep the creditor at bay as long as he could. Knowing that a verdict would go against him, he would carry the dispute as far as the trial before confessing judgment. Thomas Jefferson, who practiced law before the Revolution, once took a case with instructions to "appear for defendant and protract the matter. He acknowledges the debt." In his memorandum for another case he noted that "the def. does not deny the acct. but being piqued by the pl. will keep him out as long as he can."[8] What such incidents reveal about the role of courts in prewar Virginia in resolving disputes between creditors and debtors no doubt holds true as well for Marshall's practice in the post-Revolutionary period.

8. Jefferson's comments are from his casebook as quoted in Frank L. Dewey, "New Light on the General Court of Colonial Virginia," *William and Mary Law Review*, XXI (1979), 12–13.

1. Latham v. Gaines
1782–1789

I. Capias ad Respondendum, 27 November 1782
II. Declaration, 30 June 1784
III. Affidavit, 1 October 1784
IV. Commission, 1 October 1784
V. Deposition of Charles Davenport, 6 November 1784
VI. Deposition of John Long, 18 October 1786
VII. Agreement, ca. 24 October 1787
VIII. Plea, 7 October 1789
IX. Replication, 7 October 1789
X. Verdict and Judgment, 8 October 1789
XI. Bill of Exceptions, 8 October 1789

Editorial Note

Assault and battery, or unlawful force against a person, was a variety of trespass *vi et armis* ("with force and arms"), one of the oldest personal actions at common law. Trespass vi et armis as understood and applied in the eighteenth century had a more restricted and technical meaning than did the medieval notion of trespass, which was simply the general idea of legal wrong. The writ of trespass originally extended by fiction to cases that did not involve "force and arms." Later, new writs of trespass were formulated for such cases that omitted the phrase altogether and instead showed a cause of action by means of a detailed statement of the case. In time such actions of trespass "on the case" evolved into a distinct form called "case." In general the line between trespass and case was between forcible and nonforcible wrongs, though particular adjudications forced judges to make more precise definitions. By Marshall's day the distinction commonly made between trespass and case was that the former lay for direct and immediate injuries and the latter for consequential injuries.[1] Assault and battery presented no problem, of course, being clearly a trespass.

The case below reproduces the classic pleadings in assault and battery that had been in use for centuries. Between 1784 and 1788 Marshall recorded fees for some twenty cases of "T.A.B." ("trespass, assault and battery"), and there were undoubtedly others that were either unrecorded or not so identified by those initials. To judge from the pattern discernible in his account book, he seems to have stopped taking on assault cases after 1788.[2] Most of these cases began and ended in the General Court before 1789, and all traces of them vanished in the 1865 fire that destroyed the court building. The papers for two of Marshall's assault cases have survived: *Latham* v. *Gaines* and *Kuhn* v. *Hoomes*. They escaped destruction because the actions were pending in 1789 and were subsequently transferred to the newly established District Court at Fredericksburg.[3]

The incident that provoked the suit between Thomas Latham and Richard Gaines and others occurred in November 1782 at the tavern of James Gaines in Culpeper County. A fight broke out between Latham, an elderly man with a reputation as a wife beater, and John Camp. They were interrupted by Richard Gaines, who invited Camp to join him in whipping Latham. After administering this punishment, Gaines and his companions tried to force Latham to sign a bond that he would not prosecute them. As one witness noted, the whole company "seemed somewhat intoxicated with Liquor" (Document VI). The plaintiff, Marshall's client, was probably the Thomas Latham, formerly of Caroline County, who had married Caroline Smith in 1758. Their daughter was married to a James Gaines, apparently the same man who was the proprietor of the tavern.[4]

Besides showing representative pleadings in assault and battery, this case illustrates the procedure for taking provisional depositions of witnesses in civil actions (Documents III and IV). Also among the papers is a bill of exceptions filed by the attorney for the defendants (Document XI). This was an important device for placing on the record matters that occurred at the trial so that an appellate court could review them. The story that emerges from the documents produced by Latham's suit is one of intrinsic human interest, providing a kind of snapshot of rural society and folkways in eighteenth-century Virginia.

1. Baker, *English Legal History*, 82–85.

2. See *PJM*, I, 327–412 passim; II, 345, 435.

3. For the latter case, see *PJM*, I, 183 and n. 2.

4. *WMQ*, 2d ser., X (1930), 215; Raleigh Travers Green, comp., *Genealogical and Historical Notes on Culpeper County, Virginia* (1900; Baltimore, 1964 reprint), pt. 2, 51.

I. Capias ad Respondendum
27 November 1782

THE commonwealth of Virginia, to the sheriff of ⟨Culpeper⟩ county greeting:[1]

You are hereby commanded to take ⟨Richard Gaines, John McBargon & John Camp⟩[2] if ⟨their⟩[3] be found within your bailiwick, and ⟨them⟩ safely keep, so that you have ⟨their⟩ bod⟨ies⟩ before the Judges of the General Court, at the courthouse, in the city of Richmond, on the ⟨Eighth⟩ day of ⟨April⟩[4] court next, to answer ⟨Thomas Latham of a plea of Trespass, Assault & Battery damage five thousand pounds⟩[5] And have then there this writ: Witness, ⟨Paul Carrington⟩ Esq; Chief Justice of our said court, at Richmond, the ⟨twenty seventh⟩ day of ⟨November 1782⟩ In the ⟨seventh⟩ year of the commonwealth:

JOHN BROWN CGC[6]

Printed form, Latham v. Gaines, Office of the Clerk, Circuit Court, Fredericksburg, Va. Blanks filled in and signed by clerk; endorsed on verso: "Executed John Slaughter Shif/ RC ST."

1. The sheriff of Culpeper County at this time was John Slaughter (*CVSP*, IV, 558, 595). The writ of capias ad respondendum commenced all personal actions at common law in Virginia.

2. The will of one Richard Gaines of Culpeper was probated in Feb. 1805; that of another was probated in Feb. 1807. John Camp (d. 1801) had served as an officer in the Continental army (Green, *Notes on Culpeper County*, pt. 2, 49; Mary Stevens Jones, ed., *An 18th Century Perspective: Culpeper County* [Culpeper, Va., 1976], 33, 36). The identity of McBargon has not been established. He apparently did not attend any of the proceedings in this case.

3. The clerk obviously intended "they."

4. The return day was either the eighth or twenty-third day of the court term, which began the first day of April and of October each year (Hening, *Statutes*, IX, 403; X, 455).

5. It was necessary to lay damages sufficient to cover any possible recovery. The amount laid could far exceed what the plaintiff might actually claim (Robinson, *Practice*, I, 126).

6. The initials stood for "Clerk of the General Court." Latham originally employed Edmund Randolph to prosecute this case but was apparently nonsuited for failure to file a declaration. After the cause was reinstated at the Oct. 1783 term of the General Court, Latham hired JM to represent him (see Latham's affidavit, 10 Oct. 1783; notice, 20 Feb. 1784, Latham v. Gaines). In his account book JM recorded under Mar. 1784: "Recd. from Mr. Latham one fee T.A.B." (*PJM*, I, 301).

II. Declaration
30 June 1784

⟨Culpeper⟩ COUNTY TO WIT,[1]
⟨Thomas Latham⟩ com⟨plains⟩ of ⟨Richard Gaines John Mcbargon & John Camp⟩ in custody and so forth, for this to wit: That the said defendant⟨s⟩ on the day of in the year of our Lord with force and arms to wit: with swords, staves, knives, clubs, ropes, guns, pistols, ⟨switches cowhides, horse whips⟩[2] and fists, in and upon the plaintiff at the parish of in the county of ⟨Culpeper⟩ aforesaid, made an assault, and him the plaintiff then and there did beat, wound, and ill treat, so that his the defendant's[3] life was greatly despaired of,[4] and other outrages on him the plaintiff, then and there committed against the peace of the commonwealth of Virginia and to the damage of the plaintiff ⟨five thousand⟩ pounds; and therefore he brings suit and so forth.[5]

EDMUND RANDOLPH, for the Plaintiff.[6]

Pledges of prosecution.
JOHN DOE & RICHARD ROE.[7]

Printed form, Latham v. Gaines, Office of the Clerk, Circuit Court, Fredericksburg, Va. Blanks filled in by JM; on verso: jury verdict, clerk's statement of costs, and summary of proceedings. Filed 30 June 1784, as noted on verso.

1. This declaration in trespass for assault and battery follows the form that had long been used in English law (Henry John Stephen, *A Treatise on the Principles of Pleading in Civil Actions* . . . [3d Am. ed.; Philadelphia, 1837], 38–39; Sutton, *Personal Actions*, 76–77; Baker, *English Legal History*, 311–12). For another JM declaration in assault and battery, see *PJM*, I, 183.

2. The words inserted by JM—"switches cowhides, horse whips"—denote the actual weapons used to commit this assault and battery.

3. This should be "plaintiff's."

4. Declarations in assault and battery commonly alleged that the plaintiff's "life was greatly despaired of" whether or not the fact was true. These were formula words.

5. "He brings suit," that is, he produces his followers or witnesses. The "and so forth" at the end of a declaration stood for "and good proof" (Sutton, *Personal Actions*, 81, 82).

6. JM took over this case from Randolph after it was reinstated in Oct. 1783. He used one of Randolph's forms with Randolph's name printed on it (see Doc. I, n. 6).

7. By JM's day the plaintiff no longer actually had to give security for prosecution, though declarations continued to name the fictional (and ubiquitous) Messrs. Doe and Roe as pledges (Sutton, *Personal Actions*, 16). As noted by the clerk on the verso of the declaration, the defendants, represented by John Taylor of Caroline, pleaded the general issue of "not guilty"

at the Sept. 1784 meeting of the rules at the clerk's office. The case was then continued while the parties took depositions.

III. Affidavit

1 October 1784

Henrico County to wit[1]

Thomas Lathum personally appeard before me James Buchanan[2] one of the Magistrates for the County aforesaid & made oath that Charles Davenport is a material witness in an action of Trespass assault & battery now depending in the General Court between the said Thomas Lathum plaintiff & Richard Gaines, John Camp & John Barger[3] defendants & that the said Charles Davenport is now about to leave this state so that the said Thomas Lathum is afraid of losing the benefit of his testimony.[4] Given under my hand this 1st October 1784.

James Buchanan

AD, Latham v. Gaines, Office of the Clerk, Circuit Court, Fredericksburg, Va. In JM's hand with insertions and additions in hand of James Buchanan.

1. In trials at law, testimony was given orally by witnesses present in court. If a party believed his claim or defense depended on a single witness or if the witness was about to leave the country or was by age, sickness, or other reason unable to attend the trial, a commission, upon affidavit signed by a magistrate, was awarded to take the deposition of such witness *de bene esse* ("well done for the present" or "for what it is worth"). The affidavit for this purpose was usually drawn up beforehand by the party's attorney, to be completed and signed by the magistrate. Depositions taken de bene esse were provisional and could be admitted as evidence only if the party could prove the witness was unable to attend the trial (Hening, *Statutes*, IX, 410; XII, 747–48).

2. Buchanan here inserted his name. The magistrate was most likely the Richmond merchant of that name (*PJM*, II, 264 and n. 6).

3. The documents in the case file refer to this defendant as both "McBargon" and "Barger."

4. The remainder of the affidavit is in Buchanan's hand.

IV. Commission
1 October 1784

THE COMMONWEALTH of Virginia To James Slaughter, Samuel Clayton & Edward Stevens[1] Gent: Greeting Know ye that to your fidelity and circumspection in diligently examining Charles Davenport a material witness who is now about to leave this state on behalf of Thomas Lathum against Richard Gaines, John Camp and John Barger Defendants Command you or any two or more of you that at such certain days and places as you shall appoint you assemble yourselves and the witness aforesaid before you or any two or more of you; you call and cause to come and diligently examine on the holy evangelist of almighty god and his examination into our General Court distinctly and plainly without delay you shall send and certify inclosed returning also to us this writ witness Paul Carrington esqr. Chief Justice of our said Court at Richmond the first day of October 1784 In the ninth Year of the Commonwealth.

JOHN BROWN CGC

ADS, Latham v. Gaines, Office of the Clerk, Circuit Court, Fredericksburg, Va.

1. These names were inserted in another hand. In addition to serving as Culpeper magistrates, Slaughter and Clayton were vestrymen of St. Marks Parish. The former had fought with JM as a member of the Culpeper Minutemen Battalion in 1775 and 1776 (Green, *Notes on Culpeper County*, pt. 1, 46–48, 55; Jones, *Culpeper County*, 54, 65). On Stevens, see *PJM*, I, 303 n. 54.

V. Deposition of Charles Davenport
6 November 1784

THE Deposition of Charles Davenport being of Lawful age taken in a suit Depending in the General Court between Thomas Latham Plaintiff & Richard Gaines John Camp & John Barger Defendants, Deposeth & Saith That some time about the first of November 1782, This Deponant was Riding by James Gaines' & a Negro fellow told this Deponent that Thomas Latham had been there and that the sd. Latham & John Camp had a Quarrell, And that Richard Gaines, John Camp & John Barger had Whippd. him. The Deponent askd. the Negro What they had Whippd. him for. The Negro said they Whippd him because he Whippd his Wife. The Deponant ask'd the Negro where they were. He said they had Carried him to Richard Gaines's in order to make him give Bond not to Prosecute them. The

Deponant rode to Gaines's and saw Barger & Latham sitting some Distance from the house. The Deponant went to them & Latham said he had been Whippd And Barger or some other Person answered & said that it was Good [Enough?] that he Whipp'd his Wife & he should be Whipp'd every time he did so. The Deponent went back to the house and Latham came to this Deponent and told him he wanted to speak with him, & then told him that he had been sadly abused. The Deponent answered him that he could Expect no other but if he would stay at home those things wou'd not happen to him. Latham told the Deponent that he wanted to go home but they would not let him. The Deponent Answered that Certainly no one wou'd hinder him, and that he would go with him & When the Deponent & Latham got some distance from the house, John Camp & Richard Gaines Call'd after the Deponent & ask'd him where he was going With that Damn'd old Son of a Bitch. The Deponent said he was going home with him. They said he did not know the way home. The Deponent said he knew the way & shou'd go with him, they ordered the Deponent to bring him back, he said he Shou'd not. Upon that very high words passed between them & the Deponent ask'd Latham to give him his Stick. He refused so to do. Camp ask'd the Deponent if he meant to Defend that Damn'd old Son of a bitch with that Stick. The Deponent said no, but that he wanted to defend himself & if he had such Weapon as he had at home he wou'd Defend himself & Latham too. They went back with Latham & the Deponent went home, & further this Deponent saith not.[1]

CHARLES DAVENPORT

Taken at Culpeper Courthouse, & Sworn to the Sixth day of November 1784 in Presence of John Camp at the same Time James Branham made Oath before us that Mr Thos. Latham gave Notice to Richd. Gaines of the time & Place of taking the above Deposition.

SAM CLAYTON
EDWARD STEVENS

DS, Latham v. Gaines, Office of the Clerk, Circuit Court, Fredericksburg, Va. Clerk's endorsement noted that the deposition was returned 27 Nov. 1784.

1. That Davenport's deposition was not entered in the record book indicates that it was not read as evidence at the trial. The clerk's endorsement noted that the deposition was "Not with the Jury." His testimony may have

been excluded because his knowledge of the beating was based on what "a Negro fellow" told him.

VI. Deposition of John Long
18 October 1786

The Deposition of John Long[1] of Lawful age Taken by virtue of a Dedimus[2] from the General Court in a suit there Depending Between Thomas Latham Plt. And Richard Gaines John McBargon & John Camp Defendants

The said Deponant being Sworn on the holy Evangelist of Almighty God Deposeth & saith that some time in the Year 1782 as he and Gabriel Long[3] a nephew of his was on their way to one James Gaines's in the County of Culpeper before they got to the House he heard a Noise which alarmed him, And when they came into the Yard he saw the Plaintiff going in at the Door. And the Defendants Camp and Gaines told the Deponant that they had whiped the old fellow (Latham) That the Deft. Camp told him Latham had Struck him, And that he throwed him Down and was going to beat him, And that the Deft Gaines had pulled him off, And said dont beat him! But let us whip him as he has done his wife Many a time! The Deponant saith that Camp & Gaines Said to him, there is Basil Nooe[4] (who was one of the Company) would not Join us in Whiping of him but if there was any expence he would Agree to pay his Proportionable part; Which Nooe agreed to do.

That the Deponant told them he thought they had been doing Wrong that they might Depend Latham would not put up with it. That when he the Deponant went into the House he enquired for Latham and was informed he was gone upstairs, That he then went up stairs and found Latham Lying on a bed, And appeared to be very uneasy and told the Deponant he had been Whipped by the said Defts. and pulled up his Shirt. That the Deponant saw Several Stripes on his back that had drawn blood, And he appeared as if he had been whiped with a Switch. He further saith the whole of the Company seemed somewhat intoxicated with Liquor, that they called for more brandy and Insisted the Deponant should drink raw brandy with them as they been Drinking before, That the said Latham came down stairs and set off to go home. And that the said Deponant with the Defendants and Several others sett off Immediately after, before the said Latham had got out of Sight, to go to the Deft. Richd Gaines's, That on their way the Defendants Left the rest of the Company and went after the said Latham, that a small time after the Deponant and the rest of the Company had got to the said Gaines's, the Defendants came & Latham with them to the house. That the Deponant then heard the Defendants, propose to the said Latham that he should sign a bond, And that Latham refused to do it. He further saith that he heard the said Gaines & Camp say that the bond was to keep him from prosecuting them! He also saith he never heard Latham give any of the Company any Aggravating Language; And that he had heard the Defendants and the people in the neighbourhood say they thought (the old man) Latham Deserved a Whiping for beating his wife, & further the Deponant saith not.

JNO LONG

Culpeper sct.[5]

Sworn to before us at Culpeper Courthouse The Parties being All present except McBargen Given under our hands this 18th day of October 1786.

SAML CLAYTON
EDWARD STEVENS

DS, Latham v. Gaines, Office of the Clerk, Circuit Court, Fredericksburg, Va. Accompanying affidavit (drawn by JM) and commission, both dated 26 Sept. 1786, not printed. According to clerk's endorsement on commission, deposition was returned 24 Oct. 1786.

1. According to the affidavit, John Long was about to move to Georgia.

2. A *dedimus potestatem* ("we have given power") was the commission empowering the magistrates to take testimony.

3. This was possibly the Gabriel Long (1751–1827) who commanded a company of Culpeper riflemen at the beginning of the War of Independence and later held a commission as a captain in a Continental regiment under Daniel Morgan (*DAR Patriot Index* [Washington, D.C., 1966], 422; Green, *Notes on Culpeper County*, pt. 1, 47; pt. 2, 3, 157). In Apr. 1788 JM drew an affidavit to obtain Gabriel Long's testimony, but apparently no deposition was taken (affidavit, 9 Apr. 1788, Latham v. Gaines).

4. The will of Basil Noe (Nooe) was probated in Apr. 1809 (Green, *Notes on Culpeper County*, pt. 2, 52).

5. *Scilicet* ("to wit").

VII. Agreement
ca. 24 October 1787

Birkett Deavenport	Culpeper
James Weathers	Fauquier
John Thornton	Culpeper
William Green	Ditto[1]

We do hereby constitute & appoint the above Gentn. to settle the suit depending in the Genl Court brot. by Thomas Latham agst Richd Gains & others, & in case of Death or inability of one or more of them to attend, the survivors to appoint others in their room & if the whole of them attend & should be divided in Opinion they are to choose a fifth Man whose award is to be binding.[2] Any three may meet & a majority may make an award.[3]

THOMAS LATHAM
JOHN CAMP
RICHD. GAINES

DS, Latham v. Gaines, Office of the Clerk, Circuit Court, Fredericksburg, Va. Undated but drawn about time of accompanying General Court order (copy), 24 Oct. 1787, referring case to arbitrators.

1. For scattered references to Deavenport (Davenport), Thornton, and Green, see Green, *Notes on Culpeper County,* pt. 1, 12, 19, and passim.

2. Arbitration was a common means of settling matters in dispute concerning personal chattels, debts, or personal wrongs. The submission to arbitration occurred either through the initiative of the parties themselves, as in this case, or by the intervention of the court, as in McHaney v. George (Case No. 2). For a detailed discussion of arbitration as practiced in Virginia, see H. St. G. Tucker, *Commentaries on Va. Laws,* II, Bk. 3, 28–42; Robinson, *Practice,* I, 269–80.

3. The last sentence is in JM's hand. The following notation in another hand is on the verso: "This agreement was explained by the parties agreeably to the order previous to the rendering the order." With the dispute still undecided, JM in Apr. 1788 moved to set aside the order of reference, which was done (order [copy], 14 Apr. 1788, Latham v. Gaines). The case was continued at the Oct. 1788 term and thereafter transferred to the Fredericksburg District Court.

VIII. Plea
7 October 1789

And the said John, Richard, & John as to the Trespass aforesaid above supposed to be commited, they say that the said Thomas ought not to have or maintain his action aforesaid thereof against them, because they say that the said Thomas at the said time when the Trespass aforesaid is said to have been commited, at Culpeper aforesaid with force & arms &c on them the said John Richard & John did make an assault & them then & there would have beaten, wounded & abused if they had not then & there defended themselves against the said Thomas, wherefore they did then & there defend themselves against the said Thomas & so the said John Richard & John say that the mischief or damage, if any then & there happened To the said Thomas, was from the proper assault of him the said Thomas & in defence of themselves the said John Richard & John: and this they are ready to verify:[1] Wherefore they pray Judgment if the said Thomas ought to have or maintain his action aforesaid against them &c.[2]

AD, Latham v. Gaines, Office of the Clerk, Circuit Court, Fredericksburg, Va. Apparently in hand of John Taylor, attorney for defendants. Undated but filed 7 Oct. 1789 (Frbg. Dis. Ct. Law Ord. A, 1789–93, 65).

1. The defendants had originally pleaded the general issue of "not guilty" (see Doc. II, n. 7). Since this plea denied committing the trespass, they could not offer evidence under it to justify the deed. Such matter had to be pleaded specially by way of "confession and avoidance," as in the plea of self-defense here entered on their behalf. This plea admitted the assault but sought to avoid liability by alleging that it resulted from the plaintiff's own assault—hence the name of the plea as it was known in law French: *son assault demesne* ("his own assault"). Special pleas such as this one, which introduced new facts, always concluded with a common verification ("and this he is ready to verify") and required the plaintiff to reply. A direct denial or general issue, by contrast, concluded "to the country," that is, asked to have the issue tried by a jury. For examples of pleading in assault and battery, see Sutton, *Personal Actions*, 77–78, 86–87; Baker, *English Legal History*, 91–92, 312–13.

2. This plea and JM's replication to it (Doc. IX) were not entered in the record book, indicating that the plea was withdrawn before the case went to the jury. The defendants may have relinquished the plea after one of their witnesses, Basil Noe, was disqualified (see Doc. XI).

IX. Replication
7 October 1789

Latham v Gaines & al } in Trespass asst. & Battery

And the said plf. by his atty. comes & says that he ought not to be bard by any thing by the said defendants in pleading in their second plea alledgd from having his action against them because he says that he did not make an assault on the defendants at the time of the trespass in the said plea mentiond as is in the said plea the defendants have alledgd[1] & this he prays may be enquird of by the country[2] and the Deft like wise.[3]

AD, Latham v. Gaines, Office of the Clerk, Circuit Court, Fredericksburg, Va. In JM's hand; undated but filed 7 Oct. 1789 (Frbg. Dis. Ct. Law Ord. A, 1789–93, 65).

1. JM replied by means of a "common traverse," an express denial of a single specific allegation. He could have used a more comprehensive form of replication, the *replication de injuria*, which was the usual reply in assault and battery where the defendant pleaded self-defense. The replication de injuria would have forced the defendants to prove that they had acted in self-defense. Apparently JM saw no risk in denying only the single allegation that his client assaulted the defendants (Benjamin J. Shipman, *Handbook of Common-Law Pleading* [3d ed.; St. Paul, 1923], 367–70; Sutton, *Personal Actions*, 78, 90–91; Baker, *English Legal History*, 313).

2. The plaintiff here "tenders issue," that is, submits himself to a jury trial. JM started to write "and of this he puts himself upon the country," the proper conclusion if the defendant was tendering issue. He amended his conclusion to conform to the slightly different phraseology required when the plaintiff tendered issue (Sutton, *Personal Actions*, 78, 83, 91).

3. The preceding four words signify the defendant's "joinder in issue," also called the "similiter." They were added in another hand, probably that of attorney John Taylor. At this point the case was ready to go to trial. The plea of self-defense was withdrawn before the case went to the jury (see Doc. VIII, n. 2).

X. Verdict and Judgment
8 October 1789

This day came the parties by their Attornies and thereupon came a Jury to wit, Joseph Strother, James Vent William Smith David Olivier John Sunderland, Stephen Lacoste Zachariah Vowles, Niel McCoull,

Frans. Thornton, Peter Garts, William Wiatt & Daniel Branham who being elected tried and sworn the Truth to speak upon the Issue Joined upon their Oath do say that the Defts are guilty in manner and form as the plt against them hath complained and they do Assess the plts Damages by Occasion thereof to One hundred pounds besides his costs Therefore It is Considered by the Court that the plt: recover against the Defts his Damages aforesaid in form aforesaid and his Costs by him about his suit in this behalf expended and the said Defts may be taken &c.[1]

Copy, Fredericksburg District Court Records, 1789–92, 113 (microfilm), Vi.

1. Ill feeling between Latham and Gaines was manifested in another case between them that was also decided at this term. This was a slander action brought by Gaines against Latham, represented by JM, for calling Gaines a hog stealer. The plaintiff obtained a judgment for £25 (Frbg. Dis. Ct. Law Ord. A, 1789–93, 45; Rec., 1789–92, 55–61).

XI. Bill of Exceptions
8 October 1789

Gaines &c.
ads
Latham } T.A.B.

Memorandum[1] that upon the tryal of this cause the Defendts offered to give in evidence the testimony of Bassell Noe to which the plt. by his Attorney objected alledging that the sd Noc was interested in the event of the said suit & therefore an incompetent witness & to support his objection gave in evidence that the sd. Noe had come to the tavern of James Gaines the place where the assault was committed & joined in company with the Defendts. before the plt came, that during the transaction the Defendts. carried the plt by force about the distance of fifteen or sixteen yards from the house where the assault commenced, that as the aforesd. James Gaines was going about half way to the place where the Defendts were beating the plt the witness took him by the arm & told him that it was not worth his while to interfere as he could not prevent what was doing & that the Defendts. would probably beat him also & that the said Noe shortly after went to the place but whether the defendts had ceased to beat the plt when the said Noe got up was not certainly proved and that after the assault one of the Defendts. came to the said Noe & told him that he expected the plt woud sue them & if he did that he the said Noe must pay a fourth part of the Damages if any should be recovered and that the said Noe answered that I will. To whh. the Defendts. by their Attorney excepted as insufficient to exclude the said Noe's testimony because the plt had produced no proof to shew that the said Noe had received any consideration to support the said promise or that he was in any manner engaged in the assault except as aforesaid & that the sd. Noe used no force to prevent the interference of the sd. James Gaines, but the court being of opinion that the sd. testimony was sufficient to prove the said Noe interested & an incompetent witness & that he should not be suffered to give his testimony in evidence to the jury and did order accordingly. To which opinion of the court the Defendts. by their attorney excepted & prayed that his exceptions might be sealed & enrolled according to the statute in that case made & provided & it is done accordingly.[2]

CUTHT: BULLITT[3] [L.S.]

DS, Latham v. Gaines, Office of the Clerk, Circuit Court, Fredericksburg, Va.

1. The bill of exceptions was an expedient created by statute in 1285 (Statute of Westminster II, 13 Edw. I, c. 31; reenacted by the Virginia legislature in 1789) for the purpose of placing matters on the record that otherwise would not appear. An appellate court could not review a case on a writ of error unless the matter complained of was part of the record of the trial court. At common law this record contained only the bare proceedings and nothing of the evidence presented at the trial or the rulings made upon it. Thus, if a judge improperly admitted or excluded evidence or gave incorrect instructions to the jury, the proper remedy was to file a bill of exceptions, which after being signed and sealed by the judge was formally embodied in the record (S. F. C. Milsom, *Historical Foundations of the Common Law* [2d ed.; Toronto, 1981], 57–58; Hening, *Statutes*, XIII, 10–11; Robinson, *Practice*, I, 344–49; H. St. G. Tucker, *Commentaries on Va. Laws*, II, Bk. 3, 290–94).

2. The appeal of this case was apparently dropped. There is no record of it in the Court of Appeals order book.

3. On Cuthbert Bullitt, see *PJM*, I, 138 n. 8. Bullitt's colleague at this term of the Fredericksburg District Court, Richard Cary, was absent this day because of illness (Frbg. Dis. Ct. Law Ord. A, 1789–93, 10, 66).

2. McHaney v. George
1784–1791

Editorial Note

Like the preceding case, *McHaney* v. *George* began in the General Court and was transferred to the Fredericksburg District Court. In this case, too, the original attorney for the plaintiffs was Edmund Randolph, who upon his election as governor of the commonwealth in 1786 turned his practice over to Marshall.[1] Cornelius McHaney and his wife Mary brought suit against Reuben George, son and executor of John George, Sr., of Caroline County, at the May 1784 term of the General Court. The circumstances suggest that Mary McHaney, a daughter of John George, Sr., and her husband were provoked to take legal action on learning that she had been virtually cut out of her father's will.[2]

Widowed from a previous marriage, Mary came to live with her father in 1777. She kept his house until sometime in 1782, when she married McHaney and moved to distant Pittsylvania County. Father and daughter clearly did not part on amicable terms. The vexations of caring for an elderly parent, hinted at in the deposition of Catey Brown (Document VI), no doubt persuaded Mary to leave when the opportunity arose. Shortly before he died in February 1784, John George made his will, leaving his land to Reuben George and giving a slave to each of his eight living children. He left the remainder of the estate to be divided among just five of the children, Mary and two sisters being excluded. Because the slave bequeathed by the will had previously been deeded to her by her father, Mary in effect received nothing from the estate despite having kept house for him during his last years.[3] Reuben George, the executor, wrote to Cornelius McHaney on 22 April 1784 informing him of John George's death and of the legatees' intention to divide the estate after probate. He requested McHaney to state any demands he might have against the estate. McHaney may have then applied to the executor and been refused. In any event, on 15 May 1784 he and his wife instituted proceedings against the estate for the value of her services as a housekeeper. Later the plaintiffs added a claim for cattle and other property that Mary had left behind at her father's house.[4]

The McHaneys' case was stated in the form of a breach of an undertaking or promise; the action was called by its Latin name, *assumpsit* ("he undertook"). Technically assumpsit belonged to the category of actions known as trespass "on the case" (or simply "case"), but it had long since become a distinct form. By Marshall's day assumpsit was the most common of the actions founded on contract, and much of the modern law of contract developed from it. Assumpsit lay for the breach of any simple or unsealed contract, whether express or implied. It was the principal means of recovering money due on a simple contract, superseding the action of debt early in the seventeenth century. The chief recommendation of assumpsit was that it avoided procedural and other disadvantages associated with the action of debt.[5]

When used in place of the action of debt, assumpsit was either special or general. The former referred to actions founded on express agreements or contracts, the latter to those founded on implied contracts. The distinguishing feature of the declaration in special assumpsit was that it set out in explicit detail the transaction (the contract or agreement) giving rise to the debt. A declaration on a protested bill of exchange, for example, was usually framed in special assumpsit (Case Numbers 10 and 14). The declaration in this case is an example of general assumpsit (Document I). The plaintiff declared upon standard forms of count known as the "common counts," so called because they were applicable to debts arising from everyday transactions. For example, there were counts for goods sold and delivered, work done, money lent, and money due by an account stated. They were short general statements, comprehensive in scope, alleging indebtedness and the breach of a fictitious or implied promise to pay.[6]

The common counts fell into several classifications. The *indebitatus* count ("being so indebted") alleged a specific sum due, such as the price of goods sold and delivered or of work performed, and an implied promise to pay in consideration of the debt. If the exact sum could not be proved, or if no price had been stipulated for the benefit performed, the plaintiff could bring counts stating, for example, that in consideration of goods furnished or work done the defendant promised to pay so much as the goods were reasonably worth (*quantum valebant*) or so much as the plaintiff reasonably deserved to have (*quantum meruit*) for his services. Another type of common count was the account stated (*insimul computasset*), which set forth that the parties had "accounted together" and that the defendant promised to pay the arrears. The plaintiff normally declared alternatively on several different counts for the same debt, so that if he failed to prove one he might succeed in another. To avoid prolixity (and thus additional expense) declarations by Marshall's time combined the common counts into one—for example, one indebitatus count was laid for goods sold and delivered, money lent, work and labor performed, and so on. By this time, too, some authorities viewed the quantum valebant and quantum meruit counts as unnecessary, for it had been held that a plaintiff might recover under an indebitatus count where no specific price or sum had been agreed upon.[7]

1. See Randolph's announcement in the *Va. Independent Chronicle*, 15 Nov. 1786.

2. On the George family, see Marshall Wingfield, *A History of Caroline County, Virginia . . .* (Richmond, 1924), 433.

3. Account, John George to Mary Dudley [McHaney], 1777–82; will (copy) of John George, Sr., 7 Feb. 1784; deed (copy), 12 Dec. 1779, McHaney v. George, Office of the Clerk, Circuit Court, Fredericksburg, Va.

4. Reuben George to McHaney, 22 Apr. 1784; capias, 15 May 1784, ibid.

5. Baker, *English Legal History*, 82–85, 182–95. For a thorough analysis of this development, see A. W. B. Simpson, *A History of the Common Law of Contract: The Rise of the Action of Assumpsit* (Oxford, 1975).

6. Shipman, *Common-Law Pleading*, 153–67; Baker, *English Legal History*, 194–95; Simpson, *Common Law of Contract*, 305–7, 493–501.

7. Blackstone, *Commentaries*, III, 295; Simpson, *Common Law of Contract*, 493–501; Chitty, *Pleading*, I, 297–309.

I. Declaration
30 January 1785

County to wit;

Cornelius McHaney and Mary his wife complain of Reuben George executor of John George deceased in custody &c for that whereas the said John George deceased, in his life time, to wit, on the day of in the year of our lord at the parish of in the County of aforesaid, was indebted to the said Mary, then a single woman, in the sum of two hundred pounds for work and labor by the said Mary,[1] before that time done and performed for the said John George at his special instance and request, and he the said John George being so indebted,[2] in consideration thereof, afterwards, to wit, on the same day and year aforesaid, at the parish aforesaid in the County aforesaid, in his lifetime undertook and then and there faithfully promised,[3] that he the said John George would well and truly pay the said sum of two hundred pounds to the said Mary, when he should be thereunto required.[4] And[5] whereas also the said John George decd. was in his life time & in the county aforesaid indebted to the said Mary then a single woman for work & labor & services done before that time by the said Mary for the said John at the special instance & request of the said John & also for stock & goods by the said Mary to the said John sold & deliverd at the like special instance of the said John[6] & being so indebted he the said John undertook & faithfully promisd that he woud when thereunto requird well & truely pay to the said Mary so much money as the said work labor & services & stock & goods were reasonably worth & the plaintiffs in fact say that the said work & labor & goods & stock were reasonably worth £200 of which the said John then & there had notice:[7] Nevertheless[8] the said John George the deceased, his promises and assumptions aforesaid, so made in his life time as aforesaid, not regarding,[9] did not in his lifetime pay to the said Mary, while single, nor to the plaintiff Cornelius since the intermarriage of the said Cornelius and the said Mary either of the said sums of £200,[10] altho he the said John George in his lifetime was thereunto often requested; nor hath the defendant, since the said John George's death altho also thereunto oftimes requested paid either of the said sums of £200[11] to the plaintiffs[12] but the same to them to pay have hitherto refused and still do[13] refuse to the damage of the plaintiffs two hundred pounds; and therefore they bring Suit &c.[14]

RANDOLPH. p. q.[15]

Pledges &c.
JOHN DOE & RICHARD ROE.

DS, McHaney v. George, Office of the Clerk, Circuit Court, Fredericksburg, Va. In unknown hand, with interlineations in hands of Edmund Randolph and JM, and one long insertion by JM; filed in clerk's office on 30 Jan. 1785, as noted by clerk's endorsements on verso summarizing proceedings.

1. Mary (Dudley) McHaney sought payment for her services as a housekeeper at the rate of £20 per year, as shown by an account for the years 1777 through 1782. For 1779 the account shows a credit of £60 to John George for the slave Dinah he deeded to Mary that year. According to the deed, George sold the slave to Mary "for the Consideration of her haveing lived with me and Kept my house." As evidence that her services were worth £20 annually, Mary McHaney produced two letters from a former employer of-

fering to pay at least that rate. The clerk's endorsements on these letters state that they were admitted to be read at the trial (account, John George to Mary Dudley, 1777–82; deed [copy], John George to Mary Dudley, 12 Dec. 1779; Philip Johnson to Mary Dudley, 11 Aug., ca. Sept. 1767, McHaney v. George).

2. The phrase "being so indebted" identifies this as a count in indebitatus assumpsit.

3. The promise is fictional, implied by law from the performance of the "consideration," the work and labor done by Mary McHaney. Ostensibly the plaintiff seeks damages for the breach of the promise; the real object is to recover a debt.

4. This concludes the first count. At this point a caret was inserted, indicating where the second count, drawn by JM on a separate sheet, was to be inserted.

5. The second count, in JM's hand, begins here. The clerk omitted this count when copying the declaration into the record book.

6. John George's account with his daughter shows a debit in 1781 of £7 for four head of cattle (account, John George to Mary Dudley, 1777–82, McHaney v. George). See also Doc. IV.

7. JM's inserted count ends here. Although pleaded in the the language of indebitatus assumpsit, this count was essentially a quantum valebant. Instead of positing at the outset a precedent debt for a certain sum, £200, the count alleged that the defendant promised to pay so much as the services and stock and goods were reasonably worth. The plaintiff then would not have to prove that £200 was the agreed price but would be able to recover the value, which the jury might set at more or less than £200.

The count as drafted by JM indicates that professional opinion by his day no longer considered it essential to have separate indebitatus and quantum counts. Although there were precedents in the late seventeenth century for using an indebitatus count to recover the value rather than a stated sum, the prevailing practice that emerged during the first half of the eighteenth century was to declare alternatively: an indebitatus count, where the plaintiff claimed a fixed sum, and a quantum count, where he claimed a reasonable sum. The quantum counts continued to be necessary as long as the courts held that under an indebitatus the plaintiff had to prove a fixed price or sum (Chitty, *Pleading*, I, 301; C. H. S. Fifoot, *History and Sources of the Common Law: Tort and Contract* [London, 1949], 360–63; Simpson, *Common Law of Contract*, 496–99).

JM used the same form, combining indebitatus assumpsit and quantum counts into one indebitatus count, in other declarations. Among his Virginia colleagues, however, the older practice continued to be followed. See, for example, Case No. 15, Doc. I.

8. The text here returns to Randolph's original declaration. This is the beginning of the section in the declaration known as the "common breach" (Shipman, *Common-Law Pleading*, 258–59, 262).

9. At this point in the common breach it was usual to include the phrase, "but contriving and fraudulently intending, craftily and subtilly, to deceive and defraud the said [plaintiff] in this behalf." Randolph omitted this allega-

tion, as did JM in his own declarations in assumpsit. These form words were no longer necessary, having been originally included to justify an action on the case in assumpsit for "nonfeasance" (ibid., 262; Baker, *English Legal History*, 184–87, 191–92).

10. The text originally read "the said £200." JM inserted "either of" and "sums of" to make the wording consistent with the addition of the second count.

11. See n. 10.

12. JM changed this to the plural and made the appropriate corrections in the rest of the document.

13. The text originally read "hath hitherto refused and still doth," which made subject and verb agree in number. JM apparently made the changes under the mistaken impression that the subject, "defendant," had changed to the plural.

14. As noted on the verso, the defendant, represented by John Taylor of Caroline, pleaded the general issue, "non assumpsit," at the Jan. 1785 meeting of the rules. The cause was continued every subsequent term of court until Sept. 1790.

15. The initials stand for *pro querente* ("for the plaintiff").

II. Cornelius McHaney to Edmund Randolph
2 September 1786

Honoured Sir September 2th 1786 Pitselvana County

I woud wish to Inform you that I have Rote Several Letters to you Concerning the Sute I Emplod you in Against Mr. Rubin George and have never had answer from you. I should be glad you would sind Me answer by West Whether it will be Tryed this Cort and whether you have Sent Surpens to Sommons the witnesses to at tend this Cort as I Axedently Saw a letter from Mr george to his frinds out hear that it would be Tryd this Cort pray Sir Spar no pains to have it Tryd as Soon as you Can and give me notis that I may attend pray Send me the Surpenes to have the witneses out here sommoned Which is James DeGarnett in halafax and James Mayo George[1] in pitselvana and James Yarbrough and Elizabeth[2] his Wife in Carriline County pray Send them in Carriline to the Sherif as they are the meterel witneses pray dont fail to Send me answer how I am to porsead by Mr West as he will wat upon you for it this from your Homble Sarvant.

Cornelius McHaney

Noteb

Sir pray Consider the grat distance that I Live of and that I heant the Same oppertunety to Attend as the other party has and be Cearful how you send your Letters to me as thir is Several persons that if tha fall into thir hands I Shant Never see them. Mr West is a Safe hand pay Sir Spare No pains as you Shall be hansomly Rewared If you Git Suit if the Sepeneas hant already ishued pray Scnd them that is to Com out hear by West To me for thir is Never any Such thing Com to my hand pray send me Word What Day of the Cort you think I Must attend yurs &c.

C M

ALS?, McHaney v. George, Office of the Clerk, Circuit Court, Fredericksburg, Va. Addressed to Randolph, "Eterny in the City of Richmond"; sent "pr favor of Mr. West"; endorsed by Randolph. Since this letter and two subsequent ones to JM (Docs. III, V) appear to have been written in three different hands, McHaney's autograph is impossible to identify with certainty.

1. See Doc. IV.

2. See Doc. VII.

III. Cornelius McHaney to John Marshall
6 March 1788

Dear Sir, March 6th. 1788.

You will Receive by William Shelton[1] a Line or two Concerning my suit vs Reubin George. I beg you to inform me by Capt. Shelton wheather it is Like to com to Trial or not and to Send me some Blank spa.[2] that I may have the witnesses, & please let me know what day of the Court it will be set for Trial. I will thank you to send a Spa. in to Cariline County for James Yarbrough & his wife Elizebeth. I shall be much Obliged to you to push it and bring it to a hearing as quick as Possible, at any Rate do not let it Escape this insuing Court and Mutch Oblige Your Most Obt. & Hbl. Sevt. &c.

Cornilius McHayney

P.S. If you will bring it to Trial & gain my Cause this Spring, I will gain you a Double fee on Sight.

C. McHayney

ALS?, McHaney v. George, Office of the Clerk, Circuit Court, Fredericksburg, Va. Addressed: "Mr. John Marshell Atto. at Law/ Richmond"; endorsed by JM: "Answd. but enquire in Genl. court about [suit?]"; second endorsement by JM reads: "enquire about Mr. [Brices?] business—a bond which was lost"; immediately below second endorsement someone wrote "ER" (Edmund Randolph?); accessioned after publication of *PJM*, I.

1. William Shelton (d. 1794) was a resident of Pittsylvania County (Clayton Torrence, comp., *Virginia Wills and Administrations, 1632–1800* . . . [Richmond, (1930)], 382; Maud Carter Clement, *The History of Pittsylvania County, Virginia* [Lynchburg, Va., 1929], 173, 205).

2. Subpoenas.

IV. Deposition of James Mayo George
6 May 1788

Hallifax County to wit May 6th. 1788

The Depusion of James mayo George Being of Lawful age Deposeth & Sayeth that Soone after The marrid of Mary Dudley to Mr. McHaney he was at Mr. John Georges Seanr. in Carroline County & that The Said Mary McHaney & the Said George was on a Bargin aboute Som Cattle & Could not agre on the pris but after Som time agread that he & James Yarbrough & Rubin George Should Set a pris on four head of Cattle The property of the Said Mary McHaney & that they did Vallue the Cattle to Be worth Seven pound, & that the Said George agread to Giv it, & that he was present when the wagon was Loaded to Move the Said mary Mchaney To pittsylvani & that he help load the wagon & that The Said John Georg was present & made no demands of any thing that was brought away Nor for any thing that the Said mary was owing & farther Saith not.[1]

Edmd. King Justis[2]

ADS, McHaney v. George, Office of the Clerk, Circuit Court, Fredericksburg, Va.

1. The deponent probably testified at the trial and therefore his deposition was not entered as evidence.

2. Edmund King was appointed to the Halifax commission of the peace in June 1785 (Commission Book No. 1, Vi).

V. Cornelius McHaney to John Marshall
17 June 1788

Sir, Pittsylvania 17th. June 1788.

I shud be glad you wod let me know by Colo. Lankford[1] what is done with my Suit against Reubin George and when you think it will be tryd. When you want the Witnesses please to send a Sommons to Caroline County and have James Yarborough and Elizabeth Yarborough sommond from there. Allso please to send me a blank Supana to Pittsylvania County as I may have some Witnesses Sommoned from there & you will Oblige Sir yr. mo hbl Sevt.

CORNELUS MCHANEY

ALS?, McHaney v. George, Office of the Clerk, Circuit Court, Fredericksburg, Va. Addressed to JM and endorsed by him; accessioned after publication of *PJM*, I.

1. Benjamin Lankford (d. 1810) of Pittsylvania County served, beginning in the 1760s, as sheriff, justice of the peace, militia officer, and delegate to the General Assembly (Clement, *Pittsylvania County*, 96n, 116, 142, 159, 166, 191, 197, 286–87).

VI. Deposition of Catey Brown

7 May 1790

The deposition of Caty Brown[1] Taken by Consent of parties at the House of William Brown, in a Suit depending in the District Court of Fredericksburg, Between Cornelius McHany and Mary his wife, and Reuben George Exor. of John George decd. This deponent being first Sworn, deposeth and Saith that being at her fathers She heard Conversation pass between Mrs. McHaney, and her father Respecting a negro, which he had given to another of his daughters. This deponent Saith that Mrs. McHaney told her father, that he had Told her he woud give the negro to her, and Just as She had Learned her, to take Drudgery of her hands, he had Taken her away, & that She woud not Stay any Longer with him. In Return her father told her, you Talk of Twenty pound. I will give you forty, Rather than you Shoud Leave me. This Conversation pass'd in the year 1782, and Mrs. McHaney was marryed Some time afterwards. This deponent further Saith that She thought the above Conversation was intended Only as an aggravation to her But there was no anger between them, But Only Supposed that it might be on account of Some negroes that was given up to her mother Some little time before.

This deponent further Saith that She Remembers there was a pair of hand Irons at her fathers before Mrs. McHany came to Live there, and a Considerable time after. This deponent further Saith that Mrs. McHaney Raised Colts and Sold them while She Lived with her father. This deponent further Saith that She heard her father Say, after Mrs. McHaney was marryed, She had Ruined him, for She had stript him naked, and left him Only 3 or 4 Old plates. And further this deponent Saith not.[2]

CATEY BROWN

Caroline To witt.

The above deposition Sworn too before us, this 7th day of May 1790.

JAMES SUTTON[3]
J CHILES[4]

DS, McHaney v. George, Office of the Clerk, Circuit Court, Fredericksburg, Va. Endorsed on verso: "Caty Browns/ Deposition/recd. under Cover sealed."

1. Catey Brown was a sister of Mary McHaney. Her deposition, along with that of Elizabeth Yarbrough (Doc. VII), was taken under a commission issued 4 May 1790 (will [copy], John George, Sr., 7 Feb. 1784; commission, 4 May 1790, McHaney v. George).

2. Since Catey Brown testified at the trial, her deposition was not needed as evidence and was not entered in the record book (subpoena, 28 Sept. 1790, ibid.).

3. James Sutton had been a justice of Caroline County since July 1785 (Commission Bk. No. 1).

4. John Chiles was appointed to the Caroline commission of the peace in June 1789 (*JCSV*, V, 98).

VII. Deposition of Elizabeth Yarbrough
7 May 1790

The deposition of Elizabeth Yarbrough Taken by Consent of parties at the House of James Yarbrough in a Suit depending in the district Court of Fredericksburg between Cornelius McHaney, and Reuben George Exor of Jno. George decd.

This deponent being first Sworn, deposeth and Saith, that She believes that Mrs. McHaney Lived with her father Jno. George about Six years, that before She came there She had frequently Seen a pair of hand Irons there, & that afterwards She Saw another pair, which were Large and appeared new. Which Mrs. McHaney told this deponent was her property, which She had never Seen there before. And further this deponent Saith Not.[1]

her
ELIZA. X YARBROUGH
mark

Caroline To witt,

The above deposition Sworn too, before us this 7th. day of May 1790.

JAMES SUTTON
J CHILES

DS, McHaney v. George, Office of the Clerk, Circuit Court, Fredericksburg, Va. Endorsed on verso: "Eliz. Yarbroughs/Deposition/recd. under Cover sealed."

1. Elizabeth Yarbrough also testified at the trial, and her deposition was therefore not entered as evidence (see Doc. VI, n. 2).

VIII. Notes of Argument
[5 October 1790?]

Gave her a fortune

To build her a house

---

she his child. poverty

Told she left it more destitute
than she found [it]

---

above labor

---

other daughters.

Mrs. McHeny said it was
a gratuity &c witness
thought so

---

attempt the account
by that generous conduct[1]

AD, McHaney v. George, Office of the Clerk, Circuit Court, Fredericksburg, Va. In JM's hand. Endorsed on wrapper by Edmund Randolph, "Mchaney vs. George's exr."; second endorsement by clerk reads: "1791 Apl. Court/Jud. Accd. to award." Printed in *PJM*, II, 91, under date of 4 May 1791 but here dated according to date of first trial.

1. The case went to the jury on 5 Oct. 1790. The following day the jury reported that it was unable to reach a verdict, and the case was continued to

the next term. JM may have used these notes at the second trial and arbitration in May 1791 (Frbg. Dis. Ct. Law Ord. A, 1789–93, 162–63, 169, 235–36).

IX. Order of Reference
5 May 1791

Fredericksburg District Court May 5th. 1791

Cornelius McHaney and wife . . . . . . Plaintiffs vs. Rueben George Exor. John George decd. Defendant	In Case

By consent of the parties by their Attornies all matters in difference between them are referred to the final determination of James Blair James Somerville and William Glassell: Gents whose award thereupon is to be made the Judgment of the Court and the same is ordered accordingly.[1]

Teste

JNO. CHEW CDC[2]

ADS, McHaney v. George, Office of the Clerk, Circuit Court, Fredericksburg, Va. Attached to arbitrator's award (Doc. X).

1. The court ordered the dispute to be referred to arbitration after a second jury was unable to reach a verdict. The arbitrators were prominent citizens of Fredericksburg (Frbg. Dis. Ct. Law Ord. A, 1789–93, 235–36; *VMHB*, XXX [1922], 68; S. J. Quinn, *The History of the City of Fredericksburg, Virginia* [Richmond, 1908], 336; Hutchinson, *Madison Papers*, XIII, 137 n. 3).

2. John Chew, Jr., clerk of the Fredericksburg District Court, was also clerk of the Fredericksburg Hustings Court (Quinn, *History of Fredericksburg*, 130).

X. Award
6 May 1791

In obedience to the annexed order of the Honorable Fredg. district Court having on the 5th. Inst. attended at the House of Mr. David Blair.[1] Where Cornelius McHaney & Reuben George Parties in the suit appeard before us, & where they produced their evidences, & we heard their testimony on Oath and examined sundry papers shewn to us by the said parties, to elucidate and explain all matters in difference between them, and having maturely deliberated thereon do

Award that the said Reuben George as Executor of John George decd. shall pay to the said McHaney the sum of seven pounds Current money,[2] and it appearing to us that it is a vexatious suit we do further Award that each of the parties pay their own Costs. Given under our hands and seals this sixth day of may 1791.[3]

James Somerville [L.S.]
James Blair [L.S.]
Wm: Glassell [L.S.]

DS, McHaney v. George, Office of the Clerk, Circuit Court, Fredericksburg, Va. Follows immediately below annexed order of reference (Doc. IX); endorsed by John Chew: "Recd. under cover/sealed May 6th. 1791."

1. David Blair was a Fredericksburg merchant (William Armstrong Crozier, ed., *Virginia County Records: Spotsylvania County, 1721–1800* [New York, 1905], 425, 494).

2. This sum evidently represents the value of the four head of cattle (see Doc. IV).

3. The court on this day ordered judgment according to the award (Frbg. Dis. Ct. Law Ord. A, 1789–93, 246).

3. Payne v. Walden's Executor

1789–1795

I. Declaration, ca. October 1789
II. Pleas, March 1790
III. Special Verdict, 6 October 1791
IV. Argument in the Court of Appeals, 17 November 1794
V. Certification of Judgment, 2 May 1795

Editorial Note

This is one of a handful of Marshall cases that can be documented at both the trial and appellate level, the case file in this instance being supplemented by a published report of the appeal. Because *Payne* v. *Walden's Executor* presented an unresolved question of law, Marshall and his opposing counsel agreed before the trial to proceed on the basis of a "special verdict" (Document III). Unlike a general verdict, in which the jury determined the facts and then applied the law to those facts pursuant to the court's instructions, a special verdict limited jury participation to fact-finding alone. The court rather than the jury applied the law to the facts as stated in the special verdict and gave its judgment accordingly.

In Virginia, St. George Tucker noted, "special verdicts are the practice constantly in difficult cases." They facilitated an appeal to the Court of Appeals for definitive resolution of disputes in which the applicable law was doubtful. By stating the naked facts uncolored by the trial court's understanding of the law, special verdicts also obviated the need for a new trial in the event the appellate court disagreed with the trial court's interpretation of the governing law. In form a special verdict appeared to come from the jury, but the statement of facts was actually drawn up by counsel under the court's supervision. The jury participated only to the extent of deciding facts in dispute. In Virginia if the parties agreed on all the facts and recourse to a jury was unnecessary, counsel drafted and signed a "case agreed." Like a special verdict, the case agreed became part of the record, which enabled a dissatisfied litigant to bring an appeal by means of a writ of error.[1]

John Walden, Marshall's client, was sued as executor of Charles Walden. An executor (and an administrator of an intestate) assumed large responsibility. He had to make an inventory of the estate, collect the goods and chattels inventoried, sell so much of the estate as necessary to pay the debts and legacies, and distribute the remainder to the residuary legatees or next of kin. He was personally liable for waste, mismanagement, or negligence committed in the performance of his duties. In discharging his responsibilities, the executor at common law had at his disposal only the personal estate of the decedent. He was chargeable for the "assets," that is, whatever could be converted into money from the sale of the personal estate. He acted as a trustee of the assets for the benefit of the creditors of the estate. The executor could not sell the real estate to pay debts unless so directed by the will.[2]

After Charles Walden died in 1777, John Walden sold the personal estate, exclusive of slaves, which together with a quantity of paper money belonging to the testator became the fund for discharging the debts of the estate. Pursuant to a county court order, the executor then distributed the remaining property, consisting of slaves, to the widow and three children. To pay a bond debt owing to Daniel Payne (the plaintiff in this case), the executor twice offered paper money, which the creditor refused. Except for this paper currency, which subsequently became worthless by depreciation, no assets remained to satisfy this debt.

Payne apparently sued the estate of Charles Walden as the first step toward establishing the personal liability of the executor. He could not sustain an action against the executor personally until he first obtained a judgment against the estate and sued out execution against the decedent's goods. Payne challenged the propriety of John Walden's delivery of the slaves to the legatees before all the estate debts had been paid. Had the executor acted negligently in this regard? In the Court of Appeals this question provoked an inquiry into the nature of slave property in Virginia. Were slaves to be regarded as real or personal property? Under Virginia law an executor had no power to sell slaves except in payment of the testator's debts, and then only if the personal estate was insufficient for the purpose. Did this mean that slaves were assets in the hands of the executor, essentially no different from other personal estate? Other laws seemed to place slaves in the category of real property, not subject to the executor's broad powers of disposal.[3] As counsel for Walden, Marshall argued that slaves should be treated essentially as realty, liable for the payment of debts only if there was a deficiency of the personal estate. In this case, he contended, the personal estate was sufficient to discharge the debts and therefore the executor's distribution of the slaves was proper.

1. Tucker, *Blackstone's Commentaries*, III, 377 and n. 31; H. St. G. Tucker, *Commentaries on Virginia Laws*, II, Bk. 3, 300; Martin P. Burks, *Pleading and*

Practice in Actions at Common Law (Charlottesville, 1913), 531–34; Edith G. Henderson, "The Background of the Seventh Amendment," *Harvard Law Review*, LXXX (1966), 307–10. For an example of a case agreed, see Case No. 11, Doc. III.

2. Tucker, *Blackstone's Commentaries*, II, 507–16.

3. After an exhaustive analysis of this topic in an appendix to his edition of Blackstone, Tucker concluded that it was "difficult to assign to them [slaves] any determinate place, either under the head of real or personal property" (*Blackstone's Commentaries*, II, App., Note E, 73–97 [quotation at 96]). See also the colonial case of Blackwell v. Wilkinson, Jeff. 73 (1768).

I. Declaration
ca. October 1789

⟨Caroline⟩ County to wit.[1]

⟨Daniel Payne⟩ complain⟨s⟩ of ⟨John Walden acting Executor⟩ of ⟨Charles Walden⟩[2] lately deceased in custody &c. of a plea, that ⟨he⟩ render to ⟨him⟩ the just sum of ⟨one hundred & fifty Pounds lawful money of Virginia⟩ which ⟨he⟩ unjustly detain⟨s⟩[3] for that whereas[4] the aforesaid ⟨Charles Walden⟩ in his lifetime, that is to say, on the ⟨twenty ninth⟩ day of ⟨December⟩ in the year of our Lord one thousand seven hundred and ⟨seventy six⟩ the parish of and county aforesaid by his certain writing obligatory, sealed with the seal of the said ⟨Charles Walden⟩ in his lifetime and now here shewed to the court[5] the date whereof is the same day and year, acknowledged himself to be held and firmly bound to the above named ⟨Daniel Payne⟩ in the aforesaid sum of ⟨one hundred & fifty pounds⟩ to be paid to the said plaintiff when afterwards he should be thereto required:[6] Yet the aforesaid ⟨Charles Walden⟩ in his lifetime, and the aforesaid ⟨John Walden or any other person⟩ after the death of the said ⟨Charles Walden⟩ although often thereunto required, have not paid, neither have either of them paid the said sum of ⟨one hundred & fifty Pounds⟩ to the said plaintiff But the said ⟨Charles Walden⟩ in his lifetime and the said defendant after the death of the said ⟨Charles Walden⟩ have here⟨tofore⟩ ⟨refused⟩ to pay that to him, and the said defendant doth still deny and unjustly detain⟨s⟩ it from the said plaintiff, to the damage of the said plaintiff ⟨five⟩ pounds[7] and thereof ⟨he⟩ bring⟨s⟩ suit and so forth.

J. Doe — Buchanan ꝑ Quer.[8]

Pledges &c

R Roe

Printed form, Payne v. Walden's Executor, Office of the Clerk, Circuit Court, Fredericksburg, Va. Blanks filled in; pledges of Doe and Roe added; and signed by plaintiff's attorney Andrew Buchanan. Clerk's endorsements on verso summarize proceedings. Undated but probably filed in Oct. 1789.

1. A writ of capias, dated 3 Aug. 1789, commanded the defendant's appearance at the term commencing 29 Sept. (capias, 3 Aug. 1789, Payne v. Walden's Executor). According to the clerk's endorsement on the verso of the declaration, a conditional judgment was entered against the defendant at the Oct. 1789 rules in the clerk's office. This indicates that the plaintiff had filed his declaration and that the defendant had failed to appear.

A companion case, Allason v. Walden's Executor, in which JM represented the defendant, also began at this time. The facts were the same in both cases, and they proceeded in parallel fashion through this court and the Court of Appeals. JM recorded fees for these cases under date of 1 Oct. 1789 and Nov. 1794, when the appeal was heard (Robinson, *Practice*, I, 169; Allason v. Walden's Executor, Office of the Clerk, Circuit Court, Fredericksburg, Va.; *PJM*, II, 371, 483).

2. Daniel Payne lived in Falmouth, a Stafford County town across the Rappahannock from Fredericksburg. Charles Walden listed his residence as King George County on his bond to Payne, though his will was recorded in Stafford County. He left his estate to his widow Mary and their three children. John Walden, the executor, was apparently a brother of Charles Walden. A resident of Caroline County, he may have been the John Walden who was formerly overseer for Edmund Pendleton (Mays, *Pendleton*, II, 205).

3. The phrase "owes and unjustly detains" signifies that this is an action of debt. The words "owes and" were omitted in this declaration because the action was brought against the executor, who did not originally contract the debt. Because the debt arose from a bond, the action of debt was the only available remedy. Indebitatus assumpsit did not lie for "specialties," or instruments under seal (Blackstone, *Commentaries*, III, 156; Sutton, *Personal Actions*, 48, 97).

4. Following the introduction, the declaration in debt on a bond proceeded immediately to the statement of the contract. It differed from the declaration in assumpsit by omitting the consideration on which the contract was founded. Consideration was presumed in contracts under seal (Chitty, *Pleading*, I, 311).

5. This is the plaintiff's formal *profert in curia* ("he produces in court") of the bond, or "writing obligatory," signifying that he is prepared to give his adversary a hearing of the instrument or inspection of it before trial.

6. The bond is in the form of a conditional obligation, binding Walden to pay the penal sum of £150, to be discharged on the condition that he pay £75 (bond, 29 Dec. 1776, Payne v. Walden's Executor). The £75 was the real sum owed, even though the action was brought for the penal amount. On conditional bonds see Case No. 9, editorial note.

7. In debt on a bond, damages were nominal and the space was either left blank or filled in with a small sum.

8. The attorney *pro querente* ("for the plaintiff") was Andrew Buchanan of

Stafford County. He also represented the plaintiff in the companion case, Allason v. Walden's Executor (see *PJM*, II, 39 n. 6).

II. Pleas

March 1790

And the said John Walden exr of Charles Walden by John Marshall his Attorney comes and defends the force Injury and damages and whatever else he ought to defend, when and where the Court will consider thereof, and craves Oyer of the said writing Obligatory, and it is read to him &c. he also craves Oyer of the condition thereof which is read to him in these words &c. which being read and heard,[1] the said John saith that the said Plt ought not to have or maintain his said action against him because he saith, that he paid the said sum of £75 in the condition of the said writing Obligatory before the bringing of this Suit, together with all Interest due thereon, according to the Act in that case made and provided, and this he is ready to verefy wherefore he prays Judgment &c.[2] And the said John with the leave of the Court to plead several matters,[3] for further plea saith that the said Plaintiff ought not to have or maintain his said action thereof against him because he saith, that at the time of the said Plaintiffs Issuing the Original writ in this Suit against him to wit: the 3rd of August 1789[4]—he the said John had fully administerd all the goods and Chattles which were of the said Charles Walden his Testator at the time of his death in his hands to be administerd except the sum of four hundred & thirty pounds paper money of the value of   specie;[5] and that he the said John hath not, nor at the day of the said Plaintiffs taking out his said writ, or at any time since had any Goods or Chattles which were the said Charles Walden at the time of his death in his hands unadministerd Except the sum aforesaid whereby the said John is not able to pay to the said Plaintiff his said debt, and this he is ready to verify whereupon he prays Judgmt &c.[6] And the said John with the Leave of the Court for further plea saith that the said Plaintiff ought not to have or maintain his said action thereof against him because he saith that the non payment of the debt in the condition of the said writing Obligatory mentioned is owing to the said Plaintiff and this he is ready to verify wherefore and by Virtue of the Act Intitled "An Act directing the mode of adjusting and Settling the payment of certain Debts and Contracts and for other purposes" In that case made and provided he prays the Court to award such Judgment as to them shall appear Just and Equitable.[7]

MARSHALL for Deft.

DS, Payne v. Walden's Executor, Office of the Clerk, Circuit Court, Fredericksburg, Va. Document, including signature, is in unknown hand except for interlined phrase in JM's hand (see n. 5). Undated but filed at Mar. 1790 rules according to clerk's endorsement on verso of declaration (Doc. I).

1. In debt on a bond the defendant was allowed *oyer* ("hearing") of the instrument before pleading. This was a means of having the bond entered verbatim on the record, so that the defendant could take advantage of any variance between the declaration and the deed produced. Because the declaration recited only the penal amount of the bond, the defendant had to demand oyer of the condition as well if he intended (as JM did here) to plead performance, that is, payment of the principal sum. In this case, as shown by the clerk's endorsement on the declaration, JM "craved oyer" at the Nov. 1789 meeting of the rules, when he first made an appearance for the defendant. The conditional judgment that had been entered against his client at the Oct. 1789 rules was then set aside (Robinson, *Practice*, I, 159, 209; Shipman, *Common-Law Pleading*, 482–83; see Doc. I, n. 1).

2. The conclusion by common verification—"and this he is ready to verify"—identifies this as a special plea, one that introduced new facts to avoid liability. JM chose to plead specially rather than directly to deny the allegation in the declaration. In debt on a bond the direct denial or general issue was *non est factum* ("not his deed"), that is, the defendant denied that he had executed the instrument mentioned in the declaration. This allowed only a few defenses and in Virginia was rarely pleaded because it had to be verified by affidavit. Instead of pleading the general issue, the defendant alleged payment of the money due by the condition to show that the bond was void. Payment was thus a special plea of "confession and avoidance" (Case No. 1, Doc. VIII, n. 1).

At common law payment of the conditional amount was not allowed as a defense without a formal acquittance, or release under seal. By the statute of 4 and 5 Anne (1705) payment without an acquittance could be pleaded if at any time before the action was brought the debtor paid the principal and interest. In Virginia payment was the usual plea in actions brought on bonds for the payment of money. It was routinely pleaded when the debtor had no real defense but was trying to gain time or set aside an office judgment. Although here and in Case No. 9 payment was a special plea, the Virginia Court of Appeals in 1790 held that this plea amounted to a general issue on the ground that it expressly denied the plaintiff's allegation of nonpayment in the declaration. It then became possible in Virginia courts to plead payment as a general issue, as JM did in his British debt cases (Tucker, *Blackstone's Commentaries*, III, 306 n. 20; Robinson, *Practice*, I, 208–9; H. St. G. Tucker, *Commentaries on Va. Laws*, II, Bk. 3, 104–5; Baker, *English Legal History*, 180; Simpson, *Common Law of Contract*, 122; Hening, *Statutes*, IV, 359–60 [reenacting the English statute of 4 and 5 Anne, c. 16, sec. 12]; Henderson v. Southall, 4 Call 371 [1790]). See Case No. 12, Doc. V, for JM's pleading of payment as a general issue.

3. At common law a defendant who had several possible defenses to a count in the declaration could select only one on which to rest his case. This rule against multiplicity in pleading was altered by the statute of 4 and 5

Anne, c. 16, sec. 4, reenacted in Virginia in 1732, which allowed the defendant "with the leave of the court, [to] plead as many several matters, as he shall think necessary for his defence." In 1788 the Virginia assembly reenacted this provision, adding a phrase permitting the "several matters" to be of law or fact. This act also dropped the expression "with the leave of the court." The intent of the addition was to allow the defendant to plead or to demur. The purpose of the omission presumably was to dispense with the necessity of applying for a rule of the court to plead several matters (Shipman, *Common-Law Pleading*, 418–20; Hening, *Statutes*, IV, 324; XII, 745; Robinson, *Practice*, I, 217–18).

4. This is the date of the capias.

5. The words "except the sum . . . specie" were interlined by JM.

6. This is also a special plea, one allowed to the defendant in his capacity as executor. He could plead *plene administravit* ("fully administered") or, as here, *plene administravit praeter* ("fully administered, except") (Chitty, *Pleading*, III, 970–71; H. St. G. Tucker, *Commentaries on Va. Laws*, II, Bk. 3, 115).

7. This special plea interposed the fifth section of the act of Nov. 1781 establishing a scale of depreciation for paper money that circulated in Virginia between Jan. 1777 and Dec. 1781: "That where a suit shall be brought for the recovery of a debt, and it shall appear that the value thereof hath been tendered and refused; or where it shall appear that the non-payment thereof is owing to the creditor; or where other circumstances arise which, in the opinion of the court before whom the cause is brought to issue, would render a determination agreeable to the above table unjust; in either case it shall and may be lawful for the court to award such judgment as to them shall appear just and equitable" (Hening, *Statutes*, X, 473).

According to the clerk's endorsements on the verso of the declaration, the case continued at the rules until Nov. 1790, when the plaintiff made a general replication and issue was joined. No replication seems to have been filed, however, and JM in the appeal objected that issue had not been properly joined (see Doc. IV).

III. Special Verdict
6 October 1791

Daniel Payne
agst
Walden } in debt, Special Verdict

We of the Jury find that Charles Walden being possessed of sundry Slaves and other personal estate, departed this life on the 28th. day of September 1777 having first made his last will and testament, and thereof appointed John Walden the deffendant & other executors of whom the said John Walden alone qualified, and undertook the execution thereof.[1]

We find that the said defendant on the 27th. day of November 1778 had the said estate duly appraised, according to law, and at the same time proceeded to make sale of the whole personal estate, except slaves, having by advertisement in the public gazette previously advertised the said sale, and having then also call'd upon the creditors of the said charles Walden deceased to come in, make known their demands and receive payment.[2]

We find that the delay in proving the will, in the said appraisement, and the said sale, was owing to the prevalence of the small pox in the County of Stafford at that time, where the said Charles Walden resided, where he died of that disorder and where his property lay.

We find that the defendant had due notice of the debt in the declaration mentioned and offered to pay the amount thereof including interest to the plaintiff in the then circulating paper money, first on the first day of January 1778 and afterwards in November 1778 and that the plaintiff at each time refused to receive the money.

We find that the non payment of the debt in the declaration mentioned, has been owing to the creditor, the same having been as aforesaid Offered to and refused by him.

We find that the deffendant sold off as aforesaid sufficient of the estate of the said Charles Walden deceased, together with the money in the house and outstanding debts, to discharge his debts.

We find that on the motion of Samuel Frinsley, one of the Legatees under the said will an order was made by Stafford County Court in September 1778 directing the estate of the said Charles Walden to be divided according to his will, which said order we find in these words, Stafford County &ct.[3]

We find that the said Daniel Payne who was appointed by the said order to divide the said estate, is the plaintiff in this suit.

We find that in pursuance of the sd. order, the said estate of the said Charles Walden, not sold and disbursed in the payment of debts, or offered to his creditors, was accordingly divided on the 27th day of november 1778, which division we find in these words, pursuant &c.[4]

We find that the said property was accordingly delivered at or soon after the division aforesaid, to the several persons therein mentioned.[5]

It does not appear that the deffendant did take any bond from either of the said persons for the return of the said property or any part thereof, in case future debts shou'd appear against the sd. estate.

We find that Simon Frensley one of the legatees in the said will mentioned, has sold his part of the estate of the said Charles Walden & is insolvent.[6]

We find that the money so offered by the defendant to the plaintiff, was of the paper money then in circulation, and was liable and subject to the law for calling in and redeeming the said paper money at one for a thousand.[7]

We find that the defendant received of the same kind of money, to a larger amount than the plaintiff's demand, for debts contracted to his said testator in or before the year 1776.

We find that the defendant divested himself of the whole of the estate of the said Charles Walden deceased, before the bringing of this suit, in the payment of debts, and in obedience to the order and division aforesaid the monies excepted so offer'd by him to creditors amounting to £427 paper money.

We find that John Walden a legatee in the said will and division mentioned,[8] and the testators widow, have married and removed to parts of the State very distant from the defendant and carried their shares of the said Charles Walden's estate with them.

We find that the defendant has not paid the debt in the declaration mentioned.

If upon the whole matter the law be for the plaintiff, Then we find for him the debt in the declaration mentioned, to be discharged by payment of the principal & interest or so much thereof as to the court shall appear just and equitable, Otherwise We find for the Defendant.[9]

STEPHEN LACOSTE f.[10]

DS, Payne v. Walden's Executor, Office of the Clerk, Circuit Court, Fredericksburg, Va. Undated, but see copy under date of 6 Oct. 1791, Frbg. Dis. Ct. Law Ord. A, 1789–93, 317–18.

1. John Walden qualified as executor at the Aug. 1778 court of Stafford County. Lewis Walden, brother of Charles, was also named as an executor, but he refused to serve (Stafford County Court orders [copies], Aug. 1778, Sept. 1790, Payne v. Walden's Executor).

2. The estate inventory and appraisement were recorded in Stafford court on 14 Sept. 1778 (copy, Payne v. Walden's Executor). A notice in the *Virginia Gazette* (Dixon and Hunter), 6 Nov. 1778, announced that the sale would take place on 25 Nov.

3. The order appointed four men to divide the estate, one of whom was the plaintiff Daniel Payne. The given name of Frinsley as stated in the order was "Symon" (copy, Payne v. Walden's Executor). In a subsequent section of the special verdict he is referred to as "Simon Frensley." He was married to a daughter of Charles Walden.

4. Copy, ibid.

5. This property consisted of twelve slaves. The widow, Mary Walden, re-

ceived four for her dower; the rest went to the three children, George Walden, John Walden, and Elizabeth Frensley.

6. The slaves bequeathed to Elizabeth Frensley were sold in execution of a judgment obtained by William Allason against Simon Frensley (special verdict, 6 Oct. 1791, Allason v. Walden's Executor, Frbg. Dis. Ct. Law Ord. A, 1789–93, 319–20).

7. The legislature in Nov. 1781 passed "An act for calling in and funding the paper money of this state" at the rate of 1,000 to 1 (Hening, *Statutes*, X, 456).

8. This person is not to be confused with the John Walden who was executor and defendant in this case.

9. The cause continued to the next term for argument on the questions of law. The court postponed a decision until 5 Oct. 1793, when it gave judgment for the plaintiff in this and in the companion case. Walden then appealed both judgments (Frbg. Dis. Ct. Law Ord. A, 1789–93, 317–20, 529).

10. The "f." stands for "foreman."

IV. Argument in the Court of Appeals
17 November 1794

MARSHALL for the appellant.[1] I shall insist first, that slaves are not assets in the hands of executors, if the personal estate be sufficient to pay the debts. If so, then secondly, that the defendant has fully administered the assets. Thirdly, if these points be against the appellant, still the court may give an equitable judgment.

1st, Slaves by the act of Assembly passed in 1705, C. 3, are declared to be *real* estate with certain exceptions;[2] and tho' some of the exceptions render them like to chattels, yet, there is no law which declares them to be assets, nor can the executor dispose of them as he may of the personal estate, for the payment of debts, unless there be a deficiency of the latter; in that case only can he sell slaves. The laws passed in 1727, and in 1748 were made, because slaves having been declared to be real estate, could not, as such, have been applied by the executor to the payment of debts, and the legislature, in these laws, have been carefull to distinguish this species of property from chattels.[3] If we refer to other laws, we shall find, that slaves are always contemplated as a species of property totally unlike to personal estate. Thus, in the law respecting distributions, slaves are not comprehended under the words *goods, chattels* and *personal* estate.[4] Again, by the same law, the executors or administrators *may* distribute the personal estate after nine months from the death of the testator, taking bond and security to refund.[5] But by the act of 1748, C. 3, § 30, the slaves of a decedent are to continue on the land to finish the crop (where the testator or intestate dies between the 1st of March, and the 25th of December,) until the latter period, when they are to be delivered to those having a right to them, well cloathed at the expence of the estate, and their crops are declared to be assets.[6] Now mark the difference between slaves and personal estate. The latter *may* be distributed at one time, the former *shall* be delivered at another; in the latter, security to refund may be required, but not in the former. Why? Because they are not assets, nor as such liable to pay the debts, unless the personal estate be deficient. The obvious conclusion is, that this sort of property is made an auxiliary fund for the payment of debts, where the assets are insufficient, and the executors are empowered by a special law, to sell them *for that purpose only*. The executor in this case had no power to retain possession of the slaves, there being a sufficiency of personal estate, 1st, because the law not only imposed it as a duty upon him to deliver them up, but the judgment of a court having competent jurisdiction compelled him to do so,[7] and this order, he was bound to obey, without a power given to him of protecting himself, by taking security to refund. Let it also be remarked, that it would be exercising an unnecessary, as well as an unjust rigor against the executor, to charge him with a devastavit,[8] when the legatees may in a court of equity be resorted to. 2 *Vern.* 75, 205—1 *Vern.* 94, 162—2 *Ventr.* 360, 358—2 *P. Will.* 447.[9] Should it be contended, that an executor before he delivers or pays a legacy, may demand security to refund, and that if he neglect to require such a security, he cannot compel the legatee to refund, I answer: 1st, that the cases on this head relate to personal estate only, which are always assets, and liable to pay debts; whereas, slaves are real estate, and are liable to pay debts, only as an auxiliary fund; that the executor is obliged to deliver them up within a limited time, without security, unless there be a deficiency of the personal estate. 2dly, The delivery in this case was not voluntary.

2d point. The verdict finds, that all the estate hath been administered except the slaves which were delivered to the commissioners, to be divided under the order of court, and £427 paper money. Now this money was either funded, or it was not. If the former, it remains a debt due from the public (worth according to the scale 8/6 specie) payable at a future day, as the public acts of the legislature prove.[10] If the latter, it is taken out of circulation by an act of the government, and thereby deprived of all its value. In either point of view, it forms no part of the *assets in the hands of the executor*, being a debt due and uncollected. 2 *Bac. ab.* 417.[11]

To charge the executor with a devastavit, he should be guilty of mismanagement, misapplication, fraud, or of paying legacies when the assets are insufficient to pay the debts. 2 *Bac. ab.* 435.[12] The executor in this case did not mismanage, nor misapply the assets, by selling the personal estate and offering the money in discharge of the debts, because this was a part of his duty. Neither has he left debts unpaid, by disposing of the *assets* to legatees, if I am right upon the first point. If then, the executor is subject to no blame for delivering up the slaves under all the circumstances of the case, there is no possible ground left to charge him, unless indeed he can be chargeable with the consequences of a legislative act which destroyed in his hands the funds reserved for paying the debt; an idea too monstrous to be contended for.

3d point. The issue upon the third plea is with the defendant, the jury having found, that *the non-payment was owing to the creditor*; and therefore, the court may give an *equitable judgment* on the case. I will not repeat all the equitable circumstances which appear to favor the executor, believing that no case ever exhibited more than the present. The case of Kenner and Turner in the old General Court,[13] was not so strong in favor of the defendant as the present, for in that, the court interfered, even after a verdict rendered upon the plea of payment. The case was, that Turner, who was indebted to Kenner, *offered to pay the debt*, (without making *a legal tender*)[14] which was refused. The court scaled the debt as of the day when the offer was made, because Turner, holding the money in his own right, was presumed to have afterwards made use of it, it not being improper in him to do so; it was therefore thought just, that he should sustain the loss by subsequent depreciation. But in this case, *the executor*, acting as a *trustee*, ought not to be presumed to have used the money, because it was improper that he should have done it, and therefore, it would be unjust to make him bear any part of the loss by depreciation, but it should be born by the creditor, for whose use the trustee held it.[15]

Marshall in reply. It must be admitted, that the decision of the County Court was not made upon proceedings regularly conducted; yet as that court had *jurisdiction over the subject*, the judgment standing in force and unreversed, was obligatory upon the executor.[16]

It is true, that the 2d section of the act of 1781, is confined to contracts made after the 1st day of January 1777,[17] but it does not follow that the law is confined entirely to contracts entered into between the periods mentioned in that section. The third section (since it declares, that execution shall not issue upon *any judgment* theretofore obtained, before December 1783;) obviously is not, and why should the 5th section, which is as general as language could make it, be restrained in its operation, when the mischief intended to be remedied, is the same? If it were just, that an equitable judgment should be given upon a contract made on the 1st of January 1777, where the non-payment was owing to the creditor, is it not as much so, if it had been made on the last day of December 1776? And since the words of the 5th clause of the law, do not expressly confine the cases to particular contracts, the court will so construe the act, as to extend the relief to every case coming within the mischief.[18]

An objection which was over-looked in opening the cause, may here be mentioned; it is, that no issue is made up. The pleas conclude with an averment as it was proper they should, to which there is no replication. The case of Stevens and Taliafero (ante vol. I, page 155) is in point.[19]

Printed, Bushrod Washington, *Reports of Cases Argued and Determined in the Court of Appeals of Virginia*, II (Richmond, 1799), 2–5, 6–8.

1. The appeal was styled Walden v. Payne. JM recorded a fee of £10 for arguing the appeals on behalf of Walden against Payne and Allason. Both appeals were heard together on 17 Nov. 1794. John Walden died pending the appeals, which were revived in the name of his executor, John Taylor (*PJM*, II, 483; Va. Ct. Ap. Ord. Bk. III, 36, 38–39).

2. "An act declaring the Negro, Mulatto, and Indian slaves within this dominion, to be real estate" (Hening, *Statutes*, III, 333).

3. The 1727 act to explain and amend the 1705 act declared that "no executor or administrator hath or shall have any power to sell or dispose of any slave or slaves of his testator or intestate, except for the paying and satisfying the just debts of such testator or intestate, and then only, where there is not sufficient of the personal estate of such testator or intestate, to satisfy and pay such debts." This provision was repeated in the 1748 act concerning probates of wills and administration of intestates' estates (ibid., IV, 224; V, 464).

4. The 1748 act "for the distribution of Intestates estates" declared "that after debts, funeral, and other just expences first paid and allowed, the surplus of all and singular the goods, chattels, and personal estate, other than slaves, of every person dying intestate, shall be distributed amongst the wife and children" (ibid., V, 444).

5. Ibid., 448.

6. JM here summarized sections 31 and 32 of the 1748 act concerning the probate of wills (ibid., 464–65).

7. JM alluded to the Sept. 1778 order of the Stafford County Court (Doc. III and n. 3).

8. An executor or administrator charged with a *devastavit* ("he has wasted") was liable to heirs, creditors, or legatees for losses resulting from his waste or mismanagement of the assets of the decedent's estate. To establish the executor's personal liability, the creditor first had to obtain a judgment against the estate and sue out an execution. Upon a return of *nulla bona* ("no goods"), he could then bring an action of debt suggesting a devastavit. If he succeeded in proving waste, the creditor could then bring suit upon the executor's administration bond. See JM's argument in the 1791 case of Braxton v. Winslow (4

Call 312–14); see also Robinson, *Practice*, I, 56–57; H. St. G. Tucker, *Commentaries on Va. Laws*, I, Bk. 2, 416, 455.

9. Stiddolph v. Leigh, 2 Vern. 75, 23 Eng. Rep. 658 (Ch. 1688); Newman v. Barton, 2 Vern. 205, 23 Eng. Rep. 733 (Ch. 1690); Noell v. Robinson, 1 Vern. 94, 23 Eng. Rep. 336 (Ch. 1682); Anonimous, 1 Vern. 162, 23 Eng. Rep. 388 (Ch. 1683); Hodges v. Waddington, 2 Vent. 360, 86 Eng. Rep. 485 (Ch. 1683); Noell v. Robinson, 2 Vent. 358, 86 Eng. Rep. 484 (Ch. 1682); Edward v. Freeman, 2 P. Wms. 447, 24 Eng. Rep. 807 (Ch. 1727). The general rule arising from these cases was that a creditor could recover against a legatee in a court of equity except where the executor had voluntarily paid the legacy.

10. Using the scale established by the 1781 act, JM divided £427 by 1,000 to arrive at the sum of 8s. 6d. On delivering their paper money to the state treasury, holders were to receive a loan office certificate for the specie value, redeemable on or before 1 Dec. 1790 and to bear 6 percent interest (Hening, *Statutes*, X, 456–57).

11. Bacon, *Abridgment* (5th ed.), II, 417: "But Debts due to the Testator . . . are not Assets till they are recovered by the Executor."

12. Ibid., 435: "Legacies are properly recoverable in the Spiritual Court, yet if an Executor pays Legacies before Debts, tho' by Simple Contract, it is a *Devastavit* in him."

13. This was an unreported case, which also apparently involved the application of the 1781 act establishing a scale of depreciation for paper money.

14. In making a legal tender, as distinguished from an offer to pay the debt, the debtor actually produced the money for the creditor's acceptance at the time of the offer. A tender and refusal did not discharge the debt but operated to extinguish the interest from the time of the tender. Although Walden's executor twice offered to pay the debt in paper money, he evidently did not actually produce the money so as to make his offer a lawful tender (Hening, *Statutes*, IX, 298).

15. Andrew Ronald, for the appellee Payne, replied to JM. He contended that slaves in most respects resembled personal chattels. Although an executor could not sell them unless the personal estate was deficient, the same was true of specific legacies, which nevertheless were still regarded as assets in his hands (2 Wash. 5–6).

16. Ronald dismissed the county court order for dividing the estate as an extrajudicial proceeding, one that the executor was not bound to carry out until all the estate debts had been paid.

17. Hening, *Statutes*, X, 471. Since Charles Walden executed his bond to Payne on 29 Dec. 1776, Ronald maintained that the 1781 act did not apply to this case.

18. Ibid., 472, 473–74. JM attempted to exploit the fact that the time period was stated only by way of preamble to the second section and therefore should apply only to that section.

19. Stevens v. Taliaferro, 1 Wash. 155 (1793). In this case the plaintiff's replication concluded with a verification; the record then stated "and thereupon an issue was joined by the parties." The court held that since there was no rejoinder, issue was not properly joined and the judgment below was

therefore erroneous. As counsel for the losing appellant in this case, JM contended that "the informality in joining the issue" was cured after verdict by the statute of jeofails and the verdict should not be set aside on that account (1 Wash. 156). For the Virginia statute of jeofails, see Hening, *Statutes*, XIII, 36–38.

Ronald replied that this objection could not be raised after verdict. On 20 Nov. Judge Peter Lyons delivered the opinion of the court affirming the judgment of the district court. Adopting Ronald's reasoning, Lyons maintained that slaves were by nature chattels and assets in the hands of the executor. It was the executor's responsibility, therefore, to demand security to refund from the legatees before delivering the slaves. The executor could also have protected himself, said the judge, by making a legal tender of the paper money. Whether this inattentiveness amounted to a devastavit was "a premature enquiry at this time; when a suit is brought suggesting a devastavit, that question may properly be decided" (Va. Ct. Ap. Ord. Bk. III, 38–39; 2 Wash. 7–8).

V. Certification of Judgment

2 May 1795

Daniel Payne by his Attorney this day produced to the Court the transcript of a Judgment of the Court of Appeals in the words following to wit;[1] Virginia to wit At a Court of Appeals held at the Capital in Richmond the 20th. day of November 1794

John Taylor executor of John Walden who was acting Executor of Charles Walden deceased Pltf against Daniel Payne Deft.	}	Upon a revived appeal from a Judgment obtained by the deft.

against the said John Walden in his lifetime as Executor of the said Charles Walden decd. in the District Court held in Fredericksburg the fifth day of October 1793 for one hundred and fifty pounds & Costs to be levied of the goods and chattles of the said Charles Walden decd. in the hands of the said John Walden to be adminerstered, if so much thereof he had, but if not, then the Costs to be levied of his proper goods & Chattles, but to be discharged by the Payment of Seventy five pounds with Interest thereon to be computed after the rate of five per Cent per annum from the 29th. day of December 1776 till payment & the Costs.

This day came the parties by their counsel and the transcript of the Record of the Judgment aforesaid, having been maturely Consid-

ered, the Court is of opinion, that there is no error in the said Judgment, therefore It is considered that the same be affirmed & that the Deft recover against the Plaintiff damages according to Law for retarding the Execution thereof;[2] and his Costs by him about his defence in this behalf expended, to be levied of the goods and Chattles of the said Charles Walden decd. in the hands of the Plt to be administered if so much thereof he hath, but if not, then of the goods and Chattles of the said John Walden decd. in the hands of the said Plt to be administered, if so much thereof he hath, which is Ordered to be Certified to the said District Court,
Costs in the Court of Appeals 89 Cents,

A Copy teste J BROWN C.C.

Therefore It is considered by the Court that the Judgment aforesaid of the Court be affirmed, & that the said Daniel Payne recover against the said John Taylor exor. of John Walden who was acting Exor of Charles Walden decd. Damages according to Law, for retarding the Execution thereof, and his Costs by him about his defence in the said Court of Appeals expended, to be levied of the goods and chattels of the said Charles Walden deceased in the hands of the Plt to be administered if so much thereof he hath, but if not then of the Goods and Chattels of the said John Walden deceased in the hands of the said Plt. to be administered If so much thereof he hath.[3]

Copy, Fredericksburg District Court Law Orders B, 1794–98, 112–13 (microfilm), Vi. In margin opposite entry clerk noted costs and damages.

1. The clerk of the Court of Appeals was to certify the affirmance or reversal of the judgment to the court below (Hening, *Statutes*, IX, 524).

2. Where the defendant in any personal action appealed and the judgment was affirmed, damages were assessed at 10 percent per year on the principal sum and costs recovered in the lower court (ibid., XII, 754). In this case the damages in lieu of interest from 5 Oct. 1793 to 20 Nov. 1794 amounted to more than £15.

3. It is not known whether Payne further pursued his remedy by means of an action of debt suggesting a devastavit (Doc. IV, n. 8). He may have reached a private settlement with John Taylor, John Walden's executor.

II. The High Court of Chancery

Editorial Note

The High Court of Chancery was the superior court of equity in Virginia. Created by the constitution of 1776 and organized by a statute of 1777, the court was modeled on the English court of the same name. Until the Revolution there had been no separate equity court in Virginia; the General Court functioned as a tribunal to hear both actions at law and suits in equity. The establishment of a separate court of chancery was no doubt motivated in part by practical considerations. Besides promoting a more efficient dispatch of business, the division of jurisdiction promised to improve the quality of justice by enabling the judges to gain greater mastery of the "principles of adjudication" peculiar to their respective courts. Another likely motive for reform was a concern that blending equity and common law jurisdiction in the same judges was theoretically repugnant. As Marshall explained, "There was an apparent absurdity in seeing the same men revise in the characters of Chancellors the judgements they had themselves renderd as common law judges."[1] The county courts, however, continued to unite law and equity jurisdiction.

The High Court of Chancery originally consisted of three judges, who also sat with the General Court and Admiralty judges as the Court of Appeals. The assembly elected three of the commonwealth's most distinguished lawyers and statesmen as chancellors: Edmund Pendleton, George Wythe, and Robert Carter Nicholas. When Nicholas died in 1780, his place was filled by John Blair, later to be appointed to the federal Supreme Court. In 1788 the legislature created a separate Court of Appeals and reduced the High Court of Chancery to a single judge. Wythe thereafter served as sole chancellor.

Throughout the period of Marshall's practice, equity jurisdiction at the superior level remained centralized in one court sitting in Richmond. In 1792 the assembly conferred a measure of chancery jurisdiction upon the district court judges, empowering them to grant injunctions and to hear suits commencing by injunction. The following year, however, the General Court declared this reform measure to be contrary to the Virginia Constitution. The upshot was the postponement of decentralization until 1802, when the legislature erected three superior courts of chancery sitting in Richmond, Williamsburg, and Staunton.[2]

1. JM to Albert Gallatin, 3 Jan. 1790 (*PJM*, II, 48, 49).

2. Hening, *Statutes*, XIII, 432–33. The case was Kamper v. Hawkins, 1 Va. Cas. 20, an early precedent for judicial review. See Charles T. Cullen, "St. George Tucker and

GEORGE WYTHE

Engraving by J. B. Longacre from John Sanderson, *Biography of the Signers of the Declaration of Independence. Courtesy of Virginia State Library*

Because the dispersal of equity jurisdiction occurred after Marshall quit the bar in 1800, all his cases in the High Court of Chancery were destroyed in the Richmond fire of 1865.[3] (The survival of a significant portion of his common law cases was the happy result of the 1788 reorganization of the General Court.) The four cases presented in this section have been reconstructed from other sources. Transcripts of the records of two of them are in the British debt claims commissions papers at the British Public Record Office (Case Numbers 5 and 7). In the other two, documents generated by the litigation survive in the private papers of the parties (Case Numbers 4 and 6).

Chancellor Wythe ensured the immortality of selected cases in his court by publishing in Richmond in 1795 his *Decisions of Cases in Virginia, by the High Court of Chancery, With Remarks upon Decrees by the Court of Appeals, Reversing some of those Decisions*. The original edition reported forty-five cases decided between May 1788 and September 1794. As suggested by the title, Wythe's publication was motivated by his personal rivalry with Edmund Pendleton, who as president of the Court of Appeals reversed or modified many of the chancellor's decrees. Wythe subsequently published in pamphlet form seven additional cases heard between 1792 and 1799, which were included in an 1852 edition of his chancery decisions. Because it omitted the arguments of attorneys, Wythe's *Decisions* is of limited utility in documenting Marshall's chancery practice.[4] A better glimpse of Marshall as an equity lawyer is provided by the reports of his cases in the Court of Appeals, many of which began as suits in the High Court of Chancery (see Section VI). Marshall's equity practice was not confined to the state courts. A small number of his cases in the U.S. Circuit Court were heard on the chancery side. The few surviving equity pleadings in Marshall's hand can be found in the papers of this court (see Sections III and IV).

When Marshall entered the legal profession in 1780, equity had long since developed into a highly organized and rational system of law that operated as a kind of adjunct, or supplement, to the domi-

---

Law in Virginia, 1772–1804" (Ph.D. diss., University of Virginia, 1971), 120–27, 156–60.

3. In 1802 pending cases in the High Court of Chancery were distributed among the Williamsburg, Richmond, and Staunton superior courts of chancery. The records of the Williamsburg court survived until 1911; the Staunton chancery records are extant. See Case No. 5, editorial note, n. 2; Case No. 6, editorial note, n. 8.

4. JM has been identified from his account book fees as counsel in twenty cases reported by Wythe. One of JM's cases in the High Court of Chancery, Harrison v. Allen (1794), was reported by St. George Tucker. This report, which includes arguments of counsel, is printed in *PJM*, II, 282–89.

nant system of common law. Largely as a result of historical accident, equity in England came to be administered by a separate tribunal, the court of chancery. This court had evolved from the office of the chancellor, the most important royal official, to whom were addressed petitions by litigants unable to obtain justice through the ordinary mechanisms of the common law. As "keeper of the king's conscience" and his delegate in charge of all judicial matters, the chancellor had power to intervene and to see that justice was done in extraordinary cases. Because it offered many procedural advantages, the court of chancery was popular with litigants. By the middle of the fifteenth century it ranked in importance with the common law courts.[5]

At first separated in practice, law and equity became distinguished in theory during the Tudor period. "Equity" stood for the absolute justice that corrects general law in particular cases. It was regarded as a higher law transcending the inflexible rules of the common law. The chancellor decided cases not by fixed rules but according to the dictates of his "conscience," a human reflection of divine justice. Equity was thus discretionary; it proceeded ad hoc from case to case. An equity decree acted upon the person, not the thing or property in dispute. It compelled a person to do something he was bound in conscience to do (convey property, for example) or to refrain from doing something (such as bringing vexatious lawsuits) that was against conscience.

In theory, law and equity coexisted in perfect harmony, but in the sixteenth century open conflict broke out as the two systems vied for supremacy. The controversy reached its climax in 1616, when James I intervened to sustain the jurisdiction of the court of chancery. Thereafter conflict receded as the chancery court shed much of its discretionary character and introduced certainty into its proceedings. By the beginning of the eighteenth century equity had become a regularized system of jurisprudence with its own rules, which became known through the published reports of cases in the court of chancery. The chancellor's "conscience" was no longer his personal sense of justice (which varied, like the size of his foot, from chancellor to chancellor) but a set of known and accepted principles. At midcentury Blackstone could describe equity as "a laboured connected system, governed by established rules, and bound down by precedents." Originating as a remedy of the defects of the common law, equity developed its own peculiar flaws, notably the long delays and enormous expense of proceedings in the court of chancery.[6]

5. Baker, *English Legal History*, 38–41.

6. Ibid., 42–46; Blackstone, *Commentaries*, III, 432. For an excellent brief discussion

The rather unwieldy and highly formalized system of equity that Marshall had to master eventually collapsed of its own weight in the nineteenth century, though many of its principles and procedures survived. Perhaps the most striking characteristic of equity was its power to draw the truth and obtain evidence from the defendant. This power of "discovery," unknown at common law, compelled the defendant to answer upon oath concerning facts or documents within his knowledge that would help to sustain the plaintiff's claim. Discovery served to enforce purely legal rights where there was a defect of evidence. Through this means the court of chancery acquired concurrent jurisdiction with the courts of common law in such matters as account (including, for example, the administration of estates, partnership dealings, mercantile transactions), fraud, mistake, and accident. Equity also afforded unique means of relief that gave courts of chancery concurrent jurisdiction with courts of law over a wide spectrum of cases. A plaintiff at law, for example, could recover money damages, but this might prove to be an inadequate or incomplete remedy. Equity could provide more complete relief by decreeing specific performance of a contract or by compelling a conveyance of property. One of the most important weapons of a court of chancery was the injunction. It prevented a variety of mischiefs and injuries for which the common law remedies were ineffectual. Although there was much overlapping jurisdiction between the two systems, equity had exclusive cognizance of certain kinds of disputes, most importantly those arising upon trusts and mortgages.[7]

A brief sketch of chancery procedure follows, principally to show how it differed from the practice in the courts of common law and to note the most important ways in which Virginia modified or departed from traditional English procedure. As an aspiring practitioner in the High Court of Chancery, Marshall could consult any number of treatises and manuals on English procedure, including those by Joseph Harrison (which he purchased in 1793), Robert Hinde, and John Mitford (Lord Redesdale).[8] His purchase of William Brown's *Reports* showed his intention to keep abreast of the latest decisions of the English High Court of Chancery.[9] Marshall also di-

---

of the evolution of equity jurisdiction in England, see Stanley N. Katz, "The Politics of Law in Colonial America: Controversies over Chancery Courts and Equity Law in the Eighteenth Century," *Perspectives in American History*, V (1971), 258–61.

7. Blackstone, *Commentaries*, III, 436–40. A number of JM's cases in the Court of Appeals dealt with the question of equity jurisdiction. In addition to those included in Sec. VI, see Pryor v. Adams, 1 Call 382 (1798).

8. *PJM*, II, 456. JM cited Harrison in Jones v. Williams and Tomlinson, 1 Wash. 230 (1793).

9. *PJM*, I, 381.

gested the Virginia statutes dealing with the High Court of Chancery, the most important of which were enacted in 1777, 1788, and 1792.[10]

To begin a suit in the court of chancery the plaintiff filed his bill of complaint, which concluded with a request for process of subpoena to issue against the defendant.[11] In Virginia, except where the plaintiff requested an injunction or a writ of *ne exeat* (restraining a person from leaving the country, state, or jurisdiction of the court), the practice was to issue the subpoena before the filing of the bill.[12] Like the common law capias, the subpoena commanded the sheriff to summon the defendant to appear and to answer the complainant's bill under penalty of one hundred pounds (strictly a matter of form). If the defendant did not appear on the day stated in the subpoena, then successive processes of contempt were awarded—attachment, attachment with proclamations, commission of rebellion, search by sergeant at arms, and sequestration of the estate. The complainant's bill, the counterpart of the common law declaration, followed the style of a petition addressed to the chancellor. Like the declaration, the bill was liberally sprinkled with boilerplate phrases, though it narrated the circumstances of the case at greater length and with more concrete detail than did the formulaic common law pleading.

On making his appearance and taking a copy of the bill, the defendant had several means of defense. He could demur, as at common law, admitting the truth of the allegations but denying their sufficiency to maintain the case. If he believed that on the face of the bill there was no sufficient cause of equity shown, the proper course was to demur. If the court sustained the demurrer, the bill was dismissed and the parties were saved the expense of protracted litigation. The defendant could also enter a plea (a special answer) to the bill, denying the jurisdiction of the court, asserting some disability on the plaintiff's part, or showing some matter in bar to the demand for relief. In most instances a defendant did not demur or plead in bar to the whole bill but only to a part. In complicated bills it was not unusual for the defendant to demur to one part, plead to another, and answer the rest.[13]

If he did not demur or plead or was unsuccessful with those defenses, the defendant was compelled to answer under oath the allegations of the bill. Because of the appeal to conscience, which gave credibility to the defendant under oath, the answer was the most

10. Hening, *Statutes*, IX, 389; XII, 464; XIII, 411.

11. This summary of procedure is derived from Blackstone, *Commentaries*, III, 442–55.

12. Tucker, *Blackstone's Commentaries*, III, 443 n. 14.

13. See Case No. 7 for examples of all three defenses to a bill.

distinguishing feature of equity pleading. In the eyes of a court of chancery the defendant was a witness in his own cause, and his answer took the form of a deposition. To the extent that it responded to the bill and plainly denied its allegations, the answer was regarded as evidence of such weight that it could be overthrown only if contradicted by two witnesses or by one witness and corroborating circumstances. The defendant, of course, had to prove any new facts he affirmed in his answer to avoid the plaintiff's allegations.[14]

The usual course at this point was the joining of issues by means of the plaintiff's replication and the defendant's rejoinder. The plaintiff reaffirmed the truth and sufficiency of his bill and denied the truth and sufficiency of the answer; the defendant reaffirmed the direct opposite. As in actions at law, all the pleadings—bill, answer, replication, and rejoinder—were filed at monthly meetings of the rules in the clerk's office.[15]

The next step was to prove facts in issue by examining witnesses. In a common law trial witnesses testified orally in open court before a jury. Testimony in chancery suits was by depositions in writing taken by specially appointed commissioners (usually county magistrates) near the witness's place of residence. The English mode of taking depositions was by written questions, or interrogatories. According to Tucker interrogatories were rarely used in Virginia, "the usual way being to let the witness tell his own story, after which, a few questions, *ore tenus*, are perhaps propounded to him by the parties, or their attornies, and both questions and answers are inserted in the deposition."[16]

After the depositions had been returned to court and inspected by the parties, the cause was placed on the docket for hearing. The court without a jury decided all matters of law and fact arising upon the bill, answer, depositions, and arguments of counsel. The decree of the court was either interlocutory (provisional) or final. In complicated cases, as chancery suits often were, there might be many intervening decrees. For instance, if facts were strongly contested, the court would usually direct an issue to be tried in a court of law before a jury. Also, suits that involved mercantile accounts were referred to a master in chancery, whose report and any exceptions to it (proceedings that could take years) formed the basis of a final decree.[17]

In Virginia the prevailing party could enforce a decree either by process of contempt, as was the practice in England, or by execution, as at common law. Execution to enforce chancery decrees for "lands,

14. H. St. G. Tucker, *Commentaries on Va. Laws*, II, Bk. 3, 502.

15. Hening, *Statutes*, IX, 393; XIII, 417–18.

16. Tucker, *Blackstone's Commentaries*, III, 449 n. 24.

17. See, for example, Case No. 8.

slaves, or money, or things of a similar nature" was first allowed by a statute enacted in 1788.[18] If the decree required the losing party to perform a specific act, enforcement was by the original remedy of attachment for not performing the decree. If successive processes of contempt failed to bring him into custody, then a writ of sequestration against his estate might issue. The aggrieved party could petition for a rehearing or, upon apparent error in judgment or discovery of new evidence, file a bill of review. The last resort was an appeal to the Court of Appeals, which could be taken where the claim was valued at $150 (later reduced to $100) or involved a freehold or franchise.[19]

While Marshall was at the bar, the Virginia General Assembly reformed chancery procedure chiefly by eliminating the delays and consequent accumulation of expense that in England had become a national scandal. Declaring that justice was "greatly delayed by the tedious forms of proceedings," which obliged suitors "to waste much time and expence, to the impoverishment of themselves and the state," the legislature in 1788 substantially abridged English procedure. According to Marshall "great advantages" resulted from this reform: "There have been instances of suits depending for twenty years but under our present regulations a decision woud be had in that court as soon as any other in which there were an equal number of weighty causes."[20]

One major source of delay in English practice was the necessity of resorting to successive processes of contempt to compel the defendant to appear and to answer the bill. If the defendant did not appear or did not file his answer, the complainant had to go through each process from attachment through sequestration before his bill could be taken for confessed, unless the defendant was actually in custody and refused to answer. As early as 1748 Virginia enacted legislation allowing the complainant's bill to be taken for confessed after service of the first process of attachment. The 1788 act went a step further and eliminated the attachment. It declared that if the defendant did not file his answer within three months of the filing of the bill, the plaintiff could "proceed to take his bill for confessed, and proceed in the same manner as in the case of an attachment returned executed." This provision worked a hardship on defendants in remote parts of the state, however, and in 1790 the legislature reinstated the attachment.[21]

18. Hening, *Statutes*, XII, 465.

19. Ibid., IX, 523–24; XIII, 406; Shepherd, *Statutes*, I, 302; Tucker, *Blackstone's Commentaries*, III, 453 n. 33, 454 n. 35; Robinson, *Practice*, II, 411–13.

20. Hening, *Statutes*, XII, 464; JM to Albert Gallatin, 3 Jan. 1790 (*PJM*, II, 49–50).

21. Joseph Harrison, *The Practice of the Court of Chancery* . . . (1st Am. ed.; 2 vols.; Philadelphia, 1807), I, 168, 203–6; Hening, *Statutes*, IV, 189; V, 485; VI, 346; IX, 391–92; XII, 464; XIII, 122.

The act of 1788 further expedited chancery procedure by limiting the time for taking depositions to six months, after which either party could set the cause for hearing. That act also (as noted above) authorized common law executions to enforce chancery decrees. Perhaps the most radical departure from English practice was the introduction of trial by jury upon oral testimony in the High Court of Chancery, as provided in the act of 1777. After six years the legislature abandoned the experiment, noting that it was "found to be expensive to the parties, and inconvenient to witnesses." The expedient finally settled on, adopted in the act of 1788, was to empower the chancery court at its discretion to direct issues of fact to be tried in that or any other court. As Marshall explained, "In most chancery cases the law & fact are so blended together that if a jury was impaneld of course the whole must be submitted to them or every case must assume the form of a special verdict which woud produce inconvenience & delay."[22]

A lawyer practicing in the higher courts of Virginia had to develop a sure grasp of the relationship between law and equity. To succeed in a court of chancery it was essential to establish the "equity" of the complaining party's case, to show that he had no remedy at common law or that such remedy was inadequate. Indeed, one important measure of a lawyer's professional acumen was his ability to discern what kinds of cases properly required equitable relief.

Although the documentary record of Marshall's chancery practice has largely vanished, what remains is sufficient to illustrate the various stages of a typical suit and to convey some idea of the different kinds of disputes that came under equity jurisdiction. As attorney for the plaintiffs Marshall drafted the bills in two of the cases in this section. One sought to quiet title to a disputed tract of land in the Northern Neck of Virginia. The other was filed on behalf of merchant Robert Morris to compel his erstwhile agent to disclose his dealings in carrying out a tobacco contract with the Farmers-General of France (Case Numbers 4 and 6). In the other two cases, creditors of a decedent sued the executors, represented by Marshall, for an account of their administration of the estate (Case Numbers 5 and 7). Of the handful of bills Marshall filed on the chancery side of the federal circuit court, nearly all requested an injunction against a law judgment. Three such bills appear below in Section IV. In each instance Marshall's client claimed credits on his bond that for various accidental reasons could not be proved at the law trial (Case Numbers 16, 17, and 18).

22. Hening, *Statutes*, IX, 394; XI, 343–44; XII, 464–65; JM to Gallatin, 3 Jan. 1790 (*PJM*, II, 49).

4. Leith v. Hite et al.

1786–1790

I. Bill in Chancery, ca. November 1786
II. Deposition of Joseph White, 29 August 1787
III. Deposition of Laurence Bodkin, 1787
IV. Answer, 29 September–16 October 1789
V. Decree, 5 August 1790

Editorial Note

This was one of numerous suits growing out of the May 1786 decree of the Court of Appeals in the case of *Hite* v. *Fairfax*.[1] That decree confirmed title to a large tract of lands in the Shenandoah Valley to the heirs of Joist Hite and others. Although these lands lay within the boundaries of the Fairfax proprietary, which embraced the extensive territory between the Potomac and Rappahannock rivers known as the Northern Neck, the court ruled for the Hites on the basis of certain orders in council obtained by Joist Hite and his associates in 1731 and a subsequent promise by Lord Fairfax to confirm crown grants within the proprietary. The 1786 decree contained two reservations: (1) those persons in possession of lands derived from contracts with Hite or his associates and who subsequently obtained confirmation deeds from Lord Fairfax were to remain in quiet possession; and (2) those persons having equitable claims to land within the contested area were to state such equity to the High Court of Chancery at a session of that court "next succeeding the expiration of three months" after they received a copy of the decree.[2]

As counsel for the Fairfax family in *Hite* v. *Fairfax*, Marshall represented many claimants under the second reservation, among them James Leith.[3] They sought to be quieted in the possession and title to their lands, all of which were contained within twenty-seven surveys described in a commissioners' report for the General Court in 1771. This report was prepared under an interlocutory decree of 1769 awarding to the representatives of Joist Hite and others all lands "*actually surveyed*" before Christmas 1735 under Hite's orders in council and appointing commissioners to "examine and state a memorial of all such surveys."[4] The report, on which the 1771 and 1786 decrees in *Hite* v. *Fairfax* were founded, listed the names of all those possessing land in each of the surveys and stated the nature of their claim. All the lands included in these twenty-seven surveys lay in the counties of Shenandoah, Frederick, and Berkeley (now West Virginia). To be quieted in the possession of their lands, Marshall's clients had to prove sale contracts with the original grantees, Joist Hite and his associates Robert McKay and Robert Green, and to establish the chain of subsequent conveyances.[5] John Taylor represented Isaac Hite, John Hite, James McKay, Andrew McKay, and John Green, descendants of the original grantees. The Hites and their co-defendants believed that many of the present inhabitants were intruders and would be unable to establish clear title. Their principal line of defense was to confess ignorance of the facts alleged in the bills. This forced the complainants to establish the truth of their allegations.

Gaps in the records and the loss of papers made it necessary to obtain the testimony of witnesses to prove the various transactions regarding the contested lands. To expedite the process Marshall and other counsel for the claimants proposed that general commissions issue for taking depositions without waiting for the bills and answers to be filed. (Usually commissions issued only after the pleadings.) Taylor readily assented to this proposal, believing it would work to the advantage of his clients. The complainants, he predicted, would quickly proceed to the taking of their depositions; the defendants would thus know what testimony the other side relied on before taking their own depositions or swearing to their answers. They could at leisure consider ways to counteract this evidence or to form advantageous compromises. Because the outcome of many of these cases would be largely determined by the testimony of witnesses, Taylor advised his clients to obtain proof that those testifying for the claimants were not credible persons or that they were "immediately interested" and "united in one phalanx to oppose your claims, & swear to support each others."[6]

The suits were consolidated for the purposes of argument and apparently came to trial at the spring 1790 term of the High Court of Chancery. Taylor moved to disallow depositions where the witness appeared "in any respect interested either in the particular claim wherein he deposes or in any other claim whatever." Chancellor Wythe accepted this motion only in part, ruling that those claiming lands in the same survey or even co-plaintiffs might be witnesses for each other "if they claim by title so different & independant that the doom of both may not be the same."[7]

James Leith was one of at least seven of Marshall's clients who claimed land within the survey known as the South River tract, consisting of seven thousand acres lying on the south branch of the Shenandoah River. His claim was among the easier ones to prove; he possessed the bond for the original purchase, and one of the defendants confessed the sale. The defense unsuccessfully attempted to show that witnesses for the claimant were interested in the outcome of the suit.

1. 4 Call 42. For the earlier history of this litigation, see *PJM*, I, 150–64.

2. Va. Ct. Ap. Ord. Bk. I, 77–80; 4 Call 81–83.

3. JM's argument is reprinted in *PJM*, I, 153–64. JM kept a separate fee list for these suits (*PJM*, II, 104–7). Many papers generated by the Hite litigation are preserved in Clark-Hite Papers, KyLoF. A transcript of the record of the principal case is in Add. Mss 15317, British Museum. Excerpts from this transcript are printed in the appendix to Josiah Look Dickinson, *The Fairfax Proprietary: The Northern Neck . . .* (Front Royal, Va., 1959), i–lvii. This record formed the basis of the 1786 appeal and the cases that grew out of it.

4. One of the commissioners was Thomas Marshall, JM's father (4 Call 51–52). Copies of the report are in Clark-Hite Papers, KyLoF; Record of Hite v. Fairfax, Add. Mss 15317, British Museum.

5. JM to Corbin Washington, 23 Aug. 1789 (*PJM*, II, 37–38). Washington was also one of JM's clients in the suits against the Hites.

6. John Taylor to John Green, 2 Dec., ca. 18 Dec. 1786; to Isaac Hite, 20 July 1789, Clark-Hite Papers, KyLoF.

7. This motion is embodied in one of the decrees issued on 5 Aug. 1790 by the High Court of Chancery. Copies of the decrees are in Clark-Hite Papers, KyLoF.

I. Bill in Chancery

ca. November 1786

To the Honourable the Judges of the High Court of Chancery Humbly complaining shew unto your Honours your Orator James Leith,[1] that he is in possession of a Tract of Land lying on the South side of south branch of Shanandoh river a part thereof being occupied by himself and a part by Josiah Leith his Tenant, that he claims the same as eldest son and heir at Law of Ephraim Leith deced.[2] who purchased the said tract of his father James Leith as is witness'd by an instrument of writing hereunto annexed, and that James Leith purchased the said Land from the original Grantees as is witnessed by their bond hereunto annexed which your Orator prays may be taken as a part of this his bill, and your Orator says that tho the names subscribed to the said Bond are now torn off, yet it is known to James McKay senr. one of the parties to the suit Hites and others Complts agst. the representatives of the late Lord Fairfax defts, that the said bond was executed, and your Orator further says that the said James

Leith was an Original settler on the said Land and was reported as such in the list taken by Wolf,[3] and the bond aforementioned was for the Land on which he settled, that having this fair and equitable Title to the premises your Orator well hoped to be permitted to remain in the peaceable enjoyment of the same. BUT NOW SO IT IS may it please your Honours that a copy of the Decree obtained by the Hites and others Complts against the representatives of the late Lord Fairfax defts has been served upon your Orator, by which the Hites and others call upon your Orator to state his claim to this Honourable Court or loose his Land entirely; All which is contrary to equity. IN TENDER consideration whereof and to the end that your Orator may be quieted in the possession of and Title to the said Land. May it please your Honours &c. And your Orator shall pray &c.[4]

J. MARSHALL for Comp.[5]

Copy, Clark-Hite Papers, KyLoF. Attested by John Brown, clerk of the High Court of Chancery; endorsed on verso: "South River No. 25/Page 101 of record/heard." Taylor sent this copy to his clients, whose preliminary answers are on verso (see Doc. IV, nn. 2, 3).

1. Probably James Leith (Leeth) of Shenandoah County, whose will was probated 13 Oct. 1806 (Amelia C. Gilreath, comp., *Shenandoah County Virginia: Abstract of Wills, 1772–1850* [Nokesville, Va., 1980], 130).

2. Ephraim Leith's claim to this land was summarized in the 1771 commissioners' report, which was entered on the record of Hite v. Fairfax, 122, Add. Mss 15317, British Museum.

3. The list made by Peter Wolf in Jan. 1736 contained the names of forty-nine settlers on the land lying in the forks of the Shenandoah and its tributaries that had been granted to Joist Hite, Robert McKay, and others. James Leeth, presumably the complainant's grandfather, was on this list (Record of Hite v. Fairfax, 262–63, Add. Mss 15317, British Museum; Dickinson, *Fairfax Proprietary*, App., liv–lv).

4. The conclusion of a bill consisted largely of formal expressions that were usually omitted. The full conclusion would read: "May it please your Honours to grant unto your orator a writ or writs of subpoena to be directed to the said defendants thereby commanding them at a certain day, and under a certain pain therein to be inserted, personally to be and appear before your Honours in this honourable court, then and there to answer the premises, and to stand to and abide such order and decree therein, as to your Honours shall seem agreeable to equity and good conscience. And your Orator shall ever pray, &c" (adapted from a bill in Harrison, *Chancery Practice*, II, 212).

5. Copies of seventeen other bills drawn by JM on behalf of claimants against the Hites are in Clark-Hite Papers, KyLoF.

II. Deposition of Joseph White
29 August 1787

State of North Carolina }
Anson County }

Whereas by Virtue of a Dedimus Protestation,[1] directed to us Stephen Pace and Theoderick Webb Justices of the Peace for the said County, from the Commonwealth of Virginia, and the High Court of Chancery in Richmond, to take the examination of whatsoever Witnesses On behalf of James Leith as On behalf of John Hite Isaac Hite And others Defts. We therefore On the Twenty ninth day of August 1787 At the dwelling House of Mr Joseph White, in Anson County Aforesaid, And between the Hours of Nine O Clock in the morning And Six in the After noon Mr Joseph White was Sworn before us On the Holy Evangelist of Almighty God's and deposeth And saith, that as well as he Could Recollect in the Year 1736 at the first Settling of Shanandoah River above where Robert McKay lived, that he was Present with the Said Robert McKay and James Leith and the said James Leith Purchased 200 Acres of the said Robert McKay, And was to give three pounds a Hundred, the lands was lying on the South side of Shanandoah River, below Caleb Jobs Run, the first low Grounds below said Run, And further saith some time After, he saw the said James Leith Pay the said Robert McKay Six pounds for Said Land, And further Saith, that the said Robert McKay said he wou'd make the said James Leith a Right to the said Land as Soon as he Got a Right himself & further sayeth not.[2]
Sworn to before us this 29th. 1787

JOSEPH WHITE

STEPHEN PACE JP.
THEODERICK WEBB JP.

Copy, Clark-Hite Papers, KyLoF. Text and signatures in same unidentified hand as in Doc. III.

1. Should be "potestatem." See Case No. 1, Doc. VI and n. 2.

2. As indicated in the decree (Doc. V), John Taylor tried to prevent the admission of White's deposition. The grounds for his objection are suggested by the comment in an undated memorandum that White was "Interested in Odells claim." The memorandum, in an unknown hand but doubtless prepared for Taylor (who inserted notes in it), accompanied the papers in this suit (Clark-Hite Papers, KyLoF). White had formerly possessed South River land and sold it to Samuel Odell, who like Leith was a claimant in this survey (deposition of Adam Cunningham, 23 Mar. 1770, Record of Hite v. Fairfax, Add. Mss 15317, British Museum).

III. Deposition of Laurence Bodkin
1787

Shanandoah County Sc.[1]

Persuant to a Dedimus to us John Netherton and William Jennings directed, we have Caused Laurence Bodkin of the same County to come before us, And him have Diligently examined upon the Holy Evangelist of Almighty God, Touching Such things which either party might have Objected to, And this deponent Laurence Bodkin Aged 78 years doth Plainly say, that about the year 1754 or 1755 he heard James Leith say that he Bought the tract of Land which Ephraim Leith lived then Upon from Robert McKay the Elder and paid him a Certain Sum but how much he doth not Remember, this deponent further Sayeth that The Above named Leith Said the Bounds of the said Land was from Broad Run up Shanando River to the Mouth of Calebs Run now Call'd Adams Run. And further this deponent Saith not.

ISAAC HITE Deft Present
JOHN NETHERTON
WILLIAM JENNINGS

his
LAURENCE ʃ BODKIN
Mark

Copy, Clark-Hite Papers, KyLoF. Text and signatures in same unidentified hand as in Doc. II; date derived from memorandum accompanying suit papers (Doc. II, n. 2).

1. *Scilicet* ("to wit").

IV. Answer
29 September–16 October 1789

THE ANSWER of Isaac Hite John Hite, John Green, Andrew McKay and James McKay[1] to the bill of complaint Exhibited against them in the high court of chancery by James Leith complainant.

THESE DEFENDANTS saving and reserving to themselves all benefit of Exception to any imperfections in the said bill contained, for answer to so much thereof, as they are advised is material for them to answer, say, and first the said Isaac Hite John Hite John Green & Andrew McKay for themselves say, that they are ignorant of the facts stated by the said bill, nor can they say any thing as to the bond refered to, because it is not annexed.[2] And the defendant James McKay for himself saith, that many years ago he saw a bond to James Leith for land, being of that claimed by the bill (tho' this defendant cannot tell whether the complainant holds more or less than the bond specified) that the said bond if ever signed, was torn, and the signers names off. That from what he has heard, he believes that the said Leith did buy and pay for the land, tho' he knows it not of his own knowledge.[3] And the defendants denying all fraud and combination, pray to be hence dismissed with their costs in this behalf most unjustly sustained. Without that that &a.[4]

ISAAC HITE
JAMES MACKAY
ANDW MKAY
JOHN GREEN
JN HITE

Culpepper County Sct.[5]

John Green, Isaac Hite James McCoy three of the above mentioned defendants, appeared before me a Magistrate for the said County, and made oath and Andrew McCoy another of the above mentioned Defts made affirmation[6] that this their answer is just and true, so far as they know or believe. Certified this 29th day of September 1789.

JOHN WIGGINTON

Frederick County Sct.

John Hite one of the above mentioned defendants appeard before me a Majestrate for the said County, and made oath that this his answer was just and true so far as he knows or believes. Certified this 16th day of October 1789.

ELISHA WILLIAMS

DS, Clark-Hite Papers, KyLoF. In hand of John Taylor except for signatures and certifications; endorsed, "Filed Jany 13 1790."

1. Isaac Hite (1721–1795) of Long Meadows, Frederick County, was the third son of Joist Hite the pioneer and the father of Isaac Hite, Jr. (1758–1836), who later built Belle Grove. John Hite (d. 1792), the oldest son of Joist Hite, held a number of important civil and military offices in Frederick County during the colonial period and represented the county in the General Assembly before and during the Revolution (T. K. Cartmell, *Shenandoah Valley Pioneers and Their Descendants: A History of Frederick County, Virginia* [Berryville, Va., 1963], 253–54, 257, 278). John Green (ca. 1730–1793), a vestryman of St. Marks Parish, Culpeper County, had been a distinguished officer in the Virginia Continental Line during the Revolution. He was the fourth son of Robert Green (1695–1748), one of Joist Hite's associates (Green, *Notes on Culpeper County*, pt. 1, 61, 68–69; Dickinson, *Fairfax Proprietary*, App., xv, xxxii). Andrew McKay (1736–1804) and James McKay were, respectively, a grandson and son of Robert McKay (d. 1752), a Scotch-Irish

Quaker who was Joist Hite's partner in bringing settlers to the lower Shenandoah Valley. The family was frequently referred to as "McCoy" (Howard S. F. Randolph, comp., *The Ancestors and Descendants of Colonel David Funsten and His Wife Susan Everard Meade* [New York, 1926], 46–50; Dickinson, *Fairfax Proprietary*, 118).

2. The preliminary answers of these four defendants, written in an unknown hand on the verso of the bill in chancery (Doc. I), read as follows:

"The defendant Isaac Hite knows nothing of the Facts Set forth in this Bill and Observes that the instruments of Writing and therin refered to Are not Annexed.

"Andrew McKay knows nothing of the execution of Such a Bond.

"Same J Green.

"John Hite Knows nothing of the facts Stated in this Bill."

3. James McKay's preliminary answer follows immediately below the others on the verso of the bill in chancery (Doc. I), but is written in a different hand, also unidentified. It reads:

"James McKay says that many years agoe he saw a bond to James Leath for the Land claim'd: that the bond if ever sign'd, was torn, and the signers names off—he further says that from what he has heard he believes Leith did buy and pay for the Land."

4. The full conclusion to an answer to a bill in chancery, consisting largely of formal expressions that were usually omitted, reads: "And this defendant denies all and all manner of unlawful combination and confederacy wherewith he is charged, without that, that there is any other matter, cause, or thing in the complainant's said bill of complaint contained, material or effectual in the law, for this defendant to make answer unto, and not herein and hereby well and sufficiently answered, avoided, traversed, or denied is true, to the knowledge and belief of this defendant. All which matters and things this defendant is ready and willing to aver, maintain, and prove as this honourable court shall direct, and humbly prays to be hence dismissed with his reasonable costs and charges in the law, in this behalf most wrongfully sustained" (Robert Hinde, *The Modern Practice of the High Court of Chancery, Methodized and Digested in a Manner Wholly New* [Dublin, 1786], 207–8).

5. *Scilicet* ("to wit"). The certifications are in an unidentified hand, not that of the magistrates who signed them.

6. Andrew McKay was a Quaker. The words "and Andrew McCoy . . . affirmation" are interlined, the writer having originally included him with the other three as having sworn to his answer.

V. Decree
5 August 1790

Virginia to Wit

At a High Court of Chancery held at the Capitol in the City of Richmond August the 5th. 1790

In the case of James Leith in possession of part of the seven thousand Acres of Land called South River tract which part is stated to have been sold by Robert Mackay and his partners to James Leith and to have been transfered by him to his son Ephraim from whom it descended to his son & heir, the present possessor: the Writing which called a Bond is an exhibit and to which a reference is made by the Bill of the Possessor, hath not nor ever had a date, and the part of it wherein such writings, executed and attested obligors & Witnesses usually subscribe their names seem to have been torn off or otherwise distroyed, except that the tops of two Characters in the name of a Witness perhaps appear in what is extant but this Writing being nearly in the same form as the bonds admitted to have been executed in some other cases particularly one in the case of Benjamin Thrailkeld a Witness namely Joseph White whose Deposition notwithstanding the exception to it,[1] was admitted to be read having possitively testified that in his presence Robert Mackay agreed to sell two hundred Acres of Land which by his Deposition if it seems to be this land to James Leith and James Mackay one of the plts in the principal case having confessed by his Answer to this Bill that from what he had heard he believed, although he did not know, the sd. Leith did buy and pay for the Land. The Court doth believe that Robert Mackay made a contract for Sale of the Land described in the writing before mentioned to James Leith at the rate of three pounds for one hundred Acres but notwithstanding what James Mackay hath confessed, and Joseph White deposed concerning payment of the purchase money, that of the forty Shillings, which remained due at the execution of that Writing if indeed it was executed, no part hath been since paid, because by the terms of the contract Stated in the condition annexed to the writing it was not payable before the controversy between Mackay & others & Lord Fairfax should be determined & the Court being of Opinion that James Leith the present Possessor to whom the title of the purchaser derived, doth fall within one or other of the reservations contained in the Decree of the eighth Day of may in the year 1786 in the principal case, the first reservation, if he have a proprietors grant, the second, if not, doth therefore adjudge Order & Decree that the said Decree of the eighth day of may in the year 1786 be not carried into execution as to the two hundred

Acres of Land so purchased, but that James Leith the present Possessor thereof be quieted provided, within twenty one days after he shall have been served with a Copy of this Decision he do pay or tender unto the plts in the principal case, or unto him whom they shall authorize to demand & receive, forty Shillings with interest from the first day of January in the year 1740 and the Costs expended by them on this occasion.[2]

Copy, Clark-Hite Papers, KyLoF. Attested by Peter Tinsley, clerk of the High Court of Chancery.

1. John Taylor's exceptions to the testimony of certain witnesses are embodied in one of the numerous decrees in the Hite cases of this date. He objected to deponents who were in any way interested in the particular claim or in any other claim arising out of the same survey. In addition, the counsel for the Hites opposed the reading of depositions from North Carolina, where White's deposition had been taken, "because they had been taken by Commission, without a special Order of the Court; because the days appointed by the parties for executing the Commissions, were so near the days appointed for executing other Commissions and the places so far asunder, their agents could not attend all; & because the Commissioners had not been named in Court & approved by the Court as it is generally done where Commissions are sent out of the State" (decree [copy], Hite et al. v. Fairfax et al., 5 Aug. 1790, Clark-Hite Papers, KyLoF).

2. The Hites filed cross-bills against Leith and the other claimants seeking to quiet their titles to the disputed lands. Thus, the decree in this suit and others of this date were issued in pairs, both decrees in each pair having identical texts but with the names of the parties reversed. The decree in Leith's suit was accompanied by an identical one under the title of Hite et al. v. Fairfax et al.

The Hites appealed the decree in Leith's case, but the Court of Appeals affirmed it on 14 Nov. 1791. The High Court of Chancery certified the appellate decree on 1 Mar. 1792. Leith subsequently paid the Hites the amount of the decree, interest, costs, and fee (£13.3.9), deducting costs of the appeal (£5.6.2½) (decrees [copies], Hite et al. v. Fairfax et al., 5 Aug. 1790 [Leith's case]; Leith v. Hite et al., 1 Mar. 1792, Clark-Hite Papers, KyLoF; receipts for payments, 24 Aug. 1795, on verso of decrees).

5. Shermer v. Shermer's Executors

1787–1794

I. Bill in Chancery, 5 November 1787
II. Answer of Price Davies, 14 May 1789
III. Answer of Dudley Richardson, 15 May 1789
IV. Answer of Thomas Booth, 25 May 1789
V. Thomas Booth to John Marshall, 25 May 1789
VI. Chancellor Wythe's Opinion, 27 September 1792
VII. Decree of the High Court of Chancery, 27 September 1792
VIII. Argument in the Court of Appeals, 15 October 1794

Editorial Note

In October 1787 Marshall received the unusually large fee of twenty-eight pounds from "Shermers exrs." This payment coincided with the commencement of a suit brought by William Shermer of Great Britain in the High Court of Chancery against the executors of John Shermer, late of James City County. The plaintiff was heir and executor of his father Richard Shermer, older brother and heir at law of John Shermer. William Shermer sought to recover the half portion of John Shermer's estate that had been distributed among his widow's relatives after her death. He founded his claim on these words of John Shermer's will: "I also give her [his wife] the use and Profits of my whole Estate both Real and Personal During her natural life, and after that is ended then my will and desire is that the whole of my Estate (exclusive of that already given my wife) be Equally Divided betwixt whoever my wife shall think proper to make her heir or heirs and my loving Brother Richard Shermer."[1]

Mrs. Shermer died within a few days of her husband's death without making a will. William Shermer's bill in chancery maintained that the moiety, or half portion, which John Shermer had given to his wife's disposal represented a life estate only. As a life estate it consequently devolved on Richard Shermer as John Shermer's heir at law. The executors of John Shermer contended that the distribution of this moiety to Mrs. Shermer's relations carried out their testator's express intention. They maintained that John Shermer's words conveyed absolute ownership of one half of the estate in his wife.

As a controversy over the construction of a will, *Shermer* is representative of a large class of cases that formed a substantial portion of the work of chancery courts. In construing a will courts were to effect the testator's intentions. Such disputes, like the present one, frequently centered on establishing those intentions. The words of John Shermer's will left no doubt that the testator intended to give his wife full use of his estate for her life. It was also clear that half his estate was to pass, upon his wife's death, to the beneficiaries of her choosing. What was not clear was the effect of the language in light of Mrs. Shermer's intestacy. Did John Shermer intend that half his estate should pass to her heirs at law? The High Court of Chancery had to determine the testator's intentions with respect to a situation he had not contemplated, namely, his wife's failure to make a will designating her heirs.

A copy of the record and other documents relating to this suit were later submitted to the commissions for settling the claims of British creditors of American citizens. These sources make it possible to reconstruct the concrete circumstances, the particular human passions, that lay behind the abstract legal question of whether John Shermer's will conveyed an estate in fee simple upon his wife.[2] The story properly begins in February 1742, when John Shermer, a younger son of the English squirearchy who had settled in Gloucester County, married Ann Reade of that county. The widow of Thomas Reade, she was a daughter of the late Thomas Booth, a prominent Gloucester merchant. Shermer was an upholsterer by trade with a visible estate reportedly consisting of only one slave and two horses. By his marriage he made a first important step toward acquiring a fortune. Ann Shermer, whose family and friends opposed the marriage, brought with her thirty slaves and a life interest in her deceased husband's plantation. Her estate, though encumbered with debt, provided sufficient capital for John Shermer to set himself up as a tobacco planter and merchant. During the next thirty years he prospered, extending his interests and property from Gloucester to the counties of New Kent, King William, and James City, where he eventually settled. At his death in January 1775 Shermer's estate was worth eleven thousand pounds Virginia currency; it included some twenty-six hundred acres in James City and King William, worked by 120 slaves, as well as cattle, sheep, oxen, horses, and a chariot complete with a harness for four horses.[3]

As directed by the will, the executors of John Shermer sold all his real and personal estate in March 1775. The sale attracted a large number of buyers, mostly from the Williamsburg region but including some from as far as Norfolk, Richmond, and Petersburg. Purchasers bought on credit, giving bonds payable by 1 May 1776. In July 1776 the executors divided the liquidated estate, distributing one-half of the bonds, bills, and accounts due the estate in seven equal shares to Ann Shermer's surviving brother, sister, nephews, and nieces. The payment of Richard Shermer's half portion had to be suspended for the duration of the war. Dudley Richardson, one of the executors, acted as trustee for receiving payments on Shermer's account.[4]

The sale and liquidation of the Shermer estate coincided with the outbreak of the War of Independence, a stroke of misfortune for the legatees, especially for Richard Shermer, a subject of Great Britain. During the war paper money became a legal tender in discharge of public and private debts, and many of the estate purchasers paid off their bonds in this depreciating currency. The Virginia legatees presumably minimized their losses by applying the paper money they received to pay their own debts or to make purchases. Paper money received on Richard Shermer's account, however, accumulated in the hands of the trustee, where its value deteriorated ever more rapidly as the war progressed. The trustee administered this fund as best he could by lending it out and avoided further payments in paper by burying the unpaid bonds in the ground during the British army's invasion of the state in 1781. By the end of the war he had received twenty-seven hundred pounds in depreciated paper on behalf of the British legatee, including sixteen hundred pounds paid into the state treasury at one thousand to one under the terms of the 1781 act calling in the state's paper money. In effect, Richard Shermer's share of the estate had shrunk to about half its original value.[5]

In May 1783 William Shermer, representing his aged father Richard, came to Virginia to settle his late uncle's estate—the first of ten Atlantic crossings he made on this mission during the next fifteen years. On this first journey Shermer apparently gave no hint of any design on the Virginia legatees' half portion of the estate. Following the death of his father in February 1787, he made a second trip to Virginia, this time laying claim to the entire estate, no doubt hoping to recoup his losses from depreciated paper currency. Not surprisingly, he was unable to reach an amicable settlement with the executors and Mrs. Shermer's relatives, who considered him "a depredator aiming to wrest from them their long enjoyed property."[6] From November 1787, when he filed his bill in chancery, to his death in July 1806, William Shermer doggedly pursued his claim to his uncle's estate, first in the Virginia courts, then with the commissions established to settle the claims of British creditors of American citizens.[7]

1. *PJM*, I, 395; will of John Shermer (copy), 11 June 1766, T.79/36 (claim of William Shermer), P.R.O.

2. On the claims commissions, see Sec. IV, editorial note. Most of the docu-

ments presented in this case are taken from the copy of the record (T.79/36 [claim of William Shermer], P.R.O.). The original papers in the Shermer suit were transferred to the Superior Court of Chancery at Williamsburg in 1802. There they survived until Apr. 1911, when a fire destroyed all the old chancery papers ("House History: Courthouse of 1770," ViWC). William Carter Stubbs, a genealogist, made copies of the original Shermer papers and reproduced many of them at length in his *Descendants of Mordecai Cooke . . . and Thomas Booth . . .* (New Orleans, 1923), 238–45.

3. Deposition of Ann Jones, 19 June 1789; letters of John Shermer, 1741–70, Record of Shermer v. Shermer's Executors, T.79/36 (claim of William Shermer), P.R.O.; *Va. Gazette* (Dixon and Hunter), 18 Feb. 1775.

4. Notice of sale, *Va. Gazette* (Dixon and Hunter), 18 Feb. 1775; commissioners' report, 5 Feb. 1793; "An account of the paper money received for Mr. Richard Shermer . . . ," Record of Shermer v. Shermer's Executors.

5. Hening, *Statutes*, X, 456–57; memorial and claim of William Shermer (read 20 Nov. 1798); claim on behalf of Richard Shermer, 7 Feb. 1804, T.79/36 (claim of William Shermer), P.R.O.

6. William Shermer to J. W. Hay, 20 Sept. 1802; claim on behalf of Richard Shermer, 7 Feb. 1804; answer of William Shermer to Board of Commissioners, 19 Sept. 1805 (source of quotation); answer of William Shermer to Board of Commissioners, 31 Jan. 1806, T.79/36 (claim of William Shermer), P.R.O.

7. See Doc. VIII, n. 6.

I. Bill in Chancery
5 November 1787

To the Honorable the Judges of the High Court of Chancery. Humbly complaining sheweth unto your Honors, your Orator William Shermer heir Executor and residuary legatee of Richard Shermer his father late of Great Britain deceased. That John Shermer late of New Kent County[1] deced departed this life on the ninth day of January one thousand seven hundred and seventy five, having first made his last will and testament, to which as of Record in the County Court of James City your Orator begs leave to refer. (Of which Will he Appointed the Defendant Dudley Richardson with Thurston James, George Boothe, Thomas Boothe, and Anne Shermer since deceased his Executors and Executrix.[)][2] That the said John Shermer in and by his said Will among other things, he devised as follows, "I give to my wife the use and profits of my whole Estate both real and personal during her natural life and after that is ended, then my will and desire is that the whole of my Estate exclusive of that already given my wife, be equally divided betwixt whoever my wife shall think proper to make her Heir or Heirs and my loving brother Richard Shermer"[3] and the said Testator further directed "That his Executors as soon as the crops were finished after his wifes decease, should sell and dispose of his whole Estate both real and personal as they might think most conducive to the receivers benefit" as by the said Will may more fully appear. That on the 15th. day of the same month of January, the said Anne Shermer relict of the said Testator, departed this life intestate, and without having made any gift or Appointment whatsoever in consequence of the power given to her in and by the said Will. That after the death of the said Anne, the other Executors in the said Will named, qualified as such, and soon after proceeded to sell and dispose of the whole estate of the said testator to the amount of eleven thousand pounds and upwards on credit taking bonds with security, payable the first day of May one thousand seven hundred and seventy six. That the said Richard Shermer in the Will mentioned, was the only brother heir at law next of kin and sole legal representative of the said Testator John Shermer. That soon after the death of the said testator Dudley Richardson one of the Executors in the said Will named who has been all along the principal acting exor. and who is now the surviving executor of the said Will wrote to the said Richard Shermer informing him of the death of his brother, that he was entitled to a moiety of the estate, and requesting from him a power of Attorney to receive and remit that moiety to him, which power the said Richard being beyond sea, and unacquainted with the extent of his claim did accordingly forward to the said Richardson, but the intervention of the war put a stop to the intercourse between this Country and Great Brittain and to the said Richards acquiring further intelligence on the subject. That the said Dudley Richardson with or without the other Executors proceeded without any Warrant to divide one moiety of the amount of Sales of the said John Shermer's estate, among various persons, under the idea of their being representatives of the said usufructuary for life, altho' she never in any manner executed the power given to her in the will, and consequently the moiety of the said Testators estate over which the power was given, devolved upon the said Richard Shermer as heir at law, or next of kin to the said John Shermer the testator, that the said Dudley Richardson with or without the other Executors, paid in money or bonds to sundry persons as representatives of the said usufructuary for life, the sum of five thousand four hundred and eighty nine pounds sixteen shillings and two pence half penny of the said John Shermers estate in sundry proportions, according to the Schedule hereunto added and which your Orator prays may be taken as a part of this his bill. And your Orator further shews unto your Honors, that your Orator is the only son and heir at Law of the said Richard Shermer, brother to the testator, that the said Richard departed this life in the year one thousand seven hundred and eighty six, having first made his last will and testament, an attested copy of which, as proved approved and registered in the prerogative Court of Canterbury in the Kingdom of Great Brittain is herewith filed and refered to.[4] That your Orator is in and by the said Will appointed sole executor and residuary Legatee, and that he hath duly qualified as such executor. That the said Dudley Richardson hath never made up or settled any Account of his Administration of the said John Shermers Estate, which upon your Orators request he refuses to do, or to pay to your Orator the proceeds of the whole sales of the said John Shermers whole estate real and personal (except some specific Legacies to the said Anne and to one William Richardson[)] as he ought to do. And now so it is may it please your Honors, that the said Dudley Richardson combining and confederating with William Boothe of the County of Frederick,[5] John Perrin executor &c. of Mary Perrin deceased[6] Reverend Pryce Davis, Clerk,[7] Matthew Anderson and Anne Fox Administrators with the will annexed &c. of John Fox deceased,[8] Thomas Boothe of Gloucester Administrator &c. of Thomas Boothe deceased[9] Philip Tabb Executor &c. of George Boothe deceased commonly called George Boothe Jur.[10] Thomas Boothe of Henrico,[11] Mary Jones Widow and Administratrix &c. of Emanuel Jones deceased[12] Mordecai Boothe,[13] Thomas Boothe and Thomas Baytop Executors &c. of George Boothe of Poropotank[14] whom and their Testators or intestates have received the several sums set opposite to their names in the schedule hereunto added, and all of whom your Orator prays may be made Defendants to this his bill, and to and with divers other persons to your Orator unknown, who when discovered he also prays may be made Defendants, do wholly refuse the said Dudley Richardson surviving exor of the Will of the said John Shermer to make up and render fair Accounts of the estate of the said John Shermer, which has come to his hands, and to pay the balance due to your Orator, and the said other Defendants to return and refund the said Several sums with Interest so unjustly paid to them, or the said Richardson to make good to your Orator, any loss which may be sustained by reason of such improper conduct. In tender consideration whereof, and for as much as your Orator is remediless in the premises, save by the interposition of this Honorable Court where matters of this kind are properly cognizable. To the end therefore that the said Defendants, may upon their corporal Oaths, full true and perfect answers make to all and singular the premises, as fully as if the same were herein again repeated and interrogated; that they may declare whither themselves, or those whom they represent, did not in bonds, in money, or in some other manner receive the several sums set opposite the names in the Schedule hereunto added. That the said Richardson may also say, whither such payments were not made; That the said Richardson may before Auditors to be appointed by this Honble Court make up and render on Oath, a fair Account of his administration or Executorship of the said John Shermers Estate. That he may be decreed to pay to your Orator any balance with which he is chargeable. That the other defendants may refund the moneys by them respectively received with Interest before or after an Account has been taken thereof. That the said Richardson may be decreed to make good to your Orator any loss or losses which may be sustained on Account of the inability of such persons or either of them to refund, or otherwise by reason of the said misapplication of the said Testators Estate, or that your Orator may be further or otherwise releived in the premises according to Equity and good conscience. May it please your Honors to grant to your Orator a Writ or Writs of Subpœna to the said Defendants to be directed &c.[15]

[Schedule][16]

William Boothe (Frederick by the hands of George Boothe[)]	£ 784. 5. 2 ¾
Mary Perrin by James Hubbard (deceased)	784. 5. 2 ¾.
Pryce Davis (New Kent)	784. 5. 2 ¾.
John Fox (Gloucester) (deceased)	784. 5. 2 ¾.
Thomas Boothe (Gloster) (deceased)	784. 5. 2 ¾.
George Boothe (Gloucester) (deceased)	784. 5. 2 ¾.
Thomas Boothe (Henrico)	196. 1. 3 ½
Emanuel Jones (King William) deceased	196. 1. 3 ½
Mordecai Boothe (do.)	196. 1. 3 ½
George Boothe (Poropotank) (deceased)	196. 1. 3 ½
	£5489.16. 2 ½

Copy, Record of Shermer v. Shermer's Executors, T.79/36 (claim of William Shermer), P.R.O. Full record consists of forty-eight unnumbered pages in hand of Peter Tinsley, clerk of the High Court of Chancery, certified by Chancellor George Wythe and attested by Gov. James Wood, 3 Mar. 1798; record states that bill was exhibited in court on 5 Nov. 1787.

1. At the time he made his will in 1766, Shermer was a resident of Blisland Parish, which lay within New Kent and James City counties. His dwelling house at the time of his death was in James City.

2. Will of John Shermer (copy), 11 June 1766, T.79/36 (claim of William Shermer), P.R.O. Dudley Richardson, the only surviving executor, was a James City County planter. Thruston James (ca. 1715–1780) served with

John Shermer as a vestryman and churchwarden of Blisland Parish (C. G. Chamberlayne, ed., *The Vestry Book of Blisland Parish, New Kent, and James City Counties, Virginia, 1721–1786* [Richmond, 1935], 88–205 passim; *WMQ*, 1st ser., XII [1903], 27). George Booth (d. 1786) of Poropotank, Gloucester County, was the oldest son of Thomas Booth (1702–1756), Ann Shermer's brother. The last-named executor was Thomas Booth "the younger" (d. 1784?), also of Gloucester County and son of Dr. George Booth, oldest brother of Ann Shermer (Stubbs, *Descendants of Mordecai Cooke*, 190–96).

3. The passage as quoted in the bill varies slightly from the actual text of the will.

4. A copy of Richard Shermer's will, dated 7 Apr. 1786, was entered on the record.

5. William Booth (1723–1790), Ann Shermer's youngest brother, moved to Frederick County around 1773 (Stubbs, *Descendants of Mordecai Cooke*, 247–49).

6. Mary Perrin, Ann Shermer's sister, was the second wife of John Perrin (1690–1752) of Gloucester County. The John Perrin mentioned in the bill as her executor was apparently her stepson (ibid., 35, 242, 246).

7. Rev. Price Davies (d. 1793), originally from Wales and a graduate of Christchurch, Oxford, 1754, became rector of Blisland Parish in 1763. That same year he married Elizabeth Perry, daughter of Robert Perry and Elizabeth (Booth) Perry, who was Ann Shermer's sister (Sir David Evans, "Price Davies, Rector of Blisland Parish: Two Letters, 1763, 1765," *VMHB*, LXXIX [1971], 153–61; John Melville Jennings, "Further Notes on the Reverend Price Davies," ibid., 162–66).

8. John Fox (1740–1785), a nephew of Ann Shermer, was the son of Rev. John Fox of Ware Parish, Gloucester County, and Isabel (Booth) Fox. His widow and one of his administrators was Ann Mason Fox (Stubbs, *Descendants of Mordecai Cooke*, 231–35).

9. For the deceased Thomas Booth ("the younger"), see n. 2. The administrator was probably Thomas Booth (d. 1801), first child and only son of George Booth of Poropotank. He was a vestryman of Petsworth Parish and later served as sheriff of Gloucester (ibid., 196–97).

10. George Booth (d. 1777) of Bellville on the North River in Gloucester was the son of Mordecai Booth, brother of Ann Shermer. Philip Tabb, George Booth's executor, married his widow, Mary Mason (Wythe) Booth (ibid., 225–27).

11. Thomas Booth of Henrico was a nephew of Ann Shermer and brother of George Booth of Poropotank (ibid., 218–19).

12. Rev. Emanuel Jones of King William County had married Mary Cooke Booth (1750–1820), niece of Ann Shermer and sister of George Booth of Poropotank (ibid., 220).

13. Mordecai Booth (b. 1756) was a brother of George Booth of Poropotank and Thomas Booth of Henrico (ibid., 225).

14. The executors of George Booth of Poropotank were his son, Thomas Booth (see n. 9), and Thomas Baytop (1751–1812), who in 1782 had married Sarah, George's daughter (ibid., 204).

15. The attorney who drew the original bill was probably Jerman Baker, whose name appears on the record as signing the amended bill that was filed around Jan. 1790.

16. On the advice of attorneys Benjamin Waller and Robert Carter Nicholas, whose opinions were entered on the record (Doc. III, n. 2), the executors limited the distribution of Ann Shermer's half of the estate to her surviving brother and sister and to the children of her deceased siblings. The proceeds were divided into seven equal shares, as indicated on the schedule. One of these shares was in turn divided into four equal parts and given to the three children and a son-in-law of Thomas Booth (1702–1756). The latter was the only one of Ann Shermer's nine brothers and sisters who had more than one living child at the time of her death in 1775. This circumstance explains why his children received only quarter shares, while Ann's other nephews and nieces received full shares.

II. Answer of Price Davies
14 May 1789

The Answer in Chancery of Pryce Davis[1] to the Bill of Complaint exhibited against him and others in this Honorable Court by William Shermer. This Respondent saving to himself every benefit of exception to the Bill of the Complainants for answer to so much thereof as he is advised 'tis material for him to Answer to he answereth and saith. That he admits the death of John Shermer about the time stated in the bill and that he made a last will and testament, a true Copy of which is filed in this Cause. This Respondent also admits that Anne Shermer departed this life intestate about the time in the Bill set forth. This Respondent has ever understood that it was the intention of the said John Shermer, that one half of his estate should be divided among his wifes relations as the greater part of it came by her, and this Respondent has been advised, that such is the Operation of his Will connected with the circumstances of the case. This Respondent further Answering says, that some time about the year 17   a division of the estate was made by Dudley Richardson Attorney in fact for Richard Shermer Father of the Complainant on the one part, and by the other Executors of John Shermer on the other part, and that the sums of money mentioned in the bill, in bonds was alloted to the testators of this Respondent, some time about the year 17   . And this Respondent for his testators claims the benefit of the length of time the said property has been retained in their possession without any claim on the part of the Complainant. This Respondent denies all combination without that &c. and prays to be hence dismissed with his Costs &c. and this Respondent will ever pray.

Copy, Record of Shermer v. Shermer's Executors, T.79/36 (claim of William Shermer), P.R.O. Sworn in New Kent County, 14 May 1789.

1. Davies had married a niece of Ann Shermer (Doc. I and n. 7).

III. Answer of Dudley Richardson
15 May 1789

The Answer of Dudley Richardson Executor of John Shermer deceased to the Bill of Complaint in this Honorable Court against him and others by John Shermer exhibited. This respondent now and at all times hereafter saving and reserving all manner of benefit of exception to the said Bill for answer thereto or to so much thereof, as it is material for him to answer he answereth and saith. That true it is that his testator departed this life, about the time set forth in the Bill, having first made his last Will and testament, to a true copy of which, this Respondent refers. He admits that Anne Shermer the relict of the said John departed this life intestate and about the time in the bill set forth. That this respondent qualified as Executor to the Will of the said John Shermer and together with the other Executors therein named took on him the burthen of the Execution thereof. This respondent further Answering saith, that thereupon he wrote to the said Richard Shermer, informing him of the death of the said John Shermer, and of his wife, inclosing at the same time a copy of the Will, and the annexed opinions of Counsel thereon. That he received an Answer thereto enclosing a letter of Attorney, to true copies of which hereto annexed this Respondent refers, and prays that they may be taken as a part of this his answer.[1] He further answering saith that he joined the other Executors in a Sale of the Estate of the said John Shermer, as in the Bill mentioned, and that one moiety thereof was distributed among the next of kin to the said Anne Shermer. That this distribution was made after having consulted eminent Counsel, who gave it as their Opinion, that a just construction of the Will of the said John Shermer authorised such a distribution.[2] This Respondent further saith that in the life time of the said John Shermer, there was a very close intimacy between him and this respondent, who was well acquainted with the Situation of his affairs particularly with the circumstances of his having acquired the greater part of his fortune by intermarrying with the said Anne his wife. That he hath had frequent conversations with the said John Shermer on the subject of the disposal of his Estate and hath frequently heard him declare, that if he outlived his said wife, he would divide one half of his Estate among her relations, and that on her out living him, she should have one half of his Estate to dispose of among her relations in the manner she should think most proper. This Respondent further answering saith, that guided by the opinions of Counsel above refered to, as well as by his knowledge of the intentions of the said John Shermer he did not doubt the right of the relations of Anne Shermer to one moiety of the estate left by her Husband, that accordingly conceiving himself authorized by said Letter of Attorney, as well as the Will of John Shermer he as above set forth together with the other Executors made distribution of one Moiety of his Estate among the representatives of the said Anne Shermer, and as he thought at that time finally settled and closed their Accounts and demands he further answering saith, that an Account of the amount of Sales of the said estate of the division thereof and of the debts paid and received by him was made out, and that to the best of his knowledge it is true and exact he begs leave to refer to a true copy thereof which is hereto annexed and which he prays may be made a part of this his answer.[3] He has ever been and still is ready to come to any Just Settlement with the Complainant. He denies all manner of unlawfull combination without that &c. and prays to be hence dismissed with his costs &c. and this Respondent will ever pray &c.

Copy, Record of Shermer v. Shermer's Executors, T.79/36 (claim of William Shermer), P.R.O. Sworn in James City County, 15 May 1789.

1. The annexed documents were not entered on the record and are not among the other papers filed with William Shermer's claim before the British debt commissions.

2. The "eminent Counsel" were Benjamin Waller and Robert Carter Nicholas. Waller's legal opinion was that "Mrs. Shermers dying between the twenty fifth day of December and the first day of March I think her Husbands executors should sell his whole estate, except the Plate, Watches, and Rings particularly bequeathed her, as soon as they conveniently can without waiting till another crop is made and finished and as both real and personal estate is directed to be turned into money, I think Mrs. Shermers half part thereof, together with the Plate Watches and Rings must be equally divided among all her brothers and sisters, and if any be dead the Children of the deceased to share their fathers or Mothers part" (copy, Record of Shermer v. Shermer's Executors). The second opinion was given by Nicholas: "There may possibly be some doubt, whither the part of the estate left to Mrs. Shermers disposal, should be considered as personal estate, under the latter clause of the Will, but upon considering the whole matter I entirely concur

with Mr. Waller in his opinion" (ibid.). Nicholas added a postscript: "I think the distribution should extend to brothers and Sisters Children and no farther."

3. This account was entered on the record.

IV. Answer of Thomas Booth
25 May 1789

The answer in Chancery of Thomas Boothe exor. of George Boothe of Poropotank deceased and Administrator with the Will annexed of Thomas Boothe deceased to the Bill of Complaint exhibited against him and others in this Honorable Court by William Shermer Complainant.[1] This respondent saving to himself every benefit of exception to the bill of the Complainant, for answer to so much thereof as he is advised 'tis material for him to answer to, he answereth and Saith. That he admits the death of John Shermer about the time stated in the bill, and that he made his last will and testament, a true copy of which is filed in this cause. This respondent also admits, that Anne Shermer departed this life intestate, about the time in the Bill set forth. This Respondent has ever understood, that it was the intention of the said John Shermer, that one half of his Estate should be divided among his wifes relations as the greater part of it came by her, and this Respondent has been advised that such is the Operation of his Will connected with the circumstances of the case. This Respondent further Answering saith, that in month of July 1776 a division of the estate was made by Dudley Richardson Attorney in fact for Richard Shermer father of the Complainant, on the one part and by the other Executors of John Shermer on the other part, and that the sum of £196.1.3½ in bonds dated the month of March 1775, and due about the month of May in the year 1776, was allotted to this Respondents testator George Boothe, and the sum of £784.5.2¾ in bonds dated in the month of March in the year 1775, and due about the month of May in the year 1776, was allotted to this Respondents testator Thomas Boothe deceased, and the sum of £756. was by him received in the year 1778 in the months of June or July, all of which said sum were received by the testator Thomas Boothe deceased in the paper Currency of the said year. And this Respondent for his testators aforesaid, claims the benefit of the length of time, the said property has been retained in their possession without any claim on the part of the Complainant. This Respondent denies all combination &c. without that &c. and prays to be hence dismissed with his reasonable Costs &c. and this Respondent will ever pray &c.

Copy, Record of Shermer v. Shermer's Executors, T.79/36 (claim of William Shermer), P.R.O. Sworn in King and Queen County, 25 May 1789.

1. See Doc. I and n. 9.

V. Thomas Booth to John Marshall
25 May 1789

Glos'ter May 25th. 1789[1]

The inclosd is the answers of the Revd. Mr [Davis] & myself in the suit of Shermer against us.[2] [Pleas?]e take out commissions for the taking of [the?] following depositions James City County Mrs. [Fra?]nces Henley & Mr. Charles Hankins, in Glos'ter Mrs. Mary Tabb Mrs. Ann Jones & Mrs. Mary Booth.[3] You will also examine the notice sent & make any alteration you may think necssary & give the bearer hereof every instruction he may require. If you should make any alteration in the notice please observe the date & let it be the same. Let me heare from you if any thing should be wanting.[4] I am Sir Yr. Hble Servt.

THOS. BOOTH

ALS, Coleman v. Wyatt, Office of the Clerk, Circuit Court, Fredericksburg, Va. Endorsed on verso by JM, "Coleman v. Wyat"; published in *PJM*, II, 23.

1. Although this letter relates only to the Shermer suit in the High Court of Chancery, JM's mistaken endorsement caused it to be filed with the papers in Coleman v. Wyatt, a case JM had brought in the General Court in 1785 and which was later transferred to the Fredericksburg District Court (*PJM*, I, 143 and n. 7).

2. Docs. II and IV. The deponents first sent their rough answers, which JM put in the appropriate form. JM then returned them to be sworn before a magistrate. Booth here enclosed the sworn answers.

3. The court on 27 May 1789 awarded commissions to the parties to take the depositions of their witnesses. The depositions were taken in June and July. Three of the persons named by Booth deposed in this suit: Charles Hankins, Mary Mason Tabb, widow of George Booth of Bellville and wife of Philip Tabb (Doc. I, n. 10), and Ann Jones, widow of Dr. Richard Jones. Mary Booth was probably the widow of George Booth of Poropotank (Stubbs, *Descendants of Mordecai Cooke*, 194, 262).

The other deponents in the Shermer suit were Mary Richardson, William Hawkins, Moses Sweenny, and John James. The depositions, along with letters in the handwriting of John Shermer, comprised the evidence in the case (copies, Record of Shermer v. Shermer's Executors). The main point the defendants sought to establish by this testimony was John Shermer's intention to devise half his estate to Ann Shermer and her relatives.

4. In Aug. 1789 the plaintiff was given leave to file an amended bill and to add several persons as defendants. The amended bill, differing in only minor particulars from the original, was filed around Jan. 1790. Dudley Richardson put in his amended answer on 4 Oct. 1791, and Thomas Booth did likewise on 21 June 1792 (ibid.).

VI. Chancellor Wythe's Opinion

27 September 1792

In this cause, upon these words in the testament of John Shermer, who died in 1775, 'i give to my wife the use and profits of my whole estate, both real and personal, during her natural life, and, after that is ended, my will and desire is, that the whole of my estate, exclusive of that already given my wife, be equaly divided betwixt whoever my wife shall think proper to make her heir or heirs, and my loving brother Richard Shermer,' a question was made, whether Anne Shermer, the wife of the testator, who died, a few days after him, in the same month, without making any disposition of her estate, took a fee simple in one half of the land devised, and a property in one half of the other estate bequeathed, to her? the plaintiff, who is heir of John Shermer, and next of kindred to him, claming the half, of which she had not the ownership, as he insists, but only power to dispose; because, by her failure to exercise that power, that half was undisposed, and consequently descended and devolved upon him.

BY THE COURT, the 27 day of september 1792.

By the first section of Lyttleton's tenures we learn, that, in feoffments and grants, a fee simple, or the greatest property, in land is not conveyed to the taker, unless in the habendum after his name be inserted the words, 'and to his heirs.'[1] but these words, notwithstanding the addition of them at that time was necessary, in those acts, to augment the estate, from an estate for life, which without them it would have been, to an estate of inheritance, do not import, as an ordinary reader might suppose, a transfer of any right to the heirs. indeed if he, to whom and to whose heirs, land is conveyed, make no disposition thereof, his heir will succeed to it. yet this is not because he was indicated by the word, 'heirs,' in the deed of conveyance, for where an inheritance is acquired, not by tralatitious act, as by estopel, disseisin, abatement, intrusion, &c. the heir, if no disposition be made of it, will succede to it. it is because, where the dying owner of an inheritance hath not appointed a successor, the law appointeth one for him: but he may prevent the hereditary succession, by act taking effect in his lifetime, e g. by a sale or gift, or not until after his death, e. g by appointment of a testamentary successor or a haeres factus. the words, 'to his heirs,' therefore, even where they are requisite, are an antiphrasis: they do not restrain the ancestor from disinheriting, but instead of that, making him absolute owner, impower him to disinherit, the heir. a grant to one and to his heirs then is, in effect, a grant of power, in popular language, to dispose. so that a grant to one of a power to dispose of lands, is a form naturally as apt to convey an inheritance, as a grant of the lands to him and to his heirs.

Accordingly in some formulae the word heirs is unnecessary. in a testament technical language is dispensed with, and may be supplied by the testators intention; for if a man devise lands to one, TO GIVE, in this case a fee simple doth pass by the intent of the devisor. Cokes institutes, 1 vol. fol. 9. b. and more than a myriad of other examples to the same purpose may be quoted.[2] a devise then to one to give, is equivalent to a devise to one and to his heirs. a devise to my wife, 'and to whomsoever she shall think proper to make her heir or heirs,' is equivalent to a devise to my wife, 'to give;' and consequently equivalent to a devise to my wife and to 'her heirs.' a devise in this form, 'i make I S heir of my estate,' or 'i will that I S inherit my estate,' hath been adjudged in a multitude of cases, without an exception, to convey a fee simple; for, although, if I S be not he, whom the law denominateth the heir, the testator can no more make him heir than he can change the law, yet his intention being manifest, that I S should have the same interest in the estate, as if the characters of an heir were verified in him, the meaning of technical words, which would effectuate that intention, is transfused into the inartificial words by which the testator declared it. in like manner in a devise to my wife, with this addition, 'and my desire is that, after her death, the estate shall go to the heir or heirs whom she shall think proper to make,' the intention being manifest, she should have such a right and power that he to whom she should think proper to give the estate, or dispose of it otherwise, should have the same interest in it, as if he were in law her heir, or, if she should make no disposition that her heir should succede to it, whether she should give or dispose of it, or suffer it to descend, being a matter unimportant to the testator or his family, to the testators inartificial words shall be attributed the meaning of those technical words by which his desire will be accomplished, that is, it shall be a devise to the wife and to her heirs.

Now the words of John Shermer's testament being, 'i give to my wife the use and profits of my whole estate, during her life, and after that is ended, then my will and desire is, that the whole of my estate be equaly divided betwixt whoever my wife shall think proper to make her heir or heirs, and my brother Richard Shermer;' this devise, if for some terms in it be substituted the equivalent terms, being read thus: 'i give to my wife the use and profits of my whole estate, during her natural life, and, after that is ended, my will and desire is, that the whole of my estate be equaly divided between my wifes heirs, and my brother Richard Shermer,' would unquestionably have conveyed a fee simple in one half of the lands, and an absolute property in one half of the other estate to the wife; and such ought to be the operation of the testators own words, unless it be interdicted by the gift to her for life. if this be relied upon, two answers are given to it, either of which is sufficient to obviate the objection, if it deserve that appellation; 1 that where an estate for life is given to one, and afterwards in the same conveyance the estate is given to the heirs of the donee, the donee takes the inheritance immediately. Cokes institutes 1 vol fol. 22. b.[3] and, by like reason, where an estate for life is devised to one, and afterwards in the same testament the donee is impowered to make an heir of the estate, the donee takes the inheritance immediately. 2 that in the devise to the wife, the words, 'during her natural life,' ought not to be applied to that moiety of his estate which the testator designed for her heir or heirs, because a power to dispose, or to make an heir of the moiety, which she undeniably had, and an inheritance or property in the moiety, being synonymous terms, the words, 'during her life,' can have no effect upon her right to that moiety, which was greater than an estate during her life but ought to be confined to that moiety, which was designed for his brother, and in which her interest would cease with her life. so that the devise ought to be expounded as if it had been written thus: 'i give one half of my estate to my wife, and to whomsoever she shall think proper to make her heir or heirs, that is, i give one half of my estate to her and to her heirs, and i give the other half of it to her during her life only, and, after her death, to my brother Richard Shermer.'

This exposition of the testament fulfilleth the intention of him who made it, to divide, after the death of his wife, his estate between their two families equaly.

Dismiss the bill as to the moiety of the estate whereof the wife had a power to dispose.[4]

Printed, George Wythe, *Decisions of Cases in Virginia, by the High Court of Chancery* . . . (Richmond, 1795; Evans #29930), 6–8.

1. Edward Coke, *The First Part of the Institutes of the Laws of England; or, A Commentary upon Littleton* . . . , I (16th ed.; London, 1809), 1a. The passage

from Coke's translation of Littleton reads: "For if a man would purchase lands or tenements in fee simple, it behooveth him to have these words in his purchase, To have and to hold to him and to his heires: for these words (his heires) make the estate of inheritance."

The "habendum" is that part of a deed beginning "To have and to hold," following the granting part of the deed. "The office of the *habendum*," wrote Blackstone, "is properly to determine what estate or interest is granted by the deed" (Blackstone, *Commentaries*, II, 298).

2. Coke, *Institutes: Commentary upon Littleton*, I, 9b: "First, to *last wills* and *testaments*; for thereby, as he himselfe after saith, an estate of inheritance may passe without these words (his heires)."

3. The passage Wythe seems to have had in mind reads: "If a man make a gift in taile, or a lease for life, the remainder to his own right heires, this remainder is void, and he hath the reversion in him, for the ancestor during his life beareth in his body (in judgment of law) all his heires. . . . And this appeareth in a common case, that if land be given to a man and his heires, all his heires are so totally in him, as he may give the lands to whom he will" (ibid., 22b). Blackstone commented on this passage as follows: "The ancestor, during his life, beareth in himself all his heirs; and therefore, when once he is or might have been seised of the land, the inheritance so limited to his heirs vests in the ancestor himself: and the word 'heirs' in this case is not esteemed a word of *purchase*, but a word of *limitation*, enuring so as to encrease the estate of the ancestor from a tenancy for life to a fee-simple" (*Commentaries*, II, 242). Blackstone restated the famous rule in Shelley's Case: "Where the ancestor takes an estate of freehold, and in the same gift or conveyance an estate is limited, either mediately or immediately, to his heirs, either in fee or in tail, the heirs are words of limitation of the estate, and not words of purchase" (1 Co. Rep. 93b, 76 Eng. Rep. 208 [K.B., 1581]).

4. Immediately below his opinion Wythe wrote: "This dismission was affirmed upon an appeal."

VII. Decree of the High Court of Chancery
27 September 1792

As in and by the said Bills answers, Depositions of Witnesses and other proceedings in the said cause all of them remaining as of record in this Honorable Court relation being thereunto had may more fully and at large appear, and the said cause thus standing in Court ready for a hearing as to Dudley Richardson, Pryce Davis, Thomas Boothe and Philip Tabb, a day was appointed by this Honorable Court for the hearing thereof on which day to wit Thursday the twenty seventh day of September in the year of our lord one thousand seven hundred and ninety two. The same came on to be heard on the Bills answers exhibits and examinations of Witnesses and was then argued by Counsel. On consideration whereof, the Court is of Opinion, that in the devise to his wife by the testator John Shermer, quoted in the Bill, the words "during her natural life" ought not to be applied to that moiety of his estate of which he impowered her to dispose, because such Application would be inconsistant with his intention manifestly indicated by giving her such power, that she should have an interest in that Moiety, which would continue after her death namely the absolute property, but ought to be confined to the other moiety which he gave to his brother Richard Shermer, and in which he intended her interest should continue no longer than she should live, and consequently that the Plaintiff is not entitled to the wifes moiety, and therefore doth adjudge order and Decree, that the bill of the Plaintiff claiming the last mentioned moiety be dismissed, as it is accordingly hereby so far dismissed. And doth further order that the Defendant Dudley Richardson do make up state and settle an Account of his Administration of the estate of his testator John Shermer deceased before William Norvel Joseph Hornsbey and Robert Greenhow or any two of them to whom it is referred to examine state and settle the said Account, and the said Commissioners may proceed in the absence of either party who having reasonable notice of the time and place appointed shall fail to attend and are directed to report their proceedings to the Court, stating specially matters thought pertinent by themselves or required by the parties:[1] From which decree the Plaintiff by his Counsel prayed an Appeal from so much thereof as dismisses his bill in part, which is granted on his entering into bond with sufficient security in the penalty of twenty pounds in one month from this day.[2]

Copy, Record of Shermer v. Shermer's Executors, T.79/36 (claim of William Shermer), P.R.O.

1. Pursuant to this decree William Norvell and Robert Greenhow, two of the commissioners, along with the plaintiff William Shermer and John Brown, agent for Dudley Richardson, met at the Raleigh Tavern in Williamsburg on 5 Feb. 1793. The commissioners examined and approved Richardson's account of his administration of John Shermer's estate and also his accounts as attorney in fact for Richard Shermer (commissioners' report, 5 Feb. 1793, and accounts, Record of Shermer v. Shermer's Executors).

2. The appeal first came before the Court of Appeals in Apr. 1794, when it was continued to the next term (Va. Ct. Ap. Ord. Bk. II, 262).

VIII. Argument in the Court of Appeals
15 October 1794

MARSHALL for the appellee.[1] The devise to Mrs. Shermer, was intended to pass to her, the whole interest and absolute ownership in the moiety, given to her appointed heir. In last wills, it is not necessary that the testator should use technical words, in order to pass a fee; for however inartificially he may express himself, yet if his intention can be discovered to mean a disposition of his whole interest in the thing devised, the court will supply such words, as may be necessary to effectuate that intention. Thus, if the devise had been to the wife, to *dispose of as she pleased*, she would most unquestionably have been entitled to the fee simple, because such a power is the eminent quality of such an estate. But the case of Tomlinson and Dyghton is relied upon, to establish this principle, viz: that where an *express* estate for life is given, it cannot be enlarged by words of implication, tho' if the estate had been given *generally*, it might be otherwise.[2] I shall contend 1st, that the principle is not true, and 2dly, if it were, still the case itself is not like the present.

1st, The principle is fully contradicted by the case of King and Melling, 1 *Ventr.* 214, and the great variety of cases there cited.[3] Langly and Baldwin 1 *Eq. Cas. Ab.* 185.—Blackbourn and Edgley 1 *P. Wms.* 605.—The Attorney General *vs* Sutton, 1 *P. Wms.* 754. These cases clearly prove, that an express estate for life, may be enlarged by words of implication, if the testator's intention require it.[4] The case Tomlinson and Dyghton is consequently founded upon a mistaken principle, and ought not to be regarded.

But 2dly, If that case be law, it is unlike the present. In that, the power of disposing is limited to particular children; in this, it is to the heirs general. The distinguishing feature of a fee simple estate, is consequently discernible in this case, and not in that. Again—in that case, as well as in that cited from 3 *Leon.* 71,[5] the wife having made an appointment, the intention of the testator could not be frustrated, and consequently, the question, turning merely upon the validity of the appointment, the nature, or extent of the wife's estate, was a point only incidentally decided, and therefore, the opinion as to that point, ought not to be considered as a binding authority. Again; it will not be denied but that if an express estate for life had not been given to the wife, the latter words, would have enlarged the estate into a fee simple. In this case, the court, to effectuate the intention of the testator, will consider the life estate given to the wife, as applying, not to her moiety, but to the moiety, which after her death is devised to the brother, and this will materially distinguish the present case, from that of Tomlinson and Dyghton, & will bring it precisely within that part of the rule laid down by the court, which makes the estate to the wife a fee simple.[6]

Printed, Bushrod Washington, *Reports of Cases Argued and Determined in the Court of Appeals of Virginia*, I (Richmond, 1798), 267–68.

1. The case was argued on 15 Oct. 1794 (Va. Ct. Ap. Ord. Bk. III, 2). JM was preceded by Andrew Ronald for the appellant, who said that the principle of this case was "so conclusively settled" by Tomlinson v. Dighton (see n. 2) that it was "unnecessary to add any thing to it" (1 Wash. 266–67).

2. Tomlinson v. Dighton, 1 P. Wms. 149, 24 Eng. Rep. 335 (Ch., 1711). In this case the testator devised land to his wife for her life; the land was then to be at her disposal, provided it went to any of his children. One of the questions was whether this devise passed a fee simple estate to the wife or only an estate for life. Counsel (whose remarks JM here paraphrased) observed that "where lands are devised to one generally, and to be at his disposal, this is a fee in the devisee, but where lands were devised to one expressly for life, and afterwards to be at the devisee's disposal . . . , in this case only an estate for life passes to the devisee, with a bare power to dispose of the fee; for that (as it is said) words of implication shall not merge or destroy an express estate for life." The court was of opinion that the wife had only a life estate (1 P. Wms. 154, 171, 24 Eng. Rep. 336, 342–43).

3. King v. Melling, 1 Vent. 214, 86 Eng. Rep. 144 (K.B., 1672). This citation is only to the first hearing of the case, in which the court appeared to be of opinion that the devise in question passed only a life estate. After a second argument, however, the court ruled that the devise passed an estate tail, though the testator used the expression "for life." "The intention of the testator," said Judge Hale, "is the law to expound the instrument. . . . Tho' these words (for life) do weigh the intention that way (to an estate for life), yet they are balanced by an apparent intention that weighs as much on the other side (an estate tail)" (1 Vent. 228–32, 86 Eng. Rep. 153–55 [K.B., 1672]).

4. Langley v. Baldwin, 1 Eq. Ca. Abr. 185, 21 Eng. Rep. 976 (Ch., 1707); Blackborn v. Edgley, 1 P. Wms. 600, 24 Eng. Rep. 534 (Ch., 1719); Attorney General v. Sutton, 1 P. Wms. 754, 24 Eng. Rep. 600 (Ch., 1721). In each of these cases the testator devised "for life," but the court held that by implication he intended to pass an estate tail. JM no doubt had particularly in mind this passage from the report of Blackborn v. Edgley: "But the court exploded the notion, that words of implication should not turn an express estate for life into an estate-tail" (1 P. Wms. 605, 24 Eng. Rep. 536).

5. Anonymous, 3 Leo. 71, 74 Eng. Rep. 548 (C.P., 1578). In this case, which was discussed by counsel in Tomlinson v. Dighton, the testator devised lands to his wife for life; after her death the lands were to be given to whom she pleased. The court held that the wife had only a life estate with a power to dispose of the reversion. The testator, said the court, had devised the lands expressly to his wife for life, "and therefore by implication she should not have any further estate: but if an express estate had not been appointed to the wife; by the other words, an estate in fee-simple had passed."

6. Bushrod Washington for the appellant followed with a long rebuttal

founded on what he conceived to be the true principle of Tomlinson v. Dighton: "But the Court never will convert an *express* estate for life into an estate of inheritance, by words of *implication*, unless compelled to do so by absolute necessity; that is, where the intention is in the first place clear, and not merely a doubtful, or possible intention; and secondly where that intention *cannot otherwise be effectuated*." The cases cited by JM, he said, were consistent with this principle. There was no necessity, Washington insisted, for the court to construe John Shermer's intention—"there is no room left for construction, where there is no ambiguity in the expression." Ann Shermer either neglected or chose not "to exercise the power she had, and therefore, this attempt is made, in order to repair the consequences of this omission, by sacrificing to that end, the established principles of law" (1 Wash. 269, 270, 271).

JM's reasoning, however, proved more persuasive to President Pendleton, who on 18 Oct. delivered the opinion of the court affirming the decree of the High Court of Chancery. The cases cited on behalf of the appellant, said Pendleton, "seem to verify the saying of a judge, 'that in disputes upon wills, cases seldom illucidate the subject, which depending on the intention of the testator, to be collected from the will, and from the relative situation of the parties, ought to be decided upon the state and circumstances of each case.'" As for Shermer's will, "the intention is apparent, that the wife should have the whole estate for life, and that at her death, one half (except his specific bounty to her) should go to *her family*, and the other to *his own*. Their relative situation, and his prior declarations, only shew such intention to be liberal and just" (Va. Ct. Ap. Ord. Bk. III, 6; 1 Wash. 271, 272).

After losing in the Virginia courts, William Shermer took his case to the British debt claims commissions, seeking to recover the loss occasioned both by the adverse chancery decree and by the depreciation of paper money during the war. By 1803 the total sum he claimed, including nearly thirty years' interest, amounted to £17,000 sterling, £11,000 of which embraced that half of the Shermer estate distributed to the relations of Ann Shermer, plus law costs. The board of commissioners rejected this part of his claim, not persuaded by Shermer's contention that the Virginia court of chancery was biased against him because he was a British subject. As for the loss resulting from paper money, the board made no decision on that part of Shermer's claim before his death in 1806, and there is no indication that his widow continued to press his claim (memorial and claim of William Shermer, 16 Nov. 1803, T.79/36 [claim of William Shermer], P.R.O.; Minute Book of Board of Commissioners, 1803–4, 243–46, 343–46, T.79/104, P.R.O.; Minute Book, 1806, 228–29, T.79/107, P.R.O.; Minute Book, 1807, 470–72, T.79/108, P.R.O.).

6. Morris v. William Alexander & Company
1788–1801

I. Robert Morris to John Marshall and Others, 16 June 1788
II. Bill in Chancery, ca. July 1788
III. Deposition of Joseph Higbee, 31 January 1795

Editorial Note

The far-flung commercial activities of Robert Morris generated voluminous litigation during the lifetime of the great merchant and financier. Two of the longest and costliest of Morris's cases occurred in Virginia, where John Marshall served as his attorney. The first began in March 1787, when Morris's former associate Carter Braxton filed a bill in chancery in the Henrico County Court for the settlement of wartime commercial transactions with the firm of Willing & Morris.[1] The second commenced in the summer of 1788, when Morris sued William Alexander & Company of Richmond in the High Court of Chancery for a large balance due on their tobacco contracts between 1784 and 1787. So complicated were Morris's business dealings with Braxton and Alexander that he found it necessary to reside in Virginia from November 1787 to July 1788 in an attempt to settle his affairs. During this extended stay, which coincided with the contest over the ratification of the Constitution, the Philadelphia merchant and his Richmond lawyer no doubt began to cultivate a close professional and personal relationship. Eventually their two families would be united by the marriage in April 1795 of Hester Morris, Morris's daughter, and James M. Marshall, Marshall's brother.[2]

The Braxton and Alexander cases remained in the courts for years, following the typical pattern of chancery causes involving complicated mercantile accounts. After the Henrico court decreed for Braxton in 1791, Morris appealed to the High Court of Chancery, which overturned the county court's ruling in 1793. Braxton then took his case to the Court of Appeals. In a lengthy and complex decree of November 1795 that court reversed numerous parts of the chancery court's decree and ordered new proceedings on other parts, a decision which Morris condemned as "the most infamous act of injustice that ever man suffered."[3] Against Alexander he fared better, though by the time of his eventual victory in 1801 Morris had suffered a drastic reversal of fortune. Having overextended himself in vast land speculations, the former merchant prince had to endure the indignity and privation of debtors' prison, followed by bankruptcy proceedings on behalf of his many creditors. Measured against this calamity, the outcome of his suit with Alexander must have been of small comfort to him.[4]

To a great extent Morris's financial woes in the 1790s resulted from the failure of two large-scale tobacco contracts of the preceding decade. In both of these contracts Morris was associated with William Alexander & Company, whose partners were William Alexander (1729–1819), a prominent Scots merchant and banker, and Jonathan Williams, Jr. (1750–1815), Alexander's son-in-law and grandnephew of Benjamin Franklin.[5] Through Franklin's patronage this firm obtained a contract in September 1783 to supply the Farmers-General of France with fifteen thousand hogsheads of tobacco annually for three years at a set price. Under this arrangement Alexander established himself at Richmond early in 1784, Williams remaining in France. In March 1784 Morris became a partner with a one-third share in the venture. This contract was superseded early in 1785 by a second between Morris and Simon-Emmanuel-Julien Le Normand, receiver-general of La Rochelle, by which the Philadelphia merchant was to ship twenty thousand hogsheads of tobacco annually in 1785, 1786, and 1787 at a stated price to four French ports. To finance the scheme Morris, who now had the directing role in the operation, was to receive a large advance from a French banking house. Out of a "sence of delicacy" (Document I) he gave Alexander a one-third share in this new contract. In July 1786 Alexander agreed to give up his interest and accept a commission of one dollar per hogshead on the total to be delivered. If, as expected, Virginia and Maryland tobacco could be purchased at well below the contract price, Morris and his associates stood to reap enormous profits. For a variety of reasons, but chiefly because the anticipated drop in American tobacco prices occurred too late, this contract proved disappointing and seriously strained Morris's heavily committed financial resources.[6] Morris blamed his losses in part on Alexander's alleged mishandling of funds for the purchase of tobacco. Unable to reach an amicable settlement of their accounts, the erstwhile partners resorted to the High Court of Chancery to resolve their dispute.

In response to Morris's bill (Document II) Alexander made a counterclaim by means of a cross-bill, a tactic that defendants in chancery frequently employed. Ultimately the proceedings between these two merchants embraced no fewer than five separate suits that were decided together by the High Court of Chancery and the Court of Appeals: *Morris* v. *Alexander & Company*; *Alexander* v. *Morris*; *Griffin* v. *Alexander & Company*; *Alexander on behalf of himself and Company* v. *Griffin and Morris*; and *A. J. Alexander* v. *Griffin and Morris*.[7] The documentation of these cases is ample, including not only the published report of the appeal decided in 1801 but also a massive group of original papers arising from Morris's side of the contest. Now part of the Arents Tobacco Collection at the New York Public Library, these papers consist of pleadings, reports, and exhibits (correspondence, accounts, contracts, etc.) that were filed in the High Court of Chancery.[8] Two other important manuscripts also survive: Morris's letter of 16 June 1788 to Marshall and other attorneys, and Marshall's draft of the bill in chancery (Documents I and II). These two documents together provide an excellent illustration of the process of preparing a bill in equity.

After the filing of Morris's bill in 1788, three years passed before the pleadings phase was completed. The court then referred the business to commissioners to audit the accounts and prepare a report, a common procedure in mercantile disputes. By law the court of chancery could appoint one or more commissioners for this purpose—in this case four were named.[9] Before the commissioners could report, the two parties had to submit statements of their own claims and exceptions to each other's claims. The chief point of disagreement was a twenty-thousand-dollar credit claimed by Alexander. By the terms of his July 1786 contract with Morris, Alexander was to receive a commission of one dollar per hogshead. In the summer of 1785 the Farmers-General had permitted Morris to ship up to twenty thousand additional hogsheads—eighty thousand total—within the three-year contract period to offset losses sustained on earlier shipments. Financial embarrassments and other circumstances prevented the Philadelphia merchant from taking full advantage of this offer. By the end of the contract period Morris had shipped sixty-seven thousand hogsheads, though the Farmers-General actually accepted something less than the sixty thousand originally agreed upon. Alexander's interpretation of the various agreements and contracts was that his commission covered eighty thousand rather than sixty thousand hogsheads.[10]

Alexander's claim rested on several assumptions: that he had been a partner with a one-third share in the contract; that his agreeing to receive a fixed commission was a consideration for relinquishing his share; and that the indulgence granted to Morris in the summer of 1785 in fact extended the contractual number of hogsheads to be delivered from sixty thousand to eighty thousand. In essence, Alexander maintained that he had exchanged a one-third share of the profits on eighty thousand hogsheads for a commission of one dollar per hogshead on that number. Morris, on his part, insisted that Alexander's true situation was that of an agent rather than a partner and that the commission agreement was a compensation for services rendered and to be rendered, not for renouncing any alleged interest in the contract. As for the allowance to ship additional tobacco, this was a separate agreement affecting Morris alone, one that was purely optional and that in no way obligated him to employ Alexander beyond the sixty thousand hogsheads of the original contract.[11]

The chancery commissioners, now reduced to three, finally reported in June 1797; two of them sided with Morris, the other with Alexander. Sixteen months later Chancellor Wythe handed down a decree that emphatically upheld the Philadelphia merchant.[12] When Alexander decided to appeal, Morris may have expected the worst from President Pendleton, whom he denounced as an "old villain" for the "rascally decree" of the Court of Appeals in the Braxton suit. The appellate court let the decree stand, however, though Pendleton did not hesitate to express his strong disapproval of Morris (suggesting he was motivated by "an insatiable thirst for riches") and his methods of doing business.[13]

Marshall was one of five Richmond lawyers—the others were William Nelson, Jerman Baker, John Taylor, and James Innes—originally retained by Morris in his suit against Alexander. Marshall evidently remained actively employed on Morris's behalf until he departed on his diplomatic mission to France in the summer of 1797.[14] He returned from Europe shortly before the High Court of Chancery issued its decree on 22 September 1798. Whether Marshall renewed his attention to this case during the appeal is unknown. By the time the appeal arguments were heard in the fall of 1801, Marshall was sitting as chief justice of the U.S. Supreme Court.[15]

1. *PJM*, I, 370 and n. 62.

2. James Madison to George Washington, 18 Nov. 1787 (Hutchinson, *Madison Papers*, X, 253, 254 n. 1); Robert Morris to Marshall, 2 Nov. 1795 (*PJM*, II, 322 and n. 8).

3. Braxton v. Willing, Morris & Co., 4 Call 288–304; Morris to John Richard, Jr., 8 Dec. 1795, Robert Morris Letterbook, DLC.

4. For Morris's activities as a land speculator, see Barbara Ann Chernow, *Robert Morris: Land Speculator, 1790–1801* (New York, 1978).

5. For information on the Alexander family of Edinburgh, see Jacob M. Price, *France and the Chesapeake: A History of the French Tobacco Monopoly, 1674–1791, and of Its Relationship to the British and American Tobacco Trades* (2 vols.; Ann Arbor, 1973), I, 606–16.

6. Ibid., II, 738–87.

7. These suits, the reporter noted, were "so interwoven with each other, as in truth to constitute different points in the same cause" (3 Call 89).

8. Price cited some of these documents in his work (*France and the Chesapeake*, II, 1101). The Arents Tobacco Collection acquired the Morris papers from King V. Hostick, a Chicago manuscripts dealer, between 1968 and 1971 (Joseph T. Rankin, Curator, Arents Collections, to Charles F. Hobson, 13 Apr. 1981, Editorial Office, Papers of John Marshall). The originals once reposed in the Office of the Clerk, Augusta County Circuit Court, Staunton, Va. After the Court of Appeals decree in 1801, the Morris and Alexander suits were remanded to the High Court of Chancery for further proceedings. In 1802 these suits were transferred to the new Superior Court of Chancery at Staunton. The papers thus survived the Richmond fire of 1865, which destroyed the papers of the original High Court of Chancery. The Morris and Alexander case file, except for a bill in chancery dated 20 June 1794, was apparently removed from the Augusta Circuit Court sometime before 1912. The chancery bill was the only document from these cases still remaining (as it does today) in the clerk's office when Lyman Chalkley published his extracts from the loose papers of the Augusta court (*Chronicles of the Scotch-Irish Settlement in Virginia* [3 vols.; 1912; Baltimore, 1974 reprint], II, 117).

9. Hening, *Statutes*, XII, 767. The commissioners were Richmond merchants William Hay, Alexander Buchanan, George Weir, and John Groves. See John Richard, Jr., to commissioners, 7 Apr. 1792, Morris v. Alexander, Arents Tobacco Collection, NN.

10. Answer of Robert Morris, 6 Nov. 1789, Morris v. Alexander, Arents Tobacco Collection, NN. See also Price, *France and the Chesapeake*, II, 773–75, 783–85.

11. Memorial of William Alexander, 25 Jan. 1792; John Richard, Jr., "Observations," [3 Dec. 1796?], Morris v. Alexander, Arents Tobacco Collection, NN.

12. Report of Commissioners Buchanan and Weir, 6 June 1797; report of Commissioner William Hay, 6 June 1797; opinion of George Wythe, ca. Sept. 1798, Morris v. Alexander, Arents Tobacco Collection, NN.

13. Robert Morris to John Richard, Jr., 8 Dec. 1795; Morris to Benjamin Harrison, Jr., 13 Dec. 1795, Robert Morris Letterbook, DLC. For Pendleton's opinion, see 3 Call 94–105 (quotation at 103).

14. JM recorded a retainer fee from Morris in May 1788 (*PJM*, I, 410). Only one letter in the surviving correspondence between JM and Morris mentions the Alexander litigation (Morris to JM, 16 June 1796 [*PJM*, III, 29]).

15. Va. Ct. Ap. Ord. Bk. IV, 110–19, 126.

I. Robert Morris to John Marshall and Others
16 June 1788

Gentlemen Richmond June the 16th. 1788

The unjust, unexpected, and unprovoked Treatment which I have met with from Messieurs William Alexander & Company of this Place having compelled me, contrary to my inclination, to seek that Justice by a Course of Law which they refuse to render me unless compelled, I now sit down to give you in writing, that history of my dealings and connection with them which, at my first interview with you, I had the honor to communicate verbally, but as I have not with me the sundry Agreements, Memorandums & Letters which are necessary to enable me to do it with accuracy, I am obliged to trust, for the present, to memory, but I expect that this detail will be sufficiently so to enable you to file in the High Court of Chancery my Bill of Complaint against them in such terms as can be supported.

In the year 1783 or 1784 William Alexander Esqr: called on me at my Dwelling in the City of Philadelphia[1] & after delivering some introductory Letters, he proceeded to inform me that previous to his departure from Paris, he had made an agreement, under the Firm of William Alexander & Company, with the Farmers General of France, by which the Farm was bound to receive from them any quantity of Tobacco not exceeding Fifteen Thousand Hogsheads at the price of Thirty Livres Tournois ℔ hundred Pounds Nett weight of Tobacco delivered at the Ports of Dieppe, Havre de Grace, Bourdeaux or Morlaix, in France and, inviting me to take on third Interest in that Contract, he produced certain Articles of Agreement executed under hand & seal by himself and by Mr. Jonathan Williams, purporting, if I remember right, to be Articles of Copartnership between them for the sole purpose of executing that Contract under the Firm of William Alexander & Company. He urged me to become a party thereto, alledging many things to induce my concurrence. I suppose it may be useless to repeat here the conversation that passed between us on this subject, because finally I was prevailed on to comply with his wishes and become a party to that paper, altho' I had no expectation of his being able to do any profitable buisiness under that Contract, and on the other hand he urged that nothing could be lost as William Alexander & Company were not bound to deliver any Tobacco unless they chose to do so, and this being in their option they should only attempt it at such times as the Article could be purchased on Terms to yield a profit.[2] He produced to me a Letter of Credit signed by Messrs: Laval & Wilfelsheim Bankers in Paris, by which they agreed to honor the Bills of William Alexander & Company to the extent of either 150,000 or 300,000 Livres Tournois upon certain conditions therein expressed. This Letter was accompanied by an attestation of Doctor Franklin in his Ministerial Capacity as having been Witness to the signature of Messieurs Laval & Wilfelsheim in order to put the Credit beyond doubt in America.

After agreeing to become a Partner in this Contract, I agreed also to negotiate and endorse the Bills to be drawn by the said William Alexander & Company on Messieurs Laval & Wilfelsheim for account of the object before us. All points being thus settled, Mr. Alexander returned to Richmond and commenced his operations.

The Paper herewith No. 1 is a copy of the account which he has rendered to me of the buisiness of this Contract, by which it appears there is a loss of £1972:14:1 Virginia Currency, for one third part of that Sum, vizt £657:11:4¼ like Money, he charges me in Account Current, but as he hath not produced any vouchers in support of this Account, it appears to me that he ought to shew the actual Cost & charges of the Tobacco therein charged, the actual prices obtained for the Tobacco sold, produce the account Sales in France to ascertain the actual Nett Proceeds & actual charges and I observe that he extends the amount of the Nett Proceeds of three Cargoes 170,310lt. 6s.7d[3] at 29½ ₱ ecu[4] to reduce the Livres into Sterling Money and that Sterling at 130 ₱. ct. to bring it into Virginia Currency. Now as I sold the Bills he drew on Messieurs Laval & Wilfelsheim for the Purchase of Tobacco at an higher Exchange than that at which he credits the said Nett Proceeds, it follows that in this instance the account is erroneous. Messieurs Laval & Wilfelsheim having, since these Transactions, failed, & Mr. Laval being employed to wind up their affairs, he has transmitted to me his Power of Attorney with the state of their Accounts with Messieurs William Alexander & Compy on which a ballance remains due to the former. It is my intention, under that Power of Attorney, to bring Suit for the recovery of said ballance, but this cannot be done untill I return to Philadelphia & send hither the Accounts. It occurs here to ask, as I became a party in the Buisiness of this Contract, how far I may be liable for that ballance, the Credit being given to William Alexander & Jonathan Williams, under the Firm of William Alexander & Company previous to my Concern, which Concern is probably unknown even at this day to Messrs. Laval & Wilfelsheim. My Complaint under this Contract is that the sum of £657:11:4¼ charged to me as my third of the loss is not a just charge, & that I have not been furnished with the proper Vouchers in support of the several Articles of Debit & Credit in the Account rendered.[5]

In the year 1784 I received Letters from Mr. Le Normand & Messieurs Le Couteulx & Co: of Paris proposing a Contract with the Farmers General of France, and desiring me to specify the Terms on which I would engage to supply them with fifteen or Twenty Thousand Hogsheads of Tobacco annually, either on Commossion or at fixed price, a Correspondence ensued between those Gentlemen and myself on this subject,[6] in the progress of which I found that it would ripen into an actual Agreement, and altho' Mr. Alexander's name had never been mentioned in the Letters of my Friends in Paris, yet, from a sence of delicacy alone, I was induced to admit him into a participation of my Contract, least it might appear to him, or in the eyes of the World as if I had supplanted him in the buisiness. I, therefore, allowed him one third part of my Contract, and he was to superintend the business in Virginia. Accordingly in the Spring of the Year 1785 he commenced the purchase of Tobacco under my Contract, his own having ceased. The first Cargo [dispa]tched was by the Ship Elizabeth 530 Hhds in April or May, which on it's arrival in France was attached by Mr. Walpole of London on account of a debt due to him by William Alexander,[7] but, the Documents of this Cargo being in my name, the attachment was withdrawn & my Freinds in France wrote that if Mr. Alexander had any Interest in this Contract I must immediately disengage him from it;[8] upon the receipt of these Letters I wrote for Mr. Alexander, he came to Philadelphia and entered into a new Agreement under hand & seal, whereby he renounced all Share, Interest & Concen in my said Contract.[9] He had in the meantime been dealing in some of the Public Securities and let me know that it was his intention that those dealings should be considered as an appendage to the Contract, and that the Parties should participate therein in the same proportions as they did in the Contract itself, this I declined and refused to have any Interest, Share or Concern in any of the Securities or Funds, or in his bargains and dealings therein. But as he had purchased more Tobacco than he had Shipped and had sold again some part thereof at an advanced price, I thought it proper, as he was still to superintend in Virginia the business of my Contract there, that he should renounce all right to buy & sell Tobacco except for my account only, and accordingly he is bound by one Article of the agreement to purchase no Tobacco but on my account nor to make Sale of any but on my Account also, unless my permission should be first obtained. This Articles comprehends the purchase & Sales already made as well as those which were to be made during Continuance of my Contract, consequently the account of all Tobacco by him purchased, as well as the disposition thereof, whether sold or shipped, kept in his Books is my account of Tobacco, the Profit or Loss thereon being mine. By another article of this agreement, I agreed to allow to Messieurs William Alexander & Co: (the Members of the Firm being now William Alexander & Jonathan Williams, for I was only one so far as Mr. Alexander's Contract went & for that Concern only) one Mexican Dollar for every Hhd of Tobacco shipped under my Contract, in lieu of the Interest or Concern which he renounced and in lieu of Commission being in full Compensation for the services and assistance which he was to render me in executing the business of the Contract. This agreement being executed, Mr. Alexander returned to Virginia & contin[ued] the purchase [& shipm?]ent of Tobacco on my account and under my directions, for which I provided him with Funds from time to time as he required or represented to be necessary, by sending Specie, Bills of Exchange on Paris & on London, by permitting him to draw upon my Credits, by remitting him Drafts on Virginia & by allowing him to draw upon my Correspondents in Baltimore & New York & upon myself in Philadelphia, also by placing in his hands, to be used as occasion might require & oppertunities offer, my promissary Notes, payable on demand in Bills of Exchange or Specie, or Notes for Specie only.[10] Under these various modes of Obtaining Funds, Mr. Alexander took care from the Start to provide himself with Funds beyond what were actually necessary or what were actually employed as they ought to have been for my service, and I expect that one operation of my Bill in Chancery will be to compell him to shew the uses to which my monies were really applied; I have good reason to believe that he continued his dealings in Public Securities, that he lent out monies to great amount upon usurious Contracts taking Pledges in Public & other Securities, and that these dealings and Loans were made entirely with my money, for in fact he had none of his own nor would any other person trust him with any. Neither should I, had I not been deceived into an Opinion of him which he never deserved. He kept me constantly in such a state of Advance as forced me to draw Bills on my Friends in Europe faster than I ought, which occasioned them first to complain, and at last obliged them to protest my Bills, by which I was subjected to heavy Damages & what is of infinitely more consequence, the loss of my Credit. In the Accounts which Mr. Alexander, at various times, has rendered, he gives a List, or charges large Sums of Mony as placed by him for my account in the hands of the Sub-Agents employed by him in the Tobacco Purchase & other Sums advanced to Persons with whom he said he had contracted for Tobacco deliverable at a future day, this was done to shew me how the large ballances which appeared upon his accounts were employed, but I have reason to believe that in some instances larger sums were charged than were actually so placed, & that in others the Contracts for Tobacco on which advances were made had originated in dealings foreign to my Concerns and were afterwards converted into Tobacco Contracts for the purpose of charging the out lying Monies to my account & of exposing me, instead of himself, to the risk of loss thereby. I have been repeatedly inform'd that Mr. Alexander has placed Facilities, Indents[11] & other Public Securities, in the hands of his Sub-Agents, together with money, that so they might purchase Tobacco paying part in one and part in the other. These Securities have been bought with my Mony at 20 or 25 ℔ Ct. or perhaps a greater Discount, & the Tobacco so purchased charged to me at the price given, he pocketting the said Discount, and the price has probably been higher for payments in this way than if it had been bought, as it ought, with all ready mony, besides that the purchase must by such means have been delayed, & consequently the advance of my Funds in Europe lengthened in point of time & increased as to the amount.[12] He has, in many instancies, Charged me with Tobacco which he neither bought, or paid for, and although he has acknowledged and corrected some of his errors in this respect, yet he has not done it in all the instancies. He has charged me his Commission of a Dollar ℔ Hhd on Sixty Thousand Hogsheads of Tobacco long before the purchase was made. He has charged me the Damages on some of my Protested Bills, although he purchased them at an under rate of Exchange from those to whom they were passed in the first instance, and paid for them with my mony, for which he never accounted with me untill the Bills came back & then he charges them to me at the highest course of Exchange with Ten ℔ Cent Interest from the date. He has charged me with the amount of a sum advanced to Doctor Griffin on a Contract for the delivery of Tobacco on my account, & upon my settling for this Contract with the Doctor, he refuses to give up the Pledges he took in Security.[13] He has charged me for various other Sums said to be advanced for the purchase of Tobacco or on Tobacco-Contracts, and has refused to give me assignments on the Parties for the Same, holding those and other funds of mine in his hands, as he pretends, to endemnify him against such of my Protested Bills as bear the endorsation of William Alexander & Co., which, not being of so great amount, I requested him to pay and charge them to me instead of which he requires that I should employ another Capital in the discharge of those Bills & then he will settle with me. I beleive the general Heads of my Complaint upon the Transactions under my Contract are now comprized in this letter & will enable you to draw such a Bill to be filed in the High Court of Chancery as we shall be able to support by the Correspondence between William Alexander & Company and me, by the Contract & agreements mentioned, & by the accounts which he has rendered, together with the information and Proofs which I shall endeavour to gain from others. I have however omitted to mention in it's proper place, that although I have for near a year been calling for the General Accounts of the Tobacco as purchased, sold &

shipped by him, I have not been able to obtain it. He pretends there is a loss on it, which is not possible, because what he sold was sold to a profit, and he has charged me with all (and more than all) that he has delivered to my use at as high or higher prices than it cost and he has frequently declared that this Account would carry a profit of several Thousand Pounds to my Credit, and which it inevitably must. It will be necessary, therefore, that his Books & Papers be produced to the Inspection of the Court, or of the Auditors that may be appointed in this Cause, not only for the purpose of investigating fully this Tobacco Account, but also to examine to the bottom the uses to which my Monies have been applied, to discover the Profits arising thereon, and to see how much thereof hath been faithfully used for my buisiness. It seems to me that my Claims on William Alexander & Compy. for the Transactions under my Contract will be—
1st: For the Profit that has arisen on the Tobacco Account.
2nd: For over-charges in their accounts of every kind, particularly for purchases of Tobacco with Indents and other Public Securities & Ca. instead of the Specie put in their hands by me.
3rd: For Interest on such part of my monies as were not employed in the Tobacco purchase.
4th: For the ballance which shall be due on the Account Current when ascertained.
To these you will add such others as may in your opinion properly arise on the Facts stated, as on the other hand you will omit any of them should you deem them improper.
As to the Damages for the injuries I have sustained by the loss of my Credit, by the detention of my Ships waiting for Cargoes whilst they employed the money to other purposes; by the Damages paid on my Protested Bills occ[asioned by?] their detention of the Funds &Ca. These I am told must be [brou]ght in the other Courts & that I must wait the Issue of the Chancery Suit before such an Action is commenced. I shall leave Mr. John Richard at Richmond to collect information & Evidence in this buisiness, and he will apply for your advice & Assistance when necessary. Mr. Benjamin Harrison Junr: will be my attorney in Fact, and through them you can communicate every thing that may from time to time, become necessary on my part.[14]

The Justice due to myself and Family, as well as some spice of resentment for the ungratefull returns made to me by Mr. Alexander for putting Sixty Thousand Dollars in his Pockett, without any risk to him and in reward for very little personal labour, conspire to draw forth, and will continue to urge, my exertions to bring him to Justice; in attempting which my principle reliance is on your well known Talents and Abilities, which I have not a doubt will be used to the best advantage in support of a Cause so just as I apprehend mine to be.

With perfect Respect & Esteem I have the honor to be Gentlemen Your most Obt. hble Servant

ROBT MORRIS

LS, Jefferson Papers, MHi. Addressed to William Nelson, John Marshall, Jerman Baker, John Taylor, and James Innes; words or parts of words in brackets indicate torn portions of MS; accessioned after publication of *PJM*, I.

1. This meeting took place in late Feb. 1784 (Price, *France and the Chesapeake*, II, 743).

2. The articles of agreement forming the copartnership of William Alexander and Jonathan Williams, dated 8 Nov. 1783, provided for taking on a third partner. Robert Morris formally signed on as a partner on 2 Mar. 1784. For copies of these agreements, see Morris v. Alexander, Arents Tobacco Collection, NN.

3. Abbreviations for the French monetary units livres tournois, sou, and denier.

4. A French coin, equivalent to three livres tournois (John J. McCusker, *Money and Exchange in Europe and America, 1600–1775: A Handbook* [Chapel Hill, 1978], 4–5). The figure 29½ apparently is the number of English pence equal to the French ecu.

5. Copies of this account have not been found.

6. Extracts of Morris's correspondence in 1784 and 1785 with Le Normand and Le Couteulx & Co. were submitted as exhibits in his suits with Alexander (Morris v. Alexander, Arents Tobacco Collection, NN).

7. For the litigation between William Alexander and London banker Thomas Walpole, see Price, *France and the Chesapeake*, II, 691–700.

8. See the extracts of Le Normand's letters to Morris of 25 June and 27 Aug. 1785, reporting Walpole's attachment of this cargo; see also Le Couteulx & Co. to Morris, 25 Aug. 1785, warning that European creditors would attach any cargo that Alexander appeared to have any interest in (Morris v. Alexander, Arents Tobacco Collection, NN).

9. Agreement (two copies), 6 July 1786, Morris v. Alexander, Arents Tobacco Collection, NN. Voluminous extracts from the correspondence of the two merchants were submitted as exhibits. See Morris to Alexander, 4 June 1786, requesting Alexander to come to Philadelphia to work out a new arrangement (ibid.).

10. These promissory notes, popularly known as "Morris's notes," enjoyed general circulation. They were first issued during Morris's reign as superintendent of finance (E. James Ferguson, *The Power of the Purse: A History of American Public Finance, 1776–1790* [Chapel Hill, 1961], 136, 138–39, 164, 169–70, 173–74).

11. The term "facilities" apparently refers to a variety of warrants issued by the state auditor that were receivable as specie for taxes in Virginia (Hening, *Statutes*, XII, 418–19). Indents were certificates issued by authority of the Confederation Congress for payment of interest on public securities in lieu of specie (Ferguson, *Power of the Purse*, 223–29, 270, 277).

12. On this point, see the testimony of Joseph Higbee (Doc. III).

13. The transactions between William Alexander and John Tayloe Griffin (b. 1750) were the subject of separate suits brought by these parties against each other. Griffin, a physician educated at the College of William and Mary and the University of Edinburgh, was the brother of Samuel Griffin, a Virginia congressman from 1789 to 1795, and of Cyrus Griffin, judge of the U.S. District Court of Virginia from 1789 to 1810 (*WMQ*, 1st ser., XIII [1905], 184; XIX [1911], 155–56; 2d. ser., I [1921], 33; Wyndham B. Blanton, *Medicine in Virginia in the Eighteenth Century* [Richmond, 1931], 75, 87; *Biographical Directory of the American Congress, 1774–1949* [Washington, D.C., 1950], 1238).

JM drafted a bill on behalf of Griffin, probably at the same time as the one for Morris. (The MS bill, in JM's hand, was offered for sale by Kenneth W. Rendell of Newton, Mass., in 1974.) The real plaintiff in this suit, as Griffin himself attested, was Robert Morris (affidavit of John Tayloe Griffin, 2 June 1791, Morris v. Alexander, Arents Tobacco Collection, NN). The bill called for the return of $56,000 in "final settlement" certificates—interest-bearing securities issued by Congress beginning in 1782 to liquidate civilian and military claims arising from the war (Ferguson, *Power of the Purse*, 145, 179–80, 184–88, 252). Having contracted in 1787 to borrow a large sum of money from Alexander & Co. and to repay it in tobacco, Griffin deposited these certificates with the company as a pledge. Morris and Griffin contended that Morris was the real creditor and that the money loaned to Griffin was out of the funds advanced by the Philadelphia merchant to Alexander on their tobacco contract. Griffin failed to deliver the tobacco, but Morris later discharged him upon the physician's selling land and other property, including the certificates, to him. Alexander refused to deliver up the final settlements and subsequently sold them, justifying the sale as an indemnity for indorsing protested bills of exchange drawn by Morris. Both the High Court of Chancery and the Court of Appeals ruled that Alexander had no lien on these certificates and no power to sell them. By the decree he was ordered to make specific restitution of certain certificates and to pay the present value of the rest (answer of John T. Griffin, 16 Jan. 1792; answer of Robert Morris, 16 Jan. 1792; answer of Robert Morris, 5 Aug. 1798, Morris v. Alexander, Arents Tobacco Collection, NN; 3 Call 100–103).

14. John Richard, Jr., acted on Morris's behalf throughout the Alexander litigation. He and Benjamin Harrison, Jr. (d. 1799), son of former Gov. Benjamin Harrison and brother of future President William Henry Harrison, corresponded frequently with Morris about the Braxton and Alexander suits during the 1790s (*VMHB*, XXXV [1927], 89; Robert Morris Letterbook, DLC). They also served as agents for New York merchant William Constable, who had a case in the Virginia courts at the same time (Case No. 8).

II. Bill in Chancery

ca. July 1788

To the Honble. the Judges of the High court of chancery humbly complaining sheweth unto your Honors your Orator Robert Morris[1]

That some time in the year 1783 or 1784 a certain William Alexander esquire calld on your orator in the city of Philadelphia & after delivering some introductory letters proceeded to inform him that previous to his departure from Paris he had made an agreement under the firm of William Alexander & Co. with the farmers genl. of France by which the farm was bound to receive from them any quantity of tobacco not exceeding fifteen thousand hox heads at the price of thirty livres tournois pr. hundred pounds nett weight of tobacco deliverd at the ports of Dieppe, Havre de grace, Bourdeaux, or Morlaix in France & producd certain articles of Agreement executed under hand & seal by himself & by Mr. Jonathan Williams purporting as well as your orator recollects to be articles of agreement between them for the sole purpose of executing that contract under the firm of William Alexander & Company. He warmly urged your Orator to become a party thereto, & alledgd many inducements—in particular that nothing coud be lost as William Alexander & Company were not bound to deliver any tobacco unless they chose to do so, & this being in their option they shoud only attempt it at such times as the article coud be purchasd on terms to yield a profit. Your orator was inducd tho reluctantly to become a partner in this contract. The said Alexander producd also to your Orator a letter of credit sign'd by Messieurs Laval & Wilsesheim bankers in Paris & attested by Doctor Franklin by which they agreed to honor the bills of William Alexander & Co. to the extent of either 150,000 or 300,000 livres tournois upon certain conditions therein expressd. After agreeing to become a partner in this contract your orator also agreed to negotiate & indorse the bills to be drawn by the said William Alexander & Co. on Messieurs Laval & Wilsesheim for the object before them. Things being thus adjusted the said William Alexander return'd to Richmond to commence his operations. He has since chargd your orator with a considerable loss sustaind in this business but has producd no vouchers in support of his charge.

In the year 1784 your Orator receiv'd letters from Mr. le Normand & Messieurs le Couteulx & Co. of Paris proposing a contract with the farmers General of France & desiring your orator to specify the terms on which he woud supply them with fifteen or twenty thousand hogsheads of tobacco annually either on commission or at a fix'd price. A correspondence ensued between those Gentlemen & your Orator on this subject in the course of which he discoverd that it

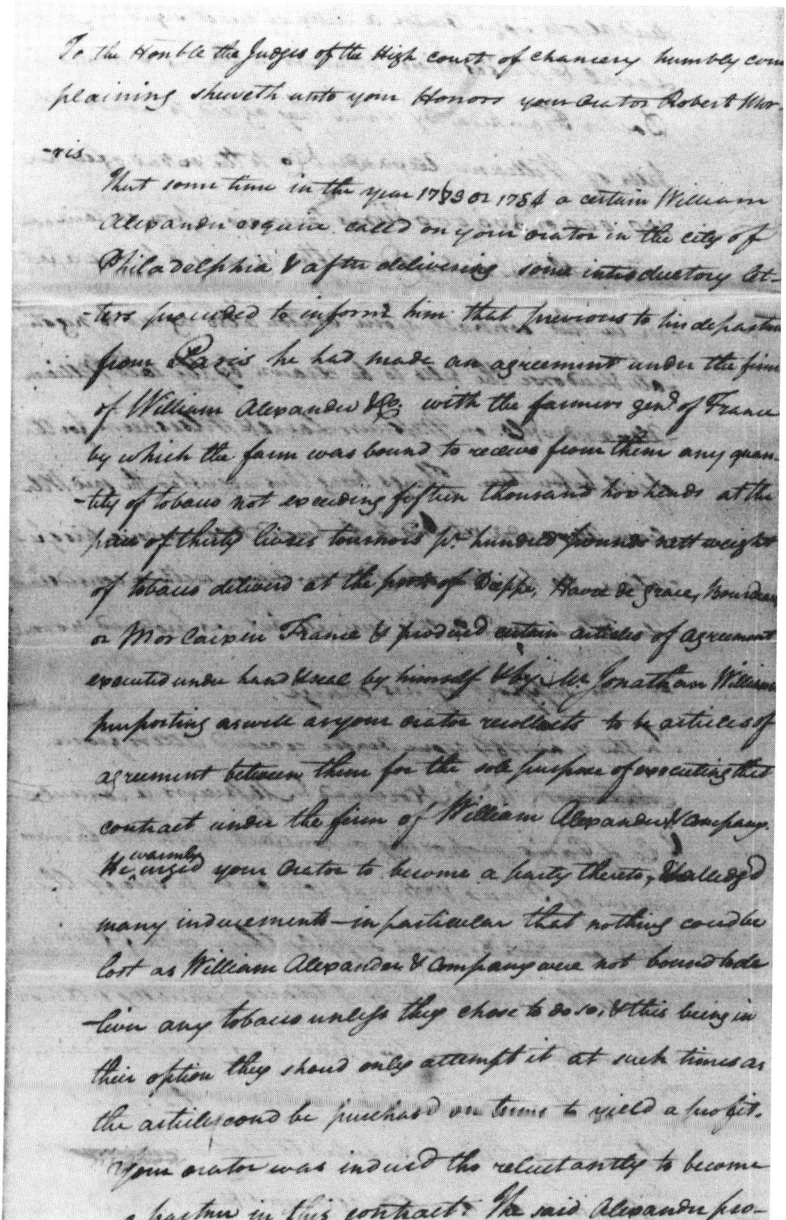

To the Honble the Judges of the High court of chancery humbly complaining sheweth unto your Honors your Orator Robert Morris.

That some time in the year 1783 or 1784 a certain William Alexander esquire called on your orator in the city of Philadelphia & after delivering some introductory letters proceeded to inform him that previous to his departure from Paris he had made an agreement under the firm of William Alexander & Co. with the farmers genl of France by which the firm was bound to receive from them any quantity of tobacco not exceeding fifteen thousand hogsheads at the price of thirty livres tournois pr. hundred pounds nett weight of tobacco delivered at the ports of Dieppe, Havre de Grace, Bourdeaux or Morlaix in France & produced certain articles of agreement executed under hand & seal by himself & by Mr. Jonathan Williams purporting as well as your orator recollects to be articles of agreement between them for the sole purpose of executing that contract under the firm of William Alexander & Company. He warmly urged your Orator to become a party thereto, & alledged many inducements—in particular that nothing could be lost as William Alexander & Company were not bound to deliver any tobacco unless they chose to do so, & this being in their option they should only attempt it at such times as the articles could be purchased on terms to yield a profit. Your orator was induced tho reluctantly to become a partner in this contract. The said Alexander pro-

BILL IN CHANCERY

The first page of Marshall's bill on behalf of Robert Morris in *Morris* v. *Alexander* (Case Number 6, Document II). *Courtesy of Swem Library, College of William and Mary* woud certainly ripen into an absolute agreement & was inducd by motives of delicacy, tho Mr. Alexander's name had never been mention'd, to admit him into a participation of the contract. *Your Orator therefor allowd him one third part of this contract* & he was to superintend the business in Virginia. Accordingly in the spring of the year 1785 the said William Alexander commencd the purchase of tobacco under this contract his own having ceas'd. The first Cargo he dispatch'd was by the ship Elizabeth 530 hogshads in April or May which on its arrival in france was attachd by Mr. Walpole of London on account of a debt due to him by Mr. Alexander; but the documents for the cargo being in the name of your Orator the attachment was withdrawn & your Orator was informd by his friends in france that if Mr. Alexander had any interest in this contract he must be immediately disengagd from it. Upon the receipt of these letters your Orator wrote for Mr. Alexander who came to Philadelphia & enterd into a new agreement under hand & seal whereby he renouncd all interest, share, or concern in the said contract. The said William Alexander had in the mean time been dealing in some of the public securities & informd your Orator that it was his intention that those dealings shou'd be considerd as an appendage to the contract & that the parties shoud participate therein in the same proportions that they did in the contract itself. This your Orator declind & refusd to have any interest, share, or concern in any of the securities or funds or in any of his bargains or dealings therein. Your Orator enterd into a further agreement with the said William Alexander by which the said William Alexander was still to superintend the business of your Orator in purchasing tobacco in Virginia for which the said William Alexander & Co. consisting of William Alexander & Jonathan Williams were to receive from your Orator one mexican dollar for every Hogs head of tobacco ship'd in full compensation for the services they were to render your orator in the execution of his contract. And as the said William Alexander had while a partner purchasd more tobacco than he had ship'd, & had sold again some part thereof at an advancd price, it was further agreed that so long as he shoud continue in the business of your Orator, he shou'd renounce all right to buy & sell tobacco except on the account of your Orator only. This article comprehended the purchases & sales then made as well as those to be made; all which will more fully appear by a true copy of the said agreement hereunto annexd to which your Orator refers & prays that the same may be taken as a part of this his bill. This agreement being executed the said William Alexander returnd to Virginia & continued the purchase & shipment of tobacco on account of your Orator & under his directions, for which your Orator provided him with funds from time to time as he requird or represented to be necessary, by sending specie, bills of exchange on Paris & on London, by permitting him to draw on the credits of your orator, by remitting him drafts on Virginia by permitting him to draw on your orators correspondents in Baltimore & New York & on himself in Philadelphia, & also by placing in his hands to be usd as occasion might require & opportunities offer, the promissory notes of your Orator payable on demand in bills of exchange or specie, or notes for specie only. Under these various modes of obtaining funds confided implicitly by your Orator to the said Alexander, he from the commencement provided himself with sums of money far beyond what were actually necessary or what were actually employd as they ought to have been for the service of your orator.

Your Orator charges that the said William Alexander continued his dealings in public securities, that he lent out monies to a great amount upon usurious contracts taking pledges in public & other securities & that these dealings & loans were made with the money of your Orator placd in his hands for other purposes. These proceedings kept your Orator constantly in such a state of advance as forcd him to draw bills on his friends in Europe faster than he ought to have done, which occasion'd them first to complain & at length to protest his bills whereby your Orator was subject to very heavy damages & to what is of infinitely more consequence, loss of credit.

The said William Alexander in some accounts render'd charges your Orator with large sums of money as placd by him on account of your Orator in the hands of subagents employd by him in the purchase of tobacco & with other sums advancd by him to persons to whom he pretends to have contracted for tobacco deliverable at a future day. Your Orator charges that in many instances such advances were not really made & that in others the contracts for tobacco on which advances were made had originated in dealings foreign to the concerns of your Orator & were afterwards converted into tobacco contracts for the purpose of charging the outlying monies to the account of your Orator & of exposing him instead of the said Alexander to the risk of loss thereby.

Your Orator further charges that the said William Alexander has repeatedly placd facilities of different sorts purchasd with the money of your Orator, together with specie, in the hands of his subagents for the purchase of tobacco thereby increasing the price given for the tobacco & chargeing the whole price given, as specie, to your Orator.

Your Orator further charges that the said William Alexander purchasd bills drawn by your Orator with the money of your Orator in his hands at an under rate of exchange, from those to whom they were first passd, & tho' he never accounted with your orator for his money so expended until the bills came back protested Yet he has chargd your orator with them as if taken up by him after the protest, with ten percent interest from the date & with the highest rate of exchange. He has chargd your Orator with various other sums pretended to have been advancd for the purchase of tobacco or on tobacco contracts & has refusd to give your orator assignments or orders on the parties for the same but holds them with other funds of your Orators in his hands under a pretext of securing himself as indorser against some protested bills drawn by your Orator to a much less amount than the funds in his hands & yet he refuses to take up the said bills, thereby exposing your orator when attackd by difficulties created by the conduct of the said Alexander to the extreme inconvenience of employing two capitals in the discharge of one debt. Your Orator further shews unto your Honors that he has repeatedly calld on the said William Alexander & Co. for a complete statement of all their dealings with him & has offerd to settle with them on the most liberal & generous principles provided they woud pay him up so much money as they coud command & secure the balance which might be due in some reasonable time, but the said William Alexander & Co. have eluded all your orators attempts to bring them to a fair settlement & have at length even denied that they are indebted to him. ALL WHICH ACTINGS & DOINGS are contrary to equity & tend manifestly to the great injury of your Orator. IN TENDER CONSIDERATION whereof & for as much as your Orator is remediless at & by the strict rules of the common law & only releivable in equity where matters of account & trust are properly cognizable. TO THE END therefor that the said William Alexander & Co. may on their corporal oaths true & perfect answer make to all & singular the premisses & especially that they may set forth precisely what the profit or losses on the first agreement between them & your Orator, that they may produce the accounts of sales in france properly authenticated & the price given for the tobacco here, & shew when & from Whom was it purchasd? That they may set forth & shew clearly what funds of your orator have come to their hands? In what & how were they receivd? In what sums & at what dates? That all the books of the said William Alexander & Co. concerning the purchase of tobacco may be laid before this Honble Court or persons to be appointed by them, That the said William Alexander & Co. may shew clearly what quantities of tobacco they have purchasd for your orator? of whom were the several quantities purchasd & at what dates? What were the prices given? When were the payments made? And in what were they made? That they may shew in what manner & in what quantities the surplus money of your orator in their hands was employd? To whom was it lent? On what terms? What profit was made upon it? What tobacco contracts has he the sd. Alexander made on account of your Orator? With what persons & at what times? State their nature with the motives & inducements leading to such contracts? How did the dealings between the several persons to whom such advances have been made under tobacco contracts & the said William Alexander & Co commence & what changes have they undergone? What securities have been taken for a compliance on the part of those with whom such contracts have been made? That they may set forth & discover what protested bills drawn by your Orator they have taken up? from whom, at what time, with what sums were they taken? When & how did the interest of the said William Alexander & Co. commence? What profit has arisen on the tobacco account? That the said William Alexander & Co. may be decreed to account fully with your Orator & to pay him whatever shall be due to him, that your Orator may in the account be allowd interest for his money in the hands of the said Alexander & not employd in the business of your Orator, that an issue may be directed to try what damages your Orator has sustaind by the conduct of the said Alexander in employing the funds of your Orator to his own purposes & thereby occasioning your Orators bills to be protested & that the said William Alexander & Co may be decreed to pay the same, & that your Orator may have such further & other relief as to your Honors shall seem proper & fitted to his case MAY IT PLEASE your Honors to grant to your Orator the commonwealths most gracious writ of subpœna to the said William Alexander & Co. to be directed commanding them &c. And your Orator will ever pray &c.[2]

J MARSHALL p q[3]

ADS, Marshall Papers, ViW. Date assigned on basis of Morris's letter of 16 June 1788 (Doc. I); probably filed at Nov. 1788 term.

1. JM used Morris's letter (Doc. I) to draft the bill.

2. Alexander's answers to this bill and to another brought by John Tayloe Griffin (also drawn by JM—see Doc. I, n. 13), and Alexander's own cross-bills, have not been found. Morris submitted his answer to Alexander's cross-bill in Nov. 1789 and an amended answer in Mar. 1792. The separate answers of Morris and Griffin to Alexander's cross-bill against them were filed in Feb. 1792. In 1796 Alexander John Alexander, brother of William, exhibited his bill against Morris, who put in his answer in June of that year (Morris to JM, 16 June 1796 [*PJM*, III, 29]). Finally, by a court order of 4 June 1798, William Alexander filed another bill against the Philadelphia merchant, which Morris answered in August of the same year. All of Morris's answers are in Morris v. Alexander, Arents Tobacco Collection, NN.

3. *Pro querente* ("for the plaintiff").

III. Deposition of Joseph Higbee
31 January 1795

A[1]

Questions to be propounded by Mr Morris to Mr Higbee[2]

Que 1st. Did you in the year 1786 carry on trade & merchandize in the city of Richmond under the firm of Lott & Higbee?

Que 2d. Did Lott & Higbee in or about the month of August or at any other time in that year sell or contract to sell to William Alexander or William Alexander & Co a quantity of Richmond or Petersburg tobacco?

Que 3d. Relate the price, the articles in which payment was made & all the circumstances of the transaction?

Que 4th. What was the difference between the value of the indents in specie & the nominal price affixd on them in the contract?

Que 5th. Woud the price at which you sold the tobacco have been proportionally lower had the whole payment been made in specie & woud you have preferd such a contract?

ROBT MORRIS

Que. 6h. Was there a considerable difference between the price of such tobacco as woud satisfy your contract & of prime tobacco.

ROBT MORRIS

B[3]

Interrogatories on the part of William Alexander & Company Defendants—

1. Do you know what Price was generally given for Tobacco in upper James River when you contracted with William Alexander in August 1786.
2. Do you know what was generally given for such Tobacco at the Time of Delivery? name these Prices.
3. Did you not buy all or part of the Tobacco for the Contract at a higher Price than that specified in the said Contract? name the prices you gave.
4 Did you not on the 15 July 1786 transact with W. Alexander & Co six hundred & twenty five Dollars Indents for Cash at the price of ten shillings in the Pound—or at what Price.
5. Did you not conceive upon the whole that the Cash & Indents paid you on the Contract was a fair & equitable Price for Tobacco to be delivered in three or four months.

6. You have said in a Letter to W. Alexander of July 4. 1794. That Indents were in Philadelphia at the Time of the Contract 7/6 to eight shillings in the Pound; But that your Inducement to take them at ten shillings was the Cash and the Time allowed for the Delivery of the Tobacco. Were not Indents at that Time higher in Richmond than in Philadelphia and were they not then received in Virginia as Cash in Payment of certain Taxes.[4]

7 Do you not know that Indents were at, or about that Time, bought in Philadelphia for the Virginia market as an object of Profit on accot. of the higher Price in the latter Place.

8 Did you buy Indents from any other Person in Richmond at the time of the Contract with W. Alexander & at what Price? If on credit name the term of Credit. If for Tobacco name the price & Time of Delivery.

In behalf of William Alexander & Co

JONA WILLIAMS

9. Did the Contract specify that the Tobaccos should be of certain Inspections & at what Inspection or Inspections were they to be delivered. In behalf of William Alexander & Co

JONA WILLIAMS

On[5] this Thirty first day of January in the year One thousand seven hundred ninety five at the City Tavern in second Street in the City of Philadelphia We James Crawford, Hugh Holmes & Clement Biddle—Commissioners named in the Annexed Commission issued from the High Court of Chancery for the Commonwealth of Virginia in a suit depending in the said Court wherein Robert Morris is plaintiff and William Alexander and Company are defendants, proceeded to the Execution of the said Commission and Joseph Higbee a Witness produced on the part of the Plaintiff named in the said suit being duly sworn according to Law to declare the whole truth in his Answers to such Interrogatories to him to be put as well on behalf of the plaintiff as of the defendants in the said suit named, the Interrogatories annexed marked A and entitled "*Questions to be propounded by Mr. Morris to Mr. Higbee*" were severaly put to the said Joseph Higbee, to which several Interrogatories on his solemn Oath,

To the first Question
or Interrogatory answering saith—I did.

To the second Question
or Interrogatory answering saith—Yes they did contract about that time to sell to William Alexander & Company about one hundred & twenty hogsheads of such Tobacco.

To the third Question
or Interrogatory answering saith—
The Contract was for twenty shillings per hundred pounds of Petersburgh Tobacco and Twenty One shillings & six pence or twenty two shillings & six pence (he dont recollect which) for Richmond Tobacco, payment was made in Advance, not wholy, four or five hundred pounds in Cash and nine hundred pounds in Indents rated at Ten shillings in the pound equal to four hundred and fifty pounds Virginia Currency, the balance in Cash at or about the delivery, the Contract was to deliver the Tobacco on time at three or four months from the time of Contract.

To the fourth Question
or Interrogatory answering saith—about Two shillings, they would not have brought Eight shillings Cash in the pound.

To the fifth Question
or Interrogatory Answering saith, Yes.

To the sixth Question
or Interrogatory answering saith—Yes.

And the Interrogatories hereunto annexed marked B entitled "*Interrogatories on the part of William Alexander & Company Defendants*," were severaly put to the said Joseph Higbee to which several Interrogatories on his solemn Oath,

To the first Question
or Interrogatory answering saith, It was generaly higher than the price which He contracted to deliver for at that time, he supposes it was at the time of Contract worth twenty five Shillings per hundred pounds but not of the Kind he was to deliver but of the Tobacco of the year before—that which he was to deliver was of new Tobacco.

To the second Interrogatory answering saith—He does not know.

To the third Interrogatory answering saith—He did not, he bought it under, does not recollect the prices.

To the fourth Interrogatory answering saith—he does not recollect that.

To the fith Interrogatory answering saith—that he was satisfied with it or should not have entered into the negociation.

To the sixth Interrogatory answering saith—That they were higher and were so received in Taxes.

To the seventh Interrogatory Answering saith, that they were.

To the Eighth Interrogatory Answering saith—that he did not.

To the Ninth Interrogatory Answering saith—The Inspections were Petersburgh and Richmond or Manchester or either of them.

And further that he knows nothing further Material to the parties Plaintiff or defendant in this Suit. And on his Oath declares the several Answers by him set forth as Aforesaid to be just and true.

JOSEPH HIGBEE

Whereupon we the said Commissioners have closed the said Commission at Philadelphia Aforesaid the day and year hereinbefore first set forth and in Testimony thereof have hereunto set our hands and Seals.[6]

JAMES CRAWFORD [L.S.]
HUGH HOLMES [L.S.]
CLEMENT BIDDLE [L.S.]

DS, Morris v. Alexander, Arents Tobacco Collection, NN. Partly in JM's hand, as noted below (n. 1). Filed with notice, 16 Jan. 1795, signed by commissioners in chancery approving commission named to take Higbee's deposition; and with commission, 16 Jan. 1795, issued by High Court of Chancery; endorsed: "Retd. Enclosed & Sealed / Feb: 16th 1795."

1. The interrogatories marked "A" are in JM's hand except for Morris's signature. JM was in Philadelphia at this time to argue Ware v. Hylton (Case No. 13) before the Supreme Court, but the appeal was postponed until the next term. Later this day Morris wrote to his agent: "This day at 12 oClock the Commissioners appointed by the High Court of Chancery of Virginia met, at the City Tavern where Mr Marshall & myself attended" (Morris to John Richard, Jr., 31 Jan. 1795, Robert Morris Letterbook, DLC).

2. Joseph Higbee, a merchant, resided in Richmond as late as 1791. He later moved to Philadelphia (Hening, *Statutes*, XIII, 175; *CVSP*, V, 58, 230; *VMHB*, VIII [1901], 293).

3. The interrogatories marked "B" are written on a separate sheet. They were prepared by Alexander's unidentified counsel and signed by Jonathan Williams on behalf of the company.

4. Indents, or certificates of interest on public securities of the U.S. (Doc. I, n. 11), were receivable in payment of taxes in Virginia, not to exceed the proportion of two-thirds (Hening, *Statutes*, XII, 95).

5. This part of the deposition begins on a separate sheet and is written in an unknown hand. Higbee signed his name at the foot of each page of his testimony, but his signatures have been omitted here except for the last.

6. Morris was pleased with the results of this testimony, writing to Richard that "our point is established by this Evidence & I hope good use will be made of it" (Morris to John Richard, Jr., 31 Jan. 1795, Robert Morris Letterbook, DLC).

In a lengthy statement prepared for the commissioners in chancery, Morris's agent contended that Alexander freely mixed his own private speculations with the purchase of tobacco on Morris's account, specifically referring to the transaction with Lott & Higbee as an example. According to the statement, Alexander, having accumulated a large quantity of indents, used his tobacco contracts as a means of selling this public paper at higher than the market rate. The commissioners subsequently allowed Morris's claim for a £90 overcharge on the tobacco bought from Lott & Higbee. "This claim is admitted," they noted in their June 1797 report, "because it appears by the deposition of Joseph Higbee that the Plaintiff sustained a loss to this amount and that the Defendants made a proffit by the transaction to which they were not entitled" (John Richard, Jr., "Tobacco Account, William Alexander & Co. with Robert Morris, with Notes of Reference &c.," 3 Dec. 1796; report of commissioners, 6 June 1797, Morris v. Alexander, Arents Tobacco Collection, NN). The £90 overcharge resulted from rating indents at 10s. to the pound rather than at the market price of 8s. Alexander & Co. should have charged only £360, not £450, as the real cash value of the £900 in indents advanced to Lott & Higbee.

After the Court of Appeals in 1801 sustained the 22 Sept. 1798 decree of the High Court of Chancery, the Morris and Alexander cases were remanded to the chancery court for further proceedings. Final decrees, affirming the original decree, were rendered on 3 Dec. 1804 and 6 Apr. 1805 in the Superior Court of Chancery at Staunton (Superior Court of Chancery, Augusta County, Order Book, 1802–5, 221, 253, 340–41, 402–4 [microfilm], Vi).

7. Wayles's Executors v. Randolph et al.

1795–1799

I. Bill in Chancery, March 1795
II. Answer of David M. Randolph, 6 June 1795
III. Plea and Demurrer of David M. Randolph, 6 June 1795
IV. Plea and Demurrer of Richard Randolph, 12 March 1796
V. Answer of Richard Randolph, 12 March 1796
VI. Answer of Brett Randolph, 12 March 1796
VII. Answer of Ryland Randolph, 12 March 1796
VIII. Bill of John Loyd and Thomas Main, ca. April 1797
IX. Answer of Richard Randolph and David M. Randolph, 23 May 1797
X. Amended Answer of David M. Randolph, ca. May 1797
XI. Amended Answer of Richard Randolph, ca. May 1797
XII. Replication of John Loyd, ca. May 1797
XIII. Order of Reference, 25 May 1797
XIV. Commissioner's Report, 26 May 1797
XV. Exceptions to Commissioner's Report, ca. 26 May 1797
XVI. Agreement, ca. June 1797
XVII. Decree of the High Court of Chancery, 5 October 1797
XVIII. Argument in the Court of Appeals, ca. 6 November 1799
XIX. Decree of the Court of Appeals, 9 November 1799

Editorial Note

John Wayles (1751–1773) and Richard Randolph (ca. 1725–1786), whose executors and heirs were parties to this complicated suit, were tobacco planters with extensive mercantile interests along the James River before the Revolution. Both men accumulated vast landed and personal estates along with large debts, owed mainly to British merchants. Wayles, born in Lancashire, studied law in England before coming to Virginia. He eventually settled in Charles City County, establishing his seat at The Forest. Married and widowed three times, Wayles had four daughters. The oldest, Martha, married Thomas Jefferson, who along with Francis Eppes (another son-in-law) acted as Wayles's executor. According to Jefferson, Wayles was "worth at least £30,000 Sterling" at his death, with outstanding debts of about ten thousand pounds sterling, most of which was owed to Farell & Jones, a Bristol merchant company. Although he died solvent, the settlement of his estate over the next thirty years caused much expense and vexation to his executors.[1]

Unlike Wayles, Richard Randolph died a virtual bankrupt in 1786. He was a grandson of William Randolph of Turkey Island, progenitor of the Randolph clan in Virginia, and had inherited the Curles estate in Henrico County from his father, the first Richard Randolph. By his marriage to Anne Meade he had four sons (the defendants in this suit) and six daughters. Randolph, too, had become heavily indebted to British merchants before the war. A substantial portion of his indebtedness, amounting to more than six thousand pounds sterling principal, is documented in this case. In addition, he owed in excess of seven thousand pounds principal to Farell & Jones, suits for which were brought in the federal court during the 1790s.[2]

During his last years Richard Randolph conveyed or devised his personal and landed estate to his sons, who subsequently disposed of portions of this property to others. As a result, no assets remained when Farell & Jones sued Randolph's estate for their debts. Randolph's executors, who employed Marshall to defend them in these suits as well as in the present case, successfully pleaded that they had "well and truly administered" the assets of their testator and thus avoided personal liability for the debts. "[A] greater villain never lived than Richard Randolph," grumbled the agent of Farell & Jones, referring to the Virginian's scheming efforts to keep his estate out of the hands of British creditors.[3]

Wayles's executors brought this suit in chancery to have the court set aside the various deeds conveying Richard Randolph's property and to decree that the property devised by his will should be applied to the discharge of the estate's debts. Although Farell & Jones was not directly involved in these proceedings, the dispute had its genesis in a commercial undertaking between the Bristol merchant firm and the two Virginia planters. In 1772 Farell & Jones arranged the consignment to Wayles and Randolph of the cargo of a slave ship, *The Prince of Wales*, owned by another Bristol concern, John Powell & Company. In return for a profitable commission on the sale of its cargo of 280 blacks from Africa, the Virginians were to remit the proceeds at stated times to Powell & Company. Farell & Jones, who regarded Wayles and Randolph as favored customers, agreed to become their security for the sale. *The Prince of Wales*, commanded by James Bivins, arrived in Virginia in September 1772, and the consignees commenced to sell the slaves on credit, taking bonds in their own names as factors.[4]

In December 1772 Randolph executed a bond to Captain Bivins, master of the vessel, probably for services performed in transporting the Africans to Virginia. John Wayles, who was Randolph's security, retained the original bond for safekeeping. The payment of this bond by Wayles's executors twenty years later under a federal court decree prompted them to bring the present suit in the High Court of Chancery against Randolph's executors.[5]

The consignment of slaves from *The Prince of Wales* also gave rise to two law actions on behalf of Farell & Jones in the federal court in 1790. After Wayles died in 1773, the remaining bonds had been turned over to Randolph for collection. Upon Randolph's default Farell & Jones, as security for the Virginians, had to pay Powell & Company the large balance due from the net proceeds of the sale. To recover this sum, William Jones, the surviving partner, sued the estates of Randolph and Wayles, with Marshall serving as counsel for the executors in both cases. At the trial of the suit against Wayles's executors in June 1797, the defendants contended that the interests and powers of the joint consignees passed completely over to Randolph on the death of Wayles and that Wayles's representatives, retaining no interest, were not answerable for Randolph's failure to pay. At a second trial in November 1797, the jury exonerated Wayles's executors. At the same term a jury returned a verdict in favor of the British plaintiff for fifty-three thousand dollars in the suit against Randolph's executors, though absolving the defendants from personal liability on the plea that the assets had been fully administered.[6]

In the chancery suit, representatives of two of Richard Randolph's other British creditors subsequently joined Wayles's executors as plaintiffs: John Loyd and Thomas Main, executors respectively of London merchants Osgood Hanbury and John Hyndman. Main later submitted a claim on behalf of his testator to the British debt claims commissions. Among the supporting papers accompanying the claim was a copy of the record of this suit. This copy, like that in the Shermer suit (Case Number 5), is now in the Treasury papers at the British Public Record Office. It provides the text for all the documents below except for the report of Marshall's argument of the appeal.[7]

Marshall, who had received a retainer fee from Richard Randolph's executors in 1787, served as their counsel in both the original chancery case and the appeal.[8] The Randolphs also employed Burwell Starke on their behalf in the chancery court, though not in the

Court of Appeals. So important was the appeal to the Randolphs that they obtained the services of no fewer than five of the Richmond bar's most distinguished attorneys: Marshall, Daniel Call, William DuVal, John Warden, and Edmund Randolph.

1. Dumas Malone, *Jefferson and His Time* (6 vols.; Boston, 1948–81), I: *Jefferson the Virginian*, 156–57, 432–33, 441–45; Jefferson to Farell & Jones, 9 July 1773 (Boyd, *Jefferson Papers*, XV, 657–61); Jefferson to John Read, 25 June 1798, T.79/30 (claim of John T. Ware), P.R.O. On Farell & Jones, see Case No. 12.

2. Gerald S. Cowden, "The Randolphs of Turkey Island: A Prosopography of the First Three Generations, 1650–1806" (2 vols.; Ph.D. diss., College of William and Mary, 1977), I, 439–54; Jones v. Richard Randolph's Executors (two suits), U.S. Cir. Ct., Va., Ended Cases (Restored), 1797, Vi; memorial of John Tyndale Ware, 1 May 1804, T.79/30 (claim of John T. Ware), P.R.O.

3. Richard Hanson to William Jones, 17 Mar. 1790, T.79/30 (claim of John T. Ware), P.R.O.

4. On this episode see the editorial discussion and documents in Boyd, *Jefferson Papers*, XV, 642–77. See also the voluminous documentation of the "African Account" in T.79/30 (claim of John T. Ware), P.R.O.

5. See Doc. I and n. 3.

6. In addition to the sources cited in n. 4, see Jefferson to Henry Skipwith, 6 May 1791 (Boyd, *Jefferson Papers*, XX, 373–76); Jones v. Wayles's Executors, U.S. Cir. Ct., Va., Ended Cases (Restored), 1797; Jones v. Richard Randolph's Executors. For JM's work as attorney for Wayles's executors, see *PJM*, II, 89–90, 413; Skipwith to Jefferson, 7 Apr. 1791 (Boyd, *Jefferson Papers*, XX, 166–67); Stevens T. Mason to Daniel C. Brent, 25 Oct. 1796, Jefferson Papers, DLC (partly quoted in Boyd, *Jefferson Papers*, XV, 648).

7. Record of Wayles's Executors v. Randolph et al., T.79/19 (claim of James Buchanan & Co.), P.R.O. For a description of the copy of this record, see Doc. I, n.

8. *PJM*, I, 373.

I. Bill in Chancery

March 1795

To the honorable George Wythe esquire Judge of the honorable the high Court of Chancery, humbly complaining, shew unto your honor, your orators Francis Eppes[1] and Thomas Jefferson executors of the last will & testament of John Wayles deceased; that on the 13th. day of December 1772, Richard Randolph esquire of Curles being indebted to James Bivins of the City of Bristol, in the sum of £740. sterling, executed a bond to the said Bivins, binding himself, his heirs &c. in the penalty of £1480. like money; to the payment of the said sum of £740. with interest from the 30th. September then next following, within twelve months from the date; the said bond was also executed by the testator of your orator as security to the said Randolph. That the said Bivins shortly after departed from this Country and left the bond aforesaid in the care and custody of your orators' testator, taking a copy and receipt for the original. That some few years after this, your orators' testator departed this life, being then in possession of the said bond, no part of the principal or interest of which had been paid off by the said Randolph, so far as they know or believe. That in the year 17 a suit in Chancery was instituted by the representatives of the said James Bivins, in the Federal circuit court for this state, against Henry Skipwith[2] and Anne his wife, late Anne Wayles executrix of the said John Wayles, for the recovery of the principal and interest due on the said bond, and at the May Session 1793, a decree nisi was entered for the sum of £740. sterling, of the value of 3288 dollars and eighty nine cents with interest at five per cent per annum from the 13th. day of September 1773, till payment, and the costs.[3] That neither the said Skipwith and his wife, nor your orators being able to shew any just cause against the decree, the same remains absolute. All which will more fully appear, reference being had to the said original bond now in the possession of your orators, and ready to be produced, and by the records of the said Federal circuit Court. That your orators having the management of the estate of their testator, have thought it belonged to them to pay, out of the assetts in their hands, the said debt, though they are not named in the decree; they have accordingly made considerable payments and are going on to make more; an account of all which will in due time be laid before this honble. Court. They further beg leave to shew unto your honor, that the said Richard Randolph, on the 21st. day of March 1786, made and duly published his last will and testament and thereby gave the residue of his estate after several devises and bequests to be equally divided between his four sons Richard Randolph, David Meade Randolph, Brett Randolph and Ryland Randolph, and he appointed his said four sons his executors.[4] That shortly afterwards, he departed this life, and the said will was duly proved and admitted to record in the County Court of Henrico, as will more fully appear reference being had to a true copy of the said will, and to the certificate of the probate thereof, which are hereto annexed.[5] That the said Richard Randolph deceased, died largely indebted, and the said executors give out in speeches that they have already sold all the slaves and the personal estate of their testator and applied the proceeds to the discharge of his debts so far as the same would extend, and that there are many debts to a large amount still due from the estate. Whether this be so or not, your orators are at present unable to say certainly, but they believe they have yet assetts in their hands. They further shew unto your honor, that on the 11th. day of October 1780, the said Richard Randolph being indebted on the bond and otherwise, to an amount equal to, if not exceeding, the whole of his estate, and being seized of a tract of land in Bermuda hundred in the County of Chesterfield, and possessed of a large number of slaves, did seal & execute a deed conveying the said tract of land and all the stocks of horses, cattle, sheep and hogs, and all the plantation utensils on the said land, together with nineteen slaves named in the said deed, unto the said David M. Randolph, his son, his heirs and assigns forever, for and in consideration of his natural love and affection for his said son, and for his advancement in life, as will more fully appear, reference being had to a true copy of the said deed which is hereto annexed (marked B.)[6] That the said Richard Randolph deceased, being indebted as aforesaid, and being seized of a large and valuable estate in the said County of Henrico called Curles, did, on the 20th. day of September 1785, execute a deed conveying the same to his son Richard Randoph, above named, his heirs and assigns forever, after the death of him, the said Richard Randolph deceased, and Ann his wife; the consideration expressed in the said deed, being a marriage shortly to be had and solemnized between the said Richard, the son, and Miss Maria Beverley, the daughter of Robert Beverley, but the said Maria was not a party to the said deed. That the same was not proved until the third day of July 1786, as will more fully appear, reference being had to a true copy of the said deed, and to the certificate of the proof thereof in the County Court of Henrico, which are hereto annexed (marked C.)[7] That the said Richard Randolph deceased, was at the time of making his said will, and at his death, seized in fee simple of two considerable tracts of land in the Counties of Cumberland and Prince Edward, the one called Sandy Ford, the other Clover Forest; as also a valuable mill and acres of land adjoining, also in the said County of Prince Edward; he was also seized as aforesaid of a tract of land containing about 130 acres, lying in the County of Chesterfield, and another tract of about the same extent lying in the last mentioned County, known by the name of Elams. That by the said will he devised the tract called Sandy Ford to his said son Brett Randolph and his heirs forever; the land known by the name of Clover Forest and the tract opposite to Curles, he devised to his said son Ryland and his heirs forever. The mill and 50 acres adjoining, he gave to his sons Ryland and Brett, in fee simple, as tenants in common, and the tract called Elams he devised to his son David M. Randolph and his heirs forever, as will more fully and at large appear, reference being had to the said will. That the said devisees entered upon and were seized of the said tracts of land respectively and are now seized of them as aforesaid. That the said Richard Randolph the younger is the eldest son and heir at law of Richard Randolph deceased. That the aforesaid deeds executed by the said Richard Randolph deceased, were made by him when he well knew that his estate in possession was insufficient to pay his debts, and with intent to defraud his just creditors and that as your orators are advised, they are void as to the creditors not only for this reason but because the conveyance to David M. Randolph was not made on consideration good in law against creditors,[8] and the conveyance to Richard Randolph was not recorded in due time according to the act of assembly in that case made and provided.[9] That they are entitled, as they are advised, to a discovery of the personal estate and slaves that have come to the hands of the said executors, and an account of the manner in which they have been disposed of, and if any should now remain in their hands to have them applied to the discharge of the debt aforesaid, or to a reimbursement of what monies your orators may have paid in discharge of the same. That if the said assetts should prove insufficient, they are entitled to a like satisfaction out of all the said lands, or any other real estate of the said Richard Randolph deceased, they being entitled in equity as they humbly conceive in respect to the real estate of the said Richard Randolph deceased, to stand in the place of the original creditor on the bond aforesaid, and of any other creditors by specialty who have been paid their debts out of the assetts in the hands of the said executors.[10] That they have in a friendly manner represented their just claims to the said executors and requested them to pay off the balance due on the said decree, and to reimburse them for such payments as they have made in discharge of the same. Your orators further charge that the said Richard Randolph, the son, hath conveyed the said estate called Curles to Anthony Singleton[11] by way of mortgage, and the said Singleton is since dead, and William Fenwick and William Berkeley are his executors; the said Richard Randolph hath also conveyed the same estate by way of mortgage to William Heath,[12] who, together with the said William Fenwick and William Berkeley, are prayed to be made defendants hereto.[13] But now so it is, that the said Richard Randolph, David M. Randolph, Ryland Randolph and Brett Randolph, altogether refuse so to do. In tender consideration whereof, and for as much as your orators are only relievable in equity; To the end therefore that the said Richard Randolph, David M. Randolph, Brett Randolph, and Ryland Randolph, who they pray may be made defendants to this their bill, may on their corporal oaths make full, true and perfect answer to all and singular the premises, and that as if the same were herein again set forth and they thereto interrogated. That they may make a true discovery of the assetts that have come to their hands of the estate of the said Richard Randolph, and make up a full and compleat account of their administration; that the demand of your orators may if the personal estate is insufficient, be satisfied out of the real estate of the said Richard Randolph and that as well the lands and other property mentioned in the deeds aforesaid as those devised may be made liable thereto, and that your orators may have such other relief as is consistent with equity; may it please your honor to grant a writ of Subpœna, commanding the said Richard Randolph, David M. Randolph, Ryland Randolph and Brett Randolph &c. and your orator &c.[14]

Copy, Record of Wayles's Executors v. Randolph et al., 1–5, T.79/19 (claim of James Buchanan & Co.), P.R.O. Full record consists of forty-eight numbered pages copied by John Brown, clerk of Virginia Court of Appeals; signed and sealed by Brown, 29 Dec. 1804, and certified by Gov. John Page, 31 Dec. 1804. Record states that bill was exhibited at chancery term beginning 2 Mar. 1795.

1. Francis Eppes (1747–1808) of Eppington, Chesterfield County, was married to Elizabeth, second daughter of John Wayles (Edward C. Carter II et al., eds., *The Virginia Journals of Benjamin Henry Latrobe, 1795–1798* [2 vols.; New Haven, 1977], II, 540–41).

2. Henry Skipwith (1751–1815) of Hors du Monde, Chesterfield County, married Anne, youngest daughter of John Wayles, in 1773 (Malone, *Jefferson the Virginian*, 433; Carter, *Latrobe Va. Journals*, II, 554).

3. A bill in chancery was filed in the federal court on 9 Apr. 1792 by Thomas Wigan, executor of James Bivins, against John Wayles's executors. On 7 June 1793, the defendants failing to answer, a decree was entered for the plaintiff. JM represented Wayles's executors in this case (U.S. Cir. Ct., Va., Ended Cases [Restored], 1793, Vi; U.S. Cir. Ct., Va., Rec. Bk. II, 491–506).

4. Richard Randolph the testator and Anne Meade Randolph had four sons: (1) Richard, married to Maria, daughter of Robert Beverley of Blandfield; he died while the appeal was pending; (2) David Meade (1758–1830), married to Mary, daughter of Thomas Mann Randolph of Tuckahoe; he served as U.S. marshal for Virginia during the 1790s; (3) Brett (d. 1828), married to Lucy, another daughter of Robert Beverley of Blandfield; and (4) Ryland (d. 1815), married to Elizabeth Frazier (*WMQ*, 1st ser., IX [1900–1901], 183; Va. Ct. Ap. Ord. Bk. III, 327; *PJM*, II, 274 n. 7).

5. A copy of the will and the certificate of probate, dated 3 July 1786, were entered on the record as exhibits (Record of Wayles's Executors v. Randolph et al., 34–37).

6. The deed of 11 Oct. 1780 was entered as an exhibit (ibid., 31–32).

7. The deed of 20 Sept. 1785 was entered as an exhibit (ibid., 33–34).

8. One of the contested points was whether the conveyance to David M. Randolph was made as a consequence of his marriage, which in law was deemed a valid consideration. As Randolph explained in his plea and de-

murrer (Doc. III), the attorney who drew the deed mistakenly omitted to express marriage as the consideration, though he insisted it was the real consideration.

9. According to the "act for regulating conveyances," adopted at the Oct. 1785 session of the General Assembly, deeds of conveyance had to be recorded within eight months after the sealing and delivery (Hening, *Statutes*, XII, 154). The deed of 20 Sept. 1785 was not recorded until 3 July 1786. The question was whether the recording of the deed within eight months of the reacknowledgment made it good.

10. Another contested point was whether Wayles's executors should be considered bond creditors or simple contract creditors. Virginia's "act for the relief of creditors against fraudulent devises," which reenacted the English statute of 3 Wm. III, c. 14, made lands passing by devise as well as descent to the heir liable for specialty debts in which the heir was expressly bound (Hening, *Statutes*, IV, 164; V, 537; XIII, 53–55; Tucker, *Blackstone's Commentaries*, II, 378 and n. 9; JM to Patrick Henry, 31 Aug. 1790 [*PJM*, II, 60–61]).

11. A copy of the mortgage deed of the Curles estate to Anthony Singleton (d. 1795), dated 1 Apr. 1794, was entered as an exhibit (Record of Wayles's Executors v. Randolph et al., 42–43). Singleton had served as an officer in the Continental army and as the agent of the sinking fund established by the commonwealth in 1787 (Hutchinson, *Madison Papers*, XIII, 64 n. 2).

12. William Heth (1750–1807), an officer in the Continental army during the Revolution, later served as commissioner to settle Virginia's account with the Union concerning the Northwest Territory and as a member of the Council of State (*DAR Patriot Index*, 319; Hutchinson, *Madison Papers*, X, 353–54 n. 1; *JCSV*, IV, 246). A copy of the mortgage deed to him was not entered on the record.

13. The Curles estate was first mortgaged to Singleton as security for a debt of nearly £2,000. Randolph subsequently made a second mortgage of Curles to William Heth. After being named defendants, Heth and the executors of Singleton filed answers to the bill; each side claimed the full benefit of its respective mortgages (Record of Wayles's Executors v. Randolph et al., 17–18).

14. At this point the record states that attachments were awarded against the defendants for failing to answer. On 30 May 1795, the defendants still not answering, the court ordered the bill to be taken for confessed unless the defendants showed cause to the contrary at the next term. On 6 June this order was set aside on motion of counsel for David M. Randolph, who proceeded to answer. The other three brothers delayed answering until Mar. 1796.

II. Answer of David M. Randolph
6 June 1795

To the honorable George Wythe, Judge of the high Court of Chancery; the answer of David Meade Randolph acting executor of Richard Randolph late of Curles deceased, to the bill of complaint exhibited against him and others in this honorable Court, by Francis Eppes and Thomas Jefferson executors of John Wayles deceased. This defendant saving to himself the benefit of exception to the errors and insufficiencies in the said bill of complaint contained, for answer to so much thereof as he is advised it is material for him to answer, he says, that as to the allegations in the said bill contained respecting the bond therein mentioned, this respondent of his own knowledge knows nothing, and therefore leaves those facts to be substanched by the complainants; he saith that the said Richard Randolph in the bill mentioned, the testator of this defendant, died about the day of in the year greatly indebted by judgments, bills of exchange, bonds, notes and simple contracts to an amount greatly beyond the assetts of the said Richard which came to the hands of this defendant. That he verily believes that these assetts will be insufficient to discharge his testator's debts of the highest to wit; debts due from the said Richard as guardian &c. which have priority by the law, Judgments rendered against the said Richard in his lifetime, and bills of exchange, besides which, there are bonds to a considerable amount, still unpaid.[1] That by an order of this honorable Court in the suit this defendant is now making up an account of his administration of the estate of the said Richard Randolph which came to his hands to be administered, and to the report in that cause whenever the same shall be returned, he begs leave to refer this honorable Court; and denying all combination, he prays to be hence dismissed with his costs &c.

Sworn to in Court, June 6th. 1795. D. M. Randolph
Starke p.q.[2]

And the said David M. Randolph the defendant, by protestation not confessing any of the matters and things in the Complainants' said bill, to be true, as they are therein and thereby set forth and alledged, doth demur to so much of the said bill as prays that the said Complainants should stand in the place of, & be considered by this honorable Court, as bond creditors, because, as he is advised, the complainants by their own shewing are not bond creditors, but simple contract creditors of the said Richard Randolph in the bill mentioned; wherefore the said defendant doth demur to so much of the said bill of complaint as prays for relief, as if the complainants were bond creditors; and prays the judgment of this honorable Court whether he shall be compelled to make any answer to such part of the said bill as is so demurred to &c.[3]

Copy, Record of Wayles's Executors v. Randolph et al., 5–6, T.79/19 (claim of James Buchanan & Co.), P.R.O.

1. Executors were required to pay the debts of their testator according to this priority: (1) funeral expenses, costs of probate, etc.; (2) debts due the state on record or bond; (3) debts preferred by particular statutes, such as those owed by the testator on account of his guardianship; (4) debts of record, such as court judgments or decrees, and those having the force of a judgment, such as a protested bill of exchange; (5) debts due by specialty or bond; and (6) simple contract debts (Blackstone, *Commentaries*, II, 511).

2. Burwell Starke was attorney for the defendant. Hence the clerk should have used the initials "p.d." for *pro defendente* ("for the defendant") instead of "p.q." After attending Donald Robertson's school in King and Queen County in 1768 and 1769 and the College of William and Mary in 1773, Starke took up the practice of law. He qualified for the bar of the Court of Appeals in Nov. 1786 (*VMHB*, XXXIV [1926], 146, 147, 232, 233; *WMQ*, 1st ser., XIV [1905–6], 26, 29; *PJM*, I, 236 n. 3; Va. Ct. Ap. Ord. Bk. I, 92).

3. The "&c." stands for these concluding words of the demurrer: "and humbly prays to be hence dismissed, with his reasonable costs and charges in this behalf most wrongfully sustained" (Hinde, *Chancery Practice*, 169).

III. Plea and Demurrer of David M. Randolph

6 June 1795

To the honorable George Wythe judge of the high Court of Chancery The plea and demurrer of David Meade Randolph in his individual character, to the bill of complaint exhibited in this honorable Court against him and others by Francis Eppes and Thomas Jefferson executors of John Wayles deceased. This defendant by protestation not confessing or acknowledging the matters and things in the complainants bill alledged, to be true in manner and form as the same are therein and thereby set forth, for plea to the said bill of complaint, he says that he hath, and took no lands or slaves, which were of the lands and slaves of Richard Randolph the elder in the said bill mentioned, at the Time of his death by the devise of him the said Richard, except one hundred and thirty acres in the County of Chesterfield called Elams, which is the only land devised to him by the said Richard; and that he took not the land aforesaid under the will of the said Richard to his own use, but has sold the same for the sum of which, as executor of the said Richard, he has applied to the use of the estate of the said Richard. And for further plea, the said David Meade Randolph saith that about the day of in the year 1780, the said David Meade Randolph having made proposals of marriage to Mary the daughter of Thomas Mann Randolph esquire deceased,[1] the said Thomas M. Randolph, wrote a letter to this defendant's father, the said Richard consenting to this defendant's marriage with the said Mary, provided the said Richard would give to this defendant, and put him into possession thereof of a decent and competent fortune. That the said letter was delivered open by the said Thomas Mann Randolph to this defendant, and by him requested to deliver it to his father the said Richard; which this defendant did, but which letter has been lost or mislaid, but the contents of which this defendant believes he can prove to this honorable Court.[2] That in consequence of that letter and of the intended marriage aforesaid, the said Richard, upon the 8th. day of August 1780, wrote a letter to this defendant to be shewn to the said Thomas Mann Randolph in which he promised that in consideration of such marriage taking place, to give to this defendant a fee simple estate in all his the said Richard's lands in Bermuda hundred, one thousand acres in Cumberland known by the name of Dry creek, with the slaves and stocks thereon and two negro carpenters mulatto Peter and Mingo, which will more fully appear to this honorable Court from the said letter hereto annexed;[3] that the said marriage afterwards took effect, some little time before which, to wit; on the 11th. day of October in the year aforesaid, in consideration of the said intended marriage the said Richard Randolph conveyed to this defendant his land and plantation in Bermuda hundred in the County of Chesterfield, & 19 slaves then on the said plantation;[4] and by letter of attorney of the same date, reciting that the said Richard Randolph had purchased the said land plantation in Bermuda hundred aforesaid of Richard Royal and Joseph Royal deceased, both of whom had departed this life before they had executed a conveyance for the same, although quiet possession had been delivered to the said Richard, and that the heir at law of the said Richard Royal and Joseph Royal was an infant, by reason whereof it had become necessary to institute a suit in the Court of Chancery for completing the title to the said land and plantation, which he had conveyed as aforesaid to the said David Meade Randolph; he the said Richard Randolph in order to enable the said David M. Randolph to obtain all the benefit of the conveyance aforesaid, & a title in fee simple to the land and plantation aforesaid, to his own use and behoof, did constitute and appoint the said David M. Randolph his attorney without power of revocation, to sue for, recover and receive from the heir at law of the said Richard Royal and Joseph Royal a conveyance in fee simple of the aforesaid land and plantation to the only use and behoof of him the said David Meade Randolph, which will more fully appear to this honorable Court by referring to the said letter of attorney hereto annexed.[5] By virtue of which said indenture and letter of attorney this defendant, on the day of in the year did obtain a decree against the heir at law of the said Richard Royal and Joseph Royal, that he should execute a conveyance in fee simple of the land and plantation in Bermuda hundred aforesaid, to this defendant which hath accordingly been done; and the said Richard on the of in the year 1780, in compliance with his letter aforesaid conveyed to this defendant acres of land situate upon Dry creek in the county of Cumberland, as will appear to this honorable Court by refering to an authenticated copy of the said indenture hereto annexed,[6] that owing to the mistake of the attorney who drew the said indenture, the said intended marriage is not expressed as a consideration although it was the real consideration. All which matters and things this defendant doth aver and plead in bar to the complainants said bill, and of the pretended demand for which he seeks relief, and he prays to be hence dismissed with his costs.

STARKE p.d.

Copy, Record of Wayles's Executors v. Randolph et al., 6–8, T.79/19 (claim of James Buchanan & Co.), P.R.O.

1. Thomas Mann Randolph (1740–1793), proprietor of Tuckahoe (Thomas Jefferson's boyhood home) and other large plantations in Henrico, Goochland, and Albemarle. Toward the end of his life he was heavily indebted to both British and Virginia creditors. JM represented him or his executors in four British debt suits (William H. Gaines, Jr., *Thomas Mann Randolph, Jefferson's Son-in-Law* [Baton Rouge, 1966], 3–38; Lidderdale's Executors v. T. M. Randolph's Executors [3 suits], U.S. Cir. Ct., Va., Ended Cases [Restored], 1797; Jones v. T. M. Randolph's Executors, ibid.; see also Case No. 18).

2. In their depositions, taken 8 Mar. 1797, Henry Randolph and Richard Randolph stated that they had seen or heard of the missing letter (Record of Wayles's Executors v. Randolph et al., 13).

3. For this letter, see ibid., 30–31. It is also printed in full in the report of the appeal (2 Call 130–31).

4. For a copy of the deed to Bermuda Hundred, see Record of Wayles's Executors v. Randolph et al., 31–32.

5. The letter of attorney was not entered on the record.

6. For a copy of the deed to Dry Creek, see ibid., 32–33.

IV. Plea and Demurrer of Richard Randolph
12 March 1796

The plea and demurrer of Richard Randolph in his individual character to the bill of complaint exhibited in this honorable Court against him and others by Francis Eppes and Thomas Jefferson executors of John Wayles deceased. This defendant by protestation not confessing or acknowledging the matters and things alledged in the complainants bill to be true for plea to the said bill says that he has or took no lands or slaves which were of the lands and slaves of Richard Randolph the elder in the said bill mentioned at the time of his death by the devise of him the said Richard, which this defendant doth aver, and plead in bar of the said bill and prays the benefit thereof in like manner as if the same had been more formally pleaded and the said defendant not admitting all or any of the allegations of the said bill to be true doth demur to so much thereof as prays that the complainants should stand in the place of bond creditors because as he is advised the complainants by their own shewing are not bond creditors. Wherefore this defendant prays the judgment of this honorable Court whether he shall be bound to make any further answer to such part of the said bill as is so demured to &c.

Copy, Record of Wayles's Executors v. Randolph et al., 8, T.79/19 (claim of James Buchanan & Co.), P.R.O. The record states that Richard, Brett, and Ryland Randolph filed their answers on 12 Mar. 1796.

V. Answer of Richard Randolph
12 March 1796

The answer in Chancery of Richard Randolph executor of Richard Randolph to the bill of complaint exhibited against him in this honorable court by Francis Eppes and Thomas Jefferson executors of John Wayles deceased. This respondant saving to himself every benefit of exception to the complainants bill for answer thereto saith. That as to the allegations in the said bill contained respecting the bond therein mentioned this respondent of his own knowledge knows nothing. Richard Randolph the testator of the defendant died about the day of in the year 178 indebted to an amount greatly beyond the assetts of the said Richard which came to the hands of his executors nor does this defendant believe that there will be assetts sufficient to discharge debts of superior dignity to[1] claimed by the complainants. David Meade Randolph has acted as executor of the said Richard the testator and by the order of this court is now making up the accounts of executorship before the commissioner of this honorable court, to that report when returned this respondent begs leave to refer, he himself never acted. He denies all combination without that &c. and p[r]ays to be hence dism[i]ssed &c. and he will ever pray &c.[2]

Copy, Record of Wayles's Executors v. Randolph et al., 8, T.79/19 (claim of James Buchanan & Co.), P.R.O.

1. The copyist omitted "those."

2. The answer was sworn before John Pendleton, a magistrate of Henrico County, on 10 Mar. 1796.

VI. Answer of Brett Randolph
12 March 1796

The separate answer of Brett Randolph to the bill of complaint exhibited against him and others in the honorable high Court of Chancery by Francis Eppes and Thomas Jefferson executors of the testament and last will of John Wayles deceased, This defendant now and at all times hereafter saving to himself all exception &c to the said bill for answer thereto, says that he knows nothing of the debt said in the said bill to have been due from the said Richard Randolph deceased to the said James Bivins, nor does he admit it. This defendant admits however that the said Richard Randolph did make such a will as that in the bill mentioned but this defendant never qualified or acted as executor thereof, or in any manner intermeddled with the administration of the testators personal estate. This defendant admits likewise that the said Richard Randolph did devise by his said will to this defendant the said tract of land called Sandy Ford, lying in the county of Prince Edward, and Cumberland, and containing by estimation eleven hundred and sixty five acres, and the said tract of 50 acres with the Mill to this defendant and the said Ryland Randolph as tenants in common as in the said bill is set forth, of which this defendant hath sold   acres including a moiety of the said Mill and fifty acres to sundry persons according to list number one hereto annexed for the sum of £   being the full value thereof as this defendant believes.[1] That the said Richard Randolph the testator was indebted by bond at the time of his debt to Thomas Pleasants in the sum of £   who hath since brought suit thereon against this defendant and the said Ryland Randolph as devisees aforesaid in the County Court of Henrico, and hath obtained judgment therein for the sum of £ and costs as by the records of the sd. County Court more fully doth appear, a moiety of which said judgment this defendant is advised he by law is now bound to satisfy.[2] That the said Richard Randolph was likewise indebted by bond at the time of his death to Benjamin Harrison junior and company in the sum of £ who also have since brought suit thereon in the County Court of Henrico against this defendant and the said Ryland Randolph as devisees aforesaid, and hath obtained judgment therein against them for the sum of £ and costs, as by the records of the said Court manifestly doth appear, on which said last mentioned judgment the said Benjamin Harrison hath sued out an execution against the whole of the residue of the said lands remaining unsold by this defendant:[3] This defendant further answering states that the said residue of the lands unsold by this[4] were naked and unimproved at the death of the testator, and that this defendant hath since put buildings & improvements thereon to the value of £ whereby the same is considerably inhanced in value.[5] That after the execution aforesaid issued he parted with the same to the said Benjamin Harrison in discharge of part of the sum due by said judgment and execution, at the price of £ being the full value thereof in their present improved state according to a fair estimation and valuation made by respectable and honest men of the neighbourhood. That Frances Jackson wife of Lewis Jackson had the fee simple in three hundred and seventy one acres of the said tract of Sandy Ford and the said fifty acres, which this deft. was obliged to purchase after the death of the said testator for which this defendant paid £ which either should be allowed him or else that Jacksons land should be considered as forming no part of the devise aforesaid.[6] That these several sums, to wit this defendants moiety of Pleasants judgment, the amount of the buildings and improvements put on the lands by this defendant, without which they would not have been estimated at near so much by the valuers, and that paid for Jacksons title as aforesaid; if the Court should be of Opinion that this should be considered as part of the devise this defendant insists are fair credits in his favor and exceed alienations made by him as far as this defendant recollects. Wherefore this defendant contends that he is not liable to be called on by the complainants in this suit in respect of the devises aforesaid to him and denying all fraud &c. prays to be hence dismissed with his costs &c. without that, that &c.

Copy, Record of Wayles's Executors v. Randolph et al., 9–10, T.79/19 (claim of James Buchanan & Co.), P.R.O.

1. The annexed "list number one" was not entered on the record. Some

additional details of this transaction are related in the commissioner's report of 26 May 1797 (Doc. XIV).

2. This was a suit brought by Robert Pleasants & Co. (in which Thomas Pleasants was a partner) in the Richmond District Court, not the Henrico County Court, on a bond executed by the elder Richard Randolph on 22 Apr. 1785, conditioned for the payment of £300 Virginia currency. A default judgment against Brett and Ryland Randolph was entered at the Apr. 1793 term of that court (Record of Wayles's Executors v. Randolph et al., 28–29).

3. Judgment in this suit was rendered at the Nov. 1795 term of the Henrico County Court. This was a special judgment in debt against an heir or devisee on the obligation of his ancestor and was recoverable on all the lands descended or devised. The execution levied on this special judgment was a rarely used common law writ known as an extent, or writ in the nature of an extent. It was levied against the whole of the lands and therefore differed from the statutory writ of *elegit*, which extended only to half the lands. It was also distinct from the virtually obsolete common law writ of *levari facias*, commanding the sheriff to take the rents of the land in satisfaction of the debt. After reciting the special judgment, the writ of extent commanded the sheriff and "good and lawful men" in his bailiwick to assess the annual value of the land (Record of Wayles's Executors v. Randolph et al., 25–28; William Tidd, *The Practice of the Court of King's Bench, in Personal Actions: With Reference to Cases of Practice in the Court of Common Pleas* [2d Am. ed.; 2 vols.; New York, 1807], II, 853–55, 953; Hening, *Statutes*, XIII, 53–55; Tucker, *Blackstone's Commentaries*, II, 378 and n. 9; III, 418, 421 n. 27).

4. The copyist omitted "defendant."

5. Brett Randolph obtained the testimony of witnesses in Cumberland County to show the value of the buildings and improvements he had made (depositions, 1 May 1797, Record of Wayles's Executors v. Randolph et al., 12).

6. Deed from Lewis Jackson and Frances Jackson to Brett Randolph, ibid., 41–42.

VII. Answer of Ryland Randolph
12 March 1796

The separate answer of Ryland Randolph to the bill of complaint exhibited against him and others in the honorable High Court of Chancery, by Frances Eppes & Thomas Jefferson executors of the testament and last will of John Wayles deceased. This defendant now and at all times hereafter saving to himself all exceptions &c. to the said bill for answer thereto says; that he knows nothing of the said debt in the said bill supposed to have been due from the said Richard Randolph deceased to the said James Bivins and therefore does not admit it. This defendant admits however that the said Richard Randolph deceased did make such a will as that in the bill mentioned; but this defendant never qualified or acted as executor thereof, or in any manner intermeddled with the administration of the testators personal estate. This defendant admits likewise that the said Richard Randolph deceased did devise by his said will to this defendant in fee simple the said tract of land called Clover Forest, containing fourteen hundred and fifty acres, the said tract opposite to Curles containing one hundred and fifty six acres (by a late survey) instead of one hundred and thirty as in the said bill is supposed, and to this defendant and the sd. Brett Randolph the Mill and fifty acres of land adjoining in fee simple as tenants in common. Of which said several tracts of land this defendant sold the said tract of one hundred and fifty six acres opposite to Curles for three hundred and seventy one pounds sixteen shillings being the full value thereof as this defendant believes, and seventy four acres of the Clover Forest tract, for seventy six pounds fifteen shillings being the full value thereof as this defendant believes.[1] That the said Richard Randolph the testator was at the time of his death indebted by bond to Robert Pleasants and company in the sum of £   who hath since brought suit thereon against this defendant & the said Brett Randolph as devisees aforesaid in the District Court of Henrico, and recovered judgment therein for the sum of £301.11.11. current money of Virginia, with interest after the rate of five percentum per annum from 22d of April 1785 and costs as by the records of the said District Court more fully doth appear;[2] a moiety of which said judgment this defendant is advised he is now bound in law to satisfy. That the said Richard Randolph the testator was likewise at the time of his death indebted by bond to Benjamin Harrison in the sum of £   who also hath since brought suit thereon in the county court of Henrico against this defendant and the said Brett Randolph as devisees aforesaid, and recovered judgment therein against them for the sum of sixty three thousand four hundred and eighty pounds of upland, James river inspected, crop tobacco with interest after the rate of five per centum per annum from the tenth day of January, 1784, till payment, and costs as by the records of the said County Court doth appear. On which said last mentioned judgment the said Benjamin Harrison junr. and company have sued out two executions against the said Mill and the whole of the said lands unsold by this defendant the one directed to the sheriff of Prince Edward and the other to the sheriff of Cumberland County were the said Mill and unsold lands lie which were not sufficient to discharge the interest of this defendants proportion of the said judgment as by the inquisitions returned by the sheriffs aforesaid into to the said County Court doth more fully appear.[3] Whereby the said Benjamin Harrison junr. and company as this defendant is advised obtained a perpetual title to the said lands under the execution aforesaid. That in the year 17 there was an arrearage of public taxes amounting to £ due on the several tracts of land belonging to the testator at his death in the county of Cumberland, to satisfy which the Sheriff of the said county of Cumberland seized one hundred and eleven and one half acres of the Clover Forest tract which this defendant redeemed on the day of sale by payment of the taxes aforesaid:[4] That this defendant bought at public sale the said Brett Randolph's moiety of the said Mill and fifty acres prior to the rendition of the judgments aforesaid at the fair and full price of four hundred pounds,[5] which moiety is also included in the said inquisition by the sheriff of Prince Edward, and this defendant insists forms a fair credit on his behalf, which together with his moiety aforesaid of Pleasants judgment far exceeds the amount of this defendants own alienation. This defendant therefore conceives that he is not liable to be called on in this honorable court by the complainants in respect to the lands devised him by the testator. And denying all fraud &c. prays to be hence dismissed with his costs &c. without that, that &c.

Copy, Record of Wayles's Executors v. Randolph et al., 10–11, T.79/19 (claim of James Buchanan & Co.), P.R.O.

1. The tract "opposite to Curles" in Chesterfield County was conveyed by two deeds: one to Eleazer Clay for 133½ acres, dated 28 Jan. 1794; the other to George Woodson for 22½ acres, dated 15 Feb. 1794 (Record of Wayles's Executors v. Randolph et al., 39–41). There is nothing in the record about the sale of the Clover Forest tract in Cumberland County.

2. See Doc. VI, n. 2.

3. See ibid., n. 3.

4. On 31 May 1794 Brett Randolph paid £46 to redeem 111½ acres taken by the commonwealth for the nonpayment of taxes charged to Richard Randolph's estate in 1788 (Record of Wayles's Executors v. Randolph et al., 44).

5. This sale was executed 15 Sept. 1794 (ibid., 44).

VIII. Bill of John Loyd and Thomas Main
ca. April 1797

And your orators John Loyd executor of the last will of Osgood Hanbury surviving partner of Capel and Osgood Hanbury, and Thomas Main executor of the last will & testament of John Hyndman surviving partner of James Buchanan and company who are severally creditors of the estate of the said Richard Randolph deceased, and who by consent of parties are admitted as parties complainant in this cause beg leave to set forth their demands against the estate of the said Richard Randolph. And first your orator John Loyd executor &c. of Osgood Hanbury surviving partner of Capel and Osgood Hanbury saith, that the said Richard Randolph being indebted to the said Capel and Osgood Hanbury in the sum of £3117 sterling did on the 16th. of July 1770 confess judgment in three suits brought against him by the said Capel & Osgood Hanbury in the County Court of York for the sum of £1039.0.8 sterling in each suit with interest from the date of the said judgments at five per centum per annum till payment as will more fully appear reference being had to the copies of the said judgments which are hereto annexed; that on the thirty first December 1773 the balance due on the said judgments amounted to £3107 Sterling, which last mentioned sum is now due with interest thereon from the 31st. December 1773.[1] And your orator Thomas Main further saith that the said Richard Randolph on the 13th day of May 1772 executed his bond to the said J. Hyndman & Richard Lancaster surviving partner of James Buchanan with Thomas Randolph surety thereto on the penalty of £5649.3.6 sterling with condition for the payment of £2824.11.9 sterling on demand on which bonds there remained a balance due on the 5th of July 1775 of £2355.11.3 sterling as will appear by the account hereto annexed which your orator Thomas Main prays may be taken as a part of this his bill,[2] which said balance with interest from the 5th. of July 1775 is justly due unto him as executor of the last will and testament of the said John Hyndman surviving partner as aforesaid and your orators pray that they may have such relief as they are severally intitled to having regard to the dignity of their debts.[3]

Copy, Record of Wayles's Executors v. Randolph et al., 14, T.79/19 (claim of James Buchanan & Co.), P.R.O.

1. For the three York County Court judgments, see Record of Wayles's Executors v. Randolph et al., 23.

2. See ibid., 24–25.

3. Thomas Pleasants, executor of Robert Pleasants, also joined as a complainant in this suit. His bill immediately follows that of Loyd and Main on the record. Except for the specific facts of his claim, Pleasants's bill is virtually identical to that of Wayles's executors. He sought to recover a judgment against the elder Richard Randolph obtained at the Henrico County Court in 1786 (ibid., 14–16). On Pleasants, see Case No. 14.

IX. Answer of Richard Randolph and David M. Randolph

23 May 1797

And the defendants Richard Randolph and David Meade Randolph by way of answer to the amendments of the bill of the complainants, so far as the same relates to the judgments, therein stated to have been recovered in the court of the County of York by Capel and Osgood Hanbury against the said Richard Randolph deceased, say; that they cannot deny that such judgments were obtained: but each for himself doth positively and expressly deny, that he, or any agent, or any one of them, before the date of the deed, under which he claims; before the execution thereof; or any other time until since the death of Richard Randolph deceased:[1] that being a purchaser for a valuable consideration, prays each for himself that his said purchase may be saved to him, as if it were now specially pleaded in the most formal manner: that the said Richard Randolph deceased, at the time of the said judgments, being rendered lived in the County Henrico and that the tract of land called Curles lies in the County of Henrico and the tract called Presque Isle; lies in the County of Chesterfield, and the tract called Dry Creek, lies in the County of Cumberland, which lies at a considerable distance from the said County of York:[2] and that they believe, that the said judgments, have been in the whole or the greater part paid and relying on the presumptions arising from the length of time, strengthened by a letter from the agents of the plaintiffs annexed & refered to, prays as they have already prayed, to be hence dismissed &c.[3]

Sworn to in Court May 23d. 1797 — RICHARD RANDOLPH
PETER TINSLEY — D. M. RANDOLPH

Copy, Record of Wayles's Executors v. Randolph et al., 16–17, T.79/19 (claim of James Buchanan & Co.), P.R.O.

1. The language is obscure, perhaps owing to the clerk's omission of some words. The two sons were apparently denying any knowledge of the York judgments until after their father's death.

2. In his appeal argument JM contended that county court judgments should not bind lands lying in another county so as to destroy intervening alienations (Doc. XVIII).

3. The reference is to a letter from James Balfour, a partner of the Hanburys, to Richard Randolph, dated 4 Nov. 1773, calling upon Randolph to pay the debt immediately or have execution served upon him (Record of Wayles's Executors v. Randolph et al., 24).

X. Amended Answer of David M. Randolph
ca. May 1797

The defendant David M. Randolph by way of amendment to his answer says that the lands conveyed to him were purchased by his father Richard Randolph subsequent to the date of the said judgments as will appear by the conveyance thereof to which he refers.[1]

Copy, Record of Wayles's Executors v. Randolph et al., 17, T.79/19 (claim of James Buchanan & Co.), P.R.O.

1. According to the commissioner's report of 26 May 1797 (Doc. XIV), the Bermuda Hundred and Dry Creek lands (conveyed to David M. Randolph on 11 Oct. 1780) were among those possessed by Richard Randolph on 16 July 1770, when the Hanburys obtained their judgments against him.

XI. Amended Answer of Richard Randolph
ca. May 1797

That Richard Randolph, the elder, was on the 21st. of March 1786, labouring under that sickness, which terminated in his death, on the 5th. of June 1786. That Mrs. Randolph the mother of the respondent immediately upon the death of the said Richard Randolph, the elder, entered upon the plantation, called Cu[r]les by virtue of the deed aforesaid of the said Richard Randolph, the elder, to the respondent, dated the 20th. September 1785; and hath continued in possession thereof uninterrupted, and without any demand from the complainants, until the bringing of this suit, which was instituted on the . That the complainants if creditors at all were so prior to the 20th of September 1785, except indeed, that such of them, as are executors of John Wayles, have become so, in the year 179 .[1] That the portion promised by Robert Beverley, in consideration of the marriage between the respondent and his daughter Maria to wit £1200 sterling hath been actually paid by the said Robert Beverley to the respondent. That the executors of the said Wayles were acquainted with the existance of the said deed of September 20th. 1785, in a very few months after its execution. That a deed was executed to this respondent in consideration of the said marriage contract, which was acknowledged by his father on the day of in the year 1786 and was recorded within eight months thereafter as will appear by the deed itself and the certificate of its being recorded.[2] That this respondent has conveyed the said land to Anthony Singleton deceased by deed of mortgage dated the day of 179 . That he has also conveyed the said land to William Heth by deed of mortgage dated the 1st. day of July 1794 and has also conveyed it to Mrs. Randolph by deed of mortgage dated the day of 179 .[3] He admits that the said deed for the tract of land called Curles was executed prior to the time of the second delivery thereof but he does not recollect whether it was delivered at the time it bears date or whether it was or was not attested by all the witnesses at the same time.[4]

Copy, Record of Wayles's Executors v. Randolph et al., 17, T.79/19 (claim of James Buchanan & Co.), P.R.O.

1. The reference is to the date of the judgment obtained by the executor of James Bivins against Wayles's executors, 7 June 1793 (Doc. I and n. 3).

2. See Doc. I and nn. 8, 9. The deed of 20 Sept. 1785 was reacknowledged on 21 Mar. 1786 and recorded on 3 July 1786.

3. See Doc. I and nn. 11–13. No copy of a deed to a Mrs. Randolph was entered on the record; nor is such a deed mentioned in the commissioner's report of 26 May 1797 (Doc. XIV).

4. The deed contains the signatures of seven witnesses, followed by James Currie's certificate, dated 25 Mar. 1794, that four of them (including himself) witnessed the deed on 21 Mar. 1786 (Record of Wayles's Executors v. Randolph et al., 34).

XII. Replication of John Loyd
ca. May 1797

The replication of John Loyd executor of the last will & testament of Osgood Hanbury surviving partner of Capel and Osgood Hanbury to the amended answer of to the amended bill of complaint exhibited by him the said John Loyd and others against them. This replicant saving to himself all benefit of exception to the said answer for and by way of replication thereto saith that the said amended bill and all & every the matters therein contained are true and sufficient in law to be answered by the said defendants and that the said amended answer is untrue and insufficient to be replied to by this defendant.[1] He further saith that he was on the 4th. of July 1776 and has been at all times since a British subject within the intent and meaning of the several acts of Assembly prohibiting the recovery of British debts. That by a treaty of peace made and concluded between the United state of America and the King of Great Britain made on the 3d. September 1783 it was agreed that creditors on either side should meet with no lawful impediment to the recovery of the full value in sterling money of all bona fide debts heretofore contracted, that the several judgments aforesaid were debts within the intent & meaning of the article above recited in the said treaty notwithstanding which the acts of Assembly aforesaid remained unrepealed by any act of the Legislature of Virginia and the Court of York County in which the said judgment was obtained refused to hold plea of debts due to British subjects till after the year 1791.[2] He further saith that David M. Randolph executor of the last will and testament of Richard Randolph deceased, and one of the defendants in this cause had due and legal notice of the said judgments on or before the 1st. of June 1791. and that from the time of the rendition of the said judgments until this time the said Capel & Osgood Hanbury during their lives and, this complainant since their deaths have constantly resided in parts beyond sea and out of the limits of Virginia[3] without that &c.[4] and this complainant prays as in his original bill he has prayed.

Copy, Record of Wayles's Executors v. Randolph et al., 18, T.79/19 (claim of James Buchanan & Co.), P.R.O.

1. The clerk should have written "replicant." Up to this point the form of the reply is that of a general replication asserting the truth and sufficiency of the allegations in the plaintiff's bill and denying the truth and sufficiency of the defendant's answer. The plaintiff then recited new matter—his being a British subject and creditor within the meaning of the peace treaty of 1783 and a resident outside of Virginia—by way of special replication. Special replications were employed whenever the defendant presented new allegations in his plea or answer. In this instance the plaintiff apparently was responding to Richard and David M. Randolph's assertion that the Hanburys' judgments should be presumed paid because of the great length of time that had elapsed (Doc. IX).

By JM's day special replications had fallen into disuse, and the usual procedure was for the plaintiff to amend his bill or to file a supplementary bill responding to new matter by the defendant. Although a special replication required the defendant to rejoin, no rejoinder was entered on the record of this suit (John Mitford, *A Treatise on the Pleadings in Suits in the Court of Chancery, by English Bill* [3d Am. ed.; New York, 1833], 17–18; Hinde, *Chancery Practice*, 283–89; Harrison, *Chancery Practice*, I, 299–300).

2. On the disabilities of British suitors in Virginia courts during and after the Revolution, see Sec. IV, editorial note. The plaintiff was attempting to show why he had been unable to revive the 1770 judgments or to bring a new action upon them.

3. The plaintiff claimed the benefit of the saving clause for foreigners to avoid the operation of the statute of limitations. By a 1792 act the revival of a judgment or the bringing of a new action on it was limited to ten years after the rendition of the original judgment (Shepherd, *Statutes*, I, 27).

4. The following general words were omitted: "that any other matter or thing whatsoever in the said answer contained, material or effectual in the

law to be replied unto, confessed and avoided, traversed or denied, is true; all which matters and things this repliant is and will be ready to aver and prove as this honourable court shall direct, and" etc. (Harrison, *Chancery Practice*, I, 301).

XIII. Order of Reference
25 May 1797

The Court doth order that one of the commissioners thereof do state an account of all the lands, tenements & hereditaments whereof Richard Randolph, father of the four first named defendants, was seized in fee simple on the sixteenth day of July, in the year one thousand seven hundred and seventy,[1] & which descended from him to his eldest son and heir at law the defendant Richard Randolph, if any, & also which were settled by Richard Randolph the father upon any of his sons, and which were devised by the said Richard Randolph the father, to any of them and do also state an account of all such of the said lands, tenements and hereditaments as have been conveyed or otherwise disposed of by the said heir & devisees respectively with the considerations paid, or secured to be paid for the same; & als[o] an account of the permanent improvements upon any of the said lands, tenements and hereditaments made by the said devisees with an estimate of the said improvements & report the same to the Court.

Copy, Record of Wayles's Executors v. Randolph et al., 18–19, T.79/19 (claim of James Buchanan & Co.), P.R.O. Date of order noted in record immediately preceding text.

1. The date of the Hanburys' judgments against Richard Randolph in the York County Court.

XIV. Commissioner's Report
26 May 1797

Commissioners Office May 26th. 1797

Agreeably to the aforegoing order, & at the instance of the parties your commissioner having examined the papers laid before him, has to report as follows. That by a copy of the will of Richard Randolph the elder among the exhibits in this cause, it appears that he devised to his son Brett Randolph the land & plantation called Sandy Ford in the Countys of Cumberland & Prince Edward, excepting the Mill & 50 acres of land. And to his son Ryland Randolph, all that tract of land called Clover Forest, or so much thereof as he should be possessed of, lying in the county of Cumberland. Also his land and plantation in the county of Chesterfield opposite to Curles. And to his sons Brett and Ryland Randolph, the Mill at Sandy Ford & fifty acres of land—also to David Meade Randolph the tract of land called Elams in the County of Chesterfield containing by estimation 130 acres. It further appears that by a deed dated the 11th. day of October 1780, Richard Randolph the elder conveyed to David Meade Randolph, 900 acres of land, lying in Burmuda Hundred in the County of Chesterfield, which deed was acknowledged and duly recorded. It also appears by the records of the General Court, that Richard Randolph the elder did on the said 11th. day of October 1780, convey to David Meade Randolph one thousand acres of land lying in the county of Cumberland, called and known by the name of Dry Creek, which was also acknowledged & recorded. It further appears that the said Richard Randolph executed a deed in fee, on the 20th. of September 1785, to Richard Randolph the younger, for a tract or parcel of land lying in the county of Henrico commonly called Curles, with the tract or tracts of land thereto adjoining or belonging, this deed was proven on the 3d. of July following: Your commissioner has further to report that of these lands, it appears the following have been sold, or otherwise disposed of. It is admitted by the defendant Brett Randolph that he had sold to John Holcombe 282 acres of land part of Sandy Ford tract, & for which he executed a deed in 1791, or 1792, for the consideration of four hundred & eighteen pounds. By a deed dated the 14th July 1792. Brett Randolph one of the defendants, conveyed to William Penick for the consideration of £300, Two hundred & eleven & three quarters, acres of land, lying in the county of Cumberland, being part of Sandy Ford & duly proved & recorded. By another deed, Ryland Randolph & Brett Randolph conveyed on the 28th. of January 1794, 133½ acres of land to Eleazer Clay, for the sum of £334.15. this land lies in Chesterfield county. On the 15th. of February 1794 Ryland Randolph conveyed to George Woodson 22½ acres of land in Chesterfield County for the consideration of £38. By deed dated the 15th. September 1794 Brett Randolph conveyed to Ryland Randolph one moiety of the Mill and fifty acres of land in Prince Edward county, for the consideration of £400. And by deed of equal date, from said Brett Randolph to Ryland Randolph, is conveyed 50 acres of land on appomatox river adjoinging Randolph's Mill, and near Sandy Ford bridge, for the consideration of £50. By deed dated January 31st. 1795 Ryland Randolph conveyed to Alexander Legrande 150 acres lying in Cumberland County, and on the south side of Clover Forest Road, for the consideration of £91.10.0. The said Ryland Randolph also conveyed on the 13th. of November 1795, 35¼ acres of land lying in Cumberland & Buckingham countys adjoining Clover Forest to Philip Gatch for the sum of £35.5.0. It appears also by the record books of the Richmond District court, that Richard Randolph the defendant did on the 1st day of April 1794 executed a mortgage in favour of Anthony Singleton, whereby he subjected the tract of land called Curles to the payment of the sum of £1989.12 on or before the first day of April 1797, which instrument is duly proved and recorded. It also appears, from the records of the General Court, that the said Richard Randolph did on the 21st of July 1794, convey unto William Heth the tract of land called Curles, to assure & secure the payment of 3333⅓ dollars on or before the first day of January 1801, which is duly proved & recorded. Your commissioner upon the subject of improvements, has to add, that from the allegation of the defendant Richard Randolph he has placed a granery and other buildings upon the plantation called Curles, which cost at least £180. That the defendant D. M. Randolph also alledges that the improvements in buildings &c. done by him at the place formerly called Burmuda Hundred costs at lea[s]t £1500.0.0. It also appears from the depositions of Benjamin Allen that the Houses &c. erected by Brett Randolph on the tract of land called Sandy Ford amounted to £482.0.0 & from the allegation of the said Brett sundry brick work & plastering was done by a person now dead, to the amount of upwards of £50.0.0.

Aw. Dunscomb M. C[1]

Copy, Record of Wayles's Executors v. Randolph et al., 19–20, T.79/19 (claim of James Buchanan & Co.), P.R.O.

1. Andrew Dunscomb, master in chancery (*PJM*, II, 198 n. 7).

XV. Exceptions to Commissioner's Report

ca. 26 May 1797

The defendants Brett Randolph & Ryland Randolph except to the commrs. report in this cause for the following reasons viz: The said Brett Randolph because it is not stated as it ought to have been that he aliened all the residue of the lands devised him including the improvements made by him to Benjamin Harrison junr. & company, to sales by a levari facias issued against him and Ryland Randolph on a judgment obtained against them by the said Benjamin Harrison junr. & company on a bond given by the testator for a bona fide debt, & therefore that he hath now nothing in his hands by devise from the testator.[1] And the said Ryland Randolph because it is not stated by the commissioner as it ought to have been that the other lands devised to him together with some of his own to a considerable value were taken by a levari facias at the suit of Benjamin Harrison junr. & company to satisfy a judgment for a bona fide debt due by bond from the testator to the said Benjamin Harrison junr & company, the interest of which was greater than the extended yearly value of the said lands, and therefore that he hath nothing by devise from the testator at this time.

Copy, Record of Wayles's Executors v. Randolph et al., 20, T.79/19 (claim of James Buchanan & Co.), P.R.O.

1. The execution was a writ of extent, not a levari facias (Doc. VI and n. 3).

XVI. Agreement
ca. June 1797

It is agreed[1] in this case that the judgment creditors are not to be considered as subject to the disadvantage attendant on their being plaintiffs in equity with the admission of their having no legal title nor are the defts. to be understood as admitting that they have a legal title, but it is agreed that the claim and defence are to be first considered as they would stand at law, & if the defendants have a defence at law they are to receive the benefit of it, if on the contrary it is the opinion of the Court, that the plaintiffs ought to succeed at law, then it is agreed that the case shall be so considered, and the defence, of the defendants as well legal as equitable shall be estimated as it would be if they were now praying to be relieved against those judgments. Any issues which the court may deem necessary may be directed, notwithstanding this agreement. It is further understood that nothing in this agreement shall bar the Court, if the right be determined in favor of the complainants from extending the remedy according to the principles of equity.

JNO. WICKHAM counsel for compts.
J MARSHALL for defts.

Copy, Record of Wayles's Executors v. Randolph et al., 22, T.79/19 (claim of James Buchanan & Co.), P.R.O.

1. This undated agreement immediately follows the text of the decree of 5 Oct. 1797 (Doc. XVII) and immediately precedes an agreement of the same

date signed by plaintiffs' counsel John Wickham concerning a proposed suit on behalf of Robert Beverley and his daughter for the specific performance of the marriage contract mentioned in this suit. JM must have signed the present document before leaving Richmond around 20 June to serve as American commissioner to France.

XVII. Decree of the High Court of Chancery
5 October 1797

In the cause, which came on the last term by consent of parties, to be heard, on the bills, demurrers, pleas, answers, replication, exhibits, examinations of Witnesses and a written agreement between the parties, & was then argued by counsel, the Court on the fifth day of October, in the year of our Lord one thousand seven hundred & ninety seven, delivered the following opinion;[1]

The indentures made the eleventh day of October in the year one thousand seven hundred & eighty, between Richard Randolph of the one part & his son David Meade Randolph, of the other part, said to be, one, 'for his advancement in life' and the other 'for his better advancement in life' may be avered to have been in consideration of the marriage of that son, and the daughter of Thomas Mann Randolph: and alliance which was then contemplated in a treaty for that purpose, & accomplished after sealing & delivery of the indenture. This averment is admissible being congruous with the consideration mentioned in the indentures. In execution of the judgment by Capel and Osgood Hanbury, of whom the surviver is now represented by John Loyd, which had not been revived, & in execution of the judgments by Charles Carter & Charles Turnbull,[2] of whom the last is now dead, which were revived against the executors of Richard Randolph the father, if they were at this time revived against his heir and devisee writs of elegit would not, by relation, defeat or impair lawful mesne acts, such as were the indentures between Richard Randolph, & his son David Meade Randolph, and proceedings in execution, & aleinations in satisfaction of the judgments recovered against the devisees of Richard Randolph the father. The indenture made between Richard Randolph, the father, and his son Richard Randolph, which beareth date in September of the year one thousand seven hundred and eighty five, if it had been cancelled, and reexecuted in March next afterwards, and if it had been altered in another part would have been an act of the latter day, in the same manner as if another conveyance had been then executed; and having been proved within eight months from that time would have been good against the creditors of the father, although the marriage of the son & Maria Beverley, in consideration of which the conveyance was executed had preceeded: for marriage is a consideration continuing. But the indenture was only acknowledged before the witnesses who proved it, which can mean nothing more than acknowledgment, that the indenture had been sealed & delivered on the day of its date, and the indenture is stated to have been made in consideration of a marriage, to be had and solemnized, whereas the marriage had been actually solemnized before; and therefore the indenture cannot be an act of the day when it was so acknowledged, & consequently not having been proved within eight months from the sealing & delivery thereof is void, against creditors, by the words of the act of General Assembly.[3] The demand made by the representative of Capel & Osgood Hanbury is not liable to the objections thereunto urged by the defendant Richard Randolph. In execution of the judgments, recovered by Capel & Osgood Hanbury, against Richard Randolph the father, if they had been revived by writs of scire facias against himself, or his heir and devisees, writs of elegit or of levari facias might by force of the statute enacted in the year one thousand seven hundred & seventy two have been lawfully directed to the sheriff of any county other than that of York,[4] the court of which awarded the original judgments, and in that case, those judgments must have been first satisfied, but not having been revived, they are not intitled to priority against creditors whose demands are of equal dignity. The executors of John Wayles, if they had taken an assignment to their trustee of the Obligation of Richard Randolph, the father, with his said surety, for payment to James Bevins of the money recovered from those executors by virtue of the said obligation, would have been intitled, by prosecuting an action in the name of their said trustee, to the same remedy as the said James Bivens might have prosecuted against the heir and devisees of the said Richard Randolph, the father and this court would have restrained the heir and devisees from pleading payment by the surety's executors, and they ought now to have the same remedy as if such assignment had been made, & have equal right to satisfaction of their demand with the judgment creditors, because the heirs were specially bound by the said Obligation. The money for which the land called Elams which was devised by Richard Randolph, the father, to his son David Meade Randolph hath been sold by him, is liable to the payment of the plaintiffs demands. And the court doth adjudge, order and decree, that the bill of the plaintiffs be dismissed as it is accordingly hereby dismissed, as to that part thereof which claimeth a satisfaction of the demands of the plaintiffs out of the lands conveyed by Richard Randolph, the father to his son David Meade Randolph in consideration of marriage as aforesaid;

that the lands conveyed by Richard Randolph, the father, to his son Richard Randolph, the son, be sold, subject to the dower of Richard Randolph the fathers widow and the proceeds of sale after a deduction therefrom of the value of permanent improvements erected on those lands, by the said Richard Randolph the son, to be allowed and paid to him in the first place, and also after a deduction of the expences of sale, be applied towards satisfaction of the plaintiffs said demand; and   are appointed commissioners to estimate the value of the permanent improvements aforesaid, and after giving three weeks previous notice in one or more of the Richmond News-papers, and to make the sale aforesaid at public auction for ready money, & report their proceedings to the Court: and the Court doth declare the lands devised to the defendants Ryland Randolph and Brett Randolph by their father Richard Randolph, which had been extended and sold for payment of that testators debts, to be exonerated from the lien, to which they would otherwise have been subject; and doth direct the commissioners, employed in examining, stating and settling the account of administration by Richard Randolph & David Meade Randolph, of their fathers goods chattels and credits, to state and report an account of the debts, with which his heir and devisees were chargeable, and of the credits, to which they, on account of payment of debts and improvements, on the lands descended, & devised, are intitled.[5]

Copy, Record of Wayles's Executors v. Randolph et al., 20–22, T.79/19 (claim of James Buchanan & Co.), P.R.O.

1. JM was absent on his mission to France at the time this decree was handed down.

2. Charles Carter, surviving trustee of William Byrd, had joined as a complainant in this suit the preceding June. He based his claim on a judgment obtained by Byrd's trustees against Richard Randolph at the July 1784 term of the Henrico County Court. This judgment had been revived against Randolph's executors at the May 1788 court (Record of Wayles's Executors v. Randolph et al., 20, 37–38).

3. Hening, *Statutes*, XII, 154.

4. The 1772 statute empowered county court clerks to issue "any legal or proper writ of execution or attachment" upon judgments or decrees in their courts to the sheriff of any other county (ibid., VIII, 516–17). Before this act only writs of fieri facias or capias ad satisfaciendum could be so issued.

5. Immediately following the text of the decree, the record states that Richard Randolph "prayed an appeal from so much of the foregoing decree as relates to the Curles estate which is allowed on his entering into bond with sufficient security in the Clerks office of this court, in the penalty of twenty pounds within one month from this day which was accordingly done" (Record of Wayles's Executors v. Randolph et al., 22).

The case, now styled Richard Randolph v. Wayles's Executors et al., first came before the Court of Appeals on 30 Apr. 1798, at which time three of the five judges declared themselves interested in the event of the suit. In this situation, Virginia law provided for a special Court of Appeals to be constituted, consisting of the remaining judges and as many judges of the General Court as would make the number at least five. This special court did not hear the case until Nov. 1799 (Va. Ct. Ap. Ord. Bk. III, 226, 274, 327, 355–56, 357; Hening, *Statutes*, XIII, 25).

XVIII. Argument in the Court of Appeals
ca. 6 November 1799

Marshall for the appellants.[1] 1. The executors of Wayles are not specialty creditors. For the original debt has been paid to the obligee and no action to recover it, is sustainable at common law; because the bond having been paid off, and not assigned, lost its obligation. It is not true that the executors are in the place of an assignee; for the assignment preserves the bond, but the payment destroys it.[2]

The principle that the court goes on, in the case of marshalling assets, is not correctly stated, by the opposite counsel; for it is not that the specialty debt, is revived in favor of the simple contract creditor, but that the specialty creditor, having two funds, has contrary to equity, taken the personal estate from the simple contract creditor, and thereby let the real estate which ought to have contributed, go quit of bearing any proportion of the debts. An act which operates as a fraud; because it relieves the land that was justly bound, to the prejudice of a fair creditor, contrary to the rule of equity, which uniformly compels the party, having two funds, to resort to that, which does not interfere with the claim of him, who has but one.[3] But that is not our case; For this is not a question concerning the unjust exercise of a right against two funds: but whether a man, who has paid off anothers debt, without taking an assignment of it, shall be permitted to the prejudice of third persons, to revive the debt which had been extinguished by his own act? It is therefore not within the principle of marshalling assets.

Moreover that principle is never applied to affect a purchaser; because he has as much equity as the claimant, and he has the law besides. But, in this case, a Court of Equity is called on to assert, to the injury of fair purchasers, a principle invented for the sake of affecting justice. An attempt contrary to the nature of that court; which always refuses to act when injustice would follow from it. But in the present case the plaintiffs had at most only an equitable claim; and therefore it would be monstrous to set it up, after it had been extinguished, in order to avoid the mesne acts of others.

The question has a great resemblance, in principle, to the case of old incumbrances in the doctrine of mortgages. For, there, an old incumbrance will protect a latter mortgage, if it has not lost its legal force; but, if it has lost its legal effect, it will not, *Pow. Mortg.* 215.[4] So in this case the bond, if it had not lost its legal effect, might have availed the plaintiffs; but having been paid off, by one of the obligors, its legal force is gone; and therefore the executors can only be considered as simple contract creditors.

2. The judgments are not specific liens on the lands.[5]

At common law lands were not bound, and the lien is only in consequence of the statute; which does not bind them, in express terms, but only by implication. The lien is a mere creature of the Court, resulting by construction from the election given to the creditor by the statute; and therefore the Court will never extend it beyond the limits of public convenience. No case has been produced where lands conveyed after the year and day were held to be bound; nor indeed can such an inference be fairly drawn, when there is no right to take an execution. For the lien is predicated on, and is only co-extensive with the right to take execution. If the case be taken by analogy to real actions it is clear. For in those the lien is gone when the right to take execution ceases; which is the same principle contended for, in the case now before the Court.[6]

It is said that the *scire facias* revives every thing. But that can only be where the right is continuing; for it cannot retroact upon a mesne act, where the right has ceased. The statute which gave the *scire facias* does not say it shall overreach mesne acts; and the lien is gone before the *scire facias* becomes necessary.[7]

The argument, that the *scire facias* is a judicial writ, and that a release of the execution will discharge it, proves nothing; for it will also be released by a release of all actions; and therefore it may as well be called an action as an execution. Relation is fair between the parties; but it would be iniquitous, that it should have effect, against third persons; and accordingly it never does, unless, in favour of one who has a superior equitable or legal right. Suppose a legal title extinguished and afterwards revived, would this revival avoid the mesne act against a third person, who had innocently acquired a title in the mean time? It would be shocking that it should; and the law would never countenance such injustice. Yet that is the amount of the principle contended for, on the other side.

It is said that since the statute, if notice is given, execution may go at any time. But this is contrary to all practice; the statute never was so understood; and the mischiefs of such a doctrine, to creditors and purchasers, would be incalculable.

It is not true that there is no difference between the case at bar, and one where the plaintiff continues his *elegit* on the roll. For the continuance is a notice to the world, as much as the original judgment, and of itself imports that the judgment has not been satisfied; whereas, when no further steps are taken, it affords a presumption that the judgment has been satisfied. This doctrine is applicable to all the judgments; but as to those of *York* Court it is entitled to still greater weight. For, as it is the case of a lien by implication merely, it will not be extended, by the court, to all judgments indiscriminately.

Generally speaking when the law obliges a man to take notice of any act, it affords the means of doing it. But how can that take place, in the case of County Court judgments? For the County Courts are so numerous that no prudence or industry could enable a purchaser to guard against them. No matter how many transfers may have taken place; no matter how many years may have elapsed since the judgment was rendered; no matter how many precautions may have been taken to guard against injury, the judgment would overreach them all, and bind the lands in the hands of the innocent purchaser. So that the shackles on property would be infinite; especially, when it is considered that judgments are always docketed in the names of the plaintiffs and not of the defendants: A purchaser therefore, before he could venture to contract, would be obliged to search through all the judgments of all the courts in the country. A labour which would be endless, and the pursuit intolerable.

The true idea therefore is, that the lien should be confined to the same courts, which the law requires the recording of deeds to be confined to. So that a man should not be obliged to search further for a judgment than for a deed: Especially as the Legislature by the record laws meant to favour and secure purchasers; and therefore the court ought not, by mere construction and implication, to raise up an inference, entirely contrary to the spirit and intent of those laws; but on the contrary should promote the object of the Legislature as much as possible. It is not to be believed, that the Legislature could intend that the implied lien should extend every where, when the express lien was confined to certain limited jurisdictions. Because the danger from implied liens, was much greater than from express liens, and therefore more to be discouraged.[8]

But the necessity of a *scire facias* against the *terretenants* is decisive; for there could be no such proceeding where the lands lay in another county; and therefore as the *terretenant* could not be brought before the court, the lien could not be revived by the *scire facias*.[9] In such a case there can be no inference of notice; because the lands could not be reached in the hands of the *terretenants*, between whom and the creditor there is no privity; although it may be otherwise as to the heir on account of the privity between him and the creditor.

Therefore whether the principles of the common law, the object of the Legislature, or the reason and convenience of mankind be consulted, it will be found to be true, that the judgments constitute no lien upon the lands in the present case.

3. There is no question, but that the policy of the record laws may be as well answered, by allowing a re-acknowledged deed to prevail, from the time of its re-acknowledgment, as by allowing an entire new deed to have effect from its date. This position has been stated by us, and has not been answered by the counsel for the appellees. Nor indeed can any just answer be given to it. For, in both cases, not more than eight months will elapse between the acknowledgment and the recording of the deed; and that is all which the policy of the law appears to have required.[10]

But, forsaking this point, the counsel for the appellees insists that the act of Assembly is express, that it shall be recorded within eight months from the execution of the deed, and that a plain man would necessarily so understand it: Therefore he concludes that a second acknowledgment will not supply the omission. He admits however, that if the deed had been given up to be cancelled and then had been re-acknowledged, it would have operated as a new deed: Which is not very consistent with the other position contended for by him, that nothing could pass by a subsequent deed; or with the words of the act of Assembly, according to the construction which he puts upon them. For how, in the case he supposes, would the estate get back to the grantor, or how could he have any thing for the second delivery to operate on, if the whole was out of him? This very admission necessarily proves that the grantor has an interest, which he may grant, so as to be effectual against creditors from the second delivery; or else the new deed would have no effect at all; which is contrary to the terms of the admission.[11]

It is said however, that the re-acknowledgment was no delivery. But for what purpose was it made then? Certainly the intention was to deliver; and here the evidence is express that it was delivered on the date of the last acknowledgment. Besides there ought to be positive evidence of the first execution of the deed; and I submit it to the court whether that be proved or not.

But it is argued that if the re-acknowledgment be a second delivery, that still the second delivery was void and *Perkins* and *Cowper* are cited in support of the position.

The case in *Cowper* was that of a re-delivery by one, who was a feme covert at the time of the original delivery, but sole at the time of the re-delivery; and, if it proves any thing, it rather supports what we contend for; because it was decided there, that the re-delivery amounted to a confirmation, and that circumstances might amount to a re-delivery.[12] The same argument would apply, with equal force, in the present case, as the first delivery has been rendered void, as to creditors and purchasers, by the statute.

The passage in Perkins is of a case where the first delivery takes effect; but we insist that the estate in the present case remained in the grantor, as to creditors and purchasers; and therefore that the second delivery did operate.[13] For our law is like the English statute of enrolments, and therefore as against creditors and purchasers the estate does not pass out of the grantor until the deed is recorded. But it is said that the 4th section makes a difference; because by that the deed is to be good between the parties.[14] The cases cited though, prove, that to be nothing more than the English Judges had, by construction implied before; and it was probably inserted, in our statute, in conformity to their decisions. The only difference therefore is, that in England the Judges declared it to be good, between the parties, upon principle and construction; but in this country the act of Assembly, pursuing the course of their decision, has declared it so in express words. If this reasoning be correct, then *Hindes case* 4. *Co.* shews that there may be a second delivery, which will not only confirm the estate between the parties themselves, but will be effectual as to every other purpose. Indeed the contrary doctrine would be intolerable; as, according to that idea, a defective deed would not be made effectual by any conveyance.[15] There is no similitude therefore between the case in *Perkins* and that under consideration. For *Perkins* supposes a case, where nothing remained in the grantor; but here we prove an existing interest which he might part with; and if he could grant it at all; he might as well convey it to his own grantee, as to any other person.

It was said that according to this argument a judgment between the date and recording of the deed would be good against the grantee; although the deed should be actually recorded within eight months from its original date. But that position is not found; for the judgment would by relation, be over-reached by the recording of the deed according to the doctrine in Hindes case, as there would be no injustice in it. For as the first purchaser would have the first right in equity, no injury would be done to those whose rights were subsequent to his. From all this, it follows, that the re-acknowledgment was clearly good; and therefore that the creditors cannot affect the lands.

4. But the mortgagees have clearly the first right; because they

had both titles, that is to say, the title under the deed, and that by descent.[16]

For 1. Their case resembles that of the alienee of a devisee, whose right will be good against creditors, although the devisee himself continues liable to them. For the statute of 3. *W. and M.* like our act for recording deeds, expressly declares that the devise shall be void against creditors;[17] but nevertheless the title of the alienee of the devisee is good, and the estate cannot be touched in his hands, *Mathews* vs *Jones*, 2. *Anstr. Rep.* 506. In that case it was expressly argued, that the devise being void as to creditors, nothing passed by it, as against them; and of course that the devisee could convey no estate to their prejudice. But the Court unanimously held, that the devise did pass the estate so as to enable the devisee to alien, and that he would only be personally liable.[18] The same doctrine applies to this case; For the conveyance here will be good except against creditors, and the alienation by the grantee will be good, altho' the grantee will be personally liable to the creditors. For the two statutes are equally strong and the principles precisely the same. Before the record laws in this country, the alienation would have withdrawn the lands from the creditors here, in the same manner as the devise there; and of course, if the alienation of the devisee there will prevail, so will the alienation of the grantee here.

But 2. If this doctrine were not true, then the consequence inevitably would be that the title of the mortgagees under the lien must prevail. For if the conveyance is void altogether, then it is the same thing as if it had never been made, and in that case Richard Randolph must, as to the creditors, take as heir necessarily. But, if he took as heir, then the mortgages by him are certainly good. Because alienations by the heir are good, although he is liable to the creditor for the value. But a mortgage is so far an alienation; and therefore necessarily good.

5. The conveyance to David Meade Randolph is not liable to exception.[19]

It is in vain to argue, that a considerable property has been conveyed, without any valuable consideration paid for it. Such an argument may be proper to the Legislature, but not to the Court: As it is no longer a question, whether a conveyance, in consideration of marriage, be sustainable or not. For the law is settled, that such a conveyance is good.

But it is said, that a voluntary conveyance to a son, about to be married, is void. As that however, is not the present case I will not say whether the position be correct or not; but there are some cases which might make it very doubtful. As for instance in the case of the

East India Company vs *Clavel*, 2. *Bac. abr.* 607. *Prec. ch.* 377. where A, agreed with the East India Company to go as president to Bengal, and entered into a bond of £2000 for performance of articles; but before he set out he made a settlement of his estate, and among other things he declared the trust of a term of 1000 years to be for the raising of £5000 as a portion for his daughter, who afterwards married I. S. a gentleman of £700 per annum, who before the marriage, was advised by counsel that the portion was sufficiently secured, and who afterwards on her death, had at her request expended £400 on her funeral, *but never made any settlement on her*; and A. having embezzled the goods and stock of the company to a considerable value, the question was, whether this settlement was voluntary and fraudulent as to them; and it was held to be a prudent and honest provision, without any colour of fraud; and though in its creation it was voluntary, yet being *the motive and inducement to the marriage*, it made it valuable.[20] This case and others which might be mentioned seem to refute the position advanced on the other side; but, deeming it altogether unnecessary, I shall not go into the argument of that point now. Because an express marriage contract has been proved in our case. The letter of *Thomas Mann Randolph* and the depositions of Richard and Harry Randolph, shew that the marriage was suspended until the conveyance was made.[21] The letter of Richard Randolph the father to *David* was clearly intended as an answer to that of Thomas Mann Randolph. For, in it he says that he had been looking out for an estate, ever since he heard of his addressing the lady; and that, in consideration of the marriage, he would give the property.[22] The conveyance was the real ground upon which the consent of the lady's parents was obtained; and without it, the marriage would not have taken place. So that it is much stronger than the case of the *India Company* vs *Clavel*; because here was an actual treaty for the property, but there was none in that case. To which may be added that without the marriage David Meade Randolph could not have compelled a conveyance.

It is objected though, that he also says, he intended to give him the same property before. But can that destroy the claim arising from the marriage? Surely not; for it is saying no more than was necessarily implied: because, before he would enter into the agreement, he must have been previously disposed to give the property. So that the objection does in fact amount to no more than this, that a man who is disposed to make an agreement ought not to make it, because he was previously disposed to do so.

It is said however that the letter from Richard Randolph to David M. Randolph does not refer to that of *Thomas Mann Randolph*. But the contrary is expressly proved. Besides, if it removed the objections of Thomas Mann Randolph, it was the same thing.

Another objection raised is, that the conveyance is to David Meade Randolph, and not to his wife.[23] But so was that in the case of the *East India Company* vs *Clavel*; and yet the settlement was held good. Besides the estate contributes to the benefit of the wife and her family; and the husband cannot deprive her of her right of dower in it. So that she in fact is benefited by it. In the common cases of settlements on marriage the remainder is generally limitted to the husband and his heirs; Which, according to the doctrine contended for by the opposite counsel, would be void; but the marriage has always been considered as protecting the whole settlement.

It is urged, that it is mockery to say, that the letter turned him into a purchaser. But in point of law it does; and although he may afterwards defeat the provision, by squandering or alienating it away, that will not alter the case. For there is a confidence that he will keep it; and as the object was the ease and comfort of the daughter and children, that end was thought to be sufficiently attained by the conveyance to the husband.

But a singular objection is raised, namely, that Thomas Mann Randolph must have known of the embarrassment, under which the affairs of Richard Randolph were, at that time. Now, besides that such knowledge is not necessarily to be inferred, from any proofs in the cause, it cannot be contended that that circumstance would make any difference in law. For most marriage settlements originate from apprehensions of that kind; and therefore the knowledge instead of operating against the conveyance would rather strengthen it. Because *Thomas Mann Randolph* would not have permitted the marriage without it, and the testimony expressly proves that to have been the consideration of the conveyance. The words of the statute of *Eliz.* are not opposed to this doctrine; in which nothing, relative to such a case, is said: Nor indeed does that statute render even mere voluntary conveyances void, unless made to deceive and defraud creditors. 1. *Eq. cas. ab.* 149.[24] But that is not important to be inquired into in the present case; because here was a sufficient consideration in law to support the conveyance.

As to the form of the deed, it is to be remembered, that Richard Randolph the father had not got the legal estate conveyed to him, as to part of the lands, when the marriage contract was entered into, but David procured it afterwards;[25] and therefore the argument contended for, with respect to the form, does not apply, as to that part. But, independent of that, if the deed does not secure the estate according to the terms of the agreement, then it is contrary to the contract, which the court will consider as still standing, and controuling the deed.[26]

Printed, Daniel Call, *Reports of Cases Argued and Adjudged in the Court of Appeals of Virginia*, II (Richmond, 1802), 161–72.

1. The appeal was in the name of the legal representatives of Richard Randolph, who was now dead. Arguments were heard on 5, 6, and 7 Nov. 1799. Preceding JM were Call and DuVal for the appellants, Hay for the appellees, and Warden for the appellants (Va. Ct. Ap. Ord. Bk. III, 327, 355–57; 2 Call 140–61).

2. JM's argument was a direct reply to that of Hay for the appellees. Hay's first point was that Wayles's executors were bond creditors, standing in the place of the original obligee or of an assignee. As creditors by a bond in which the heir was bound, Wayles's executors would have a claim upon the real estate in satisfaction of this debt. Simple contract creditors, however, could resort only to the personal estate (2 Call 156–57).

3. Hay likened this case to the principle of marshaling assets. According to this principle, if a bond creditor, who had the choice of resorting either to the personalty or realty, exhausted the personal estate, a court of equity would enable simple contract creditors to stand in place of the specialty creditor and recover from the realty the amount of what the specialty creditor had drawn from the personalty (Tucker, *Blackstone's Commentaries*, II, 512 n.; Robinson, *Practice*, II, 87–88).

4. John Joseph Powell, *Treatise upon the Law of Mortgages* (3d ed.; Dublin, 1791), 215: "But, where the prior incumbrance taken in is deficient in those requisites which are necessary to give it legal efficacy, no protection can be derived from it." An incumbrance on land made it subject to a charge or liability, as, for example, a mortgage.

5. These were the judgments obtained by the Hanburys against Richard Randolph in York County Court in 1770 (Doc. VIII and n. 1). Hay contended that these judgments were a lien upon Randolph's estates that continued to attach to the lands despite their subsequent sale (2 Call 157).

6. JM alluded to the statutory writ of elegit (Statute of Westminster II, 13 Edw. I, c. 18), which gave the creditor a right of execution against half the debtor's lands. This and other writs of execution had to be prosecuted "within the year" of the judgment. Since no execution had issued on these judgments, JM maintained that the lien expired after a year and could not bind lands sold after that time (Hening, *Statutes*, XIII, 357, 358–59).

7. A creditor who did not sue out execution within a year could revive his judgment by a writ of *scire facias* ("that you cause to know"; given by the Statute of Westminster II, 13 Edw. I, c. 45), which required the defendant to show cause why judgment should not proceed to execution (Blackstone, *Commentaries*, III, 421–22). Hay argued that the scire facias had the effect of continuing the lien.

8. The Virginia act for regulating conveyances stipulated that deeds should be recorded in the General Court or in the court of the county or city

in which the land, in whole or in part, lay (Hening, *Statutes*, XII, 154). JM contended that the York County judgments would only bind lands in that county.

9. A terre-tenant was one who was in actual possession of the land. In the law of executions, a terre-tenant was the owner of land acquired from a judgment debtor.

10. Hay insisted that the deed from Richard Randolph the father to Richard Randolph the son was void as to creditors, since it had not been recorded within eight months as prescribed by the act for regulating conveyances. The point at issue was whether the deed, which was originally executed in Sept. 1785, reacknowledged in Mar. 1786, and recorded in July 1786, met the requirements of this act (2 Call 157–59; Hening, *Statutes*, XII, 154).

11. Hay's position was that by the original sealing and delivery of the deed the estate passed out of the hands of the grantor and therefore the reacknowledgment was ineffectual. JM contended that the grantor retained an interest in the estate until the deed was actually recorded and that the reacknowledgment operated as a second delivery.

12. Hay cited Goodright v. Straphan, 1 Cowp. 201, 98 Eng. Rep. 1043 (K.B., 1774) as proving that "a re-acknowledgment, where the first delivery has actually had effect, has no operation" (2 Call 158). In this case, decided by Lord Mansfield, the court held that the redelivery by a single woman (feme sole), after the death of her husband, of a mortgage deed originally delivered while she was married (covert) was a sufficient confirmation of the deed to bind her without having the deed reexecuted.

13. John Perkins, *A Profitable Book, Treating of the Laws of England; Principally as They Relate to Conveyancing* (1827; New York and London, 1978 reprint, from 15th ed.), sec. 154, 32:

"A deed cannot have and take effect at every delivery, as a deed; for if the first delivery take any effect, a second delivery is void. As in case an infant, or a man by duress of imprisonment, make a deed, and deliver it as his deed, &c. and afterwards the infant when he comes to his full age, or the man imprisoned when he is at large, re-delivers as his deed, the same deed which he delivered before as his deed, this second delivery is void. But if a feme covert deliver an obligation or other writing as her deed, this delivery is merely void; and therefore if after the death of her husband, she being sole, delivers the same deed again as her deed, this second delivery is good and effectual."

Lord Mansfield quoted this passage in Goodright v. Straphan, as did Hay in his argument (2 Call 158).

14. JM referred to the fourth section of the conveyance law, as reenacted in 1792, which stipulated that conveyances of land were "void as to all creditors and subsequent purchasers, unless they shall be acknowledged or proved, and recorded according to the directions of this act; but the same as between the parties and their heirs, shall nevertheless be valid and binding" (Shepherd, *Statutes*, I, 84). This passage was not in the former act.

15. Hynde's Case, 4 Co. Rep. 71, 76 Eng. Rep. 1041 (K.B., 1591). JM's cocounsel Daniel Call had earlier cited this case to prove that with regard to

creditors and purchasers an estate was to be considered as remaining in the hands of a grantor until the deed was recorded (2 Call 151).

16. Though moving on to his fourth point, JM was still speaking to Hay's third point. The mortgagees of the Curles estate were Anthony Singleton and William Heth (Doc. I and nn. 11–13). JM argued that even if the deed was void, the mortgagees had a prior claim in equity to this land.

17. JM referred to the statutes concerning fraudulent devises, 3 Wm. III, c. 14, from which the Virginia act of 1789 was copied. The purpose of this statute was to make devisees as well as the heir liable for the ancestor's bond debts in which the heir was expressly bound (Hening, *Statutes*, XIII, 53–55).

18. Mathews v. Jones, 2 Anst. 506, 145 Eng. Rep. 949 (Ex., 1794). The court held that the defendants, who had purchased land from a devisee, were protected because they purchased it without notice of a creditor's claim.

19. JM was taking up Hay's fourth point, that the deed to David Meade Randolph was void because not made for valuable consideration (2 Call 159–61).

20. East India Company v. Clavel, Prec. Ch. 377, 24 Eng. Rep. 170 (Ch., 1714), summarized in Bacon, *Abridgment* (5th ed.), II, 607. JM closely paraphrased Bacon's summary.

21. The letter from Thomas Mann Randolph to Richard Randolph (the elder) was missing, but its contents were proved by the depositions of Richard Randolph (the son) and Henry Randolph (Doc. III and n. 2).

22. See Doc. III and n. 3. This letter, dated 8 Aug. 1780, is printed in Call's report (2 Call 130–31).

23. David M. Randolph explained that by a mistake of the attorney who drew the deed, marriage was "not expressed as a consideration although it was the real consideration" (Doc. III).

24. JM referred to the statute concerning fraudulent conveyances, 27 Eliz. I, c. 4, which was incorporated into the Virginia statute of 1785 (Hening, *Statutes*, XII, 160–62). In Parslow v. Weedon, 1 Eq. Ca. Abr. 149, 21 Eng. Rep. 950 (Ch., 1718), the court held that land disposed of during a testator's lifetime, whether voluntarily or not, was not subject to the claims of bond creditors. This was not a situation provided for by the statute, which looked only to protect creditors against frauds that "might be supposed in a Man's last Sickness."

25. See Doc. III.

26. JM was followed by Wickham for the appellees and Randolph for the appellants. Speaking through President Pendleton, the Court of Appeals on 9 Nov. unanimously upheld the deed from Richard Randolph the elder to Richard Randolph the son, thus reversing in part Chancellor Wythe's decree of 5 Oct. 1797 (2 Call 183–88; Doc. XIX and n. 1).

XIX. Decree of the Court of Appeals
9 November 1799

And now on this day, to wit, the aforesaid ninth day of November in the year one thousand seven hundred and ninety nine aforesaid,[1] came the parties by their Counsel and the Court having maturely considered the transcript of the record aforesaid and the arguments of Counsel is of opinion that the deed from Richard Randolph, the elder, to Richard the younger, was made upon good & valuable consideration, and was binding upon the creditors of the father, having been duly recorded within eight months from the twenty first day of March one thousand seven hundred and eighty six, when the said deed was reexecuted by sealing and delivery and attested by new subscribing witnesses, and ought to be considered to every intent and purpose as a new deed of that date: that altho' the deeds for David Mead Randolph expressed the considerations to be for natural affection and advancement in life he was nevertheless at liberty to aver and prove an additional consideration, and having established by satisfactory proof that the said deeds were made in consequence of a treaty of marriage between the fathers of him & his lady he is to be considered as a bona fide purchaser of the estates: that the said purchasers are not to be affected by the supposed lien upon the lands from the Judgments in the proceedings mentioned, such lien not existing at the time of their respective purchases for the reasons stated in the decree of the said High Court of Chancery:[2] that the appellees, executors of John Wayles, ought to stand in the place of James Bevins and be considered as bond creditors so far as may affect the distribution of remaining assetts, but not so as to charge the executors with a devastavit on account of payment, or Judgments to simple contract creditors: and that there is error in so much of the decree aforesaid as declares the deed to Richard Randolph the son void as to creditors and directs a sale of the lands by commissioners and the application of the money to the benefit of the appellees; and as to so much as subjects the money for which the land called Elam's, devised by Richard Randolph the father to his Son David Meade Randolph hath been sold by him, to the payment of the demand of the appellees, the Court being of opinion that the money for which the said Land was sold is only liable to the demand of the appellees, if it has not already been applied to the payment of debts which bound the devisee;[3] therefore It is DECREED & ORDERED that so much of the said decree as is herein stated to be erroneous be reversed and annulled, that the bill be dismissed as to the appellants, that the residue of the said decree be affirmed, with the reservation herein before stated as to the executors of John Wayles, and that the appellees pay to the appellants the costs expended in the prosecution of the appeal aforesaid here.

WHICH is Ordered to be certified to the said High Court of Chancery.

Copy, Record of Wayles's Executors v. Randolph et al., 47–48, T.79/19 (claim of James Buchanan & Co.), P.R.O.

1. The decree is recorded in Va. Ct. Ap. Ord. Bk. III, 358–59, and printed in 2 Call 188–89.

2. Pendleton noted that the creditor had taken no steps to sue out an execution or to renew his judgments by scire facias. "If he had done so," said the judge, "the *lien* would have been revived; but to operate prospectively, and not to have a retrospective effect, so as to avoid mesne alienations." Admitting that British subjects could not sue in Virginia courts between 1774 and 1791 (see Doc. XII), Pendleton pointed out that the creditor (Thomas Loyd, executor of Hanbury) had already let the judgments expire before 1774. After 1791, moreover, he let six more years pass before coming "into equity to set up his lien against purchasers. This appears, to me, to be contrary to every principle of law and equity" (2 Call 187).

3. In his plea (Doc. III), David M. Randolph said that he sold the Elams estate as executor and applied the money to the estate of Richard Randolph. The High Court of Chancery had decreed that this money was liable to the payment of the demands of Wayles's executors and of the other plaintiffs. The Court of Appeals ruled that this money was liable only so far as it had not been applied to the payment of other bond creditors.

III. The United States Circuit Court of Virginia

Editorial Note

John Marshall qualified to practice in the U.S. Circuit Court of Virginia on 26 November 1790 at the courthouse in Williamsburg. The court was then holding its second session, having met briefly in Charlottesville the preceding May.[1] During the next ten years Marshall was to be a conspicuous presence in this court, representing both his fellow Virginians and clients from outside the commonwealth. He can be identified as counsel in approximately 150 cases brought between 1790 and 1800 and was no doubt involved in dozens more for which no traces of his participation remain. In the great majority of Marshall's cases—more than a hundred—he was employed by Virginia defendants in suits brought by British creditors to recover debts contracted before the Revolution. Because of their importance in Marshall's law practice, the British debt cases have been assigned to a separate section of this volume (Section IV). The four cases presented below are a sampling of those not belonging to the special category of British debt.

The Court of the United States, Middle Circuit, District of Virginia, convened in May and November each year. Originally designated to meet alternately at Charlottesville and Williamsburg, the court settled permanently at Richmond beginning at the third session in May 1791. It was a court of general jurisdiction, having cognizance of civil suits at common law or equity where the matter in dispute exceeded five hundred dollars and a foreigner was a party or the suit was between a Virginian and a citizen of another state. The circuit court was composed of two justices of the federal Supreme Court and the judge of the federal district court, acting in their two capacities as judges of law and chancellors in equity. The Supreme Court justices who sat with the district judge changed from term to term, as they rode circuit on a rotating basis.[2] The other federal court in the state, the district court, was primarily a tribunal to hear admiralty and maritime causes. Having never practiced in the state admiralty court, Marshall rarely if ever attended the federal district court.

The federal circuit court heard essentially the same kinds of disputes that were brought in the state courts of common law and equity. On the law side the great bulk of the cases was for the recovery of a debt, either by action of debt or assumpsit. One or the other of these actions was employed in all of the British debt suits and in 80 percent of the other cases in the federal court that bear the stamp of

1. U.S. Cir. Ct., Va., Ord. Bk. I, 4.
2. *U.S. Statutes at Large*, I, 75, 78–79, 217.

Marshall's participation. Most of the debt actions were for the payment of money secured by bond (Case Number 9); the others were founded on protested bills of exchange or promissory notes. The assumpsit actions embraced unliquidated debts due by open account and also a few cases for the recovery of money due by bill of exchange (Case Number 10). Among Marshall's other common law cases in this court were four in covenant, three in ejectment (Case Number 11), one in trespass with force and arms, and one in detinue. On the chancery side, exclusive of the British debt cases, only five Marshall cases have been found. Four of these were bills of injunction to stay proceedings at law (Case Number 10). The other was a suit for equitable accounting between two merchants (Case Number 8).

Procedure and practice were the same in both the state and federal courts, as Congress had decided against adopting uniform rules in order to render a system of federal courts more palatable to the citizenry of thirteen diverse states. The Process Act of 1789 provided that "the forms of writs and executions" in the federal courts should be the same as those then in use in the highest courts of the state where the federal court was sitting.[3] In Virginia, for example, the initial process was the writ of capias ad respondendum. The same writ was used in the new federal court, identical in form except that it issued in the name of the president of the United States and was directed to the U.S. marshal rather than the county sheriff.[4] At its first session in Charlottesville the federal circuit court adopted a rule requiring bail in all civil cases in which it was requirable by the laws and usages of Virginia. The court also ordered the adoption of the same regulations governing proceedings at the rules in the clerk's office as were used in the state district courts.[5]

The records of the federal circuit court of Virginia, now deposited at the Virginia State Library, provide the best documentation extant of Marshall's practice at the trial level. These include the original papers of the ended cases—writs, pleadings, notices, depositions, mercantile accounts, bonds, bills of exchange, promissory notes, correspondence, and the like. Numerous pleadings and other documents in Marshall's hand testify to his busy practice in the federal court. Supplementing the case papers are bound volumes of order books, record books, and rule books, similar in content to books kept by the state court clerks.[6] They survive in more completeness than do

3. Ibid., 93; Goebel, *Antecedents and Beginnings*, 509–40.

4. See Case No. 12, Doc. I.

5. U.S. Cir. Ct., Va., Ord. Bk. I, 1.

6. These sources are discussed in Sec. I, editorial note.

their counterparts for the Fredericksburg District Court, particularly the record books and rule books. In the federal court rule book the clerk frequently, though not consistently, wrote the initials of the attorneys for plaintiff and defendant, making it a valuable source for identifying Marshall's cases.

Marshall's clients in the federal circuit court, aside from the Virginians he defended in the British debt suits, were mostly merchants residing in the large towns along the eastern seaboard. New Yorkers retaining Marshall included William Constable (Case Number 8), and the partners Harman Leroy and William Bayard. Other mercantile gentlemen employing him were John Vaughan (Case Number 10), Joseph Swift, and Joseph Ball of Philadelphia and Andrew Van Bibber and William Livesay of Baltimore. Marshall also represented a number of London firms—Samuel Gist, James and Bruce Wilson, Thomas Blane, Robinson, Sanderson & Rumney, among others. These suits fall outside the British debt classification, as they were brought for the recovery of debts incurred since the peace.

8. Hunter, Banks & Company v. Constable and Sargeant

1789–1801

I. Subpoena, 27 March 1789
II. Bill in Chancery, ca. April 1789
III. Answer of William Hill Sargeant, 21 May 1789
IV. Draft Answer of William Constable, ca. 11 July 1789
V. Benjamin Harrison, Jr., to William Constable, 12 July 1789
VI. Answer of William Constable, 9 February 1790
VII. William Constable to John Marshall, 13 February 1790
VIII. Petition for Removal of Suit to U.S. Circuit Court, 8 June 1791
IX. Order of Reference, 5 December 1794
X. Notice, 7 November 1797
XI. Commissioner's Report, 4 August 1799
XII. Decree, 9 May 1801

Editorial Note

Merchants residing in the large commercial cities of New York, Philadelphia, and Baltimore frequently turned to John Marshall when they needed a Virginia lawyer. Robert Morris of Philadelphia was the most prominent of such clients (see Case Number 6). Another was William Constable, Morris's onetime partner, who enjoyed a successful career in trade during and after the Revolution. He later became a leading speculator in public securities and land.[1] This suit arose from Constable's mercantile activities during the last years of the War of Independence. Although based in New York City, Constable at that time resided in Philadelphia and was in partnership with James Seagrove. The two merchants had come to this city during the British occupation and became associated with Benedict Arnold in some dubious business ventures. The firm of Constable & Seagrove carried on trade with the West Indies and France. The return trip often included stops at Wilmington, North Carolina, and Richmond, where their ships were loaded with tobacco. The company became an important supplier of this commodity to Silas Deane and Robert Morris.[2]

In 1780 two Fredericksburg merchants established at Richmond the firm of Hunter, Banks & Company. The principal partners were James Hunter and John Banks. A third partner was Henry Banks, John Banks's younger brother, who after the company's dissolution acted as its agent in settling accounts and bringing lawsuits.[3] The company suffered great losses during the British invasion of 1781, when a number of its vessels were impressed into state service. John Banks subsequently set up operations in the Carolinas, contracting to supply General Greene's army with food and rum, a venture that brought both ruin and discredit. Even before the company was dissolved in 1782, there had been a falling out between the Banks brothers and Hunter. "Want of candor, want of moral integrity, an ambitious pride to do something equal to his education and pretensions," Henry Banks later wrote of Hunter, "rendered him fit for nothing."[4]

The dispute that provoked Henry Banks to bring his bill in chancery originated in the purchase by the Richmond firm of a quantity of rum, linen, and other goods from Constable & Seagrove in August 1780. There were two attempts to settle the accounts arising from this transaction in the next two years. The first was in April 1781, when William Hill Sargeant, a resident of Petersburg who had shipped some of his own goods to Constable from the West Indies in 1780, made a settlement with Henry Banks on behalf of Constable (then serving as Lafayette's aide-de-camp). For reasons stated in his answer (Document VI), Constable considered this agreement void and entered a new one with James Hunter in May 1782. Banks, who was not present at this settlement, disregarded it on the grounds that his partner was not fully informed of the company's dealings with Constable. Apart from this basic disagreement, the settling of accounts between these two merchants was complicated by the loss of papers during the British invasion and the inevitable confusion attending payments in a rapidly depreciating paper currency.

After the war both parties seemed willing to resolve their differences through arbitration. Banks went to New York in June 1786, executed arbitration bonds with Constable, and empowered Alexander Hamilton to act on his behalf. According to Banks's later account, Hamilton neglected this business and, worse, allowed Constable to examine Banks's papers, some of which subsequently were missing. For these reasons the Richmond merchant did not wish to try another arbitration and instead brought suit in the Virginia High Court of Chancery in 1789.[5] Contrary to Constable's confident assertion in 1789 that the accounts could "be settled by a Couple of Merchants in half an hour," the final decree in this case was not issued until 1801, two years before the New Yorker's death.[6] Marshall was closely involved in the first phase of the suit, as shown by his surviving correspondence with Constable and his draft answer (Document IV). He continued to be the attorney of record when the case was transferred to the federal court in 1791.[7] His active role as Constable's lawyer ended with his diplomatic mission to France and his subsequent public service. He was apparently succeeded by Edmund Randolph.[8]

Hunter, Banks & Company v. *Constable and Sargeant* was in certain respects similar to *Morris* v. *Alexander*. Both were suits to settle mercantile accounts, begun in the Virginia chancery court in the late 1780s and concluded in the same year, 1801. In each case the accounts were referred to a commissioner in chancery, with both Morris and Constable employing Benjamin Harrison, Jr., and John Richard, Jr., as agents to prepare their claims. The timing of Banks's bill, however, allowed Constable as a defendant the option of transferring the suit to the federal court, which he chose to do. Although this change of courts may have made no difference in the outcome of the suit, one happy consequence was the survival of the suit papers. These papers, supplemented by a collection of Constable's private papers, provide excellent documentation of the case, particularly in showing how lawyer and client worked together to prepare an answer in chancery.

1. On Constable's career, see the sketch and references in *PJM*, II, 30 n. 1.

2. Carl Van Doren, *Secret History of the American Revolution* (New York, 1941), 173–76; William A. Davis, "William Constable: New York Merchant and Land Speculator, 1772–1803" (Ph.D. diss., Harvard University, 1955), 31–37.

3. Hunter (1746–1788) is not to be confused with his older cousin of the same name who was master of the celebrated iron works at Fredericksburg (R. Walter Coakley, "The Two James Hunters of Fredericksburg: Patriots Among the Virginia Scotch Merchants," *VMHB*, LVI [1948], 3–21). On John Banks (ca. 1757–1784) and Henry Banks (1761–1836), sons of Gerard and Frances Banks of Green Bank in Stafford County, see *Tyler's Quarterly*, XV (1933–34), 121–23, 237–38; Carter, *Latrobe Va. Journals*, II, 534–35.

4. *CVSP*, IV, 371–72; Commonwealth v. Banks, 4 Call 338–46; Henry Banks, *The Vindication of John Banks* . . . (Frankfort, Ky., 1826), 9–12, 68–69.

5. "Remarks of H. Banks on the Report of the Comr. dated Novr. 29. 1800," Hunter, Banks & Co. v. Constable and Sargeant, U.S. Cir. Ct., Va., Ended Cases (Restored), 1801.

6. William Constable to JM, 13 July 1789 (*PJM*, II, 31–32).

7. U.S. Cir. Ct., Va., Rule Bk. I, 43–44, 76–77.

8. JM's correspondence with Constable, with the exception of one letter, is published in *PJM*, II, 30–37; the omitted letter is presented below (Doc. VII). In the suit papers there is an undated document, consisting of notes to one of the commissioner's reports, addressed to Randolph.

I. Subpoena
27 March 1789

The Commonwealth of Virginia to the sherif of Dinwiddie County greeting: You are hereby commanded to summon William Constable and William Hill Sergeant to appear before the Judge of the High Court of Chancery, at the Capitol in the City of Richmond, on the first day of the next Court to answer a bill in Chancery, exhibited against them by Hunter Banks and Company and this they shall in no wise omit under the penalty of one hundred pounds each. And have then there this writ: Witness George Wythe, Judge, of our said Court, at Richmond, this twenty seventh day of March one thousand seven hundred and eighty nine in the thirteenth year of the Commonwealth.[1]

PETER TINSLEY CHCC

Copy, Hunter, Banks & Co. v. Constable and Sargeant, U.S. Cir. Ct., Va., Ended Cases (Restored), 1801, Vi. Taken from transcript of proceedings in state High Court of Chancery that also includes copies of bill in chancery, Sargeant's answer, and order of 8 June 1791 transferring suit to federal court.

1. An endorsement notes that the subpoena was returned on 4 Apr. The practice in Virginia was to issue the subpoena before the filing of the bill (except in cases requesting writs of injunction or ne exeat), even though the bill formally concluded with a prayer that a subpoena issue against the defendant (Tucker, *Blackstone's Commentaries*, III, 443 n. 14).

II. Bill in Chancery
ca. April 1789

To the Honble. George Wythe Esqr. Chancellor of Virginia.[1]

Humbly Complaining shew unto your honor, your Orators Hunter Banks & Co. That John Banks for Hunter Banks & Co. in the year 1780 purchased from William Constable a considerable quantity of Goods which were payable for in tobacco at £65 ℔ Ct. and Amounted to £64,997.10 Paper money, that the said Acct. remained unclosed 'till the month of February following, during which time frequent applications were made to your Orators by the said Constable and also by Capt. William Hill Sergeant his Agent or partner in the said business, that a settlement was made by Henry Banks Agent for your Orators with the said Serjeant, allowing for depreciation & Interest £13102.14 paper money. And your Orators have made sundry payments in discharge of the said Acct. reduced the ballance due to the said Constable to the Amount of his orders, which your Orators drew in favor of the said Constable or Serjeant, the first for £80 specie, which was agreed upon between your Orators, and the said Serjeant should be equal to £11200 of the said paper money debt, the said Order was drawn on William Patterson & Brothers of Baltimore.[2] Your Orators drew another order in favor of the said Constable or Serjeant on John M Nesbit & Co. of Philadelphia for £40.000 Paper Money,[3] being the ballance which your Orators owed the said Constable and Sergeant or one of them, which orders your Orators believe were not paid and are still in the possession of the said Constable or Sergeant. Your Orators state the above facts, to shew, that at the time of the said Settlement, there was no fixed rule for the Depreciation of the Paper Money,[4] that the Consent of the said parties, that an Allowance of £13102.14 of like money should be considered as equal to the depreciation of the paper Money from the time of the Original Contract to the day of Settlement should be obligatory on them, which took place in the month of 178 Your Orators further shew that after the said settlement they paid the said defendants £187.1.6 ¾ agreeable to the annexed Account, that at the several times of paying the specie there being no fixed Standard or ratio it was mutually understood by all parties, that all over the £80 Specie shou'd go towards discharging the £40.000 Paper Money at the same rate. That £80 specie shou'd be equal to the sd. £11.200 paper money as that rate of Exchange had been established by consent of all the parties, since which no further Settlement hath taken place. That in the month of May 1782 the said William Constable applied to James Hunter then acting for Hunter, Banks & Co. and who [knew][5] not the exact situation of the said Account nor the agreement of the said parties which had been previously entered into by your Orators said Agent Henry Banks touching the allowance for the depreciation of the said paper money, and the said James Hunter sold to the sd. Constable either upon his own account or on Account of himself and the said Serjeant, or for the benefit of a certain James Seagrove, your Orators one fifth part of a Brig called the Wilkes for the sum of £800 specie, and also sold him the one fifth part of her Cargo for £204.3 specie, for neither of which have the said defts. or either of them accounted with your Orators, except a pair of Carriage Guns of about the value of £50 specie.[6] Your Orators further shew that the[y] sent to the said Constable 10 Guineas by one Mitchell in the year 1781, and that one Guinea was said to be bad, & was not then entered, but is since entered at the foot of your Orators Acct. to the Credit of the said Constable;[7] Your Orators further shew, that the whole of all their dealings & transactions with the said defts.

commenced in the year 1780. and ended in 1782. most of which were transacted in this State, which may more fully appear by referring your honor to your Orators Acct. which is hereto annexed, & which they pray may be taken & Considered as part of this their bill. Your Orators charge that there is a just ballance of £790.9.10¼ Specie due to your Orators, with interest thereon, to be computed from the first day of June 1782, either from the said Constable or from the said William Hill Sergeant, or from both. Your Orators further shew, that they have frequently in a friendly manner applied to the said defts. & requested them to come to a fair settlement with your Orators, & to pay to your Orators the just ballance due to them. & that the sd. defts. have evaded & neglected to do so under various and frivilous pretences. Your Orators further charge, that many of their sd. dealings & transactions were negociated in private, between your Orators & them.

Your Orators placing confidence in their honor & justice, which is usual among merchants so to do, & that your Orators cannot establish their Accts. but by the Oaths of the defts. in Chancery. In tender consideration whereof & for as much as your Orators are remediless in the premises by the rules of the Common Law & cannot support their sd. Accts. which is just & true, without the aid of your honor in Chancery, where private transactions between parties, and matters of this sort are properly cognizable. To the end therefore, that the said defts. William Constable and W. H. Sergeant his agent or partner may on their several and respective corporal Oaths full, true & perfect answer make to all & singular the premises as fully & distinctly as if the same were to be here again repeated and they the said defts. thereunto more particularly interrogated, & more especially that they may set forth & discover, Whether in the year 1780 your Orators did not purchase of the said William Constable a considerable quantity of Goods which were payable for in Tobacco at £65 ℔ Ct. which amounted to £64997.10 paper Money? Did not the said Accts. remain unclosed until Febby. 1781. & did not the said W. H. Sergeant as agent for, or partner with the said Constable, settle the same with the said Henry Banks Agent for the said Complts. & by the consent of all parties? Did not the said Henry Banks allow the sd. defendts. in lieu of Interest & depreciation, the sum of £13.102.14 paper money? Was there any rule fixed by Law at that time settling the sd. depreciation? Was not the sd. Settlement made by the Consent of the said Banks & the said Sergeant, & was it not also agreed that £80 specie should be equal to £11200 paper money being the Amt. of the sd. Order drawn on William Patteson & Brothers in Baltimore in favor of the sd. deft. or one of them, the said order being unpaid, and did not your Orators draw on John M.

[ANNEXED

Dr	Mr. William Constable	in Account		
1780 December 10	To 5 hhds Tobacco pd C Jones 5078 lbs @ £65	3.300	14	—
1781 Mar. [2]3[a]	To J M Nisbet draft on them	40.000	—	—
1782[b] Febr 23	To Cash pd. Willm H Sargeant in part	16 871	2	—
April 7	To Cash paid Your self	3 488	—	—
[March 6	To Capt. W H Sergeant Bale. in full	805	—	—][c]
May-6	To an Error in settling your Acct with Captn Sargeant in April 1781 which I suppose.	2 495	8	—
		66 960	4	
	To Ballance paper money	11 200	—	
		78 160	4	—
		£78 160	4	—
1781 June 14[d]	To specie paid yourself	30	—	—
Decr 16	To Cash Received from Joseph North on Acct Captn Harris .... } 90			
	Sales of Cloath Petersburg .... 83.16.10¾ deduct ⅕th ...16.15. 4½ } 67.1.6[¼][e]	157	1	6¼
		187	1	6¼
	To Ballance	226	5	1¾
		£413	6	8
1782 May	To ⅕th. part of the Brig wilkes sold you	800	—	—
	To ⅕th part of her Cargo agreeable to Account furnished	204	3	—
	To Cash sent to you by M Mitchel last year 10 Guineas one of which was bad & not enterd in place	12	12	—
		1016	15	—
1782 June	To ballance due at this date as foregoing Acct	790	9	10½[f]
	To Interest till paid @ £39.10.5 ℔. Annum			

ACCOUNT]
Current with HUNTER BANKS & CO. CR

Date	Particulars	£	s	d
1780 Augt 3d	By 4 hhds Rum from mandean & smith 457½ 8 ditto from Mitchel & Gamble . . . . . 911 1368½ 1368½ Gallons @ 22.10/[g]	30.107	10	—
29	By Amount of Good Imported in the wilkes . 628.1.4 ditto on the Betsey Peggy . . . . . 664.2.5 1292.4.3 deduct 10 ℔ Cent taken out By 129.2.0 Mr Moss for freight 1163.2.3			
1781	1163 Ps of 8 100 for 1 payable in Octr in Tobacco @ £65 ℔ Cnt.	34 890	—	—
Febry 11	By Ballance of Goods bot of him sometime since @ £61693.4 payable in Tobacco at 65£ advance to £78.15	13 102	14	—
	By 2 lb of sein Twine for brig willing Lass	60	—	—
		78 160	4	
1782 Mar 6	B J M Nesbit & Co for one order on them returnd settled at 120 for 1. £40 000–is	333	6	8
	By ballance of paper money settled in specie 11200 paper	80	—	—
		413	6	8
	By ballance	226	5	1¼[h]
1782 May —	By 1 pair of Carriage guns	50	—	—
	By ballance due H Banks Co at this date with Interest from the first June 1782	790	9	10¼
		£1016	15	—

Copy Test

PETER TINSLEY CHCC[i]

Nesbit & Co. of Philadelphia for £40.000 paper money in favor of the said defts. or one of them, which said Order was also unpaid, & do not the sd. defts. or one of them hold the said Orders? Did not the sd. plts. pay the sd. defts. subsequent to the sd. Orders as ⅌. Acct. £187.1.6¾ Specie, & at the time of paying the specie, there being no fixed standard, was it not mutually understood, that all over the £80 specie the reduced value of the £11200 Paper money shou'd be applied towards discharging the other order of £40.000 paper Money? Did not the said defts. or one of them purchase the one fifth part of the Brig Wilkes, & receive the same of your Orators for £800 Specie? Did not the said defts. or one of them purchase & receive the one fifth part of your Orators Cargo belonging to the said Brig for £204.3. Specie when & to whom have the said defts. or either of them paid them same & in what manner? Did not the said Complt. send to the said defts. or one of them 10 Guineas by Major Mitchell, one of which was said to be bad, & is entered at the foot of your Orators Acct. to the Credit of the said Constable? Have the said defts. or either of them paid to your Orators since the said Settlement, any thing except the said two Carriage Guns? Does not the said Complts. Acct. contain a just & full statement of all debits and Credits between your Orators & the said defts. William Constable & Wm. H. Sergeant agent or supposed partner of the other deft.? Does not the said Sergeant live at Petersburg, & was he not an Agent or partner of the said Constable? Is there any mistake or Error in the said Acct., if so, that the said defts. or either of them do particularly point out & state in their answer such Error or Errors, Mistake or mistakes, Omission or Omissions, otherwise that your Orators Acct. be considered as fairly, justly & truly stated? Were not the debts of the said defts. or the some of them contracted in this Commonwealth. That your honor will order & Decree that the said defts. or deft. as the case may be pay to your Orators the said ballance of £790.9.10. or whatever may be found due to your Orators, with Interest thereon from the 1st. June 1782. & that the said defts. be compelled to produce their Books, & papers to be examined & inspected by auditors to be appointed by This Hble. Court, to settle & adjust the same, & that your honor may make such further Order & Decree in the premises as are agreeable to Equity & to your honor may seem meet. May it please your Honor to grant to your Orators a Writ of Subpœna &c.

PETER TINSLEY C H C C.[8]

Copy, Constable-Pierrepont Papers, NN. Endorsed: "Hunter Banks & Co. vs. Constable & Sergeant/ Copy Bill." Another copy in High Court of Chancery transcript (see Doc. I, n.).

1. The attorney representing the plaintiff was William DuVal (U.S. Cir. Ct., Va., Rule Bk. I, 43). The exact date of the filing of the bill is unknown, but Sargeant had received a copy by 14 May 1789 (William H. Sargeant to W. B. Giles, 14 May 1789, Constable-Pierrepont Papers, NN). The subpoena was issued on 27 Mar. and returned on 4 Apr. (Doc. I).

2. A promissory note of 8 Apr. 1781 from Hunter, Banks & Co. to Sargeant for £11,200, payable in specie at 140 to 1 (£80 specie), was filed with the suit papers. No bill drawn on William Patterson & Brothers of Baltimore has been found, though there is one dated 26 Apr. 1781 drawn on Smith, Johnston & Co. of Baltimore for $779 specie, payable to Sargeant (Hunter, Banks & Co. v. Constable and Sargeant). In his answer (Doc. VI) Constable denied any knowledge of a bill on Patterson & Brothers but admitted his possession of the bill on Smith, Johnston.

3. This bill of exchange, dated 25 Apr. 1781, is filed with the suit papers. The face amount was $133,333.33, or £50,000 in Pennsylvania money, where the bill was drawn. (This was equivalent to £40,000 Virginia currency.) The depreciation rate stated on the bill was 120 paper to 1 of specie.

4. Virginia established a scale for the depreciation of paper currency by an act of Nov. 1781 (Hening, *Statutes*, X, 471).

5. This word, omitted from the copy, is supplied from the High Court of Chancery transcript.

6. Hunter, Banks & Co. sold one-fifth part of the brig *Wilkes* and cargo to Constable in May 1782. In January of that year the company had purchased one-half share of the vessel for £2,000 specie from the owner, Samuel B. Cunningham. The *Wilkes* set sail for the West Indies in April and was captured by the British on her return voyage (bill of sale, 28 May 1782; deposition of Samuel B. Cunningham, 2 May 1792, Hunter, Banks & Co. v. Constable and Sargeant). At the time of the British invasion of Virginia a year earlier, the *Wilkes* had been pressed into state service. Cunningham, represented by JM, later obtained a judgment against the commonwealth for the impressment of the brig and loss of cargo (*PJM*, II, 263 and n. 3).

7. The annexed account current shows a charge of £12.12 for the guineas. This was the equivalent in Virginia currency of nine guineas.

8. The initials stand for Clerk, High Court of Chancery.

a. The "2" was omitted by the copyist. The date should be 23 Mar., as it is in the High Court of Chancery transcript.

b. The year probably should be "1781" for this and the following three entries.

c. This entry was omitted by the copyist and is supplied from the High Court of Chancery transcript. The next entry of 6 May is undated in the transcript but follows under this 6 Mar. entry.

d. Here and in the next two entries there are check marks, apparently signifying Constable's agreement with the charges. These correspond with the "7th, 8th, & 9th" charges he admitted in his answer "to be just" (see Doc. VI). There is also a check mark preceding the May 1782 entry charging one-fifth part of the cargo of the *Wilkes*.

e. The fraction was omitted and is supplied from the High Court of Chancery transcript.

f. The fraction should be "¼," as entered on the credit side and on the High Court of Chancery transcript.

g. Here someone, possibly Commissioner Hay, inserted "diffce. £683.15." This refers to the error in multiplying 1,368½ by £22.10. Whoever inserted the correction also struck through "½" on 1,368½ gallons. See Doc. XI.

h. The fraction should be "¾," as entered on the debit side and in the High Court of Chancery transcript.

i. JM received this copy of the bill and a copy of Sargeant's answer (Doc. III) from William Branch Giles on 8 July 1789 and then forwarded them with other papers to Constable on 11 July (*PJM*, II, 29, 30–31).

III. Answer of William Hill Sargeant
21 May 1789

The Separate answer of William H. Sargeant, Defendant to that Bill in Chancery, exhibited against him and William Constable by Hunter Banks & Company:[1]

This defendant now and at all times hereafter saving and reserving to himself all manner of Benifit and Advantage of exception to the manifold errors and insufficiencies in the Complainants said Bill Contained, for answer there to or to so much thereof as he is advised is material for him to answer unto, answereth and saith;[2] That he never was a partner of William Constable, but that having made a voyage to the West Indies in the year 1780, he shiped in Several Vessels from the West Indies Sundry goods to the address of William Constable, then residing in Virginia, part of the said goods on the Account of William Constable, and part on his own account, That on his arrival in Virginia in the fall of the said year, this defendant learnt that William Constable had disposed of a great part of his own goods to Hunter Banks & Co. as well as part of those in which this Defendant was Concern'd all in his own name; to William Constable therefore this Defendant looked for Payment, not to Hunter Banks & Co with whom this Defendant wished never to be Concern'd, but to the person to Whom the goods Were Consigned; Early in the year 1781. Mr. Constable being then in the Army,[3] requested that this defendant would Call on Henry Banks, who this defendant believed, then acted for Hunter Banks & Company and endeavor to make a settlement of his Accounts with that Company in behalf of the Said Constable; agreeable to such request this Defendant waited on Mr Henry Banks and some Settlement was made, the Particulars of which, this Defendant doth not recollect, only that, (as is set forth in the Bill) Sundry Drafts which were delivered to this Defendant by the said

Banks were not Honored; all of which together with Most or all the Papers relative to the Transaction, this Defendant, deliverd as far as he can recollect to Mr Wm. Constable previous to this Defendants quiting the United States Which he did in the Month of June in the same year, after which being twice Captured by the British, this defendant must have lost any papers relative to Mr Constables transactions with Hunter Banks & Co if any such Papers were retain'd by him, otherwise such Papers should Cheerfully be produced, and when ever this defendant shoud. be furnished with any papers of his that may be either in the hands of M Constable or any other person relative to the Business, this defendant aided by such papers will give such impartial testimony as truth and Honor will ever dictate; finally before the Searcher of Hearts, this defendant declares that he never Considered himself as having any thing further to do with Hunter Banks & Co than the Settling thier Accounts with Mr Constable & in his behalf alone and that he never had any interest or Concern whatever in the Brigg Wilkes & her Cargo, said to be Purchased from the aforesaid Hunter Banks & Co by the said Wm Constable, as this defendant believes Mr Henry Banks well knows & William Constable Can attest, the latter of whom long Since Settled with this defendant for the goods addressd to him by this Defendant part of which goods the said Constable sold to Hunter Banks & Co.[4] And this Defendant denying all and all manner of Combination and Confederacy wherewith he stands Charged in and by the said bill of Complaint, without that, that &c. & humbly prays to be hence dismissed with his reasonable Costs and Charges in this behalf most Wrongfully Sustain'd.

Copy, Constable-Pierrepont Papers, NN. Endorsed: "Sargeant ads Hunter Banks & Co./ Answer in Chancery." Another copy in High Court of Chancery transcript (see Doc. I, n.), noting that answer was sworn in Petersburg on 21 May 1789.

1. Sargeant enclosed a draft of his answer to William Branch Giles on 14 May. Giles put the answer in final form and sent it on to JM, who then transmitted it with other papers to Constable (Sargeant to Giles, 14 May 1789, with draft answer, Constable-Pierrepont Papers, NN; JM to Giles, 8 July 1789; JM to Constable, 11 July 1789 [*PJM*, II, 29, 30–31]).

2. From this point to the formal concluding sentences, the text closely follows Sargeant's draft, except for the change from the first person to the third person.

3. As he explained in his own answer (Doc. VI), Constable joined the Continental army late in 1780 and served until Aug. 1781. He acted as aide-de-camp to Gen. J. P. G. Muhlenberg and to General Lafayette (Boyd, *Jefferson Papers,* V, 295, 369; VI, 18–19).

4. In his letter to Giles of 14 May, Sargeant said that he had "no more to do with [this affair] than the man in the Moon."

IV. Draft Answer of William Constable
ca. 11 July 1789

The answer in chancery of William Constable to the bill of complaint exhibited against himself & others in this Honble. court by Hunter Banks & Co.[1]

This respondent saving to himself every benefit of exception to the bill of the complainants for answer thereto saith that he admits it to be true that in the year 1780, on the 5th. of August he sold to the complainants a quantity of goods a list of which is hereunto annex'd, to be paid for in tobacco at sixty five pounds per hundred to be deliverd in two months. This respondent having lost several papers relative to this transaction in the year 1781, which were destroyd by the British has it not in his power to state accurately the price of each article, but he asserts that the whole amounted to 107420 lb Tobo. & he annexes hereto an extract from the entries on his waste book, which he believes to be correct.[2] That the complainants boasted of the advantageous bargain they had made & actually sold a large part of the goods to   an agent of Mr. Samuel Beall for a much higher price than they had given this respondent for them. At the time of the sale this respondent informd the purchaser that he was about to go to Philadelphia but shoud return about the time the tobacco was payable & relied on their holding it ready for him. A few days after the return of this respondent & in the course of the month of october he applied by letter to the complainants for payment of part of the tobacco & receiv'd for answer that as he had not calld on the 10th. when the tobacco became due they had appropriated it "and did not hold their punctuality at stake in case they did not answer my future demands till perfectly convenient to them.["] This letter was immediately enclosd by this respondent to Messieurs Hunters at Fredericksburg & was answerd by Mr. James Hunter who assurd this respondent that the most pointed honor shoud be observd & every satisfaction given as will appear by his original letter ready to be produced. About this time this respondent joind the continental army & remaind with it till august 1781. In April 1781 this respondent requested William H. Sergeant in the bill namd (who was going to Philadelphia) to settle with the complainants & to deliver the money or tobacco he shoud receive from them to Messrs. Stewart & Totten of Philadelphia. Mr. Sergeant receivd from them bills on Smith Johnston & Co. of Baltimore & on messieurs John M. Nesbit & Co. of Philadelphia. These bills were drawn for specie & paper money rating the tobacco at ten shillings specie per hundred, viz 779 dollars—specie 13333 do. paper. These bills were protested the drawees having in their hands no effects belonging to the drawers. Thus disappointed this respondent considerd the settlement, which was in fact nothing more than a consent to receive the sums for which those bills were drawn, shoud they be paid, in discharge of the debt, as being void, & the debt as resting on its original principles. The complainants were of the same opinion as will appear by the extracts of their letters to this respondent which are hereunto annexd & of which the originals are ready to be producd to this Honble. court. Being however repeatedly disappointed by the complainants & finding no prospect of payment or a complete adjustment of their accounts without a personal application, this respondent in May 1782 determind to go from Philadelphia to Richmond on this business. On his way through port royal[3] he wrote to Mr. Henry Banks who, he understood, was then in Fredericksburg, informing him of his business. Soon after this respondents arrival in Richmond Mr. James Hunter sent an express for Mr. Banks requiring his attendance, as he Mr. Hunter tho one of the Copartners was not acquainted with the business, it having been transacted by Mr. Banks. Mr. Banks replied that he was lading a brig & that it woud not be convenient for him to come for some time. This respondent waited more than a fortnight in Richmond on this single business & at length, finding that Mr Banks continued to evade a meeting with him, he insisted on Mr. Hunters settling the account. On seeing the letters of Hunter Banks & Co. Mr. Hunter was perfectly convincd of the justice of his claim & came to an agreement a true copy of which is hereunto annexd & of which the original is ready to be producd to this Honble. court. This respondent says that the loss he sustaind by the protest of the bills drawn in April 1781 as is before stated is not compensated by the restoration of the original contract. This respondent admits the purchase of the one fifth part of the brig calld the Wilkes[4] which this respondent agreed to receive on Account of so much of his Demand against the said Claimants as the Cost & Outfitt of the said Vessell & her Cargo might appear to have stood in when the several Accounts of his Disbursements & Charges cou'd be collected—but at the same time averrs that the said Vessell was estimated by James Hunter Jr. as supposed to cost about Two thousand Pounds & her Cargo about One thousand pds Curt. Money of Virginia.[5]

AD, Hunter, Banks & Co. v. Constable and Sargeant, U.S. Circuit Court, Va., Ended Cases (Restored), 1801, Vi. In JM's hand, except for concluding passage in Constable's hand (noted below); endorsed (by Constable?): "Draft of an Answer to H: Banks & Cos. Bill."

1. JM wrote Giles on 8 July that he would "endeavor to prepare an an-

swer" for Constable. Three days later he sent Constable "part of an answer" (presumably the draft reproduced here), observing that he was unable to finish it for lack of information. "You will please to alter it where you think proper, complete it, swear to it & send it properly authenticated to me so soon as you can with convenience," he added (*PJM*, II, 29, 30–31). The annotation of this draft is confined to a few textual points. For substantive annotation of the answer, see Doc. VI.

2. At this point three lines are deleted, which read in part: "This respondent further says that he believes the rum was under two shillings per gallon, the irish linnen at three shillings & six pence per yard [*illegible*]."

3. Port Royal in Caroline County was situated on the southern bank of the Rappahannock, about twenty miles below Fredericksburg. The name of the town was omitted in the final form of the answer.

4. At this point the following words have been deleted: "for the price of about £400 [figure apparently inserted by Constable]—& of a part of her cargo for the price of." This deletion was apparently executed by Constable, for the remainder of the MS is in his hand.

5. The answer went through at least one more draft before the final one. Constable wrote some remarks on Banks's bill and accounts, which he intended to forward to JM. Whether he actually sent these is uncertain, but in August he did transmit a draft answer, prepared with the help of a young practitioner in New York City. Constable may have given his remarks to this lawyer, as suggested by a statement on two different drafts of these remarks: "Mr. Marshall directs that I may reply to each item of the Account which I do in the following manner." The draft answer was sent to JM on 19 Aug. "to be corrected & Returned cloathed in such form as you may deem requisite." JM added the final two clauses of the formal conclusion on Constable's draft: "prays to be hence dismissd with his costs &c and this defendant will ever pray &c" (Constable to JM, 13 July, 8 Aug., 19 Aug. 1789 [*PJM*, II, 32, 34–35, 36–37]; "Remarks on Hunter, Banks, & Co's. Bill in Chancery"; "Remarks on H: Banks & Cos. A/C" [two drafts]; "Draft of Answer to H: Banks & Cos. Bill," Constable-Pierrepont Papers, NN).

V. Benjamin Harrison, Jr., to William Constable
12 July 1789

Dear Constable Richmond 12th July 1789

I have your favor of the 30th Ult.[1] & I intend to put this Letter under cover with all the Papers that Mr Marshall has given me relative to your dispute with Banks. They are rather Bulky to go by Post, but as they appear to be of the consequence of £700 & upwards to you, I must take the safest Method of conveyance & not mind the Expence. You will find among them your statement of Facts made in 1782.[2]

This Business does not admit of Mr Banks being held to security. I had before your Letter, proposed that measure, & to become Bound for you, but Mr Marshall says that it cannot be done. I was then for your filing a Cross Bill.[3] Mr Marshall's reply to this was that it could answer no one good purpose whatever, but that of procuring him a double fee.

If Mr With[4] finds any difficulty in the Accounts annexed to the Bill & Answer, he will order them before, his Master Commissioner, Mr William Hay,[5] to be examined & to state specially the matters of difference, for him to decide on.

If it should be my hard fate to be involved in Law in N York, I shall apply to you, freely, but I have enough of it at home for any one Man. At the time of bringing this Bill vs you, Banks brought 39 others. In one of them he has done me the honor to include me, & I have myself to defend in a Charge for 3000 lb of Tobacco, which I do not owe, but my Matter will be very easily settled. It only puts me to some Trouble & Expence. Our Legal Chancery fee is £5.0.0. I have given Mr Marshall twenty Dollars with which I charge you & am very sincerly yours.[6]

BENJ HARRISON JR

ALS, Constable-Pierrepont Papers, NN. Endorsed by Constable.

1. See Constable to Harrison, 30 June 1789, William Constable Letterbook, Constable-Pierrepont Papers, NN.

2. This statement has not been found (see JM to Constable, 11 July 1789; Constable to JM, 13 July 1789 [*PJM*, II, 30–32]).

3. In chancery an answer could pray dismissal of the bill. If the defendant sought any relief against the plaintiff, he had to initiate an original bill known as a cross-bill (Blackstone, *Commentaries*, III, 448).

4. George Wythe.

5. William Hay (1748–1825), a prominent Richmond merchant, had emigrated from Scotland in 1768. He served as commercial agent of Virginia during the Revolution and afterwards as a master in chancery for the High Court of Chancery and the U.S. Circuit Court. He also acted as the agent of John Hay & Co. in that Scottish firm's attempts to recover its prewar American debts (*WMQ*, 1st ser., XV [1906–7], 85–86; *CVSP*, III, 351; William Hay, "Considerations on the various Subjects of Enquiry . . . ," T.79/97 [claim of John Hay & Co.], P.R.O.).

6. JM recorded this $20 as £6 in his account book (*PJM*, II, 366). The chancery fee of £5 was established by an act of 1761; this was later changed to its equivalent in dollars, $16.66 (Hening, *Statutes*, VII, 400; Shepherd, *Statutes*, I, 15).

VI. Answer of William Constable
9 February 1790

THE ANSWER of WILLM. CONSTABLE to the Bill of Complaint exhibited against himself & others in this Honourable Court by Hunter Banks & Co.[1]

THIS RESPONDENT saving to himself every benefit of Exception to the Bill of Complaint for Answer thereto; SAITH; That He admits it to be true, that in the Year of our Lord one thousand seven Hundred & Eighty, on the fifth day of August, when a Citizen of the state of Pensylvania & a resident of Philadelphia, in said State, He sold to the Complainants a Quantity of Goods, a list of which is hereunto Annexed, to be paid for in Tobacco at sixty five Pounds per Hundred to be delivered in two Months.[2] THIS RESPONDENT having lost several Papers relative to this Transaction in the Year of our Lord, seventeen Hundred & Eighty One, which were destroyed by the British Troops, has it not in his Power to state Accurately the price of each Article, but He Asserts the whole Amounted to One Hundred & seven Thousand, four hundred & Twenty Pounds of Tobacco, & He annexes hereunto an Extract from the Entries in his Waste Book,[3] which He believes to be Correct, & that the original Invoice of said Goods was at the time of the delivery thereof, delivered to Henry Banks, one of the Complainants in the said Bill named. THIS RESPONDENT, further says, that the Complainants frequently boasted of the Advantageous bargain they had made for the said Goods, & Actually sold a part of them to an Agent of a certain Samuel Beal[4] for a much higher price than they had given this respondent therefor, as He has been informed & verily believes to be true, and that at the time of the sale of the said Goods, this Respondent informed the Purchaser, that He intended going to Philadelphia, but shoud return about the time the Tobacco was payable & relied on their holding it ready for him. A few days after his return & in the month of October, One Thousand seven Hundred & Eighty, He Applied by letter to the Complainants for delivery of part of the Tobacco, & received for Answer, that as He had not called on the 10th. Inst. when the Tobacco was due they had Appropriated it, "and did not hold their punctuality at stake in Case they did not Answer any future demands 'till perfectly Convenient to them." This letter was immediately inclosed by this Respondent to James Hunter, one of the Complainants in the Bill named at Fredericksburg, and was Answered by him Assuring this respondent "that the most pointed honour shoud be observed & every Satisfaction given." THIS RESPONDENT further says about this time, He joined the Continl Army & remained with it untill August, seventeen Hundred & Eighty One, That in April, One

Thousand seven Hundred & Eighty One, He requested, William Hill Sargeant, in the Bill named, to settle with the said Complainants, & to deliver the Money or Tobacco He shoud receive from them to Messrs. Stewart & Totten[5] of Philadelphia that He the said William Hill Sargeant, made a Conditional Settlement with the said Complainants rating the Tobacco at Ten shillings Specie per hundred, & received from them two Bills of Exchange the One drawn on Smith Johnson & Co. of Baltimore for Seven Hundred & seventy Nine Dollars Specie the other on John M. Nesbitt & Co. of Philadelphia for, One hundred & thirty three Thousand, Three hundred & thirty three Dollars, in Paper, of which said Bill drawn on Smith Johnson & Co. of Baltimore, the Complainants in their said Bill of Complaint have made no mention, & the Bill of Exchange, said by the said Complainants, in their said Bill of Complaint to have been drawn in favour of the said Sargeant in the behalf of this respondent on William Paterson & Co. of Baltimore, ascertaining the pretended rate of Depreciation as charged in the said Bill of Complaint, this respondent is altogether ignorant thereof.[6] He allows there was no legal state of Depreciation, but totally denies all allowance and every Agreement with the said Sargeant as to the Depreciation of the said Money, in manner as is set forth in the said Bill of Complaint. AND THIS RESPONDENT further Answers that the said Bills of Exchange were duely presented for Payment & that the same were regularly protested for Non Acceptance, the Payers not having sufficient effects in their hands belonging to the drawers and that due notice of these protests were given to the said Complainants & that the said Bills of Exchange are now in the hands of this respondent. AND HE FURTHER ANSWERS, that the said Bills of Exchange being unpaid, the Conditional Agreement & Settlement made by the said Sargeant in behalf of this respondent with the said Hunter Banks & Co. became thereby void & of none effect And the dealings & Accounts subsisting between the said Parties rested again on thier Original principles, as will fully appear to have been the Opinion of the said Complainants by the Extracts of sundry Letters from the said Complainants to this Respondent No. 1, 2, 3, & 4; & by the Copy of the Settlement or Agreement No. 5, all of which are hereunto Annexed,[7] & of which the originals are ready to be produced to this Honourable Court, & which this Respondent prays may be Considered as part of his Answer to the said Bill of Complaint, & this Respondent further shews, repeated disappointments of a settlement of his Account as promised by the said Complainants induced him to make a personal Application for such settlement, that Accordingly in May, seventeen Hundred & Eighty two, He went to Richmond expressly on the Business & called on James Hunter, one of the Complainants in the said Bill named & informed him of his Business; the said James Hunter thereupon instantly dispatched an Express to Fredericksburg for Henry Banks one of the other Complainants in the said Bill named & requested his Attendance for the Adjustment of the said Account. The said Banks refusing to come,[8] Notwithstanding this respondent waited for him upwards of a fortnight in hopes a settlement might take place to the general satisfaction of all Parties, the said James Hunter thereupon in behalf, & as one of the House of Hunter Banks & Co. on seeing the several Letters of Hunter Banks & Co. being perfectly convinced in his own mind of the justice of this Respondent's Claim, did enter into a certain written Agreement with this Respondent thereby recinding the former Settlement pretended by the said Hunter Banks & Co. to have been made with the said Sargeant in behalf of this Respondent & which is sett forth & relied upon in the said Bill of Complaint, a true Copy of which Agreement is herein before refered to No. 5.[9] THIS RESPONDENT further says that the Loss sustained by him, by the Protest & non Payment of the Bills of Exchange, drawn as before stated was not nearly Compensated by the restoration of the original Contract, which if it shall be judged necessary this respondent will readily evince to this Honourable Court.

AND THIS RESPONDENT admits the purchase of one fifth part of the Brig Wilkes, also One fifth part of the Cargo thereof, but Expressly declares the Charges therefor in the Account exhibited by the said Complainant, are Erroneous & false which evidently appears by an Account transmitted to this respondent, in the hand writing of the Clerk of the said Complainants, in which Account one fourth part of the said Vessell is Charged at, Five hundred & twenty Pounds & one fourth part of the Cargo thereof, is debited to your Respondent, at Two hundred & forty three Pounds & nine Pence, Three farthings, whereas the said Complainants do not pretend by the said Account exhibited in this Honble. Court that your Respondent purchased more than One fifth part of the said Vessell & Cargo, which at the rates Aforesaid, Amount to Four hundred & Sixteen Pounds for the One fifth part of the said Vessell, & Two hundred & two Pounds ten Shillings & two Pence for the One fith part of the Cargo thereof, which several Sums this Respondents consents to be debited for. Notwithstanding He Expressly alledges that the said Vessel was Estimated by the said James Hunter, as one of the Copartners aforesaid to this Respondent at Two thousand Pounds.[10] AND THIS RESPONDENT adds that the same One fifth part of the said Vessell & Cargo were taken on account of the Debt then acknowledged to be due to this respondent by the said James Hunter as one of the Copartners Aforesaid at his Earnest solicitation, a Copy of which last above mentioned Account No. 7. are now Annexed to this Answer,[11] the originals of which are now in your respondents Custody & ready to be produced as this Honourable Court shall Award. AND THIS RESPONDENT further says, that at the time of the sale of the said Vessell & Cargo in manner Aforesaid, the said James Hunter as one of the Partnership of Hunter Banks & Co executed to this Respondent a certain writing bearing date the Twenty Eight of May, One Thousand, Seven hundred & Eighty two, called a Memorandum of an Agreement between the parties aforesaid for the sale of the One fifth part of the said Vessell & Cargo, or the Nett proceeds thereof—a Copy of which said Bill of Sale or Agreement this respondent Annexes to his Answer, being part of No. 5 & prays may be Considered as part of his Answer, the original signed by the said James Hunter in manner Aforesaid being in this respondent's Custody & ready to be produced as this Honourable Court shall award. AND HE further says, that at the time of the Execution thereof, He exhibited to James Hunter, the Copy of the Account, part of No. 5, to this his Answer also annexed by which it appeared there was due to this respondent upon the Original Contract, One hundred & five thousand, Eight hundred & thirty six Pounds of Tobacco[12] to which balance the said James Hunter in behalf of the firm of Hunter Banks & Co., Assented & executed the Agreement included in No. 5, herein before set forth & referred to, destroying the pretended settlement made with the said Sargeant.

AND YOUR RESPONDENT avers that the said Adjustment & settlement made in manner Aforesaid & the said Memorandum of the sale of the said Vessell & Cargo, are one & the same transaction executed at the same time & bearing a referance one to the other, & further avers that the said One fifth part of the said Vessell & Cargo were taken at the request of the said James Hunter on Account of the said One hundred & five Thousand, Eight hundred & thirty six Pounds of Tobacco, then Adjusted & acknowledged in form Aforesaid to be due to this Respondent. And as to the rest of the Account exhibited in this Honourable Court by the said Complainants as part of their said Bill of Complaint, this Respondent replies, that the same is false & Erroneous in many Instances. As to the first Debit therein, as to Tobacco paid C. Jones, this Respondent does not recollect, but is willing to Admit the same, provided the said C. Jones acknowledges the receipt thereof.[13] The Bill on J. M. Nesbitt being protested in manner Aforesaid the second charge in the said Account is certainly improper.

And as to the 3rd, 4th, 5th & 6th, debitts, in the said Account, this Respondent altogether denies the same. The 7th, 8th, & 9th, Charges, thereof He admits to be just, the 10th & 11th. Charges in the said Account this Respondent has already fully Answered thereto. As to the 12th. Charge therein, He admits the same, but verily believes the Complainants had Credit for the said, Ten Guineas, included in the sum of, Twenty four Pounds, seventeen shillings, passed to their Credit in an Account rendered them of the fifth day of April seventeen hundred & Eighty One. AND THIS RESPONDENT as to the Credit side of the said Account, Answereth, that there is a short Credit to him of, Three hundred & sixty two Yards of Linen, at Eleven Pounds nine shillings & two Pence ℔ yard, or Four thousand one hundred & forty seven Pounds, Eighteen shillings & four pence, as also of four Pieces of Russia Duck, the value thereof, One hundred & twenty Dollars specie which the said Henry Banks as one of the said firm of Hunter Banks & Co Acknowledged to have received as by Copy of Letter No. 8 hereunto Annexed the original whereof is in this respondents Custody & ready to be produced, as this Court shall Award, and to which for greater certainty this respondent refers himself.[14] AND THIS RESPONDENT further Answers that the Account No. 9 to this Answer Annexed, contains a full & just statement of all the Credits & Debits subsisting between him & the Complainants, And that the Balance therein specified is now justly due to this respondent with Interest therefor from the fifth day of June, seventeen hundred & Eighty two—which said Account this Respondent prays may be Considered as part of his Answer.[15] AND HE FURTHER ANSWERS, that the said Sargeant was no ways Concerned with him nor had any Interest in the Transaction between the Parties aforesaid. AND THIS RESPONDENT further answers that so far from evading a friendly & equitable settlement with the said Complainants as Charged in their said Bill of Complaint, He together with the said Complainants executed on the third day of June, One Thousand, seven hundred, & Eighty six, a certain Arbitration Bond, by which all Controversies & Accounts subsisting between the said Complainants & him were submitted to the final End & determination of two indifferent persons chosen by the said Parties a Copy of which said Bond No. 10 He annexes to this Answer & which He prays may be Considered as part thereof, the original being in his Custody duely executed & ready to be produced as this Honorable Court shall award.[16]

AND HE further Answers that since the Execution of the said Bond, He hath ever been & is yet willing & desirous to perform his part of the said Arbitration Bond, and that the Persons therein named being Men well versed in Mercantile Transactions, And consequently better qualified for determining disputes of this nature, shoud Adjust liquidate & settle all Accounts between the Parties, according to the purport & tenor of said Bond. And in hopes the said Complainants would have been equally willing to abide by their promises & Agreements and to do what is right & just this respondent hath hitherto delayed prosecuting them in a Court of Law for the recovery of the Money, now justly due to him as Appears by his said Account. And this Respondent denying all & all manner of Combination and Confederacy wherewith He stands charged in & by the said Bill of Complaint prays to be hence dismissed with his Costs. And this defendant will ever pray.

WM. CONSTABLE

Sworn at the City of New York in the State of New York this ninth Day of February 1790. Before me
RICHD. VARICK Mayor[17]

DS, Hunter, Banks & Co. v. Constable and Sargeant, U.S. Circuit Court, Ended Cases (Restored), 1801, Vi. Endorsed by JM: "Constable ads Banks/ Answer."

1. This sworn copy of the answer was enclosed in Constable's letter to JM of 13 Feb. 1790 (see Doc. VII).

2. Among the suit papers are several copies of a "Memo. of Sundries sold Hunter Banks & Co." (Hunter, Banks & Co. v. Constable and Sargeant).

3. The papers contain numerous copies of accounts between the parties (ibid.).

4. Samuel Beall was a Williamsburg merchant (see Case No. 35).

5. This was the firm of Robert Totten and Alexander Stewart (Harold C. Syrett et al., eds., *The Papers of Alexander Hamilton* [26 vols.; New York, 1961–79], II, 589 n. 1, 591–92). A memorandum by Stewart, dated 20 Aug. 1789, noted that Seagrove & Constable owed Stewart & Totten £225 Pennsylvania currency in Jan. 1782 and that the debt was paid off later that year (Hunter, Banks & Co. v. Constable and Sargeant).

6. See Doc. II, nn. 2, 3.

7. An undated memorandum by Constable that was used in drafting his answer includes extracts of Banks's letters of 22 July, 6 Sept., 2 Oct. 1781, and 20 Jan. 1782, marked Nos. 1, 2, 3, and 4. (The original letters were also filed with the suit papers.) The extract of the first of these letters (22 July 1781) reads: "'Shou'd you suppose yourself injured by our purchase of your Tobacco, I am still willing that the Bala. be again settled in that Article.'" The agreement (endorsed "No. 5"), dated Richmond, 28 May 1782, was between Constable and James Hunter on behalf of Hunter, Banks & Co. It concerned the sale of the brig *Wilkes* and her cargo. Immediately below the agreement was a memorandum signed by Hunter, Banks & Co. settling accounts with Constable by the delivery of 105,836 pounds of tobacco, "agreeable to our letters 22d. July 1781 and 20th January 1782 agreeing to return the Tobacco according to the original Sale of the 5th Aug 1780. notwithstanding the settlement made by Capt Sargeant in April 1781. which was to have been paid in Bills of Excha. which were protested and by which the disposal of the Tobacco became of Course void" (Hunter, Banks & Co. v. Constable and Sargeant).

8. Banks later explained that he was unable to leave Fredericksburg at that time because he was loading a ship. Constable, he said, promised to call upon him at Fredericksburg after settling with Hunter, but instead crossed the Rappahannock at Port Royal (see Doc. IV, n. 3) and "thus avoided an Interview" ("Remarks of H. Banks on the Report of the Comr. dated Novr. 29. 1800," Hunter, Banks & Co. v. Constable and Sargeant).

9. See n. 7.

10. By the agreement of 28 May 1782 (see n. 7), Hunter, Banks & Co. sold Constable one-fifth of the *Wilkes*, "at the first Cost of her and Cargo as she went to Sea the 21 April." The sale was originally for one-fourth part, but this was deleted and "fifth" interlined. In the account annexed to the bill (Doc. II), Hunter, Banks & Co. charged £800 for one-fifth of the vessel. The commissioner in chancery subsequently accepted this charge. The company had bought a half share for £2,000; hence a one-fifth interest was valued at £800 (Doc. XI and n. 8).

11. The account "No. 7" has not been found.

12. This was a copy of an account current (in Constable's hand) between Hunter, Banks & Co. and Constable, endorsed "delivered Jas. Hunter/ Richmd 28 May 1782" (Hunter, Banks & Co. v. Constable and Sargeant).

13. Cadwalader Jones's undated receipt for 5,070 pounds of James River tobacco from Hunter, Banks & Co. for Constable's account is in the suit papers, together with Jones's certificate, dated 5 June 1795, in these words: "This is to certify that about the year 1780. or 1781 I had a Transaction with William Constable in Consequence of which he gave me an order upon Mr. John Banks of Richmond, for some Tobacco. I think four or five Hogsheads (or Thousands pounds). I know the order was punctually paid" (ibid.).

14. The letter marked "No. 8" has not been found. Commissioner Hay subsequently allowed the credit for the linen (see Doc. XI).

15. This was apparently another copy of the account current (several survive in the suit papers) mentioned in n. 12.

16. Neither the copy nor the original of the arbitration bond has been found. Among the suit papers is a power of attorney from Henry Banks to Alexander Hamilton, dated 2 June 1786, appointing the New York lawyer to act in Banks's behalf in settling his accounts with Constable (ibid.). Constable first suggested arbitration as a means of settling the dispute in a letter to Banks in 1784. After Banks brought suit in the High Court of Chancery, Constable wrote to Benjamin Harrison, Jr., enclosing the arbitration bond for JM (Constable to Hunter, Banks & Co., 24 Feb. 1784; to Benjamin Harrison, Jr., 13 July 1789, Constable Letterbook, Constable-Pierrepont Papers, NN).

17. A separate sheet contains Mayor Richard Varick's official certification, with the seal of the mayoralty of New York City affixed, that Constable had personally appeared before him and sworn to the truth of his answer.

VII. William Constable to John Marshall
13 February 1790

13 Febry

I have not addressed you since mine of the 19 aug by Mr Stith.[1] I now inclose the Answer to Mr Banks Bill which I hope will serve to make an End of the Business. I woud have annexed the accounts but having given Mr Richards[2] the originals from wh. I made out Copies, I was fearfull that some inaccuracies might be made, & have therefore left that part to be done with you. My friend Mr Harrison will have them Copied, in Case those furnished Mr R. shoud not Answer. I have written a line to Mr Sargeant also respectg this Affair, who I doubt not will render any Aid in his power to throw light upon it that Justice to the parties may be done.[3] I am with perfect respect.

Copy, William Constable Letterbook, Constable-Pierrepont Papers, NN. Addressed to "James Marshall Esqr.," but clearly intended for JM. Not published in *PJM*, II.

1. See *PJM*, II, 36–37.

2. John Richard, Jr., who also served as Robert Morris's agent in settling his accounts with William Alexander & Co. (see Case No. 6).

3. Constable to Sargeant, 13 Feb. 1790. Constable also wrote to Benjamin Harrison, Jr., on this day, requesting his "Attention in touching up the Lawyer & obtaining me justice—or rather in defending me against plunder" (Constable Letterbook, Constable-Pierrepont Papers, NN).

VIII. Petition for Removal of Suit to U.S. Circuit Court
8 June 1791

To the honorable George Wythe, Judge of the high court of Chancery in Virginia. The Petition of William Constable of the City of New York, Sheweth, that a suit hath been brought in this honorable court against him, jointly with William Hill Sergeant of the Town of Petersburg, by Hunter Banks & Company upon a claim which he supposes to be frivolous vexatious and groundless, that he is a citizen of another state, and is desirous to remove the said suit into the Federal court, held in this state, and that no further procedings therein be had in this honorable court, he being ready to give such security as is required by the act of congress of the United States, in such cases made and provided, for appearing and defending the said suit in the court above mentioned.[1]

A Copy / Teste PETER TINSLEY C.H.C.C.

Copy, Hunter, Banks & Co. v. Constable and Sargeant, U.S. Circuit Court, Ended Cases (Restored), 1801, Vi. Date supplied from High Court of Chancery transcript (see Doc. I, n.), stating that Constable entered his appearance and filed his petition for removal on this day.

1. The reference is to section 12 of the Judiciary Act of 1789, prescribing the procedure for removing suits from the state courts. The defendant was required to file his petition for removal at the time of entering his appearance in the state court and to offer "good and sufficient surety" for appearing the first day of the next session of the federal court (*U.S. Statutes at Large*, I, 79). On 22 Nov. 1791 JM presented a certificate from the clerk of the High Court of Chancery that his client had filed a petition for removal to the federal court, and the suit was accordingly put on the rule docket. It stood continued at the rules until June 1792, when Constable's answer was filed; the suit was then further continued until Apr. 1793, when the plaintiff filed a general replication and issue was joined (U.S. Cir. Ct., Va., Ord. Bk. I, 49; Rule Bk. I, 43–44, 76–77).

IX. Order of Reference
5 December 1794

On the Motion of the Plaintiffs and for reasons Appearing to the Court, it is ordered that the former order of Reference made in this Cause[1] be set aside and that the Commissioner of this Court[2] do examine state and settle all matters and accounts between the Parties in this cause, stating such matters specially as either party may require or he may think fit and make report thereof to the Court in order to a final decree.[3]

(A Copy) Teste William Marshall Clk

Copy, Hunter, Banks & Co. v. Constable and Sargeant, U.S. Circuit Court, Va., Ended Cases (Restored), 1801, Vi. On verso: commissioner's notice of 7 Nov. 1797 (Doc. X). Date supplied from U.S. Cir. Ct., Va., Ord. Bk. I, 444.

1. The previous order of 29 May 1794 named a commission of three to settle the accounts and make a report (U.S. Cir. Ct., Va., Ord. Bk. I, 379).

2. William Hay.

3. This dispute was to remain in reference to Commissioner Hay for six years. Blackstone observed that the completion of equity decrees was retarded by settling of long accounts "and a hundred little facts to be cleared up." This business was "always . . . referred to a master in chancery to examine; which examinations frequently last for years" (Blackstone, *Commentaries*, III, 453).

X. Notice
7 November 1797

Commissioners Novr. 7. 1797

The Parties concerned are desired to take Notice that I have appointed Thursday the eleventh Day of January next for carrying into Effect the within decretal Order, upon which Day their Attendance is required at my Office in the City of Richmond, with their Papers & Accounts ready for Examination.[1]

Wm Hay M.C.

ADS, Hunter, Banks & Co. v. Constable and Sargeant, U.S. Circuit Court, Ended Cases (Restored), 1801, Vi. On verso of 5 Dec. 1794 order (Doc. IX); accompanied by sworn affidavit of George Jenkins of New York City, dated 20 Dec. 1797, stating service of notice and order on Constable.

1. The order and endorsed notice were served on Constable on 20 Dec. 1797, at which time he was given a copy of these documents. At the foot of his copy of the order and notice Constable wrote: "Served on me the 20th Decr. which may be pleaded if you want to put it off as not affording time for my attendance." He then sent this copy on to his co-defendant Sargeant (order and notice [copies], Hunter, Banks & Co. v. Constable and Sargeant).

On the appointed day the papers of both parties were filed in the commissioner's office, John Hargrave acting on behalf of Hunter, Banks & Co. and Benjamin Harrison, Jr., on behalf of Constable. Commissioner Hay's report of 8 Mar. 1798 determined that Constable owed Hunter, Banks & Co. 4,089 pounds of tobacco, or £40.18 specie (rating tobacco at 20s. per hundred pounds), bearing interest from 28 May 1782. Henry Banks then filed his exceptions to the report, protesting that the balance in his company's favor was too small (commissioner's report, 8 Mar. 1798; "Exceptions to the Report of Master Commissioner Hay," ibid.). The result was a second report, dated 4 Aug. 1799 (Doc. XI).

XI. Commissioner's Report
4 August 1799

Commissioners Office Richmd. Augt. 4. 1799

Hunter Banks and Company Pltf.
versus
William Constable and William Hill Sargeant Defts. } in Chancery

Henry Banks one of the Plaintiffs, having filed Exceptions to the Report made in this Cause the eighth Day of March one thousand seven hundred and ninety eight, accompanied with the Books of the Company and Vouchers for payments which had been made to the Defendants, together with a variety of Letters explanatory of the Transactions which had taken place between the Parties and to shew that the Defendant William Hill Sargeant was not only an Agent for but was interested in the Goods sold by William Constable, your Commissioner is obliged to restate the Accounts between them.[1] The Documents now filed, the said Henry Banks, who appears to have been the principal Agent for the Company of Hunter Banks and Company in the whole Transactions between them and the Defendants, alledged, could not have been produced before, on account of his Confinement in Philadelphia, during the Time the Parties were required to attend the Office for the final Liquidation of their Accounts.

Due Notice has been given to the Defendant William Hill Sargeant, who, by Letter to the Commissioner, declined to attend, alledging that he could not throw any new Light on the Business without having Recourse to certain Papers which he had delivered to the other Defendant William Constable, and which he could not now procure as the said Wm. Constable was in Europe, requesting at the same Time a post ponement until his Return which would be soon,[2] but your Commissioner was unwilling to delay the Settlement of the Accounts for the absence of William Constable, as the only new Debit of Consequence is fully supported by a Receipt under the Hand of the Defendant William Hill Sargeant, and which was formerly rejected for want of a Voucher, though it appeared a fair and an original Entry in the Day Book of the Plaintiffs.[3] He will now state the Account and add his Remarks thereon at the End and shall notice particularly those parts of it wherein your Commissioner cannot agree with the Plaintiff Henry Banks in his Exceptions.

William Constable
in Account with Hunter Banks and Company Cr

1780 Augt	5	By 12 Hhds of Rum 1368 Gallons at £22.10.0 ℔ Gal: (a)[4]	£30,780	0	0
		By a Case of assorted dry Goods by the Brig Wilkes cost £188.9.0 at 100 for 1 . . . . £18,845. 0.0			
		By Sundries ℔ the Betsy & Peggy as ℔ Invoice £199.6.0 at 100 for 1 . . . . 19.930. 0.0			
		38,775. 0.0			
		deduct Freight at 10 ℔ Cent 3,877.10.0	(b)34,897	10	0
		By 362 Yds of 7/8 Irish Linen at £11.9.2	(c) 4.147	18	4
		The above payable in two Months, in Tobacco at Byrds or Shockoe Warehouse at £65 ℔ Cent, 107.423 lb to New Account page 4[5]			
		107.423 lb Tobo.	£69,825	8	4

(a) Although Hunter Banks and Company credit William Constable of 1368½ Gallons of Rum at £22.10, yet they extend the Amount only £30,107.10 making an Error of £683 15. but as William Constable only charges 1368 Gal: the Error is only £672.10.

(b) Hunter Banks and Company credit only £34,890, being short £7.10, arising from their Omission of a Quarter of a Dollar in the original Cost of the Goods, which at 100 for 1 is exactly £7.10.

(c) This Linen is omitted altogether in the Account exhibited by Henry Banks, alledging that it is not credited in the Books of the Company, and it could not have been received, because upon examining their Books, he discovers no Linen sold after the Time it is said to have been received. This Objection cannot be admitted, because the Plaintiffs themselves furnished your Commissioner with the Defendant William Constable's original Account of the Goods sold, which contains the Charge of Linen,[6] and because, although the Linen is not credited in the Ledger of Hunter Banks and Company from the Inattention of their Clerk in posting their Books, yet it is found duly entered in their Day Book under the Date of the 5th. Day of August 1780, together with the Rum, as follows, to wit

"Merchandize Dr. to Seagrove and Constable for Sundries payable in Tobacco at £65 ꝑ 100 in two Months VIZ

16 ps. Irish Linen 362 Yds at £11.9.2 ꝑ Yd.

4 Hhds Rum 457½ Gal: received of Marsden & Smith at £22.10

8 do 911 . . . . of Mitchel & Gamble at Do."

The Articles in the above Entry are not extended, and it is found fairly copied into the Journal, where the Rum is extended, but instead of extending the Linen, the following Words are added in the Money column, ~~*Included below*~~ with a Line drawn through them, and then underneath, *entered forward do. do.* These Entries are in the Hand Writing of Henry Banks, and he has drawn the Pen through the Name ~~*Seagrove*~~ and added above, *William*, that the Goods may be credited to William Constable. The other Goods purchased of William Constable, are credited by Henry Banks in the Day Book on the 29th. and in the Journal on the 30th. Augt. for the Conveniency of adding other Debits to Merchandize at the same Time, and it is believed he meant to add the Dry Goods altogether but omitted it, and when the Journal was posted into the Ledger, the Memd. in the Margin, entered forward, prevented the Bookkeeper from taking in the Linen, expecting to find it entered afterwards, by which Means the Omission has been continued by him also. Your Comr. has no Doubt of the propriety of the Credit to William Constable, whether Hunter Banks and Compy. ever sold the Linen or Not.

William Constable
in Account with Hunter Banks & Company Cr.

1780 Augt	5	By Amount due in Tobacco from Accot. page 2d		. . . .	107,423 lb
Decr	10	By Interest thereon from Octr 5th. to this Date 66 Days		971	
		To payment to Cadwr. Jones ꝑ Rect		. . . .	5,078
					102,345
		By Interest to the 14th. February 1781 66 Days		921	
1781 Feby	14	To payment in paper Money to William Hill Sargeant ꝑ Rect.	16872.2.0		
		By 2 lb Twine the 11th.	60.0.0		
			£16,812.2.0		
		Tobo. at £75 . . .		. . . .	22,416
					79.929

April	5	By Interest to this Date 50 Days	547	
		To payment in Specie to William Constable, not charged in the Books of Hunter Banks & Co, but credited to them by William Constable £24.17.0.Tobo. at 20/.		2.485
				77,444
	7	By Interest to this date 2 Days.	21	
		To payment to William Hill Sargeant in paper Money £3488 Tobacco at £80		4,360
				73,084
		NB. This Debit in former Account reported was supposed on Account of the Date to be the same with the Credit given to Hunter Banks & Co, by Will: Constable in Specie but they are discovered to be very different, the one payment being Made to William Constable himself & the other to William Hill Sargeant.		
July*[7]	22	By Interest to this Date 106 Days	1,075	
		By 4 ps. Ravens Duck .... £36. 0.0 Specie		
		To 9 Guineas sent by Majr. Mitchell ... 12.12 0 23. 8.0 Tobo. 20/.		2,340
				75,424
		NB. 10 Guineas were sent by Majr. Mitchell but Wm. Constable by his letter of the 31 July, by which he acknowledges the Receipt of them, says one of them was bad.		
*June		To payment in Specie omitted above .... £30.0.0 To Interest from 14 June to 22 July 38 0.3.1¼ £30.3.1¼ Tobo. at 20/.		3,015
				72,409
		NB. This Payment is credited by Will: Constable Augt. 5. 1781,[8] but the Day Book of Hunter Banks and Co: shews the Payment to have been made to him on the 14th. June 1781		

Octr	29	By Interest to this Date 99 Days	982	
		To payment in Specie from North £90		
		To do.... in do. from Sales 67.1.6		
		£157.1.6		
		Tobo. 20/.	....	15,708
		Amount carried forward	4517 lb	56.701 lb
			Tobo.	
1781 Octr	29	By Amounts brought forward	4,517 lb	56,701 lb
Nov	5	By Interest to this Date 7 Days	54	
		By 1 pr. four Pounders £50 Tobo. at 20/.	....	5.000
				61,701
1782 Jan:	1	By Interest to this Date 57 Days	481	5,052
				66,753
		To one fifths of the Brig Wilkes fitted for Sea £800 Tobo. 20/.		80.000
				13,247
Apl.	1	To Interest to this Date 90 Days	163 lb	
		To one fifth of the Cargo of the Brig Wilkes furnished at this Date . . . £204.3.0 Tobo. 20/.	....	20.415
				33,662
				163
				33,825 lb
		Balance due Hunter Banks and Company of which 33,662 lb to bear Interest from the 1st. Day of April 1782 'till paid, to be paid in Specie at the Rate of 20/. for every 100 lb. of the Tobacco.		

Henry Banks contends in his Exceptions that all the Specie paid to William Constable should be turned into Tobacco, at ten Shillings ℔ hundred Pounds of Tobacco, alledging that the Specie would have purchased Tobacco at that Rate, and that William Constable in his Answer acknowledges that ten Shillings Specie was equal to one hundred Pounds of Tobacco. It is true that William Constable in his Answer acknowledges, that a partial Settlement had been made between William Hill Sargeant for him, and Henry Banks, in which he supposes the Parties rated the Tobacco at ten Shillings, but in this supposition he is evidently mistaken, for by the Books of Hunter Banks and Company it appears, an allowance was made to William Constable in paper Money for Depreciation, and the Paper Money due, was partly rated at one hundred and twenty and partly at one hundred and forty for one. This Settlement was not complied with on the part of Hunter Banks and Company and being evidently erroneous, has been disregarded by your Commissioner as also, the Settlement made by William Constable with James Hunter the 28th. Day of May 1782, which he contends should be the Basis of his Demand, for James Hunter had omitted to charge William Constable with considerable payments made by Henry Banks, with which it seems he was unacquainted. Both these Settlements, which were erroneous, being set aside, your Commissioner hath settled the accounts upon the Principles of Justice and Equity, rating the Payments made in Paper Money, in Tobacco at the current Price when the payments were made, and the Payments in Specie as well as the Credits in specie, in Tobacco at twenty Shillings, which was the fixed Value of Tobacco in the Estimation of the Merchants through all their paper Money Transactions during the Existence of paper Money. Specie being almost extinct in those Days, could not be a Standard for the Merchants, and Tobacco, there being no legal Scale, was therefore assumed as the least fluctuating Standard for their Transactions. Thus one hundred Pounds of Tobacco was rated as equivalent to twenty Shillings Specie, and the rise in the Price of Tobacco was to measure the Depreciation of Paper Money. Specific Tobacco was not necessary in the fulfilling of an Agreement such as the one between the Parties in this Suit, for as much paper Money as would have purchased the same Quantity of Tobacco on the fifth Day of October 1780 as the paper Money Value of the Goods would have purchased on the fifth Day of August preceding, would have discharged the Contract on the said 5th. Day of Octr. 1780. Substantial Justice to both Parties would not admit any Deviation from the mode which your Commissioner has adopted in settling the accounts, & the Balance due ought to be settled in Specie and not in Tobacco, as he hath stated at the End of the Account.

Although William Constable never finally settled with Hunter Banks and Company the Proportion which he held in the Wilkes until May 1782 when he obtained a Bill of Sale for one fifth part of her and Cargo at first Cost as she went to Sea, which was in April preceding, yet he was really interested in her from January, & therefore your Commissioner hath charged him on the first Day of that Month with one fifth part of the Vessel at what she cost the Company as appears by the Deposition of Samuel Baron Cunninghame,[9] and on the first Day of April with a fifth part of her Cargo which was laid in by Hunter Banks and Company mostly in the Month of March and partly on the tenth Day of April.[10]

WM. HAY M.C.

Commissioners fee } 32 Hours at 3/9 }	6.0.0
postages of Letter from } Wm Hill Sargeant }	0.0.6
	£6.0.6

DS, Hunter, Banks & Co. v. Constable and Sargeant, U.S. Circuit Court, Va., Ended Cases (Restored), 1801, Vi. Endorsed "No (4) A"; also endorsed: "Recd. 6th Novr. 1799 from the Commissioner into the Office." Three copies of report in Constable-Pierrepont Papers, NN.

1. Hay wrote Sargeant on 12 June 1799, informing him that Hunter, Banks & Co. was entitled to credits not admitted in the previous report and requesting his attendance at the office to settle the accounts. A copy of this letter was enclosed in Sargeant's letter to Constable of 17 Oct. 1799, along with copies of Sargeant to Hay, 6 July 1799; Banks to Sargeant, 13 Aug. 1799; and Sargeant to Banks, 20 Aug. 1799. Copies of this correspondence precede one of the copies of the report of 4 Aug. 1799 in the Constable-Pierrepont Papers, NN.

2. See Sargeant to Hay, 6 July 1799 (cited in n. 1). Benjamin Harrison, Jr., who had previously acted on behalf of Constable, had died earlier that year (Sargeant to Constable, 17 Oct. 1799 [cited in n. 1]).

3. This was Hunter, Banks & Co.'s payment of £16,871 paper money to Sargeant, recorded under date of 23 Feb. 1782 in the account annexed to the bill (Doc. II). The omission was noted in the exceptions to Commissioner Hay's first report. Banks stated the date of this payment as 23 Mar. 1781 ("Exceptions to the Report of Master Commissioner Hay," Hunter, Banks & Co. v. Constable and Sargeant).

4. See the first entry on the credit side in the account annexed to the bill (Doc. II and n. 15).

5. This is the first entry in the "New Account": "William Constable in Account with Hunter Banks & Company" (see below), which begins on p. 4 of the MS.

6. This was Constable's account current, dated Richmond 5 Aug. 1780, listing the goods sold by Seagrove & Constable to Hunter, Banks & Co. (Hunter, Banks & Co. v. Constable and Sargeant).

7. Hay placed an "x" above "July 22" and in front of "June 14" to indicate the latter entry was out of order. He had originally omitted to place this payment here because of a mistake in Constable's account. See Hay's note below the 14 June entry and n. 8.

8. Constable recorded this credit under date of 5 Aug. 1781 in his account current dated 25 May 1782 (Hunter, Banks & Co. v. Constable and Sargeant).

9. See Doc. II, n. 6. In his deposition, dated 2 May 1792, Cunningham stated that in Jan. 1782 he sold one-half of the *Wilkes* to Hunter, Banks & Co. for £2,000 specie, the value of the whole vessel being rated at £4,000. He noted further that the brig went to sea loaded with flour, arrived safely at St.

Kitt's, but was captured by a British ship on the return voyage. On the verso of this deposition, JM wrote: "This deposition is admitted under this agreement—If the defendant shall chuse to cross examine the witness he is to be at liberty at any time to do so & this is not to be usd until such cross examination be had provided the same be not unreasonably delayd by the defendant" (ibid.).

10. Henry Banks filed exceptions to this report, insisting on the validity of the settlement with William Hill Sargeant on 7 Apr. 1781. He also objected to Constable's credit for the sale of Irish linen. By his reckoning the balance in his favor should have been £719 specie plus interest. The court at the May 1800 term thereupon set aside the report of 4 Aug. 1799 and ordered the commissioner to make a new report. This report, the last of three in this suit, was issued on 29 Nov. 1800. Commissioner Hay concluded that there was no reason to alter the account stated in his previous report. He again disregarded as erroneous Banks's settlement with Sargeant in Apr. 1781 and Constable's settlement with Hunter in May 1782. This report elicited yet another response from Banks, who sarcastically remarked that the defendants would find it "highly satisfactory to them . . . that the Commissr. has protected their Interests with so much ability" ("Exceptions to the report [4 Aug. 1799] of Master Commissioner Hay"; "Statement submitted to the Consideration of the Commr."; Commissioner's Report, 29 Nov. 1800; "Remarks of H. Banks on the Report of the Comr. dated Novr. 29. 1800," ibid.).

XII. Decree
9 May 1801

This Bill[1] was brought for a settlement of accounts the complainant a Citizen of Virginia and the defendant Constable a Citizen of New York the defendant Sergeant tho a Citizen of Virginia yet standing in the Charactor of partner garnishee or factor to Constable as alleged by the Complainants, On the ground of New York Citizenship Constable had caused this suit to be removed to this Court from the High Court of Chancery of Virginia, where it had been originally instituted, We find the following facts to exist in this case.

1st That the defendant Sergeant was empowered and authorised by Constable and in vertue thereof did on the 8th day of April 1781 make a settlement with the Complainants or Henry Banks on their behalf of all transactions up to that time.

2ndly That this first settlement was not fully carried into effect and on the 28th day of May 1782 Constable on his own behalf and one of the Complainants (with due notice to Henry Banks to attend which he declined) came to a final settlement of the same accounts and transactions in which they totally disregarded the first settlement.

3rdly That the first was done away by the second Settlement but that manifest errors and omissions exist in the last settlement.
4th That it is uncertain whether Sergeant was a partner in the goods and merchandize sold to the Complainants and stated in the 1st & 2nd settlements but this fact is immaterial because the ballance of those settlements is obviously against the Complainants and their demand arises wholly on the Sale of a part of the Brig Wilkes and her Cargo.
5th That Sargeant was in no degree interested in the purchase of the Brig Wilkes and her Cargo.
6th That it is not proved that Sargeant was factor for or had any effects of Constables in his hands when this suit was first instituted or at any time since.
7th That an account between the parties was directed and taken by Commissioner Hay that it was taken and returned and exceptions filed thereto.

Upon these facts and on consideration of the Bill answer vouchers account and Argument of Counsel we aprove off ratify and confirm the report of Commissioner Hay of the fourth of August 1799 and order adjudge and decre that the Bill be dismissed with costs as to the defendant Sargeant and that the Complainants recover against the defendant Constable the quantity of thirty three Thousand eight hundred and twenty five pounds of Tobacco with Interest from the first of April 1782 which Tobacco at the election of the said Constable may be discharged in Specie at the rate of twenty shillings Virginia money for every hundred pounds of Tobacco and that the defendant pay the Costs.[2]

Copy, U.S. Circuit Court, Va., Order Book IV, 74–75, Vi.

1. This was the first session of the federal circuit court established by the short-lived Judiciary Act of 1801. The three attending judges were Philip Barton Key (chief judge), George Keith Taylor, and Charles Magill (ibid., 1, 2).

2. Banks had previously authorized David Ross to receive the proceeds of his suit against Constable (power of attorney, 13 Mar. 1798, Hunter, Banks & Co. v. Constable and Sargeant). Ross subsequently empowered New York attorney Daniel D. Tompkins to settle with Constable, who wished to discharge the decree in specie. The agreed amount was $2,480 (including interest and costs), which Constable paid to Tompkins on 1 Sept. 1802 (contract between Ross and Constable, 25 Aug. 1802, Constable-Pierrepont Papers, NN).

9. Harwood v. Lewis

1792–1794

Editorial Note

The great majority of Marshall's commercial law cases were founded upon bonds, also called writings obligatory. In the eighteenth century the bond was the most common form of a contract under seal, or "specialty." The typical bond was a money bond, committing a person to pay a certain sum of money at a certain day, a device well suited to an agrarian economy chronically short of circulating cash. A bond could be "single," obliging the debtor to pay the amount of his debt; more often it took the form of a "double," or conditional, obligation. This acknowledged a sum due, called the penalty, adding a condition that if the obligor paid a smaller sum—the principal, or amount actually owed, usually half the penal sum—then the obligation was to be discharged. A person borrowing fifty pounds, for example, would execute a bond for the penal sum of one hundred pounds.

The appropriate form of action on an unpaid bond was debt. The "debt" was the penal sum, and at common law the plaintiff was entitled to the penalty even if only a fraction of the principal remained unpaid. Defendants had to resort to equity to obtain a discharge from the penalty on paying the amount really owed. This cumbersome proceeding was eventually remedied by the statute of 4 and 5 Anne, which provided that "in all actions which shall be brought upon any bond or bonds, for the payment of any sum of money, wherein the plaintiff shall recover, judgment shall be entered for the penalty of such bond, to be discharged by the payment of the principal and interest due thereupon, and the costs of suit."[1] In declaring on a money bond the plaintiff had only to set forth the defendant's obligation to pay the penalty without mentioning the subsequent condition.[2] The penalty was the foundation of his action, though it obscured his real object, which was the recovery of the principal sum as stated in the condition. It was up to the defendant to "crave oyer" of the obligation and condition, that is, to have them read to him in court and entered on the record, and then to plead payment of the principal.

Another type of bond, distinguished from the money bond, was executed to secure the performance of some covenant or agreement, such as the transfer of property, delivery of goods, or building of a house. This was known as a bond with a collateral condition—"collateral" in the sense of requiring something other than the payment of a money debt. Here, too, debt was the proper action if the bond was forfeited, and the plaintiff could declare on the penalty without reciting the condition and assigning breaches. In Virginia, however, the recommended practice in an action of debt on a bond with a collateral condition was to state the condition and assign breaches in the declaration. By statute the plaintiff "in all actions upon any bond, or on any penal sum for non performance of any covenants or agreements, in any indenture, deed, or writing contained," could "assign as many breaches as he . . . shall think fit; and the jury . . . shall and may assess . . . damages" for those breaches proved at the trial. This statute did not embrace bonds conditioned for the payment of money.[3]

Harwood v. *Lewis* posed the problem of classifying the bond that gave rise to the action. Was it a money bond or a bond with a collateral condition? Because the plaintiffs were assignees, this was no academic question. It bore directly on the assignability of the bond and on their right to bring suit. At common law bonds were not assignable but had been made so by statute in Virginia in 1705. In the words of the 1786 act in force at the time of this suit: "Assignments of bonds, bills, and promissory notes, and other writings obligatory, for payment of money or tobacco, shall be valid; and an assignee . . . may thereupon maintain an action of debt, in his own name."[4] These words seemed to confer assignability on money bonds alone, though their meaning had not been definitively resolved at the time this case was tried in 1794. The next year the General Assembly passed a new act whose language clearly argued for a restrictive construction of the former act: "A suit may be maintained in the name of an assignee . . . on any bond, bill, or obligation, whatever, in like manner as such suit may be maintained by the assignee . . . of a bond, bill, or obligation for the payment of money or tobacco."[5] Any doubts that the old act applied only to money bonds were removed by two decisions of the Court of Appeals in 1799 and 1800, which declared that bonds with a collateral condition were not assignable before the 1795 act.[6]

Marshall represented Thomas and Benjamin Harwood of Annapolis, assignees of a bond originally executed to William Whetcroft, a merchant of the same city, by Fredericksburg merchant John Lewis on 3 February 1784 (Document II). In one respect this obligation had the appearance of a typical money bond, stating a penal sum of six thousand pounds Virginia currency to secure payment of three thousand pounds in like money. The condition contained an alternative method of discharge, however. Instead of paying three thousand pounds in money by a certain day, Lewis could pay the same amount in state certificates, with no set day for repaying the principal provided annual interest on the certificates was paid. In August 1785 and June 1786 Lewis made interest payments and discharged part of the principal in certificates; on 3 August 1790 Whetcroft assigned the bond to the Harwoods. Lewis refused to pay interest when applied to in February 1792, and the assignees brought suit at the next term of the federal circuit court in Richmond.[7]

The proceedings in this case reflect the uncertainty of counsel and judges of the true nature of Lewis's bond. On the writ of capias Marshall wrote this endorsement: "on a Bond for money/ Bail required." The words "for money" were struck out, however, suggesting that on second thought his description was inaccurate.[8] The bail requirement remained, even though by Virginia law it seemed to apply only to actions on money bonds. The statute required bail in "all actions of debt founded on any writing obligatory, bill or note in writing, for the payment of money or tobacco." In 1796, two years after the judgment in this case, the Virginia Court of Appeals determined that bonds with collateral conditions were exempt from this requirement.[9]

Marshall declared on the bond as if it were one with a collateral condition, as shown by his recital of the condition in the pleading (Document I). In Virginia payment was the customary plea in actions on money bonds; in actions on bonds with a collateral condition, the plea was performance.[10] As counsel for Lewis, Bushrod Washington submitted both pleas, a redundancy that is apparently explained by his inability to decide exactly what kind of obligation this was. After the trial Washington decided that the bond was indeed one with a collateral condition and moved to arrest judgment on the ground that it was not assignable (Document VI). The court did not find this objection persuasive and gave judgment for the Harwoods. Since they concluded that the bond was assignable, the judges must have reasoned that it was a money obligation or, if not, that Virginia law permitted the assignment of bonds with a collateral condition.

By some circuitous route that cannot now be retraced, this case reached the Supreme Court fourteen years later. That tribunal, on which the two original attorneys now sat as brethren, reversed the lower court's judgment in February 1810. Speaking for the court,

Justice Brockholst Livingston had no difficulty determining that bonds with a collateral condition were not assignable under Virginia law before 1795, following the precedent laid down by the Virginia Court of Appeals. The only real question was how to classify this bond. As Judge Roane had explained in a case decided by the Virginia high court in 1800, the true criterion of a money bond was that its condition stated a specified sum, the principal, on which judgment was to be given, and in declaring on it the plaintiff did not have to assign particular breaches. If the condition contained no ascertainable principal sum and if particular breaches had to be assigned requiring a jury to intervene to assess damages, then the bond could not be considered as one for the payment of money.[11] By this definition the bond in question did not belong to the category of money bonds. The condition, said Justice Livingston, "created an alternative by which the penalty might be discharged either by money or officers' certificates; and although the consent of both parties might be necessary to a payment in the latter way, still, as it made part of the written contract, the court cannot but perceive that, on a certain contingency, it was to be considered as a bond on which it might, as it did, become necessary to assign breaches and call in a jury to assess damages."[12]

Although recovery by surviving assignee Benjamin Harwood was denied, Lewis was of course still liable for the debt. In 1812 the instrument was returned to the representatives of William Whetcroft, the original obligee (Document II, n. 1), and Harwood was presumably reimbursed. Whetcroft's representatives may have reached an accommodation with Lewis, for there is no record of any subsequent action on this bond in the federal court.

1. 4 and 5 Anne, c. 16, sec. 13; reenacted in Virginia in 1732 and later incorporated in the 1792 code (Hening, *Statutes*, IV, 359; Shepherd, *Statutes*, I, 31–32; Robinson, *Practice*, I, 256). See also Blackstone, *Commentaries*, III, 434–35.

2. See, for example, Case No. 3, Doc. I; Case No. 12, Doc. IV.

3. Hening, *Statutes*, IV, 359 (reenacting the English statute of 8 and 9 Wm. III, c. 11, sec. 8); Chitty, *Pleading*, I, 505–6; Robinson, *Practice*, I, 153–54; H. St. G. Tucker, *Commentaries on Va. Laws*, I, Bk. 2, 278.

4. Hening, *Statutes*, XII, 359; for the earlier acts of 1705, 1730, and 1748, see ibid., III, 378; IV, 275; VI, 87.

5. Shepherd, *Statutes*, I, 366.

6. Craig v. Craig, 1 Call 483; Henderson v. Hepburn, 2 Call 232. In the latter case Judge Roane expounded at length on the differences between money bonds and bonds with a collateral condition.

7. See Whetcroft's receipts, 16 Aug. 1785, 8 June 1786, Harwood v. Lewis, U.S. Cir. Ct., Va., Ended Cases (Restored), 1794. Lewis was co-obligor on

another bond to Whetcroft, dated 13 Feb. 1784, in the same amount and on identical terms as the first. This bond was also assigned to the Harwoods in Aug. 1790 and gave rise to a companion case (Harwood v. Throckmorton and Lewis, U.S. Cir. Ct., Va., Ended Cases [Restored], 1794).

8. This endorsement appears on a writ of alias capias, 2 June 1792, Harwood v. Lewis.

9. Hening, *Statutes*, XII, 741; Ruffin v. Call, 2 Wash. 181.

10. Robinson, *Practice*, I, 209.

11. Henderson v. Hepburn, 2 Call 232, 238.

12. Lewis v. Harwood, 6 Cranch 82, 85.

I. Declaration
April 1793

United States middle circuit district of Virginia to wit[1]

Thomas & Benjamin Harwood citizens & residents of the state of Maryland assignees of William Whitcroft[2] a citizen & resident of the state of Maryland complain of John Lewis[3] a citizen & resident of the commonwealth & district of Virginia & within the jurisdiction of this court of [a plea that they render to them Six] thousand pounds current money of Virginia of the value of twenty thousand dollars which to them the plaintiffs he the defendant owes & from them unjustly detains for this to wit that the defendant John Lewis on the 3d. day of February 1784 in the commonwealth & district aforesaid by his certain writing obligatory seald with his seal & to the court now here shewn the date whereof is the same day & year acknowledgd himself to be indebted to William Whit[croft which said] William then was & has [ever since continued to be a Citizen & Resident of the State of Maryland in the Sum of Six thousand Pounds Current Money] of the state of Virginia to be paid to the said William Whitcroft his attorney his exrs admrs. or assigns when he the defendant shoud be thereunto requird, to which said writing obligatory there was a condition annexd that if the said John Lewis Alexander Dick[4] & George Lewis Copartners their exrs. or admrs. shoud well & truely pay or cause to be paid unto the said William Whitcroft his certain attorney his heirs exrs. admrs. or assigns the full & just sum of three thousand pounds current money of Virginia on or before the first day of January 1785 then the said obligation to be void.—Provided that if the said John Lewis Alexander Dick & George Lewis copartners as aforesaid on application by the said William Whitcroft[5] or his attorney to them or either of them in the town of Fredericksburg on or after the first day of Jany. 1785 shoud pay unto him the said William Whitcroft or Attorney the sum of three thousand pounds in officers certificates issued under an act of Assembly passd November 1781 for pay or arrearages of pay & depreciation[6] or shoud well & truely pay the interest of six per cent from the date [of the said Writing Obligatory on the] said certifica[tes] if not paid & shoud moreover annually & punctually pay the said six per cent when applied to as before mentiond in doing of which the condition of the said bond was dis-ch[arge]able by paying of the said three thousand pounds officers certificates otherwise the bond to have its full force & effect. Which said writing obligatory afterwards to wit on the 3d day of August 1790 was by the said William Whitcroft then a Citizen & resident [of the State of Maryland assign'd to the] plaintiffs [then Citizens and residents of the same State of Maryland of] which assignment the defendant afterwards to [wit] on the day of 1790 in Fredericksburg in the commonwealth & district of Virginia had notice, the several parts of the condition of the said writing obligatory being then totally unperformd & the said writing obligatory itself altogether uncomplied with. And the plaintiffs in fact say that the defendant hath not performd any part of the condition of the said writing obligatory but hath altogether broken the same in this that neither the defendant or Alexander Dick or George Lewis or any person for them or either of them hath paid to the said William Whitcroft his certain attorney his heirs exrs. admrs. or assigns the said sum of three thousand pounds current money of Virginia on or before the first day of Jany. 1785 or at any time since, nor hath the defendant or the said Alexander Dick or George Lewis or any person for them or either of them paid to the said William Whitcroft or attorney or to any other person having authority to receive the same, the sum of three thousand pounds in officers certificates as describd in the condition of the said writing obligatory, or paid the interest of six per cent on the said certificates from the date of the said writing obligatory, altho to pay the said certificates or [the said] interest of six [per cent upon] them the said defendant was requird in conformity with the condition of the said writing obligatory after the said 1st day of Jany. 1785 to wit on the day of 17 in the city of Fredericksburg in the said condition mentiond, Nor hath the said John Lewis or any other person for him paid the said six per cent annually & punctually when applied to as before mentiond but hath altogether refused to do the same & especially did refuse to do [so on the 6th. day of February 1792][7] in [Fredericksburg aforesaid] when & where a demand thereof was made in conformi[ty] with the condition of the said writing obligatory. By means of all which premisses an action hath accrued to the plaintiffs to have & demand of the defendants the said sum of six thousand pounds current money of Virginia of the value of twenty thousand dollars. Yet the defendant tho often requird the money aforesaid to the plaintiffs hath not paid but the same to pay hither [to] hath & still doth altogether refuse to the damage of the plaintiffs dollars whereon they sue &c.[8]

J Marshall p.q.

ADS, Harwood v. Lewis, U.S. Circuit Court, Va., Ended Cases (Restored), 1794, Vi. Clerk's endorsements and jury verdict on verso; words or parts of words in brackets obliterated in MS and supplied from copy in U.S. Cir. Ct., Va., Rec. Bk. III, 52–55. Filed at Apr. 1793 rules in clerk's office (U.S. Cir. Ct., Va., Rule Bk. I, 79).

1. After being served with a writ issued in June 1792, John Lewis gave bond to appear at the November term. The case was continued at the rules from Dec. 1792 through Mar. 1793 (alias capias, 2 June 1792; appearance bond, 10 Aug. 1792, Harwood v. Lewis; U.S. Cir. Ct., Va., Rule Bk. I, 66–67, 78–79).

2. The correct spelling is "Whetcroft." Elsewhere in the declaration JM referred to the original obligee as "Whitlock" (see n. 5).

3. Here JM deleted "& George Lewis surviving partners of John Lewis & Co" and then made the appropriate changes (in most instances) to reflect a single defendant. John Lewis (1747–1827) was the eldest son of Fielding Lewis, George Washington's brother-in-law. Originally named as a defendant in this case, George Lewis (1757–1821), half-brother of John, entered his pleas in Mar. 1794. He pleaded the general issue, denying that the bond was his deed, and also specially that he was not a copartner of John Lewis & Co. at the time the bond was executed. The case against him was dismissed by agreement at the rules in Dec. 1794 (Merrow Egerton Sorley, comp., *Lewis of Warner Hall* . . . [Columbia, Mo., 1935], 131–32, 153–57; pleas of George Lewis, 27 Mar. 1794, Harwood v. Lewis; U.S. Cir. Ct., Va., Rule Bk. I, 104–5, 118–19).

4. Alexander Dick (1753–1785), an officer in a Virginia regiment during the Revolution, succeeded his father, Charles Dick, as superintendent of the gun factory at Fredericksburg in Jan. 1783. John Lewis was then a partner in this concern, having succeeded his father. John Lewis & Co. undoubtedly grew out of this association (*Tyler's Quarterly*, VIII [1926], 138; *WMQ*, 1st ser., XVIII [1909–10], 112; *JCSV*, III, 207; Sorley, *Lewis of Warner Hall*, 131–32, 139–41).

5. JM originally wrote "Whitlock." The correction appears to be in a different hand.

6. See Hening, *Statutes*, X, 462. The states assumed the burden of paying the army after Congress abdicated this responsibility. This act provided for the issuance of certificates stating a specie sum to cover both back pay and depreciation losses. These "military," or "depreciation," certificates were payable on or before 1 Jan. 1785 and were to carry annual interest of 6 percent. They formed the largest item of state debts during the Confederation period (Ferguson, *Power of the Purse*, 50–51).

7. John Lewis gave a written acknowledgment on this date of the Harwoods' demand for interest (Harwood v. Lewis).

8. After Lewis failed to enter a plea at the rules, an office judgment was confirmed against him and a writ of inquiry awarded in May 1793. This was set aside when special bail was entered for Lewis and a continuance granted. The case was also continued by consent at the Nov. 1793 term (U.S. Cir. Ct., Va., Rule Bk. I, 78–79; Ord. Bk. I, 146; bail piece, 18 May 1793, Harwood v. Lewis; see also the clerk's endorsements on the verso of the declaration).

II. Bond and Assignment

Know all men, by these presents that we John Lewis, Alexander Dick and George Lewis Copartners of the County of Spotsylvania Virginia are held and firmly bound unto William Whetcroft of the Town of Annapolis & State of Maryland, his certan Attorney, his heirs, executors administrators or assigns in the sum of six thousand pounds Current money of Virginia, the payment whereof well and truly to be made unto the said William Whetcroft his Attorney exors: admrs. or assigns we bind ourselves, our heirs, exors: & administrators jointly and severally firmly by these presents Sealed with our seals and dated this third day of February one thousand seven hundred and eighty four.

The Condition of the above obligation is such that if the said John Lewis Alex. Dick & George Lewis copartners as aforesaid their exors: or admors. shall well and truly pay or cause to be paid unto the said William Whetcroft his certain Attorney, his heirs, exors: admors. or assigns the full & just sum of three thousand pounds Current money of Virginia on or before the first day of January One thousand seven hundred and eighty five then this obligation to be void Provided and it is to be understood that in case the said Jno. Lewis Alex. Dick & Geo. Lewis Copartners as aforesaid on application by the said William Whetcroft or his Attorney to them or either of them in the Town of Fredericksburg on or after the first day of January 1785 shall pay unto him the said William Whetcroft or Attorney the sum of three thousand pounds in Officers certificates issued under an Act of Assembly passed November 1781 for pay or arrearage of pay & Depreciation or shall well and truly pay the int. of six Per Cent from the date hereof on the said certificates, if not paid and shall moreover annually and punctually pay the said six Pr. cent when applied to as before mentioned, in doing of which the Condition of this bond is dischargeable by payment of the said Three thousand pounds Officers Certificates, Otherwise the bond shall have its full force, and effect.

Signed, Sealed & acknowledged In presence of
H Armistead
Armistead Long

John Lewis [L.S.]
for J. Lewis & Co.

For a valuable consideration to me in hand paid by Thomas & Benjamin Harwood of the City of Annapolis I do hereby assign transfer and make over unto them the said Thomas and Benjamin Harwood their heirs, executors and administrators all my right, title and interest of in and to the within bond and the principal and interest thereon due and to grow due. Witness my hand and seal this third day of August 1790.[1]

Teste Jeremiah Harwood — Wm. Whetcroft [L.S.]

Copy, Harwood v. Lewis, U.S. Circuit Court, Va., Ended Cases (Restored), 1794, Vi. Attested by William Marshall, clerk of court; copy made in 1812 (see n. 1).

1. By an order of the court of 10 June 1812, the original bond, with the endorsed assignment, was returned to the representatives of William Whetcroft (U.S. Cir. Ct., Va., Ord. Bk. IX, 120). A statement to this effect, dated 11 June 1812 and signed by Alexander Kerr on behalf of Whetcroft's representatives, appears at the foot of this copy of the bond.

III. Pleas

24 May 1794

And the said John Lewis by Bushrod Washington his Attorney comes and defends the force and injury when &c and craves oyer of the said writing obligatory and it is read to him &c and he likewise craves oyer of the Condition of the said writing obligatory which is read to him in these words "The Condition of this obligation &c["] which being read and heard the said John Lewis saith that the sd Thomas and Benjamin Harwood ought not to have or maintain their said action against him the sd John Lewis because he saith that after the making of the said writing obligatory and before the day of exhibiting the Bill of them to the said plaintiffs he the said defendant did pay to the said William Whitcroft the said sum contained in the said Condition according to the form and effect thereof together with all Interest then due thereon, and this he is ready to verify:[1]

And the said John Lewis the deft. by leave of this Court, according to the form of the laws in such case made and provided for further plea saith, that he hath well and truly observed, performed, fulfilled, and kept all and singular the matters and things specified, mentioned and contained in the sd Condition on the part of him the sd Lewis the defendant to be observed, performed, fulfilled, and kept according to the form and effect of the Said Condition; and this he is ready to verify:[2] Wherefore he prays judgment if the sd Thomas and Benjamin Harwood the plaintiffs ought to have or maintain their said action against him &c.

WASHINGTON P.D.

ADS, Harwood v. Lewis, U.S. Circuit Court, Va., Ended Cases (Restored), 1794, Vi. Date supplied from U.S. Cir. Ct., Va., Ord. Bk. I, 363. Replication (Doc. IV) begins immediately below pleas.

1. On the special plea of payment, see Case No. 3, Doc. II and n. 2.

2. This special plea of conditions performed was the customary plea in Virginia in actions on bonds with a collateral condition (Robinson, *Practice*, I, 209). Washington (as suggested in the editorial note) probably entered both pleas because of the ambiguous nature of this bond.

IV. Replication

24 May 1794

And the said Thomas & Benjamin Harwood the plaintiffs by their attorney say that they by any thing by the defendant in pleading in his first plea alledgd ought not to be bard from having & maintaining their action aforesaid against him because by way of replication to the said plea they say that the defendant hath not paid the said William Whitcroft the sum containd in the condition of the said writing obligatory according to the form & effect thereof together with all interest due thereon as in pleading he hath alledgd & this he prays may be enquird of by the country & the deft. likewise.[1]

And the said plaintiffs say that they by any thing by the defendant in his second plea pleaded ought not to be bard from having & maintaining their action against him because[2] in replication to the said plea they say that the defendant hath not performd all the things specified & containd in the said condition on the part of him the said Lewis the defendant to be performd according to the form & effect of the said condition & this they pray may be enquird of by the country & the deft. likewise.[3]

J MARSHALL p. q.

ADS, Harwood v. Lewis, U.S. Circuit Court, Va., Ended Cases (Restored), 1794, Vi. Begins immediately below pleas (Doc. III) and continues on verso; date supplied from U.S. Cir. Ct., Va., Ord. Bk. I, 363.

1. The phrase "& the deft. likewise" was added by Bushrod Washington, signifying the defendant's joinder of issue, or "similiter." Note the slight difference in phraseology when the plaintiff tendered an issue of fact. The defendant tendered issue in these words: "and of this he puts himself upon the country" (Blackstone, *Commentaries*, III, 312–13).

2. JM originally wrote "by" but appears to have deleted it and inserted "in."

3. See n. 1.

V. Verdict and Judgment

28 May 1794

This day came the parties by their Attorneys, and thereupon came also a Jury to wit, Nathaniel Anderson, John Hague, Daniel Burton, Marcus Elcan, Thomas Norvell, Jacob J. Cohen, George Pickett, Isaac Winston, Thomas Barnett, William Price, Dabney Minor and David Clopton who being elected tried and sworn the truth to speak upon the issue joined upon their Oath do say that the Deft hath not performed the condition[1] of the writing obligatory in the declaration mentioned but hath broken the same as the said Plts by replying have alledged and they do assess the Plts damages by occasion thereof to Seven thousand, six hundred and eighty dollars and forty four cents besides his Costs.[2] Therefore It is considered by the Court that the Plts recover against the Deft Six thousand pounds current money of Virginia of the Value of Twenty thousand dollars, the debt in the declaration mentioned and their Costs by them about their Suit in this behalf expended. And the said Deft in Mercy &c. But this Judgment is to be discharged by the payment of the damages aforesaid in form aforesaid assessed and the Costs.

Copy, U.S. Circuit Court, Va., Order Book I, 376, Vi.

1. Although issue was joined on payment and performance, this verdict was considered sufficiently responsive to both issues, the finding on the former being embraced in that of the latter (Robinson, *Practice*, I, 355).

2. According to Charles Lee's report (Doc. VII), the jury calculated the damages by the value of the certificates on the day the verdict was rendered. The verdict in the companion case against Lewis, also rendered this day, was for $11,279.16—the higher amount reflecting the fact that no payments had been made on that bond (U.S. Cir. Ct., Va., Ord. Bk. I, 377).

VI. Motion in Arrest of Judgment

31 May 1794

And[1] now at this day came the parties apd[2] by their attornies And the Defendant prays that Judgment upon the verdict found in this cause may be stay'd and arrested because he saith that there are divers errors in the sd verdict & proceedings[3] in this cause and particularly in this that the action is brought by Thomas and Benjamin Harwood as Assignees of William Whitcroft upon a bond which is not negotiable or in any manner assignable so as by the Laws now or at the time of the sd assignment are or were in force in this Commonwealth to intitle the sd plaintiff to mantain his said action agt. the defendant;[4] and because the bond upon which this action is founded upon the face of it appears to have been given for & upon an usurious consideration[5] for which as well as for other errors in the sd verdict & proceeding the deft prays as above.[6]

WASHINGTON for deft

ADS, Harwood v. Throckmorton and Lewis, U.S. Circuit Court, Va., Ended Cases (Restored), 1794, Vi. Date supplied from U.S. Cir. Ct., Va., Ord. Bk. I, 387.

1. Washington entered this motion in both cases, but made only one copy (headed "John Lewis ads Thos & Benjn. Harwood Assees of Wm. Whitcroft/ In debt"), which apparently was misfiled with the papers in the companion case of Harwood v. Throckmorton and Lewis.

2. Probably an abbreviation for "accompanied."

3. A motion to arrest judgment had to be addressed to errors appearing on the face of the record, which consisted of the pleadings, verdict, and judgment, but not the trial proceedings. "And this is an invariable rule with regard to arrests of judgment upon matter of law," wrote Blackstone quoting an earlier authority, "'that whatever is alleged in arrest of judgment must be such matter as would, upon demurrer, have been sufficient to overturn the action or plea.'" Judgments could not be stayed or reversed for errors cured by verdict or by the statute of jeofails (Tucker, *Blackstone's Commentaries*, III, 393–95 and n. 6; Hening, *Statutes*, XIII, 36 [for Virginia statute of jeofails]). In English practice there was an interval between verdict and judgment within which the unsuccessful party could move in arrest of judgment. There was no such interval in Virginia, but according to Tucker this motion could "be made at any time during the term when the verdict is rendered, but not *after*" (Tucker, *Blackstone's Commentaries*, III, 387 n. 1).

4. See the editorial note for a discussion of the Virginia laws concerning the assignment of bonds.

5. The defendant had the option of paying 6 percent interest on the military certificates. The legal rate of interest in Virginia was 5 percent, but the act authorizing these certificates declared that they should carry 6 percent interest (see Doc. I, n. 6).

6. The court rejected the motion and reaffirmed the judgment on 6 Dec. 1794 (U.S. Cir. Ct., Va., Ord. Bk. I, 451).

VII. Charles Lee's Report of the Case

Federal court[1]

Harwood vs Lewis, debt on bond conditioned for the payment of certificates, Jury estimated the damage by the value of certificates when their verdict was rendered—a motion for a new trial on the ground of excessive damages,[2] the rule that the jury ought to have adopted being the value when the contract was broken, authorities cited Dutch vs Warren in Strange Powel on Contracts 137—Graves vs Groves in the court of appeals[3]—new trial denied, the court saying that notwithstanding the precedents, the rule adopted by the jury was the just one.[4]

MS, "Register of Law Cases by Charles Lee (1794)," ViU.

1. Lee's MS reports, along with those of John Brown, have been published in W. Hamilton Bryson, ed., "The Reports of Charles Lee and of John Brown," *University of Richmond Law Review,* XI (1977), 691–741 (see 710 for this case). These reports are mainly of cases argued in the Virginia General Court and Court of Appeals during the 1780s and 1790s. Harwood v. Lewis is the only reported case from the federal court.

2. There is no record of a motion for a new trial in this case. The reporter was not referring to the motion in arrest of judgment (Doc. VI), for it could not be addressed to the question of excessive damages. Washington presumably made this motion at the same time he moved in arrest of judgment. Unlike the latter motion, which was concerned with errors on the record, the motion for a new trial sought to set aside a verdict on account of errors occurring at the trial. Grounds for awarding the motion included flagrant attempts by the prevailing party to influence the jury, misdirections by the judge to the jury, verdicts contrary to evidence, and verdicts giving exorbitant damages (Blackstone, *Commentaries,* III, 387–93).

3. Dutch v. Warren, 1 Str. 406 (K.B., 1729), 93 Eng. Rep. 598 (discussed in John Joseph Powell, *Essay Upon the Law of Contracts and Agreements* [2 vols. in 1; London, 1790], I, 137); Groves v. Graves, 1 Wash. 1 (1790). In both cases the court ruled that damages should be calculated according to the value of the stock or certificates at the time the contract was broken. In Groves v. Graves the jury had awarded the value of the market price of final settlement certificates at the time of the trial. The Court of Appeals held that the damages should reflect the market price as of the time the certificates were to be delivered. JM was of counsel in this case, though no arguments were reported (see *PJM,* II, 406 n. 20).

4. The appeal to the Supreme Court alleged among other errors the "im-

perfect finding of the jury," but because the Court held that the bond was not assignable, the opinion did not consider this question (Lewis v. Harwood, 6 Cranch 82 [1810] [quotation at 84]). The appellate case file has been lost, and it is therefore difficult to reconstruct the steps leading from the judgment in 1794 to its reversal in 1810. In May 1801 John Lewis obtained a temporary injunction to stay execution on both judgments against him. Four years later this injunction was made perpetual as to the judgment in the companion case (Harwood v. Throckmorton and Lewis). Presumably the injunction on the other judgment was dissolved, though no decree to this effect has been found. In any event the record of this case went up to the Supreme Court on a writ of error in Feb. 1809. It was argued on 14 Feb. 1810, and the court rendered its decision on 24 Feb. 1810 (U.S. Cir. Ct., Va., Ord. Bk. IV, 52; V, 118; Dockets of the Supreme Court of the U.S., Bk. A, 394, RG 267, DNA).

10. Vaughan v. Parker and Paine

1794–1798

I. Declaration, December 1794
II. Bill of Exchange, 29 March 1792
III. Protest of Bill of Exchange, 28 May 1792
IV. George Pickett to Elias Parker, 26 August 1792
V. Bill in Chancery, 8 January 1796
VI. Answer, 29 October 1796

Editorial Note

This case and its chancery sequel originated in a routine mercantile transaction: payment by bill of exchange. By Marshall's day the bill of exchange already had a long history as a device to facilitate commerce, particularly international commerce. In essence a bill of exchange enabled one to make a payment in a distant place without incurring the risk or inconvenience of transporting goods or gold and silver coin. For example, a Virginia planter owing money to a creditor in England might pay the money to a Richmond merchant having trade credits with a London firm. The merchant would then draw a bill of exchange on his London correspondents requesting them to pay the stipulated sum to the planter's British creditor. In law the Richmond merchant was called the *drawer*, the London firm the *drawee* (also the *acceptor* after agreeing to pay the bill), and the planter's creditor the *payee*. The great advantage of the bill of exchange was that it was negotiable, that is, it could be transferred from hand to hand. The payee might indorse the bill to another party, in which case he became the *indorser* and the new payee the *indorsee*. Such transfers could continue indefinitely, and in this way bills gained general circulation almost equivalent to cash. During the course of these transactions the various parties acquired certain legal rights and liabilities. If, as frequently happened, the drawee refused to accept or pay the bill of exchange, the present holder, no matter how remote from the original transaction, could bring suit in his own name against the drawer or any of the previous indorsers.[1]

In recovering money due by bill of exchange, the plaintiff could sue on the instrument itself or on the "consideration" for which it was given. In England the usual procedure was to set forth a count in special assumpsit on the bill itself and to add applicable common counts in general assumpsit.[2] This is what Marshall did in the declaration below (Document I). In Virginia plaintiffs had the option of bringing an action of debt in such cases, as provided by the 1748 act "for ascertaining the damage upon protested bills of exchange." A section of that act made it "lawful for any person or persons, having a right to demand any sum of money upon a protested bill of exchange, to commence and prosecute an action of debt, for principal, interest, and charges of protest, against the drawer and indorsers jointly, or either of them separately."[3] By virtue of this statute, debt became the preferred action in Virginia on protested bills. One procedural advantage for the plaintiff was that bail was demandable in an action of debt. Moreover, a default judgment in debt became final and did not have to be referred to a jury to ascertain damages by writ of inquiry.[4] For whatever reason—perhaps because of difficulties of proof under the debt action—Marshall in the present case chose to adhere to the traditional English action of special assumpsit.[5]

The damages recoverable on protested bills differed according to whether it was "foreign," drawn or payable in a foreign country, or "inland," drawn or payable in Virginia. Until 1792 foreign bills carried 10 percent, or double, interest from the date of the bill. In that year the General Assembly adopted the formula of 15 percent on the amount of the bill as damages, with 5 percent annual interest from the date of protest.[6] Under a 1786 act inland bills, by contrast, were exempt from damages and carried 5 percent interest from the date of protest. In 1795 the legislature declared bills drawn by Virginia residents on persons in another state or territory of the United States to be inland bills, which on protest were subject to 1 percent damages and 5 percent interest.[7] The bill in the present case, drawn in Richmond and payable in Philadelphia, was made before that statute. In assessing damages, however, the jury treated it as an inland bill, allowing only 5 percent interest.

Marshall represented the plaintiff John Vaughan, a Philadelphia wine merchant. Vaughan sued as indorsee of a bill drawn by Petersburg merchant Elias Parker on his brother Daniel Parker of Philadelphia. The bill was payable to Samuel Paine of Richmond, who indorsed it over to Vaughan.[8] Vaughan sought his remedy against the indorser Paine and the drawer Elias Parker. As acceptor Daniel Parker was also liable, but there was no point in suing him, since he was a bankrupt. The declaration gives the erroneous impression that this was a single action against two defendants. In fact there were two separate cases, one against Parker and the other against Paine.

Vaughan obtained judgments against Parker and Paine in December 1795. Parker thereupon petitioned the chancery side of the federal court for relief (Document V). Proceedings in this case, *Parker* v.

Vaughan, continued for another three years. Parker was represented by Daniel Call, who presumably had also defended him in the law action, and Marshall evidently continued to serve on Vaughan's behalf.[9] Parker's bill was a request for an injunction, a remedial writ specially granted by a chancery judge to prohibit a person from doing something against equity and good conscience. The writ was issued for a variety of purposes, most frequently, as in this case, to stay proceedings at law. Usually the petition in such cases came after judgment to stay execution or proceedings under execution. Injunction bills of this type commonly set forth that the plaintiff's adversary had gained some unfair advantage of him at law and that equity should interpose to restrain him from rigorously and unjustly proceeding thereon.[10] Parker's petition, for example, was grounded on the long delay in receiving notice of the protest and on the unlikely prospect of recovering the amount in case he had to satisfy the judgment.

1. For a historical introduction, see McCusker, *Money and Exchange*. Legal treatises include John Bayley, *A Summary of the Law of Bills of Exchange, Cash Bills, and Promissory Notes* (2d ed.; London, 1797); Joseph Chitty, *A Practical Treatise on Bills of Exchange . . .* (Philadelphia, 1821, from 5th London ed.); Zephaniah Swift, *A Digest of the Law of Evidence . . . and a Treatise on Bills of Exchange, and Promissory Notes* (1810; New York, 1972 reprint).

2. Bayley, *Bills of Exchange*, 94–97; Chitty, *Bills of Exchange*, 449–50, 466. On the action of assumpsit, see Case No. 2.

3. Hening, *Statutes*, VI, 85–86; first allowed in 1730, reenacted in 1792 (ibid., IV, 274; Shepherd, *Statutes*, I, 35). See also Tucker, *Blackstone's Commentaries*, III, 156 n. 9.

4. Hening, *Statutes*, XII, 741, 746; Chitty, *Bills of Exchange*, 545–47.

5. All of JM's other surviving declarations on protested bills are in debt according to the statute, as are the declarations of plaintiff's counsel in cases where JM represented the defendant. In Asselby v. Pleasants (Case No. 14) special assumpsit was also used, but in that case debt did not lie because it was against the acceptor of the bill.

6. Hening, *Statutes*, VI, 85–86; Shepherd, *Statutes*, I, 35; Tucker, *Blackstone's Commentaries*, II, 467 n. 22.

7. Hening, *Statutes*, XII, 358–59; Shepherd, *Statutes*, I, 366.

8. John Vaughan (1765–1841) served for many years as secretary of the American Philosophical Society (Sarah P. Stetson, "The Philadelphia Sojourn of Samuel Vaughan," *Pennsylvania Magazine of History and Biography*, LXXIII [1949], 459–74). On Elias Parker (ca. 1760–1799), see *WMQ*, 1st ser., VI (1897), 23. Paine was a Richmond dealer in public securities (*CVSP*, IV, 251; see also obituary of a Samuel Payne [ca. 1758–1821], *Richmond Enquirer*, 11 May 1821).

9. Only the plaintiff's attorney is listed for these two cases (U.S. Cir. Ct., Va., Rule Bk. I, 162, 252).

10. Hinde, *Chancery Practice*, 584–87; H. St. G. Tucker, *Commentaries on Va. Laws*, II, Bk. 3, 467–68, 472.

I. Declaration

December 1794

United States Middle circuit district of Virginia to wit
John Vaughan a merchant resident & citizen of the State of Pennsylvania complains of Samuel Payne & Elias Parker[1] a citizen of Virga. & within the jurisdiction of this court in custody &c. of a plea of trespass on the case for this to wit that whereas Elias Parker on the 29th. day of March in the year 1792 at Richmond within the commonwealth & district of Virginia did according to the custom & usage of Merchants[2] make his first of exchange[3] subscribd with his name & directed to Mr. Daniel Parker No. 166 South 3d. Street Philadelphia where by he directed the said Daniel Parker at forty five days sight of that his first of exchange his second unpaid to pay to the order of Mr. Samuel Paine five hundred & seventy dollars for value receivd & to place it to account of Messrs. Edward Parker & Co. of New York as per advice which said bill was afterwards to wit on the same 29th. day of March 1792 in Richmond aforesaid according to the custom of merchants indorsd by the said Samuel Paine to the plaintiff who on the 10th. day of April 1792 in Philadelphia aforesaid presented the same to the said Daniel on whom the said bill was drawn who did then & there according to the custom of merchants accept the same. And afterwards to wit on the 28th. day of May 1792 in Philadelphia the time for paying the said bill having elapsd[4] & the second being unpaid, the said bill was presented to the said Daniel Parker for payment who did then & there refuse to pay the same, whereupon the same was protested according to the custom of merchants as will more fully appear by the instrument of protest made the hand & seal of Clement Biddle Notary Public of all which the said Samuel Paine & Elias Parker afterwards to wit on the day of in the year 1792 had notice[5] by means whereof the said Samuel Paine & Elias Parker became liable to pay to the plaintiff the sum of five hundred & seventy dollars in consideration whereof he the said Samuel & Elias afterwards to wit on the said day of in the year 1792 undertook & faithfully promisd to the plaintiff that they woud when requird well & truely pay the plaintiff the said sum of five hundred & seventy dollars.[6]

And whereas afterwards[7] to wit on the day of in the year 1792 in the commonwealth & district aforesaid he the said Samuel Paine & Elias Parker were indebted to the plaintiff in one other sum of five hundred & seventy dollars for so much money before that time had & receivd by the defendants to the use of the plaintiff & being so indebted they the Defendants then & there to wit in the commonwealth & district aforesaid & on the said day of 1792 undertook & faithfully promisd that they woud when thereunto requird faithfully pay to the plaintiff the said sum of money last mentiond.[8] Yet the defendants tho often requird the sums of money aforesaid to the plaintiff have not paid or either of them but the same to pay they hitherto have & still do altogether refuse to the damage of the plaintiff eight hundred dollars where fore he sues &c.[9]

J MARSHALL pq

ADS, Vaughan v. Parker and Paine, U.S. Circuit Court, Va., Ended Cases (Restored), 1795, Vi. Clerk's endorsements and jury verdict on verso. Filed at Dec. 1794 rules in clerk's office (U.S. Cir. Ct., Va., Rule Bk. I, 162–63).

1. JM originally drew up this declaration against Paine alone and later inserted Parker's name here and at other points in the document, also changing the singular to plural at the appropriate places (though sometimes omitting to do this). He apparently made these changes so the declaration would conform to the writ of capias, which named Parker and Paine as joint defendants. Although the Virginia statute permitted the plaintiff to sue the indorser and drawer jointly in an action of debt, this was an action of special assumpsit, which at common law had to be prosecuted against each defendant separately (Tucker, *Blackstone's Commentaries*, III, 156 n. 9). Presumably separate writs should have issued against Parker and Paine. Although these proceedings began as a single case, the judgments were entered in the order book as two distinct cases (U.S. Cir. Ct., Va., Ord. Bk. II, 75, 84).

2. The rules governing bills of exchange formed part of the "custom of merchants" or law merchant (*lex mercatoria*). Originally confined to a distinct class of persons and courts, the law merchant by this time was for all practical purposes a branch of the common law (Theodore F. T. Plucknett, *A Concise History of the Common Law* [5th ed.; Boston, 1956], 657–70). Declarations usually included the phrase "according to the custom and usage of merchants," though these words were unnecessary (Bayley, *Bills of Exchange*, 102; Chitty, *Bills of Exchange*, 451).

3. Here begins the detailed description of the bill of exchange, signifying that this is a special count brought on the instrument itself. For a discussion of the various parts of the bill, see the notes to Doc. II.

4. See Doc. II, n. 1, for calculating the time when payment was due.

5. The holder was required to give notice of the protest for nonpayment to all the parties to whom he intended to resort for payment. Failure to do so discharged them from their liability. Notice had to be given with reasonable

dispatch, though the time allowed depended on the circumstances of each case (Chitty, *Bills of Exchange*, 394, 400, 402; Swift, *Law of Evidence and Bills of Exchange*, 325–26). In requesting an injunction Parker complained that he did not receive notice until three months after the protest, though Vaughan sent the protest immediately to his Richmond agent with a request to give notice (Docs. IV, V, VI). In a 1794 case the Court of Appeals construed the Virginia statute as allowing eighteen months for giving notice of the protest of a foreign bill drawn on London (Stott & Donaldson v. Alexander & Co., 1 Wash. 331; Tucker, *Blackstone's Commentaries*, II, 470 n. 27).

6. To allege an express promise was unnecessary since the law implied a promise where the party was liable. Such a statement was usually included, however, to prevent any exception to adding other counts in assumpsit (Bacon, *Abridgment* [1st Am. ed.], IV, 735; Chitty, *Bills of Exchange*, 458).

7. This phrase introduces the second count.

8. If for some reason the special count on the bill proved defective, the plaintiff could still recover on this indebitatus assumpsit count for money had and received by the defendant to the plaintiff's use. English courts had held that a bill of exchange was prima facie evidence of money lent by the payee to the drawer and consequently of money had and received to the use of the holder (Bacon, *Abridgment* [1st. Am. ed.], IV, 736; Bayley, *Bills of Exchange*, 95; Chitty, *Bills of Exchange*, 468–69). This count applied to "quasi-contractual" obligations, those created by law to cover situations where the defendant, in Lord Mansfield's words, was "obliged by the ties of natural justice and equity to refund the money" (Fifoot, *History and Sources of the Common Law*, 363–67 [quotation at 366]).

9. Neither defendant put in a plea at the rules; therefore, office judgments were rendered against them. Writs of inquiry issued, but the office judgment against Parker was set aside when he appeared in court and pleaded non assumpsit on 9 Dec. 1795. The same day a jury returned a verdict for the plaintiff, assessing damages of $672.97 plus costs. Three days later a jury assessed the same damages against Paine on a writ of inquiry (U.S. Cir. Ct., Va., Rule Bk. I, 162, 180; Ord. Bk. II, 75, 84; Rec. Bk. IV, 113–16). The sum awarded was equivalent to the face amount of the bill, $570, plus 5 percent interest from 28 May 1792 (the day of the protest). This suggests that on "foreign" bills drawn or payable in another state of the U.S., Virginia juries computed damages according to the formula for inland bills in the 1786 act (Hening, *Statutes*, XII, 358–59). Since the judgments against Parker and Paine were for the same debt, satisfaction by one of them discharged the other from liability (Chitty, *Bills of Exchange*, 443). Parker apparently assumed the obligation, as he immediately sought to enjoin the judgment (Doc. V).

II. Bill of Exchange
29 March 1792

Exchange for 570$. Richmond 29th. March 1792

At forty five days sight[1] of this my first of Exchange, second unpaid,[2] pay to the order of Mr Samuel Paine five hundred & seventy dollars for value received which place to account of Messrs. Edward Parker & Co. of New York,[3] as pr advice[4] of yr. most obedt. Servt.

To
Mr. Daniel Parker
No. 166. South 3d. Street
Philadelphia

ELS. PARKER

Accepted 10th April 1792
DANL PARKER[5]

ADS, Vaughan v. Parker and Paine, U.S. Circuit Court, Va., Ended Cases (Restored), 1795, Vi. Signed on verso, "Saml. Paine," indorsing bill; also indorsed by John Vaughan but signature struck out.

1. On a bill payable at so many days sight, the time was computed from the day of presentment for acceptance, excluding that day. Three days of grace were also allowed (Chitty, *Bills of Exchange*, 342–44; Swift, *Law of Evidence and Bills of Exchange*, 317). This bill was accepted on 10 Apr. and was therefore due on 28 May.

2. To insure against loss, several copies of the bill, known as a set, were mailed separately to the payee. Payment of any one of them voided the others (McCusker, *Money and Exchange*, 20–21). In this case two copies of the bill were sent.

3. Evidently by some prior arrangement between Elias Parker and Edward Parker, another brother, the latter was to be charged on his account for the payment of this bill. If Elias as drawer had intended to make himself debtor in this transaction, he would have inserted the words "place to my account." If, on the other hand, Daniel was being drawn on as debtor to Elias, the latter would have inserted the words "place to your account" (Chitty, *Bills of Exchange*, 115).

4. The phrase "as per advice" made the drawee's payment contingent upon further instructions from the drawer (ibid.).

5. Since this bill was payable to Paine's order, it could be transferred in the first instance only by his indorsement. A bill payable to bearer was transferable by mere delivery. Signing one's name on the back of the instrument, as Paine did, was called a blank indorsement, which according to Chitty was "by far the most common." In effect this blank indorsement constituted a new bill payable to bearer, with the indorser as the new drawer on the original drawee (ibid., 169–76 [quotation at 173], 183).

III. Protest of Bill of Exchange
28 May 1792

⟨exchange for 570D[1] Richmond 29. March 1792
At forty five days sight of this my first of Exchange second unpaid, pay to the Order of Mr. Samuel Paine five hundred & seventy Dollars for Value received which place to Account of Mesrs Edward Parker & Co of New York, as pr advice of yr most obed Servt.

ELS. PARKER

To Mr. Daniel Parker
No 166 south 3d. Street
Philadelphia

Endorsed SAML. PAINE. JNO VAUGHAN[2]⟩

ON THE ⟨Twenty eighth⟩ Day of ⟨May⟩ Anno Domini 179⟨2⟩[3] at the Request of ⟨John Vaughan⟩ I Clement Biddle, Notary and Tabellion Public for the Commonwealth of Pennsylvania, duly commissioned and qualified, dwelling in Philadelphia ⟨Presented the Original Bill⟩ whereof the foregoing is a Copy ⟨to Daniel Parker by whom the same is Accepted & demanding payment thereof Received for answer that the same Could not be paid⟩.

WHEREUPON I the said Notary, at the Request aforesaid, have and DO hereby solemnly protest against the ⟨Drawer⟩ of the said ⟨Bill⟩ and all others concerned for all Exchange, Re-Exchange, Costs, Damages and Interest already suffered and to be suffered, for Want of ⟨Payment⟩ of the said ⟨Bill⟩.

[SEAL] THUS DONE and protested in Philadelphia aforesaid, in the Presence of ⟨Thomas B. & Kenneth MacKenzie⟩ Witnesses.

IN TESTIMONIUM VERITATIS.

CLEMENT BIDDLE
Not: Pub

Printed form, Vaughan v. Parker and Paine, U.S. Circuit Court, Va., Ended Cases (Restored), 1795, Vi. Blanks apparently filled in and signed by notary Clement Biddle.

1. The protest consisted of a formal declaration by a notary public on the original bill or on a copy. In this case a copy of the bill was inserted above a printed form of a protest. Protest by a notary was indispensable in case of the nonacceptance or nonpayment of foreign bills of exchange. At common law inland bills could not be protested, but in both England and Virginia there was statutory provision for protesting bills above £5 by a notary. Such notarial protest, however, was not required for inland bills. Without it the

holder would lose his damages, interest, and costs, but his right to the principal sum remained unaffected (Chitty, *Bills of Exchange*, 278–83; Hening, *Statutes*, XII, 358–59).

2. Vaughan's name is struck out on the original bill. Its inclusion on the notary's copy suggests that the cancellation occurred sometime after the protest.

3. This date marked the end of the three-day grace period for the payment of the bill (see Doc. II and n. 1).

IV. George Pickett to Elias Parker
26 August 1792

Mr. Elias Parker Richmond 26th. August 1792

Sir

Some time ago Mr Jno. Vaughan Merchant of Phila. Enclosied your protested Bill of Exchange Drawn on your Bro Daniel Together with your Brother letter oppen to you, Requsting you to take up the Bill, as Sam Paine Esq Indorsed the Bill. I as agent to Mr Vaughan waitd on Mr Paine who took the Charge of your Bro letter to you, assuring me at the Same time, that the Bill Should be taken up. ([1]He has frequently told me sinc that you had appointed a time when you would be in Richmond with Cash to take up this Bill.) I now have to Inform you if you have any Regard for your Credit, to send the money to me and take up the Bill which is now in my hands. You will let me hear from you by Return of the post. I am your mo ob ser

GEO PICKETT[2]

ALS, Parker v. Vaughan, U.S. Circuit Court, Va., Ended Cases (Unrestored), 1798, Vi. Addressed to Parker at Petersburg and postmarked Richmond, 27 Aug. Endorsed by Parker.

1. Here Parker inserted an asterisk and wrote on the verso: "*Mr Paine was in a great error if he did tell Mr Picket any thing of the kind."

2. George Pickett (ca. 1752–1821) was a prominent Richmond merchant and dealer in public securities. Like JM he was originally from Fauquier County, and his family was connected with the Marshalls by marriage. He was the grandfather of the Confederate general of the same name (Valentine Museum, *Richmond Portraits in An Exhibition of Makers of Richmond, 1737–1860* [Richmond, 1949], 152–54; *Fauquier Historical Society Bulletin*, 1st ser., no. 2 [1922], 208–9). JM was counsel for Pickett in two reported cases in the Court of Appeals and represented Pickett's older brothers Martin and William Pickett in another (see Case Nos. 32, 39, 40).

V. Bill in Chancery
8 January 1796

To the honorable Court of the United States for the middle circuit & District of Virginia in chancery sitting, humbly complaining sheweth unto your Honors your Orator Elias Parker of the Town of Petersburg & state of Virginia

That some time on or about the 29th. day of March 1792 your orator drew a bill of exchange payable at forty five days sight in favour of Samuel Paine of the city of Richmond upon Daniel Parker of the City of Philadelphia to be placed to account of Edward Parker & Company of the city of New York as [your orator] had authority to do. That the said Bill came by assignment into the hands of one John Vaughan of Philadelphia who presented the same to the said Daniel Parker upon the 10th. day of April 1792 who accepted it according to the terms of the Bill; of all which your orator was informed and therefore made himself perfectly easy with regard to the event, confiding that the bill would be duly paid; as the said Daniel Parker had effects in his hands sufficient to discharge it, and had repeatedly assured your orator that notwithstanding his very embarrassed situation & although he expected to become a bankrupt, that Bill should be paid. That the said Bill was however afterwards protested for non payment upon the 28th day of May 1792—of which your orator received no notice from the said Vaughan untill some time on or about the 28th. day of August 1792—when your orator received a Letter from George Picket dated the 26th of August 1792 informing him thereof[1]—and that the said Picket had an open letter from the said Daniel Parker to your orator containing his reasons for the protest—which Letter & protest were afterwards in possession of said Paine, to whom your orator repeatedly wrote for a sight of them but never could obtain it. That your orator heard no more of the matter till above two years afterwards, when the said John Vaughan instituted a suit against your orator upon the said Bill in this Honorable Court at common law—and having proved by the said Picket that the notice to your orator aforesaid was much earlier than in fact it was as the letter aforesaid plainly shews. He did in absence of your orator at last term obtain a judgement for the whole amount of said Bill of exchange with costs & damages according to the direction of the act of assembly.[2]

Your orator begs leave further to shew unto your Honors that if he had received earlier notice he could have secured the amount of the said bill in the hands of the said Daniel Parker—who hath since become bankrupt & your orator if he discharges the judgement to said Vaughan, hath no prospect of recovering the same or any part thereof from the said Daniel Parker or the said Edward Parker & Company who have credit with your orator for said Bill & since as well as the said Daniel Parker have had the Benefit of the Bankrupt Laws of Pennsylvania and by force thereof are absolved from all debts prior to said acts of Bankruptcy. That your orator hath also been informed that after the said bill was accepted & became payable that the said Vaughan took a draft for the amount thereof from the said Daniel Parker on the said Edward Parker & Co payable at sight which was protested—but the said Edward Parker & Company offered to accept it payable in thirty days, in consequence of which the said Vaughan did receive that or another bill for the same amount Payable in thirty days, from the said Daniel Parker, which was accepted by the said Edward Parker & Company—and at the expiration of the thirty days it was again protested for non-payment—all which transactions & negociations calculated to indulge the said Daniel Parker, procrastinated the time & have in event produced to your orator the inconveniences before mentioned—all which is contrary to Equity—In tender consideration whereof and for as much as your orator hath no redress at common law but is only relievable in Equity—To the end therefore that the said John Vaughan may on corporal oath full true & perfect answer make to the premisses That he may forever be injoined from all further proceedings on his said judgment & that your orator may have such other & further relief in the premisses as shall be consistent with equity—and the nature of the case may require. May it please your honors to grant to your orator a writ or writs of subpœna & injunction, to be directed to the said John Vaughan his agents & attornies commanding them &c.

ELS PARKER

Town of Petersburg to wit

This day Elias Parker made oath before me an alderman of the said Town that the matters & things in the foregoing Bill are true so far as they relate to his own knowledge and as far as they relate to the knowledge of others that he believes them to be true. Given under my hand this eigth day of January 1796.

WILLIAM PRENTIS.[3]

Let an Injunction Issue, pursuant to the prayer of the above Petition, upon Security being given, as in such cases is accustomed.

March 13th. 1796.

JA. IREDELL, One of the Associate Justices of the Supreme Court of the United States.[4]

DS, Parker v. Vaughan, U.S. Circuit Court, Va., Ended Cases (Unrestored), 1798, Vi. Brackets enclose words missing owing to mutilated MS.

1. See Doc. IV.

2. As noted above (Doc. I, n. 9), the jury awarded damages according to the formula of the 1786 act on protested inland bills—the face amount plus 5 percent interest from the date of protest—even though the bill was a foreign one. See editorial note for the various Virginia statutes on protested bills.

3. Though signed by magistrate William Prentis, the text of the affidavit is not in his hand. Virginia law required petitions for injunctions to be supported by affidavit, certified at the foot of the bill, that the allegations contained in it were true (Hening, *Statutes*, XIII, 420).

4. In Virginia practice the judge's order awarding the writ of injunction was endorsed at the foot of the bill. The injunction was not to have effect until the party requesting it entered into bond for the amount of the law judgment and costs. This bond was to be filed in the clerk's office of that court where the proceedings at law had taken place (ibid.; see also H. St. G. Tucker, *Commentaries on Va. Laws*, II, Bk. 3, 467). According to the clerk's endorsements on the verso of the bill, subpoenas for Vaughan's appearance were issued at the June and Dec. 1796 terms of the court. The second of these was returned "no Inhabitant" (U.S. Cir. Ct., Va., Rule Bk. I, 252, 265, 302; subpoena, 31 Dec. 1796, Parker v. Vaughan).

VI. Answer

29 October 1796

The answer in Chancery of John Vaughan to the Bill of Complaint exhibited against him in the Honorable Court of the United States for the Middle Circuit in the District of Virginia by Elias Parker

This respondent Saving to himself every benefit of exception to the Complainants Bill for answer thereto Saith

That he admits, the Bill of Exchange came to his hands & was presented & protested for non payment about the time in the Complainants Bill mentioned, that immediately after its protest he transmitted it to Mr George Picket of the City of Richmond with a request that he would give immediate notice of the protest to the drawer & Indorser which he has been informd & believes was done. This respondent admits that from his real Solicitude to obtain payment of the Said Bill of exchange without recurring to the drawer or indorser, he did take a dft on Edward Parker & Co. which was protested & did afterwards take another Bill payable in thirty days, which was first accepted & afterwards protested for non payment, but at the receipt of these orders or Bills it was expressly Stipulated that they should in no manner affect, the right of this respondent to recieve the money due on the Bill Drawn by the Complainant, unless they should be actually paid, & this respondent also directed Mr Picket not to postpone his notice of the protest on account of the drafts so recieved as above Stated.

The Said Elias Parker, Daniel Parker, & Edward Parker & Co are Brothers & this Respondent cannot but apprehend that they are in combination with each other. He admits that having been disappointed in his endeavors to obtain the money by other means, he directed a Suit to be instituted on which judgement was render'd, but he niether admits nor believes that it was obtained unfairly or by Surprise or by any improper testimony.

This respondent denies all Combination without that &c & prays to be hence dismissed with Costs &c & he will ever pray &c.[1]

To Wit

John Vaughan made oath before me the Honorable Thomas Mc. Kean Esquire, Doctor of Laws Chief Justice of the Supreme court of Pennsylvania &c. this 29th. day of October 1796 & made oath that the allegations of the foregoing answer, So far as they are stated to be of his own knowledge are true & So far as they are Stated to be of the knowledge of others he believes them to be true.

Sworn & subscribed the twenty ninth day of October 1796 before
THOS M:KEAN[2]

JN VAUGHAN

DS, Parker v. Vaughan, U.S. Circuit Court, Va., Ended Cases (Unrestored), 1798, Vi.

1. On 5 June 1797 the court overruled Parker's motion for a permanent injunction. Once an injunction was dissolved the plaintiff still had a right to continue his cause as an original suit. At the next term Parker was awarded a commission to take the deposition de bene esse of George Pickett. The suit continued until Dec. 1798, when the court after hearing arguments by counsel dismissed the suit (U.S. Cir. Ct., Va., Ord. Bk. II, 310; III, 87, 192; see also Robinson, *Practice*, II, 248–49, for proceedings after the dissolution of an injunction).

2. The words immediately preceding the signature, beginning with "Sworn & subscribed," are in the hand of Thomas McKean. Up to this point the text of the affidavit appears to be in the same hand as that of the answer. Attached to the answer is a certification, dated 31 Oct. 1796, by Gov. Thomas Mifflin of Pennsylvania, that Thomas McKean was chief justice of Pennsylvania. The seal of the state is affixed to the certification.

11. Fairfax v. Hunter

1795–1797

I. Declaration, ca. March 1795
II. Common Rule, 30 May 1795
III. Case Agreed, 30 May 1795
IV. Judgment, 6 June 1795
V. Petition for Writ of Error, ca. 22 November 1795
VI. Petition for Postponement, 22 January 1796
VII. Writ of Error, 24 January 1796
VIII. Petition for Postponement, 29 July 1796

Editorial Note

John Marshall was as much a party to this suit as was his client Denny Martin Fairfax. At issue was Fairfax's title to the Northern Neck of Virginia, the region lying between the Potomac and Rappahannock rivers, which the family had held as proprietors since the time of Charles II. As a member of a syndicate that in 1793 had contracted to purchase a large portion of the Fairfax lands, Marshall was keenly interested in settling the question of title, preferably by means of a definitive judicial ruling.[1] If Denny Fairfax was a party to this litigation in name only, the same was also largely true of David Hunter, for his claim to the lands in this ejectment action rested on the state of Virginia's assertion of title to the Northern Neck. The real contest was between the purchasers, for whom Marshall spoke, and the commonwealth. It was fought in both the judicial and legislative arenas over the course of three decades, culminating in the famous case of *Martin* v. *Hunter's Lessee* in 1816.[2] By that time the title question was overshadowed by the constitutional issue of the Supreme Court's appellate jurisdiction under section 25 of the Judiciary Act of 1789.[3] The case presented here was a distinct action from the one that produced the 1816 Supreme Court decision. Although it too came before the high court in 1796 and 1797, *Fairfax* v. *Hunter* did not bring forth an opinion on the Fairfax title at that time because Hunter chose not to prosecute the appeal. The decision to drop the appeal came shortly after a compromise that was enacted into law in 1796 between the purchasers of the Fairfax lands and the state. This legislative settlement obviated the need for an immediate judicial determination.

The commonwealth under the compromise act of 1796 was to gain title to the lands designated "waste and unappropriated" at the time of Lord Fairfax's death in 1781; the purchasers were to be confirmed in their title to the lands "'specifically appropriated by . . . lord Fairfax to his own use either by deed or actual survey.'"[4] It was this latter category of Northern Neck lands, those reserved for the proprietor's own use, also known as the manor lands, that the Marshall syndicate was then in the process of buying from Denny Fairfax. These lands, along with the proprietor's personal share of the Northern Neck proprietary, had been devised by Lord Fairfax to Denny Martin, his nephew and a British subject, on condition that he assume the Fairfax name.[5] Although Lord Fairfax had resided for many years in Virginia and died a citizen of the commonwealth, his heir's status as not only an alien but an alien enemy gravely imperiled the Fairfax property interests in the state.

The status of the proprietary was progressively undermined by wartime laws confiscating British property and by others enacted soon after Lord Fairfax's death dealing directly with the Northern Neck. By 1785 the state formally assumed the right to issue patents under the seal of the commonwealth to lands in that region. In the meantime, however, the treaty of peace had been ratified, and Virginia in conformity with the sixth article of that pact had passed an act barring future confiscations of British property.[6] Believing that his title was good at the time of the treaty and that this pact secured him from future acts of dispossession, Denny Fairfax began to press his claims as Lord Fairfax's devisee. He eventually became a party to three distinct types of legal proceedings—actions of caveat, ejectment, and escheat—pitting his title against that of the commonwealth to the Northern Neck. This does not include *Hite* v. *Fairfax*, decided by the Court of Appeals in 1786, a dispute originating in the colonial period in which the Fairfax title was not directly in issue.[7]

The litigation over the Fairfax title began during the late 1780s when Denny Fairfax entered caveats against the issuing of patents to David Hunter (1762–1829) of Berkeley County, defendant in the present suit. Somewhat analogous to an injunction in equity, a caveat prevented the issuing of a patent until judicial proceedings determined which of the parties had a better claim. Such an action lay only where no patent for the contested land had issued. One could enter a caveat in the land office after the prospective patentee returned a plat and survey of his land to the office. The person entering the caveat then obtained a copy and delivered it to the clerk of the court of the district or county in which the land lay. The court proceeded to hear the cause upon the caveat in a summary way without pleadings or jury trial.[8]

Although David Hunter was only one of numerous speculators

who beginning in 1786 sought patents from the state for ungranted Northern Neck lands, the decision to contest his claims in particular was probably a calculated one. Most of the early state patents for these lands merely completed title proceedings that had begun in the old proprietary office, where the purchasers had obtained their warrants. Hunter was among the first to purchase warrants for Northern Neck lands from the state land office in Richmond and thus to derive his title solely from the commonwealth.[9] The grand scale of David Hunter's operations is evident from an inspection of the land office papers. In January 1788 he purchased warrants for surveys of lands in the counties of Berkeley, Shenandoah, and Hampshire, totaling more than nine thousand acres. At a price of twenty-five pounds for one hundred acres, these purchases represented a sizable investment.[10]

Fairfax took out caveats only against Hunter's Berkeley surveys, those in Shenandoah and Hampshire being allowed to proceed to patent. Entered in December 1788, the caveats came up for a hearing at the Winchester District Court in April 1790 and were then adjourned for "novelty and difficulty" to the General Court. That court dismissed them on a technicality in June 1791, but new ones were filed immediately with the register of the land office. Another hearing took place at the Winchester court in September 1791, and again the caveats were adjourned for difficulty to the General Court. Arguments were heard there in November 1792, though no decision was reached for lack of a quorum of judges. Marshall appeared for Fairfax on this occasion, having earlier received a fee of twenty-eight pounds for the caveat cases from Winchester. These cases remained undetermined at the time of the 1796 compromise.[11]

In the meantime, Hunter had initiated his own action against Fairfax, an ejectment brought at the April 1791 term of the Winchester District Court. This was a suit to try title to a 788-acre tract in Shenandoah County, for which Hunter had obtained a patent in April 1789. The Winchester court upheld the Fairfax title in April 1794, and Hunter immediately appealed to the Court of Appeals. The case was argued there in May 1796, but the appeal languished following the legislative compromise enacted later that year. Hunter subsequently revived his cause, however, and in 1810 obtained a reversal of the district court judgment. It was this decision by the Virginia Court of Appeals that gave rise to the federal Supreme Court cases, *Fairfax's Devisee* v. *Hunter's Lessee* (1813) and *Martin* v. *Hunter's Lessee* (1816), brought under section 25 of the judiciary act.[12]

Shortly before the Winchester District Court's 1794 decision in favor of Fairfax in the ejectment action, the commonwealth formally became a party to the Northern Neck litigation by means of escheat proceedings against the Fairfax manor lands. Although during the 1780s the state had assumed the right to issue patents to the unappropriated lands, the Fairfax manors—Leeds, extending over Fauquier, Loudoun, Frederick, and Shenandoah counties, and South Branch, in the counties of Hardy and Hampshire (now West Virginia)—had been left undisturbed. Leases of these lands continued to be granted in Denny Fairfax's name.[13] The move against the manor lands that began in 1793 was one manifestation of a revived and intensified anti-British posture adopted by the General Assembly, provoked in part by federal court judgments in favor of British creditors. In December of that year the legislature adopted resolutions calling for a suspension of the peace treaty and for a more rigorous execution of the act concerning escheators.[14] Although couched in general terms, the latter resolution was clearly directed at the escheators in Northern Neck counties where Fairfax manor lands lay.

As a prospective purchaser of the manors, Marshall could view this development only with alarm. He had to muster all of his legal and legislative skills to withstand the attack. In the summer of 1794 a Fauquier inquest found for the commonwealth as to that part of Leeds Manor lying within the county, a finding that was sustained by the District Court at Dumfries in October of the same year. Fairfax then appealed to the Court of Appeals—precisely at the time the state legislature was considering the proposed Eleventh Amendment to the Constitution, which threatened to prevent an ultimate appeal to the federal Supreme Court on Fairfax's part. In these circumstances the commonwealth was in no hurry to proceed with the appeal. Although arguments were heard, the Court of Appeals rendered no decision before the compromise settlement of 1796. After the compromise, which secured to the purchasers the title to the manor lands, the court quietly reversed the Dumfries District Court judgment.[15]

While all this litigation was pending—the caveats brought by Fairfax, the ejectment by Hunter, and the escheats by the commonwealth—Marshall in the spring of 1795 filed a declaration in ejectment against Hunter in the federal circuit court.[16] All along his aim had been to get the question of the Fairfax title before the Supreme Court of the United States. In particular he wanted the high court to declare the meaning of the treaty of 1783 in relation to this question. This was the proper tribunal to make such a pronouncement, he believed, which, even if unfavorable to Fairfax, would at least put a halt to costly litigation. He of course was confident that the court shared his opinion that the treaty protected the title. By initiating a new action in the federal court, Marshall apparently was trying to forestall the possibility that the appeal route to the Supreme Court for those cases then in the state court—in particular the escheat action of *Fairfax* v. *Commonwealth*—would be closed off.[17] Marshall may also have been concerned that the state appeals court would decide against the Fairfax title on common law grounds or by virtue of certain state laws, without reference to the treaty. An appeal under section 25 could be brought only on a federal question, in this instance for alleged errors in construing the treaty. If, for example, the state court determined that Denny Fairfax as an alien could not take lands by devise or that the state had completed its confiscation of the Fairfax estate before the 1783 treaty, would the Supreme Court under section 25 be able to inquire into the correctness of this ruling?[18] Bringing the case in the first instance in the federal court ensured that all aspects of the title question could be appealed on a writ of error.

The federal ejectment action was heard in June 1795, the same term in which it was brought. From the beginning of their litigation with Fairfax five years earlier, Hunter and his associates had sought support for their cause from the commonwealth. In May 1790 the state executive council had directed the attorney general "to inquire how far the right or dignity of this Commonwealth may be concerned in the dispute between . . . [Hunter] and Denny Fairfax." A few days before the hearing of this case the council, now persuaded that the commonwealth was "materially interested" in the outcome, hired Alexander Campbell and John Wickham to appear on Hunter's behalf for twenty-five guineas apiece.[19] It is not known whether Marshall had assistance in representing Fairfax on this occasion.

Although there is no report of the case as heard at the federal circuit court, the various lines of argument can be inferred from the lengthy statement of facts agreed to by the parties as the basis for the court's determination of the law.[20] On behalf of the plaintiff, Marshall contended that Denny Fairfax, though an alien, could at common law take lands by devise; that he had not been divested of those lands either by formal inquest of office or some equivalent act prior to the treaty of 1783; and that the treaty, as stipulated in the sixth article, barred the commonwealth from taking the lands of British subjects in future either by escheat or by acts of confiscation. Hunter's counsel, on the contrary, maintained that an alien had no capacity to hold lands; that even though there had been no escheat proceedings as to these lands, various acts of assembly concerning the Northern Neck were sufficient to vest the waste and ungranted lands in the commonwealth; and that the state's title to these lands was perfected before the ratification of the treaty, which therefore had nothing to do with this case.

After Judges James Wilson and Cyrus Griffin ruled in favor of Fairfax on 6 June 1795, the governor and council took out an appeal on Hunter's behalf to the Supreme Court. The Virginia legislature soon dropped its support, however, protesting the jurisdiction of the federal courts in such cases (see Document VI and n. 1). Hunter then continued the appeal on his own, hoping that the commonwealth would reconsider and employ counsel on his behalf. Marshall was prepared to argue this case along with *Ware* v. *Hylton* (Case Number 13), the British debt case (in which, ironically, he attempted to deny the applicability of the treaty of 1783), at the February 1796 term of the court. Hunter, however, obtained a postponement at this and also at the August 1796 term (Documents VI and VIII). Before the court met again, the Virginia legislature adopted the compromise settlement, and Hunter chose not to prosecute the appeal further. Marshall was keenly disappointed at losing this opportunity for the Supreme Court to decide the Fairfax title question. Although this ejectment concerned only one tract of waste and ungranted lands, a favorable decision would also have cleared title to the manor lands. Abandoning hope of an early judicial determination of the issue, Marshall as a member of the House of Delegates engineered the legislative settlement on the Northern Neck lands that was enacted into law in December 1796. Even though he did not succeed in getting a Supreme Court hearing of his case, the ejectment suit in the federal court did serve Marshall's purposes by exerting pressure on the General Assembly to reach an accommodation with the purchasers of the Fairfax lands.[21]

This is not the place to consider the later history of the legal dispute between Fairfax and Hunter. Fairfax's representatives evidently did not regard the lands contested in the ejectments with Hunter as embraced by the compromise of 1796 because these judgments were rendered before the legislature had acted. After letting his cause lie dormant for some years, Hunter revived the appeal of the Winchester decision, setting in motion the proceedings that produced *Martin* v. *Hunter's Lessee* in 1816. Marshall, then chief justice of the Supreme Court, continued to be personally interested in the outcome of this case. Until the Supreme Court made a definitive ruling, the title to the Fairfax manor lands would rest on the uncertain ground of a legislative act. Marshall always maintained that the purchasers held "not under the compromise but under the treaty," and he hoped that the highest court in the land would some day declare this to be so.[22] How important this was to him cannot be fully understood without a close study of the numerous cases in the state courts of Virginia in which he and his brother, as purchasers of the Fairfax estate, were parties—litigation that continually engaged them throughout much of their remaining lives.[23]

One who reads an old declaration in ejectment for the first time may wonder at its strange tale of two lessees with improbable names, the one being forcibly ousted from the possession of his land by the other, followed by a letter to a third person warning him to appear at the next term of court to be made defendant. The narrative and letter, of course, were part of an elaborate fiction, perhaps the most famous of those devised by the common law to reach a desired result while preserving traditional forms. In form, ejectment was a personal action in trespass brought by an ousted leaseholder for the recovery of his lease and the damages suffered by the loss. Its true function was to enable a freeholder to recover real property by trying the merits of his title against those of another claimant. Dissatisfaction on the part of freeholders with the ancient real actions, the remedies available to them for being wrongfully deprived of their land, led them to contrive means whereby they could recover land through the leaseholder's personal action of ejectment. The upshot—the full story constitutes a large and important chapter in the history of the common law—was that ejectment became the common means of trying title to real estate, virtually supplanting the old proprietary and possessory actions.[24]

To use the example of this case, Denny Fairfax, the real plaintiff, fabricated an imaginary lease to an imaginary lessee, George Goodtitle, for the land in question. Goodtitle was subsequently "ejected" by another imaginary person, Peter Plunderer, the "casual ejector" who was taken to be the tenant of David Hunter, the real defendant. As the fictional plaintiff, Goodtitle had to prove four points in order to succeed: (1) the title in his lessor, Fairfax; (2) Fairfax's lease to him; (3) his entry under that lease; (4) his ouster by Plunderer. On being notified of Goodtitle's action (by means of an imaginary letter from Plunderer), Hunter entered the "common rule"; that is, he confessed the second, third, and fourth points, which of course were fictions, so that trial could proceed on the question of title only (see Document II). Thus, what in form appeared to be only a collateral issue, the lessor's title, was in fact the real point of the suit. The courts allowed this pretense only where the situation described could actually have existed, that is, where the real plaintiff had a right of entry and could grant a valid lease. The fictions in ejectment "only enabled the plaintiff to take a short cut where he could have made the long journey." Goodtitle and Plunderer continued to flourish until the mid-nineteenth century, when the fictions were abolished by statute.[25]

1. On the Marshall purchase of the Fairfax lands and the events leading to the legislative compromise of 1796 between the purchasers and the state of Virginia, see the editorial note, *PJM*, II, 140–49. The editorial note here adds a few details, focusing in particular on the case in the federal court (discussed only briefly in the earlier note) and its connection with the simultaneous litigation in the state courts.

2. 1 Wheat. 304.

3. That section outlined the situations in which a case could be appealed from the highest state court to the Supreme Court by writ of error.

4. *PJM*, II, 148; Shepherd, *Statutes*, II, 22–23.

5. In addition to the editorial note (*PJM*, II, 140–49), see the excellent account of the dissolution of the proprietary by H. C. Groome, *Fauquier During the Proprietorship* (Richmond, 1927), 218–43.

6. These acts are recited in Doc. III.

7. *PJM*, I, 150–64; see also Case No. 4.

8. Tucker, *Blackstone's Commentaries*, III, App., Note B, 31–34; Hening, *Statutes*, X, 50–65 (58–59 on caveats).

9. Hunter's family moved from York, Pennsylvania, to the lower Shenandoah Valley of Virginia when he was a young boy in the 1760s, settling near the present site of Martinsburg. Hunter and his older brother Moses (1753–1789) became leading citizens of Berkeley County. They frequently represented the county in the House of Delegates between 1779 and 1794, and between them they held the county clerkship from 1785 to 1829. In 1792 David Hunter married Elizabeth Pendleton, daughter of Col. Philip Pendleton, who was closely associated with the Hunters in their land ventures (J. E. Norris, ed., *History of the Lower Shenandoah Valley* . . . [Chicago, 1890], 580–82; Earl Gregg Swem and John W. Williams, comps., *A Register of the General Assembly of Virginia, 1776–1918* . . . [Richmond, 1918], 390).

10. Land Office Caveats, No. 2, 1786–1814, 55–56, Vi; Northern Neck Surveys, No. 1, 1786–89, 181–84, 191, Vi; Northern Neck Grants, 1792–95, 424–29, Vi; petition of David Hunter, Moses Hunter, and Philip Pendleton, 11 Nov. 1796, Legislative Petitions, Berkeley County, Vi.

11. Land Office Caveats, No. 2, 1786–1814, 55–56, 84; Frederick County District Court Order Book, 1789–93, 48, 102, 207–8, 241 (microfilm), Vi; Fairfax v. Hunter, 1 Va. Cas. 3 (1791); Carter Braxton to unknown, 31 Dec. 1792, Wykeham-Martin Papers, Kent County Archives, Maidstone (microfilm), ViWC; *PJM*, II, 394; petition of David Hunter et al., 11 Nov. 1796 (cited in n. 10).

12. Fairfax's Devisee v. Hunter's Lessee, Appellate Case File No. 456, RG 267, DNA; Hunter v. Fairfax's Devisee, 1 Munf. 218 (1810); Fairfax's Devisee v. Hunter's Lessee, 7 Cranch 603 (1813); Martin v. Hunter's Lessee, 1 Wheat. 304 (1816).

13. Groome, *Fauquier During the Proprietorship*, 74–77, 227.

14. Shepherd, *Statutes*, I, 285; Isaac Samuel Harrell, *Loyalism in Virginia: Chapters in the Economic History of the Revolution* (1926; New York, 1965 reprint), 103–11.

15. For a detailed account of JM's role in the escheat proceedings, see *PJM*, II, 143–48. See also Va. Ct. Ap. Ord. Bk. III, 244.

16. He also instituted another ejectment on behalf of Fairfax at the Nov. 1795 term of the federal court. A default judgment for Fairfax was entered in May 1796. See Fairfax's Lessee v. Notitle [John Hunter et al.], U.S. Cir. Ct., Va., Ended Cases (Restored), 1796.

17. *PJM*, II, 145. JM attempted to circumvent this obstacle to the appeal of the escheat case by filing a traverse in his own name to the Fauquier inquest (JM to Charles Lee, ca. Dec. 1795 [ibid., 329–30]).

18. The Supreme Court later assumed the authority to make such an inquiry (William Winslow Crosskey, *Politics and the Constitution in the History of the United States* [2 vols.; Chicago, 1953], II, 790–92 [citing Smith v. Maryland, 6 Cranch 286 (1810)]).

19. *JCSV*, V, 182; Journal of the Council of the State of Virginia, 1793–95, 327, 330, Vi. Campbell and Wickham had recently been employed by the state to argue the escheat actions then pending in the Court of Appeals (Journal of the Council of the State of Virginia, 1793–95, 276, 279).

20. See Doc. III and the accompanying annotation. The cases for Fairfax and Hunter were no doubt essentially the same as those presented in the ejectment originally brought by Hunter in 1791, for which there is a report as heard in three different courts (Hunter v. Fairfax, 22 Apr. 1794, in Tucker, "Notes on Cases in the General Court, District Court, and Court of Appeals in Virginia, 1786–1811," Tucker-Coleman Papers, ViW; Hunter v. Fairfax's Devisee, 1 Munf. 218 [1810]; Fairfax's Devisee v. Hunter's Lessee, 7 Cranch 603 [1813]).

21. See, for example, the petition of the inhabitants of Hardy, Hampshire, and Shenandoah counties, 11 Nov. 1796, Legislative Petitions, Hardy County, Vi. The committee report on this petition embodied the compromise proposals subsequently adopted by the legislature (*JHDV*, Oct. 1796, 9, 25).

22. JM to James M. Marshall, 9 July 1822, Bixby Collection, MoSW.

23. Those cases that can be identified and documented will be considered at the appropriate points in subsequent volumes of *The Papers of John Marshall*.

24. Baker, *English Legal History*, 164–68; Sutton, *Personal Actions*, 52–56; F. W. Maitland, *Equity also the Forms of Action at Common Law* (Cambridge, 1926), 351–53; Blackstone, *Commentaries*, III, 199–206.

25. Baker, *English Legal History*, 168. Virginia abolished them in 1849, three years before Great Britain did so. For another ejectment case, see Case No. 27.

I. Declaration
ca. March 1795

United[1] States, Middle Circuit, District of Virginia

George Goodtitle complains of Peter Plunderer[2] in Custody &c. for that to wit, that whereas Denny Fairfax on the tenth day of May in the Year of Our Lord 1784 in the Commonwealth of Virginia & District aforesaid had demised granted & to farm let to the said George Goodtitle one Messuage, Tract and parcel of Land lying and being in the County of Shenandoah and in the District aforesaid and containing seven hundred and Eighty eight Acres[3] To have & to hold the said Tenement with the Appurtenances to the said Goodtitle and his Assigns from the said tenth day of May 1784 until the full end & term of thirty Years[4] thence next ensuing & fully to be compleated and ended; by Virtue of which said Demise the said George Goodtitle entered into the said Tenement with its appurtenances and was possessed thereof untill the said Peter Plunderer afterwards to wit, on the tenth day of May in the year 1794[5] with force and arms entered into the Tenement aforesaid with the appurtenances in and upon the possession of the said George Goodtitle and ejected and amoved the said George Goodtitle from his said Farm, his said Term not being ended & kept out the said George so ejected and amoved from his said possession and then and there did other Injuries to him against the peace of the United States & to the Damage of the said George Goodtitle five hundred pounds and therefore he sues &c. and avers that this Court has Jurisdiction of this Cause.

J. MARSHALL for the plaintiff
for the Deft.[6]

Sir,[7]

I am informed that you are in possession or claim title to the premisses in this declaration of ejectment mentioned, or some part thereof, & I being sued in this action as a casual ejector & having no claim or title to the said Premisses do advise you to appear on the first day of the next Term of the court of the United States for the middle circuit in the district of Virginia to be holden in the city of Richmond in May next by some attorney of that court and then & there by rule of the Said Court to Cause yourself to be made defendant in my Stead. Otherwise I shall suffer judgment to be entered against me & you will be turned out of possession. Your friend.

To Mr Robert Bodkins PETER PLUNDERER.[8]

1795.

Frederick County to wit[9]

Griffin Taylor—Appeared before me a majestrate for the county aforesaid this thirteenth day of april 1795. And made Oath that he did on the 4th. day of April 1795 deliver a true copy of the above declaration in ejectment to Robert Bodkins tenant in possession of the premisses in the above declaration of ejectment mentioned and at the same time informed him that it was a declaration in ejectment

& that unless he appeared on the first day of the next term of the court of the United States for the Middle circuit in the district of Virginia, to be holden in the city of Richmond in may next by some attorney of the Said Court & did then & there by rule of court cause himself to be made defendant that judgment would be intered & he would be turned out of Possession.

MATTHEW WRIGHT

Frederick County to wit[10]

Fleet Smith this day appeared before the Subscriber a Justice of the Peace in & for the said County & made Oath that he did on the 17th day of April 1795 deliver a true Copy of the Declaration in Ejectment hereunto annex'd to David Hunter (who as the said Smith has been informed Claims Title to the land therein mention'd[)] & at the same time informed him that it was a Declaration in Ejectment and that unless he appeared on the first day of the next Term of the Court of the United States for the Middle Circuit in the District of Virginia to be holden in the City of Richmond in May next by some Attorney of the said Court & did then and there by Rule of Court cause himself to be made Defendant that Judgment would be entered and he would be turn'd out of possession. Given under my hand the 26th day of the Month & year above mention'd.

GEO: F: NORTON[11]

Copy, Fairfax v. Hunter, U.S. Circuit Court, Ended Cases (Restored), 1795, Vi. The text presented here is a composite of two incomplete copies of the declaration in the case papers (see nn. 1, 7). Copies of declaration also in U.S. Cir. Ct., Va., Rec. Bk. III, 346–48; Hunter v. Fairfax's Lessee, Record on Appeal, 1–3, Appellate Case File No. 29, RG 267, DNA. Date derived from internal evidence.

1. The text from here through JM's name is taken from a clerk's copy of the record. Introductory words between the statement of venue and the beginning of the text of the declaration have been omitted.

2. In addition to Goodtitle and Plunderer, who were descendants of the notorious John Doe and Richard Roe, the names of the fictitious parties appearing in declarations in JM's ejectment cases included plaintiffs Aminidab Seekright, Simon Seekright, and Timothy Trititle and defendants Ferdinando Dreadnought, Timothy Thrustout, and Nicholas Notitle.

3. The date of the demise, or conveyance of an estate for a term of years or for life, had to be laid after the time the real plaintiff's title accrued. The declaration was in error in describing the tract of land in dispute as 788 acres in Shenandoah County. This ejectment concerned 400 acres in Hampshire County (see Doc. III, n. 15). The Shenandoah land was in fact contested in Hunter's ejectment action in the Winchester District Court. JM no doubt

consulted the Winchester proceedings in preparing his case and had the Shenandoah tract in mind when drawing his declaration. This error was of no consequence, however, for by the Virginia statute of jeofails no exception could be made to the declaration after issue was joined on the title (H. St. G. Tucker, *Commentaries on Va. Laws*, II, Bk. 3, 173–74; Fairfax's Devisee v. Hunter's Lessee, declaration [copy], Appellate Case File No. 456; Hening, *Statutes*, XIII, 37).

4. Since judgment was technically for the remaining years of the lease, the term laid should be sufficient to cover the probable determination of the suit. If the lease did expire before judgment—as happened in the Winchester case that was not decided on appeal until 1810—the court would allow a motion to enlarge the term (H. St. G. Tucker, *Commentaries on Va. Laws*, II, Bk. 3, 174; Hunter v. Fairfax's Devisee, 1 Munf. 238).

5. The date of the ouster was supposed to be after the date of the lease (H. St. G. Tucker, *Commentaries on Va. Laws*, II, Bk. 3, 174).

6. In the blank space the defendant's counsel would enter the plea of "not guilty" and sign his name after the declaration was returned and filed in court (see Doc. II, n. 3).

7. The remainder of the text is taken from what appears to be the original declaration.

8. This "letter" constitutes the required notice that was to be served upon either the person who claimed title or the one who had actual possession of the premises. In this case copies of the declaration were served upon Hunter's tenant, Robert Bodkins, as well as upon Hunter himself. The landlord had a right to be made defendant in order to prevent collusion between his tenant and the real plaintiff (Blackstone, *Commentaries*, III, 204).

9. Except for the signature of the magistrate, this affidavit is in the same hand as the notice from the casual ejector. In declarations in ejectment an affidavit of service was required (Robinson, *Practice*, I, 452).

10. The body of this affidavit is in a different hand.

11. George Flowerdewe Norton (b. 1751) was the third son of merchant John Norton and his wife Courtenay. Educated in England, he was made a partner in the firm of John Norton & Sons in 1774. He later settled in Frederick County, marrying Sarah Thruston, daughter of Charles Mynn Thruston of Winchester, in 1782 (Francis Norton Mason, ed., *John Norton & Sons: Merchants of London and Virginia* [Richmond, 1937], 515–16).

II. Common Rule
30 May 1795

David Hunter[1] On his Motion is admitted Defendant in this suit in the room of the said plunderer and thereupon by William C: Williams[2] his Attorney comes and defends the force and Injury, when

&c. pleads the general Issue, confesses the Lease, Entry and Ouster in the Declaration supposed and agrees to insist on the Title only at Trial.[3]

Copy, U.S. Circuit Court, Va., Record Book III, 348, Vi. Other copies in U.S. Cir. Ct., Va., Ord. Bk. I, 517; Hunter v. Fairfax's Lessee, Record on Appeal, 3.

1. On 22 May 1795, the first day of the term, JM filed the declaration, notice, and affidavits showing service. Hunter not appearing on that day, the court issued a conditional order stating that judgment would be confirmed against him if he failed to appear at the next term (U.S. Cir. Ct., Va., Ord. Bk. I, 462).

2. William C. Williams (1768–1817) was the fourth of eight children born to William Williams and Lucy Clayton of Culpeper County. He later settled in Woodstock in Shenandoah County and represented that county in the House of Delegates in 1789. Williams also served as Hunter's counsel at the trial of the Winchester case in 1794 and in the appeal in 1810 (Green, *Notes on Culpeper County*, pt. 1, 108; Cartmell, *Shenandoah Valley Pioneers*, 501–3; Swem and Williams, *Register*, 446; *Richmond Enquirer*, 21 Oct. 1817; John W. Wayland, *A History of Shenandoah County Virginia* [Strasburg, Va., 1927], 658–59).

3. The real defendant in ejectment was required to enter into a rule of the court, known as the "common rule," by which he pleaded the general issue in trespass ("not guilty"); admitted the three "facts" of lease, entry, and ouster; and agreed to join issue on the title only. At this point in the proceedings the name of the real defendant was inserted in place of the fictional one in the declaration (Blackstone, *Commentaries*, III, 203–4).

III. Case Agreed

30 May 1795

Denny Fairfax
vs.
David Hunter } in ejectment

We agree that the following case shall be considerd & adjudg'd in like manner as if the same were a special verdict.[1]

1st. We agree that the act of the General assembly of Virginia entitled "an act for confirming & better securing the titles to land in the northern neck held under the right honorable Thomas Lord Fairfax Baron of Cameron in that part of Great Britain called Scotland," truely recites the several grants or charters which were made by the King of Great Britain to the predecessors or ancestors of the late

Thomas Lord Fairfax of & concerning that part of the territory of the then colony now commonwealth of Virginia call'd & known by the name of the northern neck, and that all the estates rights & authorities thereby granted to them of & concerning the said northern neck were & became *lawfully* vested in the said Thomas Lord Fairfax & his heirs as in the said recited grants or charters & in the said act of Assembly is set forth previous to the year 1736 & remaind vested in him & in his possession until the time of his death, which act is in the words following to wit, "Whereas the late King Charles the second["] &c.[2]

2d We agree that the said act of Assembly shall operate to every intent & purpose in ascertaining the title of the said Thomas Lord Fairfax in like manner as if the Grants or charters themselves which are therein recited were fild as exhibits in the cause & were agreed in this case.

3d. We agree that in the year 1748 the act of General Assembly entitled, "an act for confirming the grants made by his Majesty within the bounds of the northern neck as they are now establishd["] was passd, which act is in the words following to wit "Whereas in the late dispute["] &c.[3]

4th. We agree that the said Thomas Lord Fairfax proprietor of the said territory calld the Northern neck, in the year 1748 opend & kept & conducted at his own expence an office within the said Northern neck for granting & conveying what he describd & calld the waste & ungranted lands therein upon certain terms & according to certain rules by him establishd & publishd, & that such of the aforesaid lands as were granted & convey'd by him in fee, were granted & convey'd in parcels in the following form to wit

The Right Honorable Thomas Lord Fairfax &c.[4]

and that the said grants & conveyances in fee were transcribd & enterd in books kept by him for that purpose in the said office by his own clerks or agent & were uniformly alike except as to grants & conveyances of lotts in places laid off & designd for towns. That the said Thomas Lord Fairfax kept the said office open for the purposes aforesaid from the year 1748 till the time of his death which happend in the month of December in the year 1781, during all which time as well as prior thereto from the time he became proprietor of the northern neck as aforesaid he exercis'd the right of granting & conveying in fee simple the lands calld waste & ungranted as aforesaid within the said Northern neck as proprietor thereof upon the rents conditions & reservations containd in the grants & conveyances made by him, during which time the rents reservd by him were paid to him as they annually accrued & he also exercisd the right of leasing for term of lives & for years reserving annual rents parcels of the said lands calld by him waste & ungranted which rents were also paid as they became due;[5] We agree that the said Thomas Lord Fairfax was at the time of his death & for many years before had been a citizen & inhabitant of the Commonwealth of Virginia capable of holding lands within the same & of transmitting them by devise or otherwise.

[5th.][6] We agree that Thomas Lord Fairfax, never paid or was Charged with any taxes or duties on the lands, which were claimed by him as Proprietor of the Northern Neck, from the year 177   till the time of his death whereof the lands in the declaration mentioned are a part; Nor hath Denny Fairfax the Lessor of the Plaintiff been charged with or paid any from the death of Thomas Lord Fairfax.[7]

[6th.] We agree that all other lands in the Northern Neck[8] as well those granted out by Lord Fairfax to the people as those which he granted to Thomas B. Martin and were reconveyed by him to Lord Fairfax, were subject to and did pay a tax.[9]

7th.[10] We agree that the said Thomas Lord Fairfax duly made & publishd his last will & testament in writing which will & the probate thereof are in the words & figures following to wit In the name of God &c.[11]

And that the Lessor of the Plaintiff Denny Fairfax is the same person mentiond in the said will by the description & name of "the reverend Denny Martin" and that he obtaind the name of Denny Fairfax & the Fairfax coat of arms in conformity with the directions of the said will.[12]

8th We agree that the lands in the declaration mentiond are a part of the lands known by the name of the northern neck of Virginia[13] and are also the same lands containd in a patent granted to David Hunter the defendant by   the Governor of Virginia in the words following to wit.[14]

And are of the value of two thousand dollars current money of Virginia; And the lands in the declaration mentiond are a part of the lands calld & describd as waste & ungranted within the said Northern neck by the said Thomas Lord Fairfax as aforesaid.[15]

9th. We agree that Thomas Lord Fairfax died seizd in fee of sundry tracts of land in the county of Frederick & other counties in the said Northern neck containing all together three hundred thousand acres which had been granted & conveyd by him to Thomas Bryan Martin in fee upon the same terms & in the same form of other lands conveyd & granted by him in fee as aforesaid which lands were soon thereafter reconveyd by the same Thomas Bryan Martin unto him in fee.[16]

10th. We agree that the lessor of the plaintiff was born in England a subject of the King of Great Britain in the year 1750,[17] is now & ever since his birth hath been subject to the said King & hath always inhabited within England as well during the late war between Great Britain & America which was ended by the peace made in the year 1783 as in all other times & that the said Denny Fairfax formerly Denny Martin the lessor of the plaintiff hath not made himself a citizen of the United States of America or of any of them by taking the oath of citizenship requird by any law of the said United States or of any one of them & hath never been in any of the said United States but always hath resided in England aforesaid where he now remains.

[11th.][18] We agree that a treaty of peace was finally made & concluded in the year 1783 between Great Britain & the United States of America in the words following to wit, It having pleasd &c.[19]

[12th.] We agree the several acts of the General Assembly of Virginia following to wit, one entitled an act for establishing a land office & ascertaining the terms & manner of granting waste & unappropriated lands, which act is in these words to wit, Whereas &c.[20]
Another entitled an act declaring tenants of lands or slaves in tail to hold the same in fee simple which act is in these words to wit "Whereas["] &c.[21]
Another passd in the year 1784 entitled "an act respecting future confiscations" in the words following to wit Whereas &c.[22]
Another passd in the year 1785 entitled an act for safe keeping of the land papers of the northern neck in the registers office which is in the words following to wit Whereas &c.[23]
Another passd in the year 1779 entitled an act declaring who shall be deemd citizens of this Commonwealth which is in the words following to wit Be it enacted &c.[24]
Another passd in the year 1783 entitled an act for the admission of emigrants & declaring their rights to citizenship in these words to wit, Whereas &c.[25]
Another passd in the year 1782 entitled an act concerning surveyors which act is in these words Whereas &c.[26]

[13th.] We agree another act passd in the year 1785 entitled an act concerning Escheators in these words to wit Be it enacted &c.[27]
And another pass'd in the year 1785 entitled an act to extend the operation of an act entitled an act concerning Escheators to the several counties in the northern neck in these words Whereas &c.[28]
We agree that the land in the declaration of ejectment mentiond hath not been escheated & siezd into the hands of the Commonwealth persuant to the two acts of Assembly last mentioned or either of them, & that no inquest of office of escheat hath been taken of it concerning the said lands.[29]

[14th.] We agree that the 24th. section of the act passd in the year 1782 entitled an act to amend & reduce the several acts of Assembly for ascertaining certain taxes & duties & for establishing a permanent revenue into one act is in the words following to wit And whereas no provision &c.[30]

[15th.] We agree that the defendent is a citizen of Virginia & always has been & that he enterd into the lands in the declaration of ejectment mentiond by virtue of the patent herein before mentiond purporting to be a grant of the said lands to him by the Governor of Virginia persuant to the acts above recited & that he was possessd thereof prior to this suit.

[16th.] We agree the lease entry & ouster in the declaration mentiond & if upon the whole matter the law be for the plaintiff then we agree that Judgement be renderd for him for his term yet to come in the lands in the declaration mentiond and one penny damages otherwise we agree that judgement be renderd for the defendent.

J Marshall for plf.
Wm C Williams for Def

ADS, Fairfax v. Hunter, U.S. Circuit Court, Ended Cases (Restored), 1795, Vi. Entirely in JM's hand except for points No. 5 and 6 and signature of opposing attorney. Copies in U.S. Cir. Ct., Va., Ord. Bk. I, 517–22; Rec. Bk. III, 348–57. JM's original and copies in order book and record book omit full texts of the various documents referred to. These are reproduced in their entirety in Hunter v. Fairfax's Lessee, Record on Appeal, 3–82.

1. A case agreed was like a special verdict except that in the former the parties agreed on all the facts without the intervention of a jury (see Case No. 3, editorial note). The parties had followed the same procedure in Hunter v. Fairfax, the ejectment brought in the Winchester District Court in 1791 and then pending before the Court of Appeals. JM probably consulted the record of this case when drawing up this statement of facts, for the two agreed cases are virtually identical. When JM's brother several years later was involved in an ejectment for some Winchester lots, JM advised him to consult these statements (Hunter v. Fairfax's Devisee, 1 Munf. 219–22; JM to James M. Marshall, 3 Apr. 1799 [*PJM*, IV, 9]; Marshall v. Conrad, 5 Call 364 [1805]).

2. JM omitted the end quotation marks here and elsewhere in the MS. The editors have supplied them within brackets. The act is in Hening, *Statutes*, IV, 514–23. The full text is in Hunter v. Fairfax's Lessee, Record on Appeal, 3–17. This act recited three letters patent, the first two by Charles II and the third by James II, whereby the region between the Potomac and Rappahannock was granted to Lord Culpeper. It also stated that Thomas, Lord Fairfax, as heir at law of Lord Culpeper had become the sole proprietor of this territory. JM wanted this act to be on the record as proof that title to the Northern Neck was vested in Denny Fairfax's uncle. At the trial and appeals of the state case, Hunter's counsel contended that the nature of Fairfax's title

gave him only a seignorial right to grant lands and receive quitrents, not an absolute and unconditional estate of inheritance. The proprietor's right, according to this argument, was a delegation of part of the sovereign power of the Crown; as such it devolved upon the commonwealth at the time of the Revolution. In their construction of the several letters patent, however, the judges were satisfied that Lord Fairfax had an absolute estate in the soil. Even Judge Roane was willing to concede the point. The same argument was no doubt advanced in the trial of this case.

3. Hening, *Statutes*, VI, 198–99; also in Hunter v. Fairfax's Lessee, Record on Appeal, 17–19. By this act certain Crown grants made when the Northern Neck boundaries were unsettled, and subsequently proved to be within those boundaries, were confirmed by Lord Fairfax's express consent. Lord Fairfax's refusal, in consequence of this act, to issue patents to Joist Hite and his associates precipitated the protracted lawsuit between those parties (*PJM*, I, 150–64; Case No. 4).

4. At this point there is reproduced in Hunter v. Fairfax's Lessee, Record on Appeal, 19–21, a sample Northern Neck patent. This sample patent is also in the suit papers. For a discussion of the Northern Neck grants with examples of the various forms of patents, see Fairfax Harrison, *Virginia Land Grants: A Study of Conveyancing in Relation to Colonial Politics* (Richmond, 1925), 61–121.

5. For a description of the method of granting and leasing lands in the proprietary, see Groome, *Fauquier During the Proprietorship*, 73–77.

6. Nos. 5 and 6 were written in an unknown hand on a separate sheet without any number designation. They were inserted at this point in the several transcriptions of the case agreed.

7. The following passage has been heavily deleted: "And that it ever hath been [conceived?], that such lands (so being those in the declaration mentioned are a part) were not liable or subject to the payment of any taxes."

8. The following words have been canceled: "were subject to and did pay a tax from the said year 177 till the."

9. The reference in Nos. 5 and 6 is to the land tax laid in the revenue act of Oct. 1777 (Hening, *Statutes*, IX, 349–68). The parties agreed that this tax applied to the granted lands, including the Fairfax manor lands, but not to the ungranted lands.

10. Someone (JM?) renumbered this and the next four agreed facts after Nos. 5 and 6 were inserted.

11. A certified copy of the will is in the suit papers and is entered in Hunter v. Fairfax's Lessee, Record on Appeal, 23–29. For a printed version, see Cartmell, *Shenandoah Valley Pioneers*, 134–35.

12. The will directed Denny Martin to take on the name of Fairfax by means of an act of Parliament. Although he assumed the name by royal license in Aug. 1782, Denny Fairfax did not comply with the strict terms of the will until 1797, when at JM's urging he procured a parliamentary act authorizing him to bear the Fairfax name and coat of arms (Fairfax Harrison, *The Proprietors of the Northern Neck: Chapters of Culpeper Genealogy* [Richmond, 1926], 142–43).

13. The following passage has been deleted: "& are a part of the lands

known by the name of the Northern Neck of V vested in Thomas Lord Fairfax according ["by virtue of" interlined above "according"] to the grants or charters recited in the act entitled 'an act for confirming & better securing the titles to land in the northern neck held under the right Honorable Thomas Lord Fairfax Baron of Cameron in that part of Great Britain call'd Scotland,' and are a part of the lands devisd by the said Thomas Lord Fairfax to the said Denny Fairfax the lessor of the plaintiff."

14. A copy of the grant is in the suit papers and is reproduced in Hunter v. Fairfax's Lessee, Record on Appeal, 29–31.

15. This patent, signed by Lt. Gov. James Wood on 29 Nov. 1794, was for 400 acres in Hampshire County. It was one of four grants of Hampshire lands to Hunter issued on this date by virtue of warrants purchased in Jan. 1788 and surveys made in Apr. 1794 (Northern Neck Grants, 1792–95, 424–29). In his declaration JM erroneously described the tract as 788 acres in Shenandoah County (Doc. I, n. 3).

16. Lord Fairfax employed the method of conveyance and reconveyance to secure his title to the so-called manor lands as his private property. Hunter's counsel in the 1813 Supreme Court case argued that Fairfax's process of acquiring the manor lands showed that he himself regarded his title to the ungranted lands as seignorial rather than absolute (Fairfax's Devisee v. Hunter's Lessee, 7 Cranch 615–16). Thomas Bryan Martin (1731–1798), brother of Denny Martin Fairfax, joined his uncle in Virginia in 1751 and took charge of the proprietary land office when it was established at Greenway Court (near Winchester) in 1762. According to the calculations of one Northern Neck historian, the total acreage of the Fairfax manors was about 220,000 rather than 300,000 (Harrison, *Proprietors of the Northern Neck*, 143–45; Groome, *Fauquier During the Proprietorship*, 74–77).

17. JM repeated the error in the case agreed that was made in the Winchester case. Denny Martin was actually born in 1725; he took his B.A. at University College, Oxford, in 1748 and his M.A. in 1751. He subsequently took holy orders and became parson of Loose Parish, Kent. He died in 1800 (1 Munf. 221; Harrison, *Proprietors of the Northern Neck*, 141–43).

18. Whoever renumbered the statement of facts (possibly JM) neglected to change the numbers on the last five points. The editors have accordingly altered JM's original numbering ("9th," "10th.," etc.) for the sake of clarity.

19. The entire text of the treaty is entered in Hunter v. Fairfax's Lessee, Record on Appeal, 32–41. For the purposes of this case the key article was the sixth, which stipulated that there should be no further confiscations made against any person or persons "for, or by reason of the part which he or they may have taken in the present war."

20. Hening, *Statutes*, X, 50–65; reproduced in Hunter v. Fairfax's Lessee, Record on Appeal, 41–65.

21. Hening, *Statutes*, IX, 226–27; Hunter v. Fairfax's Lessee, Record on Appeal, 66–67. This was the famous statute abolishing entails, drawn by Jefferson.

22. Hening, *Statutes*, XI, 446; Hunter v. Fairfax's Lessee, Record on Appeal, 67. This act was passed in conformity with the sixth article of the peace treaty (see n. 19). The point at issue with regard to the treaty was whether its

prohibition against future confiscations extended to estates that were liable to escheat by virtue of the ordinary laws of alienage. Hunter's counsel contended that the treaty stipulation and the act of the state passed in consequence of it applied only to confiscations that were intended as punishments of persons for their part taken during the war. The treaty had "nothing to do with the laws of alienage," according to Judge Roane, who upheld Hunter's claim in the state Court of Appeals. Fairfax's lawyers argued for a broad construction of the term "confiscation," so as to embrace every case of forfeiture. Conceding that lands acquired by an alien were liable to forfeiture, they maintained that Denny Fairfax "became an alien by reason of the part he took in the war," so that escheat proceedings against his estate would amount to a confiscation within the meaning of the treaty (Hunter v. Fairfax's Devisee, 1 Munf. 226; Fairfax's Devisee v. Hunter's Lessee, 7 Cranch 614–17).

23. Hening, *Statutes*, XII, 111–13; Hunter v. Fairfax's Lessee, Record on Appeal, 67–70. This act provided for the transfer of the Northern Neck land records to the state land office in Richmond; subjected the unappropriated lands in that region to the same regulations as those applying to the other unappropriated lands belonging to the state; and exonerated Northern Neck landholders from the payment of composition money and quitrents. The disputed point concerning this act, under which David Hunter obtained his patent, was whether it vested possession of the Northern Neck in the commonwealth. On behalf of Hunter there were two lines of argument: (1) that this act was the equivalent of a formal inquest of office under escheat proceedings and that it was unaffected by treaty, or (2) admitting the application of the treaty, that the title of the commonwealth to these lands had been perfected before the treaty and that the 1785 act was therefore not a confiscation of an estate then belonging to a British subject. The case for Fairfax rested principally on the treaty of peace, and his counsel were concerned to show that the Fairfax estate had not escheated to the state, either by an inquest of office or by some legislative act, before the treaty was ratified. They were evidently willing to concede that the 1785 act, but for the bar set up by the treaty, vested title to the Northern Neck in the commonwealth.

In his opinion on the 1813 case, however, Judge Story placed Fairfax's title within the protection of the Jay Treaty of 1794 rather than the 1783 treaty. He construed the various Virginia acts, including that of 1785, as conferring "a title inchoate and imperfect; to be consummated by an actual entry under an inquest of office, or its equivalent, a suit and judgment at law by the grantee." The 1794 treaty provided that British subjects then holding lands in the U.S. should continue to enjoy possession. Story concluded that Fairfax's title was fully protected under the compact since no steps had been taken to perfect the title before then. On this point see the comments of Judges Roane and Fleming in Hunter v. Fairfax's Devisee, 1 Munf. 228–31, 234–37; and those of Lee and Jones (for Fairfax), Harper (for Hunter), and Judge Story in Fairfax's Devisee v. Hunter's Lessee, 7 Cranch 612–14, 616, 623–27 (quotation at 626). Writing to his brother years later, JM remarked: "The case of Hunter & Fairfax is very absurdly put on the treaty of 94" (JM to James M. Marshall, 9 July 1822, Bixby Collection, MoSW).

24. Hening, *Statutes*, X, 129–30; Hunter v. Fairfax's Lessee, Record on Appeal, 70–73. This act was placed on the record by Hunter's counsel to show that Denny Fairfax was an alien and therefore by the common law incapable of holding lands in the commonwealth. A minor point offered on behalf of Denny Fairfax was that as an "antenatus" (that is, born under a common allegiance before the War of Independence), he should continue to be able to hold lands in Virginia as if he were a citizen. In his opinion delivered at the Winchester District Court in 1794, however, Judge Tucker maintained that the legislative act here cited effectively repealed this principle. The fundamental issue was whether the treaty of peace cured the defect of alienage so far as it operated on British subjects born before the Revolution (Hunter v. Fairfax, 22 Apr. 1794, Casebook, Tucker-Coleman Papers, ViW). Tucker later conducted a full investigation of the question of an alien's right to purchase and hold lands (*Blackstone's Commentaries*, II, App., Note C, 53–65).

25. Hening, *Statutes*, XI, 322–24; Hunter v. Fairfax's Lessee, Record on Appeal, 73–75. This act repealed the 1779 citizenship act, though according to Judge Tucker this repeal did not affect the question of Fairfax's alienage (see Tucker citations, n. 24).

26. Hening, *Statutes*, XI, 159–60; Hunter v. Fairfax's Lessee, Record on Appeal, 75–77. This act declared that all entries made with surveyors in Northern Neck counties and returned to the late proprietor's office should be "held, deemed, and taken, as good and valid in law as those heretofore made under the direction of the said Thomas Lord Fairfax, until some mode shall be taken up and adopted by the general assembly concerning the territory of the Northern Neck." Hunter's counsel contended that this law and another enacted at the same session sequestering the Northern Neck quitrents (see n. 23) amounted to a legislative inquest of office by which the vacant lands of the Northern Neck had escheated to the commonwealth prior to the treaty of 1783. For opposing constructions of these acts, see Hunter v. Fairfax's Devisee, 1 Munf. 228–31, 234–35; Fairfax's Devisee v. Hunter's Lessee, 7 Cranch 614, 623–24.

27. Hening, *Statutes*, XII, 158–60; Hunter v. Fairfax's Lessee, Record on Appeal, 77–80. This citation to the 1785 act appears to be an error. As Judge Fleming pointed out, counsel probably meant the 1779 act concerning escheators, which provided for the appointment of such officers in every county except those counties of the Northern Neck. The 1785 act directed the appointment of escheators in every county, but another 1785 act extended the operation of the 1779 act concerning escheators to the Northern Neck (see n. 28). By extending the operation of the 1779 act to the Northern Neck, the legislature rendered the 1785 act superfluous, and it was thereby repealed in 1786 (Hunter v. Fairfax's Devisee, 1 Munf. 233; Hening, *Statutes*, X, 115–17; XII, 117, 411).

28. Hening, *Statutes*, XII, 117; Hunter v. Fairfax's Lessee, Record on Appeal, 80–81.

29. Judge Tucker in 1794, Judge Fleming in 1810, and Judge Story in 1813 were of opinion that the commonwealth could not divest Denny Fairfax of his title to the Northern Neck except by a formal inquest of office. They

agreed that the legislature could have effected this by a special act, but insisted that such an act should be clear and explicit if its purpose was to repeal the common law procedure of escheat by inquest of office. Tucker elaborately distinguished between two kinds of escheat. One kind was equivalent to confiscation or forfeiture such as might occur in wartime. In 1779, for example, the assembly passed an act concerning escheats and forfeitures from British subjects, vesting in the commonwealth all British property within its boundaries. Under this act, Tucker observed, no inquest of office was necessary to establish the commonwealth's title to the property, and escheat proceedings were held merely to designate and place on the record the particular parcels of land confiscated. This act did not apply to Denny Fairfax, however, since he acquired his property after its passage. His case therefore fell into the second category of escheats, those resulting when lands descended upon aliens. In such cases, said Tucker, a solemn inquest of office was absolutely necessary to vest title in the commonwealth (Hunter v. Fairfax, 22 Apr. 1794, Casebook, Tucker-Coleman Papers, ViW; Hunter v. Fairfax's Devisee, 1 Munf. 233–34; Fairfax's Devisee v. Hunter's Lessee, 7 Cranch 620–22; Tucker, *Blackstone's Commentaries*, II, App., Note C, 54–60).

30. Hening, *Statutes*, XI, 128; Hunter v. Fairfax's Lessee, Record on Appeal, 81–82. This section of the 1782 revenue act sequestered in the hands of the landholders the quitrents then due "until the right of descent shall be more fully ascertained, and the general assembly shall make final provision thereon." Quitrents becoming due thereafter were to be paid into the state treasury. On the significance of this act, see n. 26 and the references cited there.

IV. Judgment
6 June 1795

The Court after mature consideration of the whole matter contained in the Case agreed in lieu of a Special Verdict in this Cause are of opinion that the Law is for the Plt. Therefore It is considered by the Court, that the Plt. recover against the Defendant his Term yet to come of and in the Messuage and Lands with the Appurtenances in the declaration mentioned and one penny damages besides his Costs by him about his suit in this behalf expended.[1] And the said Defendant may be taken &c., Whereupon the Plt: prays the Writ to the Marshal of the said District to be directed to cause him to have his Possession of his Term aforesaid yet to come &c.[2] And to him it is granted returnable here &c.

Copy, U.S. Circuit Court, Va., Record Book III, 357, Vi. Other copies in U.S. Cir. Ct., Va., Ord. Bk. I, 536–37; Hunter v. Fairfax's Lessee, Record on Appeal, 82–83.

1. In keeping with the fiction, judgment in ejectment for the plaintiff was the recovery of his lease. The basis for the judgment was that Goodtitle's lessor, Denny Fairfax, had a better title to the land than did David Hunter. Damages were nominal because the principal question was the title. To recover the profits of the land during the defendant's adverse possession, one had to bring a separate action in trespass for "mesne profits" (Blackstone, *Commentaries*, III, 205).

2. This was the writ of *habere facias possessionem* ("that you cause to have possession"). For an example, see Conway Robinson, *Forms Adapted to the Practice in Virginia*, I (Richmond, 1841), 240.

V. Petition for Writ of Error
ca. 22 November 1795

To the Honorable the Chief Justice and the associate Judges of the United States David Hunter petitions & shews to your honors[1]

That George Goodtitle Lessee of Denny Fairfax impleaded your Petitioner in the Circuit Court of the United States in the District of Virginia in a certain action of Ejectment, and in that Court obtained a Judgment against your Petitioner, for his term unexpired & to come in the Lands in his Declaration in the said Court exhibitd as will appear by the record hereto annexed; which Lands by the said Records, are shewn to be of the value of Two thousand Dollars.[2] Your petitioner is advised that in the said Record and in the Judgment rendered thereon, there is manifest error, in this, that Judgment on the declaration & pleadings in the Record set forth, ought to have been for the Defendant your petitioner, whereas the same was rendered for the plaintiff, the Lessee of the said Denny Fairfax. Your Petitioner therefore prays that a Writ of Error may issue from this Honorable Court to bring the Record of the proceedings aforesaid before your Honors: that the said proceedings may be review'd by your Honors—the judgment of the Circuit Court thereupon be reversed & annulled, or such other Judgment rendered thereupon as to your Honors shall seem right. And Your Petr. will pray &c.

I the undersigned Counsel practising in the Supreme Court of the United States, do certify the Justices to whom the foregoing petition is directed, that in my opinion the judgment thereby pray'd to be review'd is erroneous, & that the same ought to be reversed.

Alex Campbell

Let[3] a Writ of Error issue, pursuant to the above Petition: John Marshall Esquire, of Counsel for the Defendant in Error, personally appearing before me, and waiving any Security for Costs.

JA. IREDELL, one of the Associate Justices of the Supreme Court of the United States.

ADS, Hunter v. Fairfax's Lessee, Record on Appeal, Appellate Case File No. 29, RG 267, DNA. Written and signed by Alexander Campbell as counsel for Hunter. Endorsement at foot of petition in hand of James Iredell. Date assigned refers to first day of term of federal circuit court sitting in Richmond. Petition filed some time during the Nov. 1795 term, as indicated by Iredell's endorsement. Iredell was Supreme Court justice assigned to Virginia circuit for that term.

1. Appellate procedure in the federal courts was outlined in the Judiciary Act of 1789, sec. 22. That act said little about the petition for a writ of error, but this was standard practice in England and the American states. The procedure followed here was similar to that recited in the Virginia statute of 1788 establishing district courts. The party intending to apply for a writ of error first obtained a transcript of the record and then procured an attorney practicing in the appellate court—in this case Alexander Campbell—to certify that there was sufficient error for reversal (*U.S. Statutes at Large*, I, 84; Hening, *Statutes*, XII, 753–54; Goebel, *Antecedents and Beginnings*, 478–79, 666–72). The appellate case file consisted of the petition, the writ of error, a transcript of the record, and a citation to the adverse party summoning him to appear at the next session of the Supreme Court. Although no citation has been found in the present case file, the last page of the transcript of the record contains the following endorsement in JM's hand: "I acknowledge service of the citation in this case according to law/ J Marshall atty. for deft. in error" (Hunter v. Fairfax's Lessee, Record on Appeal, 83).

2. There was a minimum monetary limitation of $2,000 in appeals to the Supreme Court in cases that had been brought up to the circuit courts on appeal from the district court. This restriction, however, apparently did not apply to those cases—such as the present one—that were brought originally in the circuit court (*U.S. Statutes at Large*, I, 84; Goebel, *Antecedents and Beginnings*, 479).

3. This endorsement is in Iredell's hand.

VI. Petition for Postponement
22 January 1796

To the Honourable the Judges of the Supreme Court of the United States.

The Petition of David Hunter of the County of Berkeley in the State of Virginia Humbly Sheweth.

That a suit was lately Instituted in the Circuit Court of the united States for the District of Virginia by Denny Fairfax of Great Brittain as Devisee of the late Lord Fairfax proprietor of the Northern neck of Virginia against your Petitioner to try his Title to the unappropriated Lands of the Northern neck for disposing of which the Legislature of Virginia had in the year 1785 opened a Land office your Petitioner having obtained a Grant according to the Laws of the state for a Tract of Land within the said northern neck. This suit was an Ejectment for the recovery thereof. Your petitioner was entered Defendant & Council were employed by the executive of this State to argue the cause on behalf of the State & your petitioner hath been informed that the said cause was argued before the said Court in the month of June last & Judgment given in favour of the said Denny Fairfax. That by the direction of the executive an appeal was entered to the supreme Court of the United States before your Honours & where the said cause is now depending. Your Petitioner was informed that council woud be sent by the executive to argue the cause at the ensuing Term so that he hath given himself no concern in the business. Your petitioner hath lately been further informed that the Governor of this Commonwealth communicated to the General Assembly at their last Session the circumstances of this case & advised sending on council to argue it on behalf of the Commonwealth, which your petitioner made no doubt but woud be done. But your petitioner is now informed that the House of Delegates conceiving that the right of this commonwealth to the unappropriated Lands within the same & the validity of the Laws thereof for disposing of the same were not properly cognizable in the Courts of the united States declined giving any directions respecting the said suit[1]—and Your petitioner for the reasons aforesaid is entirely unprepared for prosecuting the said Appeal at the ensuing Term should he be advised to do so upon consulting the Governor & Council of this Commonwealth,[2] thereupon. Your Petitioner Therefore Humbly Prays that the said cause may stand over & the argument thereof be postponed untill the next Term, and your petitioner will pray &c.[3]

David Hunter,
January 22nd. 1796.

ADS, Hunter v. Fairfax's Lessee, Record on Appeal, 87–88, Appellate Case File No. 29, RG 267, DNA. Endorsed by a clerk: "filed 2 Feby. 1796."

1. Hunter was referring to a resolution of the Committee of the Whole presented to the House of Delegates on 25 Dec. 1795: "*Resolved*, That though this House does not admit, but most unequivocally denies the authority of the federal courts to decide cases affecting titles to lands under the grants of this commonwealth to the citizens thereof, and also denies all responsibility founded upon any decision in such cases, yet that the governor with the advice of council be empowered to employ counsel for the purpose of prosecuting the writ of error of David Hunter and others, against the representatives of Lord Fairfax, in the supreme federal court; and that he be authorized to draw by warrant from the public treasury as much money as will pay the expence of the same." The resolution was tabled after a third reading (*JHDV*, Oct. 1795, 129). Although it was not adopted, this resolution foreshadowed the bitter struggle between the Virginia Court of Appeals and the Supreme Court over the latter's jurisdiction in the appeal of the ejectment heard in the state court.

2. At the time he wrote this petition, Hunter may not have received a letter from Virginia governor Brooke, dated 19 Jan. 1796, informing him that the executive council declined to act further in this business, "as it has been agitated in the legislature and a decision on it postponed until their next meeting" (Executive Letterbook, Vi). In other words, the compromise adopted at the next session was already in the works.

3. The case was ordered to be continued on 14 Mar. 1796, the last day of the term. Writing to his wife at the beginning of the term, JM predicted the postponement: "My own cause I greatly fear will not be taken up & I shall be under the very disagreeable necessity of returning without any decision" (Dockets of the Supreme Court of the U.S., Bk. A, 26; JM to Mary W. Marshall, 3 Feb. 1796 [*PJM*, III, 3–4]).

VII. Writ of Error
24 January 1796

United States &c.

[SEAL] The President of the United States to the Judges of the Circuit Court holden in and for the District of Virginia Greeting: Because that in the record and process and also in the Rendering of Judgment in a Suit before you or some of you, between George Goodtitle lessee of Denny Fairfax plaintiff and David Hunter Defendant of a plea of Ejectment, a manifest error has intervened, to the great Damage of the said David Hunter as in his Complaint has been stated; And as it is just and proper that the error, if any there be should be corrected in due manner, and that full and speedy Justice should be done to the parties aforesaid, in this behalf, you are hereby commanded, that if Judgment thereof be given, then under your Seal, you do distinctly and openly send the Record and process in the Suit aforesaid, with all things concerning them and this Writ, so that you have the same before the Chief Justice and the Associate Justices of the Supreme Court of the United States on the first Monday of February next, at Philadelphia, being the present Seat of the National Government, that the record and process aforesaid, being inspected, they may cause to be done thereupon what of right ought to be done. Witness the Honourable John Rutledge Esquire,[1] Chief Justice of the said Supreme Court, at Philadelphia aforesaid, this twenty fourth day of January in the year of Our Lord One thousand seven hundred and Ninety six and of the Independence of the United States the twentieth.[2]

WILLIAM MARSHALL Clk

Allowed by
JAMES IREDELL Esqr.

ADS, Hunter v. Fairfax's Lessee, Record on Appeal, Appellate Case File No. 29, RG 267, DNA. Writ originally drawn with blank spaces for names of the parties and date, which were inserted at a later time.

1. A month earlier the Senate had refused to confirm Rutledge's appointment as chief justice. Writs continued to issue in his name until a successor was chosen (Charles Warren, *The Supreme Court in United States History*, I [rev. ed.; Boston, 1926], 127–39).

2. The writ of error issued before Hunter's petition for postponement had been received (Doc. VI and n.).

VIII. Petition for Postponement

29 July 1796

To the Honourable the Judges of the Supreme Court of the United States.

Your Petitioner David Hunter Humbly sheweth.

That a cause is now depending before your Honors on an appeal or writ of error from the Circuit Court of the United States for the District of Virginia wherein your Petitioner is appellant & Denny Fairfax devisee of the late Lord Fairfax proprietor of the Northern Neck of Virginia is Appellee,—That your Petitioner had engaged Alexander Campble Esquire an emminent attorney at Law of the State of Virginia to argue his cause.

That your Petitioner was informed on the Twenty fifth of this Instant July that on the eighteenth Instant the said Alexander Campble departed this life in Richmond so that your Petitioner is left without council & hath not time to provide for the argument of this cause by employing other council at the ensuing Term.[1]

Your Petitioner therefore most Humbly prays that the Consideration of his cause aforesaid may be postponed untill the next Term & shall pray &c. &c.[2]

David Hunter
July 29th. 1796.

ADS, Hunter v. Fairfax's Lessee, Record on Appeal, 89, Appellate Case File No. 29, RG 267, DNA. Addressed to clerk of Supreme Court in Philadelphia by Hunter, who posted it at Martinsburg on 29 July. On verso of cover Hunter wrote a note to the clerk asking him to present the petition if the cause was called for a hearing. Clerk's endorsements on cover indicate petition was received 5 Aug. and read and granted on 6 Aug. (ibid., 91, 96).

1. The "ensuing Term" began 1 Aug. Fearing that Campbell's death (a suicide) would "be usd as the instrument of delay for our cause," JM attempted unsuccessfully to get John Wickham to take Campbell's place. In late July he began his northward journey to Philadelphia, uncertain whether the case would be heard, but he evidently proceeded no farther than Mount Vernon once he received word that Hunter would seek another postponement. Before learning of Campbell's death, Hunter tried to retain Alexander Hamilton, promising him $1,000 or the land in dispute (worth about $2,000) if successful. The New York lawyer declined the offer, as it was not his "general plan" to practice in the Supreme Court (JM to Henry Lee, 18 July 1796 [*PJM*, III, 35–36]; David Hunter to Alexander Hamilton, 7 July 1796, Hamilton Papers, DLC [briefly calendared in Syrett, *Hamilton Papers*, XX, 249, with Hamilton's endorsement summarizing his reply]).

2. The Supreme Court granted a continuance on 6 Aug., not wishing a case of this magnitude to "be heard and decided *ex parte*." Charles Lee and Charles J. Ingersoll, also representing Fairfax, were present on this occasion and objected to the petition. Had they been successful, JM presumably would have made a hurried trip to Philadelphia, though perhaps he would have been content to let Lee, who had been Fairfax's lawyer in the Winchester case, handle the business (Minutes of the Supreme Court of the U.S., 6 Aug. 1796, RG 267, DNA; Hunter v. Fairfax's Devisee, 3 Dall. 305 [1796]).

Lack of representation was only the ostensible reason for Hunter's requesting a continuance. His real motive was disclosed in his letter to Hamilton (cited in n. 1): "If [the postponement] can be obtained," he wrote, "it is probable that the legislature of this state & perhaps some others will see the propriety of defending themselves against the claims of the late proprietors and their representatives." In Nov. 1796 Hunter petitioned the General Assembly for financial assistance, but his request was rejected the day before a committee reported the compromise proposals that were subsequently adopted. At the Feb. 1797 term of the Supreme Court the writ of error in Hunter v. Fairfax's Lessee was "non pross'd," short for *non prosequitur* ("he does not follow up, or pursue"), a judgment against the plaintiff for failure to take the proper steps within the prescribed time—in this instance, for not arguing the case (*JHDV*, Oct. 1796, 9, 24; Minutes of the Supreme Court of the U.S., 11, 13 Feb. 1797).

IV. The British Debt Cases

Editorial Note

Much the greater part of the docket of the federal circuit court during its first years of existence consisted of suits brought by British subjects to recover debts contracted by Virginians before the Revolution. More than a hundred such cases taken on by John Marshall during the 1790s can be identified from his account book and the case files, order books, record books, and rule books of the federal court. For whatever reasons—personal preference, political considerations, or simply because the debtors approached him first—Marshall employed his professional talents almost exclusively for the defense in British debt suits. Among those who retained him were members of the political and social elite of Virginia: the Randolphs, Harrisons, Byrds, Carter Braxton, and Thomas Jefferson (as executor of John Wayles). His clients were planters, great and small, and merchants such as the Richmond firms of Daniel L. Hylton and Pleasants & Company, the Manchester house of Trents, Crump & Bates, Roger Atkinson of Petersburg, and Williamsburg apothecary John M. Galt. As counsel for the Virginia debtors, Marshall argued the test case of *Ware* v. *Hylton* (Case Number 13), his first and only appearance at the bar of the Supreme Court.

The recovery of prewar debts was stipulated in the fourth article of the definitive treaty of peace between Great Britain and the United States, concluded 3 September 1783: "It is agreed that creditors on either side shall meet with no lawful impediment to the recovery of the full value in sterling money, of all *bona fide* debts heretofore contracted."[1] Until the federal court opened in the spring of 1790, this article remained a dead letter as far as British creditors of Virginia citizens were concerned. During the 1780s the state courts of Virginia were closed to them. Their prospects improved once they gained access to the federal court, but even there they experienced much delay and frustration. The debtors raised elaborate special defenses, grounded on the plaintiff's being a British subject, in addition to the usual common law pleas. These special defenses were the distinguishing feature of the British debt cases. Though ultimately held to be legally insufficient, the special pleas effectively postponed a decision in these cases for at least three years. Long after the federal court rejected the special defenses, British creditors continued to encounter obstacles to recovery.

1. John Bassett Moore, ed., *International Adjudications Ancient and Modern: History and Documents* (8 vols.; New York, 1929–36), III, 3. On the British debt litigation in Virginia, see Charles F. Hobson, "The Recovery of British Debts in the Federal Circuit Court of Virginia, 1790 to 1797," *VMHB*, XCII (1984), 176–200.

After the war Virginians claimed exemption from paying their British debts by virtue of legislation enacted by the General Assembly during the Revolution. The most important of these measures was the sequestration law of 1777, which allowed debtors to pay British debts into the state loan office and obtain a receipt discharging them for the amount paid.[2] Lawyers for Virginia debtors contended that loan office payments were a legal discharge of British debts despite the fourth article of the peace treaty. In addition to the sequestration law, Virginians cited the following section of a 1782 act concerning executions to deny British creditors standing in the courts: "That no debt or demand whatsoever, originally due to a subject of Great Britain, shall be recoverable in any court in this commonwealth, although the same may be transferred to a citizen of this state, or to any other person capable of maintaining such action, unless the assignment" was made before 1 May 1777.[3] The prevailing view in Virginia during the decade after the peace was that this law continued in full force as a general prohibition against the recovery of all British debts. Not only Virginians but many creditors as well acted on the assumption that until the assembly expressly repealed this law, no court in the commonwealth would hear a suit for the recovery of a British debt.

Although immediately after the promulgation of peace in 1783 the Virginia legislature seemed disposed to give effect to the treaty, the citizens of the commonwealth could not be reconciled to opening the courts of justice to their former enemies. An invading British army had recently caused widespread devastation in the state, but no action had angered Virginians more than the carrying off of their slaves and the subsequent refusal in the spring of 1783 of British Commanding General Carleton to return them. Retention of the slaves, along with continued British occupation of the Northwest posts, constituted in the eyes of Virginians a clear violation of the seventh article of the treaty and helped turn the majority of the citizens against payment of British debts. Beginning in 1784 the legislature defeated successive attempts to remove legal impediments to recovery, in each instance making it clear that no steps would be taken on the debts until Britain made satisfaction for the slaves.[4]

The courts showed little inclination to resist the legislative will on the subject of British debts. When the courts reopened in 1777 (having been closed since 1774), suits brought before the war for the recovery of British debts were placed on the "British docket." There

2. Hening, *Statutes*, IX, 379–80. This is fully discussed in Case No. 12, editorial note.

3. Hening, *Statutes*, XI, 76; see discussion in Case No. 13, editorial note.

4. Emory G. Evans, "Private Indebtedness and the Revolution in Virginia, 1776 to 1796," *WMQ*, 3d ser., XXVIII (1971), 358–67.

they languished until well into the 1790s.[5] While the old cases remained suspended and the legislature refused to repeal its wartime acts preventing recovery, British creditors saw little point in bringing new suits. One agent for a British merchant firm stated that it would have been irresponsible to put his clients "to the expense of prosecuting suits, which at the very moment of instituting them, I knew would not be tried." Only in the rare instances in which the defendant agreed not to plead British debt did creditors bother to sue.[6]

The attitude of Virginia judges was summed up by Judge John Tyler, who at the Fredericksburg District Court in 1790 declared "that he would preside at the Trial of no Cause, where a British Subject was plaintiff, and the Plea was such." Tyler refused even to hear cases between two Virginians that indirectly involved debts owed to British subjects.[7] One Virginia judge who did express an opinion in favor of the legal rights of British creditors was George Wythe, who presided over the High Court of Chancery. In the case of *Page* v. *Pendleton*, decided in May 1793, Chancellor Wythe forthrightly declared that payments made by the plaintiff's testator into the state loan office under the sequestration law of 1777 did not discharge the testator's debts to British creditors. This case established no precedent, however, as it was not brought by a British subject for the recovery of a debt owed by a Virginian. Both parties were Virginians, and the purpose of the decree was to instruct the plaintiff as executor not to distinguish between British and other creditors in distributing the assets of the estate. The chancellor, indeed, was rebuked for "having officiously given Opinions on Points, which he was not bound in that Case, to decide."[8]

The opening of the federal court in the spring of 1790 gave British creditors renewed hope for legal redress. The restriction of federal jurisdiction to $500, or £150 Virginia currency, was a serious drawback, particularly to the Scottish merchants engaged in the retail trade at stores located throughout the Piedmont countryside. Nevertheless, the accumulated interest and rate of exchange on many smaller debts brought them up to the required sum. A bond to secure payment of £75 also qualified because the suit was brought

5. Hening, *Statutes*, IX, 368, 380; John Warden to William Hay, 22 June 1799, T.79/27 (claim of John Hay & Co.), P.R.O.

6. Deposition of Benjamin Waller, Jr., 12 Sept. 1810, 2, T.79/3 (claim of Robert Cary & Co.), P.R.O.; William Hay to William Moore Smith, 3 Feb. 1799, T.79/27 (claim of John Hay & Co.), P.R.O.

7. John Warden to William Hay, 22 June 1799, T.79/27 (claim of John Hay & Co.), P.R.O.

8. Wythe 211; William Hay to William Moore Smith, 3 Feb. 1799; John Warden to William Hay, 22 June 1799, T.79/27 (claim of John Hay & Co.), P.R.O.

for the penal sum of £150.[9] Among the most conspicuous plaintiffs at the first term of this court was William Jones, surviving partner of Farell & Jones, merchants of Bristol (Case Numbers 12, 13, and 18). Although Jones and other English consignment merchants were well represented on the federal court docket, more numerous were the Scottish houses centered in Glasgow, a distribution that reflected how completely the Scots had captured the Virginia tobacco market during the generation preceding the war.[10] Representative of this class of litigants was James and Robert Donald & Company (Case Number 17).

Progress in the federal court was painfully slow for British plaintiffs. Marshall and other attorneys for the debtors employed every device at their disposal to drag out the proceedings. The most effective delaying tactic proved to be the special British debt defenses, for the judges were in no hurry to decide the controversial issues raised in them. Arguments were not heard until November 1791, with *Jones* v. *Walker* as the selected case (Case Number 12). A second hearing took place at the May 1793 term, when the court in the case of *Ware* v. *Hylton* rejected three of the four British debt pleas. Three more years passed before the Supreme Court—in the appeal of *Ware* v. *Hylton*—struck down the last of the special defenses: that payment into the loan office was a valid discharge of the debt (Case Number 13). After these judicial rulings, British creditors began to obtain judgments with increasing frequency. Still, however, they complained bitterly that justice was denied them. Virginia juries routinely deducted interest on their debts for the eight years of the war (Case Number 16). Creditors obtaining judgments were often unable to collect because their debtors had died, moved away, become insolvent, or distributed their property so as to make it impossible to levy an execution. In debts arising from unpaid bills of exchange or upon open accounts, they unhappily discovered that Virginia's statute of limitations could be successfully pleaded against them and that the rules for proving book debts were much stricter than before the war (Case Numbers 14 and 15).

Ultimately the question of British debts, as part of the larger problem of relations between the United States and Great Britain, was

9. Evans, "Private Indebtedness," *WMQ*, 3d ser., XXVIII (1971), 349–50; William Hay, "Remarks on the Answer of the Attorney General of the United States to the Memorial of William Cunninghame & Company . . . ," 15 May 1798, 24, T.79/27 (claim of John Hay & Co.), P.R.O.; Richard Hanson to William Jones, 10 July 1790, 17 Aug. 1791, T.79/30 (claim of John T. Ware), P.R.O.

10. During the first three terms, Farell & Jones brought thirty cases; James and Robert Donald & Co. brought forty-eight (U.S. Cir. Ct., Va., Rule Bk. I, 1–51). On Farell & Jones, see Case No. 12, editorial note and n. 3.

resolved at the negotiating table. The Jay Treaty of 1794 established an arbitration commission for hearing claims of British creditors for losses allegedly arising from the operation of lawful impediments to recovery and for which full compensation could not be obtained "in the ordinary course of justice." Composed of three British and two American members (the fifth seat fell by lot to a British subject), the commission met at Philadelphia beginning in May 1797. British plaintiffs immediately shifted their attention from the courts to this quasi-judicial body, which was to determine cases according to "justice and equity." After two years of hearing claims, however, the board was dissolved by the withdrawal of the American commissioners, who had consistently dissented from a series of rulings favorable to the claimants. Further negotiation, in which Marshall was briefly involved as secretary of state, led to the Convention of 1802. By this agreement the United States paid Britain an indemnity of six hundred thousand pounds sterling. The money was distributed by a British commission that heard claims between 1803 and 1811. The Convention of 1802 also declared that the fourth article of the peace treaty of 1783 was "to be binding and obligatory" in its future operation. British creditors could continue to seek recovery in American courts, more secure in their footing as plaintiffs than they had been during the preceding two decades.[11] The federal court in Virginia heard and decided cases for the recovery of pre-Revolutionary debts until well into the nineteenth century.

11. For the proceedings of the British debt claims commissions, see Moore, *International Adjudications*, III. For the Jay Treaty provisions, see ibid., 6.

12. Jones v. Walker

1790–1797

I. Capias ad Respondendum, 9 June 1790
II. Bail Bond, 11 November 1790
III. Recognizance of Special Bail, 23 December 1790
IV. Declaration, 27 December 1790
V. Pleas, 27 February 1791
VI. Replications and Demurrer, 26 July 1791
VII. Amended Pleas, 23 November 1791
VIII. Amended Replication, 23 November 1791
IX. Rejoinder, 23 November 1791
X. Demurrer, 23 November 1791
XI. Joinder in Demurrer, 23 November 1791
XII. Scire Facias, 10 July 1794
XIII. Verdict, 27 May 1797

Editorial Note

A large number of Marshall's clients in British debt cases were sued by William Jones, surviving partner of the Bristol merchant firm of Farell & Jones. Jones was plaintiff in more than twenty suits instituted immediately after the U.S. Circuit Court for the district of Virginia opened for business in the spring of 1790.[1] Thomas Walker retained Marshall on several occasions between 1787 and 1794.[2] Other debtors to Farell & Jones who employed Marshall included members of various branches of the Randolph family, the executors of John Wayles, and Richmond merchant Daniel L. Hylton, whose case he later argued before the Supreme Court.

Farell & Jones carried on an extensive business in Virginia before the Revolution, chiefly among the larger Tidewater planters and merchants. In return for its correspondents' shipments of tobacco or other produce, the firm sold the produce, shipped goods and paid insurance on return cargoes, and accepted and paid bills of exchange drawn on them. One year's credit was allowed on the purchase of goods, with 5 percent interest charged after the expiration of the credit.[3] These terms were typical of the consignment, or commission, trade that was gradually displaced during the generation preceding Independence by the system of direct purchase of tobacco within the colony by Scots factors. Accounts were customarily settled each year. This usually meant carrying over the planter's indebtedness to a new ledger or, if the accumulated balance against him had become too large, requiring him to give his bond for the outstanding amount. The bond in this case, executed by Walker to Farell & Jones in May 1772, probably originated in this way. If the planter was long overdue in paying off his bond, the British creditor might demand a mortgage or deed of trust as a security.[4]

Jones v. *Walker* is representative of suits for the recovery of debts on bonds, which formed the largest category of Marshall's British debt cases. It also exemplifies those cases in which the defendant pleaded wartime payments into the state loan office in discharge of the debt. The case papers provide ample documentation of the pleadings used in virtually all the British debt suits heard in the U.S. Circuit Court for Virginia between 1790 and 1796.

As closely identified as he was with defending Virginians indebted to British merchants, Marshall unquestionably had major responsibility for drafting the elaborate special pleas that he and other lawyers entered in these cases. The British debt pleas raised matters of law and were thus referred to the court for determination before the case went to the jury. In addition to these special defenses, the defendant always pleaded the general issue. If the court decided against him on the special pleas, then the debtor would be sure of having his case tried by a jury of his Virginia peers. In the anti-British political climate of Virginia during the 1790s, juries could be expected to bestow every advantage within their power upon the defendant—for example, by withholding interest on these debts for the period of the war.

Marshall soon found it convenient to have the special British debt pleas printed up in two sets of forms, one for actions of debt, the other for actions of assumpsit. These forms began with the plea of the general issue. Thus, the first plea in a case of debt on a bond was payment, which in Virginia was considered to be a general issue in this action.[5] Immediately below payment came the plea of *nil debet* ("does not owe"), the general issue in debt on a simple contract. Depending on whether the debt action was on a specialty or simple contract, Marshall would delete one or the other of these general issues. The British debt pleas then followed in turn. In assumpsit cases the first plea was non assumpsit, the second the act of limitations, after which came the British debt pleas.[6]

At first there were only two British debt pleas. One recited the defendant's payment of all or part of the debt into the state loan office according to the terms of the 1777 sequestration law. The other declared that the debt was originally due to British subjects and not recoverable "by virtue of the Laws in that case made and provided" (Document V). These two pleas were eventually superseded by four new British debt pleas. The first two were expanded versions of the original pleas. The other two were entirely new. One alleged British infractions of the peace treaty and continuing hostile acts amounting to a state of war between the United States and Great Britain. The other declared the plaintiff's right to be totally annulled by the dissolution of the existing government on 4 July 1776 (Document VII). Once the defendant put in these pleas, the case followed a set pattern. The plaintiff took issue on the plea of payment, nil debet, or non assumpsit, and the British debt pleadings terminated in demurrers. The arguments on the points of law, when they finally came to be heard, proceeded on these demurrers.

Jones v. *Walker* was one of twenty-odd cases handled by Marshall in which the defendant pleaded payment into the state loan office under the sequestration act of 1777. This plea of course could be made only where the debtor to a British subject had actually paid money into the loan office, the other three pleas being routinely entered in all cases of British debt. Although the motives behind the sequestration act are not entirely clear from its language, the Virginia legislature evidently had in mind a money-raising scheme, not unlike a public loan, to bolster the state's depleted wartime finances. Moreover, since paper money was a legal tender, the assembly hoped to maintain the value of that currency by allowing debtors to pay this money into the loan office.

In this regard the act was a notable failure. Relatively few citizens chose to pay off their British debts in this manner, and the expected financial boon did not materialize. Unless moved by patriotism, debtors in theory had no incentive to make use of the act, since British creditors as alien enemies could not recover their debts during the war. The great depreciation of the paper money, however, soon made it possible for them to pay off these debts at a fraction of their real value. The scale went from 4 to 1 in January 1778 to 60 to 1 by May 1780, when the act was finally repealed. Not surprisingly, most of the payments occurred during the last two months of the act.[7] Nevertheless, even at the height of the depreciation, the number of debtors taking advantage of the sequestration law was strikingly small. Of those who did pay in this fashion there were some, to be sure, who saw an easy opportunity to escape their indebtedness. Others simply tried to protect themselves by depositing in the loan office the depreciated paper which they as creditors were by law required to accept from their own debtors. Thomas Jefferson, for example, made two payments in discharge of John Wayles's debts to Farell & Jones totaling £2,666, equivalent to about £90 specie.[8] This amount, as he later explained to Jones, was identical to that he had received in greatly depreciated currency for lands sold in 1776 "before a shilling of paper money was issued." Jefferson at that time had offered to assign the bonds taken for the lands to Jones's agent but was refused.[9] Another Virginian informed his British creditor that he did not wish "a farthing advantage" by his loan office payment but only to make good the currency he had been obliged to receive for real value.[10]

That so many Virginians refrained from paying off their British debts under the terms of the sequestration law perhaps reflected their concern that such payments would not remove their legal liability. Would the courts allow these payments to bar recovery by the British creditor? The legislature provided no clear signals. The act said nothing about compensation for either creditor or debtor. In 1788 the assembly declared the state's liability for sums paid into the loan office to be the actual specie amount when reduced by the scale of depreciation plus interest at 6 percent. To whom the state was to be liable the legislators pointedly refused to say, explaining that "it belongs not to the legislature to decide particular questions, of which the judiciary have cognizance, and it is therefore unfit for them to determine whether the payments so made into the loan office as aforesaid, be good or void between the creditor and debtor."[11] Although the federal circuit court upheld the loan office plea in the case of *Ware* v. *Hylton* (Case Number 13) in June 1793, the Supreme Court overturned that decision three years later. The Virginia assembly soon after reenacted the principles of the 1788 legislation in providing for the reimbursement of citizens who had paid money into the loan office.[12]

Jones v. *Walker* was the original test case for determining the validity of the loan office plea and of the other three British debt pleas as well. The first hearing began 24 November 1791 and continued for more than a week before Associate Justices Thomas Johnson and John Blair of the Supreme Court and District Judge Cyrus Griffin. Each of the contending parties was represented by four of the ablest counsel of the Virginia bar: Andrew Ronald, Jerman Baker, John Wickham, and Burwell Starke for the plaintiff; Patrick Henry (who had just qualified to practice in the federal court), Marshall, Alexander Campbell, and James Innes for the defendant.[13] Henry's speech on behalf of the Virginia debtors—the last of his oratorical masterpieces—is the only surviving record of the arguments on this occasion.[14] Exploiting his knack for translating dry questions of law into personal terms, Henry for three successive days held the rapt attention of the large audience that crowded into the courtroom of the Capitol in Richmond. His defensive strategy was to turn this private dispute over a debt into a public controversy between Great Britain and America. In this view of the subject the plaintiff's right of recovery was forfeited by the perfidious acts of his king during the war and since the peace. "Those animosities which the injustice of the British nation hath produced, and which I had well hoped would never again be the subject of discussion, are necessarily brought forth," he remarked at the outset of his impassioned address.[15] By the time he sat down, the debtors in attendance must have been fully persuaded that they did not owe a shilling to their British creditors.

Although Henry and the other counsel conducted an exhaustive investigation of the topic at this hearing, their efforts were wasted because the court was not prepared to rule on the pleas. Blair left before the term ended because of his son's death; he was also reportedly unwilling to sit in the case because of a personal stake in the loan office payments. The other two judges declined to give their opinions.[16] When the pleas came to be argued a second time in May 1793, *Jones* v. *Walker* was temporarily off the court docket, and *Ware* v. *Hylton* accordingly became the new test case.[17] Final judgment in the suit against Walker, and of all those in which loan office payments were pleaded, was suspended until after the Supreme Court's determination of *Ware* v. *Hylton*.

1. U.S. Cir. Ct., Va., Rule Bk. I, 1–51.

2. Thomas Walker (1715–1794) of Castle Hill in Albemarle County led a notable career as a physician, soldier, explorer, land speculator, and legislator. See *PJM*, I, 240 and n. 4, 372; II, 29–30, 43–44, 130, 157, 366, 375.

3. Farell & Jones to Virginia correspondents, 10 Aug. 1771, printed in W. E. Minchinton, *The Trade of Bristol in the Eighteenth Century* (Bristol, 1957), 170–71; memorial of John T. Ware, 16 Oct. 1798, T.79/30 (claim of John T. Ware), P.R.O.

4. For a succinct discussion of the consignment and the Scottish factor methods of trading in colonial Virginia, see Richard B. Sheridan, "The British Credit Crisis of 1772 and the American Colonies," *Journal of Economic History*, XX (1960), 168–69, and sources cited therein.

5. See Case No. 3, Doc. II, n. 2.

6. For the debt form, see Doc. V; for the assumpsit form, see Case No. 14, Doc. II.

7. Evans, "Private Indebtedness," *WMQ*, 3d ser., XXVIII (1971), 354–57; Hening, *Statutes*, X, 473–74.

8. See Richard Hanson's memorandum of "Paper Money Paid in at Loan Office on Account of Farell & Jones," 7 Dec. 1787, T.79/30 (claim of John T. Ware), P.R.O.

9. Thomas Jefferson to William Jones, 5 Jan. 1787 (Boyd, *Jefferson Papers*, XI, 14–18).

10. Robert Hart to George Anderson, July 1784, T.79/32 (claim of Anderson & Daiziell), P.R.O.

11. Hening, *Statutes*, XII, 529–30. In Ware v. Hylton, Jay cited this act to show that Virginia considered these as subsisting debts.

12. Shepherd, *Statutes*, II, 17.

13. William Wirt, *Sketches of the Life and Character of Patrick Henry* (3d ed.; Philadelphia, 1818), 318–19.

14. Wirt had access to David Robertson's stenographic report (ibid., 312–13).

15. Ibid., 321.

16. Ibid., 321–69; James Monroe to Thomas Jefferson, 1 May 1792 (*American State Papers: Documents, Legislative and Executive, of the Congress of the United States . . . , Class I: Foreign Relations* [38 vols.; Washington, D.C., 1832–61], I, 234); Richard Hanson to William Jones, 29 Jan. 1792, T.79/30 (claim of John T. Ware), P.R.O.; William Madison to James Madison, 3 Dec. 1791 (Hutchinson, *Madison Papers*, XIV, 136).

17. See Case No. 13, editorial note.

I. Capias ad Respondendum
9 June 1790

The PRESIDENT *of the* UNITED STATES,
to the MARSHAL *of the District of Virginia*, GREETING:

YOU are hereby commanded to take ⟨Thomas Walker⟩ if ⟨he⟩ be found within your District, and ⟨him⟩ safely keep, so that you have ⟨his⟩ bod⟨y⟩ before the Judges of the Court of the United States for the middle Circuit, at ⟨Williamsburgh⟩[1] in the District of Virginia, on the ⟨22nd. day of November Next⟩ to answer ⟨William Jones Surviving partner of Farrell & Jones late Merchants in the Kingdom of Great Britain⟩ of a plea of ⟨Debt for Two Thousand Nine hundred & Three pounds Fifteen Shillings & Eight pence Sterling of the Value of three thousand eight hundred twenty one pounds 14-2 current money Damages Fifty Pounds⟩

[SEAL] *And have then there this writ. Witness,* JOHN JAY, *Esquire, Chief Justice of the United States, at* ⟨Williamsburgh⟩ *this* ⟨9th⟩ *day of* ⟨June⟩ *in the year* ⟨1790⟩ *and of the Independence of the United States the* ⟨Fourteenth⟩.[2]

WILLIAM MARSHALL C C C[3]

Printed form, Jones v. Walker, U.S. Circuit Court, Va., Ended Cases (Restored), 1797, Vi. Blanks filled in and signed by clerk William Marshall. Endorsements on verso in hand of U.S. Marshal Edward Carrington and plaintiff's attorney Jerman Baker.

1. This court originally was to meet alternately at Williamsburg and Charlottesville. In 1791 Richmond became the permanent meeting place (*U.S. Statutes at Large*, I, 75, 217).

2. Plaintiff's attorney Baker endorsed the capias, "on a Bond for money." In personal actions the true species of action had to be endorsed on the writ so that the sheriff (or marshal) would know whether to take bail for the appearance of the defendant (Hening, *Statutes*, XII, 740). Since bail was required in this case, U.S. Marshal Carrington took bail, or appearance, bond (Doc. II) on executing the capias, endorsing on the writ the names of the bail. Carrington noted that he served the writ on 11 Nov. 1790.

3. The initials stand for "Clerk, Circuit Court." William Marshall was JM's brother.

II. Bail Bond

11 November 1790

KNOW *all men, by these presents, that we* ⟨Thomas Walker, John Walker & Francis Walker⟩[1] *are held and firmly bound unto Edward Carrington, Marshal of the district of Virginia, in the just and full sum of* ⟨Two thousand, Nine hundred & three pounds fifteen Shillings & 8d. Sterling of the value of Three thousand eight hundred & twenty one pounds 14/2 Current money⟩ *to be paid to the said Edward Carrington, his executors, administrators, or assigns; to which payment, well and truly to be made, we bind ourselves, our heirs, executors, and administrators, jointly and severally, firmly by these presents. Sealed with our seals, and dated this* ⟨Eleventh⟩ *day of* ⟨November⟩ *in the year of our Lord* 179⟨0⟩.

THE Condition of the above obligation is such, that if the above bound ⟨Thomas Walker⟩ shall appear before the Judges of the court of the United States for the middle Circuit at ⟨Williamsburg⟩, on the ⟨Twenty Second⟩ day of ⟨this month to answer William Jones surviving Partner of Farrell & Jones late Merchants in the Kingdom of Great Britain of a Plea of Debt for Two thousand Nine hundred & three pounds fifteen shillings & 8d Sterling of the value of £3821. 14.2 Currency, damage Fifty pounds.⟩
Then the above obligation to be void, otherwise to remain in full force and virtue.[2]

Sealed and delivered in the presence of,
Test JNO. LENOX as to Jno. Walker
HARRY HETH as to F.W. for him self and Father

FRS WALKER atty for THOS WALKER [L.S.]
JN. WALKER [L.S.]
FRS WALKER. [L.S.]

Printed form, Jones v. Walker, U.S. Circuit Court, Va., Ended Cases (Restored), 1797, Vi. Blanks filled in by U.S. Marshal Edward Carrington.

1. John Walker and Francis Walker were sons of the plaintiff. Francis Walker acted for his aged father under a power of attorney (*PJM*, II, 44 n. 5, 124–25, 130, 157).

2. This form of the bail bond follows that printed in Blackstone, *Commentaries*, III, App., No. 3, xix–xx. The law required appearance bail for all actions of debt on bonds, bills, or notes for the payment of money or tobacco, covenant, and detinue (Hening, *Statutes*, XII, 741).

III. Recognizance of Special Bail
23 December 1790

⟨Henrico⟩ County to wit[1]

Memorandum that on the ⟨twenty third⟩ day of ⟨December⟩ One thousand seven hundred and ⟨ninety⟩ personally appeared before me ⟨Nathl Wilkinson⟩ one of the Justices of the Peace within the said County ⟨John Walker and Francis Walker⟩ and undertook for ⟨Thomas Walker⟩ at the suit of ⟨William Jones surviving partner of Farrel & Jones⟩ in an action of ⟨Debt⟩ now depending in ⟨the circuit court of the united states for the middle circuit in Virginia⟩ that in case the said ⟨Thomas Walker⟩ shall be cast in the action aforesaid, ⟨he⟩ the said ⟨Thomas Walker⟩ shall satisfy and pay the condemnation of the Court or render his body to Prison in Execution for the same or that ⟨t⟩he⟨y⟩ the said ⟨John Walker & Francis Walker⟩ will do it for him. Given under my hand the day and year aforesaid.

NATHL. WILKINSON

MS form, Jones v. Walker, U.S. Circuit Court, Va., Ended Cases (Restored), 1797, Vi. In an unknown hand, with blanks filled in later by another hand.

1. The appearance of the defendant in cases where bail was required was effected by putting in special bail, or bail to the action. The appearance bail, who usually became the special bail, was thereby discharged from the first obligation. Any justice of the peace could take recognizance of special bail, which had to be transmitted to the court and filed with the suit papers (Tucker, *Blackstone's Commentaries*, III, 290–91; Robinson, *Practice*, I, 168; Hening, *Statutes*, XII, 742).

IV. Declaration
27 December 1790

United States, Middle Circuit.
District of Virginia, Albemarle County to wit[1] }

William Jones, surviving partner of Joseph Farell & William Jones, late Merchts. & partners, in the Kingdom of Great Brittain, complains of Thomas Walker, of the County of Albemarle, in the District & Commonwealth of Virginia, one of the united States of America, in the middle Circuit, and within the Jurisdiction of this Honorable Court, in custody of the Marshall of the said District &c. of a plea that the said Thomas Walker the defendant, render to the said William Jones the Plaintif Two thousand nine hundred and three pounds, fifteen shillings and eight pence Sterling, which to him the said Defendant owes, and from him unjustly detains:[2] For that whereas the said Defendant on the eleventh day of May in the year of our Lord one thousand seven hundred and seventy two, at the Parish of   in the County of Albemarle aforesaid in the then Colony and Dominion, now Commonwealth and District of Virginia, one of the united States of America, in the middle Circuit and now within the Jurisdiction of this Honorable Court, made his certain writing obligatory[3] sealed with his Seal dated the same day and year aforesaid and now to the Court here shewn wherein and whereby the said Defendant did bind and oblige himself, in the life time of the said Joseph Farell, to pay to them the said Joseph Farell & William Jones, the aforesaid sum of Two thousand nine hundred and three pounds fifteen shillings and eight pence Sterling, when thereunto afterwards required. Nevertheless the said Defendant altho often afterwards required, did not pay to the said Joseph Farell & William Jones, in the life time of the said Joseph Farell, the aforesaid Sum of Two thousand nine hundred and three pounds fifteen shillings and eight pence Sterling, nor hath he paid the same to the Plaintiff, (who is the surviving partner) since the death of the said Joseph Farell altho: often required so to do, and particularly on the   day of   in the year of our Lord one thousand seven hundred & eighty and at divers days and times since, at the Parish and in the County aforesaid, within the Commonwealth and District aforesaid and within the Jurisdiction of this Honorable Court, but the same to him to pay hath hitherto refused and still doth refuse to pay (and detains the same) to the Damage of the said Plaintiff Fifty Pounds and therefore he brings suit & so forth.

Pledges to prosecute
John Doe }
Richd. Roe }

Baker ℘ Pltf.

ADS, Jones v. Walker, U.S. Circuit Court, Va., Ended Cases (Restored), 1797, Vi. Presumably filed in clerk's office on 27 Dec. 1790 (see n. 1). Verso contains jury verdict (Doc. XIII) and clerk's endorsements summarizing the proceedings at the rules.

1. The plaintiff had to "file his declaration in the clerk's office, at the next succeeding rule day after the defendant shall have entered his appearance." The appearance day in this case was 27 Nov. 1790, the day after the rising of the Nov. 1790 term of the court, though special bail, or appearance, on behalf of Walker was postponed until the December rules. The "next succeeding rule day" was one month later. At the Jan. 1791 rules the plaintiff obtained a rule to plead, which he could do one month after filing his declaration. Thus, the plaintiff must have filed his declaration at the Dec. 1790 rules (Hening, *Statutes*, XII, 745; U.S. Cir. Ct., Va., Rule Bk. I, 9, 10).

2. See the notes to Case No. 3, Doc. I, for a discussion of some of the characteristic features of the declaration in debt on a bond. The declaration in this case differs slightly from that in Case No. 3 because the defendant is the debtor himself rather than the executor of the debtor. Therefore it states that the defendant "owes" as well as "detains" the debt.

3. The bond, with an account stating the cumulative interest and credits as of 30 Sept. 1775, is in the suit papers.

V. Pleas

27 February 1791

AND the said ⟨Thomas Walker⟩ by JOHN MARSHALL his Attorney,[1] comes and defends the force and injury when and where, &c. and says that the Plaintiff[2] ought not to have and maintain his said action against him, because he says that he has paid the debt in the declaration mentioned, and of this he puts himself upon the country.[3]

And the said ⟨Thomas Walker⟩ with special leave of the Court to plead as many several matters as may be necessary for his defence, for further plea saith, that he doth not owe the debt in the declaration mentioned, or any part thereof, and of this he puts himself upon the country.[4]

And the said ⟨Thomas Walker⟩ by the special leave of the Court, for further plea saith,[5] that the Plaintiff ought not to have or maintain his action aforesaid against him, because he says that throughout the year 1777, the Plaintiff ⟨was⟩[6] British subject, and this Defendant was a citizen of this Commonwealth, and that on the day of in the year 177⟨9⟩ this Defendant being then a citizen of this Commonwealth, did pay into the Loan-Office of this Commonwealth, on account of the debt in the declaration mentioned, the sum of ⟨seven thousand one hundred & seventy three dollars⟩ and did take out a certificate of the same in the name of the ⟨said Farrell &

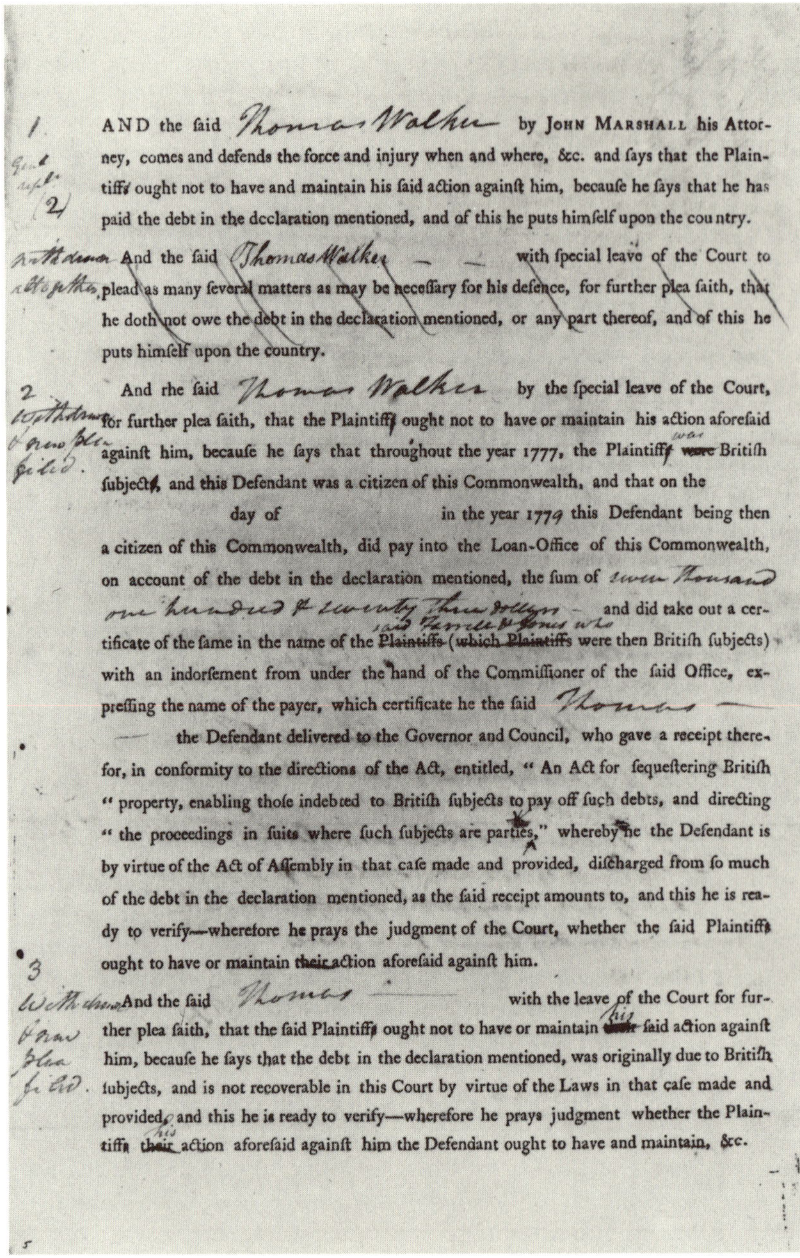

1 AND the said Thomas Walker by JOHN MARSHALL his Attorney, comes and defends the force and injury when and where, &c. and says that the Plaintiffs ought not to have and maintain his said action against him, because he says that he has paid the debt in the declaration mentioned, and of this he puts himself upon the country.

And the said Thomas Walker — — with special leave of the Court to plead as many several matters as may be necessary for his defence, for further plea saith, that he doth not owe the debt in the declaration mentioned, or any part thereof, and of this he puts himself upon the country.

2 And rhe said Thomas Walker by the special leave of the Court, for further plea saith, that the Plaintiff ought not to have or maintain his action aforesaid against him, because he says that throughout the year 1777, the Plaintiff ~~were~~ was British subject, and this Defendant was a citizen of this Commonwealth, and that on the day of in the year 1779 this Defendant being then a citizen of this Commonwealth, did pay into the Loan-Office of this Commonwealth, on account of the debt in the declaration mentioned, the sum of seven thousand one hundred & seventy three dollars — and did take out a certificate of the same in the name of the ~~Plaintiffs (which Plaintiffs~~ said Farrell & Jones who were then British subjects) with an indorsement from under the hand of the Commissioner of the said Office, expressing the name of the payer, which certificate he the said Thomas — — the Defendant delivered to the Governor and Council, who gave a receipt therefor, in conformity to the directions of the Act, entitled, "An Act for sequestering British "property, enabling those indebted to British subjects to pay off such debts, and directing "the proceedings in suits where such subjects are parties," whereby he the Defendant is by virtue of the Act of Assembly in that case made and provided, discharged from so much of the debt in the declaration mentioned, as the said receipt amounts to, and this he is ready to verify—wherefore he prays the judgment of the Court, whether the said Plaintiff ought to have or maintain ~~their~~ action aforesaid against him.

3 And the said Thomas — with the leave of the Court for further plea saith, that the said Plaintiff ought not to have or maintain ~~their~~ his said action against him, because he says that the debt in the declaration mentioned, was originally due to British subjects, and is not recoverable in this Court by virtue of the Laws in that case made and provided, and this he is ready to verify—wherefore he prays judgment whether the Plaintiff ~~their~~ his action aforesaid against him the Defendant ought to have and maintain, &c.

BRITISH DEBT PLEAS

The original pleas submitted by Marshall in *Jones* v. *Walker* (Case Number 12, Document V). *Courtesy of Virginia State Library*

Jones⟩ (⟨who⟩[7] were then British subjects) with an indorsement from under the hand of the Commissioner of the said Office, expressing the name of the payer, which certificate he the said ⟨Thomas⟩ the Defendant delivered to the Governor and Council, who gave a receipt therefor, in conformity to the directions of the Act, entitled, "An Act for sequestering British property, enabling those indebted to British subjects to pay off such debts, and directing the proceedings in suits where such subjects are parties,"[8] whereby he the Defendant is by virtue of the Act of Assembly in that case made and provided, discharged from so much of the debt in the declaration mentioned, as the said receipt amounts to, and this he is ready to verify—wherefore he prays the judgment of the Court, whether the said Plaintiff ought to have or maintain[9] action aforesaid against him.

And the said ⟨Thomas⟩ with the leave of the Court for further plea saith,[10] that the said Plaintiff ought not to have or maintain ⟨his⟩ said action against him, because he says that the debt in the declaration mentioned, was originally due to British subjects, and is not recoverable in this Court by virtue of the Laws in that case made and provided,[11] and this he is ready to verify—wherefore he prays judgment whether the Plaintiff ⟨his⟩ action aforesaid against him the Defendant ought to have and maintain, &c.[12]

Printed form, Jones v. Walker, U.S. Circuit Court, Va., Ended Cases (Restored), 1797, Vi. Blanks filled in by JM; filed at 27 Feb. 1791 rules. Endorsed on verso by JM: "three pleas, two withdrawn & new pleas filed. The first stands."

1. JM recorded a fee of £9 "From Mr. Walker (federal)" under date of 1 Feb. 1791 (*PJM*, II, 411).

2. This word is in the plural on JM's printed British debt forms. Here and elsewhere in the answer JM deleted the "s" and also changed "their" to "his."

3. In all his British debt cases JM pleaded payment as a general issue in debt on a bond. On this plea, see Case No. 3, Doc. II, n. 2. Opposite this plea JM wrote in the margin: "1. Genl. repl. (2)." As he noted on the verso, this was the only one of the original pleas retained when new ones were filed in Nov. 1791 (Doc. VII).

4. The plea of nil debet, which was the general issue in debt on a simple contract, could not be used in this case. JM should have deleted it before filing his answer. He subsequently crossed it through and wrote in the opposite margin: "withdrawn altogether."

5. In the opposite margin JM wrote: "2 withdrawn & new plea filed."

6. JM omitted "a."

7. The inserted words replaced "Plaintiffs (which Plaintiffs."

8. Hening, *Statutes*, IX, 377–80. JM here inserted an asterisk and wrote on the verso: "*which receipt is in these words & figures, following to wit." He then copied the receipt. In the amended answer (Doc. VII) the receipt is embodied in the text of the loan office plea.

9. JM deleted "their" but forgot to insert "his."

10. JM wrote in the opposite margin: "3 Withdrawn & new plea filed."

11. These laws are fully identified in the amended pleas (Doc. VII).

12. After the pleas were filed, the plaintiff demanded oyer of the loan office receipt and time was given him to reply. Further time was granted in March and April, and at the next two monthly meetings of the rules the case was continued (U.S. Cir. Ct., Va., Rule Bk. I, 9–10, 21–22).

VI. Replications and Demurrer
26 July 1791

Jones surviving partner &c of Farell & Jones vs Thomas Walker.	in Debt. repl:[1]

And the said plaintif as to the plea of the said Defendant,[2] by him first pleaded, in bar, saith, that he by reason of any thing in that plea alledged, ought not to be barred from having, or maintaining his said Action against the said Defendant, because the said Plaintif as before, saith, that the said Defendant hath not paid the Debt in the Declaration mentioned, as in the Said plea he hath alledged, and this he also prays may be inquired of by the Country.[3]

And the said Plaintif, as to the plea of the said Defendant,[4] by him secondly above pleaded in Bar, saith, that he by reason of any thing in that plea alledged ought not to be barred from having or maintaining his said Action against the said defendant, because the said Plaintif saith, that he the said Defendant doth owe the Debt in the Declaration mentioned to the said Plaintif, and this he prays may be inquired of by the Country.[5]

And the said Plaintif, as to the plea of the said Defendant[6] by him thirdly as above pleaded,[7] in Bar, Saith that he by reason of any thing in that plea alledged, ought not to be barred from having or maintaining his action aforesaid against the said Defendant, because protesting that that plea, and the matters therein contained, are not sufficient in Law to bar the said plaintif, from having his said Action in this behalf, against the said defendant, to which the said plaintif hath no need, neither is he bound in any wise, by the Law of the Land to answer;[8] Yet for replication in this behalf the said plaintif saith, that after the day, on which the said Debt in the said Declaration mentioned was contracted, and also after the day on which the said receipt in the said plea mentioned, was granted, that is to say on the third day of September, in the year of our Lord one thousand seven hundred and eighty three, it was, by the fourth article of the Definitive Treaty of peace, between the united States of America, and his Brittanick Majesty made & done in the City of Paris, that is to say in the then Commonwealth, now District of Virginia and now within the jurisdiction of this honorable Court, stipulated and agreed that creditors on either side, shou'd meet with no lawful impediment to the recovery of the full value in Sterling money of all bona fide Debts theretofore contracted. And the said Plaintif farther saith, that he on the said third day of September in the year of our Lord one thousand seven hundred and eighty three, and long before, was, ever since hath been, and still is a subject of his Brittanick Majesty, and a creditor within the intent and meaning of the said fourth article of the said Definitive Treaty, and that the Debt in the Declaration mentioned, was bona fide contracted before the said third day of September one thousand seven hundred and eighty three to wit in the County and Commonwealth aforesaid, now the District of Virginia and now within the jurisdiction of this honorable Court, and then was, and still is, due, owing, and unpaid.[9]

And the said Plaintif for farther replication saith, that after the making of the writing obligatory in the Declaration mentioned; by the said Defendant; and also after the third day of September in the year of our Lord 1783, that is to say on the 17th day of September in the year of our Lord 1787, in the then Commonwealth, now the District of Virginia, and now within the Jurisdiction of this Honble: Court, it was, by the constitution of the united States of America, among other things, expressly declared, that Treatys which were then made, or which shou'd thereafter be made, under the authority of the united States, shou'd be, the Supreme Law of the Land, any thing in the said constitution, or of the Laws—of any State, to the contrary notwithstanding: And the said Plaintif doth in fact aver, that the said constitution of the united States, was made, subsequent to, and after the ratification of the said Definitive treaty of peace, between the united States of America, and his Brittanick Majesty, whose subject the said Plaintiff, then was, & still is. Wherefore for that the Debt in the Decla: mentioned was bona fide contracted, before the making, and ratification, of the said definitive treaty of peace, and the said constitution of the united States, and by the operation thereof, he the said plaintif is entituled to have demand and recover, of, and from the said defendant, the aforesaid Debt in the Declaration mentioned, Without that, that[10] the Governor & Council did give a receipt, for a certificate of the payment into the loan office of this Commonwealth of the sum of Seven thousand, one hundred and seventy three Dollars, in the name of the plaintiff and in conformity to, the directions of the Act, entituled an Act sequestering Brittish property, enabling those indebted to British Subjects, to pay off such Debts, and directing the[11] proceedings in suits, where such Subjects are Creditors, as in the said plea of the said Defendant is alledged, and this he is ready to verify. Wherefore the said Pltff as before prays Judgment of the Court, and his Debt aforesaid, and Damages for the detention of that Debt to be adjudged to him.[12]

And the said Plaintif as to the said plea of the said Defendant fourthly as above pleaded in Bar,[13] saith, that he by any thing in that said plea alledged, ought not to be barred from having or maintaining his Action aforesaid, against the said Defendant, because the said Plaintif saith, that that plea, and the matters therein contained, are not sufficient in Law[14] to bar the said plaintif, from having or maintaining his said action, in this behalf against the said Defendant, to which said plea, in manner and form as the same is above pleaded, he the said Plaintif hath no need, nor is he in any manner, bound, by the Law of the Land to answer, and this he is ready to verify, wherefore for want of a sufficient plea in this behalf, the said Plaintif, as before prays Judgment for his Debt and Damages, for the detention of that Debt, to be adjudged to him.[15]

BAKER ℘ Pltff.

ADS, Jones v. Walker, U.S. Circuit Court, Va., Ended Cases (Restored), 1797, Vi. Filed at rules 26 July 1791. Baker enclosed his interlineations within parentheses to mark them as insertions. The editors have ignored these marks, while incorporating the additions. Endorsed on verso in unknown hand: "this withdrawn as to the plea now standing as the second, originally the 3d & new repl: filed, & also as to the other pleas withdrawn."

1. Baker originally wrote "& Demr:," which was deleted.

2. In the opposite margin someone wrote "1t repl."

3. Baker replied to the plea of payment as if it had been pleaded specially. JM, however, pleaded payment as a general issue, in line with a recent decision of the Virginia Court of Appeals. Since the defendant had already tendered issue (by putting himself upon the country), the plaintiff presumably needed only to join issue rather than reply (see Case No. 3, Doc. II and n. 2; Case No. 9, Doc. IV and n. 1).

4. In the opposite margin someone wrote "2 repl."

5. JM forgot to delete the plea of nil debet, which was not applicable to this case, and Baker compounded the error by replying to it (Doc. V, n. 4).

6. In the opposite margin someone wrote "3 repl."

7. This is the replication to the plea of payment into the loan office.

8. Up to this point the pleading follows almost exactly the language of a demurrer. However, instead of demurring, Baker replied with a *protestando* ("protestation"). He introduced the replication by protesting the legal sufficiency of the plea, and in so doing saved to the plaintiff the right to demur to this plea in any future action. The effect was to confess the sufficiency of the plea, but only for the purposes of the existing suit. Although employed here

as an alternative to a demurrer, the protestation was more frequently used by a plaintiff to protest allegations in the opposing plea that he could not directly deny. The rule against double pleading forced him to choose only one allegation to deny, which had the effect of tacitly admitting others that might be contained in the plea. By protesting, the plaintiff reserved his right to dispute the other allegations on some future occasion (Blackstone, *Commentaries*, III, 311–12; Edward Lawes, *An Elementary Treatise on Pleading in Civil Actions* [1st Am. ed.; Portsmouth, N.H., 1808], 141–43; Sutton, *Personal Actions*, 177–79).

9. At this point Baker deleted eight lines, inserted "(a-)," and then began a new page, placing "(a)." in the opposite margin.

10. The phrase "Without that, that"—more properly, "without this, that"—identifies this pleading as a special traverse. The phrase is more commonly known by its Latin form *absque hoc* ("without this"). The purpose of a special traverse, as distinguished from a direct denial or common traverse, was to make an indirect or qualified denial by setting up an affirmative case. That part of the special traverse stating the affirmative matter—in this instance the treaty of peace and the Constitution—was called the "inducement." This was the real substance of the pleading. The next part, the absque hoc, was the formal denial necessary to prevent the pleading from being dismissed as argumentative. Since it introduced new facts, the special traverse concluded with a verification and prayer of judgment rather than a tender of issue (Stephen, *Principles of Pleading*, 165–89; Sutton, *Personal Actions*, 170–77).

11. At the bottom right-hand corner of the page below "the," Baker inserted "(-b)." At the top of the next page, he deleted the first three lines, and in the margin opposite "proceedings," he wrote "a to b."

12. Counsel for both parties no doubt agreed beforehand to extend the pleadings on the loan office plea to several stages to ensure that certain questions would come squarely before the court for adjudication. The replication, for example, set up the peace treaty and the Constitution in support of the plaintiff's claim. The defendant, for his part, could then rejoin (Doc. IX) by reciting British infractions of the treaty and raise the question of whether the treaty continued in force. Only in this cumbersome way could these issues be submitted to the court for determination.

13. In the opposite margin someone wrote what appears to be "n. 1 demr."

14. The phrase "not sufficient in Law" identifies this pleading as a demurrer. By demurring, the plaintiff admitted the truth of the facts recited in the defendant's plea and signified his readiness to let the court decide on the legal effect of those facts. As a traverse concluding to the country tendered an issue in fact, so a demurrer tendered an issue in law (Stephen, *Principles of Pleading*, 54–55). For another example of a demurrer, see Doc. X.

15. At the August rules the defendant was ordered to rejoin to the replication to the loan office plea and join in the demurrer to the plea of British debt. Since the defendant did not respond at the next monthly meeting, an office judgment was entered against him in October. This judgment was set aside at the November term of the court, when JM filed amended pleas (U.S. Cir. Ct., Va., Rule Bk. I, 21–22; Doc. VII).

VII. Amended Pleas
23 November 1791

2nd plea[1]

And the said defendant[2] defends the force & injury when &c & with the special leave of the court & according to the act of Assembly in that case made & provided for further plea saith that the plaintiffs ought not to have or maintain their action aforesaid against him as to seven thousand one hundred & seventy three dollars equal to £2151-18 virga. money[3] part of the debt in the declaration mentiond because he says that on the 4th. day of July in the year 1776 he the said defendant became a citizen of the state of Virginia & hath ever since remaind a citizen thereof & a resident therein & that the plaintiffs on the said 4th. day of July in the year 1776 were & from the time of their nativity had ever been & always since have been & still are british subjects owing yielding & paying allegiance to the King of Great Britain, which said King of Great Britain & all his subjects as well the plaintiffs as others were on the said 4th. day of July 1776 & so continued until the 3d. day of September 1783 enemies of & at open war with the state of Virginia & the united states of America, & that being so enemies & at open war as aforesaid the legislature of the state of Virginia did at their session begun & held in the city of Williamsburg on Monday the 20th. day of October in the year 1777 pass an act entitled "an act for sequestering british property, enabling those indebted to British subjects to pay off such debts & directing the proceedings in suits where such subjects are parties," whereby it is enacted "that it shall & may be lawful for any citizen of this commonwealth owing money to a subject of Great Britain, to pay the same or any part thereof from time to time as he shall think fit, into the said loan office taking thereout a certificate for the same in the name of the creditor with an indorsement under the hand of the commissioner of the said office expressing the name of the payer, & shall deliver such certificate to the Governor & Council whose receipt shall discharge him from so much of the said debt."[4] And the defendant says that he did on the day of in the year 177 in the county of & within the state of virga. while the said recited act continued in full force, in pursuance thereof, pay into the loan office of this commonwealth on account of the debt in the declaration mentiond the sum of seven thousand one hundred & seventy three dollars & did take out a certificate for the same in the name of Farrell & Jones in the declaration mentiond as creditors, with an indorsement under the hand of the commissioner of the said office expressing the name of the payer which certificate he the defendant then deliverd to the Governor & council who gave a receipt therefor in conformity to the directions of the said act in the words & figures following to wit

Williamsburg May 25th. 1779

Receivd from the hands of the Honble Thomas Walker a loan office certificate for seven thousand one hundred & seventy three dollars being so much money due from the said Thomas Walker esquire to Farrell & Jones of the kingdom of Great Britain & sequesterd according to the act of Assembly for that purpose made. Given under my hand date above

£2151-18 P HENRY[5]

whereby the defendant is by virtue of the said act of Assembly dischargd from so much of the debt in the declaration mentiond as the said receipt specefies & amounts to. And this he is ready to verefy—Wherefore he prays the judgement of the court whether the said plaintiffs ought to have or maintain his action aforesaid against him for the said sum of £2151-18 parcel of the debt in the declaration mentiond.[6]

3rd. plea[7]

And the said Thomas Walker with the special leave of the court & according to the act of assembly for that purpose made & provided defend the force & injury when &c for further plea saith that the plaintiff ought not to have or maintain his action aforesaid against him because he says that on the 4th. day of July in the year 1776 he the said defendant became a citizen of the State of Virginia & hath ever since remaind a citizen thereof & resident therein & that the plaintiff and the said Farrel on the said 4th. day of July in the year 1776 & from the time of their nativity had ever been & always since have been british subjects & plf still is a british subject yielding & paying allegiance to the King of Great Britain, Which said King of Great Britain & all his subjects as well the plaintiff & the said Farrel as others were on the said 4th. day of July 1776 & so continued untill the 3d. day of September in the year 1783 enemies of & at open war with the state of Virginia & the United States of america & that being so enemies & at open war as aforesaid the legislature of the state of Virginia did at their session commencd & held in the city of Williamsburg on the third day of May in the year 1779 pass an act entitled "an act concerning escheats & forfeitures from British subjects" whereby it was among other things enacted, "that all the property real & personal within this commonwealth belonging at this time to any british subject, or which did belong to any british subject at the time such escheat or forfeiture may have taken place, shall be deemd to be vested in the commonwealth, the lands slaves & other real estate by

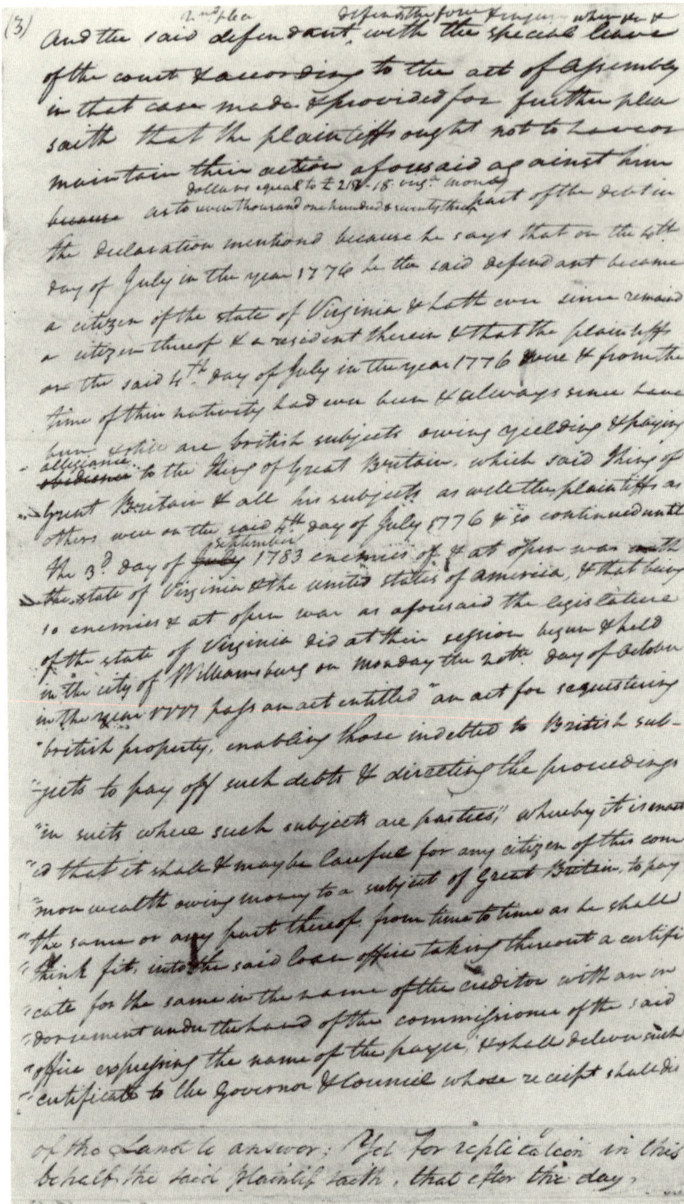
(3) And the said defendant, with the special leave
of the court & according to the act of Assembly
in that case made & provided for further plea
saith that the plaintiffs ought not to have or
maintain their action aforesaid against him
because as to seven thousand one hundred & seventy three dollars equal to £ 2151-18 curr. money part of the debt in
the declaration mentioned because he says that on the 4th
day of July in the year 1776 he the said defendant became
a citizen of the state of Virginia & hath ever since remained
a citizen thereof & a resident therein & that the plaintiffs
on the said 4th day of July in the year 1776 were & from the
time of their nativity had ever been & always since have
been & still are british subjects owing yielding & paying
allegiance to the King of Great Britain, which said King of
Great Britain & all his subjects as well the plaintiffs as
others were on the said 4th day of July 1776 & so continued until
the 3d day of September 1783 enemies of & at open war with
the state of Virginia & the united states of America, & that being
so enemies & at open war as aforesaid the legislature
of the state of Virginia did at their session begun & held
in the city of Williamsburg on monday the 20th day of October
in the year 1777 pass an act entitled "an act for sequestering
british property, enabling those indebted to British sub-
-jects to pay off such debts & directing the proceedings
in suits where such subjects are parties," whereby it is enact
-ed that it shall & may be lawful for any citizen of this com
-mon wealth owing money to a subject of Great Britain to pay
the same or any part thereof from time to time as he shall
think fit, into the said loan office taking thereout a certifi
-cate for the same in the name of the creditor with an in
-dorsement under the hand of the commissioner of the said
office expressing the name of the payer, & shall deliver such
certificate to the Governor & Council whose receipt shall dis
of the Land to answer; Yet for replication in this
behalf the said Plaintiff saith, that after the day

LOAN OFFICE PLEA

Marshall's revised "2nd plea" in *Jones* v. *Walker* and the first of the four British debt pleas (Case Number 12, Document VII). *Courtesy of Virginia State Library*

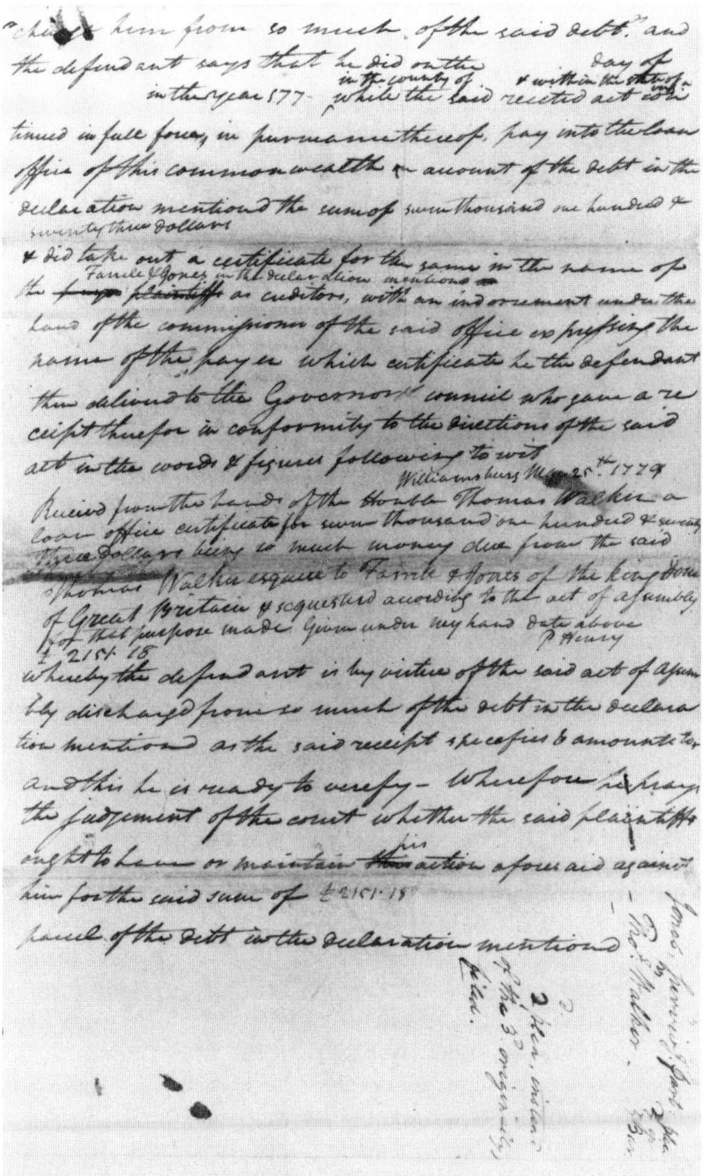

"charge him from so much of the said debt." and the defendant says that he did on the day of in the year 177_ in the county of & within the state of while the said recited act continued in full force, in pursuance thereof, pay into the loan office of this commonwealth on account of the debt in the declaration mentioned the sum of seven thousand one hundred & seventy three Dollars & did take out a certificate for the same in the name of the ~~plaintiffs~~ Farrell & Jones in the declaration mentioned as creditors, with an indorsement under the hand of the commissioner of the said office expressing the name of the payer which certificate he the defendant then delivered to the Governor & council who gave a receipt therefor in conformity to the directions of the said act in the words & figures following to wit

Williamsburg May 25th 1779

Received from the hands of the Honble Thomas Walker a loan office certificate for seven thousand one hundred & seventy three Dollars being so much money due from the said Thomas Walker esquire to Farrell & Jones of the Kingdom of Great Britain & sequestered according to the act of assembly for that purpose made. Given under my hand date above

P Henry

£ 2151.18

Whereby the defendant is by virtue of the said act of assembly discharged from so much of the debt in the declaration mentioned as the said receipt specifies & amounts to and this he is ready to verify — Wherefore he prays the judgement of the court whether the said plaintiffs ought to have or maintain ~~their~~ his action aforesaid against him for the said sum of £2151.18 parcel of the debt in the declaration mentioned

Jones surv. of Farrell & Jones v. Thos. Walker.

2 Plea [illegible]

way of escheat & the personal estate by forfeiture["][8] and that the legislature of the state of Virginia did in their session begun & held in the town of Richmond on Monday the 6th. day of May in the year 1782 pass an act entitled "an act to repeal so much of a former act as suspends the issuing of executions upon certain judgements until December 1783" whereby it is enacted "that no demand whatsoever originally due to a subject of Great Britain shall be recoverable in any court in this commonwealth, altho' the same may be transferd to a citizen of this state or to any other person capable of maintaining such action, unless the assignment hath been or may be made for a valuable consideration bonafide paid before the 1st. day of May 1777.["][9] Which said acts are unrepealed & still in full force. And the defendant in fact says that the debt in the declaration mentiond was personal property within this Commonwealth belonging to a british subject at the time of the passing of the said act entitled "an act concerning escheats & forfeitures from British subjects" & the defendant also in fact says that the debt in the declaration mentiond is a demand originally due to a subject of Great Britain not transferd to any person whatever. And these things he is ready to verefy—Wherefore he prays the judgement of the court whether the said plaintiffs ought to have or maintain their said action against him.[10]

4th. plea[11]

And the said defendant with the further leave of the court & according to the act of assembly in that case made & provided comes by[12] his Attorney & further defends the force & injury &c & for further plea says that the plaintiff ought not to have or maintain his action aforesaid against him because he says that the plaintiff is a subject of the King of Great Britain & that a definitive treaty of peace between the United States of America & his Britannic Majesty was done at Paris on the 3d. day of September one thousand seven hundred & eighty three & that by a part of the 7th. article of the said treaty it was expressly agreed to on the part of his Britannic Majesty with the united States among other things that his said Britannic Majesty shoud with all convenient speed & without causing any destruction or carrying away any negroes or other property of the American inhabitants withdraw all his armies garrisons & fleets from the said United states & from every post[13] place & harbor within the same which may more fully appear reference being had to the said treaty, and the said defendant avers that on the said 3d. day of September 1783 & from his birth to this day he has been a citizen of these united States & of the State of Virginia & that the plaintiff has ever been a british subject & that the plaintiff ought not to maintain his action because his britannic Majesty hath wilfully broken & violated the sd treaty in this that his Britannic Majesty hath from the day of the said treaty & ever since continued to carry of[f] the negroes in his possession the property of the American inhabitants of the United States & hath & still doth refuse to deliver them or permit the owners of the said negroes to take them,[14] and the defendant avers that his Britannic Majesty hath & still doth refuse to withdraw his armies & garrisons from every post place & harbor of the United States which his said Britannic Majesty was bound to do by the said treaty & the defendant avers that from the day of the treaty his Britannic Majesty by force & violence with his army retains possession of the forts Detroit & Niagara & a large territory adjoining the said forts & within the bounds & limits of the United States of America. And the defendants say that in further violation of the said treaty of peace concluded as aforesaid certain nations or tribes of Indians known by the names of the Shawanese, Tawas Twightwees, Pontawatamies, Quicapoos, Wyandots, mingos Piankashaws & Naidonesses & others being at open publick & known war with the inhabitants of the United States & living within the limits thereof & for the purpose of aiding the said Indians in such war & hostility at certain posts forts & garrisons held & kept by the troops & garrisons of his said Britannic Majesty, to wit at Detroit, Michilimachinac & Niagara within the limits of the said united states on the 4th. day of September 1783 & at divers times after the said 4th. of Septr. 1783 up to the institution of this suit, by orders & directions of his said Britannic Majesty & his officers commanding his said troops & armies at the said garrisons of Detroit Michilimachinac & Niagara & at other forts & stations held by the said troops & armies within the limits of the said United States are supplied & furnishd with arms ammunition & weapons of war, to wit with guns gun powder, lead, leaden bulletts, Tomahawks & scalping knives for the purpose of enabling them to prosecute war against the citizens of these United States & also giving & paying to the said Indians money goods wares & merchandizes for booty & plunder taken in such war & for persons citizens of these United States made prisoners by the said Indians in such their warfare against these United States and the King of Great Britain is an enemy of these United States & this he is ready to verefy. Wherefore he prays the judgement of the court whether the plaintiff ought to have or maintain his action aforesaid against him.

5th plea

And the said defendant with the leave of the court and according to the act of Assembly in that case made & provided further defends the force & injury when &c. and for further plea saith that the debt in the declaration mentiond was contracted before the 4th day of

July 1776 to wit on the day of in the year 17 & that when the said debt was contracted & from thence to the said 4th day of July 1776 & on that day & until this day the said plaintiff was & is a subject of the King of Great Britain & the defendant was also a subject of the King of Great Britain residing in Virginia until the said 4th. day of July 1776 on which day the people of North America among whom was this defendant who had theretofore been subjects of the King of Great Britain dissolvd the till then subsisting government whereby the right of the plaintiff to the debt in the declaration mentiond was totally annuld. And this he is ready to verefy wherefore he prays the judgement of the court whether the plaintiff ought to have or maintain his action aforesaid against him.

AD, Jones v. Walker, U.S. Circuit Court, Va., Ended Cases (Restored), 1797, Vi. In JM's hand. Each plea written on separate sheet and individually endorsed. Entered in court on this date as were subsequent pleadings—replication, rejoinder, demurrer, and joinder in demurrer (Docs. VIII–XI) (U.S. Cir. Ct., Va., Ord. Bk. I, 54–55).

1. JM withdrew all his original pleas except for that of payment, on which issue stood joined. He then substituted four new British debt pleas in place of the original two. The first of these, a revised version of the loan office plea, thus became the second plea in the amended pleas. The other three British debt pleas were designated as the third, fourth, and fifth pleas. JM had these revised pleas printed up, though not in time to use in this case.

2. JM wrote out the pleas, leaving blank spaces for the particular details which he filled in later.

3. The sum in Virginia currency was calculated by dividing the sum in dollars by 3⅓ (£1 Virginia currency equaled $3.33).

4. Hening, *Statutes*, IX, 379–80.

5. At the time Walker presented his loan office certificate, the rate of depreciation was 20 to 1. The sum of £2,151.18 Virginia currency was thus equivalent to £107 specie. Walker's payment was one of nine made by Virginians to the account of Farell & Jones between Nov. 1778 and May 1780 (see Hanson's memorandum of "Paper Money Paid in at Loan Office on Account of Farell & Jones," 7 Dec. 1787, T.79/30 [claim of John T. Ware], P.R.O.).

6. An endorsement in the lower margin reads: "2d. plea, instead of the 3d. originally filed."

7. JM's heading, stating the name of the case and the cause of action, has been omitted.

8. Hening, *Statutes*, X, 67.

9. Ibid., XI, 75–76.

10. An endorsement on the lower margin reads: "3d plea, instead of the 4th. originally filed."

11. JM's heading has been omitted (see n. 7).

12. JM originally wrote "Patrick Henry," which he deleted. Henry was one of four lawyers who argued Walker's case at this term of the court.

13. Appears as "port" in the printed British debt pleas here and in the same phrase repeated below; but in the printed rejoinder appears correctly as "post."

14. Virginia had long complained about the carrying off of slave property during the British evacuation. Only a few days before JM submitted this new plea, the Virginia General Assembly adopted a resolution declaring that British violation of the seventh article "has been highly injurious" to Virginians and calling upon the federal government to enforce that article (*JHDV*, Oct. 1791, 21, 42, 58).

VIII. Amended Replication

23 November 1791

Jones surviving partner &c
vs
Thomas Walker } In Debt.

And the said plaintiff as to the plea of the said Defendant, by him secondly as above pleaded in Bar saith,[1] that he by reason of any thing in that plea alledged ought not to be barred from having or maintaining his said Action against the said Defendant, because protesting that that plea, and the matters therein contained are not sufficient in Law to Bar the said plaintif from having or maintaining his said Action in this behalf against the said Defendant, to which the said plaintif hath no reason, neither is he, in any wise bound by the Law of the Land to answer: Yet for replication in this behalf he the said plaintif saith That after the Debt in the said Declaration mentioned was contracted, and after the said fourth day of July, 1776, in the said plea of the said Defendant mentioned, & also after the said 20th. day of October 1777, and the passing of the Act of General Assembly,[2] in the said plea also mentioned, and also after the day in which the said receipt in the plea stated is said to have been granted, to wit on the third day of September in the year of our Lord one thousand seven hundred and eighty three, it was by the definitive Treaty of peace, between the united States of America, and his Britanick Majesty, made and done in the City of Paris, that is to say in the Commonwealth, now the District of Virginia, and now within the Jurisdiction of this Honorable Court, stipulated and agreed, among other things "that Creditors on either side shoud meet with no lawful impedement, to the recovery of the full value in Sterling money of all bona fide Debts, theretofore contracted." And the said Plaintiff in fact saith, that he on the said third day of September in the year 1783 and for a long time before, (as well as the said Joseph Farell, in his life time) were, then was, and ever since hath been, and still is, a subject of his Brittanick Majesty, and a Creditor within the intent and meaning of the fourth article of the said definitive Treaty, and that the Debt in the Declaration mentioned was contracted before the said third day of September 1783, that is to say, in the County and Commonwealth aforesaid, now the District of Virginia, and now within the Jurisdiction of this Honorable Court, and then was, and still is due, owing and unpaid. And the said Plaintif for farther replication saith, that after the contracting of the Debt in the Declaration mentioned, by the said Defendant, and also after the said 4th day of July in the year of our Lord 1776, and after the said 20th. day of October in the year of our Lord 1777, and also after the said third day of September in the year of our Lord 1783, that is to say, on the day of , 1787, in the then Commonwealth, now the District of Virginia, and now within the Jurisdiction of this Honble Court, it was by the constitution of the united States of America, among other things, expressly declared, that Treatys which were then made, or which shou'd thereafter be made, under the authority of the united states shou'd be the supreme Law of the Land, any thing in the said constitution, or of the Laws of any State, to the contrary notwithstanding. And the said plaintif doth in fact aver, that the said constitution of the united States, was made and accepted subsequent to, and after the ratification of the said definitive Treaty of peace, between the said united States of America, & his Britanick Majesty whose subject the said plaintiff then was, and still is, and after the said 4th day of July in the year 1776, and also after the said 20th day of October 1777. Wherefore for that the Debt in the Declaration mentioned was bona fide contracted before the making of the said definitive Treaty of peace, and bef[ore] the making of the said Constitution of the united States, he the said plaintif is entituled to demand, have, and recover of the said Defendant the aforesaid Debt in the Declaration mentioned, Without that that the Governor & Counsil did give a receipt for a Certificate of the payment into the Loan office of the sum seven thousand one hundred & seventy three Dollars, equal to Two thousand one hundred & fifty one pounds eighteen shillings Virginia money in the name of the sd. Farell & Jones, and in conformity to the directions of the Act of General Assembly entitled, "An Act for sequestering British property, enabling those indebted to British subjects to pay off such Debts, and directing the proceedings in suits where such subjects are partys" whilst the said Act was in force as in the said plea of the said Defendant is alledged, and this he is ready to verify. Wherefore the said plaintif as before, prays Judgment of the Court, and his Debt aforesaid, and Damages for the detention of that Debt to be adjudged to him.

BAKER ℘ repln.[3]

ADS, Jones v. Walker, U.S. Circuit Court, Va., Ended Cases (Restored), 1797, Vi. Baker enclosed his interlineations within parentheses to mark them as insertions. The editors have ignored these marks, while incorporating the additions. Endorsed on verso: "Repl. to 2d plea"; entered in court on this date (see Doc. VII, n.).

1. This is the replication to the loan office plea. It is essentially the same as the original replication (Doc. VI), with some additions and changes to make it conform to the amended plea.

2. The sequestration act (Hening, *Statutes*, IX, 377–80).

3. Baker also entered demurrers to the third, fourth, and fifth pleas, which have been omitted. In subsequent British debt cases printed forms were used for the plaintiff's replication and demurrers.

IX. Rejoinder
23 November 1791

Walker
ads } in debt[1]
Jones surviving partner &c

And the said defendant, as to the replication of the plaintiff to the second plea by him the said defendant above pleaded saith that the said plaintiff for any thing in his said replication containd ought not to have or maintain his said action against him because he by way of rejoinder in this behalf says that in the same definitive treaty of peace between the United states of America & his Britannic Majesty by the plaintiff in his said replication mentiond & which is now to the court shewn it was among other things stipulated & contracted as follows, "there shall be a firm & perpetual peace between his Britannic Majesty & the said States & between the subjects of the one & the citizens of the other, wherefore all hostilities both by sea & land shall from henceforth cease; all prisoners on both sides shall be set at liberty, & his Britannic Majesty shall with all convenient speed & without causing any destruction or carrying away any negroes or other property of the American inhabitants withdraw all his armies garrisons & fleets from the said United states & from every post place & harbor within the same." And the defendant in fact says that his said Britannic Majesty hath not performd those things which by the said treaty of peace he was bound to perform but hath altogether faild to do so & hath broken the said treaty in this, that on the fourth day of September in the year 1783 & on the day of 179 [2] & at divers times between the said 4th. day of September in the year 1783 & the said day of in the year 179 his Britannic Majesty at Detroit & other posts within the boundaries of the united States to wit within the commonwealth of Virginia & the jurisdiction of this Honble court, in open violation of the said treaty & the articles thereof excited persuaded & stird up the Shawanese & divers other tribes of Indians to make war upon the United States of America & the commonwealth of Virginia & gave them the said Indians aid in the prosecution of the said war & furnishd them with arms & ammunition for the purpose of enabling them to prosecute the same, and his said Britannic Majesty hath not with all convenient speed & without causing any destruction, or carrying away any negroes or other property of the American inhabitants withdrawn all his armies garrisons & fleets from the said United States & from every post place & harbor within the same but hath carried away five thousand negroes the property of the American inhabitants on the 4th. day of September in the year 1783 from New York to wit in the Commonwealth of Virginia & within the jurisdiction of this court & hath refusd to withdraw, with all convenient speed, his armies & garrisons from these United States & from every post & place within the same, but hath with force & violence & in open violation of the said treaty of peace on the said 3d. day of September in the year 1783 & since maintaind his Armies & Garrisons in the forts of Niagara & Detroit which are posts & places within these United States & still doth maintain his Armies & garrisons within the said forts. And the defendant further says that the debt in the declaration mentiond or so much thereof as is equal to the sum of £2151-18.0 was not a bona fide debt due & owing to the plaintiff on the said 3d. day of September 1783 because the defendant had on the day of 177 in Virginia aforesaid paid in part thereof the sum of £2151-18- & had afterwards obtaind a certificate therefor according to the act of the General Assembly entitled an act for sequestering British property, enabling those indebted to British subjects to pay off such debts & directing the proceedings in suits where such subjects are parties which payment was made while the said act continued in full force. Without that that[3] the said treaty of peace & the constitution of the United States entitle the said plaintiff to maintain his said action against this defendant for so much of the said debt in the declaration mentiond as is equal to £2151-18. And this he is ready to verefy wherefore he prays the judgement of the court whether the plaintiff ought to have & maintain his action aforesaid against him for so much of the debt in the declaration mentiond as is equal to the said sum of £2151-18.

AD, Jones v. Walker, U.S. Circuit Court, Va., Ended Cases (Restored), 1797, Vi. In JM's hand. Endorsed on verso: "rejoinder to 2d plea"; entered in court on this date (see Doc. VII, n.).

1. In the printed pleadings that were used in later British debt cases, the plaintiff's replication to the loan office plea and the defendant's rejoinder were printed together on the same form.

2. JM omitted filling in the date this suit commenced, 9 June 1790, the day the writ of capias issued (Doc. I).

3. The rejoinder, like the replication, is in the form of a special traverse, so identified by the absque hoc (Doc. VI and n. 10).

X. Demurrer
23 November 1791

Jones surviving partner }
vs
Thomas Walker }

And the said Plaintif as to the rejoinder of the Defendant to the replication of the sd. plaintif to the second plea of the said Defendant, by him, as above pleaded in Bar saith, That he by reason of any thing in that rejoinder alledged ought not to be barred from having or maintaining his Action aforesaid against the said Defendant, because the said plaintif saith, that the said rejoinder, and the matters therein contained are not sufficient in Law to bar the said plaintif from having, or maintaining his said Action in this behalf against the said Defendant, to which said rejoinder, as the same is above pleaded, in manner and form, the said plaintif hath no need, neither is he bound by the Law of the Land to answer, and this he is ready to verify, wherefore for want of a sufficient rejoinder in this behalf the said plaintif as before, prays Judgment and his Debt aforesaid, and Damages for the detention of that Debt to be adjudged to him.[1]

BAKER ℘ Pltff.

ADS, Jones v. Walker, U.S. Circuit Court, Va., Ended Cases (Restored), 1797, Vi. Endorsed on verso: "Demurrer to rejoinder to repl: to 2 plea"; entered in court on this date (see Doc. VII, n.).

1. The language of this demurrer is exactly the same as that in Doc. VI, except that here the plaintiff is demurring to defendant's rejoinder rather than to an initial plea.

XI. Joinder in Demurrer
23 November 1791

And the said defendant saith that the plea by him pleaded by way of rejoinder to the replication of the plaintiff to the plea of the defendant by him secondly pleaded in bar and the matter therein contained as the same is therein in manner and form pleaded are good and sufficient in law to bar him the said plaintiff from having & maintaining his Action aforesaid against him which said plea & the matter herein contained he the said deft. is ready to verify & prove as the Court here shall think fit and because the said plaintiff doth not answer to that plea nor doth in any manner deny it he the said deft. again prays Judgment whether the said plaintiff his Action aforesaid against him ought to have or maintain.[1]

MS, Jones v. Walker, U.S. Circuit Court, Va., Ended Cases (Restored), 1797, Vi. In an unknown hand. Endorsed on verso: "Joinder in demurrer to the rejoinder to the repl: to the 2nd. plea"; entered in court on this date (see Doc. VII, n.).

1. A joinder in demurrer was analogous to a joinder of issue, or similiter, on a tender of issue of fact. In the former the issue was submitted to the court for decision in the first instance; in the latter the issue went to the jury, subject to the instructions of the judge (Stephen, *Principles of Pleading*, 55, 238–39; Case No. 9, Doc. IV and n. 1).

Arguments on the demurrers to the British debt pleas commenced the next day, 24 Nov., and continued into December. No decision was forthcoming either at this term or the next two succeeding ones of May and Nov. 1792. In the meantime William Jones died, and his numerous suits had to be revived in the name of his administrator, John Tyndale Ware, by writs of scire facias. This could not be accomplished in time for the May 1793 term, but to prevent further postponement of a second hearing, the court, with the defendant's consent, ordered one of the cases to be revived in Ware's name. This was the suit against Daniel Hylton, which then became the test case (U.S. Cir. Ct., Va., Ord. Bk. I, 141).

XII. Scire Facias
10 July 1794

The PRESIDENT *of the* UNITED STATES *of* AMERICA,
to the MARSHAL *of the* VIRGINIA DISTRICT, Greeting:

[SEAL] WHEREAS in an action ⟨of Debt⟩ lately depending in the court of the United States, for the middle circuit in the Virginia district, between ⟨William Jones surviving partner of Farrel & Jones late Merchants in the Kingdom of Great Britain Plaintif and Thomas Walker defendant⟩ and whereas, since ⟨the commencement of the said Action⟩ but before any judgment entered therein, the said ⟨William Jones⟩ departed this life, having first made ⟨his⟩ last will and testament, and appointed ⟨John Tyndale Ware⟩ executor thereof, who have taken on ⟨him⟩sel⟨f⟩ the burthen of the administration thereof; nevertheless, this cause remains undetermined, and the said ⟨John Tyndale Ware⟩ have applied for a proper remedy in this behalf, and being willing that right and justice may be done agreeable to the acts of the Congress of the United States in such case made and provided, command you, that by good and lawful men of your district, you make know[1] to the said ⟨Thomas Walker⟩ that ⟨he⟩ be before the Judges of the Court of the United States for the middle circuit in the Virginia District, at the Capitol in the city of Richmond, on the twenty-second day of ⟨November⟩ next, to shew if any thing for ⟨himself he⟩ can say why the cause may not be enquired in and a judgment entered up thereon against ⟨him⟩, if to the ⟨said Ware⟩ it seems expedient, and further to do and receive what the said court on their part shall consider; and have then there the names of those by whom you shall make known, and this writ. Witness, JOHN JAY, Esq; Chief Justice of the United States of America, this ⟨10th⟩ day of ⟨July⟩ in the year 179⟨4⟩ and in the ⟨nineteenth⟩ year of the independence of the United States of America.[2]

WM MARSHALL Clk

Printed form, Jones v. Walker, U.S. Circuit Court, Va., Ended Cases (Restored), 1797, Vi. Blanks filled in by clerk. Executed 30 Oct. 1794, by Deputy Marshal Thomas Lewis, whose endorsement on verso reads: "Executed in presence of Edward Fearneyhough a free holder in the County of Albemarle and Charles Merewether a free holder in the County of Bedford."

1. At common law, suits abated if one of the parties died before judgment, but by statute could be revived by or against the executor or administrator of the deceased party. This was done by a writ of scire facias requiring the defendant to show cause why the suit should not proceed to final judgment (*U.S. Statutes at Large*, I, 90).

2. Writs of scire facias in this and twenty-one other suits originally brought by William Jones were awarded 4 Dec. 1793. These were returnable at the May 1794 term, but the one against Walker apparently was not executed in time and another had to be sued out. By the Nov. 1794 term the defendant Walker was dead; a scire facias was accordingly awarded against his executor at this term and again in May 1796. Final judgment in this suit was postponed until after the Supreme Court's decision in Ware v. Hylton (U.S. Cir. Ct., Va., Ord. Bk. I, 241–43, 401; II, 105).

XIII. Verdict
27 May 1797

We of the Jury find for the Plaintiff the debt in the declaration mentioned to be disharg'd by the payment of Five Thousand three Hundred & 8 Dollars & 8 Cents with Interest from septr 30th 1775[1] till paid deducting Eight Years Interest during the War.[2]

Wm Dabney
May 27th 97

ADS, Jones v. Walker, U.S. Circuit Court, Va., Ended Cases (Restored), 1797, Vi. On verso of declaration (Doc. IV).

1. An account filed with the bond showed a balance against Walker of £1,195.13.8 sterling as of 30 Sept. 1775. The sterling amount was converted to dollars by multiplying by $4.44, the rate of exchange established by law (*U.S. Statutes at Large*, I, 167).

2. On the deduction of war interest, see Case No. 16, editorial note. The plaintiff agreed to stay execution of judgment until 27 May 1798. When executor Francis Walker failed to pay by then, Ware sued out a fieri facias (an execution writ) for the sum of $9,574.29—the full amount of principal, interest, and costs. This was levied on seventeen slaves and one hundred head each of cattle and sheep. The executor then gave a forthcoming bond to keep the property until the day of the sale, scheduled for 22 Nov. 1798. The property was not delivered on that day, and the plaintiff accordingly moved for judgment on the forfeited forthcoming bond. Final judgment was rendered on 25 May 1799 (U.S. Cir. Ct., Va., Ord. Bk. II, 221–22; III, 121, 204; Jones's Executor v. Walker, U.S. Cir. Ct., Va., Ended Cases [Unrestored], 1799).

13. Ware, Administrator of Jones, v. Hylton

1790–1796

I. Argument in the Circuit Court, 29–30 May 1793
II. Writ of Error, 6 June 1794
III. Appeal Bond, 24 June 1794
IV. Citation, ca. 28 June 1794
V. Argument in the Supreme Court, 9 February 1796
VI. Judgment, 7 March 1796

Editorial Note

After hearing arguments in *Jones* v. *Walker* in November 1791, the federal circuit court suspended proceedings in the case at the next two terms. During the interval the plaintiff William Jones died, which meant that his many suits had to be revived by writs of scire facias in the name of his administrator, John Tyndale Ware. Since these writs could not be returned in time for the May 1793 term, the parties, to prevent further delay, agreed to have one of the cases revived by court order without a scire facias. This was the suit against Richmond merchant Daniel L. Hylton.[1] Thus *Ware, Administrator of Jones,* v. *Hylton* replaced *Jones* v. *Walker* as the test case for deciding the British debt pleas. The facts of the two cases were the same: both were actions of debt on a bond in which the defendant pleaded all four of the special British debt pleas.

Daniel Hylton had the distinction of being party to two early constitutional cases decided by the Supreme Court.[2] Before the Revolution he had established himself as an importing merchant at Bermuda Hundred on the James River just below Richmond. In July 1774 Hylton & Company executed a bond to Farell & Jones to settle an account balance of nearly £1,500 sterling. Six years later Hylton, as provided by Virginia's sequestration law, paid £933 in depreciated paper currency (equivalent to £15 specie) into the state loan office in partial discharge of his company's debt to the Bristol firm. Jones sued for payment immediately on the opening of the federal court in the spring of 1790.[3]

The original lawyer for Hylton was not Marshall but James Innes, attorney general of Virginia. The defendant first retained Marshall in April 1793, a month before his case became the occasion for the second hearing of arguments on the British debt pleas.[4] Hylton also engaged Patrick Henry and Alexander Campbell to join Innes and Marshall as his counsel—this was the same team that had argued the case of the Virginia debtors eighteen months before in *Jones* v. *Walker*. The court at the May 1793 term was composed of Chief Justice John Jay, Associate Justice James Iredell, and District Judge Cyrus Griffin. The hearing of Hylton's case took place between 24 May and 7 June. On the latter day the judges unanimously rejected three of the British debt pleas, but on the loan office plea Iredell and Griffin overruled Jay, holding that payments under Virginia's sequestration law were a legal discharge of debts to British creditors. The plaintiff carried an appeal on this point to the Supreme Court, which in 1796 reversed the circuit court's judgment and struck down the last of the special pleas.[5]

The documents selected for this case include previously unpublished notes of Marshall's arguments as heard in the circuit court in May 1793 and the Supreme Court in February 1796. In neither instance did Marshall himself write the notes—no manuscript in his hand survives. The source for his circuit court argument is a manuscript notebook by Justice Iredell, now at the Law Library of the Library of Congress. This is the second of at least two notebooks (the first is missing) Iredell compiled during the trial of *Ware* v. *Hylton*. It begins on 29 May 1793, with "Mr. Henry's recapitulation"; hence the missing first notebook must have contained the opening statements by one or more of the plaintiff's counsel, followed by Henry for the defendant. After Henry came Marshall (29–30 May), Campbell (30 May), and Innes (31 May). The notebook concludes with John Wickham's reply for the plaintiff (31 May–1 June). Whether Iredell entered further arguments in a third notebook is uncertain.[6]

Document I is extracted from that part of the surviving notebook that summarizes Marshall's speech of 29 and 30 May. Iredell wrote in a minute scrawl that is difficult to read when not illegible. The notes are in rough form, consisting of disconnected words and phrases whose meaning is not always clear even when the transcription is complete. The judge kept his notebooks for his personal use, to jog his memory when writing his opinion. He obviously did not intend them to be comprehensible to anyone but himself. Defective as they are from the standpoint of today's reader, Iredell's notes are the only extant record of Marshall's argument on behalf of the Virginia debtors at the trial stage of *Ware* v. *Hylton*. The annotation attempts to clarify and amplify the notes, though some passages remain hopelessly obscure. The notes also make greater sense when read along with the report of Marshall's argument in the Supreme Court.

In his report of the appeal of *Ware* v. *Hylton*, Alexander J. Dallas, who was not present during the arguments of counsel, acknowledged using the notes of William Tilghman, a leading practitioner at the bar of the Supreme Court. Tilghman's notes came to light at the Historical Society of Pennsylvania, where for years they had reposed in oblivion.[7] This discovery provides a rare opportunity for a historical edition to collate a printed text with its manuscript source. Document V presents in parallel columns Tilghman's summary of Marshall's argument and the corresponding section of Dallas's report. A comparison of the two texts shows that Dallas, except for omitting two brief passages, adhered to the substance of Tilghman's notes while improving their readability by stylistic embellishments and interpolations. His version is thus not a literal rendition of Marshall's remarks. In the absence of other sources it is impossible to know how faithful Tilghman was to the wording and style of the speech as actually delivered.

Although the circuit court proceedings in *Ware* v. *Hylton* were not reported, the opinions delivered by Iredell and Jay survive in published form. These, along with Iredell's manuscript notebook of attorneys' arguments, provide adequate documentation of the trial below. Iredell did not sit in the appeal, but his circuit court opinion was included in Dallas's report. Jay's opinion, though published more than a century ago, has escaped scholarly attention because it appeared under another title in a volume of reports of cases in the federal circuit court of New York.[8]

Unlike the justices who decided the appeal, Iredell and Jay had to consider all four of the special British debt pleas, not just the one interposing payments into the state loan office. Some of the defenses they quickly dismissed with little comment, such as the plea alleging that the debt was annulled by the dissolution of the former government. Counsel for the defendant in fact gave this up during the course of argument, inconsistent as it was with the acts recited in the other pleas that explicitly recognized the continued existence of British debts. They also abandoned the defense grounded on the 1779 act "concerning escheats and forfeitures from British subjects," vesting in the state the real and personal property of British subjects. By the very words of this act the confiscation was not to "extend to debts due to British subjects, and payable into the loan office." As Jay charitably remarked, this act "must have been inadvertently pleaded."[9] A more difficult point confronting the judges was the charge of British infractions of the peace treaty. If the charge was true, did it mean that a state of war existed or that the treaty was void and of no effect? After carefully distinguishing political from judicial matters, both Iredell and Jay concluded that these were policy questions that fell outside the province of the judiciary.

With the treaty declared to be in force, the two remaining props supporting the debtors' cause were the sequestration law of 1777 and the 1782 law prohibiting the recovery of debts originally owed to British subjects unless the debts had been assigned to a citizen before 1 May 1777. Jay disposed of the latter on the ground that the legislature intended it to operate only during the war and for the purpose of preventing alien enemies from recovering their debts by fraudulent assignments. He insisted that the plaintiff's right to sue was good after the war even without the express stipulation in the fourth article. Iredell contended that the supremacy clause of the Constitution in effect repealed the 1782 law. At the same time, however, the North Carolina jurist believed the treaty as "supreme law" had only a prospective operation—it could not nullify the payments into the loan office under the 1777 sequestration law. These payments, he held, exonerated the debtor, though he conceded that the British creditor still had a good claim against the commonwealth. Jay, in dissent, allowed the fullest operation to the treaty to annul loan office payments and went even further to suggest that independently of the treaty the sequestration law did not bar the creditor's right to recover from the Virginia debtor. He construed the act to show that the legislature intended only to prevent payment to British creditors during the war. When the appeal came before the Supreme Court three years later, Jay was no longer on the bench, but he had the satisfaction of seeing his dissent receive the unanimous endorsement of the high court.

In stating the case for the debtors on the loan office plea, Marshall was at pains to avoid the constitutional question raised by the apparent conflict between the Virginia law and the treaty of peace. His strategy was to reconcile the two by a "fair and rational construction" of the treaty itself without venturing onto the controversial ground of the treaty's effect on contrary state laws (Document V). The result was an ingenious piece of advocacy, demonstrating a highly developed skill in manipulating language that he frequently called upon in later years in writing his judicial opinions. Although he gained his point on circuit, perhaps largely owing to the accidental circumstance that Iredell was Jay's judicial companion at that term, Marshall was unable to persuade the four sitting justices in the appeal—Samuel Chase, William Paterson, James Wilson, and William Cushing—that Virginia's sequestration law lay outside the scope of the 1783 treaty. His "ingenious, metaphysical, reasoning and refinement upon the words, debt, discharge, extinguishment" were rejected as defeating the plain meaning of the fourth article and contrary to the accepted maxims of construing treaties.[10]

Biographers have not failed to note the irony that in his only appearance at the bar of the Supreme Court Marshall had to argue a cause that ran counter to his deeply felt nationalist sentiments. One has suggested that the court's decision must have "soothed his conscience."[11] This should not imply that his defense of the Virginia debtors was halfhearted. The legal strategy he chose did allow him to fulfill his duty to his client without sacrificing his personal views. However, if Marshall shied away from the constitutional issue in *Ware v. Hylton*, he did so not because he found the doctrine of state sovereignty personally repugnant, but because his informed professional judgment convinced him that a case depending on that doctrine would surely lose.

1. U.S. Cir. Ct., Va., Ord. Bk. I, 141.

2. The other was Hylton v. U.S., on the constitutionality of the carriage tax, also decided in 1796 (3 Dall. 171).

3. *Va. Gazette* (Purdie and Dixon), 8 Jan., 20 Aug. 1767; bond and account, Ware v. Hylton, U.S. Cir. Ct., Va., Ended Cases (Restored), 1794; Hanson's memorandum of "Paper Money Paid in at Loan Office on Account of Farell & Jones," 7 Dec. 1787, T.79/30 (claim of John T. Ware), P.R.O.

4. U.S. Cir. Ct., Va., Rule Bk. I, 9, 23. Innes in fact used JM's printed pleas, crossing out JM's name and inserting his own (Ware v. Hylton). JM recorded a fee of £7 from "Mr. Hylton—retainer" (*PJM*, II, 457).

5. James Iredell to Mrs. Iredell, 20 May 1793 (Griffith J. McRee, *Life and Correspondence of James Iredell*, II [New York, 1858], 394–95); *Virginia Gazette and Richmond Manchester Advertiser*, 10 June 1793; Ware v. Hylton, 3 Dall. 199 (1796).

6. A rough transcription by J. A. C. Grant accompanies the surviving MS notebook (Law Library, DLC). The editors are indebted to John Semonche of the University of North Carolina and to James R. Perry of the Documentary History of the Supreme Court of the United States, 1789–1801, for directing them to this source.

7. 3 Dall. 207 n. Credit for discovering these notes belongs to James R. Perry and James Buchanan of the Documentary History of the Supreme Court of the United States, 1789–1801.

8. Hobson, "Recovery of British Debts," *VMHB*, XCII (1984), 189 and n. 36.

9. Hening, *Statutes*, X, 70; Fed. Cas. No. 7507, 1064.

10. 3 Dall. 282 (Cushing's opinion). See also *PJM*, III, 4–7.

11. Francis N. Stites, *John Marshall, Defender of the Constitution* (Boston, 1981), 59.

I. Argument in the Circuit Court

29–30 May 1793

Mr Marshall—For the Defendant.
1. Acts of Assembly form a bar.
2. Nothing to remove the Bar.
  1. Acts of Assembly form a bar
    1. Acts such as an Independent Nation at War had a right to pass.
    2. That V.[1] *quoad*[2] this was Sovereign & Independent
    3. Acts sufficiently express for the purpose
1st. point. Such as a Nation at War had a right to pass.
  1. If contrary to the Laws of War. Acts *de facto* valid.
  Gov. may pass any law *not inconsistent with its Constitution.*
  Principle of Society—
    Each Party to have a Will of its own.
    Some Power to express it.
    L.[3] to express it.
    L. will bind, unless in something they cannot act upon.
Will of Society *commensurate with its object.*
Constitution must express an exception (if any)
This not a *natural right.*
  Surrenders a right to acquire & hold by force, for a right to acquire & hold by law.
  Strange to permit rights—allow a Recovery—and not to restrain.
  Obj. L. can't pass an Act contrary to Justice. Great lines of Justice & Injustice—Many intermediate gradations—often nearly approach.
      Judges appointed *to judge of the law.*
    1 Bl. Comms. p. 45, to 49.[4]
  No distinction between this court and a court of Virginia.
  At that time the G.[5] could only legislate *by means of the State Legislatures.*
  2. But not contrary to the Laws of War
  That which may be done against *a Nation* may be against *an Individual of that Nation.*
  Property of G. being seizable   That of the People might be.
  No way of attacking the Nation but by attacking Individuals.
    Grotius, 3 Book, 2 Chapter, 2 Section. 9 i.[6]
    Vattel 2 B. s. 80, 81, 82
        3 B. s. 70, 71, 72.[7]

Laws of N. authorise *seizing property of the Enemy during the War to carry on the War.*
First principle—self preservation—its very existence might be at stake.

Duty will not only justify but order. Duty to one's self, & others in competition—prefer the first.
Who shall judge? Must not the Nation? Sole Judge of its necessity.
Thing justified in one situation may not in another. Expediency.

2 upon a plank at sea

Situation of a Nation may be the same.
If justified at the time—can a subsequent Power judge and over-rule?
Wickedness to abandon—Folly of the one measure (that of forbearing at first) could only be equalled by the vice of the other.

Right to go to war. to take away the property of the Enemy in battle. No rule for the exercise of it. If Gov. can authorise a General to act *as necessity shall* require, why may not the L. itself.
Any inferior Legislation binding. If Confiscation permitted, may diminish—influence the degree of necessity required—

might have remitted—or abolished totally—or deny its exercise.
Debt—Property, as well as that visible & tangible—

Owing to the Laws of Society.
Equally convertible to use
Distinction not authorised—Contrary laid down.[8]
Grotius 3 B. 2 Ch. 2 Sect.[9]
2 Burl. c. 8. sect. 1, 2, 3.[10]
Vatt. 3 B. Ch. 5. s. 77.[11]

Principle not to be [reserved?] *to the particular illustration.*
Vattel—2 principles

1. a right to all goods. Debts among them.
2. a right to any sum due from Neutral Nations to our Enemies.

Vatt. c. 9. s. 160, 161, 162.[12]
Bynk. (refers to Innes).[13]

Explicit declaration—complained of—but the Confiscation & the right maintained.

Recognized in the case from Parker.

Legatee—like a Creditor. Chose in Action.

Choses in Action forfeitible.[14]

Would shew—*forfeitible by the War itself.* (if carried into effect)—
Answer to P's[15] arguments

Members of the social Compact unnecessary. Where a division—& effected by a War—*all the rights of War devolve on each Party.*[16]

Argument would go to other things as well as Debts.
Vattel's P.D. s. 11, 17, 20[17]—1 Burl.[18] Cases cited by P.

Don't apply to a state of War

Contract *during War*—laws of War suspended—not to apply where no faith is pledged—If pledged during War, as to any thing, *faith ought to be observed*—

Rights of Commerce—

Modern Books as well as ancient warrant confiscation. National Debts depend on the faith of Government. Individual Debts contracted *in society*, & with the knowledge as to the Laws of War.

1 Chan. Ca. 123.[19] Case not applicable to shew a distinction between Debts & other property—Instance of Confiscation—sanctioned by Treaty—Payment produces an Equity. If intelligible it supports the power of Confiscation.

Cases from Dallas—

p. 71. If Debt not acted upon during the War—Debt revived—Admitted—[20]

403. opinion of Shippen.[21]

If any weight—conclusive in his favour. What is confiscated is the *right of the creditor*—not the *property of the Debtor*. If an Individual by an offence forfeits a Debt—why not in a state of enmity, from the nature of the thing?

Things in which they inhere to be in possession.

Puffendorff.[22]

Rivers, Forts & [Countries?] &c.

Necessary appendages—can't exist independent.

don't inhere in the Person—Debts due by account—by Bond &c.

If inhering [at all?]—they do in the Debtor—and where power over the Debtor—power over the Debt.

Right to legislate over Foreigners. This goes to rights of all kinds. (Lands—other personal property, besides Debts.)

Report on the Prussian Memorial.[23]

distinctions between Silesia Loans & British Debts.

dependent on Will of G. to pay.

solemn treaty to pay.

by confiscating the Debt he violated his own Treaty.

Would have [returned?] the B. creditors to the original Debtors, contrary to his own agreement

a doubt even in this case.

a threat

Arguments, not on the Powers, but on the Circumstances—admits therefore, with the exception of the latter.

Gov. substituted itself—*without consent of the creditor*.

Debts becoming due *during the War* subject to confiscation. Rule generally laid down—particular exception not allowable—Distinction between Debts *during the War*, & *after the War*—No other rational distinction—Each payable—Each recoverable substantially alike.

Upon what principle [but State of necessity?]. kill the Enemy—take other property.

Suppose an order to a Gen. to put Prisoners to death—Can he be punished for Murder?

Ransom Bills. No difference between that & other Property.[24]

Customary Law

Authorities admit the right.

Power recognized—forbearance from mutual policy[25]

Debt Not subject to Inquisition—Parker's Case—Chose in Action—

Is not the power of L. equal? *Tho' a creature, above the Creator.* No other mean—

Inquisition of [*illegible*].

No law authorizing another mode—If L. had authorized another mode sufficient P. shews he is within the description. May be ascertained before a Jury. Decision against his right by L.[26]

Obj.—Clothed with rights—equally applicable to other property.

2d. point. Virginia an Independent State &c.

Several Provinces no connexion before the War but as Subjects of a common Sovereign—

Declaration of Independence

Congress—Power to advise.

No power to controul till confederation—(after 1777)[27]

Confederation. No restriction from legislating—No power to Congress to legislate on the Subject—

Power of Confiscation in time of War necessary for a Nation to possess.

No sufficient power of self defence otherwise.

Deposit of some Powers—not of this.[28]

Congress. Power to make Peace.

therefore V. not competent to confiscate

Congress must attend to the manner in which they can act.

K. of G.B. may make peace. But L. must confiscate.

Act of that part of the G. which it was necessary to employ.

3. Words & operation of the Acts of Assembly.

Payment—

words sufficient to discharge.

bar a recovery, if nothing to remove it.

1st. Act 1777—p. 65.[29]

Receipt *discharge from so much of the debt.* If now liable, *are they discharged from the Debt?* meant—discharge *during the War.*

real meaning perhaps—payment during the War.

When words are general, they mean *forever.*

In various arguments [press?]—*no necessity for the temporary discharge by law.*

Discharge to fail *when most wanted*
If not intended to deprive the Creditor—intended to discharge the Debtor.
Intended to be applied to the purposes of the War.
Confiscation exercised so as to discharge the Debtor.
No payments would have been made but on the faith of the discharge.
No promise to indemnify. Says they shall never recover.
Binding forever on Gov. & Party, if rightly confiscated, &c.
Law declared the discharge as to its nominal amount.
Sacredness of National faith. Solemn pledge not to violate—
Nothing but the more direful necessity.
Acts, p. 64, 65

1777—only operates on payments into the Treasury.

p. 99— This does not operate—[30]

Act of 1782 } No debts &c. recoverable, altho' transferred &c.
p. 65. } Law calculated for both objects—originally due or assigned—[31]

unless as *if* (P.'s construction)
unless *nor shall* (D's).[32]

refer to a temporary Law of 1782—this to be [expressed?] in the perpetual Law just read—[33]

Introduce—clause. "All British Debts."
general prohibition—
guard against elusion.
other cases not comprehended before by which the Law might be eluded.[34]

Enumeration of Special cases don't confine the general prohibition—not less solicitous to guard against British Subjects than against assignees.
Act Oct. 1783.

1. Relates to Oct. 1782—
2. Act concerning Exon's.
No repealing Clause as to those Laws
No intention shewn.
L. supposed the laws were not perpetual
opinion not to controul the real operation
Constitution denies the L. a power to judge.

Act—May 1782. perpetual
Oct. 1782. temporary.
Oct. 1783. consider *both temporary*.[35]

Thursday May 30th.

Mr. Marshall, in continuation—

Acts would operate after War as well as before until a Repeal.

Treaty *not operating*, nor intending to operate, on payments—but *on general claims*.

Treaty—

Acknowledges its obligation on all the People of America as on other Nations.

1. Non-compliance by G.B.
2. Treaty did not comprehend Payments.
3. Treaty will not repeal a legislative Act.[36]

1st. point. Non compliance.

1. Being a compact between Sovereigns—*quid pro quo*.
2. Every article conditional.

Gr. 3 B. 14 Ch. 19 Sect.[37]

Because Courts not introduced to decide.

Part in Independent Covenants different

Because no Court of Justice.

Condition precedent (in case of a breach).

If the breach by G.B. was caused by a breach by L.—that might have been shewn.[38]

Power of discharging—or receiving Compensation—In the U.S.

Obj. This Court cannot notice the breach

Necessary for the Court to judge on what is brought before them.

Cases cited *inapplicable to this*.

If no Acts in the way—upon a peace the Creditor might have recovered without considering the Treaty.

P. cannot maintain his Action but upon the Treaty.

Qu. Whether Treaty did in fact repeal; or *an actual Repeal* was necessary.

Required some time to repeal

Evacuation of Territory first article to be performed—

Congress has not remitted &c.

Therefore British C no right to recover—*broke as to them*—[39]

our right entire—*void as to them*.

Rejoinder fortifies the Bar—[40]

Compensation could be no otherwise made, or remitted, but by a Treaty—

Treaty the law of the Land, & Judges bound to take notice.

A refusal to render Judgment for P. no cause of War to G.B.

Deny only a present right of the P.

Vattel 2 Book s. 257.[41]

Whole Treaty must be looked into—If broke not sanctioned.

Gov. adopted the Treaties as they stood—not understood *as a remission.*

Payments into the Treasury.[42]

Could not comprehend—not as if in contemplation.

Debtor completely discharged—

Creditors on either side

Who Creditors?

Those at the time.

Debts—*now due*—not *formerly existing heretofore.*

meant to provide for *previous* Debts, not for any future ones—

might exclude future Confiscation.

Debts once subsisting, tho' paid off.

Not Debt if paid off to the Plaintiff—

Nor if paid in any other manner.

Same as if Creditor had received payment—

Impediment by *law*—not by *fact*—

Payment a fact its operation by Law lawful discharge.[43]

Recovery—From whom?

From him who owes nothing.

From him who does not owe *the Debt.*

Does it create a right not subsisting before?

If he has a Debtor it is not he whom the Law has declared is discharged—

It is the Government. G. Debtor.[44]

Being of an European Nation in Europe not at stake.

Necessities therefore greater here—

G. in the same situation as if substituted by the Debtor himself.

Treaty operates on the Act of 1782.[45]

Law of 1782. No Creditor shall recover—says nothing about the discharge.

Act of 1777 makes Gov. a Debtor.

one operates on the right: the other on the remedy.

Treaty to apply to cases where there was a prohibition to recover.

not imposing a new burthen.

Implication from the 5th. Article.[46]

ackn. that where G. had actually exercised a right over the property.

Where there was only *a bar to the Recovery* that shall be removed—

But where, *not bar merely*, but *the right* destroyed—

If words doubtful—principles—

1. Where there is a plain & positive law no measure to be construed against but from absolute necessity.[47]

It is not to be presumed these Laws should be unknown.

If intention to create a retrospect, the expression should have been plain.

G.B. ought to have required full words for the purpose.[48]

2. Not to be construed to violate the public faith—upon doubtful construction.

Exemption purchased by a fair consideration.

3. Not such a construction as would imply an excess of power in Congress.

If for public safety indispensably necessary to sacrifice a private Individual &c.—will not say—

Nothing but the last necessity could justify it.

Individual stood as if he had owed nothing.

Implies a power to select one who never owed.

Where doubtful, the impropriety of the thing ought to prevent such a construction.

If Creditors to receive the money—Why not by the Government?

Repeal could affect nothing done under the Act before the Repeal.[49]

Constitution—

Formerly Treaty the same force as in other Govs.

A Person making a Treaty not having a Legislative Authority cannot effect an actual Repeal.

Some Powers have Legislative Powers.

Repeal of a Law completely Legislative

If by the Executive under the form of a Treaty—if repeal—why not enact?

If of every sort—discrimination unnecessary.

Cannot operate on the *Domain* not parted with.

Pledges the public faith that a Law shall pass &c.[50]

If the aid of any department of G. is wanted—that aid shall be afforded—

Constitution of the U.S. Legislative Power vested in Congress. (In the U.S.)

Some of the Legislative Power to be vested in President & Senate.

4th. Plea—Positive acts of Hostility.

Act of Declaration not necessary.

Cro. Eliz. 142[51]

2 Stra. Levy vs—.[52]

1777—Produce of Lands &c. also to be deposited.[53]

MS notebook of James Iredell, Law Library, DLC. For discussion of MS, see editorial note.

1. Virginia.

2. As to, or with respect to.

3. Legislature.

4. Blackstone, *Commentaries*, I, 45–49. In this passage the commentator defined municipal, or civil, law and made his celebrated remark that the sovereign power of society resides in the legislature.

5. Government.

6. Hugo Grotius, *The Rights of War and Peace*, Bk. III, chap. II, sec. 2, Classics of International Law, ed. James Brown Scott, II (trans. of 1646 ed.; Oxford, 1925), 624–25. In the cited passage Grotius said that according to the law of nations the property of subjects was liable for the debts of the sovereign.

7. Emmerich de Vattel, *The Law of Nations, or the Principles of Natural Law Applied to the Conduct and the Affairs of Nations and of Sovereigns*, Bk. II, secs. 80–82; Bk. III, secs. 70–72, Classics of International Law, ed. James Brown Scott, III (trans. of 1758 ed.; Washington, D.C., 1916), 138, 259. In the first passage Vattel observed that "the property of individuals, taken as a whole, is to be regarded as the property of the Nation with respect to other Nations . . . and that if a Nation has a right to any part of the property of another Nation it has an indiscriminate right to the property of the citizens of that Nation to the amount of the debt." In the second he said that when two nations were at war, all the subjects of one nation were enemies of all the subjects of the other.

8. JM alluded to opposing counsel's contention that the law of nations authorized confiscation of a person's visible estate but not incorporeal rights such as debts (see also Henry's speech in Jones v. Walker [Wirt, *Patrick Henry*, 365–66]).

9. Grotius, *Rights of War and Peace*, Bk. III, chap. II, sec. 2, 624. According to Grotius, the voluntary law of nations sanctioned the principle "that for what any civil society, or its head, ought to furnish, . . . there are held and made liable all the corporeal or incorporeal possessions of those who are subject to such a society or its head."

10. The reference is apparently to J. J. Burlamaqui, *The Principles of Natural and Politic Law* (5th ed.; 2 vols. in 1; Dublin, 1791), II, pt. I, chap. viii, secs. 1–3, 230. The title of the chapter is "Of the right of sovereignty acquired over the conquered."

11. Vattel, *Law of Nations*, Bk. III, chap. v, sec. 77, 260. In this passage the author defined enemy property as including "incorporeal things—rights, titles, debts." A nation, he said, could confiscate debts if payment fell due during the war or could at least prevent its subjects from paying such debts during the war. He went on to say that in the interest of promoting commerce among nations, the modern practice was to refrain from confiscating debts. See Justice Chase's comment on this passage (3 Dall. 227).

12. Vattel, *Law of Nations*, Bk. III, chap. ix, secs. 160–62, 291.

13. Cornelius van Bynkershoek (Bijnkershoek), *A Treatise on the Law of War* (Philadelphia, 1810). Iredell's notes indicate that James Innes, JM's co-counsel, cited Bynkershoek in his argument on 31 May.

14. A "chose in action" (thing in action) is a personal right not reduced to possession but recoverable by suit at law. Examples would be money due by bond or damages for some wrong or injury. The case of Attorney-General v.

Weeden and Shales, Parker 267, 145 Eng. Rep. 776 (Ex., 1699), established that "choses in action belonging to an alien enemy are forfeited to the Crown: but there must be a commission and inquisition to intitle the King; and a peace before inquisition discharges the cause of forfeiture." This case was also cited by Chase and Iredell in their opinions (3 Dall. 227, 264).

15. Plaintiff's.

16. The plaintiff contended that the right of confiscation should not be exercised where creditor and debtor originally belonged to the same government. See the argument of Edward Tilghman in the appeal (3 Dall. 207–8).

17. Vattel, *Law of Nations*, Introduction, secs. 11, 17, 20. In the older editions the introduction was entitled "Preliminaries" or "Preliminary Discourse."

18. Burlamaqui, *Principles of Natural and Politic Law*.

19. Weymberg v. Touch, 1 Chan. Cas. 123, 22 Eng. Rep. 724–25 (Ch., 1669). The plaintiff filed a bill in equity for relief against an action of debt for money due to the defendant, a merchant who had sold wares to the plaintiff in Denmark. During hostilities between England and Denmark, the plaintiff was compelled to pay the money owed to commissioners authorized for the purpose by the king of Denmark. The terms of peace stipulated that subjects on each side who had paid debts in this way should be discharged against creditors. The defendant was ordered to answer the bill.

20. Wilcox et al. v. Henry, 1 Dall. 69, 71 (Pa. Supreme Court, 1782). "An alien enemy," said Chief Justice Thomas McKean in his charge to the jury, "has no right of action whatever during the war; but by the law of nations, confirmed by universal usage, at the end of the war, all the rights and credits, which the subjects of either power had against the other, are revived."

21. Camp v. Lockwood, 1 Dall. 393, 403 (Pa., Court of Common Pleas, Philadelphia Co., 1788). Camp, formerly an inhabitant of Connecticut, had his real and personal estate confiscated during the war because of his adherence to the British. He brought suit after the peace to recover a debt from a citizen of Connecticut then residing in Pennsylvania. President Edward Shippen denied the plaintiff's right to bring suit on the ground that the debt was vested in the state of Connecticut.

22. Samuel Pufendorf, *On the Law of Nature and Nations*, Classics of International Law, ed. James Brown Scott, II (trans. of 1688 ed.; 2 vols.; London, 1934). The reference is apparently to Bk. VIII, chap. vi, sec. 22, 1311: "On the acquisition in war of non-physical things, this special point should be noted, namely, that they can only be acquired along with the subject in which they inhere, whether that be persons or things. Now certain rights inhere in things, such as lands, rivers, ports, cities, territories, and even more to persons, in so far as they possess those things, there belong specific rights over other things or men." Apparently plaintiff's counsel objected that incorporeal rights such as debts attached to the subject in which they inhere, that is, the right of the British creditor could not be confiscated without seizing the person of the creditor.

23. The reference is to the *Report of the Law Officers of the Crown* (London, 1753), protesting the refusal of Frederick II of Prussia to repay loans made by British merchants to the Hapsburgs for mining operations in Silesia.

After Prussia conquered Silesia, Frederick agreed to assume the loan as part of the peace settlement, but he later withheld payment because of losses suffered by Prussian subjects at the hands of British privateers (Richard Lodge, *Great Britain and Prussia in the Eighteenth Century* [New York, 1972], 39–40, 64, 88). For information on the *Report* and its availability to American lawyers, see Henry J. Bourguignon, *The First Federal Court: The Federal Appellate Prize Court of the American Revolution, 1775–1787* (Philadelphia, 1977), 182 and n. 6.

24. A ransom bill was a contract by which a captured vessel, in return for its release and safe-conduct, was to pay a certain sum as ransom. In the appeal, plaintiff's attorney Tilghman observed that an action could be "maintained on a ransom bill, even during the continuance of the war" (3 Dall. 208).

25. Plaintiff's counsel urged that the customary law of nations did not sanction confiscation of debts. JM countered that the right of confiscation was recognized, though the policy of modern nations was to refrain from exercising it.

26. In response to plaintiff's contention that there could be no forfeiture of a debt without a formal inquest by a jury, JM insisted that the legislature, possessing the right of confiscation, could authorize any means it wished to accomplish this object. On this point, see the remarks of Henry and Iredell (Wirt, *Patrick Henry*, 366–67; 3 Dall. 263–65).

27. The Articles of Confederation were adopted by Congress in Nov. 1777 and sent to the states for approval. Ratification was not completed until 1781.

28. The plaintiff maintained that if the right of confiscation existed, only Congress, which had the power of war and peace, could exercise it. JM replied that the states retained a general right of legislation and did not delegate the power of confiscation to Congress. On this point, see the remarks of Lewis (plaintiff's counsel in the appeal) and Justice Chase (3 Dall. 219–20, 222–23, 231–33).

29. JM begins his analysis of the third section of the sequestration law (Hening, *Statutes*, IX, 379–80). The page numbers cited here and below refer to the compilation of Virginia laws enacted between 1768 and 1783: *A Collection of all Such Public Acts of the General Assembly* . . . (Richmond, 1785). This work was commonly known as the Chancellors' Revisal.

30. The "act concerning escheats and forfeitures from British subjects," Chancellors' Revisal, 98–100 (Hening, *Statutes*, X, 66–71). Although this act was pleaded in bar to the plaintiff's claim, the third section specifically excepted British debts from the confiscation. JM apparently here conceded that this law did not apply to the present case.

31. The reference is to the act of May 1782 suspending executions in certain judgments, Chancellors' Revisal, 165 (not 65) (Hening, *Statutes*, XI, 75–76). The second section of this act declared "that no debt or demand whatsoever, originally due to a subject of Great Britain, shall be recoverable in any court in this commonwealth, although the same may be transferred to a citizen of this state, or to any other person capable of maintaining such ac-

tion, unless the assignment hath been or may be made for a valuable consideration, *bona fide* paid before the first day of May" 1777.

32. This apparently refers to the opposing constructions by counsel for the plaintiff ("P") and defendant ("D") of the section of the 1782 act quoted in n. 31.

33. The "temporary" law was that of Oct. 1782 to amend the "perpetual" law of May 1782. The language of the amending law, JM suggested, showed that the legislature intended a general prohibition against the recovery of all British debts, not just those assigned to citizens. Though the Oct. 1782 law had expired, JM argued that its expression of legislative intent also applied to the May 1782 law (Hening, *Statutes*, XI, 176–80).

34. JM here summarized the first three sections of the Oct. 1782 act.

35. JM attempted to show that the May 1782 law concerning executions was still in force. An act of Oct. 1783 revived both the May 1782 and Oct. 1782 laws and continued them through the next session of the assembly, that is, until 30 June 1784. Counsel for the plaintiff therefore argued that both acts had expired. JM maintained, however, that the May 1782 act, not having an expiration clause, was perpetual and that the amending act of Oct. 1782, which was to expire 1 Dec. 1783, was temporary. Although the Oct. 1783 act showed that the legislature assumed that both laws were temporary, JM contended that this legislative opinion should not "controul the real operation" of the act. The May 1782 law remained in force by virtue of the doctrine that if a perpetual law (May 1782) is repealed by a temporary one (Oct. 1782), when the repealing law expires, the original law continues to exist. (For the 1783 law, see Hening, *Statutes*, XI, 349.) JM's construction of these three laws was undoubtedly similar to that presented by lawyer William Nelson in a letter to Thomas Jefferson of 4 Feb. 1791 (Boyd, *Jefferson Papers*, XIX, 244–45). If the peace treaty was held to be in force, then the May 1782 law, supposing it to have been unrepealed by the Virginia legislature, would have to yield to the treaty.

36. The second major division of JM's argument concerned the effect of the peace treaty. He would first try to show that the treaty had become void by repeated infractions of it on the part of Great Britain. If he failed on this point, then he would contend that loan office payments either were not within the scope of the treaty or could not be affected by it.

37. Grotius, *Rights of War and Peace*, Bk. III, chap. xix, sec. 14, 800 (Iredell reversed chapter and section numbers). According to Grotius,"The individual items of one and the same agreement seem to be related in respect to the two sides after the manner of a condition For this reason, whenever the intent is different, it is usually expressly stated that if anything is done contrary to this or that provision the other nevertheless will remain valid."

38. The plaintiff argued that Britain's refusal to evacuate the posts and return the slaves was a response to the failure of the U.S. to comply with the stipulations of the fourth article.

39. Because the formalities of pleading required him to demur, the plaintiff technically admitted the truth of the allegations of British infractions of the treaty. Since Congress had not expressly "remitted," or pardoned, the

infractions, so the argument ran, the treaty was to be regarded as broken and the plaintiff's right of recovery suspended. The important question was whether the court could take notice of these infractions and declare the treaty void, as urged by counsel for the defendant. While agreeing that the treaty had become "voidable," both Iredell and Jay denied that the court could declare it void. Such a declaration, they observed, involved policy questions of "extreme magnitude" that fell outside the province of the judiciary (3 Dall. 258–62; Fed. Cas. No. 7507, 1062).

40. The allegations of British infractions were set forth in a separate plea and in the defendant's rejoinder to the plaintiff's replication to the loan office plea (see Case No. 12, Docs. VII ["4th. plea"] and IX).

41. Apparently the citation should be to Vattel, *Law of Nations*, Bk. III (not II), sec. 257, which discusses relations between subjects of belligerents during a truce.

42. This is the second of the three points on the treaty that JM enumerated at the beginning of this day's remarks.

43. The treaty, argued JM, was intended to remove lawful impediments to the recovery of existing debts, not to undo the new factual situation created by the loan office payments. British debts paid off in this manner were to be considered in the same light as if paid to the original creditor.

44. The government of Virginia, by receiving payment from the original debtor, has now become the debtor. The British creditor should apply to the commonwealth for payment of the debt.

45. JM conceded that the treaty, if held to be in force, applied to the May 1782 law prohibiting the recovery of British debts. This was a lawful impediment within the meaning of the fourth article.

46. By the fifth article of the peace treaty Congress was to recommend to the state legislatures that they make restitution for confiscated estates belonging to British subjects and loyalists (Moore, *International Adjudications*, III, 3). Since the confiscated estates were not restored by the treaty itself, by implication (said JM) the treaty did not revive debts paid into the loan office. On this point see the opinion of Justice Cushing (3 Dall. 283–84).

47. The treaty of peace should not be construed to operate against Virginia's sequestration law ("a plain & positive law"), unless dictated by the necessity of the case.

48. The commissioners who negotiated the treaty, JM maintained, must have been aware of Virginia's sequestration law. If the treaty was to have a retrospective reach and destroy loan office payments, there should have been an express stipulation to that effect.

49. This is the last of the three points that JM proposed to discuss at the beginning of this day: "1. Non-compliance by G.B. 2. Treaty did not comprehend Payments. 3. Treaty will not repeal a legislative Act."

50. JM argued that Congress under the Confederation had no authority to repeal state legislative acts by means of a treaty. The fourth article was to be understood as calling upon the states to pass laws to carry out its purposes. As to the effect of the treaty as "supreme law" under the Constitution of 1787, JM presumably expressed views similar to those Iredell presented in his opinion: that the treaty repealed conflicting state laws, but such repeal

was prospective only. It could not affect anything done under the act while in force, e.g., loan office payments under Virginia's sequestration law.

51. Anonymous, Cro. Eliz. 142, 78 Eng. Rep. 398 (K.B., 1588). The plaintiff, a subject of Philip, King of Spain, brought an action of debt, to which the plea was that the plaintiff was an alien enemy. This was held to be a good plea even though no war had been proclaimed between England and Spain.

52. Openheimer v. Levy, 2 Str. 1082, 93 Eng. Rep. (K.B., 1737). The defendant pleaded in abatement that the plaintiff was an alien under the allegiance of the Holy Roman Empire. On a demurrer, it was held that as by law an alien friend could maintain a personal action, it was necessary to abate the writ to show that the plaintiff was an alien enemy.

53. The second section of the 1777 sequestration law authorized commissioners to deposit the profits of sequestered British estates in the state loan office. JM's point, apparently, was that the treaty did not touch these payments and therefore should also leave unaffected payments of British debts made in this manner (Hening, *Statutes*, IX, 378–79).

After counsel completed arguments, the court on 7 June 1793 ruled for the plaintiff on the demurrers to three of the British debt pleas (the third, fourth, and fifth pleas) and for the defendant on the demurrer to the defendant's rejoinder to the plaintiff's replication to the loan office plea (the second plea). It then referred to a jury the issue of payment (the first plea) of that portion of Hylton's debt that had not been paid into the loan office. Despite Chief Justice Jay's instructions to bring in a verdict for the principal and full interest, the jurors could not agree on whether to allow interest for the period of the war. On 8 June the court ordered the issue to be retried at the next term. Without a verdict, Ware's agent was unable to prosecute an immediate appeal to the Supreme Court on the loan office plea. Finally, on 31 May 1794, a jury returned a verdict for the plaintiff on the unpaid portion, deducting interest for the eight years of the war (*Va. Gaz. and Richmond Manchester Adv.*, 10 June 1793; Richard Hanson to John T. Ware, 9 June 1793, T.79/30 [claim of John T. Ware], P.R.O.; Phineas Bond to Lord Grenville, 25 June 1793 ["Letters of Phineas Bond, British Consul at Philadelphia, to the Foreign Office of Great Britain, 1790–1794," *Annual Report of the American Historical Association for the Year 1897* (Washington, D.C., 1898), 534]; U.S. Cir. Ct., Va., Ord. Bk. I, 161, 162, 381, 386). On the question of war interest, see Case No. 16.

II. Writ of Error
6 June 1794

United States Sct

[SEAL] The President of The United States To The Judges of The Circuit Court Holden in the District of Virginia Greeting.[1]

Because in the Record and process and also in the rendering of Judgment in a suit before you or some of you between John Tyndale Ware Administrator of all and singular the goods and chattels rights and credits which were of William Jones who was surviving partner of Farel and Jones of the Kingdom of Great Britain late Merchants & partners acting under the firm of Farrel and Jones Plaintiff and Daniel Lawrence Hylton and Company of Henrico County and Francis Eppes Gentleman of Charles City County[2] in the District of Virginia Defendants in a plea of Debt manifest error hath intervened to the great damage of the said John Tyndale Ware, as in his complaint has been Stated,[3] And as it is just and proper that the error if any there be should be corrected in due manner and that full and speedy Justice should be done to the parties in this behalf, You are hereby commanded that if Judgment thereof be given then under your seal you do distinctly and openly send the Record and process in the suit aforesaid with all things concerning them and this Writ so that you have the same before the Chief Justice and the Associate Justices of the Supreme Court of the United States on the first Monday in August next at Philadelphia that the Record and process aforesaid being inspected they may cause to be done thereupon what of right ought to be done. Witness the Honorable John Jay Esqr. Chief Justice of the said Supreme Court at Philadelphia aforesaid this Sixth day of June in the [year of our] Lord One Thousand seven hundred and Ninety four and of the Independence of The United States the Eighteenth.

William Marshall Clk C.C.V.D.[4]

ADS, Ware v. Hylton, Appellate Case File No. 4, RG 267, DNA. Verso endorsed by Justice John Blair: "I herewith send the record and process in the suit in the within writ mentioned, as by the said writ I am commanded." William Marshall noted on verso, "Returnable to August Court 1794."

1. On federal appellate procedure, see Case No. 11, Doc. V, n. 1.

2. Hylton executed his bond to Farell & Jones in the name of his merchant firm. Francis Eppes was his surety (Case No. 7, Doc. I and n. 1).

3. A fragment of the plaintiff's petition, in the hand of attorney Andrew

Ronald, is among the papers in the appellate case file. For an example of such a petition, see Case No. 11, Doc. V.

4. The initials stand for Clerk, Circuit Court Virginia District.

III. Appeal Bond
24 June 1794

Know all men by these presents that We John Tyndale Ware of the Kingdom of Great Britain, Richard Hanson[1] of the State of Virginia and Alexander Horsburgh of the said State aforesaid are held and firmly bound unto Daniel Lawrence Hylton and Company and Francis Eppes of the aforesaid State of Virginia in the Just and full sum of Five hundred Dollars to be paid unto their certain attorney their Heirs, Executors, Administrators or Assigns: To which payment, well and truly to be made We bind ourselves, our Heirs, Executors and Administrators, firmly by these presents. Sealed with our Seals and dated this Twenty Fourth day of June In the year of our Lord One thousand Seven hundred and Ninety Four.

The Condition of the above Obligation is such that Whereas the above bound John Tyndale Ware hath Obtained from the honorable the Supreme Court of the United States of America a Writ of Error to a Judgment of the Circuit Court for the district of Virginia against him as Administrator of William Jones deceased who was surviving partner of Farrell and Jones, by the said Daniel Lawrence Hylton and Company and Francis Eppes on the day of May last upon a demurrer. Now if the said John Tyndale Ware shall prosecute the said Writ with effect, then the above Obligation to be Void, Otherwise to remain in full force and virtue.[2]

Sealed and Delivered in presence off

Patr: Hannay — John Tyndale Warre [L.S.]
Andrew Gray — by
Richard J Munford — Richard Hanson his Attorney in fact
Richard Hanson [L.S.]
Alexr. Horsburgh [L.S.]

DS, Ware v. Hylton, Appellate Case File No. 4, RG 267, DNA.

1. Richard Hanson was the agent of William Jones (and subsequently of John T Ware) for collecting debts owed to Farell & Jones by Virginians. He also served as agent for other British creditors (see Case No. 18, editorial note).

2. The Judiciary Act of 1789 required the judge or justice signing a

citation on a writ of error to "take good and sufficient security, that the plaintiff in error shall prosecute his writ to effect, and answer all damages and costs if he fail to make his plea good" (*U.S. Statutes at Large*, I, 85).

IV. Citation
ca. 28 June 1794

To Daniel Lawrence Hylton and Company of Henrico County and Francis Eppes Gentleman of Charles City County in the District of Virginia Greeting Wheareas there is filed in the Office of the Clerk of the Circuit Court for the District of Virginia in the middle Circuit a Writ of Error Issued from the Supreme Court of the United States bearing date the Sixth day of June in the year of our Lord One Thousand Seven hundred and Ninety four and directed to the Judges of the Circuit Court holding Pleas in the middle Circuit wherein it is suggested that in the record and proceedings and also in the rendering of the Judgment in a Plea of debt brought in which John Tyndale Ware Administrator of all and Singular the Goods and Chattels Rights and Credits which were of William Jones who was surviveing partner of Joseph Farrel was Plaintiff and Daniel Lawrence Hylton and Company of Henrico County and Francis Eppes Gentleman of Charles City County in the District of Virginia were Defendants. A manifest Error hath happened to the great Injury of the said John Tyndale Ware Administrator as Aforesaid, as on his complaint the said Supreme Court have understood and the said Judges of the said Circuit Court are by the said Writ commanded if Judgment has thereon been given that under their Seal distinctly and Openly, they send the Record and proceedings with all things concerning the same, together with the said Writ so that they the same Judges have the same at the City of Philadelphia in the Supreme Court on the first Monday in August Next, that the Record and proceedings aforesaid being inspected there may be further done to correct that Error what of right and According to the Laws and Customs of the united States should be done, You therefore the said Daniel Lawrence Hylton and Company and Francis Eppes are hereby Notified of the said Writ of Error and of the fileing the same as aforesaid and Cited to appear if you see cause at the Supreme Court aforesaid to be held at Philadelphia on the First Monday in August next to make Answer thereto.[1]

JOHN BLAIR

Wmsburg,[2] July 10th. 1794. Andrew Gray this day made oath on the Holy Evangelists of Almighty God that on Saturday the twenty-eighth day of June last he did serve Daniel Lawrence Hylton with the within citation at his own house, by first shewing him the original, & then giving him a copy of the same; Also that on Monday the thirtieth day of June last he did serve Francis Eppes with the same citation, at his mill in Chesterfield county, by first shewing him the original, & then giving him a copy thereof. Sworn to before me,

JOHN BLAIR

DS, Ware v. Hylton, Appellate Case File No. 4, RG 267, DNA.

1. A citation to the adverse party, signed by a judge of the circuit court or justice of the Supreme Court, was among the papers required to be filed in an appeal to the Supreme Court. The adverse party had to have at least thirty days' notice (*U.S. Statutes at Large*, I, 84).

2. This affidavit, in the hand of John Blair, is on a separate sheet.

V. Argument in the Supreme Court
9 February 1796

Tilghman	Dallas
Tuesday Feb. 9. 1796[1]	
Marshall, for Deft. in Error 1. Act of Virga. Assy. a bar, independt. of the Treaty. 2. The treaty does not remove the bar.[3] 1st. pt resolved into 2—1st whether the Assembly had power, & 2d. whether they have exercised the power to extinguish the debt.	*Marshall*, (of *Virginia*) for the Defendant in error.[2] The case resolves itself into two general propositions: 1st, That the act of Assembly of *Virginia*, is a bar to the recovery of the debt, independent of the treaty. 2d, That the treaty does not remove the bar. I. That the act of Assembly of *Virginia* is a bar to the recovery of the debt, introduces two subjects for consideration: 1st. Whether the Legislature had power to extinguish the debt? 2d. Whether the Legislature had exercised that power?
1. It has been conceded, that independt. nations have in *general*, the right of confiscation—& that Virga. was an independt. Nation. It is contended, that from special circumstances, Virga. had no right to confiscate—the citizens of each	1st. It has been conceded, that independent nations have, in general, the right of confiscation; and that *Virginia*, at the time of passing her law, was an independent nation. But, it is contended, that from the peculiar circumstances of the war, the citi-

State, having been members of same Governmt.[4]

Not necessy. to shew parallel case in history. In order to impair sovereignty of Virga. a case shd. be shewn on the other side.

Virga. being engaged in War, necessarily possd. the powers of war—confiscation is one of these powers—it weakens the Enemy, & strengthens oneself. War is a state of force—no tribunal can decide between belligerent powers. Didn't Virga. hazard as much by the War, as if she never had been a member of the British Empire—*she hazarded much more, from the nature of civil war.*

Nations have equal powers—What wd. have been the situation of American property, if Britain had conquered?

Suppose a suit brot. during War, by a British subject agt. an Amern.—it cou'd not have been supported—if there was power to suspend the recovery, there must have been power

zens of each of the contending nations, having been members of the same government, the general right of confiscation did not apply, and ought not to be exercised. It is not, however, necessary for the Defendant in error to shew a parallel case in history; since, it is incumbent on those, who wish to impair the sovereignty of *Virginia,* to establish on principle, or precedent, the justice of their exception. That State being engaged in a war, necessarily possessed the powers of war; and confiscation is one of those powers, weakening the party against whom it is employed, and strengthening the party that employs it. War, indeed, is a state of force; and no tribunal can decide between the belligerent powers. But did not *Virginia* hazard as much by the war, as if she had never been a member of the *British* empire? Did she not hazard more, from the very circumstance of its being a civil war? It will be allowed, that nations have equal powers; and that *America,* in her own tribunals at least, must from the 4th of *July* 1776, be considered as independent a nation as *Great Britain*: then, what would have been the situation of *American* property, had *Great Britain* been triumphant in the conflict? Sequestration, confiscation and proscription would have followed in the train of that event; and why should the confiscation of *British* property be deemed less just in the event of the *American* triumph? The rights of war clearly exist between members of the same Empire, engaged in a civil war. *Vatt. B.* 3. *s.* 292. 295. But, suppose a suit had been brought during the war by a *British* subject against an *American* citizen, it could not have been supported; and if there was a to extinguish the debt. They are portions of the same power, emanating from same source.

Vatt. Book 3d. § 292 id. § 295[5] } rights of war exist between members of same empire, in civil war.

The legislative power in every country can only be restrained by its own constitution—this springs from nature of Society.

The Judiciary can have no power to question the validity of a law—unless it is authorized to do so by the constitution.

Property is the creature of civil Society & subject to its controul.

Will not say how the Judiciary might Act if the laws of God were evidently infringed by the legislature.

No weight in the argumt. arising from the *understanding of the parties*, where debt was contracted—the power of confiscation arises, not from understandg. of parties, but from nature of Governmt.

Contended, that as the party had not the power of extinguishing the debt he could not confer it on the Society[6]—*ansd.* the laws of property spring from a state of Society, & not from the rights of nature—it is under the controul of the laws of Society—*but the fact is we were not in a state of nature by the revolution*—If we were reduced to a State of nature there would be an end of the plaintiffs claim.

Contended that a debt can't be confiscated, contracted between subjects of belligerent powers in a neu-

power to suspend the recovery, there must have been a power to extinguish the debt: they are, indeed, portions of the same power, emanating from the same source. The legislative authority of any country, can only be restrained by its own municipal constitution: This is a principle that springs from the very nature of society; and the judicial authority can have no right to question the validity of a law, unless such a jurisdiction is expressly given by the constitution. It is not necessary to enquire, how the judicial authority should act, if the Legislature were evidently to violate any of the laws of God; but property is the creature of civil society, and subject, in all respects, to the disposition and controul of civil institutions. There is no weight in the argument, founded on what is supposed to be the understanding of parties at the place and time of contracting debts; for, the right of confiscation does not arise from the understanding of individuals, in private transactions, but from the nature and operation of government. Nor does it follow, that because an individual has not the power of extinguishing his debts, the community, to which he belongs, may not, upon principles of public policy, prevent his creditors from recovering them. It must be repeated, that the law of property, in its origin and operation, is the offspring of the social state; not the incident of a state of nature. But the revolution did not reduce the inhabitants of *America* to a state of nature; and, if it did, the Plaintiff's claim would be at an end. Other objections to the doctrine are started: It is said, that a debt, which arises from a contract, formed between the subjects of two belligerent tral country[7]—this is not true—a right exists for Society to apply to its own use, the property of the Enemy wherever found.

powers, in a neutral country, cannot be confiscated; but the society has a right to apply to its own use, the property of its enemy, wherever the right of property accrued, and wherever the property itself can be found. Suppose a debt had been contracted between two *Americans*, and one of them had joined *England*, would not the right of confiscation extend to such a debt? As to the case of the ransom bill, if the right of confiscation does not extend to it, (which is, by no means, admitted) it must be on account of the peculiar nature of the contract, implying a waiver of the rights of war. And the validity of capitulations depends on the same principle. But, let it be supposed, that a government should infringe the provisions of a capitulation, by imprisoning soldiers, who had stipulated for a free return to their home, could an action of trespass be maintained against the gaoler? No: the act of the government, though disgraceful, would be obligatory on the judiciary department.

Suppose a debt contracted between 2 citizens of America, & then one shd. remove to England—wd. not a right of confiscation of that debt exist.

Case of Ransom bill mentioned—I contend that even there a right of confiscation exists—if it does not, it's because of the nature of the contract, which is founded *on a waiver of the rights of War.*

Vatt. book 3. § 263. 264. was cited to prove the validity of capitulations—this depends on same principle as a Ransom bill[8]—but suppose Governmt. shd. infringe capitulation, by imprisoning soldiers who had capitulated for liberty to go home—Wou'd an action of trespass lye agt. the Goaler—no—the Act of Governmt. tho disgraceful wd. be obligatory on its own Judiciary.

Decision of Chancery of Virginia has been cited—with great respect for the Chancellor, I think he was mistaken—the decision was appeald from & is now depending—The adverse Counsel confess the Chancellor was mistaken, in denying the power of Confiscation.[9]

2d. subdn. of 1st. point—

Sect. 3d. of Act of Assy. of 1777—*discharges* the debtor—If *discharged*, how can he remain *charged*? The expression is, *he shall be discharged from the debt*—& yet tis contended he remains *liable to the debt.*

2d, But it is now to be considered, whether, if the Legislature of *Virginia* had the power of confiscation, they have exercised it? The third section of the act of Assembly discharges the debtor; and, on the plain import of the term, it may be asked, if he is discharged, how can he remain charged? The expression is, he shall be discharged from the debt;

Suppose the law had expressed, that the debtor shd. be discharged from the Commonwealth, but not from the creditor—would not this have been an Act of Insanity—who wd. have paid a farthing under such a law—& yet this construction is attempted, against the expressions of the Act.

It is contended that the Act of Assy. does not make a confiscation & that they had no power to make the substitution they have done.

What is a confiscation? Suppose the Act had ordered the debtor to pay, & the money to be applied to public uses? The State had a right to modify the confiscation as they pleased—they have thought proper to extinguish the claim of Cr. agt his Dr. & retain the money subject to their own discretion.

The power of doing the *greater*, includes that of doing the *less*.

The extinguishmt. of the dt. & the application of the money, are seperate Acts which the Governmt. may exercise separately—they may totally extinguish the claim of the Cr. agt. the Dr. & yet apply the money as they please, even repay part or the whole to the Cr.

It has been urged that the payment was *voluntary*, & thus differing from confiscation.[10]

Law is the will of Society, ex-

and yet, it is contended, he shall remain liable to the debt. Suppose the law had said, that the debtor should be discharged from the commonwealth, but not from his creditor, would not the Legislature have betrayed the extremest folly in such a proposition? and what man in his senses would have paid a farthing into the treasury, under such a law? Yet, in violation of the expressions of the act, this is the construction which is now attempted. It is, likewise, contended, that the act of Assembly does not amount to a confiscation of the debts paid into the treasury; and that the Legislature had no power, as between creditors and debtors, to make a substitution, or commutation, in the mode of payment. But what is a confiscation? The substance, and not the form, is to be regarded. The state had a right either to make the confiscation absolute, or to modify it as she pleased. If she had ordered the debtor to pay the money into the treasury, to be applied to public uses; would it not have been, in the eye of reason, a perfect confiscation? She has thought proper, however, only to authorise the payment, to exonerate the debtor from his creditor, and to retain the money in the treasury, subject to her own discretion, as to its future appropriation. As far as the arrangement has been made, it is confiscatory in its nature, and must be binding on the parties; though in the exercise of her discretion, the state might chuse to restore the whole, or any part, of the money to the original creditor. Nor is it sufficient to say, that the payment was voluntary, in order to defeat the confiscation. A law is an expression of pressed—Is this will when expressed, less binding, because no penalty is imposed? Are there not many laws, without penalty. Banks are founded on voluntary subscriptions—Canal, & road Companies, the same—The Nation wishes for banks, & companies of various kinds—So she wanted to get hold of British debts—why are the laws more obligatory in one case than the other?

Suppose an Act of Confiscation had passed, after the Act of Oct. 1777, with orders to sue all British debtors, & the Atty. Genl. had sued the present defendt.? Would it have born an Argumt.? & yet, if the Cr. retained any right, why might not the dt. have been recovered.

At the time of the Treaty, defendt. *owed nothing* to pltff.

2d. Pt. Construction of Treaty—Art. 4th. *Creditors* shall meet with no lawful impedimt. to recovery of *debts* heretofore contracted.

the public will; which, when expressed, is not the less obligatory, because it imposes no penalty. Banks, Canal Companies, and numerous associations of a similar description, are formed on the principle of voluntary subscription. The nation is desirous that such institutions should exist; individuals are invited to subscribe on the terms of the law; and, when they have subscribed, they are entitled to all the benefits, and are subject to all the inconveniences of the association, although no penalties are imposed. So, when the government of *Virginia* wished to possess itself of the debts previously owing to *British* subjects, the debtors were invited to make the payment into the treasury; and, having done so, there is no reason, or justice, in contending that the law is not obligatory on all the world, in relation to the benefit, which it promised as an inducement to the payment. If, subsequent to the act of 1777, a law had been passed confiscating *British* debts, for the use of the state, with orders that the Attorney General should sue all *British* debtors, could he have sued the Defendants in error, as *British* debtors, after this payment of the debt into the treasury? Common sense and common honesty revolt at the idea; and, yet, if the *British* creditor retained any right or interest in the debt, the state would be entitled, on principles of law, to recover the amount.

II. Having thus, then, established, that at the time of entering into the Treaty of 1783, the Defendant owed nothing to the Plaintiff, it is next to be enquired, whether that treaty revived the debt in favour of the Plaintiff, and removed the bar to a recovery, which the law of *Virginia* had

Who are *Creditors*? Can there be a *Cr.* where there is *no debt.*

Confined to *debts bona fide existing* at the time of making the Treaty. An argumt. has been raised, (in the trial in Virginia) on the word *recovery*[11]—but this word can't be construed so as to *create* a debt, where none existed.

I rely on the construction of the treaty, without discussing the power of Congs. to take away a vested right by Treaty.

The words ought to be extremely plain, to justify a construction, obliging a man to pay a debt which had been before extinguished.

Does this Treaty point out any *particular person who is to be made a debtor*? Treaties to be construed as applicable to the existing state of things.

Contended that the article has no meaning, unless it applies to present case—*not true*—there was an existing law of Virga. prohibiting the recovery of British debts, not paid into the Treasury—these were bona fide existing debts—to do away this law, was one effect of the Treaty, on any construction of it.[12]

There existed in many states, laws authorizing discharge of British debts in paper money—or by tender of property—to guard agt. these, was an important Object of the Treaty.

interposed? The words of the fourth article of the Treaty are, "that creditors on either side, shall meet with no lawful impediment to the recovery of the full value, in sterling money, of all *bona fide* debts heretofore contracted." Now, it may be asked, who are creditors? There cannot be a creditor where there is not a debt; and *British* debts were extinguished by the act of confiscation. The articles, therefore, must be construed with reference to those creditors, who had *bona fide* debts, subsisting, in legal force, at the time of making the Treaty; and the word *recovery* can have no effect to create a debt, where none previously existed. Without discussing the power of Congress to take away a vested right by treaty, the fair and rational construction of the instrument itself, is sufficient for the Defendant's cause. The words ought, surely, to be very plain, that shall work so evident a hardship, as to compel a man to pay a debt, which he had before extinguished. The treaty, itself, does not point out any particular description of persons, who were to be deemed debtors; and it must be expounded in relation to the existing state of things. It is not true, that the fourth article can have no meaning, unless it applies to cases like the present. For instance;—there was a law of *Virginia*, which prohibited the recovery of *British* debts, that had not been paid into the treasury; these were *bona fide* subsisting debts; and the prohibition was a legal impediment to the recovery, which the treaty was intended to remove. So, likewise, in several other states, laws had been passed authorising a discharge of *British* debts in paper money, or by a tender of property at a valuation, and the treaty was calculated to guard against such impediments to the recovery of the sterling value of those debts. It appears, therefore, that at the time of making the treaty, the state of things was such, that *Virginia* had exercised her sovereign right of confiscation, and had actually received the money from the *British* debtors. If debts thus paid were within the scope of the fourth article, those who framed the article knew of the payment; and upon every principle of equity and law, it ought to be presumed, that the recovery, which they contemplated, was intended against the receiving state, not against the paying debtor.

The State of things at time of treaty was that Virga. had exercised her right of confiscation, & recd. the money—if they had meant to affect those debts, the Treaty must be so construed as to give the recovery *agt. the state of Virginia.*

Virginia possessing the right of compelling a payment for her own use, the payment to her, upon her requisition, ought to be considered as a payment to the attorney, or agent, of the *British* creditor. Nor is such a substitution a novelty in legal proceedings: a foreign attachment is founded on the same principle. Suppose judgment had been obtained against the Defendants in error, as Garnishee in a foreign attachment brought against the Plaintiff in error, and the money had been paid, accordingly, to the Plaintiff in the attachment; but it afterwards appeared that the Plaintiff in the attachment had, in fact, no cause of action, having been paid his debt before he commenced the suit: If the treaty had been made in such a state of things, which would be the debtor contemplated by the fourth article, —the Defendants in error, who had complied with a legal judgment against them, or the Plaintiff in the attachment, who had received the money?

Virginia possessing the right of compelling the paymt. of the money for her own use, it is the same thing as if the money had been paid to the Attorney of the British creditor.

This power of *substitution*, is familiar in practice.

The process of *foreign Attachmt.* is founded in this principle.

Suppose Judgmt. had been obtained & the money pd. by defendant on a foreign Attachmt. agst. the present pltff, & in fact the person suing the Attacht. had had no just claim (it being afterwards proved that he had recd. paymt. before he sued the Attacht.) & in that State of things the Treaty had been made—who wd. have been the *debtor*, contemplated by the treaty—the present defendt. or the man who had recd. the money from him under the Judgmt. on the Attachmt.

This act of *Virginia* must have been known to the *American* and *British*

The Act of the Virga. Assy. must have been known to the British, &

the Amn. Comms—it cannot therefore be repealed without plain expressions pointed to that object.
Public faith should be preserved—it was plighted by the Act of the Virginia Assembly—To revive the debt, would be a shameful violation of the faith of Virginia—the treaty should be so construed if possible, as not to make this violation of faith to our own citizens.
The power of Governmt. to take away vested rights, was questionable *in the minds of the American Comms.* They would not exercise the power to restore confiscated real property—& debts stand on same footing.[13]

I will not deny the *power of Congs.* but there is weight in the *Ideas of the Comms.* who negotiated the Treaty—They thought they had no such powers. If Congs. had the power to take away vested rights, it must arise from the *Necessity* of the case—if the necessity had existed, it would have been avowed by the American Comms. & wd. have justified them to the Nation.
The Comms. could have had no object to make a treaty of the kind contended for—they should have agreed at once that the public should pay the debt, for the *U S.* must have been answerable to the Virginia debtor whom they sacrificed for the sake of Peace.

The case cited from Jenkins has no application, because in this case there is no article of the treaty, making the law of Virginia *void.*[14]

No weight in the argumt. that England had no such clause in her trea-

commissioners; and, therefore, cannot be repealed without plain and explicit expressions directed to that object. Besides, the public faith ought to be preserved. The public faith was plighted by the act of *Virginia*; and, as a revival of the debt in question, would be a shameful violation of the faith of the state to her own citizens, the treaty should receive any possible interpretation to avoid so dishonorable and so pernicious a consequence. It is evident, that the power of the government, to take away a vested right, was questionable in the minds of the *American* commissioners, since they would not exercise that power in restoring confiscated real estate; and confiscated debts, or other personal estate must come within the same rule. If Congress had the power of divesting a vested right, it must have arisen from the necessity of the case; and if the necessity had existed, the *American* commissioners, explicitly avowing it, would have justified their acquiescence to the nation. But the commissioners could have no motive to form a treaty such as the opposite construction supposes; for, if the stipulation was indispensable to the attainment of peace, the object was national, and so should be the payment of the equivalent: the commissioners, in such case, would have agreed, at once, that the public should pay the *British* debts; since the public must, on every principle of equity, be answerable to the *Virginia* debtor, who is now said to be the victim. The case cited from *Jenkins*, does not apply; as there is no article of the treaty, that declares the law of *Virginia* void. See *Old Law of Evidence* 196.

ties with Spain, Holland, & France, because I have shewn particular reasons for this provision, with regard to the U.S. which did not exist, as to other countries, on my construction of the Treaty.[15]

Old Law Evid. 196.[16]

MS, William Tilghman Papers, PHi; printed, Alexander J. Dallas, *Reports of Cases Ruled and Adjudged in the Several Courts of the United States, and of Pennsylvania*, III (Philadelphia, 1799; Evans #35374), 210–15. For discussion of Tilghman MS, see editorial note.

1. After continuances were granted at the Feb. and Aug. 1795 terms, the Supreme Court heard arguments from 6 through 12 Feb. 1796. Tilghman's notes, written in a cramped hand on both sides of long, narrow sheets, show that JM's speech took up most of this day's session.

2. This text is also printed in *PJM*, III, 7–14, fully annotated. Those annotations, along with the ones accompanying Doc. I, cover most of the substantive points of JM's argument and will not be repeated here.

3. JM's outline is the same as that followed in his circuit court argument, except that here he is concerned with only one Virginia law—the sequestration act of 1777.

4. JM alluded to the argument of Edward Tilghman (cousin of William), who had led off for the plaintiff (see *PJM*, III, 8 nn. 7, 8).

5. See *PJM*, III, 9 n. 9.

6. Edward Tilghman argued that "on the Declaration of Independence, the American debtor might choose his political party, but he could not dissolve his obligation to his British creditor; and if he had no power to dissolve it himself, it follows, that he could not communicate such a power, to the society of which he became a member" (3 Dall. 208).

7. See Tilghman's argument (3 Dall. 208).

8. Citing Vattel, Tilghman contended "that capitulations, made in time of war, though they embrace the security of debts, as well as other property, must be held sacred" (3 Dall. 208; Vattel, *Law of Nations*, Bk. III, chap. xvi, secs. 263, 264, 329–30).

9. As shown by William Tilghman's notes, Edward Tilghman cited the opinion of Chancellor George Wythe in the case of Page v. Pendleton, decided in the Virginia High Court of Chancery in May 1793, which had recently been reported in Wythe's *Decisions of Cases in Virginia by the High Court of Chancery* . . . , 127. Dallas omitted this citation in reporting Tilghman's argument and also JM's response to it. Wythe asserted that the right of an alien enemy to recover a debt could not be confiscated. The decree was appealed to the Court of Appeals, but after three of the judges disqualified themselves, the case was referred to a special court of appeals. After several continuances, the appellant declined further prosecution and the appeal was dismissed on 11 Nov. 1799 (Va. Ct. Ap. Ord. Bk. III, 57, 134, 174, 242, 244, 278, 361; see also Sec. IV, editorial note).

10. Tilghman: "The money, when paid by the debtor into the treasury, was simply, to remain there, subject to the direction of the Legislature; and as the debtor was not bound so to pay it, the provisions of the act could not amount to a confiscation; but were merely an invitation to pay, with an implied promise, that whoever accepted the terms of the invitation, should be indemnified by the state" (3 Dall. 208).

11. This point is not mentioned in Iredell's notes of JM's circuit court argument, though Chief Justice Jay refers to it in his opinion. Jay observed that the word "recovery" had a precise, technical meaning in regard to debts: "recovery by process and course of law." Thus, all British creditors, including those whose debtors made loan office payments, had a right to sue their original debtors—their remedy should not be limited to petitioning the state for compensation (Jones v. Walker, Fed. Cas. No. 7507, 1069).

12. The reference is to the May 1782 act concerning executions. It had originally been pleaded in bar but was overruled by the circuit court in 1793 (Hening, *Statutes*, XI, 76; Doc. I, n. 31).

13. JM alluded to the fifth article of the treaty (see Doc. I, n. 46).

14. See *PJM*, III, 14 n. 9.

15. Tilghman: "Had the treaty meant to obviate only a part of the impediments, the meaning would have been expressed in qualified terms. But as it could not be supposed, that, after the peace, laws would be passed creating impediments to the recovery of British debts; the treaty cannot be construed merely to intend to prevent the passing future laws, but to annihilate the operation of such as were previously enacted. There is no such clause in the treaties, which England made at the same period with France, Spain, and Holland, and for this obvious reason, that those countries had passed no law to impede the recovery of British debts" (3 Dall. 209–10).

16. William Nelson, *The Law of Evidence* . . . (3d ed.; London, 1744), 196 (citing an anonymous case in John Clayton's *Reports and Pleas of Assises at Yorke* . . . [London, 1651], 129). Iredell summarized the case in his opinion: "The case cited from the Law of Evidence, I think is an authority substantially in point, to show the complete discharge of the debtor. 'In debt upon a lease, the defendant pleaded payment, and in evidence showed, he paid it to sequestrators of the commonwealth, the plaintiff being a delinquent; and it was ruled this was good payment to prove the issue, which was a payment to the plaintiff himself.' . . . This case is certainly very strong, for it was not deemed necessary to plead it in bar, but it was admitted in evidence, upon a plea that he paid the money to the plaintiff himself" (3 Dall. 269).

VI. Judgment
7 March 1796

Whereupon all and singular the premises being seen by the Court here and fully understood, and mature deliberation had thereon, because it appears to the Court now here, that in the record and process aforesaid and also in the rendition of the Judgment aforesaid upon the demurrer to the rejoinder of the defendants in error to the replication to the second plea, it is manifestly erred;[1] it is considered that the said Judgment, for those errors and others in the record and process aforesaid, be revoked annulled and altogether held for nought And it is further considered by the Court here, that the plaintiff in error recover against the defendants two thousand nine hundred and seventy six pounds eleven shillings and six pence good British Money commonly called Sterling Money his debt aforesaid and his Costs by him about his Suit in this behalf expended and the said defendants in mercy &ca: But this Judgment is to be discharged by the payment of the Sum of five hundred and ninety six dollars and interest thereon to be computed after the rate of five per Cent per Annum from the seventh day of July one thousand seven hundred and eighty two till payment besides the Costs and by the payment of such damages as shall be awarded to the plaintiff in error on a writ of Enquiry to be issued by the Circuit Court of Virginia to ascertain the sum really due to the plaintiff exclusively of the said Sum of five hundred and ninety six Dollars which was found to be due to the plaintiff in error upon the Trial in the said Circuit Court of the issue joined upon the defendant's plea of payment at a time when the Judgment of the said Circuit Court on the said demurrer was unreversed and in full force and vigor; and for the execution of this Judgment of the Court the cause aforesaid is remanded to the said Circuit Court of Virginia.[2]

Minutes of the Supreme Court of the U.S., 7 Mar. 1796, RG 267, DNA.

1. The four sitting justices—Chase, Paterson, Wilson, and Cushing—unanimously reversed the judgment of the circuit court. Iredell did not participate in the appeal (3 Dall. 256 n.).

2. A mandate incorporating the writ of error, citation, assignment of errors, record on appeal, and proceedings in the Supreme Court was issued on 14 Mar. 1796. This was filed by the plaintiff in the circuit court on 23 May, and a jury was ordered to ascertain the additional sum due the plaintiff. At the May 1797 term the jury assessed damages of $5,418 in addition to the $596 (plus interest) previously awarded. Execution was thereupon levied on thirty-six slaves, five horses, two mules, thirty head of cattle, twenty-four head of sheep, and three hundred barrels of Indian corn. The defendants Hylton and Eppes executed a forthcoming bond, on which judgment was rendered by their default at the Nov. 1797 term (Ware v. Hylton, U.S. Cir. Ct., Va., Ended Cases [Restored], 1797; U.S. Cir. Ct., Va., Ord. Bk. II, 97–98, 214–15; III, 69; Rec. Bk. V, 386–421).

Satisfaction of this and other judgments eventually exhausted all of Hylton's property. The Richmond merchant later entered debtor's prison as a result of legal process instituted by his creditors. In his last years his only means of support was his salary as clerk of the Council of State, a post he held from 1801 to his death in 1811 ("Remarks on the Claim of Gibson Donaldson & Hamilton," 14–15, T.79/11 [claim of Gibson Donaldson & Hamilton], P.R.O.; Carter, *Latrobe Va. Journals*, II, 543).

14. Asselby v. Pleasants

1790–1794

I. Declaration, 27 December 1790
II. Pleas, 27 February 1791
III. Replication, 27 March 1791
IV. Rejoinder, 27 June 1791
V. Surrejoinder, 26 August 1791
VI. Judgment, 2 December 1793
VII. Confession of Judgment, 6 December 1793
VIII. Capias ad Satisfaciendum, 7 June 1794
IX. Forthcoming Bond, 2 July 1794
X. Notice, 11 October 1794
XI. Fieri Facias, 19 January 1795
XII. Thomas Pleasants, Jr., to Richard Hanson, 4 February 1795

Editorial Note

Suits on unpaid bills of exchange formed another category of British debt cases. In this case the British creditor was the payee of a bill of exchange drawn by planter Thomas Mann Randolph, Sr., on Robert Pleasants & Company, merchants at Curles, on the James River just below Richmond. This firm consisted of Robert Pleasants (1723–1801), a prominent Quaker (see Case Number 42), and Thomas Pleasants, Jr., his son-in-law. Randolph drew the bill on 14 May 1775, and Pleasants & Company accepted it for payment the next day. The payee, Thomas Asselby of Bristol, was well known in Virginia, having been for thirty years a master of ships trading between his home city and the colony.[1]

Of particular interest in this suit is the defendant's attempt to bar the creditor's claim by interposing the act of limitations. The pleadings on this act extended far enough to include a rare surrejoinder (Document V). Virginia's general statute of limitations of 1705 declared that certain actions at law, including trespass, detinue, trover, case (assumpsit), and debt on simple contract had to be brought within five years after the cause of action accrued. A saving clause allowed persons "beyond the sea, or out of the country" at the time to bring such actions on their return. By a 1755 act foreign merchants with resident factors were removed from the protection of this saving clause. During the war the courts of justice were closed much of the time, and the General Assembly consequently took several periods out of the computation for the act of limitations, amounting in the whole to about five years.[2]

When British creditors began to sue for recovery of their debts in Virginia courts during the 1790s, Virginians frequently and successfully pleaded the statute of limitations in cases arising on bills of exchange, promissory notes, and, especially, unsettled accounts. One attorney discouraged his British clients from bringing suits where there was no evidence of an assumption of the debt since the peace. The plaintiff's attempt to set up the treaty of peace against the act was unavailing, and even the saving clause in favor of foreign creditors was held not to cover British merchants who employed agents in Virginia.[3]

However much the experience of the war vitiated Virginians' sense of honor or concern for reputation with respect to their British debts, not all debtors rushed to take the utmost advantage of the statute of limitations. In numerous instances they most likely pleaded the statute, or threatened to do so, not to escape payment altogether but to obtain favorable terms from their creditors. One of Marshall's clients, for example, declined his advice to plead the act of limitations because his creditor "seemed willing at least to settle . . . upon amicable terms and at the same time such as would not effectually ruin us."[4] In the present case Pleasants & Company successfully pleaded limitations, but subsequently chose to confess judgment after working out a compromise with the Asselbys' agent.

The pleadings in this case disclose that the plaintiffs, executors of Captain Asselby, sought to avoid the statute of limitations by claiming the benefit of the saving clause for persons resident "in parts beyond the seas" (Document III). The defendants rejoined that Asselby had been in Virginia at the time the cause of action arose, a fact that was admitted by the plaintiffs' surrejoinder (Documents IV and V). Since Asselby remained in Virginia until June 1775, that is, for some days after Pleasants & Company accepted the bill of exchange, Marshall could argue that the statute had begun to run against Asselby before he departed the colony and that more than five years had elapsed (taking into account suspensions of the act during the war) before the bringing of the suit in 1790. The plaintiffs countered that Asselby's presence in Virginia occurred at a time that was later removed from the operation of the statute, that British plaintiffs were prevented from bringing suits in Virginia after the peace, and that the recovery of the debt was stipulated by the fourth article of the peace treaty.

The judgment in this and other cases made it clear that only those

British creditors who never set foot in Virginia and did not employ resident factors or agents could claim the protection of the saving clause. Most creditors, of course, did not fall into this category. If they failed to bring suit immediately after the peace or to obtain a new promise to pay the debt, their claims could be barred by the statute of limitations. Throughout the 1790s the courts in Virginia, both state and federal, rejected the creditors' contention that the statute of limitations in effect operated as a lawful impediment to the recovery of their debts and as such was prohibited by the fourth article of the treaty of peace. This question was later reopened by the Convention of 1802, which reaffirmed the fourth article of the 1783 treaty, and in time came before Marshall sitting as a judge of the U.S. Circuit Court in Richmond. The case was *Hopkirk* v. *Bell*, one of many pending actions founded upon open accounts or notes without seal in which the act was pleaded. After being heard at the May 1805 term, the case was certified to the Supreme Court on a division of opinion between Marshall and District Judge Cyrus Griffin. In March 1806 the high court declared that the fourth article prohibited the operation of Virginia's act of limitations upon British debts contracted less than five years before the outbreak of war in 1775. No time previous to the war could be added to any time subsequent to the peace treaty to bar a recovery of the debt. The court further held that an agent for collecting debts was not a factor and therefore that British merchants who employed such agents fell within the protection of the saving clause for foreign creditors.[5]

In addition to the pleadings on the statute of limitations, the case papers in *Asselby* v. *Pleasants* document some of the ways a creditor could enforce his judgment and in turn how his debtor could delay final execution of that judgment. Pleasants & Company confessed judgment in return for a six-month stay of execution (Document VII). When they failed to pay by the end of this term, the plaintiffs' agent immediately instituted proceedings to satisfy the judgment. As the representative of a judgment creditor he could choose among several writs of execution, depending on whether he wished to have it levied upon the goods and chattels (fieri facias), lands (elegit), or body (capias ad satisfaciendum) of the debtor. The agent elected to proceed upon a capias ad satisfaciendum, which commanded the sheriff to keep the debtor in custody and produce him at the next court to satisfy the plaintiff (Document VIII). Robert and Thomas Pleasants did not have to go to prison, however, because the law provided that a debtor could be discharged from custody by tendering personal property or slaves to the value of the debt and costs or by giving bond to have such property "forthcoming" at the day of sale. Debtors under execution by capias ad satisfaciendum or fieri facias routinely executed forthcoming bonds if they could find someone to act as security for them. This allowed them to keep the property until the day of sale (Document IX).[6]

After obtaining a second judgment against Pleasants & Company on a forfeited forthcoming bond, the Asselbys' agent this time sued out a fieri facias (Document XI). Marshall's clients thus took full advantage of the law in postponing the day of reckoning. As this case illustrates, a Virginia debtor could withhold payment and keep possession of his property for at least a year following the original judgment against him. At each stage of the proceedings, to be sure, interest and costs swelled the amount owed, but to the planter or farmer who saw salvation in the next crop, this was a reasonable price to pay for an extension of credit.

1. Betsy August, "Robert Pleasants Letterbook, 1771–1773" (M.A. thesis, College of William and Mary, 1976); "Letters of Robert Pleasants of Curles," *WMQ*, 2d ser., I (1921), 107–13; Adair P. Archer, "The Quaker's Attitude Towards the Revolution," ibid., 168–82; "Letters of Robert Pleasants, Merchant at Curles, 1772," ibid., II (1922), 257–75; Kenneth L. Carroll, ed., "Robert Pleasants on Quakerism: 'Some account of the first settlement of Friends in Virginia . . . ,'" *VMHB*, LXXXVI (1978), 3–16; Henrico County Will Book No. 2 (1787–1802), 371–74 (microfilm), Vi; *Va. Gazette* (Purdie and Dixon), 4 July 1745, 13 Oct. 1774.

2. Hening, *Statutes*, III, 381–84; VI, 481; Shepherd, *Statutes*, I, 29; Tucker, *Blackstone's Commentaries*, III, 307 n. 32.

3. Affidavit of James Webb (attorney for Archibald McCall & Co.), 14 Jan. 1804, T.79/7 (claim of McCall & Shedden), P.R.O.; Record of Jamieson & Co. v. Newton's Executor, 1797–99 (Fredericksburg District Court), T.79/26 (claim of Neil Jamieson & Co.), P.R.O.; Moore, *International Adjudications*, III, 66.

4. Roger Atkinson, Jr., to Robert Fearon, 3 Feb. 1794, T.79/17 (claim of Richard Hanson), P.R.O.

5. Certificate of William Marshall, 20 Mar. 1805; statement of Thomas Wilson, 14 June 1805, T.79/11 (claim of Speirs, Bowman & Co.), P.R.O.; Hopkirk v. Bell, 3 Cranch 454 (1806); 4 Cranch 164 (1806).

6. Hening, *Statutes*, V, 526; XIII, 357; Tucker, *Blackstone's Commentaries*, III, 413–20.

I. Declaration

27 December 1790

United States, Middle Circuit }
District of Virginia to wit[1] }

Mary Aselby, of the Kingdom of Great Brittain Executrix of the last Will & Testament of Thomas Aselby deceased,[2] of the said Kingdom of Great Brittain, Complains of Robert Pleasants & Thomas Pleasants of the County of Henrico, and District aforesaid, in the middle Circuit of the United States, and in the Commonwealth of Virginia, one of the united States of America; and within the Jurisdiction of this Honorable Court, in custody of the Marshall of the said District &c. For that whereas on the fourteenth day of May in the year of our Lord one thousand seven hundred & seventy five, at the parish of Henrico in the County of Henrico, in the now Commonwealth & District, (then Colony & Dominion) of Virginia one of the now united States of America, in the middle Circuit, and now within the Jurisdiction of this Honorable Court, a certain Thomas Mann Randolph, made his Bill in writing, signed with his proper name, & subscribed with his proper hand writing, and to the said Robert Pleasants, & Thomas Pleasants, by the firm & stile of Robert & Thomas Pleasants, Merchants in Henrico directed, by which Bill said Thomas Mann Randolph desired the said Robert & Thomas Pleasants to pay to the said Thomas Aselby, in his life time, (by the stile of Capt Thomas Aselby) or to his order, One hundred & sixty three pounds, ten Shillings & three pence half penny, which said Bill in writing, being presented to the said Robert Pleasants, & Thomas Pleasants, afterwards, to wit on the fifteenth day of May, in the year aforesaid, at the parish of Henrico, & County aforesaid, within the then Colony & Dominion aforesaid now the Commonwealth, & District of Virginia, & within the Jurisdiction of this Honble: Court, they the said Robert & Thomas Pleasants, according to the usage & Custom of merchants, accepted the same, by a writing on the back of the said Bill, in their proper name, & in their proper hand, (by the name & stile of Robert Pleasants & Co:)[3] by which they promised to pay the same, according to the tenor thereof, to wit at the parish & County aforesaid, within the then Colony & Dominion (now the District) of Virginia as aforesaid, and within the Jurisdiction of this Honorable Court, by force of which acceptance, the said Robert & Thomas Pleasants became liable according to the usage & Custom of Merchants, to pay to the said Thos: Aselby in his life time, the aforesaid sum of One hundred & sixty three pounds, ten Shillings & three pence half penny according to the tenor of the said Bill, and of their acceptance thereof, and being so liable, they the said Robert Pleasants, & Thomas Pleasants, by the firm & name of Robert Pleasants & Company, in consideration thereof afterwards, to wit on the said fifteenth day of May in the year aforesaid, at the parish & County aforesaid, within the then Colony & Dominion (now Commonwealth & District) aforesaid, and within the jurisdiction of this Honorable Court, and then and there undertook, and faithfully promised the said Thomas Aselby in his life time, that they wou'd well & truely to him the said Sum of money mentioned in the said Bill, according to the tenor and effect of the said Bill, and of their acceptance thereof as aforesaid.[4]

And whereas also afterwards, to wit on the said fifteenth day of May, in the year of our Lord 1775 aforesaid at the parish, and in the County aforesaid, within the then Colony & Dominion (now District & Commonwealth) of Virginia, aforesaid, one of the united States of America, in the middle Circuit, and now within the Jurisdiction of this Honorable Court, the said Robert Pleasants & Thomas Pleasants, by the firm & stile of Robert Pleasants & Company were indebted to the said Thomas Aselby in his life time, in One hundred and sixty three pounds, ten Shillings & three pence half penny Current money of Virginia, for so much money by the said Robert Pleasants, & Thomas Pleasants, by the firm & stile, of Robert Pleasants & Company before that time had & received to the use of the said Thomas Aselby in his life time, and being so indebted they the said Robert Pleasants, & Thomas Pleasants, by the firm & stile aforesaid, in consideration thereof, afterwards, to wit on the same day & year aforesaid, at the parish and in the County aforesaid, within the then Colony & Dominion (now District & Commonwealth) of Virginia aforesaid, one of the united states of America, in the middle Circuit, & within the Jurisdiction of this Honorable Court, assumed upon themselves, and then & there faithfully promised the said Thomas Asselby in his life time, to pay to him the said sum of One hundred & sixty three pounds, ten shillings & three pence half penny current money last mentioned, whensoever they the said Robert Pleasants, & Thomas Pleasants, shou'd be thereto afterwards required.[5] Nevertheless the said Robt: Pleasants & Thomas Pleasants, not regarding their aforesaid several promises & undertakings, with the said Thomas Asselby, in his life time, in manner & form aforesaid made, but contriving, & craftily, fraudulently & subtily intending the said Thomas Aselby in his life time to defraud & deceive, in that behalf, did not pay to the said Thomas Aselby in his life time, the aforesaid several sums of money, or either of them, althoh often afterwards required, to wit on the same day & year last aforesaid, at the parish &

County aforesaid, within the then colony & Dominion, (now Commonwealth and District) of Virginia, one of the united States of America, in the middle Circuit, and within the Jurisdiction of this Honorable Court. Nor have the said Robert Pleasants, & Thomas Pleasants, or either of them, paid the said sums of money, or any part thereof to the plaintif, since his death, althoh often required & particularly on the   day of   in the year of our Lord one thousand seven hundred & eighty at the parish & County aforesaid, in the Commonwealth & District aforesaid, & within the Jurisdiction aforesaid, But the same to pay, to the said Thomas Aselby in his life time, and to the said Mary Aselby the plaintif since his death, altogether refused; and to the said plaintif since the death of the said Thomas Aselby, and particularly on the day & year last aforesaid, at the parish & in the County aforesaid, within the Commonwealth & District aforesaid, and within the Jurisdiction aforesaid, & at divers days & times since altogether refused & still do refuse to pay the same, to the Damage of the said plaintif Three hundred pounds, & therefore she brings suit &c, And the said Plaintif brings here into Court the Letters Testamentary of the said Thomas Aselby whereby it appears &c.

BAKER ꝑ Pltff.

Pledges of prosecution[6]
JOHN DOE, }
RICHD. ROE }

ADS, Asselby v. Pleasants, U.S. Circuit Court, Va., Ended Cases (Restored), 1793, Vi. Attorney for the plaintiff, Jerman Baker, enclosed his interlineations within parentheses to mark them as insertions. The editors have ignored these marks, while incorporating the additions. Clerk's endorsements on verso summarize proceedings. Filed in clerk's office 27 Dec. 1790 (see n. 1).

1. The capias, dated 9 June 1790, was executed on the defendants on 7 Oct. The declaration was filed at the rules on 27 Dec., at which time the defendants prayed a special imparlance (requesting a delay in pleading) and oyer of the writ (U.S. Cir. Ct., Va., Rule Bk. I, 1, 2).

2. Thomas Asselby died in May 1783, having entrusted his Virginia business to Richard Hanson (Thomas Asselby to Richard Hanson, 3 May 1783; William Asselby to Richard Hanson, 8 July 1783, T.79/37 [claim of William Asselby], P.R.O.). On Hanson, who served as agent for William Jones and other British creditors, see Case No. 18, editorial note.

3. The original bill of exchange is in the suit papers.

4. This first count is in special assumpsit founded on the custom of merchants, the appropriate action against the acceptor of a bill of exchange. Since this was an inland bill, no protest for nonpayment was necessary (Robinson, *Practice*, I, 46; Bayley, *Bills of Exchange*, 75–76). On special assumpsit and bills of exchange, see Case No. 10.

5. It was customary to add applicable common counts in general assumpsit to the special count on the bill itself. The courts had held that acceptance was evidence of money had and received by the acceptor to the use of the holder. This count was accordingly an indebitatus assumpsit for money had and received (Bayley, *Bills of Exchange*, 96; Chitty, *Bills of Exchange*, 470–71).

6. This phrase was written sideways along the left-hand margin.

II. Pleas

27 February 1791

AND the said ⟨Robert Pleasants & Thomas Pleasants⟩ the Defendant⟨s⟩[1] by JOHN MARSHALL ⟨their⟩ Attorney come and defend the force and injury when and where, &c. and say that the Plaintiff ought not to have or maintain ⟨her⟩ action aforesaid against ⟨t⟩h⟨e⟩m, because ⟨t⟩he⟨y⟩ say that ⟨t⟩he⟨y⟩ did not assume upon ⟨t⟩h⟨e⟩msel⟨ves⟩ in manner and form as the Plaintiff against ⟨t⟩h⟨e⟩m have declared, and of this ⟨t⟩he⟨y⟩ put ⟨t⟩h⟨e⟩msel⟨ves⟩ upon the country.

And the said ⟨Robert & Thomas⟩ the Defendant⟨s⟩ with the special leave of the Court to plead as many several matters as ⟨t⟩he⟨y⟩ may think necessary for ⟨t⟩h⟨eir⟩ defence, say that the Plaintiff ought not to have or maintain ⟨her⟩ action against ⟨t⟩h⟨e⟩m, because ⟨t⟩he⟨y⟩ say that ⟨t⟩he⟨y⟩ did not at any time within five years next before the day on which the original writ in this suit was issued, undertake in manner and form as the Plaintiff against ⟨t⟩h⟨e⟩m ha⟨th⟩ declared, and this ⟨t⟩he⟨y are⟩ ready to verify[2]—wherefore ⟨t⟩he⟨y⟩ pray judgment if the Plaintiff ⟨her⟩ action aforesaid against ⟨t⟩h⟨e⟩m ought to have or maintain, &c.[3]

And the said ⟨Robert & Thomas⟩ with the leave of the Court for further plea saith, that the said Plaintiff ought not to have or maintain ⟨her⟩ said action against ⟨them⟩ because he says[4] that the debt in the declaration mentioned, was originally due to British subjects, and is not recoverable in this Court by virtue of the Laws in that case made and provided, and this he is[5] ready to verify—wherefore ⟨They⟩ pray judgment whether the Plaintiff ⟨her⟩ action aforesaid against ⟨them⟩ the Defendant⟨s⟩ ought to have and maintain, &c.[6]

Printed form, Asselby v. Pleasants, U.S. Circuit Court, Va., Ended Cases (Restored), 1793, Vi. Blanks filled in by JM. Filed at rules on 27 Feb. 1791 (U.S. Cir. Ct., Va., Rule Bk. I, 1, 2).

1. Here and throughout JM changed the singular to plural when referring to the defendant and the plural to singular when referring to the plaintiff.

2. The printed form for cases brought in assumpsit included the plea of limitations because it was frequently pleaded along with the general issue in

assumpsit. It was omitted from the debt form, however, because the statute of limitations did not apply to actions of debt on bonds.

3. At this point the two original British debt pleas follow exactly as on the debt form (Case No. 12, Doc. V). JM, however, struck out the first of these, the loan office plea, which was inapplicable to this case.

4. JM forgot to change this to "they say."

5. JM forgot to change this to "they are."

6. As in Jones v. Walker and the other British debt cases, the defendants in this suit later submitted new British debt pleas in place of the original ones (see Case No. 12, Doc. VII; U.S. Cir. Ct., Va., Ord. Bk. I, 229).

III. Replication
27 March 1791

And the said Plaintif as to the plea of the said Defendants, by them as above secondly pleaded in Bar saith,[1] that she by any thing in that plea alledged, ought not to be barred from having or maintaining her said Action against the said Defendants, because protesting that that plea, and the matters therein contained, are not sufficient in Law to Bar the said Plaintif from having her said Action against the said Defendants;[2] For replication in this behalf the said Plaintif saith, that the said Thomas Aselby the testator of the Plaintif, at the time of making the promise and undertaking aforesaid by them the said Defendants, was a resident in the Kingdom of Great Brittain, in parts beyond the Seas, to wit in the City of Bristol, and a Subject of his Brittanick Majesty, and so continued until the day of his death, and was not on that day, or at any time thereafter, in his life time, a resident in this Country, or State, or of any of the united States of America; but always continued in parts beyond the Seas. And that the said Plaintif, at the time of the death of the said Thomas Aselby, her testator, to wit on the day of in the year of our Lord one thousand seven hundred and was out of this Commonwealth, in parts beyond the Seas, and was resident in the said City of Bristol, in the said Kingdom of Great Brittain, and hath not since been resident in this, or any other of the united States of America, but always was, and now is a resident in the said City of Bristol.[3] And the said Plaintiff in Fact saith that neither her Testator, the said Thomas Aselby, or she the said plaintiff, were resident in this Country, at the time of making the promise an[4] assumptions aforesaid, nor at any time since, nor were they, or either of them resident in this, or any of the united States of America, on the first day of January, one thousand seven hundred and seventy seven,[5] or at any time since, until the day of the establishment of this Honble: Court, and this she is ready to verify. Wherefore the said Plaintiff prays Judgment, and her damages aforesaid sustained by the nonperformance of the promises and assumptions of the said Defendants, in manner aforesaid to be adjudged to her.

ADS, extract, Asselby v. Pleasants, U.S. Circuit Court, Va., Ended Cases (Restored), 1793, Vi. In hand of Jerman Baker. Replication to first plea, demurrer to third plea, and Baker's signature omitted (see n. 1). Filed at rules on 27 Mar. 1791 (U.S. Cir. Ct., Va., Rule Bk. I, 1, 2).

1. This is the replication to the plea of the act of limitations. The omitted replication and demurrer are standard in form and follow closely the first and last paragraphs in Case No. 12, Doc. VI.

2. As with the loan office plea, the plaintiff replied with a protestation (see Case No. 12, Doc. VI and n. 8).

3. The plaintiff claimed that the saving clause for foreigners prevented the statute of limitations from running against her.

4. Baker meant to write "and."

5. This is evidently a reference to the proclamation of Gov. Patrick Henry of 1 Jan. 1777, ordering all British merchants, their agents, factors, and storekeepers to leave the commonwealth within forty days. This proclamation implemented a resolution adopted by the House of Delegates on 18 Dec. 1776 (*JCSV*, I, 303; Harrell, *Loyalism in Va.*, 75–77).

IV. Rejoinder
27 June 1791

Pleasants
ads
Aselby } rejoinder

And the said defendants by their attorney come & say that they ought not to be chargd by any thing by the said plaintiff in her replication to the second plea of these defendants above pleaded because they say that the said Thomas Aselby the testator of the plaintiff at the time of making the several promises & undertakings by these defendants in the declaration chargd was within the commonwealth (the then colony) of Virginia, & hath often since to wit on the day of in the year 17 & at divers other times been within the commonwealth (the then colony of) virginia & this they are ready to verefy wherefore they pray judgement &c.[1]

AD, Asselby v. Pleasants, U.S. Circuit Court, Va., Ended Cases (Restored), 1793, Vi. In JM's hand. Filed at rules on 27 June 1791 (U.S. Cir. Ct., Va., Rule Bk. I, 19, 20).

1. JM started to sign the rejoinder but then crossed out what he had written. Immediately following in another hand is the defendant's joinder in demurrer to the third plea. It has been omitted, along with the rejoinder to the replication to the first plea (written on a separate sheet). The subsequent pleadings on the first plea were presumably unnecessary since the defendant tendered issue with that plea.

V. Surrejoinder

26 August 1791

Mary Aselby Erx of Thos. Aselby deceas'd vs Pleasants } surrejoinder.

And the said Plaintif saith, that she by anything in the rejoinder of the Defendts: to her replication to the second plea of the said Defendants ought not to be barred from having or maintaining her said Action, against the said Defendants, because she saith that after the Debt in the Declaration mentioned was contracted, and after the promises and undertakings of the said Defendants in the Declaration also mentioned, and within 5 years next after the making of the said promises and undertakings by the said Defendants, & in the life time of the said Thomas Aselby,[1] and after the 12th day of April, which was in the year 1774,[2] that is to say, on the day of June 1775, the said Thomas Aselby, in the Declaration mentioned, being a Mariner, commanding a Ship, employed in commerce, between the City of Bristol, in the Kingdom of Great Brittain, of which said City the said Thomas was a resident and the then Colony & Dominion, now district of Virginia, departed from the said then Colony, to parts beyond the seas, to wit, to the City of Bristol aforesaid, where he remained for all his life time afterwards, until the day of his death, after which, said day of June 1775,[3] it was by the third section of the Act of General Assembly passed at a session begun & holden in the City of Williamburg, in the month of October 1776, entituled "An Act to restrain the operation of the Acts, for the limitation of Actions, and recording Deeds in certain cases", enacted, "That in all questions which might arise in any Court of record for limitation of Actions, making entrys into Lands, or limitation of evidence, in the computation of time, the period between the 12th day of April 1774, and the end of that Session of Asembly shoud not be accounted as any part thereof, so as to bar such Action, entry, or evidence, but in all such computations, the progression shou'd be from the said 12th day of April 1774, to the day after the end of that Session, as one day."[4] And also afterwards, to wit, at a session of General Assembly, begun & holden at the Capitol in the City of Williamsburg, in the month of October 1777, it was by this second section of an Act, entituled, "an Act to restrain the operation of the Acts, for the limitation of Actions, and recording of Deeds in certain cases", enacted, "that in all questions which might arise in any Court of record, upon any Act for limitation of Actions, making entrys into Lands, or limitation of evidence, in the computation of time, the period between the 12th day 1774, and the 12th day of April next (following) shou'd not be accounted any part thereof, so as to bar such action, entry, or evidence, but in all such computations the progression shou'd be from the said 12th day of April 1774, to the 12th day of April next, [(]following) the passing of the said Act, as one day.["][5] And afterwards, to wit at a session of General Assembly, began and holden at the public buildings in the City of Richmond, on Monday the 7th day of May 1781, and from thence continued by adjournment, to the Town of Staunton, in the County of Augusta, it was, by an Act, entituled, "an Act preventing a discontinuance of the General Court, and suspending the proceedings of certain Courts, in particular cases," among other things enacted, "That until a Declaration shou'd be made by the Genl. Asembly to the contrary, neither the Court of Appeals, the High Court of Chancery, the General Court, nor any County Court, shou'd hear or determine any matter, cause, or thing, except those pleas of the commonwealth, private questions brot: on by consent, suits instituted for the division of Estates, contestation of Wills, and such other cases, in which the Law requires not a Declaration, or Bill in Equity, to be filed, and that of the time, between the first day of January in the year aforesaid, to the last day of that Session of the General Assembly, at which the foregoing suspension of the Courts judiciary proceedings shall be removed, no account shall be made in any computation upon the Act of Limitations".[6] And also afterwards, to wit, at a session of General Assembly, begun & holden at the public buildings in the City of Richmond, in the month of October 1782 (in the life time of the said Thomas Aselby,) it was, by an Act, entituled, An Act to repeal so much of a former Act as suspends the issuing of executions, on certain Judgments, until December 1783 among other things enacted, That no Debt or demand whatsoever, contracted with, or due to any british subject, or contracted with, or due to any other person, for the use of, or in concern with, any British subject, and still remaining due, and unpaid, shou'd be recoverable in any Court within this Commonwealth.[7]

And also afterwards, to wit, at a session of General Assembly, begun & holden at the public buildings, in the City of Richmond, in the month of May 1781,[8] it was by an Act, intituled, "an Act to give further time for the probation of Deeds, and for other purposes", enacted, "That in all questions which may arise in any Court of record, upon any Act for limitation of Actions, making entries into Lands, or limitation of evidence, in the computation of time, the period between the 10th day of April 1771, and the 10th day of April 1784, shall not be accounted any part thereof, so as to bar such Action, entry or evidence, but in all such computations, the progression shall be from the said 10th day of April 1771, to the 10th day of April 1784, as one day.["][9] And for that also, afterwards, to wit, on the third day of September, in the year of our Lord 1783, (before which time, to wit on the 20th day of May 1783, the said Thomas Aselby the testator of the plaintif, in the Declaration mentioned, had departed this life in parts beyond the seas, to wit in the City of Bristol, in the Kingdom of Great Brittain, being then a Subject and Citizen of Great Brittain, and not a Citizen of the united States of America, or any of them) it was by the 4th Article of the definitive treaty of peace, made between the united States of America, on the one part, & his Brittanic Majesty on the other part, (in the City of paris, that is to say, in the Commonwealth aforesaid and now within the jurisdiction of this Honorable Court) stipulated and agreed, "that Creditors on either side, shou'd meet with no lawful impediment, to the recovery of Debts bona fide contracted before the said third day of September 1783." And the said plaintif in fact saith, that she was then resident in the said City of Bristol, in the said Kingdom of Great Brittain, subject to the King of Great Brittain, and being appointed by the said Thomas Aselby executrix, of his last Will and Testament, & having taken upon herself, the burthen of the execution thereof, she was, a creditor within the meaning and intention, of the said fourth article, of the said definitive treaty, and that the Debt in the declaration mentioned, was bona fide contracted, and the promises, and undertakings, and the Assumptions of the said Defendants, in the Declaration also mentioned, made, before the said third day of September 1783, and in the life time of the said Thomas Aselby. And for that also, afterwards, to wit on the 17th day of September, in the year of our Lord 1787, it was, by the constitution of the united States expressly Declared, that Treatys, which were then made, and which shou'd thereafter be made, shou'd be the supreme Law of the Land, any thing in the said constitution, or of the Laws of any State to the contrary notwithstanding; without that, that the said Thomas Aselby, in his life time, at any time after the said day of June 1775, until the time of his death; or the said Plaintif, since the death of the said

Thomas Aselby, until the day of suing forth the original writ in this suit was, or were either of them, within this Country, or within any of the united States of America, and this she is ready to verify, wherefore the said Plaintif, as before, prays Judgment and her damages aforesaid sustained, by reason of the nonperformance of the promises and assumptions of the said Defendants, in manner and form aforesaid made to be adjudged to her.[10]

BAKER ℘ Pltff.

ADS, Asselby v. Pleasants, U.S. Circuit Court, Va., Ended Cases (Restored), 1793, Vi. Baker enclosed his interlineations within parentheses to mark them as insertions. The editors have ignored these marks, while incorporating the additions. Clerk's endorsements on verso note judgment and costs. Filed at rules on 26 Aug. 1791 (U.S. Cir. Ct., Va., Rule Bk. I, 19, 20).

1. At this point the MS is marked "(a)," indicating the place for inserting a passage that Baker wrote on a separate sheet. The editors have made the insertion.

2. On 12 Apr. 1774 the act regulating the fees of the officers and clerks of the courts expired, which in effect closed the courts for business. The act was not renewed before the Revolution (Hening, *Statutes*, VIII, 515–16; Mays, *Pendleton*, I, 244–48; George M. Curtis III, "The Role of the Courts in the Making of the Revolution in Virginia," in *The Human Dimensions of Nation Making: Essays on Colonial and Revolutionary America*, ed. James Kirby Martin [Madison, 1976], 121–46).

3. The insertion ends here.

4. Hening, *Statutes*, IX, 215. Baker's quotations from this and subsequent acts contain minor variations from the originals.

5. Ibid., 430.

6. Ibid., X, 422–23.

7. Ibid., XI, 176.

8. The year should be 1783.

9. Ibid., 294. This law was repealed in Oct. 1783 (ibid., 340). An act of 1792 brought together the various periods excluded from the running of the act of limitations: 12 Apr. 1774–12 Apr. 1778; 1 Jan. 1781–5 Jan. 1782; 5 May–20 Oct. 1783 (Shepherd, *Statutes*, I, 29).

10. JM failed to file a demurrer or rebutter to the surrejoinder, and an office judgment accordingly issued against the defendant at the Oct. 1791 rules. However, this suit abated on Mary Asselby's death. A new suit in the names of William and Mary Asselby, executor and executrix of Mary Asselby, was instituted in Feb. 1792. The plaintiffs filed a declaration in the clerk's office in Sept. 1792. When JM made no appearance for the defendant, the Asselbys obtained an office judgment at the Nov. 1792 rules. This was set aside when the defendant put in his pleas at the Nov. 1793 term of the court. In addition to bringing a new suit, the Asselbys also revived the original one by scire facias. As a result, there were two judgments at the Nov. 1793 term. The new capias, dated 25 Feb. 1792, and the second declaration of Sept.

1792 are in the suit papers, as is the scire facias, dated 15 Aug. 1792, reviving the original suit (see also U.S. Cir. Ct., Va., Rule Bk. I, 19–20, 66–67; Ord. Bk. I, 228, 229).

VI. Judgment
2 December 1793

This day came the parties by their Attornies and thereupon the Defts filed their Demurer to the Plaintiffs Surrejoinder to the Defendants rejoinder to the replication to their second plea and the Plaintiffs joined in the said Demurer,[1] and thereupon all and singular the premises in this cause having been seen and inspected by the Court and mature deliberation had thereon, it seemeth to them that the said Surrejoinder and the matters therein contained are not good and sufficient in Law to enable the Plaintiffs to support their action aforesaid in this behalf against the said Defendants. Therefore It is considered by the Court that the said Defendants go hence without day and recover against the Plaintiffs their costs by them about their defence in this behalf expended. And that for their false clamor the said Plaintiffs be in Mercy &c.[2]

Copy, U.S. Circuit Court, Va., Record Book I, 455–56, Vi.

1. The demurrer, in JM's hand, is in the suit papers. By entering this demurrer in court, JM set aside the office judgment of Oct. 1791.

2. This was the judgment in the original suit, which had been revived by scire facias. Judgment in the second suit, brought in Feb. 1792, was rendered the same day, after the defendant again put in the pleas of non assumpsit and limitations, along with three British debt pleas (identical to the third, fourth, and fifth pleas in Case No. 12, Doc. VII). The pleadings proceeded exactly as in the first case, with judgment for the defendant on his demurrer to the surrejoinder (U.S. Cir. Ct., Va., Ord. Bk. I, 228, 229).

VII. Confession of Judgment
6 December 1793

This day came the parties by their Attornies, and by their consent It is Ordered that the Judgment rendered in this suit on Monday last be set aside;[1] and thereupon the parties agree that the Plaintiffs have sustained damages by the occasion in the declaration specified to

Seven hundred and Seventy eight dollars and ninety two Cents, besides their costs.[2] Therefore It is considered by the Court that the Plaintiffs recover against the Defendants their damages as agreed aforesaid, and their costs by them about their suit in this behalf expended. And the said Defendants in Mercy &c. And the Plts agree to stay the execution of this Judgment six Months.[3]

Copy, U.S. Circuit Court, Va., Record Book I, 456, Vi.

1. There were, of course, two judgments on 2 Dec., but since these concerned the same debt, only one was to have effect.

2. This sum was somewhat less than the amount of principal and interest (deducting eight years for the war) due on the bill of exchange.

3. A letter from Richard Hanson (the plaintiffs' agent) to Robert and Thomas Pleasants, dated 11 May 1789, was entered as evidence in this suit, though for what purpose is not clear. The letter requested Pleasants & Co. to pay the bill and implied that they had recently expressed a willingness to pay. Presumably, however, this letter by itself did not constitute sufficient evidence of a renewed promise to pay the debt (U.S. Cir. Ct., Va., Rec. Bk. I, 457).

VIII. Capias ad Satisfaciendum
7 June 1794

THE PRESIDENT of the UNITED STATES of AMERICA, to the Marshall of the Virginia District, Greeting;

[SEAL] You are hereby commanded to take Robert & Thomas Pleasants if they be found within your District and them safely keep so that you have their bodies before the Judges of the Court of the United States for the middle Circuit in the Virginia District at Richmond on the twenty second day of November next to satisfy William Asselby and Mary Asselby Executor and Executrix, of Mary Asselby deceased who was Executrix of Thomas Asselby deceased Seven hundred and seventy eight dollars and ninety two cents, also Forty one Dollars and ninety cents which to the said Executor and Executrix lately in the same Court were adjudged as well for their damages which they sustained by occasion of the non performance of a certain promise and assumption by the said Robert & Thomas Pleasants to the said Thomas Asselby deceased lately made as for their Costs by them about their Suit in that behalf expended. Whereof the said Robert and Thomas Pleasants are convict as appears to us of Record. And have then there this Writ Witness John Jay esquire cheif Justice of the United States at Richmond aforesaid this seventh day of June 1794 and in the eighteenth year of the independance of the United States of America.[1]

Wm Marshall Clk

ADS, Asselby v. Pleasants, U.S. Circuit Court, Va., Ended Cases (Unrestored), 1794, Vi. David M. Randolph's return of writ on verso. Filed with papers in subsequent suit by plaintiffs to recover judgment on forfeited forthcoming bond.

1. U.S. Marshal David M. Randolph executed this writ on 2 July, at which time he took the defendants' forthcoming bond (Doc. IX). His return is in these words: "Executed on the bodies of the within defendants, who were discharged upon executing with security, a bond for the forthcoming of six negroes to wit: Ben, Peter, Saunders, Aubrey, Ned and Wiltshire as will appear by referrence to the bond herewith returned." Randolph also listed his fees.

IX. Forthcoming Bond

2 July 1794

Know all Men by these Presents, that we Robert Pleasants and Thomas Pleasants Junior together with Richard Randolph of Curls,[1] are held and firmly bound unto William Aselby and Mary Aselby, Executor and Executrix of Mary Aselby deceased, who was Executrix of Thomas Aselby deceased in the just and full sum of One thousand six hundred and sixty two dollars and fifty four cents, to be paid unto the said William Aselby Executor &c and Mary Aselby, Executrix &c &c their certain Attorney, their heirs Executors, Administrators or assigns; to which payment well and truly to be made, we bind ourselves jointly and severally, our joint and several heirs, Executors and Administrators, firmly by these presents: Sealed with our seals, and dated this Second day of July One thousand seven hundred and ninety four.

The Condition of the above obligation is such, that whereas William Aselby and Mary Aselby, Executor and Executrix above said, hath sued out of the Court of the United States, for the Middle Circuit, in the district of Virginia, a writ of Capias ad Satisfaciendum against the bodies of Robert Pleasants and Thomas Pleasants Junior for the purpose of satisfying the said William Aselby Executor and Mary Aselby Executrix, of Mary Aselby deceased, who was Executrix of Thomas Aselby deceased, for the sum of Eight hundred and thirty one dollars and twenty seven cents, including interest, costs and

Marshal's commissions,[2] which Writ hath been duly executed by David Meade Randolph, Marshal of and for the District of Virginia aforesaid, on the bodies of the said Robert Pleasants and Thomas Pleasants Junr.; where upon, the said defendants availing themselves of the relief of an Act of Assembly of the Virginia Legislature, in such cases made and provided; and by the Laws of the United States recognizing the said recited Act;[3] they the said Robert Pleasants and Thomas Pleasants Junior hath made immediate delivery of sundry negroes in discharge of their several bodies so taken in execution, to wit: Ben, Peter, Saunders, Aubrey, Ned, & Wiltshire[4] to be sold according to the true intent and meaning of the aforesaid Act of the Virginia Legislature and the Laws of the United States; And moreover, the said Robert Pleasants and Thomas Pleasants Junior desirous of keeping the aforesaid property in their possession until the day of sale of the same, hath tendered the above bound Richard Randolph as their joint and several security for the forthcoming and delivery of the same, at the place, and on the day of Sale, agreeable to Law: Now if the said Robert Pleasants and Thomas Pleasants Junior and Richard Randolph or either of them, do and shall deliver the aforesaid property to me the said Marshal at Richmond on the tenth day of Octobr.[5] next, then and there to be disposed of according to Law, for the discharge of the debt, interest, costs and Marshal's commissions, specified in and incident to the aforementioned Writ of Capias ad Satisfaciendum, then and in that event, the above obligation to be void, or else to remain in full force, Virtue and Effect.[6]

Sealed, acknowledged and delivered in the presence of Thomas Eston Randolph as to the first and last	Robert Pleasants [L.S.] Thomas Pleasants jr [L.S.] Richard Randolph [L.S.]

DS, Asselby v. Pleasants, U.S. Circuit Court, Va., Ended Cases (Unrestored), 1794, Vi. Filed with papers in subsequent suit by plaintiffs to recover judgment on forfeited forthcoming bond.

1. Randolph was the surety, or guarantor, of the bond. Here and throughout the document his name was inserted at the time of taking the bond. Randolph was one of the defendants who were represented by JM in Case No. 7.

2. U.S. Marshal David M. Randolph filed a statement with the execution writ listing the amount of the judgment, costs, fees, and commission. By mistake he charged only $21.90 instead of $41.90 for the costs. His fees for delivering the writ and taking the forthcoming bond came to $5.33. Adding the costs and fees to the amount of the judgment, $778.92, he obtained the sum of $806.15. Out of this sum he took a commission of 5 percent on the first $300 and 2 percent on the balance, amounting to $25.12. Thus, the

total came to $831.27, $20 less than it should have been. Immediately below this statement, which is in the suit papers, is a notation that the bond be credited by $470, paid on 30 Nov. 1794.

3. The latest Virginia statute concerning executions was enacted in 1792. The federal process acts of 1789 and 1792 provided that the forms of writs and executions issuing from the federal courts should be the same as those used in the respective states (Hening, *Statutes*, XIII, 357; *U.S. Statutes at Large*, I, 93–94 and n.).

4. The names of the slaves were inserted at the time of taking the bond, possibly by Robert Pleasants.

5. The date was filled in at the time of taking the bond.

6. In addition to forthcoming bonds, judgment debtors in Virginia also had recourse to "replevy" (redelivery) bonds. If at the time of execution or on the day of the sale the debtor gave bond with security, the sheriff would restore to him the goods taken in execution. Until 1787 replevy bonds were for three months, conditioned to pay the debt at the end of this period; or if no security was offered and if the goods could not be sold for three-fourths of their value (in the sheriff's opinion), the sheriff might sell the same on three-months credit, taking the bond of the buyer with security to pay it to the creditor. In 1787 the term of replevy bonds was extended to twelve months, but the debtor could replevy only if in the opinion of specially appointed commissioners the property levied upon would not sell for three-fourths of its value. In 1795 the legislature abolished replevy bonds, leaving forthcoming bonds as the debtor's only means of postponing immediate execution. As JM observed, replevy and forthcoming bonds were unknown in England, where money was plentiful and "easily procured by those who can secure the repayment of it." In Virginia, where wealth consisted principally of landed property, these expedients were "induced by necessity" (Hening, *Statutes*, V, 534; XII, 458–60; XIII, 367–71; Tucker, *Blackstone's Commentaries*, III, 422 n.; *Rev. Code* [1819], I, 530–31 n.; Ross v. Poythress, 1 Wash. 122 [1792]). For JM cases arising upon forthcoming bonds, see Johnston v. Meriwether, 3 Call 523 (1790) and Hewlett v. Chamberlayne, 1 Wash. 367 (1794).

X. Notice

11 October 1794

To Robert & Thomas Pleasants and Richard Randolph

Gentlemen

Take notice that I shall on Monday the twenty fourth day of November next it being the Second day of the next Court of the United States to be held at the Capitol in the City of Richmond for the Middle Circuit in the Virginia District, move the Said Court for a Judgment on your Forthcomeing Bond dated the Second of

July 1794 and payable to William Aselby and Mary Aselby Executor & Executrix of Mary Aselby decd. who was Executrix of Thomas Aselby deceased; taken by the Marshal of this State for the delivery of property in the City of Richmond on the tenth day of October 1794 upon a writ of Capias ad Satisfaciendum sued out of the Said Court of the United States for the Middle Circuit in the Virginia District by the said William Aselby & Mary Aselby Executor & Executrix of Mary Aselby decd. who was Executrix of Thomas Aselby deceased against Robert & Thomas Pleasants, which Bond was forfeited by the property not being deliverd.[1]

October 11th: 1794 WILLIAM ASSELBY. MARY ASSELBY.
by
RICHARD HANSON, their Attorney in fact

City of Richmond st.[2]

Personally Appeared before me Charles Grimes and made Oath that he Did deliver a Copy of the Within Notice to Richard Randolph on the 17th. of last Octr. and that he Also Deliverd a Copy of the Same to Thomas Pleasant Jnr. on the 23d. of Said Octr. — that he also Deliverd a Copy of the Same to Robt. Pleasant on the 5th. day of Novr. being this present Month — Given Under my hand this 24th. of Novr. 1794.[3]

ROBT. MITCHELL Mayor

DS, Asselby v. Pleasants, U.S. Circuit Court, Va., Ended Cases (Unrestored), 1794, Vi. Endorsements on cover note delivery of notice and copies to defendants and surety. Filed with papers in subsequent suit by plaintiffs to recover judgment on forfeited forthcoming bond.

1. Once forfeited, the forthcoming bond was to be returned to the office of the clerk of the court, to be kept there and to have the force of a judgment. On the plaintiff's motion and upon ten days previous notice to the obligors, the court then gave judgment to allow the plaintiff to proceed to execution. In this case the Asselbys recovered judgment on the forthcoming bond on 2 Dec. 1794 (Hening, *Statutes*, XIII, 364; U.S. Cir. Ct., Va., Ord. Bk. I, 428).

2. *Scilicet* ("to wit"). This affidavit, in a different hand, appears on the verso of the notice.

3. The plaintiff was required to prove by the testimony of a witness in court or by an affidavit that the defendants had ten days legal notice of his motion for judgment on the forthcoming bond (Robinson, *Practice*, I, 598).

XI. Fieri Facias
19 January 1795

The PRESIDENT *of the* UNITED STATES *of* AMERICA,
to the Marshal of the Virginia District, greeting:

[SEAL] You are hereby commanded that of the goods and chattels of ⟨Robert Pleasants, Thomas Pleasants Junr. and Richard Randolph⟩ late of your district, you cause to be made ⟨One thousand six hundred and fifty[1] two dollars and fifty four cents⟩ which ⟨William Asselby and Mary Asselby Executor and Executrix of Mary Asselby decd. who was Executrix of Thomas Asselby deceased⟩ lately in the court of the United States, for the middle circuit in the Virginia district, ⟨have⟩ recovered against ⟨them⟩ for debt; ⟨on a bond for the forthcoming of property also eleven dollars and nineteen cents which to the said Executors⟩ in the same court were adjudged for ⟨their⟩ costs in that ⟨behalf⟩ expended, whereof ⟨they are⟩ convict, as appears of record, and that you have the said ⟨Debt and Costs⟩ before the judges of the said court at Richmond, in the district of Virginia, on the ⟨twenty second⟩ day of ⟨May⟩ next, to render to the said ⟨Executor & Executrix⟩ of ⟨their⟩ debt and costs aforesaid. And have then there this writ. Witness, John Jay, Esq; chief justice of the United States of America, in the city of Richmond, this ⟨seventh⟩ day of ⟨January⟩, in the year 179⟨5⟩, and in the ⟨19th⟩ year of the independence of the United States of America.[2]

Wm Marshall Clk

⟨Memo.

The above Execution is to be discharged by the payment of Three hundred and seventy eight dollars and forty five cents with interest thereon to be computed after the rate of five per centum per annum from the thirtieth day of November 1794 'til payment and the Costs.⟩[3]

Wm Marshall

Printed form, Asselby v. Pleasants, U.S. Circuit Court, Va., Ended Cases (Unrestored), 1794, Vi. Blanks filled in by clerk. Endorsed on verso by William Marshall: "No Security to be taken." Verso also contains Richard Hanson's receipt for payment, dated 3 Apr. 1795. Filed with papers in subsequent suit by plaintiffs to recover judgment on forfeited forthcoming bond.

1. Should be "sixty."

2. As the clerk noted, no security was to be taken on this writ. In other words, once a debtor had forfeited on a forthcoming bond, he could not take out another to delay execution (Hening, *Statutes*, XIII, 364).

3. On the preceding 30 Nov. Pleasants & Co. made a payment of $470, leaving $361.27 of the original debt plus $17.18 additional costs as the balance due to satisfy the execution (Doc. IX, n. 2; U.S. Cir. Ct., Va., Ord. Bk. I, 428).

XII. Thomas Pleasants, Jr., to Richard Hanson
4 February 1795

Mr. Richard Hanson Raleigh[1] 4th. Feby. 1795
sir

I wrote you yesterday, informing you that I had made a sale of flour at sixty days—and that I would procure you Mr James Heron's acceptance, paiable at that period for the ballance due upon the Judt.[2] and this day I have recieved your letter of the 22nd. ult informing me that you are in Want of the Money and Must not be disappointed.

As I have not pointedly Complied with my promise to you; I have less Confidence in asking, or expecting farther indulgence, but as the payment may now be placed upon a Moral Certainty, and you will obtain it sooner, than by rigorous Meassures, I hope you will Come into this proposition, with an assurance that if I Can make out the Money sooner I will do it—or I will allow you any reasonable discot. for the sixty days.[3] I am, Yr Mo. ob Hble st

THOS. PLEASANTS JR

ALS, T.79/37 (claim of William Asselby), P.R.O. Addressed to Hanson at Petersburg and endorsed by Hanson.

1. Pleasants's home in the Southside county of Mecklenburg, bordering North Carolina.

2. The letter of "yesterday" was that of 2 Feb. 1795, which along with this letter was among the papers filed on behalf of the Asselbys in support of their claim before the commissions under the Jay Treaty and the Convention of 1802. James Heron was a Richmond merchant (*PJM*, I, 408 n. 7).

3. Hanson's endorsement on the verso of the letter reads: "Answerd I would wait till the 1st: April on receiving Mr: Heron's acceptance," Pleasants made the final payment on 3 Apr., as Hanson noted on the verso of the fieri facias: "Received the 3d· April 1795 the Contents of the within." The Asselbys sought to recover lost war interest on this debt before the claims commissions. According to an account filed with the claim papers, this amounted to £88 sterling as of 1 Mar. 1798 (T.79/37 [claim of William Asselby], P.R.O.).

15. Dobson & Daltera v. Trents, Crump & Bates

1790–1798

I. Declaration, 27 January 1791
II. Commission, 27 June 1792
III. Notice, 28 June 1792
IV. Deposition of Richard Hardman, 25 March 1793

Editorial Note

This suit is representative of another large class of British debt cases: those brought on open account for goods sold and delivered. The common law action for recovery of these unliquidated debts (not reduced to a specialty) was assumpsit. The suit papers include an excellent example of the classic declaration in general assumpsit setting forth the common indebitatus and quantum counts (Document I).[1]

Because of the need to obtain witnesses and papers, open account debts were more troublesome and expensive to prosecute than those founded on written instruments such as bonds or bills. To British plaintiffs recovery of such debts in Virginia courts seemed to impose extraordinary hardships on them even after the British debt pleas were thrown out. In addition to the obstacle arising from the statute of limitations (see Case Number 14), these "book debts" might be lost for want of the necessary proofs. Creditors complained that the courts enforced much stricter rules for proving their accounts than had been the practice previous to the war. Proof of the merchant's books by his own oath, for example, was no longer admitted as evidence. Such ex parte proof had been routinely accepted in the courts before the Revolution and indeed was sanctioned by law, which particularly benefited the Scottish merchants employed in the retail trade.

Under the Virginia statute "prescribing the method of proving book debts," enacted in 1748, the Scottish factor could submit his store books, proved by his oath, as good evidence if he brought his action within two years of delivering the articles charged.[2] This statutory departure from common law rules of evidence greatly facilitated the retail trade by promoting easy credit. The merchant, confident of proving his debts, liberally extended credit from year to year, demanding a bond (regarded as a "mark of distrust") only in "perilous cases." The courts, in turn, equitably interpreted the law, customarily ignoring the two-year limitation on bringing suit as long as the merchant proved his books before a magistrate within that time. Indeed, this was the usual means of proving such debts, and the courts even disallowed costs for witnesses because the plaintiff could prove his accounts by his own oath.[3] English merchants who resided in the mother country and did business by the older consignment method could prove their books in the same way by virtue of an act of Parliament adopted in 1732.[4]

Scottish merchants bringing suit after the war continued to have the benefit of Virginia's 1748 act concerning book debts, though the assembly in 1779 had eliminated the merchant's oath as admissible proof for debts contracted after 1 May 1780.[5] The old law was of little use to them, however, for the courts, both state and federal, now strictly enforced the two-year limitation on this kind of evidence. Nor did the courts, in cases brought by the English consignment merchants, regard the parliamentary act of 1732 as having any authority, even though the debts were originally contracted while that act was in force.[6] In effect, plaintiffs had to fall back on common law rules of evidence, either by proving the delivery of the articles or by proving the handwriting of the factors, clerks, storekeepers, or agents (many of whom were now dead or had departed to distant places) who kept the books before the war. Without these proofs or a positive acknowledgment of the debt, suits brought on open account would not succeed in the state or federal courts.[7] Since the same rules governing book debts applied as well to American merchants, they could not easily be classified as a lawful impediment to recovery within the meaning of the treaty. "To support an action for a British debt requires the same & no greater evidence than woud be requird from an American merchant instituting a suit of the same kind," Marshall informed Secretary of State Edmund Randolph in 1794. British creditors complained nevertheless that the strict enforcement of the rules for proving book debts in effect discriminated against them and discouraged them from bringing suits.[8]

In this case, however, the plaintiffs produced ample proofs of their account with the defendants, including original letters and bills of lading, and they eventually obtained a judgment. The open account suit was one of two brought by John Dobson and Joseph Daltera, surviving partners of the Liverpool house of Dobson, Daltera & Walker, against the Virginia merchant firm of Trents, Crump & Bates; the other was an action of debt on a protested bill of exchange. At the same time the plaintiffs instituted a similar pair of suits against Trents & Calloway. Marshall was defense counsel in all four cases, representing Richard Crump and Daniel Bates of Powhatan

County and James Calloway of Bedford County. All of this litigation originated in the same factual situation, one that throws light on the commercial relationship between English and Virginia merchants in the late colonial period.

The brothers Alexander and Peterfield Trent were principal partners in eight or nine Virginia mercantile concerns operating in the James River region before and after the Revolution. Originally from Cumberland County, the Trents were trustees of the new town of Manchester, which was established in 1769 across the James from Richmond and which became the headquarters of their various enterprises.[9] In the early 1770s they began trading with Dobson, Daltera & Walker, which at that time was doing "much Business" on the James River, having acquired a reputation among Virginians as a prosperous and well-managed company.[10] The Liverpool concern traded with Virginia planters and merchants on a consignment, or commission, basis. As frequently happened under this system and was true in the present instance, the proceeds from the consigned tobacco crop fell short of the outlays of money expended by the British merchant on behalf of his Virginia correspondents. Before the war put a stop to trade, the books of Dobson, Daltera & Walker showed large balances against the Trents' companies—in excess of four thousand pounds sterling against Trents, Crump & Bates, and twenty-eight hundred pounds against Trents & Calloway.[11]

In the fall of 1772 Peterfield Trent went to England on business, probably at the request of his creditors and in response to the financial panic then spreading through Great Britain. This "credit crisis" of 1772 precipitated numerous bankruptcies among British firms trading with America, and in its aftermath "debtor-creditor relations between the thirteen colonies and the mother country underwent marked deterioration."[12] Trent felt the repercussions of the crisis during his visit to Liverpool in the winter of 1773, when Dobson, Daltera & Walker compelled him under threat of arrest to liquidate his accounts by drawing bills of exchange for large sums in the names of his various houses. Although these bills were actually drawn in Liverpool in February 1773, they were dated in Virginia, 1 November 1772. In June 1773 the bills in the names of Trents, Crump & Bates and of Trents & Calloway were protested for nonacceptance.[13]

Trent's partners remained in the dark concerning these transactions until several years after the war, when John Dobson went to Virginia to collect the debts owed his company. Crump, Bates, and Calloway refused to pay their portions of the debts, having made payments into the loan office and suspecting error and fraud in the accounts. In 1789 Dobson settled separately with Alexander and Peterfield Trent, exonerating them from further claims by the Liverpool company.[14] This release apparently explains why the Trents made no appearance and entered no pleas in the suits against Trents, Crump & Bates and Trents & Calloway. Since the bills of exchange were originally drawn to cover the indebtedness on the open accounts, the two suits against each of these companies did not represent distinct debts. Dobson could not have expected to recover the full amount in both the debt and assumpsit actions. No doubt he hoped to succeed in the debt action on the protested bills in order to get 10 percent interest.[15] However, at the trial of the suit against Trents, Crump & Bates on the protested bill, Marshall produced evidence to show that the bill of exchange was in fact made and drawn in Great Britain, though dated in Virginia. The court thereupon instructed the jury that Trent's draft was not a good bill of exchange within the meaning of the Virginia act "for ascertaining the damage upon protested bills of exchange." Since the plaintiff was suing under this act, this ruling meant that he could not maintain his action on the evidence of the protested bill, and he was accordingly nonsuited.[16] The open account suit continued to November 1798 when judgment was given for the British plaintiff.

1. See Case No. 2, editorial note.

2. Hening, *Statutes*, VI, 53–55.

3. *The Reply of William Cunningham & Co. to the Answer of the United States . . .* (Philadelphia, 1798), 25–28; William Hay, "Considerations on the various Subjects of Enquiry . . . ," 19 Feb. 1798, 6–9, T.79/27 (claim of John Hay & Co.), P.R.O.

4. "An Act for the more easy Recovery of Debts in his Majesty's Plantations and Colonies in *America*," 5 Geo. II, c. 7.

5. Hening, *Statutes*, X, 133.

6. Edmund Randolph to James Madison, 4 Apr. 1787 (Hutchinson, *Madison Papers*, IX, 364); JM to Patrick Henry, 31 Aug. 1790 (*PJM*, II, 60–61).

7. Bowman v. Patteson, U.S. Cir. Ct., Va., Ord. Bk. II, 321, 341; III, 31; report, T.79/11 (claim of Speirs, Bowman & Co.), P.R.O.; see also St. George Tucker to William Davies, 9 Dec. 1798, T.79/27 (claim of John Hay & Co.), P.R.O.; opinion of David Robertson, 4 Apr. 1806, T.79/25 (claim of Buchanan, Hastie & Co.), P.R.O.

8. Randolph to JM, 19 Oct. 1794; JM to Randolph, 27 Oct. 1794 (*PJM*, II, 293, 294).

9. *Tyler's Quarterly*, VII (1925), 54, Hening, *Statutes*, VIII, 421–22.

10. Robert Pleasants to Samuel Pleasants, 22 Nov. 1771 (August, "Pleasants Letterbook," 54). For Robert Pleasants's letters to the firm between 1771 and 1773, see ibid., 60, 66–68, 80, 121–23, 131–32, 149, 158–59.

11. See Doc. I and the declaration in Dobson & Daltera v. Trents & Calloway, U.S. Cir. Ct., Va., Ended Cases (Restored), 1801.

12. Richard B. Sheridan, "The British Credit Crisis of 1772 and the American Colonies," *Journal of Economic History*, XX (1960), 161.

13. Original bills and protests in Dobson & Daltera v. Trents, Crump & Bates, U.S. Cir. Ct., Va., Ended Cases (Restored), 1794; Dobson & Daltera v. Trents & Calloway, U.S. Cir. Ct., Va., Ended Cases (Restored), 1795; William Marshall to David M. Randolph, 12 Feb. 1799, in Reports of Special Agents, No. 247, 5–8, T.79/78 (report on claim of Mathew Dobson and Joshua Dobson), P.R.O.; Richard Crump to C. F. Bates, 28 Jan. 1800, in Reports of Special Agents, No. 247, 171–75, T.79/86 (report on claim of Mathew Dobson and Joshua Dobson), P.R.O.

14. Reports of Special Agents, No. 247, 176–80, T.79/86 (report on claim of Mathew Dobson and Joshua Dobson), P.R.O.

15. William Marshall to David M. Randolph, 12 Feb. 1799 (cited in n. 13); Richard Crump to C. F. Bates, 28 Jan. 1800 (cited in n. 13).

16. U.S. Cir. Ct., Va., Ord. Bk. I, 405–7; bill of exceptions, 26 Nov. 1794, Dobson & Daltera v. Trents, Crump & Bates, 1794; also same result in suit against Calloway; Hening, *Statutes*, VI, 85–87.

I. Declaration
27 January 1791

United States Middle Circuit,
District of Virginia, to wit,[1] }

John Dobson, & Joseph Daltera, of the Kingdom of Great Brittain, surviving partners of John Dobson, Joseph Daltera and John Walker, late merchts: and partners, of the said Kingdom, commonly called Dobson, Daltera & Walker complains of Alexander Trent, Peterfeild Trent, Rich: Crump, and Daniel Bates, Merchants and partners, by the form and Stile, of Trents, Crump & Bates, of the County of Henrico, in the district, and commonwealth of Virginia, one of the united States of America, in the middle circuit and within the jurisdiction of this honble Court, in custody of the Marshall of the said district, and so forth: For that w[h]ereas the said defendants on the first day of November in the year of our Lord one thousand seven hundred & seventy six at the parish of Henrico in the County aforesaid in the now commonwealth and district of virginia, one of the United States of America, in the middle circuit, and now within the jurisdiction of this honorable Court, were indebted to the said Dobson, Daltera & Walker, in the life time of the said John Walker, in the sum of Four thousand, one hundred pounds Sterling money, of the value of Five thousand four hundred and sixty six pounds thirteen Shillings, and four pence Current money of Virginia for divers goods, wares, and merchandizes before that time shipped sold & delivered to the said Trents, Crump & Bates for their use, and at their special instance and request; and being so indebted, they the said defendants in consideration thereof afterwards, to wit, on the said first day of November, in the year aforesaid, at the parish, and in the County aforesaid, in the now commonwealth, and district of virginia, one of the United States, of America, in the middle circuit, and now within the jurisdiction of this honble. Court, Assumed upon themselves, and to the said Dobson, Daltera & Walker, in the life time of Jno: Walker, then & there faithfully promised, that they would well, & truly pay, to the said Dobson Daltera and Walker the aforesaid sum of Four thousand one hundred pounds Sterling, of the value of Five thousand, four hundred, and sixty six pounds, thirteen Shillings, and four pence Current money whensoever afterwards they should be thereunto required:[2] And whereas also afterwards, to wit, on the same day, & year, aforesaid, in the parish and county aforesaid in the now commonwealth, and district, of virginia; one of the united states of america, in the middle circuit, and now within the jurisdiction of this honble. court, in consideration that the said Dobson, Daltera, and Walker, had shipped, sold, & delivered to them, divers other goods wares & merchandizes of the value of other Four thousand one hundred pounds Sterling money of the value of five thousand, four hundred and sixty six pounds thirteen Shillings, and four pence Current money of Virginia, at the like special instance, and request, and to and for the use of the said Trents, Crump and Bates the defendants they the said Trents, Crump and Bates afterwards, to wit, on the same day & year aforesaid at the parish, & in the County aforesaid, in the now Commonwealth and district, of virginia, one of the united states of america, in the middle circuit, and now within the jurisdiction of this Honble. court assumed upon themselves, and to the said Dobson, Daltera & Walker, in the life time of the sd: Walker, faithfully promised, that they would well & truly pay to the said Dobson Daltera and Walker so much money, as the said goods, wares, and merchandizes, last above mentioned, were reasonably worth, at the time of the shipping, sale and delivery thereof; and the said plaintiffs in fact say, that the goods wares and merchandizes, last above mentioned, at the time of the Shipping, sales, & delivery thereof, to the said Trents, Crump and Bates were reasonably worth, other Four thousand, one hundred pounds Sterling money, of the value of Five thousand, four hundred, and sixty six pounds thirteen Shillings & four pence, Current money of Virginia that is to say at the parish aforesaid, in the County aforesaid in the now commonwealth, and district, of Virginia; one of the united States of america, in the middle circuit, and now within the jurisdiction of this Honble. Court, of which the said Trents, Crump, and Bates the defendants, afterwards, to wit, on the same day & year last aforesaid, at the parish and in the county aforesaid, in the now commonwealth, & district, of virginia one of the United States of America, in the middle circuit, and now within the jurisdiction of this Honble. court, then & there had notice:[3] And whereas the said defendants afterwards, to wit, on the day and in the year last aforesaid, at the Parish and in the County aforesaid in the now commonwealth, and district of Virginia, one of the united States of America, in the middle circuit; and now within the jurisdiction of this honble. court were indebted to the said Dobson, Daltera & Walker, in the life time of sd: Walker, in another sum of Four thousand, one hundred pounds, Sterling money, of the value of other five thousand, four hundred and sixty six pounds, thirteen Shillings, and four pence, Current money, of Virginia, for so much money by the said Dobson, Daltera and Walker, in the life time of sd: Walker, to the said defendants for their use, and at the like special instance and request, before that time, lent, paid, advanced, laid out, & expended; and being so indebted they the said defendants, in consideration thereof, afterwards, to wit, on the day and in the year aforesaid, at the parish & in the county aforesaid, in the now commonwealth, and district, of Virginia; one of the United States of america, in the middle circuit, and now within the jurisdiction of this honble. court assumed upon themselves, and to the said Dobson, Daltera and Walker, in the life time of sd: Walker, then, & there faithfully promised that they would well, & truly pay, to the said Dobson Daltera and Walker the said sum of Four thousand, one hundred pounds Sterling money, of the value of Five thousand, four hundred, and sixty six pounds, thirteen Shillings, and four pence, Current money of Virginia last mentioned, whensoever afterwards they should be thereunto required:[4] And whereas the said defendant afterwards, to wit, on the day, and in the year last aforesaid, at the parish and in the county aforesaid, were indebted to the said Dobson, Daltera and Walker, in the life time of sd: Walker, in another sum of Four thousand, one hundred pounds, Sterling money, of the value of Five thousand, four hundred, and sixty six pounds, thirteen Shillings, and four pence, Current money of Virginia for so much money by the said defendant before that time had and received, to, and for, the use of the said Dobson, Daltera, and Walker, in the life time of sd: Walker, and being so indebted they the said defendants, in consideration thereof, afterwards, to wit, on the day and in the year last aforesaid, at the parish & in the county aforesaid; in the now commonwealth, and district of, virginia; one of the united states of America, in the middle circuit, and now within the jurisdiction of this Honble. Court assumed upon themselves, and to the said Dobson, Daltera, and Walker, in the life time of sd: Walker, faithfully promised, that they would well & truly pay to the said Dobson, Daltera, and Walker the said sum of Four thousand, one hundred pounds, Sterling money, of the value of Five thousand, four hundred, and sixty six pounds, thirteen Shillings, and four pence Currt: money of Virga:, last above mentioned, whensoever afterwards they should be thereunto required:[5] And whereas also afterwards, to wit, on the day & in the year last aforesaid, and at divers times before that day, the said Dobson, Daltera, and Walker, in the lifetime of the sd: Walker, at the like special instance, and request, of them the said defendants, had done and performed, certain work, labour, & services, for the said defendts. in the way of their business as Merchants, for which the said Dobson, Daltera, and Walker were intitled to receive, certain Commissions, and allowances, for the same, they the said defendants in consideration thereof, then and there undertook, & faithfully promised the said Dobson, Daltera & Walker, in the life time of sd: Walker that they the said defendants whensoever afterwards they should be thereunto required, would well & truly pay to the said Dobson, Daltera, and Walker all such sums of money as they the said Dobson, Daltera and Walker reasonably deserved to have, for such work, labour, & services whensoever afterwards they the said defendants, should be thereunto required: and the said Plaintiffs in fact say that they the said Dobson, Daltera, and Walker reasonably deserved to have, for the said Work, labour, & services, so done and performed, by them, another sum of Four thousand, one hundred pounds Sterling money, of the value of Five thousand, four hundred and sixty six pounds, thirteen Shillings, and four pence Current mony of Virginia of which the said defendants afterwards, to wit, on the day, & in the year aforesaid, at the Parish, & in the County aforesaid, in the now Commonwealth, and district of virginia, one of the united States of America, in the middle Circuit; and now within the jurisdiction of this honorable Court; then, & there had notice:[6] And whereas, also afterwards, to wit, on the day and in the year last aforesaid at the parish and in the County aforesaid in the now Commonwealth, & district of, Virginia; one of the United States of America; in the middle circuit; and now within the jurisdiction of this hoble. Court the said Trents, Crump, and Bates and the said Dobson, Daltera, and Walker, in the life time of the said Walker, had accounted together, between themselves, of, and concerning, divers other goods, wares, and Merchandizes; before that time Shipped, sold, and delivered; to the said defendants, and of and concerning divers other sums of Money, lent, paid, advanced, laid out & expended by the said Dobson, Daltera, and Walker, in the lifetime of sd: Walker, to, & for the use of, the said defendants and at their like special instance, & request, and of and concerning divers other sums of money, before that time had & received, by the said Defendants, but to & for the use of the said Dobson, Daltera, and Walker and of and concerning, divers other work, labour, and services performed by the said Dobson, Daltera and Walker, in the life of sd: Jno: Walker, in the way of their trade, & business, as Merchants, for the benefit and at the like special instance and request of them the said Trents, Crump & Bates all which said sums of Money were then due in arrear, & unpaid to the said Dobson, Daltera, and Walker and upon such accounting, the said Trents, Crump and Bates, the Defendants, were found indebted and in arrear, to the said Dobson, Daltera and Walker, in the life time of sd: Walker, in another sum of Four thousand, one hundred pounds Sterling money of the value of five thousand four hundred sixty six pounds, thirteen Shillings, and four pence Currt: money of Virga: and being so found indebted and in arrear, they the said Trents, Crump & Bates in consideration thereof afterwards, to wit, on the day & in the year last aforesaid at the parish & in the County aforesaid within the now Commonwealth, and district of Virginia, one of the United States of america, in the middle Circuit; and now within the jurisdiction of this Honble. Court assumed upon themselves and to the said Dobson, Daltera, and Walker in the life time of the said John Walker faithfully promised that they would well & truly pay to the said Dobson, Daltera, and Walker, the sum of Four thousand one hundred pounds, Sterling money, of the value of five thousand, four hundred and sixty six pounds, thirteen Shillings, and four pence Current money of Virginia, last mentioned whensoever afterwards they the said Trents, Crump and Bates should be thereunto required:[7] NEVERTHELESS the said Trents, Crump and Bates, the Defendants, in no wise regarding their several promises and undertakings, with the said Dobson Daltera, and Walker, in manner and form aforesaid made, but contriving, and craftily, fraudulently, and subtilly, intending, to defraud, and deceive, them in that behalf, did not pay to the said Dobson, Daltera & Walker, in the life time of the said John Walker, altho' often required, the said several sums of four thousand, one hundred pounds, Stirling money of the value aforesaid, or any part thereof, nor have they paid the same to the Plaintifs, who are the surviving partners of the said Dobson, Daltera, and Walker, and who are legally authorized to receive the same, since the death of the said John Walker, but the same to pay, altho' often required, and particularly on the   day of   , in the year of our Lord one thousand, seven hundred, and eighty   at the parish, and in the County aforesaid, in the now Commonwealth, and District of Virginia, one of the united States of America, in the middle Circuit, and now within the Jurisdiction of this Honorable Court, but the same to pay the said Defendants, did refuse, have refused, and still do refuse to the Damage of the said

Plaintifs, Eight thousand pounds, and therefore they bring suit, and so forth.[8]

BAKER for Pltfs.

DS, Dobson & Daltera v. Trents, Crump & Bates, U.S. Circuit Court, Va., Ended Cases (Restored), 1798, Vi. In an unknown hand, with insertions in hand of Jerman Baker. Verso contains jury verdict and clerk's endorsements summarizing proceedings at rules.

1. The capias was issued 4 June 1790. At the Nov. 1790 rules Crump and Bates requested a special imparlance and oyer of the writ. After being given a rule to declare, the plaintiffs filed their declaration at the Jan. 1791 rules (U.S. Cir. Ct., Va., Rule Bk. I, 1, 2).

2. This is the first of six common counts laid in this declaration in general assumpsit: an indebitatus for goods sold and delivered. All of the counts are for the same debt, and most of them no doubt were unnecessary to make the plaintiff's case. According to Fifoot, "Pleaders sought to avoid the necessity of selection by telling the same tale in as many different ways as there were types of count" (Fifoot, *History and Sources of the Common Law*, 369–70). On the action of assumpsit and the common counts, see Case No. 2, editorial note.

3. The second count is a quantum valebant for goods sold and delivered. If unable to prove the exact price of the goods alleged in the first count, the plaintiff under this count could recover this sum by proving that they were "reasonably worth" so much.

4. The third count is for money paid to the defendant's use. This was one of the counts employed to recover debts founded on "quasi-contractual" liability (Simpson, *Common Law of Contract*, 489–96; Fifoot, *History and Sources of the Common Law*, 363–67).

5. The fourth count, for money had and received to the plaintiff's use, also applied to situations in which the debt arose on a quasi-contractual obligation.

6. The fifth count is a quantum meruit for work and labor.

7. The sixth and final count is on an account stated.

8. JM, representing Crump and Bates, put in five pleas at the Feb. 1791 meeting of the rules: (1) non assumpsit, (2) statute of limitations, (3) loan office payment, (4) British debts not recoverable, and (5) release of the debt. The plaintiffs eventually obtained an office judgment on the defendants' failure to join issue on one plea and to rejoin to another. This judgment was set aside at the Nov. 1791 term, when JM withdrew the original two British debt pleas (three and four) and submitted four new ones (see Case No. 12, Doc. VII). At the next term the plaintiffs were awarded commissions to take depositions of witnesses residing in Liverpool (U.S. Cir. Ct., Va., Rule Bk. I, 1, 2, 19, 20; Ord. Bk. I, 79–80, 96). JM recorded a fee in this case under date of 10 Mar. 1791 (*PJM*, II, 414).

II. Commission

27 June 1792

The President of the United States of America.[1] To James Maury,[2] William Bolden, Alexander Lafone & George Venables in the Kingdom of Great Britain Greeting.

[SEAL] Know ye that trusting to your fidelity & provident Circumspection in diligently examining of all such Witnesses as may reside in the Town of Liverpool in the Kingdom of Great Britain on the part of John Dobson & Joseph Daltera Surviving Partners of Dobson Daltera & Walker late Merchants & Partners in an action on the Case now depending in the Court of the United States for the Middle Circuit in the Virginia District between the said Dobson & Daltera Plaintiffs & Trents Crump & Bates Defendants. Command you or any two of you that on such certain Day & at such place as you shall appoint you assemble yourselves & call & cause to come the Witnesses aforesaid before you & them diligently examine on the Holy Evangelist of Almighty God & their examinations into the said Court distinctly & plainly without delay you shall send & certify enclosed returning also this Writ. Witness John Jay Esqr: Chief Justice of the United States of America this Twenty seventh Day of June in the Year 1792 & in the Sixteenth Year of the Independance of the United States of America.[3]

William Marshall Clk.

ADS, Dobson & Daltera v. Trents, Crump & Bates, U.S. Circuit Court, Va., Ended Cases (Restored), 1798, Vi.

1. The court on 25 May 1792 awarded the plaintiff general commissions to take the depositions of witnesses residing in Liverpool for this and the other cases brought by Dobson and Daltera (U.S. Cir. Ct., Va., Ord. Bk. I, 96).

The Judiciary Act of 1789 gave the federal courts power to issue such commissions to take depositions "according to common usage, when it may be necessary to prevent a failure or delay of justice." Thus, the procedure for taking depositions in this case was governed by the laws of Virginia (*U.S. Statutes at Large*, I, 90; for the relevant Virginia statute, see Hening, *Statutes*, XII, 747). Depositions of foreign witnesses, whose attendance at the trial could not be enforced, were to be admitted as good evidence as long as the proper procedures were followed (H. St. G. Tucker, *Commentaries on Va. Laws*, II, Bk. 3, 301).

2. James Maury (1746–1840) was a Fredericksburg merchant who in 1790 was appointed U.S. consul at Liverpool, where he served for forty years (Hutchinson, *Madison Papers*, I, 114 n. 8; XII, 429–30).

3. At the foot of the commission below the clerk's signature, Maury and Venables made the following endorsement: "The Execution of this commis-

sion appears by the Paper writings or Schedules hereunto annexed." The annexed papers consisted of the deposition of Richard Hardman (Doc. IV) and bills of lading, accounts, and correspondence.

III. Notice
28 June 1792

Richmond 28 June 1792

Messrs. Alexander & Peterfeild Trent Richard Crump & Daniel Bates late Merchants & partners, acting under the Firm of Trents Crump and Bates.[1]

Please to take notice that on the tenth day of October next at the house commonly called the Hotel, in Lord Street in the Town of Liverpool in the Kingdom of Great Britain, between the hours of ten in the forenoon, and Six in the evening, of the same day, and on such of the following days as the execution of the Commission herein after mentioned shall be adjourned to, We shall proceed to take the examination of sundry persons, Witnesses on our behalf in the suit which we have instituted against you, and is now depending and undetermined in the Circuit Court of the United States of America, for the middle Circuit in the Virginia district, by Virtue of a Commission send out of the said Court for that purpose, where you may attend, by yourselves, or your Agent, and see the Same executed if you please.[2] We are Sirs Your humble Servts For self & Joseph Daltera

John Dobson

DS, Dobson & Daltera v. Trents, Crump & Bates, U.S. Circuit Court, Va., Ended Cases (Restored), 1798, Vi. Endorsed on verso: "to be preserved & proven."

1. The party to whom the commission was awarded was required to give "reasonable notice" to the adverse party of the time and place of taking the deposition (Hening, *Statutes*, XII, 747).

2. The following affidavit, signed by Robert Gamble, is on the verso: "City of Richmond to wit. This day John Tinsley Jr. Came before me an alderman for the said City and made Oath that he did on the 9th. day of July 1792 deliver to the within named Peterfield Trent a true Copy of the within notice Given under my hand this 13th. day July 1792."

IV. Deposition of Richard Hardman
25 March 1793

Depositions of Witnesses residing in the Town of Liverpool in the County of Lancaster and Kingdom of Great Britain produced sworn and examined the twenty fifth day of March in the year of our Lord one thousand seven hundred and Ninety three at the House of John Leigh in Basnett Street in Liverpool[1] aforesaid Gentleman by Virtue of a Commission from the president of the united States of America to us James Maury and George Venables together with Alexander Lafone deceased and William Bolden directed for the examination of Witnesses resident in the Town of Liverpool on the part of John Dobson and Joseph Daltera surviving partners of Dobson Daltera and Walker Merchants and partners in an action on the Case now depending in the Court of the united States for the middle Circuit in the Virginia District between the said Dobson and Daltera Plaintiffs and Trents Crump and Bates Defendants the same witnesses being first sworn on the Holy Evangelists of Almighty God to speak the truth the whole truth and nothing but the truth.

Richard Hardman of Liverpool aforesaid Merchant a witness produced sworn and examined on the part of the plaintiffs under and by Virtue of the said Commission deposeth and saith that he was a Clerk in the Countinghouse of the plaintiffs Dobson and Daltera and of their late partner John Walker now deceased then carrying on Trade as general Merchants in Liverpool aforesaid under the firm of Dobson Daltera and Walker on and before the thirty first day of May one thousand seven hundred and seventy two and that he continued in such employment until in or about the month of April one thousand seven hundred and seventy Eight saith he was privy to and well acquainted with the several transactions in trade between the said house and the persons composing the firm of Trents Crump and Bates in the united States of America Merchants. That it was principally in his this Deponents department in the said Countinghouse of Dobson Daltera and Walker to make [out] or superintend the making out of Orders for Goods ordered by their [said] Correspondents abroad so as to enable and direct the Tradesmen [in] this Country to furnish the said house of Dobson Daltera and Walker with such Goods. And also to make out or superintend the making out of Invoices to be sent out to America with such Goods when furnished by the said House of Dobson Daltera and Walker for their Correspondents in America and also to attend and take care of the Shipping of such Goods to their Correspondents in America and that from such his situation and from the General knowledge he had of the business so transacted in that Countinghouse of which he had a general superintending power he is enabled to depose to the truth of the Account current now produced and signed by him and certified by the Commissioners present being an account Current between the said house of Dobson Daltera and Walker and the house of Trents Crump and Bates in America.[2] AND the said Richard Hardman further saith that the several Goods on the Debit side of the said account Current were shipped by the said house of Dobson Daltera and Walker in and on board of the several Ships or Vessels in such account mentioned[3] and that the several other Items on the same side of the same account were paid incurred or sustained by the said house of Dobson Daltera and Walker for or on account of the said Trents Crump and Bates. AND that the Interest charged on the same side of the said account is a Charge which was generally made by the said house of Dobson Daltera and Walker to their Correspondents abroad for whom [they were in advance.][4] AND that the several Sums charged for Insurance were paid by the said house of Dobson Daltera and Walker for Insurance of the property of the said Trents Crump and Bates so sent as aforesaid and that such Insurances were made in Consequence of Orders given for that purpose by the said Trents Crump and Bates or some or one of them or by some person on their behalf.[5] AND this Deponent further saith that from his situation in the said Countinghouse of Dobson Daltera and Walker he was privy to and well acquainted with the several Sales made by the said house of Goods sent or consigned to them by the said Trents Crump and Bates for Sale. AND that he hath examined the Credit side of the said account so certified as aforesaid with the Books of the said Dobson Daltera and Walker to which Books he had general access and of which Sales he had a General Knowledge and that according to the best of his Knowledge remembrance Information and belief and in which he speaks with a Considerable Degree of Confidence the several Sums carried to the Credit of the said account with the said house of Trents Crump and Bates as the proceeds of G[oods] consigned or sent to the said house of Dobson Daltera and Walker for sale are the whole of the neat proceeds of such Goods and so far as he knows or believes he saith that the several other Items on the Credit Side of the said account are all the Items and the whole amount of the Money for which the said Trents Crump and Bates are intitled or ought to have Credit with the said House of Dobson Daltera and Walker.[6] AND therefore he saith that on the first day of January one thousand seven hundred and seventy Eight there appears to have been due and this Deponent verily believes there was then due to the said House of Dobson Daltera and Walker the Sum of Four thousand seven hundred and fourteen pounds eleven Shillings and Eleven pence three farthings on the Ballance of the said Account. AND this Deponent further saith that he had access to the Letters of the said Trents Crump and Bates sent to the said house of Dobson Daltera and Walker and was privy to the Correspondence between the said two houses of trade and that the several Letters signed by this Examinant and certified by the Commissioners present marked with the figures 1, 2, 3, 4. are as this Deponent doubts not the Original Letters which were written and sent by the said house of Trents Crump and Bates in America or some or one of them or some person or persons on their behalf to the said house of Dobson Daltera and Walker in Liverpool.[7] AND he further saith that the several other paper writings signed by himself and [certified] by the Commissioners present purporting to be bills of lading of goods and merchandizes shipped by the said house of Dobson Daltera and Walker in Liverpool to the said House of Trents Crump and Bates in America are one part of the Original Bills of Lading made out on the Shipping such Goods on board of the several Ships and vessels by which the said Bills of Lading purport the same to have been sent.[8] AND that he constantly attended not only to the Packing in the Warehouse but to the Shipping of such Goods. AND this Deponent further saith that he knew the Captains of the said Ships and vessels whose names appear to be subscribed to the said Bills of Lading and was also acquainted with the Character and manner of their hands writing respectively and having examined such hands writing he doth verily believe that the same are and every of them is of the respective proper hand writing of the several persons whose hand writing they respectively purport to be.[9]

RICHD. HARDMAN

We whose names are subscribed do hereby Certify that what is herein before contained is the Deposition of Richard Hardman of Liverpool in the County of Lancaster Merchant in an action on the case now depending in the court of the United States for the Middle Circuit in the Virginia District between the said Dobson and Daltera Plaintiffs and Trents Crump and Bates Defendants, taken before us by virtue of the Commission hereto annexed, he [the] said Richard Hardman having been first by us duly sworn on [the] Holy Evangelists of Almighty God to speak the truth the whole truth and nothing but the truth. IN TESTIMONY whereof we have subscribed our names the Twenty fifth day of March One thousand Seven hundred and Ninety three.

JAMES MAURY
GEO: VENABLES

I John Leigh Notary Public by Royal authority duly admitted and Sworn dwelling in Liverpool in the County Palatine of Lancaster and Kingdom of Great Britain do hereby certify that the Examination of Richard Hardman of Liverpool aforesaid Merchant hereunto annexed was duly taken in my presence before James Maury and George Venables two of the Commissioners named in the Commission from the president of the United States of America for that purpose and annexed to the same Examination (the said Richard Hardman being first Sworn on the Holy Evangelists of Almighty God to speak the truth the whole truth and nothing but the truth); that the name "Richd. Hardman" subscribed to each Sheet of the said Examination, as the Person deposing to the truth thereof, is of the proper hand writing of the said Richard Hardman; and that the names "James Maury Geo. Venables" also so subscribed to the same Examination as the Persons before whom the same was taken are of the respective proper hand writing of James Maury and George Venables both of Liverpool aforesaid Merchants two of the Persons to whom the said Commission appears to be directed.

[SEAL] In faith and Testimony whereof I have caused my Seal of Office of Notary Public to be hereunto affixed the Twenty fifth day of March in the Year of our Lord one thousand Seven hundred and Ninety three. Which I attest

Jno Leigh Not Pub

DS, Dobson & Daltera v. Trents, Crump & Bates, U.S. Circuit Court, Va., Ended Cases (Restored), 1798, Vi. Wrapper enclosing deposition and other suit papers endorsed: "depn opened in Court 22nd May 1793." Deponent's signature is at foot of each sheet and signatures of two commissioners (Maury and Venables) in left margin of each sheet. Brackets enclose words or portions of words obscured by obliterations in MS. Missing letters or words are supplied from a similar deposition given by Hardman on this day for another case (Dobson & Daltera v. Fowler, U.S. Cir. Ct., Va., Ended Cases [Restored], 1798).

1. According to the notice (Doc. III) the examination was to take place on 10 Oct. 1792 at the Hotel, Lord Street, Liverpool. Presumably another notice, giving the new time and place, was delivered to the defendants, though none has been found in the suit papers.

2. The account current, stating a balance of £4,714.11.11¾ sterling against Trents, Crump & Bates as of 1 Jan. 1778, is in the suit papers, signed by Hardman and certified by Maury and Venables at the time of taking the deposition.

3. The debit side lists charges for goods shipped by Dobson, Daltera & Walker to Trents, Crump & Bates between 31 May 1772 and 1 Aug. 1774.

4. There are five entries for interest charges between 1 Aug. 1772 and 1 Jan. 1778.

5. There are nine separate charges for insurance on tobacco shipped by Trents, Crump & Bates to the Liverpool firm.

6. The credit side of the account current lists proceeds of sales of tobacco and wheat between 2 July 1773 and 1 Nov. 1776. Among the papers filed on behalf of the defendants in this suit are (1) bills of lading of tobacco and wheat shipped by Trents, Crump & Bates to Dobson, Daltera & Walker between Jan. 1773 and May 1775, along with statements of the sales of this produce, and (2) an account listing the Virginia firm's credits between 1 Nov. 1773 and 28 Dec. 1789, with receipts of cash payments to Dobson between 1784 and 1789.

7. The dates of these letters from Trents, Crump & Bates to Dobson, Daltera & Walker are 12 Mar. 1773, 1 Aug. 1773, 8 June 1774, and 20 Dec. 1774. They are signed on the verso by Hardman and certified by Maury and Venables.

8. The bills of lading, endorsed by Hardman and certified by Maury and Venables on the day this deposition was taken, cover shipments by the Liverpool merchants to Trents, Crump & Bates between 31 May 1772 and 20 Aug. 1773.

9. Trial of this suit was postponed pending the appeal of Ware v. Hylton. After the Supreme Court struck down the last of the British debt pleas in 1796, the circuit court ordered the trial of this case upon the issue of non assumpsit. Further delay occurred owing to Dobson's death and the revival of the suit in the names of his executors. On 26 Nov. 1798 a jury awarded the plaintiffs damages of $5,400 against Crump and Bates (the Trents were no longer parties to the suit). This sum represented their proportion of the debt and interest, with a deduction of interest for the war years. Crump satisfied execution of this judgment on 12 Feb. 1799 (U.S. Cir. Ct., Va., Ord. Bk. II, 139, 205; III, 1, 112; William Marshall to David M. Randolph, 12 Feb. 1799; Benjamin Hatch to A. B. Venable, 12 Feb. 1799, in Reports of Special Agents, No. 247, 5–8, 9, T.79/78 [report on claim of Mathew Dobson and Joshua Dobson], P.R.O.; Richard Crump to C. F. Bates, 28 Jan. 1800, in Reports of Special Agents, No. 247, 171–75, T.79/86 [report on claim of Mathew Dobson and Joshua Dobson], P.R.O.).

The parallel open account case against Trents & Calloway was tried in 1801, with a verdict and judgment for the plaintiffs for $19,000. Calloway, however, applied for an injunction, charging fraud in the account and insisting that the goods, bills, and tobacco consigned by Trents & Calloway to Dobson, Daltera & Walker had not been sold to the best advantage. This chancery suit eventually came before JM as judge of the circuit court. In 1811 the court decreed that the injunction against half the amount of the law judgment should be perpetual, being that portion of the debt owed by the Trents and having been previously satisfied (Calloway v. Dobson, 1 Brock. 119–25; U.S. Cir. Ct., Va., Ord. Bk. VIII, 350–51).

16. Banks v. McCall & Shedden

1792

I. Bill in Chancery, 23 May 1792
II. Order, 5 December 1792
III. Subpoena, 8 December 1792

Editorial Note

Marshall brought this suit in chancery on behalf of William Banks of Essex County. The bill (Document I) sought to enjoin a judgment obtained by McCall & Shedden, a mercantile firm that had operated stores in that county before the Revolution. Archibald McCall, a member of a wealthy merchant family of Glasgow, had settled in Tappahannock, a town on the Rappahannock River about forty miles below Fredericksburg. He established several flourishing enterprises in the region, and in 1770 he formed a partnership with William Shedden. Soon after the war began McCall departed for Scotland, leaving Shedden to manage the business. The partner subsequently was ordered out of the commonwealth as a British sympathizer. McCall returned to Virginia in 1783 and resided there until his death in 1814. Shedden set up as a merchant in New York City after the war.[1]

The action at law was debt on a bond for £180 Virginia currency to secure payment of £90. Since no pleas were filed at the rules, a conditional order was confirmed against Banks in July 1791. If Banks or his attorney had appeared at the November 1791 term of the federal court and put in an issuable plea, this office judgment could have been set aside. The judgment became final, however, on the defendant's failure to appear. The judgment against Banks was for the principal and interest from the date of the bond. In order to stay execution of this judgment, Banks claimed equitable relief on grounds that he should not be compelled to pay interest for the war years and that certain payments on the bond had not been credited to him. In December 1792 the court granted a partial injunction, refusing, however, to allow it for war interest.[2]

Banks stated in his bill that he had engaged an attorney (Marshall?) for the law action and assumed that it would be defended like other British debt cases. The failure to put in pleas, for whatever reason, proved costly to Banks. Had the suit gone to trial, a jury would have deducted interest for the eight years of the war. At 5 percent on a principal of ninety pounds, the deduction would have amounted to thirty-six pounds. Although in certain actions office judgments were automatically referred to juries to ascertain damages on writs of inquiry, the judgment was final in this case because it was a debt action founded on a "specialty, bill, or note in writing." In such actions the plaintiff had the option of proceeding on a writ of inquiry, but in this one he understandably waived it.[3]

Marshall's petition for an injunction declared that charging war interest on British debts was "manifestly iniquitous." This was the prevailing American opinion and nearly a universal one among Virginians—even those who favored paying British debts believed they were morally and legally absolved from paying war interest. To citizens of the commonwealth the carrying off of their slaves by the evacuating British army in 1783 was justification enough for suspending war interest. British creditors themselves often relinquished it in private settlements when there was a good prospect of receiving the principal. Those who were forced to pursue their debtors into court for payment, however, refused this indulgence, regarding war interest as a just penalty for being kept out of their debts for so long.[4]

The most elaborate exposition of the Virginia point of view came from Secretary of State Thomas Jefferson in a diplomatic note to the British minister on the subject of infractions of the peace treaty, communicated about the time Marshall drew his bill on behalf of Banks.[5] A trained lawyer, Jefferson put forward an array of legal and equitable arguments to justify the denial of full interest to British creditors. His main contention was that "interest is not part of the debt, neither comprehended in the thing, nor in the term," a maxim he insisted held true in every country, even a commercially advanced one like England. Citing numerous precedents from English law, he observed that the allowance of interest in that country was not based on express law, "but rests on the *discretion of judges and juries*, as arbiters of damages." They awarded or withheld interest according to the particular circumstances of each case. The "universal devastation" that occurred in many of the states during the war and the consequent destruction of profits from lands were circumstances that weighed heavily in American minds in favor of suspending interest, the secretary explained. He then cited as additional reasons the interdiction of commerce during the war, the withdrawal of British merchants and agents from America, and the absence of an express stipulation concerning interest in the treaty.[6]

In the federal circuit court of Virginia the question of interest was first presented to a jury at the trial of *Ware* v. *Hylton* (Case Number

13) in June 1793. Chief Justice Jay instructed the jurors to return a verdict for the principal and full interest, but they were unable to agree on whether to allow interest for the period of the war. At the succeeding term in November 1793 presiding judge William Paterson gave a like instruction to the jury in another British debt case, and this time they unanimously struck off interest for eight years. The judge at first refused to accept this verdict, sending the jurors back repeatedly, each time with the same result. After this incident, juries in the federal court routinely deducted war interest in all British debt cases.[7]

Although justices like Jay and Paterson could instruct juries that British plaintiffs were in law entitled to full interest, they were virtually powerless to overrule general verdicts. All they could do was order a new trial, which answered no good purpose because the outcome would probably be the same. In *Ware* v. *Hylton* the plaintiff's counsel proposed a special verdict, which would have referred the matter of interest to the court, but the jurors refused.[8] Since at common law errors in a general verdict could be corrected only by a new trial, the disallowance of war interest that formed part of the verdict could not be appealed to a higher court. This weighty question thus never came before the Supreme Court for adjudication. The appeal in *Ware* v. *Hylton* concerned only the issue of law arising from the plea of loan office payments.[9]

1. Memorial, 15 Nov. 1798, T.79/7 (claim of Archibald McCall and William Shedden), P.R.O.; Joseph S. Ewing, ed., "The Correspondence of Archibald McCall and George McCall, 1777–1783," *VMHB*, LXXIII (1965), 312–53, 425–54 (see 312–16 and n. 33 for biographical information on McCall and Shedden).

2. U.S. Cir. Ct., Va., Rule Bk. I, 31, 32, 36; Rec. Bk. I, 40–42; Ord. Bk. I, 138.

3. Hening, *Statutes*, XII, 746.

4. Boyd, *Jefferson Papers*, XV, 675; Phineas Bond to Lord Grenville, 12 Oct. 1792 ("Letters of Phineas Bond," *Annual Report of the American Historical Association for the Year 1897*, 518–19).

5. Jefferson to George Hammond, 29 May 1792 (*Amer. State Papers: For. Rel.*, I, 201–37), originally published as an appendix to *A Message of the President of the United States to Congress Relative to France and Great-Britain, Delivered December 5, 1793* . . . (Philadelphia, 1793).

6. *Amer. State Papers: For. Rel.*, I, 213–14. Jefferson went on to show that deduction of interest was a general practice in American courts, though not a universal one. In Virginia the practice of abating war interest was sanctioned by the Court of Appeals in the 1797 case of McCall v. Turner (the same McCall who was a party to the present suit) (1 Call 133).

7. John Hamilton to Lord Grenville, 11 Dec. 1793, Foreign Office 5/2, P.R.O.; "A Brief State of the Case of the British Merchants Trading to North America Previous to the Year 1776," 18 Mar. 1794, Foreign Office 95/512, P.R.O.

8. Richard Hanson to John T. Ware, 9 June 1793, T.79/30 (claim of John T. Ware), P.R.O.

9. Lawyers presumably could have contrived some means of bringing the question up to the high court, but no case embracing this issue was decided. See the remarks of Justice Bushrod Washington in the case of Conn v. Penn, decided in 1818 in the federal circuit court of Pennsylvania (Peters C.C. 523–24).

I. Bill in Chancery

23 May 1792

To the Honble the Judges of the fœderal court for the middle circuit in the district of Virginia humbly complaining sheweth unto your Honors your orator William Banks

That some time in or about the year 1774 your orator gave his bond to McCall & Shedden merchants for the sum of £180 to be dischargd by the payment of £90 on account of goods before that time sold & deliverd by the said McCall & Shedden to your orator. Since the constitution of this Honble court the said bond was put in suit & your orator applied to counsel to defend him & did suppose that he was defended in like manner as other persons in a similar situation untill he was informd that an office judgement had been renderd against him & confirmd in court for the whole principal & interest without any credit or deduction whatever.[1] Your orator humbly states that the plaintiffs in the said suit are British subjects as will appear by the record in the said suit & as your orator is advisd the same objections existed to the recovery in this suit as to the other suits instituted in this Honble. court by the same plaintiffs to which sundry pleas have been fild in bar as the records will shew. And your orator is further advisd that however the determination of this Honble. court may be concerning the principal of the said debt yet that it is manifestly iniquitous that he shoud be chargeable with interest thereon during the late war when property yielded scarcely any thing & your orator coud not have paid the principal as the laws forbid it & as the creditor was not in America but in England with which nation all intercourse was prohibited. Your orator further shews to your Honors that he made before the commencement of the late war several payments to William Shedden one of the obligees in the said bond which are not credited on the said bond. Your orator deliverd to the said William Shedden sixteen barrels & three bushels of corn at fourteen shillings per barrel amounting to £11.12.2.¾—also about nine barrels at ten shillings per barrel amounting to £4-10, also one hoxhead of tobacco weighing something more than one thousand pounds the price of which was not ascertaind. Your orator also furnishd him with six hundred bundles of fodder at three shillings per bundle & ten or twelve bushels of wheat at 4/6 per bushel. These several payments were estimating the hoxhead of tobacco at eight pounds woud amount to £27.5.2.¾ which was paid by your orator in part discharge of the said bond & for which he is not credited. Your orator humbly states that relying on the integrity of the said McCall & Shedden he took no receipts for these payments & well hopd that the same woud have been credited to him as in common honesty ought to have been done BUT NOW SO IT IS May it please your Honors that the said McCall & Shedden who your orators pray may be made defendants hereto in order to injure & oppress your orator have actually sued out execution on the said judgement which has been servd on the property of your orator who has given a bond to have the same forthcoming on the day of sale & your orator is apprehensive that the same will be sold to an amount sufficient to satisfy the whole of the said judgement[2] ALL WHICH IS contrary to Equity. IN TENDER CONSIDERATION whereof & for that your orator is only releivable in equity TO THE END therefore that the said defendants may on oath true answer make to all & singular the premisses & that the interest on the said bond for eight years together with so much of the principle as your orator has dischargd may be for ever injoind & that your orator may have such other releif as is proper MAY IT PLEASE YOUR HONOR to grant to your orator the United States most gracious writs of Subpœna & injunction to the said defendants to be directed commanding them &c. And your orator will ever pray &c.

Henrico Sc.[3]

This Bill was Sworn to before me in the Usual Form by William Banks this 23rd. day of May 1792.[4]

JOHN HARVIE

AD, Banks v. McCall & Shedden, U.S. Circuit Court, Va., Ended Cases (Restored), 1792, Vi. In JM's hand except for affidavit signed by John Harvie. Endorsed: "As to £27.5.2¾—Injunction &c. As to Interest the Court do not agree to an Injunction."

1. U.S. Cir. Ct., Va., Rule Bk. I, 31, 32, 36; Rec. Bk. I, 40–42. There is no

evidence to identify JM as the lawyer applied to by Banks in the law action. The rule book lists Alexander Campbell as counsel for McCall & Shedden, but no one for the defendant.

2. A writ of fieri facias was issued in Mar. 1792 to satisfy the judgment and was levied upon four slaves. Banks gave a forthcoming bond to deliver this property on the day of sale. On that day, however, he withheld one of the slaves, the other three being sold. The sale yielded £55.10.3, which was paid to McCall (U.S. Cir. Ct., Va., Rule Bk. I, 36). A copy of the fieri facias and endorsement is in T.79/7 (claim of Archibald McCall and William Shedden), P.R.O.

3. *Scilicet* ("to wit").

4. In petitioning for an injunction the plaintiff was required to swear to the truth of the allegations in his bill (Hening, *Statutes*, XIII, 420).

II. Order
5 December 1792

On the aplication of William Banks for an Injunction to stay proceedings on a Judgment obtained against him in this Court by McCall & Sheddin who having filed his Bill sworn to upon consideration of the said Bill & exhibits and the argument of Counsil the Court do order that an injunction issue as to Twenty Seven pounds five shillings and two pence three farthings with Interest from the first day of January in the year 1775 until it can be heard in a Court of equity on his giving bond & Security in the clerks Office according to law.[1]

Copy, U.S. Circuit Court, Va., Order Book I, 138, Vi.

1. The injunction was awarded on the credits claimed by the sale of corn, fodder, wheat, and tobacco to McCall & Shedden, as stated in the bill, but not for interest during the war. While pursuing his remedy on the equity side, Banks was also attempting to have the law judgment set aside and a new trial ordered. This, however, was denied two days before the partial injunction was granted (U.S. Cir. Ct., Va., Ord. Bk. I, 113, 133).

III. Subpoena
8 December 1792

The PRESIDENT *of the* UNITED STATES,
to the MARSHALL *of the District of Virginia*, GREETING:[1]

YOU are hereby commanded to ⟨summon McCall & Sheddin to appear before the Judges of the Court of the United States for the Middle⟩ Circuit, at ⟨Richmond⟩ in the District of Virginia, on the ⟨twenty Second day of May next⟩ to answer ⟨a Bill in Chancery exhibitted against them in the said Court by William Banks and this they shall in no wise omit under the penalty of one hundred pounds each.⟩

And have then there this writ. Witness, JOHN JAY, *Esquire, Chief Justice of the United States, at* ⟨Richmond⟩ *this* ⟨8th⟩ *day of* ⟨December⟩ *in the year* ⟨1792⟩ *and of the Independence of the United States the* ⟨Seventeenth.⟩

[SEAL]

WILLIAM MARSHALL Clk[2]

Printed form, Banks v. McCall & Shedden, U.S. Circuit Court, Va., Ended Cases (Restored), 1792, Vi. Blanks filled in by clerk. Returned, "No Inhabitant." Originally endorsed, "Executed on Archbd. McCall," but deleted.

1. The chancery practice in Virginia was to issue the subpoena before the filing of the bill, but not on requests for injunctions (Tucker, *Blackstone's Commentaries*, III, 443 n. 14). The printed form used in this case was actually a capias ad respondendum (the writ used to initiate proceedings at law), which the clerk altered to conform to the style of a subpoena in chancery.

2. William Marshall made the following endorsement on the verso of the writ: "To Injoin the within mentioned McCall & Sheddin from proceeding farther as to Twenty seven pounds five shillings and two pence three farthings with lawfull Interest thereon from the first day of January in the year 1775 on a Judgment obtained against the said William Banks in the Circuit Court of the United States for this District until the farther Order of the said Court, but this Injunction is to have no effect until William Banks enters into Bond with sufficient surety to obey the decree of the Court which Bond is to be given in the Clerks Office of said Court."

There were no further proceedings in this chancery suit. Presumably, by Archibald McCall's failure to answer the bill, the partial injunction became perpetual, though no decree to this effect appears in the records.

17. Burton's Executors v. J. and R. Donald & Company

1793–1797

I. Bill in Chancery, 10 December 1793
II. Answer, 11 February 1794
III. Jesse Burton to John Marshall, 11 April 1794

Editorial Note

Like the preceding case this chancery suit was brought to enjoin a judgment at law. The papers provide excellent documentation of the commercial dealings between a Piedmont planter and a Scottish firm employing resident factors in the colony of Virginia. During the twenty-five years preceding Independence the Scottish merchants had largely succeeded in engrossing the tobacco trade of Virginia, though English consignment merchants still traded extensively with the larger Tidewater planters. The great majority of British debt cases in the state courts and in the federal circuit court of Virginia were those for the recovery of debts contracted by the smaller and middling planters at the stores run by Scottish factors.[1]

James and Robert Donald & Company of Glasgow operated a network of stores throughout the Piedmont and central Southside regions of Virginia. The principal stores were located at Warwick and Manchester in Chesterfield County and at Richmond in Henrico County, with subsidiary outlets in the counties of Cumberland, Mecklenburg, Prince Edward, Albemarle, and Amherst. The company was plaintiff in numerous cases in the federal court, including more than a dozen in which Marshall represented the debtors.[2] The debtor in this case was William Burton of Albemarle County, who before the war did much business at the Albemarle and Henrico stores. In his last settlement with the firm before his death early in 1776, Burton executed a bond, on which an action of debt was brought against his executors in 1791. Judgment for J. and R. Donald & Company was rendered at the November 1793 term, and immediately afterwards Marshall drew a petition for an injunction. The pleadings raised the important question of the relationship between law and equity. The company, now the defendant in chancery, protested that Burton's executors had an adequate remedy at law, in which case equity was not supposed to interfere. Andrew Ronald, attorney for the defendant, waived this objection, however, possibly in hopes that equity would restore eight years of interest on the bond that the jury had deducted in the law action.

1. Evans, "Private Indebtedness," *WMQ*, 3d ser., XXVIII (1971), 349–50.
2. Memorial of Robert Donald, Sr., Andrew Donald, and Alexander Donald, Sr., surviving partners of J. and R. Donald & Co., 18 May 1799, T.79/15 (claim of J. and R. Donald & Co.), P.R.O.; U.S. Cir. Ct., Va., Rule Bk. I, 1–51.

I. Bill in Chancery
10 December 1793

To the Honble. the Judges of the United States for the middle circuit in the district of Virginia humbly complaining shew unto your Honors your orators Jesse Burton & Robert Burton exrs. of the last will of William Burton deceasd

That the testator of your orators had in his life time considerable dealings with James & Robert Donald & Co. & did in the year 1775 execute his bond to them for £914.13.2.[1] This bond was executed at a time when he was very ill of that sickness of which he died & when he was not in a situation to investigate the accounts between them. It was given on the account annexd[2] without examination & as your orators beleive under a perfect confidence in the honor of the said James & Robert Donald & Co. that they woud correct any error which might afterwards be discoverd. Some time about the date of the bond whether before or after it was executed your orators do not recollect your orator Jesse Burton sold to a certain Matthew Woodson a tract of land lying in Goochland county for the sum of £200 of which your orator receivd £100 & directed the said Woodson to pay the residue of purchase money to James & Robert Donald & Co. which he has informd your orators as they beleive truely that he did actually pay but they have no credit therefor on the bond. Some time in the year 1775 your orator Jesse put into his testator's hands four hoxheads of tobacco to be sold on his own account. This tobacco as your orator is informd & beleives was deliverd to James Miller who was collector for James & Robert Donald & Co. & the testator of your orators receivd as they beleive no payment therefor & consequently is entitled now to a credit on that account.[3] There was also a payment of £100 sterling made in January 1776 as will appear by the annexd account No. 2. for which your orators testator is entitled to a credit of £140.[4] Early in 1776 the testator of your orators departed this life. A sufficient sum was paid into the loan office of this state according to the act of Assembly for that purpose in discharge of the debt due to James & Robert Donald & Co. Your orators thought it their duty to do so. The certificate of this payment was put into the hands of Mr. Patrick Henry who was engagd by your orators as counsel to defend the suit & has been by him lost or mislaid so that it cannot now be producd by your orators tho they can as they beleive furnish an authentic copy thereof.[5] He omitted to plead the said certificate & it coud not be given in evidence on the plea of payment which was put in by a gentleman not employd by your orators because before the issue came on for trial the certificate was lost or mislaid. A judgement was therefore obtaind without any credit whatever and your orators are apprehensive that an execution may issue thereon.[6] Your orators further state that after the payment of the said money into the treasury a suit in chancery was instituted against them by the legatees of their father for distribution & the same was decreed so that all the estate of their testator was taken out of their hands. IN TENDER CONSIDERATION whereof and for that your orators are remediless in the premisses at and by the strict rules of the common law & only releivable in this Honble court. To the end therefore that the said James & Robert Donald & Co. may be made defendants hereto & may on oath true answer make to the premisses & that they may be perpetually enjoind from proceeding on their said judgement & that your orators may have such other releif as is proper MAY IT PLEASE your Honor &c And your orators will ever pray &c.[7]

JESSE BURTON

City of Richd. to wit

Jesse Burton appeard before me a magistrate for the aforesaid this City 10th day[8] of Decr. 1793 & made oath that the allegations of the foregoing bill are true so far as he has stated them to be of his own knowledge & so far as he has stated them to be of the knowledge of others he beleives them to be true.[9]

A H ROBERT

Wmsburg. Decr. 27th. 1793.

Let an injunction issue according to the prayer of the bill.

JOHN BLAIR
CYRUS GRIFFIN

AD, Burton's Executors v. J. and R. Donald & Co., U.S. Circuit Court, Va., Ended Cases (Unrestored), 1797, Vi. In JM's hand except for signatures and the endorsement of the judges granting the injunction.

1. The original bond, dated 28 Aug. 1775, is in the suit papers of J. and R. Donald & Co. v. Burton's Executors, U.S. Cir. Ct., Va., Ended Cases (Restored), 1793.

2. This account has not been found. According to the answer (Doc. II), it was not annexed to the bill.

3. These transactions are recorded in a memorandum enclosed in Jesse Burton to JM, 11 Apr. 1794 (Doc. III, enclosure no. 2).

4. See Doc. III, enclosure no. 1.

5. A new receipt for the loan office certificate was issued by order of the Council of State on 30 Nov. 1792. The receipt was for a certificate dated 17 May 1780, for $3,193 paid into the treasury by William Burton's executor in account with J. and R. Donald & Co. Jesse Burton sent this receipt to JM in his letter of 11 Apr. 1794 (Doc. III). The receipt was removed from the suit papers in 1806, when Jesse Burton's executor requested the clerk of the circuit court to deliver it to a Capt. Benjamin Rice (U.S. Cir. Ct., Va., Rec. Bk. IV, 439; Alexander Burton to William Marshall, 27 Nov. 1806, Burton's Executors v. J. and R. Donald & Co.).

6. See J. and R. Donald & Co. v. Burton's Executors. Judgment was rendered on 25 Nov. 1793, for $2,647.82, with 5 percent interest from 28 Aug. 1783. This suit commenced in Mar. 1791. A default judgment confirmed at the rules in July 1791 was set aside at the Nov. 1791 term when the defendant entered a plea of payment and three British debt pleas. The "gentleman not employd by your orators" was apparently JM, for he filled in the blanks in the printed British debt pleas (U.S. Cir. Ct., Va., Ord. Bk. I, 68–69, 185–86; Rec. Bk. II, 122–28).

Although the federal court in June 1793 had dismissed three of the British debt pleas, the plea of loan office payments remained good until the Supreme Court's 1796 decision in Ware v. Hylton.

7. JM recorded a fee for this suit under date of Nov. 1793 (*PJM*, II, 469).

8. JM should have written: "for the City aforesaid this 10th day."

9. The affidavit is also in JM's hand.

II. Answer

11 February 1794

The Answer of Alexander Donald one of the constituent members of the house of James and Robert Donald and Company, to the Bill of Complaint against them exhibited in the honorable the Circuit Court for the middle Circuit by the Executors of William Burton deceased, for and on behalf of the said Alexander Donald junior and the other surviving partners of the said house of James and Robert Donald & Co.[1]

The said respondent now and at all times saving and reserving to himself and to the other constituent members of the firm of James and Robert Donald and Company, all manner of advantage of exception to the errors and untruths in the said Complainants bill contained, for answer thereunto, or to so much thereof as he is advised it is any way material or necessary for him or his aforesaid company to make answer unto, he for himself and them answering saith, that true it is that the said James and Robert Donald and Company have recovered judgment at law in this honorable Court against the Complainants as Executors of the last Will and Testament of their late father and testator William Burton deceased, upon his bond bearing date the 28th. August 1775, for the sum by them stated, but altho at the time of rendering the verdict by the Jury no credit was endorsed upon the said bond, yet this respondent is informed and believes it to be true that in a few hours subsequent thereto, an account was filed with the Clerk of the Court stating the payment of the Bill of Exchange mentioned by the Complainants, shewing some deductions to be made therefrom, for monies advanced to and paid away for their testator, and striking a balance of £120.6.5 which was to be deducted from the amount of the verdict as a payment made by the said Bill in part of the bond aforesaid, on the 4th. day of January 1776, so that judgment was to be entered up for the amount found by the Jury to be due, after reducing it by the said £120.6.5 with interest;[2] and therefore upon this point the said company have practised no injustice, nor affected any concealment, their sole object on that occasion being to get a judgment for the sum actually and bona fide due to them, and this defendant is firmly persuaded they have not got judgment for more. To the account now alluded to, the Complainants themselves refer.

Upon this or any other part of the business relative to the dealings between the testator of the Complainants and the said James and Robert Donald and Company, this Respondent does not, and he believes no other member of his said Company does, possess any other knowledge or information touching the transactions which heretofore took place between the deceased William Burton in the bill mentioned, and James and Robert Donald and Company, or any credits to which the former may be intitled, than what may be derived from the books of the latter, which the defendant affirms and believes were honestly and accurately kept by agents employed for that purpose and the general management of the said Company's affairs, at their different stores in Albemarle and Henrico Counties, and else where. And upon an examination of these books it appears that the dealings between the said Company and the testator of the Complainants at the Stores in the two before mentioned Counties had been continued for several years, and been pretty considerable; that at different periods payments had been made, settlements had taken place, and bonds had been granted for the balances then due to the company at their aforesaid Stores, to wit, 25th. Septemr. 1772, bond was executed for £927.7.11. the balance then due to the Albemarle Store; 30th. July 1771, bond was executed for £295.1.5 then due to the Richmond Store in Henrico County; and 25th. Septemr. 1772 another bond was granted for £181.4.3¾ for dealings at the same Store subsequent to the date of the former bond at that Store. Posterior to the dates of these bonds sundry debits, and various credits are entered to the said Burtons account, among which is a credit the 15th. June 1775 for four hogsheads tobacco Nt. 4169 lbs. which if the fact be as stated by the Complainants, this defendant supposes may be the same four hogsheads spoken of, as having been delivered to James Miller who was one of the Company's Agents.[3] This defendant confiding as he rationally may, more in the Company's books than in the conjectures of the Complainants, does not admit it to be true that the bond granted by their testator upon which the judgement complained of is founded, was executed either during his last illness, or without a previous and attentive investigation of his account; because it is a fact apparent from the companie's books, that the balance for which that bond was granted, was the result of a settlement made the day it bears date in which the former bonds were included; and on that very day sundry credits are entered to their testator's account previous to the execution of the bond proving as far as circumstances can demonstrate, that the said adjustment was not made at the testator's place of residence, and that it was made upon a full and fair examination. This settlement appears to have been made with the aforenamed James Miller; and when the Complainants refer to an account upon which they affirm the bond was founded, they ought to have annexed that account to their bill, a thing which they have omitted to do, consequently this respondent has no opportunity of comparing it with the books.

This Respondent is advised that he might with propriety demur to any inquiry in this Court in it's present capacity, into facts, the authenticity of which might have been established, if they were capable of proof on the trial at law. But this respondent on behalf of his company wishing for nothing more than what is justly and equitably due, waves every objection to the jurisdiction of this honorable Court, submitting the right of exercising such jurisdiction to the Court itself. The defendant here alludes to the allegation in the Complainant's bill relative to the payment of £100 stated to have been paid by Mathew Woodson who is yet living, and who it is probable would not have paid any sum of money for another person without taking a receipt for it. Prior to the date of the last bond the aforesaid William Burton has credit at various times for payments in tobacco and cash, but no money is stated as having been received on his account from the said Woodson, neither does the respondent know or believe that any such payment was made, and trusts that no such credit will be admitted unless supported by legal testimony.

The several allegations in the Bill, touching the payment into the Loan Office in satisfaction of the claim of the aforesaid Company; the loss of the Certificate of such payment; and the conduct of the defence at law; are matters resting in the knowledge of the Complainants themselves, but of which this respondent is entirely ignorant. He can only therefore submit it as a question proper for the decision of this honorable Court, whether the defendants at law having failed to plead that payment, and having witheld the evidence of it which they might then have produced, shall now be permitted to avail themselves of it in a Court of Equity; this defendant being advised (supposing them ever to have possessed such a Certificate as the Act of Assembly requires, a thing which is by no means here admitted) that an authentic copy of a lost paper which is admissible evidence in a Court of Equity, is equally proper as evidence in a Court of Law.[4] And this defendant farther submits it as a question, whether as a payment into the Loan Office, if a satisfaction at all, is such only by a strict legal construction of the Act of Assembly, it will in a Court of Equity be deemed any satisfaction whatsoever; more especially when no particular Act of Assembly under which the supposed satisfaction is pretended to have been made is pleaded by the complainants, so as to enable the defendant if he should be so advised, to demur regularly to it, or if more eligible, to reply.

What application the Complainants may have made of the estate of their testator it is impossible for this respondent to say. They admit that before the suit was instituted against them for distribution, they had full knowledge of the existence of the debt which they now seek to injoin; and if they have administred all the assets they should have put in their plea at law accordingly, and might have protected themselves against the present demand in the suit which was brought against them by the Legatees. This respondent conceives it to be a principle of justice, that those who pursue equity for themselves shall do equity to those of whom they complain;[5] to the application of that principle this respondent submits the rights of himself and partners, trusting that upon such ground, the interest upon their debt for the space of eight years which was deducted or denied by the Jury will here be added to the judgment of the Court;[6] but confiding at the same time, and as far as is consistent with respect, demanding that in case of an adherence to rules of strict law against them, there will be an application of the same rules when operating in their favour. Without that that &ca. This defendant denies all combination & fraud, and prays to be dismissed with his costs & [ca.].

ALEX. DONALD

Chesterfield County sc.

Before the Subscriber as Magistrate of the said County personally appeared the above subscribing Alexander Donald, and made oath that the Contents of this his answer, so far as relates to his own knowledge are true; and so far as relates to the knowledge of others, he believes them to be true.

Given under my hand this 11th day of february 1794[7]

BERNARD MARKHAM

AD, Burton's Executors v. J. and R. Donald & Co., U.S. Circuit Court, Va., Ended Cases (Unrestored), 1797, Vi. In hand of Andrew Ronald, attorney for defendants, except for signatures. Verso contains clerk's summary of proceedings.

1. James Donald of Greenock and Robert Donald of Glasgow were the principal partners of the firm, which originally consisted of nine constituent members, including agents and factors resident in Virginia. Alexander Donald, Sr., and Alexander Donald, Jr., came to Virginia shortly after the peace, joining resident partners James Buchanan and Robert Donald, Jr., in attempting to collect the company's debts (memorial of Robert Donald, Sr., Andrew Donald, and Alexander Donald, Sr., surviving partners of J. and R. Donald & Co., 18 May 1799, T.79/15 [claim of J. and R. Donald & Co.], P.R.O.).

2. This account is in the papers of J. and R. Donald & Co. v. Burton's Executors. At the foot of the account attorney Andrew Ronald wrote the following note, dated 27 Nov. 1793, to the clerk of the court: "The above sum of £120.6.5 to be placed to the credit of the bond on which Judgment was obtained this term by James & Robt. Donald & Co. agt. Wm. Burton's Exrs." The judgment for the principal amount of $2,647.82 (Doc. I, n. 6) included the deduction of this credit.

3. See Doc. III, enclosure no. 1. The account supplied by the defendants showed the sale of the four hogsheads under date of 4 May 1776 (Doc. III, enclosure no. 2).

4. The "Act of Assembly" is the sequestration law of 1777. Jesse Burton sent a new receipt to JM in his letter of 11 Apr. 1794 (Hening, *Statutes*, IX, 379–80; Doc. I, n. 5).

5. "He that will have equity done to him, must do it to the same person" (Richard Francis, *Maxims of Equity* . . . [1727; New York, 1978 reprint], 1).

6. Interest on the judgment commenced as of 28 Aug. 1783, eight years after the bond was executed (U.S. Cir. Ct., Va., Ord. Bk. I, 185–86). On the deduction of war interest, see Case No. 16, editorial note.

7. The affidavit is also in Ronald's hand except for the date, which was filled in by Markham.

III. Jesse Burton to John Marshall

11 April 1794

Sir, April 11th 1794

I have enclosed the Loan Office Certificate respecting the Payment made to James & Ro Donald & Co[1] al[s]o James Buchanans List of Credits, which will shew that they Omited giving my Father Credit for a Bill of Exchange of 140£ made by Edward Carter, I have also sent a Memo of George Thompsons who did a great Part of my Fathers Business in his time—To shew that Mathew Woodson has paid a 100£. I expect Thompson will be at the Federal Court, tho he lives at present in Kentucky, he sent me word he would be in at that time & prove that Point, the 4 Hogsds Tobo mentioned in his Memo. I suppose will be lost, as James Miller who received them is now out of the Cuntry & the inspectors Books Burnt by the British in the time of War, which Puts it out of my Power to fix that Matter. I hope sir you'll do every thing in your Power Respecting the Business as I cannot attend on account of the Smallpox. You shall be thankfully rewarded for Your Trouble.[2] Please to let me know if you receive the Certificates & whether you think them Suficient, & in so doing You'll Greatly Oblige Your Most Obt Sev't

JESSE BURTON

[Enclosure No. 1][3]

Dr William Burton deceased in account wh. James & Robert

1773 July.	8	By 21 hhds. Tobacco at Byrds vizt			
		9 hhds. . . *WRB* . . . . . wg		9972	nt Wm Burton
		3 hhds. . . *Œ*		3710	. . . Ed. Carter
		6 hhds. . . *Œ*		7079	. . . Do.
		2 hhds. . . $I^{A}B$		2214	. . . Jesse Burton
		1 hhd. . . . *WRB*		1015	. . . Wm Burton
		21			
		By 4 hhds. Do. a[t] Shockoe		4445	Jesse Burton
				28,435	. . . . @ 18/
		By Byrds Inspectors Transfer Tobco.		638	. . . . .2d
October.	7.	By 5 hhds. Tobacco at Shockoe		5946	John Harris @ 2
		By 5 hhds. Tobacco at Byrds	ℭ	5914	Edward Carter 17
1774 May.	20	By 22 hhds. Tobacco	ℭ	19986	Edward Carter 2
1775 June.	15	By 4 hhds. Tobacco at Byrds		4169	
		By 2 hhds. . . . Do. . . at Do. .		2297	6466 Nt @ . . . . .
	20	By Cash of Geo. Divers			

Donald & Co.			Cr
£255	18	3½	
5	6	4	
49	11	0	
51	14	11	362.10. 6½
166	11	0	
80	16	6	
66	13	4	314. 0.10

I hereby certify, that the above is a true Copy of the payments made by William Burton deceased to James & Robt Donald & Co as they stand to his Credit on the books kept by James Miller their Collector, from July 8. 1773. till January 4. 1776. and that no other payments, to my knowledge, were made within that Period, nor since. As I had then no concern with the Books or the Collection, further than as I was occasionally consulted as a partner, I cannot affirm or contradict Colo. Edward Carters having by note or verbally assumed to pay James Miller the money, which on a settlement, he should owe the said Wm. Burton. I recollect since I wrote Jesse Burton lately, that his father mentioned to me something of the money he would have in Colo Carters hands, and that he intended it should go towards discharging his debt to J. & R. Donald & Co, and, if I am not mistaken, in a transaction so long past, he in-

July.	27.	By Thomas Napier . . .
Augt	23.	By Cash . . . . . of John McKindlay. . .
	28.	By Carter & Trent 100 Bushl. Wheat wh Interest . . .
		By a further allowance on 6466 Tobco. @ 2/6 . . .
		By Sum to debit June 15th. for Interest paid a. McCaul . . .
		By Discount on prizing Tobacco in 1774 . . .
1776		
Janry.	4	By Edward Carter for a Bill of Excha £100 Sterlg. Excha. . . . . . 40 . . .

[Enclosure No. 2][4]

Mem: for Col. P. Henry. Respecting the Claim of Jas. & Ro. Donalds agt. the Estate of Cap. Wm Burton. The business to G. T. appears thus.

On 1t. day Sept. 1775. Cap. Burton gave his Bond[5] to Jas. & Rob. Donalds for	£914:13: 2
This Carrys Interest till 4. Jany 1776—£15.6—	15. 6
	929.19. 2
By Bill of Exchange as appears from under Mr. Buchanans hand 4. Jany 1776 . . £140—	140. 0. 0
	789.19. 2
To Interest till 4. May 1776	9.17. 6
	799.16. 8
℔ Mathew Woodson £100	100. 0. 0
	699.16. 8
By 4 Hhs. Tobo. 4. May 76	55. 0. 0
	644.16. 8
To Interest till 17. May 1780.	129. 5. 6
	£774. 2. 2
By Cash to the Treasurer 17. May 1780	958. 0. 0
	£183:17.10. Over paid

By looking over the Acct. Which Donalds &c. had agt. Capt. Burton they have Charged Interest on Interest & Interest on Interest, & in this way they have Made Interest Carry Interest fore or five times.[6]

33	6	8		
3	2	6		
27	1	8		
8	1	7		
11	5	1		
6	2	6	89. 0. 0	
. . . .			140. 0. 0	
			£905.11. 4½	

formed me, that he had spoke to Colo Carter on the Subject, and seemd anxious to come to a settlement of this Balance; he (Burton) was to pay our Company, I think, about £400; I was told by James Miller that the Bill of Exchange, Credited above, was paid in part of Mr Carters debt to Mr Burton I mean in part of the account Unsettled. Certified under my hand this 22d. Octobr 1785.

James Buchanan

ALS, Burton's Executors v. J. and R. Donald & Co., U.S. Circuit Court, Va., Ended Cases (Unrestored), 1797, Vi. Addressed to "John Marshall Esqr Attorney at Law Richmond." Below address Burton wrote, "Mr. Ball will please Deliver this & take Mr. Marshalls Receipt for the papers it contains." Endorsed by JM: "To be filed in the suit Burtons Exrs vs James & Robt Donald & Co." Another endorsement by JM: "Qu if answer fild." Printed in *PJM*, II, 264–65.

1. See Doc. I, n. 5.

2. Arguments on the bill and answer were heard on 29 May 1794, when the court overruled the defendant's motion to dissolve the injunction. A final decree had to await the Supreme Court's determination of Ware v. Hylton on the question of the validity of loan office payments. On 7 June 1797 the court rejected the plaintiff's motion to make the injunction permanent and dismissed the bill. Burton's letter to JM was entered on the record, though he was not identified as the recipient (U.S. Cir. Ct., Va., Ord. Bk. I, 379; II, 363–64; Rec. Bk. IV, 430–39).

Execution on the judgment against Burton's estate was returned "no effects." The plaintiffs later brought suit against the legatees in the High Court of Chancery and against Jesse Burton's executor in the U.S. Circuit Court. The disposition of the former suit is unknown, but in May 1807 the case against the executor of Jesse Burton in the federal court was dismissed (statement of debts in suit, T.79/15 [claim of J. and R. Donald & Co.], P.R.O.; U.S. Cir. Ct., Va., Ord. Bk. VI, 143).

3. This enclosure is James Buchanan's list of credits. Though entered on the record of the chancery suit, the original document is filed with the papers in J. and R. Donald & Co. v. Burton's Executors (see U.S. Cir. Ct., Va., Rec. Bk. IV, 438).

4. This is the memorandum of George Thompson, filed with the chancery suit papers.

5. The bond was dated 28 Aug. 1775.

6. Virginia law allowed compound interest only in special cases. It was not considered usury if a bond with interest running over a long period of time was converted into a new bond whose principal included the interest on the former bond. This operation was not to be repeated at short intervals, however (H. St. G. Tucker, *Commentaries on Va. Laws*, I, Bk. 2, 378–79).

18. Scott v. Jones's Administrator

1795–1812

I. Bill in Chancery, 23 November 1795
II. Answer, 3 December 1795
III. Thomas Mann Randolph, Jr., to John Scott, 16 May 1795
IV. John Scott to Richard Hanson, 5 November 1795
V. John Scott to Richard Hanson, 13 November 1795
VI. Affidavit of William Vannerson, 4 December 1795
VII. Affidavit of John Marshall, 7 December 1795
VIII. Deposition of Samuel G. Adams, 7 December 1795
IX. Deposition of Thomas Mann Randolph, Jr., 7 December 1795

Editorial Note

Equity cases are far more revealing of the human dimensions of a legal dispute than are actions at law, whose pleadings reduce the particular cause to the abstract formulas of the common law. This chancery suit—another petition for an injunction—recreates in vivid detail the story of one Virginia debtor's efforts to satisfy his British creditor. The ample documentation brings into remarkably clear focus the personalities of the principals and supporting cast. Ironically, this suit—and the papers documenting it—would probably not have arisen but for Marshall's failure to present a key piece of evidence at the preceding trial at law. As it happened, the request for an injunction languished on the chancery docket for seventeen years. To compound the irony, the judge who finally issued the decree was Marshall, and he ruled against the executors of his former client.

The case of John Scott of Albemarle County illuminates the intricate network of indebtedness that spread across Virginia, linking not only debtor and creditor but also debtor and debtor. One man's default could ensnare others who were only remotely connected with him. Something like this happened to Scott, who was not originally a debtor to a British subject. His legal entanglement with William Jones can be traced to a transaction twenty years earlier in which he had not the slightest concern. In May 1772 Archibald Cary, a prominent planter and burgess of Chesterfield County, executed a bond to Farell & Jones. Thomas Mann Randolph, Sr. (Case Number 7, Document III, n. 1), and Richard Randolph (Case Number 7) were bound with Cary as sureties in case of his default.[1] After Cary died in distressed circumstances in 1787, Jones attempted to collect the enormous sum due (forty-seven hundred pounds sterling as the principal) from Thomas Mann Randolph.[2] Randolph was himself deeply mired in debt toward the end of his life, having "constantly lived in a style of elegant and expensive hospitality." Before he died in 1793 he had distributed the bulk of his real and personal estate among his family and two creditors who held mortgages on his property. As a result other creditors, including Jones's representative, were unable to recover from the estate, the executors successfully pleading that they had fully administered the assets.[3]

Thomas Mann Randolph did make one payment as surety on Cary's bond: in 1789 he assigned to Jones a bond for six hundred pounds Virginia currency, which had been executed to Randolph in 1776 by Virginia merchants Alexander and Peterfield Trent (see Case Number 15). John Scott, it turned out, was one of several sureties for the Trents, against whom Jones brought suit in the federal court in 1790. The usual British debt pleas were filed (except the loan office plea), and at the November 1794 term a jury returned a verdict for the plaintiff. The Trents having died in the meantime, judgment was entered against Scott and the other two sureties.[4] Scott, who was a creditor in account with Randolph, had intended to apply his claim against Randolph as a discount on the bond. He gave Randolph's written acknowledgment of this debt to Marshall, who forgot to produce it at the trial and then mislaid it. The purpose of Scott's bill in equity was to enjoin part of the judgment on the basis of this acknowledgment, which Marshall found shortly before instituting chancery proceedings.

With no prospect of recovering his debt from Randolph's estate, Scott hoped to compensate by setting it off against his liability to Jones. Like all Virginia debtors to this Bristol merchant, Scott had to deal with Richard Hanson, the agent for collecting the prewar debts owed to Farell & Jones. Hanson had settled in Petersburg before the Revolution and established himself in the mercantile line. When war broke out, he refused to take the oath of fidelity to the commonwealth and returned to England. He came back to Petersburg after the peace and spent the next seventeen years attempting to recover the claims of Jones (and later of Jones's administrator, John Tyndale Ware).[5] Despite his advanced age (he was sixty when he returned to Virginia in 1784), Hanson carried out his agency with great vigor, relentlessly pursuing hard-pressed debtors and earning a reputation as a "rigid Creditor" (Document VI). Thomas Jefferson, as executor of John Wayles, was "haunted nightly by the form of . . . Hanson." A Richmond merchant described him "as one of the worst of all the human race."[6] For his part Hanson, frustrated in his efforts to recover the full amount of his employer's debts in the courts, denounced Virginia as a "rascally State" where judicial proceedings were conducted by "Villainous Lawyers and Packed Juries." Hanson represented other British creditors besides Jones and also brought a number of suits in his own name. In the summer of 1801 he went "home" to England, retiring to Bath. For his services on behalf of Farell & Jones Hanson was paid an annual salary, which by the time of his retirement accumulated to nearly seven thousand pounds sterling.[7]

1. On Archibald Cary, see Robert K. Brock, *Archibald Cary of Ampthill, Wheelhorse of the Revolution* (Richmond, 1937).

2. Co-security Richard Randolph had died bankrupt in 1786.

3. Doc. II, n. 3; affidavit of John Wickham, 13 May 1809, T.79/19 (claim of James Buchanan & Co.), P.R.O.

4. Jones v. Trent et al., U.S. Cir. Ct., Va., Ended Cases (Restored), 1794; U.S. Cir. Ct., Va., Ord. Bk. I, 402; Rec. Bk. III, 68–73.

5. 4 Call 259, 262, 263; deposition of Richard Hanson, 1 Apr. 1803, T.79/30 (claim of John T. Ware), P.R.O.

6. Jefferson to Daniel L. Hylton, 17 Mar. 1792; Daniel L. Hylton to Jefferson, 25 Mar. 1792 (quoted in Malone, *Jefferson and His Time*, III: *Jefferson and the Ordeal of Liberty*, 177).

7. Richard Hanson to John T. Ware, 28 June 1796, 13 Dec. 1800; deposition, 1 Apr. 1803, T.79/30 (claim of John T. Ware), P.R.O.

I. Bill in Chancery

23 November 1795

To the Honble. the Judges of the Fœdl. court for the middle circuit & district of Virginia humbly complaining sheweth unto your Honors your orator John Scott

That some time in or about the year 177   Peter Field Trent being indebted to Thomas Mann Randolph in the sum of £600 executed to him his bond therefor which bond was also executed by Alexander Trent John Harris William Gay & your orator who were the securities of the said Peter Field.[1]

The said Thomas Mann Randolph was indebted to your orator in the month of October 1767 in the sum of £150-12-10 as will appear from the settled account & acknowledgement annexd to which your orator refers & which he prays may be considerd as part of this his bill.[2] Your orator had repeatedly requested Thomas M. Randolph to institute a suit on the bond which he declind doing & he also applied to Trent for leave to take it up which he refusd [and said?] that he shoud not pay it. In or about the month of April or May 1789 the said bond was assignd by the said Thomas Mann Randolph to [3] & a suit thereon was soon after instituted in this Honble court & a judgement was renderd for the bond against John Harris William Gay & your orator on which an execution has been issued which has been levied on the property of your orator who has given a replevin bond on which judgement was renderd by this Honble. court at its may session in the year 1795.[4] It was always contended by Peter Field Trent & your orator beleives truely that he had considerable discounts against the said bond but during the term in which the original judgement was obtaind & before it was renderd the said Peter Field Trent departed this life so that the suit as to him coud not proceed nor were his discounts producd nor can your orator yet have access to them as he is without any legal representative. The settled account & acknowledgement herein before stated & referd to which your orator conceives to have been a legal discount for him against the said bond was placd by him in the hands of his counsel to be usd on the trial, but your orator is informd by him that either the paper was mislaid or the suit was mistaken as it stood in the name of Trent on the docket & the paper was not produc'd, so that by this accident your orator has been prevented from availing himself before a jury of a discount to which he thought himself legally as well as equitably entitled.[5] Your orator further states that Thomas Mann Randolph has also departed this life leaving his sons Thomas Mann Randolph & William Randolph his exrs. who have taken upon themselves the burthen of the execution of his will but who state that they have not assets to pay the money which their Father acknowledgd himself to owe your orator.[6] Your orator has since applied to Richard Hanson to credit him for the debt herein before mentiond in like manner as if the same had been exhibited before a jury which may be done without injury to the creditor as he has a larger claim against the estate of the said Thomas Mann Randolph of such dignity that its payment is secure & as your orator beleives is only bound to credit thereon so much as shall be actually recover'd on the bond executed as aforesaid by your orator, this reasonable request the said Hanson does not think himself at liberty to comply with unless directed so to do by this Honble court. To THE END THEREFOR that the said Richard Hanson & Thomas Mann Randolph & William Randolph exrs. of Thomas Mann Randolph decd. may be made defendents hereto & may on oath true answer make to the premisses & that so much of the judgement obtaind against your orator as he ought to have had credit for originally may be perpetually injoind & that he may have such other relief as is proper May it please your Honors &c & your orator will ever pray &c.[7]

City of Richmond ss.[8]
Sworn to before me, by John Scott this 23d. Novr. 1795
Aw. Dunscomb Mayor

AD, Scott v. Jones's Administrator, U.S. Circuit Court, Va., Ended Cases (Restored), 1812, Vi. In JM's hand except for certification at foot of bill.

1. The original bond is in the suit papers. It was executed 7 Oct. 1776 and payable 25 Apr. 1783.

2. The account, also in the suit papers, is confined principally to transactions between 1763 and 1767. Accumulated interest and a sale of corn in 1788 augmented Randolph's debt to £360.9.2 by 1791, when the account was settled. Under date of 2 Sept. 1791 Randolph entered the following acknowledgment at the foot of the credit side of the account: "I do hereby acknowledge myself and bind myself, and my Hiers To John Scott esqr. of Albemarle, indebted to him, and his Hiers the Sum of three hundred and Sixty pounds 9/2—to be paid by me [*illegible*] in the Course of three years, from this date." This acknowledgment was attested by John Brown.

3. Randolph assigned the bond to William Jones on 7 May 1789, as indicated by the endorsement on the verso of the bond.

4. William Jones's administrator, John Tyndale Ware, obtained a judgment at the Nov. 1794 term for £600 Virginia currency ($2,000), with interest from 25 Apr. 1783. Before judgment, the suit abated as to the Trents on their deaths. When execution was levied, Scott gave a forthcoming (not "replevin," as stated in the bill) bond in order to retain his property until the day of sale. On 30 May 1795 the court gave judgment on this forfeited bond, to be discharged by payment of $3,385.84 and interest from 20 Feb. 1795, with execution suspended until 30 Sept. 1795 (U.S. Cir. Ct., Va., Rec. Bk. III, 68–73; Ord. Bk. I, 502).

5. See JM's affidavit (Doc. VII). Jones sued under the Virginia act permitting an assignee of a bond to bring an action of debt in his own name, provided that he allowed "all just discounts, not only against himself, but against the assignor, before notice of the assignment was given to the defendant" (Hening, *Statutes*, XII, 359).

6. Most of Randolph's real and personal estate had been conveyed to his wife and sons by virtue of marriage settlements made in 1790 and 1791. The remainder was mortgaged to creditors (affidavit of John Wickham, 13 May 1809, T.79/19 [claim of James Buchanan & Co.], P.R.O.; Moore, *International Adjudications*, III, 226–28).

7. Under date of Oct. 1795 JM recorded a fee of £4.16 from "Scot (Fedl.)," which presumably refers to this case (*PJM*, II, 496).

8. *Scilicet* ("to wit").

II. Answer
3 December 1795

The Answer of Richard Hanson to the bill of complaint exhibited in the honorable the Circuit court for the district of Virginia by John Scott against the executors of Thomas Mann Randolph deceased and this respondent.

The said defendant now and at all times hereafter reserving to himself all manner of benefit of exception to the errors and misrepresentations in the said complainant's bill contained, for answer thereunto saith, that the late house of Farrel & Jones, of whom Mr. Jones was the survivor, having very large demands on divers persons in Virginia, and amongst others against the late Thomas Mann Randolph esqr., this defendant was appointed an agent for the collection of these demands, not upon a commission, but at a fixed annual sallary, which is still continued to him; that some years agoe upon an application made by this defendant to the said Randolph for payment of the said debt, the said Randolph assigned to the said Farrel and Jones the original bond spoken of by the complainant in his bill, in part of the said debt, and delivered it to this defendant, telling him at the same time it was the last of six bonds granted by the said Scott and others, five of which had been paid off and taken up. Some time, but not very long after receiving it, this defendant informed the complainant of the said assig[n]ment, and requested payment; the complainant replied, it was all right, and should be paid in a short time; similar applications and similar promises were afterwards made, but as they produced no good effect, this defendant directed a suit to be brought on the said bond.[1] Soon after this, the complainant upon seeing this defendant addressed him thus "So you have sued me, I will keep you out of the money as long as I can," to which this defendant replied, he had no doubt of that; but it was not until some months after this, that the complainant for the first time intimated to this defendant, that he had any pretence to credits or discounts against the said bond; and he does not even now profess in his bill that he ever did notify such a claim to this defendant, tho' this defendant admits he did in general terms after, but not before the institution of the suit aforesaid. Whether the allegations of the complainant's bill with respect to his claim against the late Mr. Randolph, and his intention to oppose such claim to a recovery on the bond, and the cause for it's not having been done, are or are not true, is not within this defendant's knowledge; but if the complainant really had any well founded claim to a deduction from the said bond, good conscience seemeth to require that he should have brought it forward, before he had carried the plaintiff in the original suit thro' all the labyrinths of the law at a very heavy expence.

This defendant begs leave to refer to and annex as part of this answer two letters written by the complainant to this defendant, the one dated the 5th, the other the 13th. day of November last,[2] each containing assurances of the complainant's determination to pay off the last judgment on his replevin bond, but neither of them pretending a right to any discount.

True it is that the estate of Thomas M. Randolph deceased is very largely indebted by bond to the late house of Farrel and Jones; but this defendant cannot discover that it would be no injury to his employer to augment that debt by reducing any credit which may have been given, more espescially as the executors of the said Randolph have a few days since by their Counsel in this court signified their intention to plead "fully administred" to the action on the said bond.[3]

This defendant prays to be permitted on behalf of his constituent to avail himself of the judgment now sought to be enjoined, and to be hence dismissed with his costs &ca.

Sworn to before me this 3rd. day of Decr. 1795

ROGER GREGORY Jus.

AD, Scott v. Jones's Administrator, U.S. Circuit Court, Va., Ended Cases (Restored), 1812, Vi. In hand of defendant's attorney Andrew Ronald except for certification at foot of answer.

1. See Jones v. Trent et al. The capias, dated 5 July 1790, is in the chancery suit papers, apparently because it was submitted as an exhibit to establish the date Scott received notice of the assignment of Trent's bond (see also Doc. I and n. 4).

2. Docs. IV and V.

3. See Jones v. Thomas Mann Randolph's Executors, U.S. Cir. Ct., Va., Ended Cases (Restored), 1797. This was an action of debt against Randolph as surety on a bond executed by Archibald Cary to Farell & Jones in May 1772 for £4,700 sterling. After Cary died insolvent, Hanson applied to the surety for payment. Randolph, except for assigning Trent's bond, refused to pay, having determined to discharge his personal debts before paying those for which he was security. In 1790 Hanson, on Jones's behalf, sued Randolph in the federal court. As attorney for the defendant JM filed the usual British debt pleas; after the suit was revived against the executors he added the plea of "fully administred." In June 1797 the court gave judgment for the plaintiff for $20,500, with interest from Dec. 1785, but at the same time accepted as good the plea that the executors had fully administered the assets of the

estate. Thus, no execution could be levied on the judgment (U.S. Cir. Ct., Va., Ord. Bk. II, 296–97; Rec. Bk. VI, 162–72; Richard Hanson to William Jones, 8 May 1789; Richard Hanson to John T. Ware, 24 May 1793, 30 Nov. 1795, in extracts of Richard Hanson's letters concerning Archibald Cary's account, T.79/30 [claim of John T. Ware], P.R.O.).

III. Thomas Mann Randolph, Jr., to John Scott
16 May 1795

Dear Sir, Monticello[1] May 16, 1795

Within these fifteen minutes your son handed me your letter with the papers you mention therein. I have carefully examined them and returned them safe to him except the general statement of your accompt which I suppose you meant to be left with me. I am truly distressed at the trouble you are brought into and no one wd. feel more pleasure than me to see you extricate yourself or more willingly give you aid in doing it. I am sorry to perceive your memory did not exactly preserve what passed between us when we were last together respecting Hansons judgement and your intended prayer for injunction. I declared I could not join you in the bill you proposed to file. I told you that my answer as I was to be a party shd. be put in immediately to serve you and that it wd. be favorable to you as far as it respected the paper signed by my Father and drawn on the back of a letter of credit of David Ross bearing date March 29. 1788, for I really believed you then paid him a sum of money expressed therein, in part of your bond assigned to him (which was afterwards transferred to Hanson) which sum he promised to refund in a certain case allso expressed therein which never happened.[2] As to the other claim I could say nothing till I saw a paper you had lodged, you said, with Mr. Marshall, an acknowledged accompt between you and my Father on which it was founded.[3] I observed I could at once make known to Mr. Marshall who wd. draw my answer what the tenor of it should be as far as I have said. You thought it better I should first see the accompt that I might tell Mr. Marshall at once what I could say on both subjects and you promised to send me the paper immediately. I understood I was not to write to Mr. Marshall till I saw it & expected to receive it daily. It is more important now than before that I should see it as you acknowledge a small payment & large assumpsit of Mr. James Brown on account of my Father.[4] Besides you send me a certificate by yourself that there was due you on 2. September 1791. 360.£.2.2.[5] I beg your pardon the date of the fieri facias from the court of Cumberland for the costs, to which I recurr, explains this as you had not a right then to resume the deposit. I must however hear from Mr. Brown before I can answer to any allegation in your bill respecting that sum of 360.2.2.

It is not possible for me to have an answer drawn & swear to it till I see a certified copy of your bill—you know I must swear it is an answer to such a bill, which wd. be perjury if the bill did not exist. As to the tenor of my answer this letter shewn to Mr. Marshall will be sufficient. Wd. it not be best for you to go down immediately, draw and file your bill, send me a certified copy and an answer prepared for me by Mr. Marshall, by express? If the answer be such as I approve I will return it sworn to by your messenger—if I cannot admitt all it allows I will prune it & then send it in 6 days and with it the a/c. spoken of above. It will be necessary allso for you to get a letter from James Brown to me and allso from David Ross; the former to explain the expression in your A/c. "assumed by Jas. Brown"[6] and the other to assure me that the sum paid in 1788 by you will not be claimed as a payment on certain bills of D. Ross held by us, or in other words whether D. Ross does not mean to prosecute farther the suit against you—I am not lawyer enough to know that he cannot. If you fail in your injunction you can appeal afterwards, I suppose. I cannot by any means promise you payment of one farthing of your claim—the Crs. come in slowly. I cannot even conjecture concerning the circumstances of the Estate.

Wd. that my power to serve you equalled my inclinations! I am Sir with respect, your most sincere wellwisher & hble Servt.

TH: M. RANDOLPH

ALS, Scott v. Jones's Administrator, U.S. Circuit Court, Ended Cases (Restored), 1812, Vi. Addressed to Scott at "New-Scotland Albemarle."

1. Thomas Mann Randolph, Jr. (1768–1828), was Thomas Jefferson's son-in-law (Gaines, *Thomas Mann Randolph*).

2. The details of this claim are unclear, for Scott said nothing of it in his bill. Nor are the circumstances clarified by Randolph's references to it in his deposition (Doc. IX).

3. See Doc. I, n. 2.

4. Randolph referred to the "general statement" of the account that Scott left with him. This paper is not among the suit papers. The account containing the elder Randolph's acknowledgment was at this time lost or mislaid among JM's papers. As he noted in his affidavit (Doc. VII), JM found this account sometime in Sept. or Oct. 1795.

5. The correct sum is £360.9.2.

6. This phrase must also appear in the "general statement" (see n. 4). An endorsement on the original account (then lodged with JM) notes a payment of £14 by James Brown on 23 Jan. 1792, to be placed to Randolph's credit on the account.

IV. John Scott to Richard Hanson
5 November 1795

Dear Sir Novr. 5th. 1795.

Your messenger[1] has this day returned my order on Mr. A. Freeland[2] which I am much supprised at. I shall set out on Sunday, waiting now for a Coat to put on my Back. I shall never return home till I discharge the Exn.[3] I have not been able to get from home till albe.[4] Court to see Thos. Randolph, about the Debt, his Father owes me, he told me as you before had done, he was to be in Richd. 20th and on the 22d. if he could get ready, he should put in his answer to my Bill, to be argued that day. Do Sir run me to no more cost. The Debt is now full large to loose, the Gent. Say Mr. Harris has never payd you a shilling nor has he ever seen you, I did not think Colo Harris would have used me so Ill.[5] Add to this Sir Mr Freelands disappointment & the [Braking?] of the [Court?] & is enough to put you out of Temper but suspend your ill opinion (if you have any), till you see me. I am still Weak and low I must ride slow. I am Sir yr. Hble Srvt

JNO SCOTT

ALS, Scott v. Jones's Administrator, U.S. Circuit Court, Va., Ended Cases (Restored), 1812, Vi. Addressed to Hanson at Petersburg and conveyed by "Mr. Vanerson."

1. William Vannerson (see Doc. VI and n. 1).

2. Archibald Freeland, a Manchester merchant (*VMHB*, VIII [1901], 295).

3. The execution on the forfeited forthcoming bond (Doc. I, n. 4).

4. Albemarle.

5. John Harris, along with Scott and William Gay, was a surety on the bond assigned by Randolph to William Jones. The judgment was rendered against all three sureties, though execution was apparently rendered only against Scott. If Scott discharged the entire judgment, he had a remedy against the other sureties for their proportion, and the sureties in turn had a claim on the estate of the deceased Peterfield Trent. In Virginia, cases between a surety and the principal debtor and between one surety and a co-surety proceeded upon motions for summary judgment, that is, without a trial (Hening, *Statutes*, XII, 268–70; Shepherd, *Statutes*, I, 295; Tucker, *Blackstone's Commentaries*, III, App., 61–62).

V. John Scott to Richard Hanson
13 November 1795

Dear Sir Manchester, Novr. 13th. 1795.

I have Just got from my Horses much Tired with my long ride in my Weak State. I have been waiting three days for Colo Harris who is from home & will not return 'its suppose till Tomorrow. I would have stay'd till then, had I not have wrote you a line, I would be down Thursday or Friday. Mr. John Harris informs me his Father has drawn his money & he has money by him which he say's he Supposes his Father (Colo. Harris) keeps it for that purpose. I have Just Spoke to Mr Freeland Who says he Expects a Gent. up here this evening Who will bring your Receipt for the £300. I go to Mr Cox in the morning to see for the cash he was so good to say he Would lend me, and then shall return to the manakin Town to Colo Harris for his Share of the money & make sale of my Wheat & What Flour I had landed yesterday & in Ten days I shall have 60 barrels more. I hope to please you in the payt. which you have been Ill used in, more I believe from accident, than from intention, Colo Harris might have payed you, but I suppose he waited for my coming down, which my indisposition prevented. I shall hope to see you 20th. of this instant at Richd. and shall in the mean time Exert myself to be with you before that, if I can ride, as I never intend, to see my House again, till you are compleatly Satisfied with my Conduct as a Gent. I am Dear Sir Your Hble Srvt

JNO SCOTT

ALS, Scott v. Jones's Administrator, U.S. Circuit Court, Va., Ended Cases (Restored), 1812, Vi. Addressed to Hanson at Petersburg and conveyed by "Mr. Freeland." Endorsed by Hanson.

VI. Affidavit of William Vannerson
4 December 1795

Wm Vannerson[1] Maketh Oath before me that some time previous to the May Session of the Federal Circuit Court in this present year he went to the House of John Scott in the County of albemarle and there gave him notice that a Motion would be made against him at the succeding term of the said Court for an award of Execution upon his delivery bond[2] in favor of John Tyndale Warre Executor of William Jones decd. with the Condition of which bond he had failed to

Comply. This Deponant was ready in Court to prove such notice at the may term, but was prevented from so doing by a personal confession of Judgment on the part of the said Scott upon which confession it was understood by this deponant that Richard Hanson agent for the plaintiff had agreed to stay Execution until the first day of September[3] then next and he thinks that the first intimation which he received of such Compromise was from Scott himself; for he well remembers a Conversation which he happend to have with him about that time, in which Mr Scott spoke to this deponant of the liberallity of Hanson in agreeing to wait so long for the debt in terms to this effect. Vizt. that he had heard much of Mr Hanson as being a rigid Creditor, but did not believe it, for with him he had been extremely liberal, and such indulgence should not operate to the injury of Mr Hanson, for he would find him punctual in Payment &c.

This deponant heard not much more about the Matter until sometime he thinks in the month of October last when in the Course of business as the assistant of Mr Hanson, he found him in possession of an Order drawn by Scott in Hansons favor on Mr Archibald Freeland in Manchester for the sum of three hundred pounds. This deponant believes that Various Missives passed betwen Hanson and Freeland on the subject of payment of the Order until about the begining of November last when Hanson sent this deponant with Orders to return the Order to Scott and deliver the Execution to the Marshall or lodge it for him at the Clerks office. This deponant thinks it was the 5th. or 6th. of November when he arrived at the House of Scott and returned him the Order, at the same time shewing him some letters or missives from Mr Freeland to Mr Hanson stating reasons why the money was not paid.

Mr Scott expressed much surprize at Mr. Freelands not paying the Order, and wrote to both him and Mr. Hanson by this deponant desiring this deponant also to give Mr Hanson every assurance that the amount of the debt should be paid in a short time, and that he was about following this deponant down for the express purpose of making the payment. Accordingly it was not long before Mr Scott made his appearance at the House of this deponant in the absense of Mr Hanson, and repeated his assurances of payment saying he never intended to see his Family again until the debt was paid, which assurances have been repeated by Scott to this deponant within these few days here, and furthur that the Money was ready. In all which Conversations about payment this deponant understood Mr Scott to mean paying the whole debt, for he heard no pretentions by him to any Claim to a discount until yesterday, when he understood to his surprize that Mr Scott had got a bill drawn with a View of praying an injuntion. Frequent Mention has been made by Mr. Scott to this deponant of a Claim which he had against the Estate of Thomas Mann Randolph decd. and the hardship of Randolphs assigning away his bond notwithstanding that claim, and he generally spoke of his remedy against Randolphs Estate as depending much upon Mr Hanson, his answering a bill in chancery which he (Scott) meant to exhibit, and he shewed to this deponant the bill, but was fearful that Mr. Hansons Claims upon that Estate, being of superior dignity he might not answer his bill favourably, lest by admiting his (Scotts) Claim, he might barr his own through a defect of assets.[4] And in the Course of Messages delivered to Hanson from Scott by this deponant on that subject Mr Hanson has generally answered that he had no objection to answering Mr Scotts bill so as not to defeat his own claims against Randolphs Estate.

Given under my hand a Magistrate for the County of Henrico this Fourth day of December 1795.

MILES SELDEN.

AD, Scott v. Jones's Administrator, U.S. Circuit Court, Va., Ended Cases (Restored), 1812, Vi. In hand of Vannerson except for signature of magistrate.

1. William Vannerson, Hanson's assistant, was formerly employed by merchants David Ross and Thomas Pleasants, Jr., in settling their affairs (Thomas Pleasants, Jr., to James Madison, 23 Apr. 1789 [Hutchinson, *Madison Papers*, XII, 105]).

2. Forthcoming bond.

3. Execution was to be suspended until 30 Sept. (U.S. Cir. Ct., Va., Ord. Bk. I, 502).

4. The claim of Jones's administrator was founded on a bond. It was therefore of superior dignity to Scott's claim, a simple contract debt based on a promise to pay.

VII. Affidavit of John Marshall
7 December 1795

John Marshall deposes that either just before or during the sitting of the court which renderd Judgement against Scott & others on a bond assignd as well as he recollects to Farrell & Jones by Colo. Thomas M. Randolph decd. John Scott calld at his office engagd him to defend the suit & deliverd to him to be usd as a discount at the trial of the cause the paper which is now producd for the purpose of obtaining an injunction to a part of the judgement & which paper exhibits an acknowlegement signd with the name of Thomas M. Randolph decd. of an account due from him to the said Scott. The cause stood on the dockett against Trent & others & Mr. Duval was markd for the defendants.[1] That Gentleman was not then at the bar & Trent departed this life just before the judgement as well as this deponent recollects so that the suit abated as to him. This deponent did not recollect the application of Mr. Scott to him & altho he appeard for Mr. Duval did not produce the discount or recollect its being deposited with him until he was, after the court had risen, applied to on the subject by Mr. Scott. The paper was then mislaid. This deponent advisd Mr. Scott to apply for an injunction at the last may term & gave it as his opinion that a certificate or affidavit of the exr. of Thomas M. Randolph decd. stating what sum appeard on the books of his testator to be due to the said Scott accompanied with the affidavit of this deponent that an acknowledgement of the debt signd by Colo. Randolph had been placd in his hands & mislaid by him woud as effectually secure an injunction as the production of the paper itself. But the said Scott informd this deponent that the exrs. of Colo. Randolph woud not give the certificate requir'd. It was then proposd to obtain a writ of error to the judgement which shoud be renderd on the forthcoming bond in order to suspend any execution thereon until this deponent might in the recess of the courts search for the paper he had mislaid but this deponent advisd Scott first to inform Hanson of this & to tell him that if he woud for a time suspend his execution he woud confess judgement & drop the appeal. Scott had a conversation with Hanson & then informd this deponent that Hanson had agreed to stay his execution & that at this term the bill & answers might be exhibited together to the court for the purpose of a final decree. Some time in September or October this deponent searchd for & found the paper he had mislaid & transmitted it to Mr. Scott he beleives about the beginning of Novr. In conversation with Mr. Scott he has uniformly understood him to be preparing to discharge the balance of the judgement & to consider it as certain that the discount now claimd was to abide the judgement of this court.

Sworn to in open Court 7th Decr 1795.

William Marshall Clk

AD, Scott v. Jones's Administrator, U.S. Circuit Court, Va., Ended Cases (Restored), 1812, Vi. In hand of JM except for certificate at foot of affidavit.

1. William DuVal was the attorney of record in the case of Jones v. Trent et al. (U.S. Cir. Ct., Va., Rec. Bk. III, 69).

VIII. Deposition of Samuel G. Adams
7 December 1795

Samuel G. Adams of lawful age saith, That on the 18th. or 19th. Day of November last [he] went to a plantation of Col. John Scott to Levy an Execution on [his] property to satisfy John T. Warre Exor of Wm. Jones decd. That he [lev]ied the said Execution on Eighteen negroes & some cattle & [h]orses & intended to have carried the property off the plantation so a[s to?] have secured it, but upon Col. [Scott] assuring him that the mon[ey] should certainly be paid before [the] Day of sale or that the property should then be produced he agreed to leave it on the plantation, That Col. Scott requested him to put off the Day of sale as long as he could for that he had a Bill to present to the Judges, but did not inform him as he recollects of the particular object of the said Bill; he also informed him that he intended to pay the money early in the Session of the Court in order to move for a Judgment against a Mr. Gay one of the pers[ons] [against w]hom the former Judgment was obtained;[1] Interrogotary by [Col.] Scott; Had I informed you that I would not pay the s[um] of the amount of the Execution would you not have carried the property off the plantation; Answer; I should not have considered myself safe without doing it had you informed me of this. Question; Had I an offsett against the Judgment obtained by J. T. Warre Exr. &c. did you ever hear me say that I meant to give up any right that I had in Law or equity against the said Judgment; Answer I did not, farther he saith not.

SAML. G. ADAMS

Henrico sc.[2]

Sworn to before me Richd. Adams a Magistrate for sd County this 7th Day of Decr. 1795.

RICHD. ADAMS

ADS, Scott v. Jones's Administrator, U.S. Circuit Court, Va., Ended Cases (Restored), 1812, Vi. In Adams's hand except for certification at foot of deposition.

1. At the May 1796 term the court dismissed Scott's motion for summary judgment against Gay and Harris "to recover their proportion of a debt paid by the plff to Wm. Jones as joint security for Alexr. and Peterfield Trents." In 1801 Scott's executors brought a similar motion against Harris's executor, which was dismissed in 1804 on the plaintiffs' declining to prosecute it further (U.S. Cir. Ct., Va., Ord. Bk. II, 99, 101; IV, 68; V, 7). Apparently the federal court lacked jurisdiction in these cases since the parties were Virginians.

2. *Scilicet* ("to wit").

IX. Deposition of Thomas Mann Randolph, Jr.

7 December 1795

Very soon after the death of my Testator T. M. Randolph John Scott informed me of a claim he had against his estate and asked if I thought the Assets sufficient to reach the said claim, I told Him then & have uniformly held out to him the same since that I did not believe he wd. ever get payment. He informed me that Richard Hanson had obtained a judgement against him on a bond assigned to him by my Testator and declared a resolution to endeavor by all means to secure his debt by procuring it to be allowed as an offset against so much of the said bond, to effect which he meant to bring a bill in Chancery against Richard Hanson and wd. make me a Defendant therein allso. I allowed that the case was hard & told him I wd. aid him all I cd. towards procuring relief by puting in my answer immediately and acknowledging (provided he could make it appear to me) the justice of his claim. He took much pains after that to convince me of the justice of his sd. claim and to explain the nature of it to me. I allways understood it to rest upon two different grounds. One part upon a recept granted him by my Testator for so much money to be repaid to him in case David Ross should recover from him in a suit which the said D. Ross was then prosecuting against him but if D. Ross did not recover to be placed to the Credit of that bond which afterwards came into the hands of Richard Hanson. I acknowledged the Signature of my Testator in this recept.[1] Another part upon an acknowledged account against my Testator—I confessed the sum of a bond at the foot of that A/c to be in the hand-writing of my Testator & the signature to be his but observed to Jno Scott that my Testator was very careless and inaccurate in his account, that the one he then shewed me was not examined by him. When he acknowledged it I was convinced. There appears on the books of my Testator an account against Jno. Scot ballanced, ballance against J. Scot 4 or 5 pounds, the amt. somewhere between twenty & thirty pounds. John Scot shewed me on the twenty fifth of Nov. last a bill drawn by Mr. Marshall against Richard Hanson and myself, it remained with me till the second or third instant for my consideration in order to my answering as I had promised, then I returned it & beged to retract my promise as I had discovered I shd. give umbrage to one of the creditors of my Testator by giving a voluntary & fav-able answer.

Question by[2] John Scott. Did not Jno. Scott shew you an Acknowledged A/c for £360.9.2 which he ment to offer as an ofset agt. the Bond he was security to for 600—given by Mr Peter Field Trent to Mr Thos Mann Randolph & endorsed to Richd. Hanson for the use of Farrel & Jones Mercht. & partners in Brintain which Hanson has Obtained a judgement on in the Federal Court of Virga. answer, he did.[3]

John Scott did shew me the Account he spoke of, viz. one by him against T. M. Randolph with a ballance against T. M. Randolph of 360.9.2 acknowledged by the sd. T M. Randolph and I understood he meant to endeavor to pro[cure] it to be allowed as an offset against the bond assigned by the sd. T. M. Randolph to Richard Hanson.

TH: M. RANDOLPH.

Henrico To wit

This day came Thomas M. Randolph before me a Magistrate for the same & made oath that the foregoing writing, & answer to the interrogatory put by John Scott contains the truth so far as he knows or believes. Given under my hand this 7th. day of December 1795.[4]

WM. MAYO JR.

ADS, Scott v. Jones's Administrator, U.S. Circuit Court, Va., Ended Cases (Restored), 1812, Vi. In hand of Randolph except for one passage in hand of John Scott (noted below) and certification at foot of deposition.

1. As noted in Doc. III, this claim did not form part of Scott's bill.

2. Here begins the passage in the hand of John Scott.

3. Randolph possibly wrote "he did." The remainder of the deposition is in his hand.

4. The court on 9 Dec. granted a temporary injunction as to $187.50, with interest from 12 May 1788, but a final decree on the merits of the bill was delayed until 1812. From 1796 to 1805 the case stood continued on the docket. In 1806 it was revived by scire facias in the name of Scott's executors, Charles A. Scott and Edward Scott. The executors filed a bill of revivor at the Nov. 1807 term, to which John Wickham, as attorney for John Tyndale Ware (Jones's administrator), put in an answer in June 1809. There were no further proceedings until JM, speaking for the court, decreed on 25 Nov. 1812 that the plaintiffs' bill should be dismissed (see the suit papers and U.S. Cir. Ct., Va., Ord. Bk. II, 70; IX, 150).

In his opinion JM held that Scott, his former client, could not have set up his claim on Randolph's estate as a discount either at law or in equity. It was not a legal discount, he maintained, because the settlement of the account and Randolph's acknowledgment occurred after Scott had notice of the assignment of the bond. Moreover, Scott allowed Randolph a credit of three years. "A debt payable in future," said JM, "cannot be pleaded in bar of a present demand; and, therefore, when this acknowledgment was given, it could not have been set up against the bond." Nor could the acknowledgment be of any use in a court of equity: "The mere circumstance of giving the credit amounts to a taking the debt upon himself, and relinquishing the power to make it the debt of a third person." The circumstances of the settlement and acknowledgment, JM concluded, plainly showed that Scott was to look to Randolph or his executors for payment (Scott v. Jones, 1 Brock. 244, 246, 247).

V. Reports of Cases in the General Court

Editorial Note

From the time he began to practice in the General Court in 1786, St. George Tucker, later to become a distinguished jurist and teacher of law, took notes of cases that interested him. Two years later he was appointed to the bench and continued reporting cases in the General Court and other courts he attended for many years thereafter. These notes, covering cases in the General Court, district courts, and the Court of Appeals from 1786 to 1811, eventually filled three manuscript volumes, which have been preserved in the voluminous Tucker-Coleman Papers at the College of William and Mary.

The cases Tucker reported were mainly appeals from the county courts, over which the General Court and subsequently the district courts had appellate jurisdiction. Tucker also reported original cases in which some point of law was referred to the judges by a special verdict, case agreed, motion in arrest of judgment, or by some other means. John Marshall's arguments were reported in twenty-eight of the cases included in the bound volumes, most of them heard between 1786 and 1788. These have been published with extensive annotations in the first three volumes of *The Papers of John Marshall.*[1] The cases presented below (Case Numbers 19–31) are published for the first time, having recently been discovered among Tucker's loose papers. For some reason Tucker did not insert these reports in his bound volumes, though he did include abbreviated versions of some of them, omitting the attorneys' arguments. Ten of the thirteen cases were argued at the October 1788 term of the General Court. The bound volumes contain no reports for this term, which gap suggests that Tucker inadvertently omitted them.

With one exception these cases were heard and decided at the October 1788 and June 1789 terms of the General Court, the last two in which that court operated under the constituting statute of 1777. Thereafter, the district courts assumed the greater portion of its jurisdiction, both original and appellate.[2] Eight of the cases in this section were appeals from the county courts. Another case was referred to the General Court from the High Court of Chancery. The remain-

1. Eighteen cases, heard between Apr. 1786 and Apr. 1788, are presented in the first volume; eight cases (three in 1789, four in 1793, and one in 1794) appear in the second; the remaining two, one in 1796 and one in 1797, appear in the third.

2. The General Court continued to sit as a fiscal court and as a court to try impeachments of high government officers and indictments of court clerks for misconduct and attorneys for malpractice. Civil and criminal cases in the district courts could also be adjourned to the General Court for decision (Tucker, *Blackstone's Commentaries*, III, App., 14–16).

ing four apparently were original jurisdiction cases. Since most of the reports are quite brief, annotation has been confined to footnotes to the reports, omitting introductory editorial notes. In the appellate cases the editors have attempted to reconstruct the earlier history for those where Tucker identified the lower court and the records of that court survive.

Titles and dates of suits as written in by Tucker have been omitted from the transcriptions and instead have been uniformly rendered in the case headings. Tucker entered the suits chronologically, so dates for some cases have been supplied from the order in which they appear or from Tucker's notation of "Same day."

ST. GEORGE TUCKER

This engraving by C. B. J. Fevret de St.-Mémin serves as the bookplate in Tucker's working copy of Blackstone's *Commentaries. Courtesy of Tucker-Coleman Papers, Swem Library, College of William and Mary*

19. Pollard v. Schofield Argument

7 October 1788

Sups. to a Judgt. of Lancaster Court.[1] Suit brot. to indemnify plt, for becoming Security for one Angel the Deft's Intestate in a Bond. Plea non ass. & plene Adm. Judgt. confessed if assets—Sci. fa. to revive. Oyer. plene Admt. & Issue.[2] Verdict that the Decedent *did owe, as in Declon contained.*[3]

no averment of assets in the Sci: fa:

Marshal for Pollard—the verdict is immaterial to the point in Issue, that being whether Assets or not.

Taylor[4] produced a copy of the record, varying from that on which sups. awarded.

Certiorari[5] awarded, & clerk to be summoned.

But upon examination this appeared to be a mistake in Taylor, it being another Judgt. viz on the Sci. fa.

Taylor—the court will not open the record preceeding the sci: fa:—if so the Ct. will concieve Judgt. well described in the writ of sci. fa.—therefore to take up Cause at the Sci. fa. consequently Assets admitted. Had debt been brot. on the first Judgt. plene Adm. could not have been recieved as a plea. The worst to be apprehended is a reversal up to the sci: fa.

Reversed & sent back.[6]

MS, Tucker-Coleman Papers, ViW.

1. A writ of *supersedeas* commanded the sheriff to stop proceedings on a judgment and to give notice to the party who prevailed below to appear before the appellate court for a rehearing of the matter. In Virginia a supersedeas was the process normally used to remove a judgment of an inferior to a superior court for revision. In practice it was a substitute for a writ of error, which was never used for this purpose except where security was dispensed with (Robinson, *Practice*, I, 660 [citing White v. Jones, 1 Wash. 118 (1792); Burwell v. Anderson, 2 Wash. 194 (1796)]). See JM's petition for a supersedeas calendared in *PJM*, I, 126.

2. The case below was William Schofield v. Thomas Pollard, administrator of Samuel Angell, brought on a scire facias in Sept. 1778. Schofield in May

1773 had obtained a judgment by confession against the administrator, to be levied *quando acciderint,* that is, when assets of the estate should come to hand. If there was reason to believe that assets had come into the representative's hands, the plaintiff proceeded, as Schofield did, upon a scire facias alleging assets and requiring the representative to show cause why the plaintiff should not have execution upon them. No further proceedings took place upon the scire facias until Aug. 1782, when the defendant pleaded non assumpsit and that he had fully administered (plene administravit) the assets of the estate (Lancaster County Orders No. 15, 1770–78, 322; No. 16, 1778–83, 14, 112, 115 [microfilm], Vi; Robinson, *Practice*, I, 577–78).

3. A jury returned a verdict on 20 June 1783 that the decedent (Angell) "did owe to the said plaintiff in form as he hath declared" (Lancaster Co. Ord. No. 17, 1783–85, 14 [microfilm], Vi). On a plea of non assumpsit, however, the verdict should have stated that the decedent "had assumed." As JM noted, the verdict did not respond to the issue joined on the plea of fully administered.

4. John Taylor of Caroline, who represented Schofield.

5. A writ of *certiorari* was issued by a superior to an inferior court requiring the latter to produce a certified record of a case.

6. No further proceedings have been found in this case after it was returned to the county court.

20. Cassels v. Scott
Argument
7 October 1788

Sups. for want of a Declon. in suit where Judgt. on reference by Consent of parties.[1]

Marshal—Difference between award & Confession. In one Case he admits full extent of Judgt. agt. him—here he contests plts claim, only waves the mode of trial—therefore whatever Error after Verdict, will be after an award.[2]

But the court were of opinion that by the submission the Deft confess'd Judgt. for whatever sum the arbitrators should find agt., which brot. this within the reason of the Determination in Picket & Claiborne—Dubitante T.[3]

Judgt. affirmed

MS, Tucker-Coleman Papers, ViW.

1. The case had been referred to arbitration. Presumably the appellant Cassels was the defendant below and was seeking a reversal of the award on the grounds that Scott had failed to file a declaration.

2. Representing Cassels, JM attempted to distinguish this case from Pickett

v. Claiborne (Case No. 32), in which the Court of Appeals in 1787 held that a confession of judgment cured the omission of a declaration.

3. "Dubitante T."—that is, Judge Tucker doubted that this case fell within the scope of Pickett v. Claiborne. JM made a similar (and also unsuccessful) argument in a case decided by the Court of Appeals in 1794: "Tho' it has been determined in this court, in the case of Picket and Claiborne, that the want of a declaration is cured by a confession of judgment, yet no decision of this, or of any Court in England, has ever gone so far, as to extend this rule to judgments entered in pursuance of awards." JM perhaps conveniently forgot the General Court's decision in Cassels v. Scott, which also went unmentioned in the opposing counsel's argument and in the opinion of the court (Leftwich v. Stovall, 1 Wash. 303, 304).

21. Shackleford v. Thornton
Argument
7 October 1788

Reference by order of Court without Consent of Parties—[1]

Marshall—an order of reference without consent of parties is of itself Error. The Court will not presume consent where it does not appear of record.

Reversed unanimously.

But Taylor wishing to try to have the consent of parties ascertained, a Certiorari was awarded.[2]

MS, Tucker-Coleman Papers, ViW.

1. An order of reference, by which a case was submitted to arbitration, was supposed to state that such reference was "by consent of the parties." These words were omitted in the present case. For an example of an order of reference, see Case No. 2, Doc. IX.

2. As indicated by a fee listed in JM's account book, Thornton took this case to the High Court of Chancery in 1789 (*PJM*, II, 367).

22. Green v. Montgomery
Argument
7 October 1788

Sups. to a Judgt. of Washington Court. Declon. upon a Colloquium about keeping a stud horse to account for profits & to return horse at end of season. & that horse was kept in Consequence thereof—but not delivered up—but kept another season—& sold—& that he sued out an attachment wrongfully. plea not guilty.[1]

2. Lev. 101.
1. Ba. 29. 30.
3. Wilson 348.
2. Wilson 319.

Marshall—Error, in that plt has joined different Matters which can not be joined.[2]

Taylor—cited 3. Wilson in Margine,[3] which seems in point except as far as relates to the Attachment, which seems to me to bring in Question the Judgt. on the Attachment.

Marshall. Tort & assumpsit can not be joined—but they are united here—for there is both *misfeasance* & *nonfeasance* charged together.[4]

Cur. of the same opinion

Cro. Car. 20. Trover & contract joined; but good after Verdict.[5]

MS, Tucker-Coleman Papers, ViW.

1. Green sought to overturn a judgment against him at the county court of Washington on two grounds: (1) that the plaintiff below (Montgomery) erroneously joined two distinct actions in his declaration and (2) that he obtained his judgment by wrongfully suing out an attachment. In Virginia a writ of attachment could be issued against the estate of a debtor who was secretly moving out of the country or absconding and concealing himself, "so that the ordinary process of law" could not reach him. After the attachment was served and returned, the debtor could appear and defend himself as in any other case. As Tucker indicated below, the argument of the appeal proceeded only upon the first point, the misjoinder of actions (see Hening, *Statutes*, V, 492).

2. JM contended that the plaintiff's declaration erroneously joined actions founded on contract (assumpsit) and tort (possibly trover in this instance), citing Bacon, *Abridgment* (5th ed.), I, 30: "But Actions founded upon a *Tort* and upon a Contract cannot be joined." A marginal note to this passage in Bacon cites the case of Holms v. Taylor, 2 Lev. 101, 83 Eng. Rep. 469 (K.B., 1674), in which the plaintiff joined assumpsit and trover, with judgment for the plaintiff in assumpsit and for the defendant in trover. Judge Hale held that the declaration was bad and the judgment void, but Judge Twysden questioned whether the verdict cured the misjoinder of actions.

3. Mast v. Goodson, 3 Wils. K.B. 348, 95 Eng. Rep. 1094 (K.B., 1772). The court in this case held that the statement of a written agreement in the declaration did not mean the action sounded in contract; rather, the agreement was set forth merely to show that the plaintiff had a right to the enjoyment of his property, the denial of which constituted a misfeasance, or tort. At the same time the court rejected a subsidiary argument by plaintiff's counsel that

a declaration could join counts of assumpsit and trover. In an earlier case (cited by counsel), Dickson v. Clifton, 2 Wils. K.B. 319, 321, 95 Eng. Rep. 834, 835 (K.B., 1766), Chief Justice Wilmot declared that "the true test to try whether two counts can be joined in the same declaration, is to consider and see whether there be the same judgment in both, and not whether they both require the same plea, and wherever there is the same judgment in both, I think they may well be joined." The court in Mast v. Goodson held that this rule "is rather too large, and is not universally true, though it may be one good rule or test among others to try this point by" (3 Wils. K.B. 354, 95 Eng. Rep. 1097).

4. JM used the distinction between misfeasance, wrongly doing something one may lawfully do, and nonfeasance, not doing something that one ought to do, as means of distinguishing between actions founded on tort and those founded on contract. For a discussion of these terms in relation to the evolution of the law of contract and torts, see Baker, *English Legal History*, 184–89, 224–26.

5. Whyte v. Rysden, Cro. Car. 20, 79 Eng. Rep. 623 (C.P., 1625). The declaration joined counts of nondelivery of a horse according to a contract, abuse of the horse, and trover and conversion. On the plea of not guilty, the jury found a verdict for the plaintiff. The court said that the defendant might have demurred to the declaration, but that the verdict cured the defect in pleading.

23. Calvert v. Shropshire
Argument
8 October 1788–11 June 1789

General Court Octr. 8. 1788.

Appeal—Detinue for a Slave. plea non dett:[1] Security for costs—Exception to reading a Deposition for want of notice &c: & for that it was not made to appear that the witness whose Depon. was taken de bene, was not able to attend. Special Verdict. Judgt. for plt.

Marshall for app:[2]—The admission of proof of notice by the security for costs was Error. Court also refused to let a Depon. be read. Exception thereto.

Lies over for Argt. tomorrow.[3]

[Extract from Casebook]

June 11th. 1789.

Detinue for a Slave. On appeal from Culpeper. Special Verdict found that Eliza. Shropshire was siezed of two Slaves in 1718, & being so siezed married Robert Peck, by whom she had issue & died in 1722. That Peck lived until 1771. That suit was brought within two years &c. Two points were made on the merits:

1. Whether Robert Peck was entituled to the Slaves in right of the Marriage, but this was not insisted on.

2. Whether plaintiff barred by Act of Limitation.

This question resolved itself into two points.

1st. Whether Peck might be Tenant by Curtesy.[4]

Act of Lim. may be given in evidence on nil debet pleaded to debt for rent. See Salk 278.[5]

2d. Whether the Defts not having pleaded the Act of Limitations, it ought not to appear that it was given in Evidence, as in that Case it might have been rebutted.

Two other points were also made:

1. That the notice of taking certain Depositions which were read in the Case, was proved to have been given to the Defendant, by a person who was the plaintiff's Security for Costs (he being no Inhabitant).[6]

2d. That a Depon. taken de bene Esse was read *without proof*, that the witness who resided in the County was unable to attend.[7]

Both these points were objected to at the Trial, & the Exceptions over-ruled by the Court, but the Benefit thereof saved to the Defendant.

3. A third point arose upon examination of the record. The notice mentioned that the Deposition would be taken at the House of one Chandler in Pyttsylvania County—but the Depon. was certified from Henry County—This probably happened from the Division of the County,[8] but it did not appear that it was taken at the House of Chandler so

that for ought that appeared to the Contrary it was taken at a different place.

Henry, Judge. As to the first point—doubted whether his Interest was such as to disqualify him—but if it were, he conceived it would have been but fair for Deft to have given plt notice of the objection, before the Trial—for he was discharged from his Suretyship a long time before the trial.

As to the third—it might have been true that the Deposition was taken agreeably to notice—but it does not appear, & for ought that appears to the contrary it was taken at a different place, though at the same Time.

Cary, Parker, & Mercer Judges. Were of Opinion that the Witness was disqualified by the Interest he had in the Event of the suit.

Tucker—doubted, how far an eventual Interest amounted to such disqualification—but by the witness being relieved from his Suretyship, he became capable of being an unexceptional Witness, at the Trial. He therefore concurred with Mr Henry in thinking Deft should have given notice of the intended Objection. He thought under such Circumstances the Court were right in overruling it, as a matter of surprise on the plaintiff.

June 11th. 1789. The whole court were unanimous on the third point—

The Judgement reversed, and the verdict set aside & new trial to be had in the County Court.

MS and Casebook, Tucker-Coleman Papers, ViW.

1. Detinue was the common law action for the recovery of specific personal property and damages for its detention. The general issue was *non detinet* ("he does not detain"), which applied either to the case where the defendant intended to deny detaining the property or to the case where he intended to show the plaintiff's lack of title to the property. "The usual method of trying title to slaves, in Virginia," Tucker noted, "is by action of *detinue*; the reason, probably, is the great predilection for that species of property, and inasmuch as the specific thing cannot be recovered in any other action, recourse has

been had to this, in which not only the damages are recoverable for the detention, but the specific slave is also recovered" (Tucker, *Blackstone's Commentaries*, III, 152 n. 5). For other JM cases brought in detinue for the recovery of slaves, see Case No. 30; Dandridge's Executor v. Allen and Bailey v. Morris's Administrator, decided by the General Court in 1787 (*PJM*, I, 207–9, 211–12); and Burnley v. Lambert, decided by the Court of Appeals in 1794 (1 Wash. 308).

2. JM represented the appellant Calvert, who was defendant below. JM received fees for this case in Apr. 1787, when the appeal was initiated, and in Oct. 1788, when it was finished (*PJM*, I, 376; II, 374).

3. The only other known notes on this case appear under the date of 11 June 1789 in Tucker's Casebook, a transcription of which follows below.

4. A husband enjoyed his wife's inherited real property during the marriage. If she died first, he became tenant by courtesy (Baker, *English Legal History*, 147–48).

5. Anonymous, 1 Salk. 278, 91 Eng. Rep. 243 (N.P., Hertford, 1690). The court in this case held that on the plea of nil debet in debt for rent, the statute of limitations could be given in evidence, "for the statute has made it no debt at the time of the plea pleaded, the words of which are in the present tense; but in case on *non assumpsit*, the Statute of Limitation cannot be given in evidence, for it speaks of a time past, and relates to the time of making the promise." This ruling applied by analogy to Calvert v. Shropshire because the plea of non detinet was also in the present tense.

6. A plaintiff not residing in Virginia had to give security for costs (Hening, *Statutes*, XII, 355).

7. A deposition taken de bene esse, or provisionally, could be read in evidence only if the witness was unable to attend the trial (see Case No. 1, Doc. III, n. 1).

8. Henry County was formed from Pittsylvania in 1776 (Hening, *Statutes*, IX, 241–42).

24. Thorpe v. Thorpe's Legatees
Argument
9–17 October 1788

Contestation of a Will—appeal from Southton.[1]

Timothy Thorpe the Testator, made his will bearing Date the 27th. Day of Janry. 1776. proved by the oath Sarah Atkinson (now Barron) who swears that one Moore a subscribing witness since dead was witness & subscribed the will with her.[2]

The points of contest are

1. Testators minority—2d. a revocation.

Mary Waller.— Mary Wallers depon.—she remembers Testor born in April or May that she had a son named Drury whose was born Decr. 12. month, before Testor.[3] that Drury would be 32. years old in Dec. 1785. her knowledge of the year of her sons birth arises from her *sons writing* in a prayer.[4]

Samuel Edmunds— From an Entry in his fathers new Testt. his sister Lucy born 22. April 1755. & Testor born either that night or about that time as Depots. mother who is dead used to say.

Sarah Baron als. Atkinson Testors will written the day of the Date & then executed in her presence. Testor went into the Service—after his return put the paper into Witness's hands, but without saying any thing to her. It appeared to have been sealed but was open when Testor gave it her. That he lived 7 or 8. years after & never said any thing to her about the Will. That when she reced. this will she had no place to keep it.

James Jones— In 1781. Testor came to his house & requested him to witness a paper which he told Witness was his will, & that 2 other witnesses subscribed with him. That he read the beginning of the will.

Joshua Thorpe— Some time after Testor's death Jno. Applethwaite hinted to Witness that a Will of Testor might be produced. Some time after he picked up some papers. (Observe the Contents). That on Tuesday before Testors. death Ter. told witness he had not settled his Business & being asked if he had a Will, answd. *he had not*, or *not that he knew of*. The Day before he died very anxious to make a will.

Mary Reese— Has a Daur. born Oct. 1755. saw Testor when her Daur. 4 Wks old & supposed him 15. or 18 months old.

Jesse Cooper— When a boy heard his & Testor's mother's say Testor was the oldest by almost a year. that himself was born Feb. 1755.

Margaret Bruce—	That she had a Child born in Janry 1757. While with child she saw Testor & supposes him three or 4. years old.
Mary Scott.	Testor while she lived with Mr. Jones came to Jones's & executed a paper which he called his will in presence of herself, Jones & Mary Voper.
Lucretia Simmonds } Memo.	Of the Ages of[5] Timothy Thorpe the elder, places, the Age of Testor April 1755. proved by the oath of Lucretia Simmonds to be the writing of James Jones, who married Testors mother.[6]
Eliza Jones—	Was present when Testor's mother desired her Husband to enter Ages of her Children, who did so in Witness's presence. The above is a summary of the Depositions taken in County court. Several witnesses were sworn in Court viz.
Jesse Cooper.—	Born Feb. 8. 1755.—when 7. or 8 years old, playing with Testor who was the strongest boy, heard his & Testors mother say Testor was a year or two older than witness. Does not remember whether this determination made by comparing *the Time* of their respective births—*or their sizes* only. Knows his own Age from an Entry in his mother's prayer book. but does not[7] whose writing—read in 1769. his father cod. not write. *NB. Witness is a small man & rather slender.*
Joshua Thorpe.	Picked a Copy of the will now exhibited in a Letter directed to himself & signed *Nobody*, which Letter directing him how to proceed led to the production of the will now produced, by one Harris.
Col. Simmons—	Timothy Thorpe sold his Brother's Estate.[8] Does not recollect the Age of Testator's heir at law, whether born after will made or not. His Wife a Daur. of T. Thorpe Senr. has a prayer book with her age correspondent to Lucretia Simmons's [hand?].
Mr. Taylor.	Benj. Thorpe, heir of Testor & son of P. Thorpe, born 21. April 1776.—3 months after will dated.

Mr Starke[9] for the heir at Law. Testor under 21.

years, of course will void as to Lands. Testor wanted *a few months* of being of age. *Mary Wallers* Depon. strong for him. So is that of *Samuel Edmunds. Lucretia Simmons's* also material. A remarkable Circumstance in it, *that her mother insisted the Entry* was right. *Eliza Jones* to the same effect; *but she says they were not all right. Mary Reese & Margaret Bruce* make the Testator *considerably* over 21. years. Jesse Cooper's Testimony very slight, depending on the recollection of a boy of 8. years.

2. point—revocation.

Act of assembly & Statute of wills correspond—[10]therefore all authorities will apply. The Intention with which certain Acts are done must be the guide. When Testor gave *S. Atkinson* his Will she had no Chest, Desk, or other place of safe custody for it. He never after enquired after or mentioned—*Jones* proves the actual Execution of a subsequent will. Remarks on the mode of bringing will to light; see *Joshua Thorpes* Depon.

Parsons & Lanoo 1. Vezey 189 — Col. Lanoo going over to Ireland devises in these words, (if I *do not return from Ireland.*)[11] He return'd & adjudged that by his return & by his having children, the Will revoked. applies this to the present Case. [p. 850:]

5. Ba: 524. — Revocations may be implied, notwithstanding the express words of the Statute.[12]

5. Ba. 525. 526. — Hyde & Hyde. Tearing off seals not being done Animo Cancellandi no revocation—see the Case.[13]

Ib: 523. . . . . — Surrender of a Lease & taking a new one a revocation[14]

5. Ba: 527. — Earl of Lincoln's Case.[15]

3: Bur. 1491. — Constructive revocations contrary to the Intention of Testor. ought not to be indulged.[16]

Cowper 49. — Burtenshaw v Gilbert—Intention must govern in Cases of cancelling wills.[17]

Innes—Contra.

1. As to Testators minority. *Mary Waller's Depon.*, vague & uncertain, founded on no fixed fact. She can not read writing. the Age of her son not set down until himself could

write. *Edmunds* Depon. He knows nothing of his Sisters Age, but by recurrence to the memo. of her birth. *Lucretia Simmonds's* Testimony only refers to Entries made many years after. Correspondence between Mrs. Simmon's prayer book & Jones's bible of no validity, as applying only to her own age. These are the evidences to prove minority. *Mary Reese* speaks of her own recollection, not of uncertain entries by persons unknown. *Jesse Cooper* speaks from circumstances within his own Knowledge. Testor. larger & stronger than him: mothers on comparing ages mentioned the difference between them. *Mrs. Bruce* very positive & particular. *Mrs. Jones* proves the entry in Jones's Bible not correct, & made at a distant date.

NB. compare this with M. Waller's Depon.

2d. point. Revocation.

Sarah Barron's Depon. She was the friend & intimate of the family. Testor said nothing to her: nothing from which his Intentions could be inferred. Provision in the will for his mother, is it presumable he means so soon to revoke that provision? The testimony relative to the subsequent will is weak: making a second will does not of course revoke the former, it must appear that they are contradictory & repugnant to each other.

Swinburne 502. Sir Henry Killegrews Case. Two wills *may* stand together.

Ib: 503. . . . . *Republication* may revise a former Will, though there be a later.[18]

5. Ba. 529. 1. Eq. Ca: 407. 5. Ba. 540. prove the solemnity requisite to be used for cancelling a will.[19]

Swinburne 511. Swinburne 511. to the same Effect.

Ib: 512. Will not duly executed, no revocation, for it must be an express revocation, of equal solemnity with the Execution.[20]

Cowper 49. . . . . . . Burtenshaw v Gilbert in favor on this point.[21]

NB. The words of the Stat: 34. Hen. 8. ch: 5. Sect. 14. are—Wills or Testaments made of any Manors &c. by any woman covert, or person within the Age of 21. years &c. shall not be taken to be good or effectual in the Law.—vi: Hob. 225. 6. Co. 23. Dyer 354.[22]

Mr. Marshall—on the same side.[23]

1. As to Infancy. Testimony strong on both sides—a decision by a court to Whom witnesses known.

2. Revocation.

Act of ass. pa: 160.[24] very explicit. Nothing in the Evidence amounts to a revocation in Law. Testor has neither burnt, or torn will, if the Will be done away it must by cancel-

2. Blacks. Com. 309.

ling. Blackstone speaking of cancelling says it must be by some[25] done upon the face of a Will, as by drawing Lines across it, tearing off the Seals &c.[26]

3. Burr: 1244. 1256.

By the decisions in England upon the Stat: of frauds nothing done by Testor in this Case has been adjudged a revocation. Revocations are not favoured now—*Burrow. arguendo.* An Intention to revoke by a future Act is no re-

Cowper 52.

vocation. Ib. 1256.[27] *Cowper* 52, since the Stat: of frauds no revocation without an Act

2. Blacks. rep. 1043.

of equal solemnity with the Will.[28] The same position laid down in 2d. Blacks. rep. 1043. Where Testor tore the will, & threw it on the fire—but it was not consumed—See the Case.[29] Here the Act demonstrated quo animo it was done. Verbal will can not re-

Gilbert's Devises 107.

voke a will in writing—Gilbert 107. Revocation written on the same paper if not signed by Tester is no revocation—Ib. Revocation must be in writing.—Ib:[30]—parol Testimony unsupported by apparent Acts can be no revocation; after born Children a strong circumstance to prove an Intention of revocation—yet until the late act of Assembly even that Circumstance not sufficient to establish

2. Blacks. 937.
3. Wilson 497.
Cowper 87.

a revocation.[31] 2. Black. 937. the Case Goodright v Harvey—reversed—vi. Cowper 87. 3. Wilson 497.[32] Title of an heir at Law not to be defeated by Conjecture or Uncertainty. 1. Vez. 189. does not apply at present, nor does

5. Ba. 523. to 526. in any of the Cases cited.[33] Revocation in Law must be performed by a very different Act, from any done by Testor in this Case.

Taylor, for the Appellant.

Case before the court divisible into 3. Questions

1. Whether a Will in existence may yet be revoked.

2. Whether the facts proved amount to such revocation.

3. Whether Testor. of Age or not.

5. Ba. 529. Where a man destroys a duplicate, yet this does not amount to a revocation of the existing Counterpart—5. Ba. 529. (a mistake).[34]

Cowper 49. The Case in Cowper 49.[35] supports this doctrine. Parol proof may be let in to prove Testor's Intention as to revocation. *Parallel between the Case in Cowper & Case at Bar.* The

2. Vernon 743. court will consider *quo animo* Testor gave his will to Sarah Barron; this may be as strong an Act as tossing it into the fire. The Intention must govern—vi. Cowper. vi. etiam 2. Vern. 743.[36] Parol Evidence must be let in to explain any act of cancelling. Cowper. Testor.'s Intention in delivering Will to M. Waller, fully explained by his Declaration to Joshua

1. P. Wms. 345. Thorpe that he had no will at that time. 1. P. Wms. 346. A second will executed accordg. to the Stat: but not *subscribed in his presence*, no revocation. Nor will a cancellation by mistake revoke a will. As if a Man having two wills & intending to burn the first by accident or mistake destroys the last—1. P.W. 345. Cancelling a duplicate with an Intention to

1. P. Wms. 346. destroy it, revokes both—Ib. 346.[37]—1. Wil-

1. Wilson 310. son 310. Determinations in Cases of revoca-

Richardson on Wills 290. tion have always been in favor of the heir.[38] Devise of Lands in fee—afterwards he leases the same Lands to Devisee for sixty years, to commence from Testors death, adjudged a Revocation.[39]

2. point—as to the facts relative to revocation.

1. as to the quo animo—Testor. when he dd. paper to Sarah Baron, did it animo revocandi. When made, a mere temporary provision agt. Intestacy. Sarah Barron's not destroying the will was a fraud upon him. In 1781. Testor. executes another will—Testor. lived eight years after giving S. Br. his will in all that time he said nothing about it. Testor's situation in Life had changed, by the birth of the *heir at Law*. (NB. The heirs father[40] was heir at law at the time of making the Will.) If not a revocation as to the Lands, certainly sufficient as to the Chattels.

3. point—Infancy.

The recollection of mothers very correct as to their Children. Written Testimony to be preferred to oral. Gilbert.[41]

MS, Tucker-Coleman Papers, ViW. Endorsed by Tucker: "Argts. at Bar." Filed with Tucker's opinion, dated 17 Oct. 1788, which is here omitted.

1. This was an appeal from the Southampton County Court. County courts had jurisdiction over the probate of wills, with the General Court exercising appellate jurisdiction (Hening, *Statutes*, IX, 412; XII, 142).

The parties to this suit were Benjamin Person Thorpe, heir at law of Timothy Thorpe, and the legatees of Timothy Thorpe. Timothy Thorpe died unmarried in 1784, having executed his will on 27 Jan. 1776. He named as legatees his nephews John T. Richardson, John Person (son of William), John Person (son of Philip), and his nieces Peggy Ridley, Patsy Thorpe, and Dorothy Atherton. Benjamin Person Thorpe, son of Timothy Thorpe's older brother Peterson Thorpe, was not named in this will, having been born several months after the will was written. Although witnesses testified that Timothy Thorpe subsequently wrote a second will, the question was whether this constituted a revocation of the original will. Another disputed point was the testator's age at the time of executing the first will. If he were proved to have been under the age of twenty-one, the will was invalid as to the devise of lands (see wills of Timothy Thorpe [father of testator], 3 Sept. 1763; and of Timothy Thorpe [testator], 27 Jan. 1776, Southampton County Will Book I, 59; IV, 310; Southampton County Order Book, 1778–84, 59, 443 [all Southampton County will books and order books cited are on microfilm at Vi]; Hening, *Statutes*, XII, 140–41).

2. Sarah Atkinson exhibited the will in the county court on 10 June 1784, deposing that William Moore had also witnessed the will in the presence of the testator. The statute required that a will "not wholly written" by the testator himself should be witnessed by two persons in his presence. The court then ordered Benjamin Person Thorpe, the heir at law, to appear at the next court to contest the validity of the will. The method of contesting

the will was by a bill in chancery, with a jury trying the issue of whether the writing produced was the testator's will or not. In this case the bill was brought by Martha Thorpe, guardian of the heir at law (and presumably his mother). At the Nov. 1784 court depositions were ordered to be taken, but at the next monthly court the bill was dismissed on the plaintiff's motion. Although a new suit may have been instituted following the dismissal of this bill, no further proceedings in this case at the county court level have been found (Southampton Co. Ord. Bk., 1778–84, 59, 443, 517; Ord. Bk., 1784–89, 2; Hening, *Statutes*, XII, 140, 142).

3. That is, Drury Waller was born in Dec. 1753, more than twelve months before the birth of Timothy Thorpe.

4. Tucker should have added "book."

5. Tucker should have inserted "the children of."

6. Lucretia Simmonds (Simmons) was a sister of the testator. Their mother, Martha Thorpe, married James Jones sometime after the death of Timothy Thorpe, Sr., in 1763. According to Tucker's summary of the deposition in his accompanying opinion, Jones made a memorandum in a Bible of the birth dates of his wife's children by Timothy Thorpe, Sr. (see the wills of Timothy Thorpe, Sr., 3 Sept. 1763; and of James Jones, 5 Dec. 1771, Southampton Co. Will Bk. I, 59; II, 469).

7. Tucker omitted "know."

8. Timothy Thorpe (testator) was administrator of the estate of his older brother Peterson Thorpe, who died intestate in 1777 (*Va. Gazette* [Purdie], 21 Nov. 1777; Southampton Co. Will Bk. III, 273). Peterson Thorpe was the father of the plaintiff in this case.

9. Burwell Starke.

10. The Virginia act was taken from the English Statute of Wills, first enacted in 1540 (32 Hen. VIII, c. 1) (Hening, *Statutes*, XII, 140).

11. Parsons v. Lanoe, 1 Ves. Sen. 189, 27 Eng. Rep. 974 (Ch., 1748): "Colonel Charles Lanoe, intending to go to *Ireland*, made a paper-writing in 1732, declaring it to be his last will in manner following: 'If I die before my return from my journey to *Ireland*.'"

12. Bacon, *Abridgment* (5th ed.), V, 524. This is not a paraphrase of any passage appearing on that page, though other references leave no doubt that the fifth edition of Bacon was being cited.

13. Ibid., 525–26 (citing Hyde v. Hyde, 1 Eq. Ca. Abr. 409, 21 Eng. Rep. 1139 [Ch., 1708]). *Animo cancellandi* ("with intention to cancel").

14. Ibid., 523 (citing Marwood v. Turner, 3 P. Wms. 166, 170, 24 Eng. Rep. 1013 [Ch., 1732]).

15. The earl of Lincoln's case is set out ibid., 528–29, with citation to 1 Eq. Ca. Abr. 411, 21 Eng. Rep. 1140–41 (Ch., 1695) and 2 Freem. 202, 22 Eng. Rep. 1160 (Ch., 1695).

16. Swift v. Roberts, 3 Burr. 1491, 97 Eng. Rep. 942–43 (K.B., 1764), argument of plaintiff's counsel quoting Lord Mansfield: "that constructive revocations, contrary to the intention of the testator ought not to be indulged; and that some over-strained resolutions of that sort had brought scandal upon the law."

17. Burtenshaw v. Gilbert, 1 Cowp. 49, 52, 98 Eng. Rep. 961, 963 (K.B.,

1774), Lord Mansfield: "It is the intention, therefore, that must govern in such cases."

18. Henry Swinburne, *A Treatise of Testaments and Last Wills* (6th. ed.; London, 1743), 524. Sir Henry Killigrew in 1644 made a will in writing devising lands. In 1645 he made another will but did not devise lands by it. The court adjudged that the second will did not revoke the first "because both may be consistent and stand together, for a Revocation must always be taken according to the Subject-Matter." In another case the testator devised lands in tail to W. D. By a subsequent will he devised the same lands to his eldest daughter for life, remainder to her first, second, and third sons in tail male, and gave W. D. a rent-charge of £1,000 a year for life. Both wills were published, but the testator shortly before his death declared the first to be his will. The court held that "this *Republication* of the first Will was a Revocation of the last."

19. Bacon, *Abridgment* (5th ed.), V, 529 (citing Pollen v. Husband, 1 Eq. Ca. Abr. 412, 21 Eng. Rep. 1142 [Ch., 1712]); Onions v. Tyrer, 1 Eq. Ca. Abr. 407, 21 Eng. Rep. 1138 (Ch., 1716) (see n. 34); Bacon, *Abridgment* (5th ed.), V, 540 (citing Bransby v. Kerridge, 1 Eq. Ca. Abr. 406, 21 Eng. Rep. 1136 [Ch., 1728]).

20. Swinburne, *Treatise of Testaments and Last Wills* (6th ed.), 533. The reference is apparently to the case in which the testatrix devised her lands by one will and then by a subsequent will devised the same lands to the same person. The second will was not subscribed by three witnesses in her presence and was therefore void. It was argued, however, that the second will was a good revocation of the first. The court ruled otherwise.

21. See n. 17. Lord Mansfield in this case declared that a will could not "be revoked, but by an instrument executed according to the solemnities required by the statute [Statute of Frauds]; or by burning, cancelling, tearing, or obliterating the same by the testator himself, or by his directions" (1 Cowp. 52, 98 Eng. Rep. 962).

22. Needler v. Bishop of Winchester, Hob. 225, 80 Eng. Rep. 372 (K.B., 1615); Marquess of Winchester's Case, 6 Co. Rep. 23a, 77 Eng. Rep. 287 (K.B., 1599); Sir George Caverlye's Case, 3 Dy. 354b, 73 Eng. Rep. 795 (K.B., 1576). These cases reiterated the statutory provisions disallowing wills made by persons of unsound mind or by married women.

23. JM represented the legatees, recording fees in this case (styled by him as "Thorp v. Richardson") in Apr. 1788 and Mar. 1789 (*PJM*, I, 407; II, 357).

24. JM cited the 1748 act concerning wills, taken from the revisal of 1769 (*Acts of the Assembly, Now in Force, in the Colony of Virginia* [Williamsburg, 1769; Evans #11511], 160; Hening, *Statutes*, V, 454).

25. Tucker should have added "act."

26. Blackstone, *Commentaries*, II, 308–9.

27. Wright v. Littler, 3 Burr. 1244, 1256, 97 Eng. Rep. 812, 818 (K.B., 1761).

28. See n. 21.

29. Bibb v. Thomas, 2 Black. W. 1043, 96 Eng. Rep. 613 (C.P., 1776). This was held to be a sufficient revocation.

30. Sir Geoffrey Gilbert, *Law of Devises, Revocations, and Last Wills* (3d ed.;

London, 1773), 107: "An estate in land was devised by will in writing, afterwards the testator made a verbal will to revoke it; this is *no* revocation. . . . A revocation *must* be in writing, operating as a will, or by a writing by which the testator declares his intention, to revoke the first will."

31. By the 1785 act a will made when the testator had no children and that did not provide for future children was void if the testator died leaving a child, unless the child died unmarried or before he reached twenty-one (Hening, *Statutes*, XII, 140–41).

32. Goodright v. Harwood, 2 Black. W. 937, 96 Eng. Rep. 553 (C.P., 1774); full report in 3 Wils. K.B. 497, 95 Eng. Rep. 1177 (K.B., 1774); Harwood v. Goodright, 1 Cowp. 87, 98 Eng. Rep. 981 (K.B., 1774). In the reversal the court held that "a subsequent will, though it be found to contain a different disposition from a former, if the particulars of that difference be unknown, is no revocation of such former will."

33. See nn. 11–14.

34. Tucker's parenthetical comment apparently refers to the error in citing the page number. The correct citation is to Bacon, *Abridgment* (5th ed.), V, 525, summarizing the case of Onions v. Tyrer, 1 Eq. Ca. Abr. 407, 21 Eng. Rep. 1138 (Ch., 1716). In this case a man executed a will and a duplicate. He later made a second will devising lands to the same person as in the former and revoking all former wills. He then canceled the duplicate of the original will. The second will was not properly subscribed and was therefore not good. The court held that neither the second will nor the canceling of the duplicate of the first will was a revocation of the first will. If, however, a man canceled or revoked either the duplicate or original will with the intention of destroying the will, he effectually voided both.

35. See nn. 17, 21.

36. The case of Onions v. Tyrer (see n. 34) was also reported in 2 Vern. 741, 23 Eng. Rep. 1085 (Ch., 1716).

37. Taylor paraphrased Onions v. Tyrer as reported in 1 P. Wms. 345, 346, 24 Eng. Rep. 418, 419 (Ch., 1716).

38. Parsons v. Freeman, 1 Wils. K.B. 310, 95 Eng. Rep. 634–35 (K.B., 1751).

39. Robert Richardson, *The Law of Testaments and Last Wills* (2d ed.; London, 1769), 290 (citing Coke v. Bullock, Cro. Jac. 49, 79 Eng. Rep. 41 [K.B., 1603]).

40. Peterson Thorpe (see n. 8).

41. Sir Geoffrey Gilbert, *Law of Evidence* . . . (Dublin, 1754), 4–5. The arguments of counsel end at this point. Tucker's opinion follows, beginning on a separate sheet. Tucker upheld the will on both points, the infancy of the testator and the revocation of the existing will. On the first point he said that the burden of proof was on the party contesting the will and concluded that the plaintiff (the heir at law) failed to establish that the testator was under twenty-one when he executed the will. On the second point he maintained that nothing done by the testator in this case constituted a revocation under the Virginia statute of wills. At the end of his opinion Tucker wrote: "Octo: 17. 1788. The will was established by the unanimous opinion of the Court—& adjudged no Revocation. absent, Tazewell, Prentis & Winston."

At the foot of Timothy Thorpe's will as recorded in the county court, the clerk made the following entry: "At a Court held for the County of Southampton the 9th. day of April 1789. A transcript of the record from the general court was produced from which it appears that the last will & testament of Timothy Thorp decd. in contestation before that Court was established. Whereupon the same was ordered to be recorded . . . " (will of Timothy Thorpe, 27 Jan. 1776, Southampton Co. Will Bk. IV, 310).

25. DuVal v. Reynolds
Argument
11 October 1788

Caveat.[1] claim founded on prior Entry. Aug. 27. 1773. Date of Duval's Entry.—Land warrt. dated nov. 29th. 1783. Another in Febry 25. 1785. Reynolds's Entry 1783. in novr.[2]

Duval[3]—Reynolds' Entry made under act of 1783.[4] which was repealed in 1784.

Act of May 1784. fo. 7. chap. 7. Sect. 3. repeals a former act & all entries under it. made in 1779.[5]

Taylor[6]—2. points.

1. Land for which Duval entered, contains some high Lands. which the Entry.
2. Tho nullity of Entries made under act of 1779. as declared in Act of 1783. Entry not within a year. Therefore both Entries of 1773 & 1785. will both be good.[7]

NB. Reynolds holds the Land adjacent to the swamp.

Marshall—contra.

Caveator must prove 2. things

1. That Deft has no right
2. That he has a right himself.

In 1773. no person had a right to enter for swamp Lands adjoining the high Lands of other persons—*Consult the Act of 1748. Virginia Laws 150.*[8] The Entry could only be supported by the Act of 1779. The Act of 1784. avoids it as done before May 1786. & after the Act of 1784.[9]

Taylor—An Entry upon the eastern waters is always in force, & not necessary for survey to be made.

All entries made of sunken ground void, under 1784. without any exception as to adjacent proprietors.[10]

Witnesses—viz:

Mr. Allen—All the high Lands generally believed & supposed to be comprehended in a patent to a Mr Woodson.

Court suspended giving an opinion at the request of Duval who wished to consult his client about having a Survey agreeably to Woodson's patent.[11]

MS, Tucker-Coleman Papers, ViW.

1. A caveat prevented the issuing of a patent for land until judicial proceedings decided who had the better claim (see Case No. 11, editorial note; Tucker, *Blackstone's Commentaries*, III, App., Note B, 31–34).

2. The facts of this case can be better understood by quoting the words of the caveat, which was entered in the land office on 10 Jan. 1787: "Let no Grant issue to William Reynolds Assignee of Hutchings Matthews for 127 Acres of Land lying in the County of Henrico, on the main Run of Chickahominy Swamp, Survey'd for the said Matthews On the 18th day of February 1784, by virtue of a Land Office Treasury Warrant and Assign'd unto the said Reynolds on the 6th. day of March 1786. Samuel DuVall junr. claiming the same by Virtue of a prior entry made with the County Surveyor of Henrico on the 27. day of August 1773, and also claiming the same for the following cause (to wit) the failure of the said Matthews & Reynolds to return a Platt & Certificate of the Survey thereof to the Land Office, within the time prescrib'd by Law" (Land Office Caveats, No. 2, 1786–1814, 15, Vi). JM represented the defendant Reynolds (*PJM*, II, 343).

3. William DuVal represented the plaintiff, his younger brother (Bessie Berry Grabowskii, *The DuVal Family of Virginia* . . . [Richmond, 1931], 187–93).

4. The reference is probably to the "act for reducing the several acts of assembly concerning surveyors, into one act" (Hening, *Statutes*, XI, 352).

5. Ibid., XI, 371–73. The third section of this act voided all entries for swamp lands made under the 1779 land act. The 1779 act gave proprietors of high lands adjacent to swamps, marshes, or sunken ground preemption for such lands from one year after the passage of the act, after which any other person could enter and obtain a grant for this land.

6. John Taylor of Caroline.

7. As counsel for the plaintiff, DuVal and Taylor attempted to show that the entry under which Reynolds claimed was void and that their client's two entries of 1773 and 1785 were good.

8. JM referred to section 38 of "An Act for settling the Titles and Bounds of Lands," which required the party intending to patent swamp lands to give notice (attested by witnesses) to the proprietors of the contiguous high lands and to allow one year to pass after such notice. The plaintiff's 1773 entry evidently did not meet this requirement (Hening, *Statutes*, V, 421–22). JM used the 1769 revisal (*Acts of Assembly of Virginia*, 150).

9. The act of 1784 gave the proprietors of high lands—in this instance, Reynolds possessed such lands—preemption to make entries for contiguous

swamp lands until 1 May 1786. Samuel DuVal's 1785 entry was therefore nullified by this act (Hening, *Statutes*, XI, 372).

10. Taylor apparently contended that all entries for swamp lands had been voided by the 1784 act, including the one under which Reynolds claimed, even though the law was passed for the convenience of the proprietors of adjacent high lands.

11. On the next line Tucker wrote: "Motion to alter plea—from payt. to special non est factum." This was obviously a reference to another case.

26. White v. Letcher Argument

17 October 1788–12 June 1789

In the general[1] Court, oct. 17. 1788.

On supersedeas.[2] Declon. in debt as upon a Bond. Oyer of Writ, Declon. & Bond. Penal bill variant from Declon—plea nil debet.[3] Demurrer (a curious one). Demurrer adjudged insufficient—Exception to the court's Opinion, but not sealed—replication & Issue on the plea—Verdict that Deft. *hath not paid.* Judgt. for the Condition, not the penalty of the penal bill.[4]

Muroe.[5] Declon. states debt due on demand. But the penal bill makes a *day certain, in future.* Issue improper. Verdict insufficient
5. Ba. 315. 305. it only finds the money not paid[6]—Judgt. for less than penalty—Act of assembly page 181. requires Judgt. to be entered for penalty.[7] Verdict finds no Damages or Interest. Judgt. for principal & Interest.

vi. 1. Ld. Ray. 515. Marshall[8]—Contra. The bond & Declon. not agreeing he thinks dangerous[9]—but perhaps cured by oyer & Issue.

To be argued—memo. to enquire & examine how far the Court can take notice of the variance between the Bond & Declon. upon the Demurrer.[10]

[Extract from Casebook]

June 12. 1789. Sups. to Pyttsylvania Court. Declaration as on a Bond. Deft prayed oyer, whereupon the Action appeared to have been brought on a penal Bill—plea nil debet. Demurrer and joinder—Demurrer over-ruled, & other proceedings to Verdict.

The court were unanimously of opinion that the penal bill, which was the ground of the Action being spread on the record, the Declaration was insufficient to maintain the Action, & therefore, that on the demurrer Judgement should have been given against the plaintiff who had committed the first fault in pleading.

Judgement reversed.

MS and Casebook, Tucker-Coleman Papers, ViW.

1. Tucker inadvertently crossed through the first two words and part of the third.

2. This case began in the Pittsylvania County Court as John Letcher, assignee of William Nall, v. Rawleigh White. Judgment below was rendered on 16 Aug. 1785 (Pittsylvania County Court Records, No. 5, 1783–87, 226 [microfilm], Vi).

3. Since this action was brought on a sealed obligation, the proper plea was payment rather than nil debet, which was the general issue in debt on simple contract.

4. The plaintiff demurred unsuccessfully to the defendant's plea, and the case proceeded to verdict. The jury found "no part of the within bond paid." Although the facts as summarized by Tucker indicate that judgment was rendered for the condition rather than the penalty of the bond, the judgment as recorded in the county court order book states that the plaintiff was to recover 36,346 pounds of tobacco, "the debt in the declaration mentioned," to be discharged by paying 18,173 pounds of tobacco with legal interest from 1 June 1781 (see n. 2). Evidently the record sent up from the county court misstated the judgment. There was no other case between these two parties in the Pittsylvania court.

5. James Monroe.

6. Bacon, *Abridgment* (5th ed.), V, 315: "If the Jury find one Thing contrary to some other Thing, that is confessed, or not denied, in the Pleadings, the Verdict is as to so much bad; because the Jury had nothing to do with that which is confessed, or not denied, in the Pleadings." In this case the jury found that the defendant had "not paid," though the defendant had pleaded "does not owe" rather than payment. Bacon summarized cases where the verdict varied from the issue (ibid., 305).

7. *Acts of Assembly of Virginia* (the 1769 revisal), 181, contained the act providing that in actions of debt on a bond, judgment was to be for the penal sum of the bond, to be discharged by the payment of the principal and interest (Hening, *Statutes*, IV, 359; V, 511). On this act, see Case No. 9, editorial note.

8. JM, representing Letcher, recorded a fee in "Letcher ads. White (old appeal)" under date of Mar. 1789 (*PJM*, II, 358).

9. The danger of ignoring a variance between the bond and the declaration was that a defendant might be sued again on the same bond. The case cited from the reports of Lord Raymond has not been identified. The page reference is to an earlier edition (with apparently different pagination) than that reprinted in English Reports (the 1792 edition).

10. Apparently no further proceedings took place in the county court. Letcher revived the case in the district court at New London, where it abated in 1793 on his death (Franklin County District Court Order Book, 1789–93, 329 [microfilm], Vi).

27. Bruce v. Chapman
Argument
24–28 October 1788

Sups. to a Verd. & Judgt. in Court of—in Ejectment.[1]

Declon. blank except as to a demise of Lands of *864. acres in Culpeper.* Lease Entry and ouster confess'd. Verdict, Defts guilty & that plt is entituled to the Land & 1 d. Damages.

Lee—If there were any Term mentioned in the Declon. I should not contend that the other blanks were fatal. But there must be a Term set forth. This is a substantial thing—for Judgt. is that plt. recover his Term &c.

If a Term mentioned in a Declon. in Ejectt. expires, it is necessary to amend the Declon. by enlarging the Term.

No Case comes up to the present.

Runnington's Eject. 96. — If a Lease stated in Declon be uncertain the plt can not recover.[2]

Ib. 103. 104. 105. — If Cause be adjourned for Difficulty into Exch. Chamber, the Court will enlarge the Term. no amendt. but in matters of form.[3]

4. Burr. 2449. — A Demise held to be *mere matter* of form.

Runnington 105.[4]

But Difference between matter of form in regard to the Conduct of the suit, & matter of form in respect to the Title.

The Lease having neither commencement nor End set forth is a void Lease.

Taylor—Contra.

Ejectt. to be considered with great liberality. mere fiction—former Errors now exploded.

vi. Pugh et ux v D. of Leeds

Later cases settle the point that it is not necessary to lay the demise on the day before Entry & ouster, as was formerly supposed.[5]

Runn: 29.
1. Burr. 629. 2673

Sheriff deliver's possession according to plts shewing, and at his peril.[6]

Run. 125.

Declon. mere matter of form throughout—Lease Entry & Ouster being confess'd Deft cannot avail himself of want of form. Verdict fixes the plts title to recover the *premises* in Declon. Verdict in Eject. is the ground of the Judgt.[7]

Run. 105. }
4. Burr. 2449. }

In a modern Case demise held to be *mere matter of form.*[8]

Run: 91.

As Date & day of the Date. Pugh & Duke of Leeds—Douglas.[9]

Ib. 95. Cro. Eliz. 606. 773.

Day of Date of Demise omitted, yet good after Verdict.[10]

This Demise was at least for *two* years—the words being ______ years. Verdict within 2 years from Comt. of suit.

Marshall—on the same side.

Lee has said Court could not judge whether the Jury had they assess'd Damages had been extravagant therein—But Court can never judge upon this point.

If Declon. not sufft. court will permit it to be now amended. Amendment of a Declon

2. Burr. 1159.

Confession of a Lease is of a subsisting Term. *See the Case. & the Authorities there cited.*[11]

2. Strange 807.

Declon amended after Verd. though nothing to amend by.[12]

Eject. can not be amended—because original process—vi Ld. Rayd.

2. Burrow 1161.

Date of Demise impossible—said by Dennison to be only a Title defectively set out.[13]

Lee, in reply.

Admits Eject. fictitious action, yet hath it's essentials. A particular period of Time must be set forth as the Term, as a guide to Jury in assessing Damages.

An impossible day considered as the day of delivery—So if there be no date.

☞ Though a confession of a Lease subsisting at the time of plea pleaded—yet this no confession of a subsisting Term at the Time of the Verdict.

True that Intendment will go as far as possible to support a verdict—but it shall not be carried so far as to do injustice.

If Amendment by inserting the Comt. of Term were admitted he may go back 20. years, & recover mesne profits accordingly.

4. Burrow 2449. will not warrant present application on part of Appellees.[14] There Amendt. made because plts wd. have been barred by a fine & recovery.

2. Burr. 1162. Comes nearer to support the Appellees than any other.[15] But there a subsisting Lease con-

Run: 98. 99. strued to commence from time of delivery—but here is no Lease, nor time of Delivery laid in Declon—*Lease need not be proved.* R. 98. 99.[16]

Cur. adv. Oct. 24. 1788.

Marshall, next day.

Cowper 841. Amendment after writ Error, by Court of Error. *See the Case.*[17]

vi. Chambers v. Williams
Farrar & Randolph — In this Court.[18]
Irby &. Taft

Judgt. reversed ⅌ Cur. unanimously.

MS, Tucker-Coleman Papers, ViW. Endorsed: "arg. Oct. 24. 1788. Judgt. reversed, Oct. 28. 88."

1. On the action of ejectment, see Case No. 11.

2. Charles Runnington, *A Treatise on the Action of Ejectment* (London, 1786), 96: "But where the limitation in the lease is altogether uncertain, the plaintiff cannot recover; because where the commencement of the lease is uncertain, the lease is void in itself, and then the plaintiff cannot have a title."

3. Ibid., 103–5. This passage discussed the amendment of declarations in

ejectment. According to Runnington, "If the cause be adjourned for difficulty into the *Exchequer Chamber*, since the court itself delays the plaintiff, they will upon a rule delivered to the defendant to shew cause to the contrary, enlarge the term, unless the defendant can shew very good cause to the contrary." He concluded that "at present, the general rule of amending declarations in ejectment seems to be, that no such declaration can be amended *before* appearance; nor *afterwards*, except in matter of *form*."

4. The case cited by Runnington was Doe, Lessee of Hardman, v. Pilkington and Russel, 4 Burr. 2449, 98 Eng. Rep. 284 (K.B., 1769). In this case Lord Mansfield declared that "an ejectment is a mere fictitious action. The demise is mere matter of form: it does not exist. It is not like a real title."

5. Pugh v. Duke of Leeds, 2 Cowp. 714, 98 Eng. Rep. 1323 (K.B., 1777).

6. Runnington, *Treatise on Ejectment*, 29–30: "It is said to be the design of the law in this action, to have the thing demanded so particularly specified, that the sheriff may certainly know what to give the possession of, if the plaintiff should recover; for the judgment is in order to execution, and the judgment would be vain if execution could not be had of the thing specifically demanded: and yet, at this day, the practice is for the sheriff to deliver possession, according to the direction of the plaintiff, who therein acts at his peril." In the margin Runnington cited the cases of Cottingham v. King, 1 Burr. 629, 97 Eng. Rep. 481 (K.B., 1758); and Connor v. West, 4 Burr. 2673, 98 Eng. Rep. 404 (K.B., 1770).

7. Runnington, *Treatise on Ejectment*, 125.

8. See n. 4.

9. Runnington, *Treatise on Ejectment*, 91 (citing Pugh v. Duke of Leeds [see n. 5]): "This distinction . . . between *the date* and *the day of the date*, was lately abolished by the court of *King's Bench*, who very justly determined, after great deliberation, that both these expressions should be construed indifferently, either inclusively or exclusively, so as to give effect to the deed in which they are used." The reference to Douglas is apparently to the reporter of that name, though the case cited was reported by Cowper.

10. Runnington, *Treatise on Ejectment*, 95; Darrel v. Middleton, Cro. Eliz. 606, 78 Eng. Rep. 848 (K.B., 1598); Hall v. Denbigh, Cro. Eliz. 773, 78 Eng. Rep. 1003 (K.B., 1600).

11. Small, ex dimiss: Baker, v. Cole and Skinner, 2 Burr. 1159, 97 Eng. Rep. 765 (K.B., 1761).

12. Muttit v. Denny, 2 Str. 807, 93 Eng. Rep. 861 (K.B., 1728).

13. In the case cited in n. 11 Judge Denison remarked: "To be sure, you cannot alter the title, if it be defective: but this is only a title defectively or improperly set out. There can be no doubt but that a proper title was proved at the trial" (2 Burr. 1161, 97 Eng. Rep. 766).

14. See n. 4

15. See nn. 11, 13.

16. Runnington, *Treatise on Ejectment*, 98–99: "Though by the modern practice the plaintiff is not obliged to prove the lease mentioned in the declaration, for that is confessed by the rule, and by that means the mischief of any variance, between the lease declared on and the lease produced and

proved on the trial, is avoided,—which was a danger the plaintiff was exposed to, and often miscarried in, by the old method of proceeding;—yet in the modern practice the plaintiff must take care to declare on such a lease as suits with his lessee's title."

17. Vicars v. Haydon, Lessee of Carroll, 2 Cowp. 841, 98 Eng. Rep. 1391 (K.B., 1778). The court after affirming a judgment in ejectment from Ireland amended the declaration by enlarging the term.

18. Tucker did not report these cases.

28. Franks v. Ladds
Argument
24–28 October 1788

Appeal from N.K.[1] Debt on Bond dated Feb. 6. 1777. Plea payt. penalty of the Bond £40. Verd. that Deft *doth owe £34.7.0.*[2]—which overgoes the value of the penalty, which by the Scale is £26.13.4. only.[3]

NB. The Condn. of the Bond (of which there was no oyer) was for payt. of a sum of money by Instalments—whereas Declon. states it as due presently.[4]

Duval for Appellant—Contended these Errors fatal.

Marshall Contra—The Court will if possible mould this verdict so as to support the Judgement. The Jury have calculated Interest on £26.13.4. the Amt. of the £40. according to the Scale, & have added that Interest by way of Damages. The Court will understand the Verdict as giving the Interest by way of Damages.

Parker, T——, Fleming, Lyons, Carrington,

The Court were of opinion that the Judgt. was erroneous in this only, that the Judgt. should have been entered for the penalty, to be discharged by the payment of the value of the £34.7.0. as reduced by the Scale; saying the Verdict though in the present Tense & delivered in 1783. amounts only to saying that Deft *hath not paid*, £34.7. part of the Debt—which sum must be supposed to

relate to the same kind of money as the plt has declared for, viz. paper money.
Judgt. Oct. 28. 1788.
Mercer for reversing in toto.

MS, Tucker-Coleman Papers, ViW.

1. New Kent.

2. The proper verdict for the plaintiff in debt on a bond, where the plea was payment, was that the defendant had not paid the debt alleged in the declaration, that is, the penal sum. Judgment would then be entered for the principal and interest (see Case No. 9, editorial note).

3. The bond was executed after 1 Jan. 1777 and therefore fell within the 1781 statute establishing a scale of depreciation for paper money. The sum of £26.13.4 was calculated by dividing £40 by 1½, which was the ratio of paper to specie in Feb. 1777 (Hening, *Statutes*, X, 472). Whether the plaintiff had a remedy at law in cases where the principal and interest exceeded the penal sum seemed to be an unsettled question at the time. In the early nineteenth century the Virginia Court of Appeals held that the jury could give damages for the detention of the debt equal to the difference between the penal sum and the full amount of the principal and interest (Bacon, *Abridgment* [1st Am. ed.], V, 156; Robinson, *Practice*, I, 364).

4. Had oyer been demanded the bond would have been entered on the record, and the defendant could take advantage of any variance between the declaration and the instrument (see Case No. 3, Doc. II, n. 1).

29. Adams v. Pickett and Currie
Argument
23–24 June 1789

On a Case referred from the Ct of Chany.[1] The Question for the opo. of the Court was—whether, a bond for 1000 lbs of Tobo. being executed when Tobo. worth 18/. and discharged by another bond for £18. when Tobo. was at 36/. ℔ 100, the latter bond was an usurious contract.

Virga Laws 256. Marshall—the word *Exchange* in the Act of usury comprehends this Case, founded on Currency of Tobo.[2]

Where principal & Int. are put in *hazard* there is no injury by taking more than common Interest (as for Example Bottomree & respa. bonds.)[3]

Cowper 793.

If the contract be a Loan, no shift or device can take it out of the Statute.[4]

Baker, contra.

1. Lutw. 273.
Sid: 27. 1. Do. 182.
Lex mar: 363.
Jenk: 249.
Cro: Jas. 253.
2: Lev: 7.
2: Strange 816. 1243.

An usurious contract must be so, *at its commencement.*

The word *Exchange* is in the Statute of usury.

No usury unless there be a *Loan*[5]—Qu: he refers to the Act.

2: Str: 816. Rex v Upton. an Indt. for usury—mo. in arr: of Judgt. that it was only a corrupt agreement. Judgt. arr.

2. Str: 1243. Change of a note. *See the Cases.*[6]

Douglas 708.

Douglas 708. States fully what is & what is not usury.[7]

[Extract from Casebook]

June 24. 1789.

This was a Case from the Chancery, stated for the opinion of the court, in these words—viz: "A Bond for 1000. lbs of Tobo. was executed when that Commodity was 18/. ℔ 100. lbs. another is executed for the payt. of £18. when Tobo. was worth 36/. ℔ 100. lbs. payable in twelve months after the date. Whether this latter be usurious is referred by the Judge to the general Court for their opinion to be certified thereon."

℔ Parker, Cary, Tyler & Tucker, dissentientibus
Mercer & Bullitt
The contract on the second Bond is usurious, being an Exchange within the Act.[8]

MS and Casebook, Tucker-Coleman Papers, ViW. MS of report of arguments accompanied by Tucker's opinion, which is here omitted.

1. In Virginia the High Court of Chancery could refer "any matter of law to the general court, for their opinion to be certified thereon" (Hening, *Statutes*, XII, 768).

2. JM referred to the 1748 Virginia statute of usury, which provided that every person who "shall upon any contract . . . take, accept, and receive, by way or means, of any corrupt bargain, loan, exchange, shift, or interest, of

any monies, wares, merchandize, or other thing, or things, whatsoever, or by any deceitful way or means, or by any covin, device, or deceitful conveyance . . . above the sum of five pounds for the forbearing of one hundred pounds, for a year . . . shall forfeit and lose . . . the double value of the monies, wares, merchandizes, and other things so lent, bargained, exchanged, or shifted" (Hening, *Statutes*, VI, 102). JM's page reference was to the 1769 revisal (*Acts of Assembly of Virginia*). The assembly had recently (1786) enacted a new usury law (Hening, *Statutes*, XII, 337).

3. Bottomry and respondentia bonds pledged a ship and its cargo as security for a loan of money to carry out a voyage. The lender on such bonds received nothing if the ship and cargo were lost but was repaid with high interest (exceeding the legal rate) if the voyage ended safely.

4. JM paraphrased counsel's argument in Jestons v. Brooke, 2 Cowp. 793, 795, 98 Eng. Rep. 1365, 1366 (K.B., 1778): "If the contract is a loan, and the intention is to get more than legal interest, no shift or contrivance can take it out of the statute."

5. Wyndham Beawes, *Lex Mercatoria Redivivus, or a Complete Code of Commercial Law* (6th ed.; 2 vols.; Dublin, 1795), I, 400: "There can be no *usury* without a loan; and the court hath distinguished between a bargain and a loan." Beawes cited Yeoman v. Barstow, 1 Lut. 273, 125 Eng. Rep. 143 (C.P., 1701); and Soome v. Gleen, 1 Sid. 27, 82 Eng. Rep. 949 (K.B., 1658). In Rowe v. Bellaseys, 1 Sid. 182, 82 Eng. Rep. 1044 (K.B., 1664), the court held that the contract in question was not usurious but a purchase of an annuity.

6. Barnes v. Wolwitch, Jenk. 249, 145 Eng. Rep. 176 (Ex., 1603); Fountain v. Grymes, Cro. Jac. 253, 79 Eng. Rep. 216 (K.B., 1609); and The King v. Drury, 2 Lev. 7, 83 Eng. Rep. 427 (K.B., 1671), were cases in which the contract was ruled not to be usurious. In Rex v. Upton, 2 Str. 816, 93 Eng. Rep. 868 (K.B., 1728), after a verdict on an indictment for usury, judgment was arrested on the ground that the defendants had made only a corrupt agreement, without any loan or excessive interest. In Massa v. Dauling, 2 Str. 1243, 93 Eng. Rep. 1158 (K.B., 1745), a contract was held to be a loan rather than a purchase of notes and therefore usurious as exceeding the legal rate of interest.

7. Lowe v. Waller, 2 Doug. 736 (Tucker cited an earlier edition), 99 Eng. Rep. 470 (K.B., 1781). In this case a lender furnished goods rather than advanced cash to the borrower, who then sold the goods. The court held that if the security given by the borrower was made payable at a future day for a sum exceeding the value of the goods and the legal rate of interest, then this was a usurious loan.

Immediately below his summary of the arguments, Tucker wrote some memoranda to himself on the questions involved in this case. He subsequently wrote out an opinion, which years later he published in an appendix to his edition of Blackstone. He contended that the second bond in this case was an evasion of the statute of usury. Reviewing the English cases, Tucker distinguished between transactions in which there was a genuine risk, or contingency, and those in which the risk "was merely colourable." Where the reward was for risk, he observed, there was no usury even though it exceeded the legal rate of interest; but where the reward was for "forbearance" (payment at a future day) only, then the contract was usurious. Although in Virginia tobacco was "both a vendible commodity, and very frequently a medium of exchange," Tucker concluded that the transaction in this instance was clearly a loan of money, not a bargain for the purchase of tobacco. The first bond was evidence that the real value of the debt was £9. Executing a second bond worth £18 in discharge of the first was, in Tucker's words, "a *shift* with a view to the obtaining a greater interest for the forbearance of a loan than the statute allows" (Tucker, *Blackstone's Commentaries*, II, App., Note F, 106–11 [quotations at 107, 108, 111]).

For another case of JM's concerning usury, see Price v. Campbell, 2 Call 110 (1799). The question in this case was whether the drawing of a bill of exchange that would almost certainly come back protested (and therefore carry 10 percent interest) was a device for evading the statute of usury. Tucker commented briefly on this case (*Blackstone's Commentaries*, II, App., 112).

8. In the margin Tucker noted that on 26 June the court on motion ordered a new argument to take place at the next term. The final disposition of the case is not known, as Tucker himself noted in his edition of Blackstone: "The Editor is not acquainted with the decision of the chancellor, in this case; he has some reason to believe that no opinion upon it was given by the judges of the general court, officially" (ibid., 111 n.).

30. Gouldman v. Tayloe's Executors
Argument
23–25 June 1789

In Detinue. Sp'l verdict finds[1]

1. F.G.[2] father of plt being siezed of certain Lands, supposed to be intailed & 2. Slaves, sold to J. Tayloe all the Land within certain bounds containing by estimation 50. with clause of warranty—& covenants for quiet enjoyt. &c. & for further assurances. But Whereas Grantors title is supposed to be intail, he gives to his eldest & second son, or whoever the Land wod. descend to, two Slaves (one of them the Slave in contest) to the now plt. And in Case such person to whom the negroes shall go by virtue of this Deed shall interrupt Tayloe, then he gives the negroes to Tayloe. duly ac-

knowledged & recorded. This was a Deed of Feofft. & Livery of siezin proved.[3]

2. That E.G. eldest son of F.G. died in his father's Lifetime, & left plt his heir at law.[4]

3. That[5]

Taylor

3. Ba. Abr: 511.
Ib: 510.

A demand & delivery of part an acknowledgment of title

Col. Tayloe to be considered as a Trustee.[6]

3. Salk. 422. 423.
3. Ba. 518.

The Act of Limitation was neither *pleaded* nor *given* in *Evidence*,—If it had possibly plt might have admitted it by other Tistimony—Court cannot take notice of it on view of the facts.[7]

Royal Assent not obtained until 1773.[8] Suit brot. in 1771.

Marshall—Contra.[9]

1. The Deed does not convey a title. (examine it.) it is not *found* that he was heir in Tail of F.G.
2. No possion. in Defts found in spl verdict. (but as Exors.) Qu.[10]
3. It is evident Jury meant to find the Act of Limitation.

4th. Col: Tayloe no trustee—for Slaves never pass'd to him under the last deed.[11]

Hannah et al v Davis.
Qu: a Case in Gen. Court among my papers
1. Salk. 278.

Nelson—

1. Slaves not found with sufft certainty—they are said only to be *descended* from Bess—but whether *before* or *after* Date of the Deed is not found.[12]
2. Facts set forth in spl. verd. shew operation of Act of Limitation (Qu: a Case on this point also.)[13]

If a person may be concluded by a Deed he may be benefited by it—this r[em]ains a consideration in the D.

[Extract from Casebook]

June 25. 1789.

Detinue for slaves—along special verdict—which, together with the Arguments at Bar are among my papers.

The Question turn'd upon two points.

1. Whether the plt could take an Interest in Slaves by a Conveyance to which he was not a party, though named therein.

2. Whether the Act of Limitations, being neither pleaded, nor given in Evidence (for ought that appears in the Verdict) the court are bound to take notice of the length of time which has elapsed since defts possession commenced.

1. On the first point, the court on perusal of this Deed (see the Tenor of it in my papers) thought that the plt did take an Interest under this Deed.[14]

2. On the second point, they thought that they were not bound to take notice of the length of Time, unless the Act of Lim: had been pleaded or found expressly in the verdict.

Judgt. for plt. for the Slaves & £85. Damages & costs.[15]

Tucker, mentioned a Difficulty which occurred to him as to the mode of entering up the Judgt. for Damages whether to be levied de bonis testatoris, or de bonis propriis.

vi: Bull: ni: pr: 50. 51.

Bullitt & Tyler, thought it must be for the Damages to be levied of their own goods.[16] Absents. Mercer & Parker.

Tucker & Cary—Contra.

Cur: adv:

Steptoe v. Lee &c Exors. of Carr. April Term 1768.

Mr. Brown[17] shewed a precedent of a Judgt. in the Gen. Court April 1768. where the Damages & costs are to be de bonis testatoris if any—otherwise the costs de bonis propriis.

Mr. Henry who doubted before now assented to the opinion of Tucker & Cary. Wherefore

The Judgt. was entered according to that precedent.

MS and Casebook, Tucker-Coleman Papers, ViW. MS endorsed: "Arguments &c. Judgt. for plt." Copy of special verdict filed with MS.

1. The full title of this case, as indicated on Tucker's copy of the special verdict, was Thomas Gouldman v. Ralph Wormeley, Mann Page, and Warner Lewis, executors of John Tayloe. The special verdict was returned in the General Court on 12 Oct. 1785. Tucker's copy of the special verdict is endorsed "For Mr. Marshall."

2. Francis Gouldman.

3. This deed was executed to John Tayloe, father of the defendants' testator, in July 1724.

4. Edward Gouldman died in 1726, leaving his brother Thomas Gouldman (the plaintiff) his heir at law.

5. At this point Tucker left a blank space of about ten lines, apparently intending to complete his summary of the special verdict at a later time.

6. Bacon, *Abridgment* (5th ed.), III, 510–11. Taylor, representing the plaintiff, was attempting to get the case out of the statute of limitations. A trust, said Bacon, did not come under the statute.

7. In Virginia the limitation for bringing an action of detinue was five years. The special verdict found that the testator John Tayloe "was in quiet possession" of the disputed slaves from 1764, when the plaintiff first demanded them, until 1771, when the first suit was instituted. According to Bacon, one who wished to take advantage of the statute of limitations had to plead it positively and could not give it in evidence (*Abridgment* [5th ed.], III, 518). Tucker's citation to Salkeld is apparently an error, as Bacon cites in support of this point 2 Salk. 422, 423. The reprint of Salkeld in *English Reports* is of the 1795 edition, which has a different pagination from the edition cited by Bacon. The proper citation to the 1795 edition is 3 Salk. 227–29, 91 Eng. Rep. 792–93.

8. Another fact recorded in the special verdict was that an act of assembly had passed in 1732 confirming certain entailed lands—the same as those deeded by Gouldman to John Tayloe in 1724—in fee simple to John Tayloe. The special verdict further stated that the royal assent was not given to this act until 1 Nov. 1773 (see Hening, *Statutes*, IV, 378–79).

9. JM represented Tayloe's executors, from whom he received a payment "in full" of £11.6 in Apr. 1789 (*PJM*, II, 359; "Tayloe" is there erroneously rendered as "Taylor").

10. In detinue the plaintiff had to prove actual possession in the defendant. The special verdict stated that the disputed slaves were in the possession of the defendants "as executors of John Tayloe the son at the time of bringing this suit."

11. As stated in the special verdict, Francis Gouldman executed a second deed in May 1725, conveying four slaves to John Tayloe, including the two mentioned in the first deed of 1724.

12. The two slaves mentioned in the 1724 deed were Bess and Sue. Around the year 1764, according to the special verdict, the plaintiff Thomas Gouldman demanded from John Tayloe the son (testator of the defendants) all slaves descended from Bess and Sue. Tayloe delivered the descendants of Sue to Gouldman but not those of Bess. In 1771 Gouldman brought suit for

the slaves descended from Bess. For the case of Hannah v. Davis, mentioned in the margin, see *PJM*, I, 218–21. This was a suit for freedom by slaves claiming descent from an Indian woman, who was also named Bess.

13. Tucker probably had in mind the case of Calvert v. Shropshire, also an action of detinue for a slave, which had been decided earlier at this term of the General Court. In that case, too, the anonymous case in 1 Salk. 278, 91 Eng. Rep. 243 (N.P., Hertford, 1690) was cited to show that the act of limitations, though not pleaded, could be given in evidence under the general issue in detinue (see Case No. 23 and n. 5).

14. Tucker wrote his opinion on this point on his copy of the special verdict: "This Deed would operate as a Discontinuance of said Estate & therefore the heir in tail might elect whether he will enter for the Discontinuance, or claim the Slaves. It is a covenant on the part of F.G. (poss[ess]ion not appearing to have been delivered of the Slaves) to stand siezed for the use of plt, to which Covt. Defts ancestor was a party."

15. The judgment, as stated on the special verdict, was for six slaves valued at £380 and damages of £83.6.8.

16. Sir Francis Buller gives a brief summary of the action of detinue, though nothing is said on the specific question whether damages should be levied on the testator's goods (*de bonis testatoris*) or on the goods of the executor (*de bonis propriis*) (*An Introduction to the Law of Trials at Nisi Prius* [7th ed.; 1817; New York, 1979 reprint], 50–52).

17. John Brown, clerk of the General Court.

31. Mercer v. Beall
Argument
21 June 1791

in Covt.—Motion to set aside an Award, made in pursuance of an order of Ref. made in Gen. Court Novr. Term 1790, whereby the parties, inter alia "agreed that the Arbrs. or any three of them may award in such manner as they may deem just & equitable without regard to the strict rules of Law, & that their Award shall be the Judgt. of the Court, & bind the parties &c.["]

The Arbitrators made their Award and returned the Same into Court.

Ronald ꝑ the plt. stated the following objections to the award.

1st. That it is such an award as a Court of Law cannot make a Judgt. of Law; contain-

3. Bl. Com: 16.

ing an award to convey Lands.—he cited 3d. Bl: Com: page 16—the right of real property can not now be the subject of an Award—but a Conveyance of Lands may be awarded, & that in Case of refusal an Action would lie on the Bond, *but not on the Award itself.* 1. Ld. Ray. 114.[1] Things in the realty may be *submitted,* but can not be *recovered* upon the *award.*[2]

1. Ld. Ray. 114.
1. Bacon 149. 141.
Danv. Abr: 515. 516.

2d. It awards a matter not submitted to the parties—this was an Action of Covt. for Damages for not allotting certain Lands. The suit brought by plt *dissaffirmd* the contract; (since had he wish'd to carry it into Exo. I presume he would have brought a Bill in Chancery).[3] The Action sounded altogether in Damages. 3. Burr: 1637. No Excuse can be admitted for not performing an express covenant.[4]

3. Burr. 1637.

3d. The Award is conditional—Giving Deft an *election* to do a certain Act, or to pay Damages. 1. Ld. Raymd. 247. An election given in an award is ill. 1 Roll. 271. there cited.[5] Award can not be made on Condition Shephard Touchstone 116. 1. Bacon 147. s.p.[6]

Hardress 45.
1. Ld. Ray. 247.
1. Roll. Rep. 271.
Shep. Touch: 116.
1. Ba. 147.
5. Co: 78.

Wickham—Contra.

1st. Objection—not answered.

2d. Objection—part vicious doth not avoid the whole—1. Bacon 148.[7] Here is an award as to some matters within the submission & for those it is good.

8. Co. 98. cited.

3d. Objection—This is not an election, but something in nomine pœnæ, imposed on Deft on failure to comply with the award.

Marshall—on the same side.[8]

Suppose the award had gone no farther than that part which awards that plt shall take nothing by his Bill, would not this have been final—or if a verdict in the same Terms, had been rendered, would not the Court have rejected the rest as surplusage.[9]

MS, Tucker-Coleman Papers, ViW. Endorsed: "On mo: to set aside an award." Tucker's opinion, filed with attorneys' arguments, omitted.

1. Blackstone, *Commentaries*, III, 16: "But the right of real property cannot thus pass by a mere award: which subtility in point of form (for it is now

reduced to nothing else) had it's rise from feodal principles; for, if this had been permitted, the land might have been aliened collusively without the consent of the superior. Yet doubtless an arbitrator may now award a conveyance or a release of lands; and it will be a breach of the arbitration-bond to refuse compliance." Blackstone cited Marks v. Marriot, 1 Raym. Ld. 114, 91 Eng. Rep. 972 (K.B., 1696).

2. The page references to Bacon, *Abridgment* (5th ed.) are to the general section on "Arbitrament and Award," though the specific passage Tucker had in mind is not clear. The other reference is Knightley D'Anvers, *A General Abridgment of the Common Law* . . . (3 vols.; London, 1705-37).

3. Chancery was the proper court to bring a suit for the specific performance of a contract.

4. Shubrick v. Salmond, 3 Burr. 1637, 97 Eng. Rep. 1022 (K.B., 1765), held that an express covenant shall bind to performance.

5. In Hunter and Younger v. Bennison, Hardres 45, 145 Eng. Rep. 372–73 (Ex., 1655), Hardres, attorney, argued that an award was void because, among other reasons, it was not definitive but conditional. In Freeman v. Bernard, 1 Raym. Ld. 247, 91 Eng. Rep. 1061 (K.B., 1697), the plaintiff's attorney contended that an award was void for uncertainty and that an "election given in an award is ill," citing Lumley v. Hutton, 1 Rolle 271, 81 Eng. Rep. 483 (K.B., 1615).

6. William Sheppard, *Touchstone of Common Assurances* (5th ed.; London, 1784). This was probably the edition cited by Tucker. Bacon, *Abridgment* (5th ed.), I, 147: "A conditional Award not good, because not final to determine Matters in Difference." Samon's Case, 5 Co. Rep. 78, 77 Eng. Rep. 172 (K.B., 1594), was adjudged against the plaintiff because the award was void for uncertainty.

7. Bacon, *Abridgment* (5th ed.), I, 148: "It is an established Rule, that an Award may be good in Part, though void as to other Parts of it." Bacon cited Baspole's Case, 8 Co. Rep. 98, 77 Eng. Rep. 625 (K.B., 1610).

8. JM, representing Samuel Beall, received two fees in this case: £12 in Feb. 1790 and £33 in Mar. 1791 (*PJM*, II, 383, 415). On Beall, see Case No. 35.

9. In his opinion Tucker agreed with plaintiff's counsel that the award should be set aside. He also noted that Judge Tyler concurred in this opinion.

VI. Selected Arguments in the Virginia Court of Appeals

Editorial Note

The Court of Appeals, like all the superior courts of Virginia, was created by the constitution of 1776. First organized under an act of May 1779 (an organizing act of the preceding session of October 1778 never went into effect), this court had no separate judges but was composed of the three judges of the High Court of Chancery (who had precedence over the others), the five judges of the General Court, and the three judges of the Court of Admiralty, any five of whom made a quorum. It had appellate jurisdiction in cases brought by appeal and writ of error to reverse decrees of the High Court of Chancery, judgments of the General Court, and sentences of the Court of Admiralty where the matter in controversy was valued at fifty pounds or involved a freehold or franchise. It met for six days twice a year.[1]

The appellate court as thus constituted—it was later referred to as the "old" or "first" Court of Appeals—remained in existence for a decade. In December 1788 the assembly established a separate Court of Appeals as part of a general reorganization of the judiciary. The new Court of Appeals was the direct result of a protest by the judges of the former court against the district court law of the preceding year. This act added to the existing duties of the judges by requiring them to attend the district courts. At their spring term in May 1788, the judges refused to give effect to the act, setting forth their opinion of its unconstitutionality in a "Remonstrance" addressed to the legislature. Their chief objection to the law was that it threatened the independence of the judiciary by imposing heavy new burdens without a corresponding increase in salary. For Edmund Pendleton, author of the "Remonstrance" and presiding judge of the court from its inception, the law would have effectively ousted him from office (by the constitution judges held office during good behavior), since he was too infirm to withstand the continual travel to different courts. The assembly accordingly backed down; at the succeeding session it amended the district court law and separated the Court of Appeals from the other superior courts.[2]

The new Court of Appeals was composed of five judges, with three making a quorum. It also met twice a year (April and October were the terms eventually settled upon), but unlike the old court it was authorized to sit for an indefinite period.[3] The judges elected by the

1. Hening, *Statutes*, X, 89–92.

2. Mays, *Pendleton*, II, 273–74; "Cases of the Judges of the Court of Appeals," 4 Call 135.

3. Hening, *Statutes*, XII, 764–66; XIII, 405–11.

EDMUND PENDLETON

Miniature by William Mercer. *Courtesy of Virginia Historical Society*

assembly to serve on this court were Edmund Pendleton and John Blair from the High Court of Chancery, and Paul Carrington, Peter Lyons, and William Fleming, senior judges of the General Court. George Wythe continued to sit on the High Court of Chancery, now reduced to a single chancellor. Four of the Court of Appeals judges—Pendleton, Carrington, Lyons, and Fleming—served throughout the period of Marshall's practice. The other seat was occupied successively by Blair (soon to be appointed to the federal Supreme Court), James Mercer, Henry Tazewell, and finally, Spencer Roane. Roane, at thirty-three the youngest of the judges by more than a quarter of a century, began his illustrious career on the supreme bench of Virginia in April 1795.[4]

As presiding judge (called "The President"), Pendleton was the dominant figure on the appellate bench while Marshall was at the bar. "He was the mind and the voice of the Court," wrote Nathaniel Beverley Tucker a generation after Pendleton's death. "If he went wrong they all went wrong together, for without him they could not go at all." Tucker surely exaggerated, but even contemporaries acknowledged his eminence, likening him to the great English jurist Lord Mansfield, whose judicial opinions Pendleton held in "very high respect . . . as if he had an innate sense of congeniality." Impatient with the technicalities and formalities of the law, Pendleton "always made it his study to ascertain the very right and justice of every case, that came before him, and then to hunt up law to support it." If not learned in the law, he nevertheless possessed a deep knowledge of its substance. "Perfectly acquainted with the statute and common law, as well as with the doctrines of equity," observed lawyer and reporter Daniel Call, "he knew, remarkably well, how to apply them to the habits and exigencies of this country; which he understood not only from observation and experience; but almost by intuition." Give him a case in which justice was indifferent to the outcome, said Tucker, "and nothing could exceed the profundity of his researches, or the ability with which he collected and applied his authorities."[5] From this very model of a judge, the future chief justice of the United States learned a style of leadership in which the court most often spoke through the presiding judge and a practical approach to the art of judging that emphasized substance over technicalities.

All that remains of the manuscript records and papers of the

4. "Biographical Sketch of the Judges of the Court of Appeals," 4 Call vii-xxix. See also Mays, *Pendleton*, II, 297–99.

5. B. Tucker, *Principles of Pleading*, 57–59 (passage reproduced in Mays, *Pendleton*, II, 279–80). For Call's comments, see his "Biographical Sketch of the Judges," 4 Call vii–ix.

Court of Appeals are the order books, which somehow escaped destruction in the fire of 1865. These are complete from the beginning of the court in 1779 through the period of Marshall's practice. No longer extant are the appellate case files, containing the record of the case from the lower court and accompanying petitions and writs, and the briefs filed by the attorneys. By law counsel were required to submit a "clear and concise state of the case . . . with the points intended to be insisted upon." These statements were to be signed by counsel and printed up for delivery to each of the judges in time for their consideration before the hearing.[6]

Much of this rich storehouse of original material, along with the notes and memoranda of the lawyers and judges, is fortunately preserved in the published reports of cases in the Court of Appeals. Marshall's cases are to be found in the reports of Bushrod Washington and Daniel Call, his colleagues at the bar of this court. These reports were not available to Marshall himself until the very end of his practice. The first volume of reports, compiled by Washington, was published in 1798 and included cases from October 1790 to October 1794. A second volume embracing the period from October 1794 through October 1796 followed in 1799. Call (whose wife was Marshall's sister-in-law) assumed the task of reporting after Washington's appointment to the Supreme Court in 1798. He published three volumes in 1801, 1802, and 1805, which reported cases from April 1797 through October 1803. Call appended to his third volume some reports prepared by Marshall of cases in 1790 that had not been reported by Washington.[7] Years later, in 1833, Call brought out three more volumes of reports. The fourth volume published for the first time cases in the old Court of Appeals that existed between 1779 and 1789, as well as unreported cases in the new court from 1789 to 1803. (The fifth and sixth volumes contained the most important unreported cases from 1803 down to 1818 along with several cases in the U.S. Circuit Court.)

For the greater part of his practice Marshall had to rely on his own notes to keep abreast of the latest rulings of the Court of Appeals. Indeed, while the cases remained unreported and unpublished, the lawyers and judges had to be their own "reporters," jotting down the facts of the case, summarizing the arguments of counsel, and, most important, preserving a memorandum (or perhaps obtaining a copy) of the court's opinion. As Washington noted in the preface to his first volume, his reports were simply an extension of the notes he kept for his own use, "without any view to a publication." All that remains of

6. Hening, *Statutes*, X, 92; XIII, 410.

7. See Case No. 33, editorial note. No MSS of these reports have survived.

Marshall's "reports," which must have been voluminous, are the fifteen borrowed by Call for his third volume and one for his fourth.

Marshall's arguments in 125 cases between 1786 and 1800 are preserved in Washington's two volumes and in the first four volumes of Call. Most of these are concentrated in the years 1793 (17), 1794 (24), 1795 (20), and 1799 (24). Only two arguments are reported for 1797, when Marshall went abroad on his diplomatic mission, and just one for 1800, when he served in the Adams administration. The arguments vary in length from a few sentences to fifteen printed pages. The longer arguments were most likely written down by Marshall himself either in draft or outline, though no manuscripts survive.[8]

By all accounts Marshall enjoyed great success in the appellate tribunal, though there is no objective way of measuring how successful he was. A record of wins and losses is a crude if not meaningless yardstick of performance. The best lawyers take on the most difficult cases, for the prestige to be gained in losing outweighs that to be gained in winning a simple cause. Marshall, as it happened, won slightly more of his reported cases than he lost, a record that was apparently no better or worse than that of any other lawyer who regularly attended this court.[9] When he represented the appellee (the party who won below), which he did in a small majority of his cases, his winning percentage was higher than his total average. This is not surprising, since it is usually easier to persuade an appellate court to uphold than to overturn a judgment or decree. For the same reason, he lost more cases than he won as attorney for the appellant (the party who lost below).

The reports of Washington and Call furnish abundant proofs of Marshall's outstanding professional abilities and confirm contemporary estimates that placed him in the top rank of the Virginia bar. He did not occupy this eminence by himself, however, but shared it with a half-dozen or so practitioners who along with him monopolized the business of the Court of Appeals during the 1790s. The bar of this court was reputed "to be the most enlightened and able on the continent."[10] Its leading lights all possessed in more or less equal measure a sound knowledge and understanding of the law, along with highly developed skills in the lawyerly arts of stating a case, of applying and distinguishing precedents, and of interpreting statutes.

8. The reports contain approximately thirty additional cases identified as JM's in which no argument was reported. See the Appendix for a complete list of his reported cases.

9. A sampling of the reported cases of John Wickham (another eminent counsellor) during the 1790s reveals approximately the same record as JM's.

10. William Wirt, *The Letters of the British Spy* (1803; Upper Saddle River, N.J., 1970 reprint, from 8th ed.), 153.

In this arena Marshall most often found himself in combat with John Wickham and Edmund Randolph. These three were the generally acknowledged leaders of the bar.[11] Eight years Marshall's junior, Wickham was a New Yorker who had been imprisoned in Virginia with his parents during the Revolution. He later studied law at the College of William and Mary and began to practice in Williamsburg. He moved to Richmond in 1790, was admitted to practice in the Court of Appeals, and began his rapid ascent to the top of the profession. As early as 1789 Marshall had recommended Wickham as "a young man of great cleaverness."[12] At the age of forty, in 1803, Wickham was described as combining "a greater diversity of talents and acquirements, than any other at the bar of Virginia." He had "a genius quick and fertile; a style pure and classick; a stream of perspicuous and beautiful elocution; an ingenuity which no difficulties can entangle, or embarrass; and a wit, whose vivid and brilliant coruscation, can gild and decorate the darkest subject."[13]

Randolph had left the bar in 1786 on his election as governor of the commonwealth, turning his practice over to Marshall. He returned briefly to the law after leaving this office, but again gave it up to serve in Washington's administration as attorney general and secretary of state. After resigning from federal service in 1795, he returned to Virginia and rebuilt his practice with great success. A man of wide reading and "of close and elaborate research," he had a reputation as an eloquent speaker, with a pleasant, musical voice. To William Wirt, who contrasted him unfavorably with Wickham and Marshall, Randolph too often buried his essential points beneath a copious flow of words.[14]

Among Marshall's other formidable adversaries in the appellate tribunal were John ("Jock") Warden, Andrew Ronald—both natives of Scotland—and Alexander Campbell. Warden was greatly respected for his talents, wit, and good humor, which more than compensated for his homely appearance. He was "one of the best read and worst featured, most good tempered and most ill formed; but among the most well informed members of the Richmond bar—his mind and body were a bundle of contrasts." Ronald represented the plaintiff in the British debt case of *Jones* v. *Walker* in 1791 (Case Number 12). Campbell joined Marshall in defense of the Virginia debtors in that case and in *Ware* v. *Hylton* (Case Number 13) and accompanied

11. John Taylor of Caroline would also have been accorded this honor had he not retired from the profession in 1790.

12. JM to Percival Butler, 16 Aug. 1789 (*PJM*, II, 36).

13. Wirt, *British Spy*, 168–69.

14. Ibid., 154–63. See also sketch by Benjamin Latrobe (Carter, *Latrobe Va. Journals*, I, 132–33).

him to the Supreme Court in February 1796 to argue the appeal of the latter case.[15] The reporters Washington and Call also belonged to the select circle of lawyers who had a large practice in the Court of Appeals.

Marshall lacked Wickham's versatility, and his oratory was inferior to Randolph's. His speeches were devoid of ornament and were frequently accompanied by awkward gestures. Yet he commanded attention by the cogency of his arguments, which progressed logically from initial premise through conclusion without a superfluous thought or word. "He possesses one original, and, almost, supernatural faculty," wrote Wirt, "the faculty of developing a subject by a single glance of his mind, and detecting at once, the very point on which every controversy depends. . . . Possessing while at the bar this intellectual elevation, which enabled him to look down and comprehend the whole ground at once, he determined immediately and without difficulty, on which side the question might be most advantageously approached and assailed. In a bad cause his art consisted in laying his premises so remotely from the point directly in debate, or else in terms so general and so specious, that the hearer, seeing no consequence which could be drawn from them, was just as willing to admit them as not; but his premises once admitted, the demonstration, however distant, followed as certainly, as cogently, as inevitably, as any demonstration in Euclid."[16]

Throughout all his cases, despite their great diversity of subjects, Marshall displayed a characteristic style of argumentation, one that he carried with him to the bench of the Supreme Court. Rigorously logical, analytical, and enumerative, his arguments, as Wirt suggested, reveal an almost mathematical structure. Invariably he began by resolving the case into two or more points, which he then proceeded to dispose of in proper order. He liked to frame his arguments so that if he lost on one point he could still prevail on another. Thus, in *Shermer* v. *Shermer's Executors* he began: "I shall contend 1st, that the principle is not true, and 2dly, if it were, still the case itself is not like the present." Marshall employed this opening, with variations, on numerous occasions.[17] Eschewing rhetorical flourishes, not "stopping to weave garlands of flowers, to hang in festoons around a favourite argument," he followed the straight and narrow path of

15. Samuel Mordecai, *Richmond in By-Gone Days* (Richmond, 1856), 81; E. Lee Shepard, "Sketches of the Old Richmond Bar: Andrew Ronald," *Richmond Quarterly*, III (1980), 38–41.

16. Wirt, *British Spy*, 117–18. See also Francis Walker Gilmer, *Sketches, Essays, and Translations* (Baltimore, 1828), 22–24; Carter, *Latrobe Va. Journals*, I, 133.

17. Case No. 5, Doc. VIII. For other examples in this volume, see Case No. 13, Doc. V; Case Nos. 40, 43.

logic, presenting his case like a geometric proof.[18] In one exceedingly complicated will construction case, for example, Marshall had to show that his clients' ancestor took an estate tail. The "proof" hung on the following logical structure:

> 1st, That upon authority, the male issue of the non-surviving sons of James must take before Muscoe.
> 2dly, That according to the intention of the testator, they must take before him.
> 3dly, That they must take by descent, and cannot take by purchase.
> 4thly, That if they take by descent, the estate must be in the ancestor, and therefore that James took an estate tail.[19]

The reports indicate that Marshall had a special knack for speaking in rebuttal. When paired with another lawyer on the same side, he almost never gave the opening statement but waited until the other party had presented its case. This suggests that he was quick on his feet, an effective counterpuncher in close legal combat. He showed great facility in meeting opposing counsel on his own ground and turning his case against him. If there was the slightest flaw in a tightly woven case, Marshall would detect it and proceed to unravel the fabric.

In plying his craft in the Virginia Court of Appeals, Marshall, like any lawyer, had one essential task: to find the rule or rules of law that governed his particular case and to apply them in a way that was persuasive to the judges. In some cases positive, or statute, law supplied these rules, but the principal source was the unwritten, or common, law of England, embodied in the voluminous reports of cases dating back to the sixteenth century. The political separation from Great Britain in 1776 did not—and could not, as a practical matter—mean the overthrow of English law and jurisprudence. An ordinance of the Virginia Convention of 1776 declared that "the common law of England, all the statutes or acts of parliament made in aid of the common law prior to the fourth year of the reign of James the first, and which are of a general nature, not local to that kingdom . . . shall be considered as in full force, until the same shall be altered by the legislative power of this colony." Important parliamentary statutes enacted after 1607 had been reenacted by successive colonial assemblies and so passed into the law of the new commonwealth in 1776. After 1776 the legislature began to move toward a comprehensive revision of the laws. In some instances it radically altered the com-

18. Wirt, *British Spy*, 119.
19. Roy v. Garnett, 2 Wash. 23 (1794).

mon law, notably by the abolition of entailed estates in 1776 and of the rule of primogeniture (inheritance by the eldest son) in the 1785 act "directing the course of descents."[20]

The great body of English law nevertheless remained intact in post-Revolutionary Virginia. Its rules and principles were the predominant authority relied upon in arguing and deciding cases until well into the nineteenth century. An indigenous Virginia law had begun to develop, to be sure, in the form of statutes that consciously departed from English models and in the adjudications of the Court of Appeals. Although each year brought a new harvest of laws and cases that Marshall and his colleagues cited with increasing frequency, the number of Virginia precedents remained but a small fraction of those cited from English sources.

This reliance on English precedents was not inconsistent with the spirit of exuberant independence that animated the Virginia Court of Appeals under Pendleton. Its judgments by no means reflected an unthinking, mechanical deference to English authority. The Virginia judges viewed their tribunal as equivalent to the superior courts of England and claimed the same privilege enjoyed by their English counterparts of detecting and correcting errors pronounced in earlier cases. A Pendleton no less than a Mansfield was capable of this task. English cases were the starting point for analysis or inquiry, but the judges felt free to follow or depart from them as reason dictated. Indeed, Pendleton and his brethren assumed that the common law embodied a standard of right reason, which every case had to meet before it could be considered as a controlling authority. English cases served as a source of enlightenment, an invaluable guide leading to the discovery of the true doctrines of the law. As Judge Roane declared in 1806, English precedents were not to be received as "binding authority" but "merely as affording evidence of the opinions of eminent Judges as to the doctrines in question, who have at least as great opportunities to form correct opinions as we have, and are influenced by no motives but such as are common to ourselves."[21]

If not deferential, the attitude of the Court of Appeals toward the authority of English cases was always respectful and somewhat conservative. Chancellor Wythe of the High Court of Chancery showed himself to be a bolder spirit, as shown by a case involving the construction of the will of William Aylett. The issue was whether Aylett's devise of "all my lands" in King William County included both his

20. Hening, *Statutes*, IX, 127, 226; XII, 138. The 1785 act, which took effect on 1 Jan. 1787, fundamentally changed the common law rules of descent (Tucker, *Blackstone's Commentaries*, II, App., Note B, 11–51). In most of JM's cases the old rules continued to apply.

21. Baring v. Reeder, 1 H. & M. 162.

freehold and leasehold (for a term of 999 years). The chancellor concluded that Aylett intended to devise them both, and his decree of May 1793 expressly overruled an English decision holding that a devise of this kind passed only the freehold lands. Declaring himself "emancipated from a servile obsequiousness to the authority of adjudications in some particular instances," Wythe was unwilling to "wait for leave from english judges . . . to reject an english determination," which he believed was "clumsy, bungling, [and] unfinished."[22] In the appeal to the Court of Appeals in October 1794, Marshall argued to uphold the chancellor's decree: "If the weight of authorities were out of the way, there could be no question, in cases of this sort, about the intention, which certainly is, to pass all the testator's land, whether freehold or leasehold." The court thought otherwise, however, and reversed the decree. Pendleton could "discover no such intention" on the part of the testator and insisted that the English decision had "become a rule of property, which the court cannot depart from, without disturbing perhaps many titles, enjoyed under this long established principle."[23]

Marshall's reported arguments in the Court of Appeals contain references to more than two dozen collections of cases in the English courts of King's Bench, Common Pleas, Exchequer, and the High Court of Chancery, dating from the reign of Elizabeth I to his own time. For cases in the common law courts he used among others the reports of Coke, embracing the period from 1572 to 1616; Yelverton, Ventris, Levinz, Salkeld, covering the seventeenth and the early part of the eighteenth century; and Lord Raymond, Strange, Hardwicke, Wilson, Burrow, Cowper, Douglas, extending over the eighteenth century. On the chancery side Marshall had recourse to *Cases in Chancery*, *Precedents in Chancery*, *Equity Cases Abridged*, Vernon, Peere Williams, Talbot, Atkyns, and Brown. These contained cases from the late seventeenth century to the contemporary. All the reports he cited were available in recent editions, which he either owned or borrowed.

In researching his cases Marshall did not plunge immediately into the reports. Like lawyers today he made use of the available shortcuts to save time. His starting point might have been Blackstone or one of the digests and abridgments such as those by Comyns, Viner, and Bacon, which were alphabetically arranged by topic and consisted mainly of summaries of reported cases. In many instances Marshall probably did not venture farther than these handy compilations. He

22. Aylett v. Minnis, Wythe 219, 225, 232, 233.

23. Minnis v. Aylett, 1 Wash. 300, 301, 302. This reversal provoked a lengthy and angry commentary from the chancellor (Wythe 234).

could also turn to treatises that brought together all the cases on a particular topic. To keep abreast of the most recent decisions, which had not yet been digested or incorporated into the treatise literature, he had to go directly to the reports. These all had copious indexes to facilitate research.

Finding the relevant cases was absolutely essential, but the most thorough research went for nought if a lawyer did not also possess the skill to analyze and interpret past decisions and to extract from them the applicable rules of law. To argue effectively, one had to be able to reason by analogy and to make fine distinctions. In a typical argument, counsel on one side would attempt to bring his case within the rule laid down in previous adjudications. Opposing counsel would then endeavor either to deny that the rule was law or to distinguish the precedents from the case at hand, emphasizing the different conditions or circumstances and showing that these differences rendered the former cases inapplicable to the present one.

Marshall had to be prepared to adduce, reject, or distinguish cases as the situation demanded. Since no two cases were exactly alike, the advocate had to show that the similarities were strong enough to come within the same rule. One common tactic employed to undermine the authority of a case was to show that its principle was "fully contradicted" by a train of other decisions. If this did not work and the case stood as law, the alternative was to distinguish it by showing that it was "unlike the present." Resourceful lawyers like Marshall found many ways to distinguish cases. He might, for example, contend that the main point of the present case had been only "incidentally decided" in the former, which therefore "ought not to be considered as a binding authority." Or he might show that none of the past cases had "gone so far as the present."[24]

Virginia lawyers and judges might also justify a departure from English rules and practice by pointing to the different circumstances and customs of that country, which typically were ascribed to its "highly commercial character."[25] Marshall adopted this strategy in a 1792 case: "The cases read by Mr. Ronold, only prove that there are certain rules observed by the Chancellor in England, which neither are, or ought to be guides for us; and this necessary departure from those rules, results from the very nature of our situation, compared with that country. In that, much of the wealth of the nation consists in money; it is easily procured by those who can secure the repayment of it. . . . In this country, the wealth of the people consists principally in real property—there is so much of that, and so little money

24. Case No. 5, Doc. VIII; Case No. 43.

25. See the remark of Judge Roane in Baring v. Reeder, 1 H. & M. 162 (1806).

at market, that the latter cannot be procured on loan, with any security." Similarly, in a 1799 case he argued against the negotiability of military certificates, which the state had issued to soldiers for their pay in lieu of money. Although it was the "policy of England, which is a commercial country," to give currency to such paper, "no such policy ever obtained here."[26]

Virginia cases were also cited, including an occasional one from the colonial General Court. The Virginia decisions mostly reiterated those of the English courts, but a lawyer's argument was that much stronger if he could show that the English cases had been previously ratified by a Virginia court. Thus, after reciting a series of English cases in arguing a will construction case in 1794, Marshall remarked: "But above all, I rely upon the decision of this court in the case of Shermer *vs* Shermer."[27] At the time there were no published reports, and he had to depend on his own notes to keep track of the Virginia cases. In this instance the case cited was fresh in his mind, as he had argued it himself at the same term. On another occasion he had to admit ignorance of a case decided at the previous term, in which he had not participated.[28] The fact that the Virginia cases were unpublished could be asserted to deny their authority. This happened in 1792, when Marshall cited a decision of the "old general court" and one in the Court of Appeals. Pendleton casually brushed them aside: "These never having been published, were necessarily, known only to very few of the profession; and perhaps, hardly to any practising in the country only."[29]

Most of Marshall's appellate cases involved the application of common law rules or equity principles derived from English precedents. He also had ample opportunity to employ his skill in the art of statutory construction in litigation arising under the positive laws of the commonwealth. Among the laws he was required to construe were an act of 1779 for proving book debts and one of 1781 for settling contracts made during the period of paper money. In another of his arguments he interpreted the rules issued by Lord Fairfax for patenting land in the Northern Neck.[30]

The largest class of cases Marshall argued in the Court of Appeals concerned disputes over the ownership of land and slaves. Usually the dispute was about the proper disposal of a decedent's estate among heirs, devisees, legatees, and creditors. A creditor, for example, sued an executor for a testator's debt, insisting that the slaves

26. Ross v. Poythress, 1 Wash. 122; Wilson v. Rucker, 1 Call 503–4.

27. Roy v. Garnett, 2 Wash. 25.

28. Lawrason v. Davenport, 2 Call 99 (1799).

29. White v. Jones, 4 Call 257 (1792).

30. Case Nos. 35, 38, 39.

that had been distributed among the legatees should be considered assets of the estate and therefore liable to the payment of his debts. In another case, the creditor's executors filed a bill in chancery to set aside conveyances and devises of land and slaves made by a testator who was deeply in debt.[31]

Many such cases involved the construction of a will, the parties—usually the heir at law against other descendants or devisees—claiming the same property under a disputed provision of the instrument. Owing to their great complexity, will construction cases came before the appellate court in disproportionate numbers. They afforded numerous occasions for the bar and bench to display their mastery of the abstruse doctrines of property law and the technical rules for construing wills that had evolved with ever greater refinement in a multitude of cases. Not surprisingly, the string of English citations was longest in will cases.[32] Typically the court was required to reconcile the "intention" of the testator with the laws of property and the "settled and fixed" rules of construction. In many instances a testator drew up his own will in informal and nontechnical language, and his words might have a legal import or effect that he never intended. Ironically, the more precedents that could be adduced to aid the construction of a will, the less useful they were. On more than one occasion President Pendleton quoted with approval the remark of an English judge " 'that cases on wills serve rather to obscure, than illuminate questions of this sort.' "[33]

In will cases the court strove to give effect to the testator's intention—this was "the governing rule," said Pendleton, "to which all other rules of construction must yield."[34] There was a danger, of course, that the court might rewrite the will despite disclaiming "all authority to mould testator's wills into any form which fancy, whim, or worse passions might suggest."[35] Cases frequently followed the same dialectical pattern: one party contended that a strict and technical interpretation of the will would defeat the intention, the other that the intention had to be collected from the words of the instrument itself and had to be consistent with the law and settled rules of construction. At one time or another Marshall had to argue both positions. In *Shermer* v. *Shermer's Executors*, for example, he argued

31. Case Nos. 3, 7.

32. The best example is Roy v. Garnett, 2 Wash. 9 (1794), in which JM cited about twenty English decisions.

33. Kennon v. McRoberts, 1 Wash. 102–3 (1792); Shermer v. Shermer's Executors, 1 Wash. 271 (1794).

34. Kennon v. McRoberts, 1 Wash. 102. JM was counsel in this important case, but no arguments were reported.

35. Kennon v. McRoberts, 1 Wash. 99.

against a strict interpretation: "In last wills, it is not necessary that the testator should use technical words, in order to pass a fee; for however inartificially he may express himself, yet if his intention can be discovered, . . . the court will supply such words, as may be necessary to effectuate that intention" (Case Number 5, Document VIII). Similarly, in *Crump* v. *Dudley* he remarked: "In the present case the will is obviously pen'd by a person not accustomed to legal forms. . . . The writer, therefore, cannot be presumed to have known the legal construction of particular expressions, and to have intended that construction" (Case Number 33).[36] In *Pendleton* v. *Vandevier*, however, he took the opposite line: "The testator may have blundered, but I cannot perceive upon what principle this court can correct it. It would be to *make* not to *interpret a will*."[37]

Pendleton summed up the court's pragmatic approach to will cases in his *Shermer* opinion when he declared "that where a testator's intention is apparent to me, cases must be strong, uniform, and apply pointedly, before they will prevail to frustrate that intention."[38] In that case the precedent relied on by counsel for the heir at law failed to meet this test. The implication of Pendleton's dictum was that if the testator's intention was not clear, the court would follow the rules laid down in the old cases. This was the rationale for his reversal of Wythe's decree in the case of Aylett's will, rendered at the same term as *Shermer*.

The sharp difference of opinion between Pendleton and Wythe over Aylett's will reflected in part their long-standing personal rivalry, which had begun before the Revolution when both were at the bar of the General Court. The judicial reorganization of 1789 left Chancellor Wythe in the position of having his decrees subject to final review by a separate appellate court presided over by his old adversary. From that time until Pendleton's death in 1803, more than 150 cases (according to the count of Pendleton's biographer) were appealed from the High Court of Chancery to the Court of Appeals, with a majority of the decrees being reversed or revised.[39] It is misleading, however, to explain the large number of chancery appeals and revisions of decrees in terms of a clash of personalities. A losing suitor in chancery was more likely to take a chance on an appeal because there was usually much at stake (money or property) in the outcome. Moreover, owing to the inherently complicated nature of equity decrees, there was greater room for error. The record of a chancery suit, much more copious than that of a case at common law,

36. See also JM's argument in Guthrie's Lessee v. Guthrie, 1 Call 11 (1797).

37. 1 Wash. 388 (1794).

38. 1 Wash. 272.

39. Mays, *Pendleton*, II, 290.

contained all the evidence submitted below. The appellate court was thus not confined to one narrow point of law but was free to review the entire case and fashion its own decree.

Appeals from chancery constitute a large proportion of Marshall's reported cases in the Court of Appeals.[40] Many of these in turn were suits in which a party had sought relief after a judgment at law. Such cases raised the perennially vexing question of the relationship between law and equity, forcing the judges continually to define the boundaries between the two jurisdictions.[41] More often than not, Marshall found himself in the position of arguing for restricting equitable intervention after a case had been heard at law. These arguments repeated certain familiar refrains—that the party had a competent remedy at law, that the case had been fully and fairly decided by jury trial, and that if error had occurred, the proper resort was to an appellate tribunal, not to a court of equity. Thus, in *Barrett* v. *Floyd* (Case Number 34) he played on the fears of allowing a chancery court to substitute its discretion for that of a jury, transforming "itself into an appellate Court from general verdicts and judgments thereon, both as to law and fact." In *Pickett* v. *Morris* (Case Number 40) he admitted that courts of law and equity had concurrent jurisdiction over certain subjects, but he insisted that if the whole case had been decided at law, equity could "no more re-examine it, than the courts of law in a similar case could re-examine a decree of the court of chancery." On another occasion he contended that the matter stated in a plaintiff's bill in chancery "was but a plain assumpsit; and therefore properly triable at law."[42] In every instance such arguments failed to sway the judges, for the court under Pendleton favored a liberal and expansive view of equity jurisdiction.[43]

One other group of cases merits brief mention: those that turned on questions of procedure, pleading, and practice rather than on the doctrines of substantive law. Because the lower courts of Virginia, particularly the county courts, often failed to observe the correct forms and procedures, the Court of Appeals had to consider numerous appeals based on irregularities occurring below. In deciding these cases the Pendleton court strove to distinguish between defects of form and substantive errors, adopting the sensible rule that the

40. Nine of the twelve cases in this section plus Case Nos. 5 and 7 came up from the High Court of Chancery. Case No. 6 also began in chancery but JM did not participate in the appeal.

41. See Case No. 34, editorial note.

42. Pryor v. Adams, 1 Call 385 (1798).

43. For other cases in which JM argued against equity jurisdiction, see White v. Jones, 4 Call 256–57 (1792); Foushee v. Lea, 4 Call 283–84 (1795). For a case in which he supported the jurisdiction, see Hooe v. Marquess, 4 Call 419 (1798).

former could not bring about a reversal. This distinction was not always easy to make, since in law form and substance often blended together.

The court's unwillingness to allow a technical rule to defeat a party's right was nowhere better stated than in *Pickett* v. *Claiborne* (Case Number 32). The rule was that failure to file a declaration would result in a nonsuit. The defendants had already agreed to confess judgment, however, and sought to take advantage of the omission. On behalf of the plaintiff, Marshall appealed to the higher law of reason and justice. "All pleading," he observed, "is founded in reason, and the object is to promote, not to prevent, the attainment of justice." The court fully accepted this premise and therefore had little difficulty affirming the judgment. In a like spirit the court held in other cases that the plaintiff did not have to prove present possession in the defendant to maintain an action of detinue and that a declaration in trover did not need to state the price of the thing sued for.[44]

In some instances, nevertheless, the court concluded that there were sound reasons for upholding the technical rule. For example, in a declaration upon an administration bond, failure to state that the plaintiffs sued in their capacity as county court justices was held to be a fatal variance. The court affirmed a district court judgment rejecting the bond as evidence upon the declaration. Marshall, for the appellants, admitted that the pleadings were "not in all respects strictly correct, yet they were sufficient to have prevented the rejection of the testimony." Although Pendleton was inclined to agree and would have allowed the plaintiffs to amend the declaration, his brethren overruled him. They reluctantly concluded that the judgment should stand and that the plaintiffs would have to commence an entirely new action. They were more concerned about setting a dangerous precedent, about removing "landmarks; which, in other cases, may produce infinite uncertainty and injustice." Affirming the judgment was the better course, "especially as it will tend to produce more certainty and prevent a loose kind of practice, which has been gaining too much ground, throughout the country."[45] In all the cases of this kind, the court inquired into the reasons or policy that lay behind the rule, weighing them against those that favored dispensing with the rule.

Each of Marshall's cases arose from unique circumstances, and for that reason they exhibit so great a variety as to defy all but the most general classifications. Even then, reducing them all to a few descriptive categories is impossible. The twelve cases in this section, along

44. Burnley v. Lambert, 1 Wash. 308 (1794); Pearpoint v. Henry, 2 Wash. 192 (1796).
45. Cabell v. Hardwick, 1 Call 345, 349, 352, 356 (1798).

with three appearing elsewhere in the volume and two published in earlier volumes, provide a representative sampling of Marshall's arguments covering the entire period of his practice.[46] Because space limitations preclude reproducing the entire report, the cases selected are those in which the statement of facts, the arguments of other counsel, and the judges' opinions can be conveniently summarized in the notes. Many of the omitted cases are also discussed or mentioned at appropriate points in the annotation.

46. Three arguments have been included as documents in Case Nos. 3, 5, and 7. For JM's arguments in Hite v. Fairfax and Bracken v. College of William and Mary, see *PJM*, I, 150–64; II, 67–81. For a complete listing of his reported cases, see the Appendix to this volume.

32. Pickett v. Claiborne

1787

Editorial Note

Originating as a routine assumpsit action in the Henrico County Court, *Pickett* v. *Claiborne* followed the full appellate route, first to the General Court, then to the Court of Appeals. On appeal the case called forth a brief but important discussion of the nature of pleading, the extent to which adherence to forms and procedures was necessary, and the effect of a confession of judgment in curing mistakes or omissions in the proceedings. George Pickett, a Richmond merchant and close friend of Marshall's, brought suit in the county court in 1783 to recover a debt owed by the brothers Herbert and William Claiborne of King William County, offspring of a prominent family that had settled in that region in the seventeenth century. (They were direct descendants of William Claiborne, secretary of state for the colony.)[1] After the Claibornes entered their appearance in court, the parties agreed to settle the dispute without the expense of a trial. The cause was continued to the next term with the understanding that the defendants would confess judgment in return for a brief stay of execution. Pickett in the meantime did not file a declaration, presumably because he saw no need to after this agreement.

The Claibornes confessed judgment at the May 1783 Henrico court but subsequently obtained a reversal in the General Court, which nonsuited Pickett for failing to file a declaration. Pickett, represented by Marshall, then took the case to the highest court on a writ of error.[2] Was the plaintiff's omission of a declaration where the defendant confessed judgment fatal to his cause? Under Virginia law the plaintiff was to be nonsuited if he did not file a declaration after the defendant's appearance.[3] At the same time Virginia had adopted the various English statutes of jeofails, which precluded objections to matters of form after a certain stage of the proceedings in a lawsuit. These statutes, as President Pendleton noted, "were intended to prevent captious exceptions, where the defendant acknowledged, that justice had been done, or left it to be presumed, from his silence. Accordingly they provide, in substance, that such judgments shall not be reversed for any defect, or omission, which does not go to the right of the cause." In *Pickett* the issue was whether the want of a declaration was a mere defect of form that was cured by judgment or a substantive error that went "to the right of the cause."[4]

The Court of Appeals decided that the absence of a declaration in this case was not a sufficient reason to reverse the original judgment.

This was a conscious departure from the prior practice of the General Court, which had considered "the want of a declaration fatal in every case, whether the judgment was adversary, or confessed."[5] Having contributed to the making of the new rule that judgment by confession cured the omission of a declaration, Marshall later found himself in the uncomfortable position of having to deny its applicability to the cause he was then arguing.[6]

1. On Pickett, see Case No. 10, Doc. IV and n. 2. On the Claiborne family, see Malcolm Hart Harris, *Old New Kent County* (2 vols.; West Point, Va., 1977), II, 582–84, 594–96. Herbert Claiborne was financially distressed at this time, as shown by a subsequent case of JM's in the Court of Appeals (see Case No. 37).

2. Va. Ct. Ap. Ord. Bk. I, 40, 107; 4 Call 99–102.

3. Hening, *Statutes*, V, 496; IX, 408.

4. Virginia enacted its first statute of jeofails in 1789 but earlier had declared the English statutes of jeofails to be in force (ibid., VI, 339; XIII, 36–38). For Pendleton's comments, see his opinion in this case (4 Call 105).

5. 4 Call 104–5. According to Pendleton, forty General Court precedents were mentioned, a circumstance that nevertheless did not prevent the Court of Appeals from exercising its appellate jurisdiction over that court. See his comments on Pickett v. Claiborne in a 1792 case, Thornton v. Smith, 1 Wash. 83.

6. See Case No. 20 and Leftwich v. Stovall, 1 Wash. 303, 304 (1794).

Argument

30 October 1787

Marshall for the plaintiff in error.[1] The want of a declaration was cured by the confession of judgment;[2] for the rule is, that there should be a declaration; and not that a confession of judgment will be unavailing to supply the want of it. All pleading is founded in reason, and the object is to promote, not to prevent, the attainment of justice: but that principle will be subverted, if a solemn agreement like this, where the parties liquidate their disputes, and one grants time in consideration that the other will confess a judgment, is to be disregarded. The usual argument, of surprize, has no weight upon the present occasion; for the defendants stipulated the sum for which judgment should be entered against them; and, therefore, could be at no loss for information with regard to the nature of the demand.[3] If a release of errors had been entered, at the time of the judgment, it would have barred the writ of *supersedeas* from the general court; and there is no difference, in principle, whether the release be of record, or, *in pais*,[4] only; for, in both cases, it is nothing more than an agreement, not to bring a writ of error. But a release in law is as effectual, in all cases, as a release in deed. Thus a feoffment by one jointenant to his companion will not pass the estate, but it may operate as a release.[5] So a covenant not to sue upon a bond, does not extinguish the bond; but the agreement releases the remedy. *Holt*, 170.[6] And so, in the present case, the warrant of attorney amounted to an undertaking to relinquish all errors in the rendition of the judgment; and barred the defendants from alledging the want of a declaration; for the meaning was, that there should be an effectual judgment, in order to settle the claim, finally, on both sides: and, with that in view, it would have been absurd, if the parties had intended, that either of them should have it in his power to elude the agreement, by taking advantage of an oversight to destroy the judgment, and set all to sea again.[7]

Printed, Daniel Call, *Reports of Cases Argued and Decided in the Court of Appeals of Virginia*, IV (Richmond, 1833), 102.

1. The General Court reversed the Henrico judgment in Apr. 1784. The Court of Appeals awarded a writ of error to the General Court's judgment on 2 May 1785. The appeal was argued on 30 Oct. 1787, JM speaking first (Va. Ct. Ap. Ord. Bk. I, 49, 102–3, 106).

2. The confession of judgment in this case was effected by a note in writing addressed by the Claibornes to attorneys practicing in the Henrico court, authorizing any one of them to confess judgment in Pickett's action. This "warrant of attorney," as the note was called, was the usual means of confessing judgment where the defendant would not be present in court and had no attorney to do it for him. In England warrants of attorney were routinely executed as a security for a debt without any action depending. Virginia law, however, expressly prohibited such authorization before the bringing of a suit. The purpose of this prohibition, first enacted in 1744, was to remedy a situation in which debtors had no notice of the time and place of judgments against them, forcing them to incur unnecessary law charges and to institute expensive chancery proceedings for obtaining relief (Tucker, *Blackstone's Commentaries*, III, 397 and n. 9; Hening, *Statutes*, V, 240–41, 511–12).

3. Opposing counsel William DuVal urged that a declaration, by establishing the identity of the claim on the record, was an essential protection for the defendant, preventing him from being sued again for the same thing. John Taylor, JM's co-counsel, replied that the problem of identity also applied to declarations in general assumpsit setting forth the common counts. President Pendleton reiterated this point and added that if the defendant in a new suit pleaded a previous judgment, the plaintiff would have to show two subsisting debts at the time of the earlier judgment to sustain his action (4 Call 103, 104, 106).

4. *In pais* ("in the country") applies to a legal transaction, such as a convey-

ance of land, that has taken place without formal legal proceedings. Matters in pais are opposed to matters of record.

5. In the law of real property the proper means of conveyance by one joint tenant to another was by release. It could not be done by "feoffment," or grant of a freehold in possession, since both were already in possession. However, if this had in fact been done, then the grant amounted to a release (Bacon, *Abridgment* [1st Am. ed.], III, 694).

JM's point was that a joint tenant who had conveyed in this faulty manner would be precluded from reasserting his interest in the land at a later time. By analogy, the Claibornes' warrant of attorney should operate as a release of errors.

6. The page number is incorrect, probably a printer's error. The correct citation is Lacey v. Kinnaston, Holt, K.B., 178, 90 Eng. Rep. 996 (K.B., 1701). The court held in this case that a covenant not to enforce a deed effectively released the obligation contained in the deed and that the obligor could block an action brought on the deed by pleading the covenant.

St. George Tucker also reported this case. His notes of JM's argument, which end at this point, read as follows: "The Case of pickett & Claiborne stands on the single point of the want of a Declon: such a Confession of Judgt. as made by Deft, takes away the Error of the want of a Declon.—very few Cases in point: not any of such wt. as to overturn reason & Justice. He compared this Warrant of Atty to a release of Errors—at least he said it was substantially so; Feoffment from one joint Tenant &c to another will operate as a release. So is a Covenant never to bring suit on a bond" (Pickett v. Claiborne, 30 Oct. 1787, Casebook, Tucker-Coleman Papers, ViW).

7. DuVal followed for the defendants, citing two English cases in support of his contention that a confession of judgment did not cure error: Dawbeney v. Bannester, Cro. Jac. 32, 79 Eng. Rep. 25 (K.B., 1604), where the defendant in debt on a bond confessed judgment, which was reversed because the declaration omitted "profert" of the bond; Wade v. Rogers, 2 Black. W. 780, 96 Eng. Rep. 458 (C.P., 1771), in which the court held that consent to confess judgment on terms did not imply consent not to bring a writ of error. Taylor replied to DuVal, insisting that the warrant of attorney amounted to a release of errors (4 Call 103–4).

On 1 Nov. Pendleton delivered the unanimous opinion of the court in favor of Pickett, reversing the General Court's judgment and upholding that of the Henrico County Court. Placing great emphasis upon considerations of public policy, the president described the agreement to confess judgment almost in contractual terms. The advantages gained by the defendants saving the expense of pleading, being allowed to appear without bail, and especially obtaining further time to pay the debt—ought to be binding upon them, he said. Requiring a declaration in this instance "would have served no other purpose than to swell fees and papers," he concluded (Va. Ct. Ap. Ord. Bk. I, 107–8; 4 Call 104–6).

33. Crump's Executors v. Dudley

1790

Editorial Note

Like *Shermer* v. *Shermer's Executors* (Case Number 5) this case resulted from a family squabble over a will—always a fertile source of litigation. Such disputes usually pitted the heir at law against other members of the family and centered on establishing the intention of the testator. The parties to this suit, which began in the High Court of Chancery as *Dudley and Wife* v. *Crump's Executors*, were descendants of Elizabeth Pinchback of New Kent County, who died in 1750 shortly after making her will. She was the daughter of Thomas Massie, a landed gentleman and burgess from that county, and widow of Thomas Pinchback. She had four children at the time she executed her will: Thomas, John, Mary, and Sarah. To John she devised a five-hundred-acre tract of land in Goochland County, which she had inherited from her father. To Sarah she bequeathed a slave named Sarah for life, and if she died before her brother John, then the slave girl was to go to him. The remainder of the estate after the debts were paid was to be divided equally among all four children.[1]

The property in contest was the slave Sarah and her increase. The contingent bequest to John Pinchback never took effect, because he died during the lifetime of his sister Sarah, who had married Charles Crump. Who would get the slaves when Sarah Crump died? When the other brother and eldest son Thomas died, one of his two daughters, Anne, went to live with her Aunt Sarah Crump. After reaching the age of twenty-one, Anne Pinchback became engaged to William Dudley of King and Queen County, a future magistrate and sheriff of that county. They were married on 13 February 1773. The day before the ceremony Anne sold her interest in the slaves (which had greatly increased) to Sarah Crump for thirty pounds without Dudley's knowledge, though apparently without any attempt to conceal the sale from the prospective husband. After Sarah Crump's death (about 1786) William Dudley and his wife filed a bill in chancery for one-half of the slaves, claiming them by right of descent from the eldest son of Elizabeth Pinchback (the other half descending to the other daughter) and alleging that the deed of sale was void.[2]

The central issue in this suit, and the only one decided by the Court of Appeals, was the validity of the sale by Anne Pinchback Dudley to Sarah Crump. As counsel for the Dudleys, Marshall turned to the law of husband and wife, attempting to bring this sale (whose circumstances raised a suspicion of fraud) within that class of acts and agreements by the wife before marriage that were voided by the marriage. "Equity," Marshall had written in his student notes, paraphrasing Bacon, "will set aside the intended wife's contracts enterd into before marriage when they appear to have been made with an intent to deceive & cheat the husbd. & are in derogation of the rights of marriage."[3] He devoted part of his argument to a short disquisition on the nature of marriage that necessarily emphasized property over romance as the motive for matrimony. Fortune, he said, was an important underlying inducement growing "out of the nature of the case," although no gentleman could mention it in his professions of love for his betrothed.

The Dudleys' claim to the slaves through descent was based on the alleged intestacy of Elizabeth Pinchback with respect to this property—her will did not expressly declare where the slaves were to go upon Sarah Crump's death. The property in question was in law called a "reversion," that is, after Sarah Crump's life interest ceased at her death, it reverted to the estate of Elizabeth Pinchback. This raised the question of whether the intestacy laws extended to cases of partial intestacy. By the law then in force slaves as well as lands of an intestate passed by descent, and if the descent was from a parent, the heir (in this instance, the eldest son Thomas) was required to pay an equal share of their value to his siblings. If these laws applied, then Sarah Crump's estate independently of the sale was entitled to a share of the appraised value of the slaves.[4]

Another possibility was that the reversion passed to all the children by virtue of the "residuary clause," which disposed of all the property not specifically devised or bequeathed. If the slaves did so pass, then Sarah Crump's estate would again have a claim to an equal share. Thus, even if the sale was void, the Dudleys were not entitled to the half share they were claiming.[5] What was Elizabeth Pinchback's intention in this regard? Marshall's reasoning was largely negative: the testator could not have meant to include these slaves, whose reversion at the time was a mere possibility, in the residuary clause; therefore, by default they descended to the heir and through him to his children.

Marshall prevailed in the High Court of Chancery, where the case was argued 16 November 1786. The court decreed that the Dudleys were entitled to half the slaves. Crump's executors then brought an appeal.[6]

The report of *Crump* v. *Dudley* and the reports of fourteen other cases heard at the June and November 1790 terms of the Court of Appeals are appended to the third volume of Call's *Reports*, the body of which covers the years 1801 to 1803. In a note preceding this appendix, Call wrote: "The following Cases were reported by a gentleman high in the practice at the time, and by whose permission they are now published." The unnamed reporter was John Marshall, who was identified as such in at least two places.[7] St. George Tucker cited "Marshall's reports 3: Call 556" in a note to one of his General Court cases.[8] The anonymous correspondent who supplied information on Virginia law to the compiler of a yearbook on American law published in 1822 also identified Marshall as the reporter of the cases at the end of Call's third volume.[9] Call had occasion to use Marshall's notes again in his fourth volume, acknowledging him by name in one case.[10]

1. On the Massie and Pinchback families, see *WMQ*, 1st ser., XIII (1905), 196; 2d ser., IX (1929), 66. The will is reproduced in the case report (3 Call 507–8).

2. 3 Call 507–8. On William Dudley, see Alfred Bagby, *King and Queen County, Virginia* (New York, 1908), 373–75; *JCSV*, III, 124; V, 270.

3. See JM's "Law Notes" (*PJM*, I, 74).

4. See Argument, n. 1. The other daughter Mary had died unmarried; hence this share was now one-third.

5. Their share would be one-sixth (one-half of Thomas Pinchback's one-third interest).

6. St. George Tucker took notes of the chancery court argument, which are printed in *PJM*, I, 186–88. The executors of Sarah Crump were John Pinchback Crump (her son) and John Meade (Va. Ct. Ap. Ord. Bk. II, 1).

7. 3 Call 506. Besides Crump v. Dudley, three other cases reported by JM are presented in this volume: Barrett v. Floyd (Case No. 34), Beall v. Edmundson (Case No. 35), and Ross v. Pynes (Case No. 36). For another of these cases, Bracken v. College of William and Mary, see *PJM*, II, 72–81.

8. Gordon v. Bates, 13 Oct. 1786, Casebook, Tucker-Coleman Papers, ViW.

9. William Griffith, *Annual Law Register of the United States*, III (Burlington, N.J., 1822), 313–14.

10. Turberville v. Self, 4 Call 590 (1795).

Argument

21–22 June 1790

MARSHALL for the appellees.[1] The acts of Assembly refered to by Mr. Taylor, apply only to cases of total intestacy. The words are, "when any person dies intestate, leaving several children["] &c; and not when any person shall die intestate with respect to any part of his property.[2] The distinction between a total and partial intestacy, which the law seems to have made, is not entirely without reason. A total intestacy is seldom designed. Where it is accidental, the justice and humanity of the law gives to younger children a share of the appraised value of slaves; altho its policy makes them descendable as real estate. But where a will is made, it can seldom happen that much property will be omitted, unless the omission be designed. If however, we suppose the provision of the law to extend to a partial intestacy, can the section be construed to extend to a possible reverter, as in this case? The slave is given in the will. If John had survived Sarah, the slave is given for ever. What is to be inventoried and appraised? Is it a mere possibility? Is the heir at law to have a mere possibility inventoried and appraised, and to pay a proportionate value of that appraisement to the younger children? It is plain that the sections cited do not comprehend the case.

The slave did not pass by the residuary clause.[3]

It is true, that in the construction of wills the rules of law must be adhered to; but it is not less true, that it has become a rule of law, to obey the plain intention of the testator. It is admitted that general words may in the residuary clause of a will pass a reversion, or remainder; but it is contended that such words will not pass such an interest, if there be accompanying words, shewing the intention of the testator to be, to limit the operation of the general words to a particular property. An effect has been given to such words in a will, which they have not in deeds, to promote, and not to frustrate, the intent of the testator. In the present case the will is obviously pen'd by a person not accustomed to legal forms. As one evidence of this, each sentence of the will commences with the word *Imprimis*.[4] The writer, therefore, cannot be presumed to have known the legal construction of particular expressions, and to have intended that construction. It may well be doubted in such a case, even had there been no restraining words in the residuary clause, whether a mere possibility could be designed to pass by it; and that too in a thing before mentioned, and given away in the same will. But here are restraining words.

The property is to be kept together till debts are paid.[5] It is to be then divided. How mix a mere possibility, such as this, with other visible and tangible estate? How divide it? Why keep it for debts when it could not be productive? To me it appears, obviously, to have been the intention of the testatrix, an intention evidenced by the descriptive words of the clause, to pass, by this residuary clause, only such property as could be useful in the immediate payment of debts, and as would be susceptible of immediate partition.[6]

Marriage is to be considered as a civil contract.[7] It is an union of fortunes, as well as of persons. It is of consequence to the happiness and peace of society that it should be fair, and without deception. A person possessed of a visible fortune, who contracts matrimony, impliedly contracts to unite that fortune as well as her person, to her husband. To dispose of it secretly is a palpable fraud; immoral in itself; and productive of consequences extensively injurious. It is a breach of the contract, and has been discountenanced by courts 1 *Eq. ca. ab.* 59.[8] This case is stronger than those there cited, in as much as circumstances, not appearing in those cases, attend the transaction. The deed was executed the day before the marriage, and therefore would not probably be known to the intended husband, until the ceremony should be actually performed.

It was executed to a person whose situation probably gave her an influence over the mind of the seller, which no other person possessed. It was for an estate not in possession, but expectancy; and therefore to be the more readily parted with, at an under value; and the consideration was so inadequate as scarcely to distinguish it from a gift.

It cannot be necessary to shew, by testimony, that fortune was an inducement to the marriage. It results from the nature of the contract, that the inducements to it are various; and that fortune is not to be excluded from its share in producing it. Of course it is not to be expected that other proof is to be adduced; since it is not to be expected that declarations, to that effect, could be made by a gentleman, who is endeavouring to obtain a lady's affections. That fortune is not stated in the bill to have been an inducement cannot affect the right; since the bill is drawn, not by the party, but by his counsel; and the existence of the inducement does not depend upon the statements of the bill, but grows, necessarily, out of the nature of the case.[9]

Nor is it material that the court would not decree the appellees to refund if the right should appear to have been against them, independant of the contract. All unfair contracts bind the party who has committed the fraud; and yet the injured person may be relieved against them.[10]

It is admitted that family disputes may be compromised, but the persons compromising them ought to be in a situation to part with their property. An unequal compromise is as objectionable, if not more so, as a sale on a very inadequate consideration: Of either, the intended husband, considering the time and circumstances of the case, ought to have been informed. It would not have been withheld from him, had no fear existed of his preventing its completion.

The situation of the parties and the complexion of the case, renders it impossible, that Sarah Crump could have been ignorant of the intended marriage; nor is it pretended, by her representatives, that she could have been ignorant of it.

If then the acts directing shares of the appraised value of the slaves of intestates to be divided by the heir among the younger children, do not extend to the case: If the possibility of the reverter[11] of the slave Sarah did not pass by the residuary clause of the will of Elizabeth Pinchback And if the sale from Anne Pinchback to Sarah Crump was void as being a fraud upon the husband; then the appellees, in right of the said Anne as one of the coheiresses of the said Elizabeth Pinchback, are clearly entitled to a moiety of the slaves, according to the decree of the Chancellor; which ought to be affirmed.[12]

Printed, Daniel Call, *Reports of Cases Argued and Adjudged in the Court of Appeals of Virginia*, III (Richmond, 1805), 511–14. This was one of the 1790 cases reported by JM that Call appended to his third volume (see editorial note).

1. Arguments took place on 21 and 22 June, John Taylor speaking first for Sarah Crump's executors (Va. Ct. Ap. Ord. Bk. II, 1, 2).

2. Taylor cited acts of 1705 and 1727 in support of his first point, that even if the slaves in question descended to Anne Dudley (as the child of the heir at law) and she had not given up her right by the sale to her aunt, the estate of Sarah Crump was entitled to a share of the appraised value of the slaves. The act of 1705, which declared slaves to be real estate, directed that when a person died intestate, the slaves should descend to the heir, who was to inventory and appraise them and then divide their value equally among all the children. The act of 1727, which amended the earlier one, contained the same provision in the case of a mother dying intestate. According to Taylor these acts applied to a partial as well as a total intestacy (3 Call 509; Hening, *Statutes*, III, 334; IV, 224).

3. The residuary clause in Elizabeth Pinchback's will gave the remainder of her estate (after the specific bequests and devises) to be divided equally among her four children. Taylor argued that this clause passed the slave Sarah and her increase to all the children. While conceding that the testator's intention should govern in construing wills, Taylor maintained that the rules of law should be followed in determining that intention. One such rule was "that the remainder or reversion will pass by a general devise of the residuary estate" (3 Call 509).

4. Latin for "in the first place."

5. This stipulation was included in the residuary clause of the will.

6. In other words, the disputed slaves did not pass by the residuary clause but descended to the oldest son, Thomas, father of Anne Dudley.

7. JM next took up Taylor's principal argument, that Anne Dudley had relinquished all interest in the slaves by the sale to Sarah Crump on 12 Feb. 1773. As a single woman of full age at the time of the sale, said Taylor, she had complete control over her property; and even though the sale took place the day before the marriage, there was no evidence of fraud (3 Call 510–11).

8. 1 Eq. Ca. Abr. 59, 21 Eng. Rep. 872, is a collection of cases under the heading, "What Acts of the Wife's Before Marriage Shall the Husband Avoid, as Done in Derogation of the Rights of Marriage." Among those cited

are Howard v. Hooker, 2 Rep. Ch. 81, 21 Eng. Rep. 622 (Ch., 1673), in which the court set aside as fraudulent a widow's deed of settlement, made before marrying her second husband, who was not privy to the deed and who (it appeared to the court) had married her in confidence that she possessed such estate; Lance v. Norman, 2 Rep. Ch. 79, 21 Eng. Rep. 621 (Ch., 1673), which voided a recognizance privately executed by a woman to her brother the day before her marriage; Carleton v. Earl of Dorset, 2 Vern. 17, 23 Eng. Rep. 622 (Ch., 1686), which declared a deed of trust made without the future husband's privity to be in derogation of the rights of marriage. JM, of course, sought to have the sale voided on the same grounds.

9. Taylor noted that William Dudley had not alleged in his bill in chancery that the disputed slaves were an inducement to his marriage with Anne Pinchback (3 Call 510).

10. If, said Taylor, the court decided that Sarah Crump had a right to the slaves before the sale contract, the Dudleys could not be decreed to refund the sale price (£30); likewise, if the right was in the Dudleys, they should still be bound by the contract (3 Call 510).

11. A possibility of reverter is the interest that may return to the original grantor if the specified contingency—in this instance, Sarah Pinchback's predeceasing her brother John—does not occur.

12. On 23 June the court reversed the chancery decree, ruling that the sale was valid. It did not decide the first point, whether the statutes of 1705 and 1727 applied to cases of partial intestacy; or the second, whether the slaves passed by the residuary clause, though it was "rather inclined to consider the reversion . . . as passing by the residuary clause" (Va. Ct. Ap. Ord. Bk. II, 3; 3 Call 514).

On the second point, the court in a 1794 decision held that the dower slaves of a widow passed after her death under a sweeping residuary clause in which the testator devised the remainder of his slaves and personal estate. JM also represented the heir at law in that case, making a similar argument in favor of a restrictive reading of the residuary clause (Cole v. Clayborn, 1 Wash. 262, 264).

34. Barrett v. Floyd

1790

Editorial Note

This case followed a circuitous route from the Court of Admiralty to the Northampton County Court, the High Court of Chancery, and finally the Court of Appeals. Though it began in the state admiralty court (which remained in operation until 1789, when the federal Constitution took effect), the dispute as heard on appeal had nothing to do with admiralty law. Marshall himself was "but little versd in marine law" and "never practisd in the courts of admiralty." He took on the case, representing David Barrett, when it reached the High Court of Chancery late in 1785.[1]

In September 1779 the schooner *Polly*, a British trading vessel, ran aground in one of the inlets on Virginia's Eastern Shore, sprang a leak, and was abandoned by her crew, five of whom were taken prisoner. The schooner, formerly in the possession of a citizen of Connecticut, had recently been taken by a privateer out of New York. Berry Floyd of Accomac County (on the Eastern Shore) and a company of men proceeded to salvage the cargo, consisting principally of rum, sugar, and cocoa. Soon thereafter Barrett and another group arrived and agreed to help under the following conditions: if the *Polly* was condemned as a prize to Floyd's group, Barrett's men would be allowed 11/17 of what they saved; if the vessel was not declared a prize, then they would have a right to all they saved. Barrett's crew then joined the salvage operation, saving the greater part of the cargo.[2]

Whether the *Polly* was decreed to be a prize or a wreck, the salvage award would presumably be the same—that is, one-half of the value of the vessel and its cargo.[3] The distribution of this award, as agreed by the two salvage parties, hinged on the admiralty court's adjudication. Floyd and his men had as strong a motive for libeling the *Polly* as a prize as Barrett and his men did for having her declared a derelict. As it happened, Floyd's party successfully libeled the schooner and its cargo before Barrett, who intended to contest the condemnation, arrived at the admiralty court in Williamsburg. The court decreed the sale of the vessel and cargo in October 1779 and in November awarded one-half of the proceeds to the libelants, with 11/17 of the portion saved by Barrett's crew going to them.[4]

Barrett accepted his part of the award, but after returning home to the Eastern Shore he became convinced that the admiralty decision had been illegal. He subsequently brought an action of assumpsit against Floyd in the Northampton County Court, seeking to recover the difference between what he had received by the admiralty decree and the proceeds of the sale of that part of the cargo saved by his crew. Barrett obtained a verdict and judgment in January 1785. To satisfy execution Floyd took out a forthcoming bond, on which judgment was rendered in November of that year. He then obtained an injunction in the High Court of Chancery, which was made perpetual by decree of 29 May 1788. Barrett sought to overturn this decree.[5]

Why Barrett did not appeal the admiralty decree to the Court of Appeals is not clear from the report. Possibly he waited too long to bring an appeal and then decided to seek relief by suing Floyd in the county court. Also unexplained is why Floyd did not appeal the county court judgment as void for want of jurisdiction. When the case finally did reach the Court of Appeals, neither the correctness of the admiralty court's decree nor the county court's assumption of jurisdiction was in issue. The only question before the appellate court in *Barrett* v. *Floyd* was the propriety of equitable intervention by the High Court of Chancery in the judgment at law rendered by the Northampton County Court.

Barrett was the first of a series of cases decided during the 1790s in which the Virginia Court of Appeals grappled with the difficult problem of drawing the line of jurisdiction between law and equity. By this time the conflict between law and equity had long since ceased to be a burning political question, as it had been in England during the seventeenth century and in several of the American colonies during the eighteenth century.[6] In post-Revolutionary Virginia the jurisdiction of equity courts was accepted as a necessary means to secure the ends of justice. Although Chancellor George Wythe and President of the Court of Appeals Edmund Pendleton were frequently at odds with each other, their personal rivalry had nothing to do with competing jurisdictional claims. Pendleton, indeed, was more inclined than Wythe to extend the reach of chancery. "The jurisdiction of the Court of Chancery has regularly increased," said Pendleton speaking for the court in *Barrett*, "and is found to be beneficial to society: it should rather be enlarged, than circumscribed."[7]

At the core of the relationship between law and equity in Virginia were questions of high policy that posed an intractable dilemma for judges in their attempts to maintain the proper boundaries of jurisdiction. Everyone agreed that equity courts had a legitimate and necessary function to remedy defects and supply omissions in the common law. At the same time the methods and procedures of a court of equity, where the chancellor decided cases solely on the basis of written evidence without the presence of the parties, witnesses, and jury, were regarded as inherently inferior to those of a court of law. One

Virginia jurist, himself a chancellor, noted that in a common law trial, "justice can scarcely ever fail: because, the parties, the witnesses, the Jury, and a disinterested Court are, or may be, looking at each other, at the same time; and the smallest deviation in a witness, can be detected in a cross-examination upon the spot: nay, to see a witness, is often of more importance, than to hear him; for his looks sometimes conduct our senses to a conclusion, which his words would not." This jealousy to preserve trial by jury from interference by a court of equity, where justice resided in the discretion of a fallible chancellor, was consonant with the spirit of republican government and received explicit sanction in the Virginia Declaration of Rights: "That, in controversies respecting property, and in suits between man and man, the ancient trial by jury is preferable to any other, and ought to be held sacred."[8]

For the judges of the Virginia Court of Appeals the problem of preserving the distinction between law and equity was made more difficult by the need to rectify abuses occurring at the lowest level of the judicial system, the county courts. Most of the Virginia cases involving a clash of jurisdiction between law and equity originated there, with the aggrieved party then seeking relief in chancery. County court judges and lawyers were notoriously incompetent, and their conduct of cases frequently resulted in procedural and substantive errors. In this respect, said one Virginia lawyer, Virginia differed from England and hence required a greater role for chancery courts: "In England the trial is always had under the direction of able judges who can explain the law fully to the jury; but here it is for the most part before County Courts, who are not acquainted with the law, and therefore the judgment is frequently contrary to the plain principles of law."[9]

In Virginia, chancery assumed a special function of supervising the practice and administration of law at the county court level, one that blurred the traditional boundaries between law and equity. Beginning with *Barrett* and continuing through the decade of the 1790s, the Court of Appeals looked with favor upon this enlargement of equity jurisdiction, though the judges were careful to justify equitable interposition on traditional grounds and to distinguish between chancery's function in relieving against injustice resulting from county court mismanagement or misconduct and that of an appellate court in correcting errors of law. Other cases in which the court sustained chancery interference with a county court law judgment included *Cochran* v. *Street*, 1 Wash. 80 (1792), *Ambler* v. *Wyld*, 2 Wash. 36 (1794), *Foushee* v. *Lea*, 4 Call 279 (1795), and *Pickett* v. *Morris*, 2 Wash. 255 (1796), the last of which is also presented in this volume (Case Number 40). In each of these the court found some exceptional circumstances depriving the party of a full and fair hearing in the county court.

With the case of *Terrell* v. *Dick* in 1799, however, the Court of Appeals drew the line against a further extension of equity jurisdiction to remedy county court judgments. The county court in this case gave judgment for the defendant on the plea of British debt; the plaintiff applied to the High Court of Chancery, which decreed payment of the debt and interest. The Court of Appeals, while agreeing that the county court judgment was erroneous in law, rejected equitable intervention on the ground that the plaintiff had a remedy at law and neglected to pursue it. Pendleton, who was otherwise predisposed to favor equity jurisidiction in such cases, reluctantly concluded that the court could not "sustain the jurisdiction in this case, without fixing a dangerous precedent, wholly destructive of all distinction in the Common Law and Chancery jurisdiction." The effect of this decision was to diminish the force of *Barrett* and its successors, which were cited by counsel to support the chancery decree.[10]

1. JM to Charles Simms, 12 Dec. 1794 (*PJM*, II, 301). He recorded fees in this case under the dates of 4 Dec. 1785 and 26 Mar. 1787 (*PJM*, I, 344, 373).
2. 3 Call 531. A notice of the wreck appeared in the *Va. Gazette* (Dixon and Nicolson), 25 Sept. 1779. On Berry Floyd, see Stratton Nottingham, *Wills and Administrations of Accomack County, Virginia, 1663–1800* (Onancock, Va., 1931), vii–viii, 345.
3. Francis B. Dixon, *Abridgment of the Maritime Law . . .* (New York, 1857), 111–12; Theophilus Parsons, *A Treatise on Maritime Law . . .*, II (Boston, 1859), 617–19, 633, 636.
4. 3 Call 531; *Va. Gazette* (Dixon and Nicolson), 23 Oct., 18 Dec. 1779.
5. 3 Call 531–32. For the proceedings in the county court, see Northampton County Order Book XXX, 45, 221, 225, 240, 320, 363 (microfilm), Vi. For the date of the chancery decree, see Va. Ct. Ap. Ord. Bk. II, 20.
6. Stanley N. Katz, "The Politics of Law in Colonial America: Controversies over Chancery Courts and Equity Law in the Eighteenth Century," *Perspectives in American History*, V (1971), 257–84.
7. 3 Call 536.
8. See the opinion of Creed Taylor, judge of the Richmond Superior Court of Chancery, in the 1809 case of Alderson v. Biggars, 4 H. & M. 471–72.
9. See the remarks of John Wickham in Terrell v. Dick, 1 Call 548 (1799).
10. 1 Call 554; see the opinion of Creed Taylor (cited in n. 8).

Argument

2 July 1790

Marshall for the appellants,[1] admitted that whatever sentence the Court of Admiralty ought to have rendered, still that which they did render not having been appealed from, was binding on the parties, and the verdict in the county court ought to have conformed to it; but admitting this, he insisted on the binding force of that verdict, and on the total incapacity of a Court of Chancery to control it.[2] A verdict ought always to consist with the very right of the case, but it often happens that a Court of Chancery would have determined the cause otherwise than a jury has determined it; yet when this does happen, the Court of Chancery cannot, unless there be some unfair ingredient to give them jurisdiction, fashion the verdict according to its opinion of the right of the case.

It is not easy to conceive a case, which affords less cause, for the interposition of a court of equity, than the present. The trial has been a full, and a fair one; from the complexion of the whole case, it is obvious, that the defendant, in the court of law, was not, and could not be surprised.[3] He knew the claim of the plaintiff; he came prepared to contest it. It is not pretended that any unfair practice was used; nor is it even alledged, by the party himself in his bill, that he was not fully prepared, or that the whole case was not before the court and jury. The action was an equitable action.[4] The plaintiff could only recover on the equity of his case. The defendant could not possibly resort to a single principle for defence in a court of equity, which was not of equal avail in a court of law.[5] The cause comes on to be tried in Chancery precisely on the same facts, which have already been decided on in a court of law, and a jury. Nothing is, or can be alledged, but that the court of law decided against the law of the case. If this be sufficient ground for equitable interposition, then does the Court of Chancery erect itself into an appellate court from general verdicts and judgments thereon, both as to law and fact.[6] The decision of a county court, unappealed from, as entirely binds the subject, as the decision of the Court of Appeals. As well therefore may a Court of Chancery correct legal errors in this court, as legal errors in another court, whose judgment the parties have made final, by taking no exception, and praying no appeal. If that court may interpose in this case, there is no point of law which may not be carried into it. Suppose an action of detinue,[7] where the only question was the legal title to the thing sued for, should be determined in a court of law against the law of the case, would it be a sufficient cause, for going into Chancery, to say, that although the whole case came fully before the court and jury, yet they misunderstood the law, and the counsel for the defendant permitted the point of law to be buried under a general verdict? If that would not be a proper case for a Court of Chancery, still less is the present. In that case the legal title would, generally speaking, give its possessor some equity; in this case the legal title gives him none. If there be any original equity in either of the parties, it is only produced by the labor expended in saving the cargo. Each party then had an equitable title to the portion saved by itself. Barret and others have now only what they saved: Each party then is now possessed of that, and of that only, to which with respect to each other, each party was originally equitably entitled. The sentence of the court of Admiralty it is admitted gave to Floyd and others a legal right to that which was adjudged to them; but it gave them only a legal right; it did not enlarge their equity. They had then a legal title, but of that legal title, which the admiralty sentence gave them, the judgment of the county court has deprived them. The law which was once in their favour, is now against them, and they have not even the pretext for coming into this court, which the person would have in common cases, who had lost a good title by a general verdict; because they never had, in their favour, any thing, but positive law.

If the jurisdiction of a Court of Chancery be so extensive, as it must be, to comprehend this case, then surely, some authority for it may be produced, either from some treatise on the general principles of that court, or in some adjudged cases. If there be such let them be adduced. It is believed, however, that none exist: On the contrary, those which have been consulted assign much more limited powers to a court of equity, than must be assumed in order to support this decree, 3 *Black. Com.* 430[8] 1 *Eq. ca. ab.* 130, 2 *Eq. ca. ab.* 243, 524, 162.[9]

But the case of *Langdon against the African company and Dock, Prec. ch.* 221, is the very case: In that case, as in this, the vessel was condemned by the sentence of a court of admiralty: In that case, as in this, a court of law rendered a judgment in direct opposition to the sentence of the court of admiralty: In that case, as in this, application was made to the Court of Chancery to be relieved against the judgment; but, in that case, the relief was refused.[10]

Upon authority then, as well as upon principle, the decree of the Chancellor ought to be reversed.[11]

Marshall in reply. It has never been contended that inferior tribunals may draw before themselves subjects which have been determined in superior courts. It is admitted that had the counsel for the defendant spread the case upon the record, the judgment of the county court might have been reversed at law. The question is not, whether the county court erred, but whether the error be of such a sort as to give jurisdiction to a Court of Chancery? The judgment was against law, but not necessarily against the justice of the case; because it was contrary to the sentence of the court of admiralty. However, admitting it to be unjust, does by no means admit the cognizance of a court of equity. Juries, under the direction of a court of law, judge upon the justice, as well as law of a case; and it would erect a Court of Chancery into still more than a Court of Appeals, if their verdicts might be set aside for injustice.[12]

This case does not resemble the case of relief granted to an executor.[13] It is the admitted province of a Court of Chancery to relieve against the rigor of the law, as in case of penalties; and, in the case cited, a heavy penalty was incured by accident. It is true that equity will relieve against judgments on usurious and gaming contracts:[14] But if in either case, the whole fact had been fairly tried in a court of law and judgment rendered, no case can be shewn, where such a judgment was enjoined upon the same testimony, and merely because a court of law had decided against law.[15]

Printed, Daniel Call, *Reports of Cases Argued and Adjudged in the Court of Appeals of Virginia*, III (Richmond, 1805), 532–35, 535–36. This was one of the 1790 cases reported by JM that Call appended to his third volume (see Case No. 33, editorial note).

1. The appeal was argued on 2 July 1790 (Va. Ct. Ap. Ord. Bk. II, 17).

2. As JM shaped the issue, the case did not involve the impropriety of the county court's assumption of jurisdiction in an admiralty court matter, but rather the impropriety of the chancery court's assumption of jurisdiction in a matter that had been fairly tried at law in the county court.

3. Barrett's action at the county court was for money had and received to the plaintiff's use, one of the common counts in assumpsit. In his chancery bill Floyd evidently complained of surprise because the statement of indebtedness in the common count was too vague to give him proper notice of the nature of the claim. Perhaps for this reason Floyd failed to plead the admiralty decree as a bar to the action. On the common counts, see Case No. 2, editorial note; for an example of a count for money had and received, see Case No. 15, Doc. I.

4. JM used the term "equitable" to describe a right derived from considerations of fairness or justice rather than a course of action cognizant in a court of equity. Hence an action at law could be "equitable." JM's point was that Floyd had the same scope of defense in the county court as he was attempting to assert in the equity court.

5. Certain defenses were available only to a party in equity, as when an obligor on a bond sought relief on the ground that he was defrauded into making it. Fraud was not a defense available in a law action to enforce the bond. JM contended that no such situation existed here.

6. The most effective argument JM could make—one that he also employed in Pickett v. Morris (Case No. 40)—was to raise the specter of the equity court's becoming an appellate tribunal. This was a clever strategic tack, alerting the judges of the Court of Appeals to the dangerous consequences of upholding the chancery injunction. By sanctioning equity interference, they would override a jury determination reached at law. This was not to be lightly undertaken in a system that venerated trial by jury as a sacred right.

7. On the action of detinue, see Case No. 23, Argument, n. 1.

8. In this passage Blackstone objected to setting law and equity in sharp opposition to each other. He recited numerous examples, including the case of bond creditors whose debtor devised away his real estate, in which equity was powerless to mitigate the rigor of the common law (*Commentaries*, III, 430).

9. 1 Eq. Ca. Abr. 130, 21 Eng. Rep. 935, is a note on the jurisdiction of equity courts, with a subsection entitled: "A Cause shall not be examined upon Equity in the Court of Requests, Chancery or other court of Equity after judgment at the Common Law"; 2 Eq. Ca. Abr. 243, 22 Eng. Rep. 206, is another commentary on chancery jurisdiction and abstracts the case of Langdon v. African Company and Dockwray, which JM discussed immediately below (see n. 10); 2 Eq. Ca. Abr. 524, 22 Eng. Rep. 442, is a note on injunctions with an abstract of a case in which a request for an injunction was denied because the defendant had a defense at law; 2 Eq. Ca. Abr. 162, 22 Eng. Rep. 138, discusses when bills in equity properly lie, noting that a bill for relief after verdict where the plaintiff in equity could have defended himself at law would lie only in exceptional circumstances—e.g., discovery of new evidence.

10. In Langdon v. African Company and Dockwray, Prec. Ch. 221, 24 Eng. Rep. 108 (Ch., 1703), the defendant Dockwray, after his ship was condemned in admiralty, brought trover and conversion against the plaintiff and recovered. The plaintiff then filed a bill in chancery for relief, which the court refused to grant on the ground that he might have defended himself at law. The Court of Appeals distinguished this case in upholding the chancery injunction against Barrett's judgment. "A proper distinction," said the court, "is, where the defence comes to the knowledge of the party after the judgment." In the English case the declaration in trover gave sufficient notice of the cause of action, so that a proper defense at law could be set up (3 Call 537).

11. William Nelson followed, arguing for the appellee. He insisted that the county court judgment was unjust, being contrary to that of the admiralty court, which properly had cognizance of the dispute and where it had been fairly tried. He also cited precedents for equitable relief after a judgment at law.

12. Again, JM was trying to shift the issue away from the illegality (which he conceded) or even injustice of the county court judgment to the single question of whether the chancery court could intervene. If a party had a remedy at law and neglected to use it, he could not then seek relief in equity.

13. Nelson cited 1 Eq. Ca. Abr. 237, 21 Eng. Rep. 1016, abstracting cases

in which equity gave relief against an executor on the plea of *ne unques executor* (law French for "never executor"). In these cases the defendants denied they were executors, but judgment went against them on proof at the trial that some small items of the decedent's property had come into their hands.

14. Nelson likened this case to those of usury and gaming, where equity had often relieved against judgments at law.

15. The Court of Appeals on 6 July unanimously affirmed the chancery decree. The opinion of the court (presumably delivered by Pendleton) approved the enlargement of chancery jurisdiction as "beneficial to society" and noted that courts of chancery had interfered after law judgments on numerous occasions. The court was particularly impressed by the cases of the executors (see n. 13) as justifying a departure from the rule against interference after judgments at law (3 Call 536–37).

35. Beall v. Edmundson

1790

Editorial Note

Marshall's ingenious use of syllogistic reasoning, his knack for making his conclusion appear to follow inevitably from his initial premise, is superbly illustrated in his argument of this appeal. The case began in the General Court as an action of assumpsit for the recovery of money due on open account for goods sold and delivered. The plaintiff, represented by Marshall, was Samuel Beall, a prominent merchant of Williamsburg who had been in partnership with John Hatley Norton during the Revolution. A frequent litigant, Beall retained Marshall's services on numerous occasions.[1] The defendant was James Edmundson, a magistrate and former sheriff of Essex County who had served in the House of Burgesses before the Revolution.[2]

Beall had delivered merchandise to Edmundson on 20 July 1781. Almost two years later, on 10 March 1783, the Williamsburg merchant, not having received payment, obtained an express promise from Edmundson to pay for the articles and then immediately instituted a suit. The jury returned a special verdict, finding for the plaintiff if Edmundson's promise "takes the debt out of the act . . . 'for discouraging extensive credits and repealing the act prescribing the method of proving book debts.'" The General Court judges were divided in opinion on this question, three for the plaintiff and three for the defendant, with St. George Tucker doubting. After hearing arguments on 25 June 1789, the court the next day adjourned the case to the Court of Appeals for "novelty & difficulty," as provided by the law giving the appellate court jurisdiction in such situations.[3]

The legislation in question, enacted in 1779, was a direct reaction to the easy credit policies that prevailed before the Revolution and that Virginians believed were largely responsible for placing them in ruinous debt to British merchants. It repealed the 1748 law for proving book debts, which allowed the merchant's own books proved by his oath to be admitted as evidence of the debt. In addition, it drastically reduced the time limit for bringing suits on open account from two years to six months and hence was commonly known as the "six months" law.[4] The law was also designed as a war measure, Edmund Randolph later recalled, "conceived in the ardor of self-importance and the deficiency of political knowledge." Great Britain, so the Virginia legislators believed, "would be alarmed into some relaxation of hostility or some favorable overture by a demonstration that she was in danger of losing the facility of proving book debts, which had enabled her to engross by long and extensive credits" the trade of the former colony.[5]

By restricting credit and thus inhibiting the retail trade, the law became increasingly less popular with Virginians once the war had ended. Indeed, the circumstances of this case suggest that Virginia merchants and their customers tried to evade it. The way in which the case came before the Court of Appeals, by adjournment from a divided General Court, suggests further that *Beall* v. *Edmundson* was intended to bring forth a definitive statement as to how strictly the courts of the commonwealth were to enforce the law. Beall brought his suit more than six months after the delivery of the goods. Did Edmundson's subsequent promise create a new six-month period in the same way that a new promise took a debt out of the statute of limitations? Or did his promise take the case completely out of the 1779 law and place it on the same basis as actions whose limitation was five years? Either way, if such promises were enforced by the courts, merchants in effect could extend credit well beyond the limit imposed by the 1779 law.

Marshall employed two different strategies to persuade the court that the 1779 law should not bar Beall's suit. The first was to construe the law as an ordinary act of limitation whose bar to recovery could be removed by a new promise. If this did not succeed, he was ready with a more subtle argument. He posited two distinct contracts in this case, each founded on a different promise and consideration. The first originated in the implied promise raised by the account for goods sold and delivered. A suit on this contract was barred by the 1779 law. But Beall's suit, Marshall plausibly contended, was actually brought on a second contract created by Edmundson's express promise to pay. What was the consideration? Not the goods themselves (the consideration in the first contract), but Edmundson's "moral obligation" to pay for them. In return for his promise, Edmundson gained a clear conscience. The principle that a moral obligation was a sufficient consideration to support a contract had by this time been settled, as indicated by Marshall's citation to Buller. Blackstone had written that "any degree of reciprocity" would render a contract enforceable at law, "even if the thing be founded on a prior moral obligation, (as a promise to pay a just debt, though barred by the statute of limitations)." The principle had also been broadly stated by Lord Mansfield in recent decisions.[6]

1. On Beall, see Stubbs, *Descendants of Mordecai Cooke*, 247, 249; Mason, *John Norton & Sons*, 457–58, 462, 470, 475, 483; *Virginia Gazette and General Advertiser*, 8 May 1793. JM was also Beall's attorney in three other reported

cases: Braxton v. Beall, General Court (1787) (*PJM*, I, 221–30); Beall v. Cockburn, Court of Appeals (1790) (4 Call 162); Mercer v. Beall, General Court (1791) (Case No. 31 in the present volume). JM recorded fees from Beall in his account book for Mar. 1788, Mar. 1789, July 1789, and Aug. 1789, which probably covered this case and Beall v. Cockburn (*PJM*, I, 404; II, 356, 367, 368).

2. *Tyler's Quarterly*, VII (1926), 188–89; *CVSP*, IV, 340; *JCSV*, II, 191; IV, 361–62.

3. 3 Call 514–15. Tucker briefly reported the General Court proceedings. See Beall v. Edmundson, 25 June 1789, Casebook, Tucker-Coleman Papers, ViW. For the Court of Appeals' jurisdiction in cases of "difficulty," see Hening, *Statutes*, IX, 523.

4. Hening, *Statutes*, X, 133–34. For a discussion of the prewar legislation concerning book debts, see Case No. 15, editorial note. Tucker referred to the 1779 act as the "six months" law in his reports of cases (see Shore & McConnico v. Ferguson, 11 Oct. 1786; Beall v. Edmundson, 25 June 1789, Casebook, Tucker-Coleman Papers, ViW).

5. Edmund Randolph, *History of Virginia*, ed. Arthur H. Shaffer (Charlottesville, 1970), 279.

6. Blackstone, *Commentaries*, II, 445; Fifoot, *History and Sources of the Common Law*, 406–10.

Argument

3 July 1790

MARSHALL for the plaintiff.[1] The act of 1779 is in fact nothing more than an act of limitations.[2] The act of 1705, which is the general act of limitations declares, "that all actions of trespass &c. shall be brought within the time therein after expressed and not after; that is to say, the said actions upon the case &c. within five years next after the cause of such action has accrued, and not after:"[3] And the act of 1779 declares, that all actions or suits, founded upon account for goods, wares and merchandize sold and delivered, or for any articles, charged in any store account, shall be commenced and sued within *six months* next after the cause of such action or suit, or the delivery of such goods, wares and merchandize, and not after; except that, in case of the death of the creditors or debtors before the expiration of the said term of six months, the further time of twelve months, from the death of such creditor or debtor, shall be allowed for the commencement of any such action or suit. The object and effect of each act is, to prevent the institution of suits in certain cases after a time, limited by the wisdom of the legislature, shall have elapsed. In the operative words of the two principal clauses which have been cited, there is little other distinction than the difference of time allowed for bringing the action. It will not be contended that a longer, or a shorter time, makes the act more or less an act of limitations. The leading and important distinction between the two laws is, that the first must be pleaded, whereas the second is to be noticed by the court and jury, although the defendant should not seek to avail himself of it.[4]

The latter law does not, for this reason, cease to be an act of limitations. If a similar clause had been introduced into the first law, it would have been an act of limitations notwithstanding. That clause does not affect the right of action: It only relates to the manner in which the subject, to be decided on, is to be brought before the court. But the decision of the court will be the same in the one case, as in the other. In a cause, depending on the latter law, which comes before the court without pleading the act, the court must decide precisely in the same manner as it would decide the same case brought before it by pleading, if the act had required that it should be pleaded. This clause in the act therefore does not change its character, or make it less an act of limitations. If it be, in essence, an act of limitations, then it will be admitted that the fresh assumpsit rescues this case from the operation of the act, as the suit was brought immediately after the new assumpsit was made. But whatever may be the opinion of the court on this point, the action is clearly maintainable on other ground.[5]

The suit is instituted, not on the contract raised by the delivery of the goods, but on a new contract, for which the delivery of the goods was a sufficient consideration.[6]

Altho the declaration is in the usual form, yet the assumpsit, laid in it, may be considered, either as an implied, or an actual assumpsit.[7] Upon demurrer to the Declaration, or after a general verdict, it would be considered as founded on an express assumpsit, if it was necessary so to consider it, in order to support it: Therefore *a fortiori*, the declaration, in this case, where the verdict shews a special assumpsit, will be considered as charging that special assumpsit.[8] The suit, then, being instituted, not on the delivery of the goods, but on a subsequent agreement to pay for them; the only question is, whether the consideration, on which that agreement was made, be sufficient to support it?

A moral obligation to do a thing is a sufficient consideration for an assumpsit, *Bull. ni. pr.* 147.[9]

Can a stronger moral obligation exist than to pay for property purchased?

No clause in the act does, or can, destroy this moral obligation; nor does any clause make it an unfit consideration for a new contract.

The act designed to prevent the inconsiderate incurment of debt, by taking up goods without enquiry; not to disable the individual from making a contract upon a conscientious consideration. The act goes no further than to absolve the debtor from the legal obligation created by the original purchase of the goods: It does not disable him from making a subsequent contract concerning them. Cases innumerable might be adduced, where a promise will bind a man to do that, which he was not bound by law to do before the promise was made. Money advanced to a son, without request on the part of the father, is yet a sufficient consideration to give validity to a promise of the father to repay it. A debt barred by the act of limitations, is a sufficient consideration for an assumpsit: A bankrupt, whose legal discharge is as complete as it would have been had he never owed a shilling, will yet be bound by his promise, made after the bankruptcy, to pay a debt contracted before it.[10]

Printed, Daniel Call, *Reports of Cases Argued and Adjudged in the Court of Appeals of Virginia*, III (Richmond, 1805), 515–17. This was one of the 1790 cases reported by JM that Call appended to his third volume (see Case No. 33, editorial note).

1. The appeal was heard on 3 July 1790, JM speaking first (Va. Ct. Ap. Ord. Bk. II, 18).

2. Hening, *Statutes*, X, 133. This act is discussed in the editorial note.

3. Ibid., III, 381–82. See Case No. 14, editorial note.

4. The third section of the 1779 law required courts and juries, "*ex officio*, to take notice of this act, and determine accordingly, although the defendant shall not have pleaded it" (Hening, *Statutes*, X, 134).

5. As was to be expected, opposing attorney John Taylor stressed the differences between the two acts. By requiring courts and juries to take notice of the 1779 law even though it was not pleaded, the legislature, Taylor contended, obviously intended something more than an act of limitations: "The act of limitations does not destroy the debt, but may, or may not, bar its recovery: This act destroys the debt itself; and therefore, need not be pleaded." To treat it as a mere act of limitations would defeat its express purpose, which was to discourage easy credit (3 Call 517–19).

The Court of Appeals ignored this question in deciding the case. JM's construction of the 1779 law, however, was ratified by subsequent legislative action. In 1789 the assembly repealed the section directing courts and juries to take notice and extended the six-month period to one year. Three years later the revised law was incorporated into a general statute of limitations (Hening, *Statutes*, XIII, 5; Shepherd, *Statutes*, I, 27–28).

6. JM began his second line of argument, that the plaintiff's action was not brought on the account, to which the 1779 law applied, but on a second contract. His problem here was to establish the consideration on which the second contract was founded.

7. JM cleverly exploited the vagueness of the common counts in assumpsit

to suit his purposes. The declaration was "in the usual form," that is, it alleged that the defendant was indebted to the plaintiff for "goods, wares and merchandizes sold and delivered" (3 Call 514). In this form, JM contended, it was impossible to determine whether the count in indebitatus assumpsit was brought upon the implied promise to pay for goods received on account or upon the defendant's later express promise to pay the debt. On the common counts in assumpsit, see Case No. 2, editorial note. For a declaration containing a count for goods sold and delivered, see Case No. 15, Doc. I.

8. JM maintained that if the declaration did not clarify which contract was being sued upon, the appellate court must presume the one that could rationally support the jury's verdict. Had the jury returned a general verdict for Beall, the court would consider the suit as brought to enforce the second promise, or contract. Since in this case the jury returned a special verdict showing that Edmundson had made an express promise to pay, there was an even more compelling reason, said JM, to consider that promise as the foundation of the suit. The purpose of the special verdict, however, was to have the court decide what effect the promise had on the case; it did not necessarily show that Beall's action was brought on that promise. JM in effect was asking the court to presume what it was supposed to decide.

9. Buller, *Nisi Prius*, 147: "If in consideration of a thing already done, without my request, not for my benefit, and where I was under no moral obligation to do it, I promise to pay money, that is *nudum pactum*, and void. But if I were under a moral obligation to do a thing, and another person does it without my request, and I afterwards promise to pay, that is good."

10. JM cited no authorities, but his examples are similar to those recited by Lord Mansfield in Hawkes v. Saunders, 1 Cowp. 289, 98 Eng. Rep. 1091 (K.B., 1782), also reprinted in Fifoot, *History and Sources of the Common Law*, 433–35: "Where a man is under a moral obligation, which no court of law or equity can enforce, and promises, the honesty and rectitude of the thing is a consideration. As if a man promise to pay a just debt, the recovery of which is barred by the Statute of Limitations; or if a man, after he comes of age, promises to pay a meritorious debt contracted during his minority, but not for necessaries; or if a bankrupt, in affluent circumstances after his certificate, promises to pay the whole of his debts."

Taylor protested that if this suit could be maintained on the special promise, independent of the account, the 1779 law would be constantly evaded, for "such promises might always be obtained." The court, speaking through President Pendleton on 7 July, found JM's reasoning more persuasive and decided in favor of his client Beall. The 1779 law, said Pendleton, operated only where the plaintiff had to produce an account to support his action. In this case the action was maintainable without the account, the debtor having made a later special promise to pay in consideration of a moral obligation. This promise took the debt out of the reach of the law for discouraging extensive credits (Va. Ct. Ap. Ord. Bk. II, 21; 3 Call 519–21).

For another case involving the construction of the 1779 law, in which the court's opinion cited Beall v. Edmundson, see Tomlin, Mitchell and How v. Kelly, 1 Wash. 190, 192 (1793).

36. Ross v. Pynes

1790

Editorial Note

This case provoked a discussion at the bar concerning the extent to which jury verdicts should be subject to the superintending control of judges, who had the power of ordering a new trial when they disagreed with a verdict. Legal strategy in this instance required Marshall and co-counsel Jerman Baker to emphasize the need for such control in tempering the excesses and checking the mistakes "juries may sometimes commit." Opposing attorney John Taylor, on the other hand, maintained that the power of ordering new trials was subject to abuse and could seriously undermine the cherished institution of trial by jury: "For, if a court will perpetually grant new trials until a completely satisfactory verdict is obtained, the effect is the same, as if the court, without the intervention of a jury, should decide the cause and assess the damages."[1] The situation became more complicated when, as happened in this case, the verdict was to be certified to the High Court of Chancery to enable that court to make a final decree. Chancery courts frequently directed issues to be tried in a court of law. If court and jury disagreed on such "issues out of chancery," was the chancellor compelled to order a new trial, or could he accept the verdict or not at his discretion?[2]

The decision of the appeal in *Ross* v. *Pynes* marked the conclusion of a dispute that had begun twenty-three years earlier. In 1767 Benjamin Pynes, a resident of King and Queen County, became heavily indebted in consequence of being security for an insolvent debtor. To satisfy the demand against him he was obliged to sell most of his slaves under execution at a public auction to be held at Rocky Ridge (soon to become the new town of Manchester) in Chesterfield County. Before the auction Pynes negotiated a private sale of part of his slaves to David Ross, a prominent Petersburg merchant who was then actively engaged in the purchase of such property. This sale was not consummated, however, because Pynes's creditors demanded cash rather than a bill of exchange, the means of payment proposed by Ross. According to Pynes, Ross then agreed to bring cash to Rocky Ridge on the day appointed for the sale and take the slaves he previously had attempted to buy. Ross did not attend the sale but sent his storekeeper, John Davis, with instructions to purchase. These instructions were in a letter dated 7 December 1767, which concluded in these words: "If you think the Negroes look well you need not stand on five or ten pounds more—there has been some disputes raised about the title, they say Mann Page setts up a claim to them but I believe there is but little danger."[3]

On the day of the auction Davis decided not to purchase on Ross's behalf because only part of the slaves his employer had wanted were there. While conversing with another man about his business at the sale, Davis showed him the letter from Ross. This careless act gave rise to a rumor of the defectiveness of Pynes's title to the slaves, which spread quickly among the prospective bidders. The upshot was that no one would buy without a bond and security for warranting the title, which Pynes, being an "utter stranger" in that county, could not obtain. He was forced to sell the slaves privately the next day at a much lower price, so he claimed, than he would have received at the public auction.[4]

Soon thereafter Pynes sued Ross for slander of title, an action on the case for injury resulting from words falsely and maliciously casting doubt or suspicion on one's title to real or personal property. It was essential in such an action for the plaintiff to show some particular damage to have happened in consequence of the words, which in themselves were not slanderous.[5] After many delays the case was tried at the King William County Court in October 1783, the jury awarding Pynes five hundred pounds damages. Ross appealed the case to the General Court, which in April 1785 sustained the lower court's judgment. He then applied for an injunction in the High Court of Chancery, claiming surprise because of the absence of his chief witness, Davis, at the county court trial. Chancellor Wythe awarded a temporary injunction in May 1788 and ordered a new trial at law. At the second trial, held at the King and Queen District Court, Ross demurred to Pynes's evidence, denying that it was sufficient to maintain the action. The jury returned a conditional verdict for one thousand pounds. The district court did not decide on the demurrer but certified it and the verdict to the High Court of Chancery, also certifying its opinion that the "weight of testimony" was in Ross's favor and the verdict therefore "not satisfactory."[6]

Despite the law court's disapproval of the verdict, Chancellor Wythe upheld it in his final decree of 6 November 1789, though he reduced the damages to five hundred pounds, the amount of the first verdict. The chancellor reasoned that Ross's letter to Davis was the only source of the rumor causing Pynes's loss and that Ross should therefore "make reparation" even though he apparently had no malicious intent.[7] The Court of Appeals sustained the chancery decree in *Ross* v. *Pynes*, but later adopted a general rule concerning issues out of chancery: If the trial court certified that the verdict was against evidence, the chancellor ought not to be satisfied with the verdict and should grant a new trial.[8]

The pronouncement of this rule in the 1794 case of *Southall* v. *M'Keand* provoked an indignant commentary from Wythe in his chancery reports published the following year. In this case the district court, as in *Ross* v. *Pynes*, certified its opinion that the weight of evidence was contrary to the verdict, and again Chancellor Wythe declared the verdict satisfactory. The appellate court overruled him, stating that a verdict so certified could not be considered as settling the dispute. What, asked Wythe, was he to do if the same evidence was before him that was before the district court and he happened to differ with the opinion of the district court certifying its disapproval of the verdict? The chancellor believed the Court of Appeals should defer to him whenever he disagreed with the district court, but President Pendleton, observing that it was "unusual for the Chancellor to be satisfied with such a verdict," contended that the appellate court in this situation had complete discretion to reconsider the case on its merits.[9]

1. For Taylor's remarks, see 3 Call 572.

2. See Argument, n. 3.

3. Copies of some of the chancery suit papers in Ross v. Pynes are preserved in the Tucker-Coleman Papers, ViW. These include Ross's bill in chancery; Pynes's answer, 25 Sept. 1785; and the deposition of John Davis. The quotation from the letter is taken from Davis's deposition. The letter is reproduced in its entirety in Wythe's report of the chancery proceedings (Wythe 70–71).

4. Deposition of John Davis; Pynes's answer, Ross v. Pynes, Tucker-Coleman Papers, ViW; Wythe 70.

5. Blackstone, *Commentaries*, III, 124–25.

6. Pynes's answer; Ross's bill in chancery, Ross v. Pynes, Tucker-Coleman Papers, ViW; Wythe 69–71.

7. Va. Ct. Ap. Ord. Bk. II, 45; Wythe 71–72. St. George Tucker noted that Wythe's opinion was contrary to the rule laid down by Lord Mansfield in Hargrave v. Le Breton, 4 Burr. 2425–26, 98 Eng. Rep. 271 (K.B., 1769), that "to maintain such an action as this is, there must be malice, either express or implied; and the words spoken must go to defeat the plaintiff's title." In Ross v. Pynes, said Tucker, "There was neither malice expressed nor implied . . . and the words went rather to affirm, than to defeat the plaintiff's title" (Tucker, *Blackstone's Commentaries*, III, 124 n. 10).

8. Pleasants v. Ross, 1 Wash. 156 (1793); Southall v. M'Keand, 1 Wash. 336 (1794).

9. Wythe 99–102; 1 Wash. 337. The court had allowed the decree in Ross v. Pynes to stand because there had been two concurring verdicts.

Argument

4–5 December 1790

For the appellant[1] it was insisted.

That the original verdict having been notoriously obtained on an exparte hearing which the defendant at law could not have prevented as he could not have had notice of the illness of his only material witness, the cause came properly into Chancery for relief against that verdict.[2] Being thus properly in a court of Chancery the decree which was made on the hearing might perhaps have been final and the cause returned to a court of law, for a new trial and judgment at law, in which case the court of common law could have controlled the verdict, or it might direct as it has directed, the verdict to be certified to the court of Chancery in order to enable the chancellor to give a final decree. When the verdict is to be returned to that court, it has all the qualities of an issue directed out of chancery, and its object is to inform the conscience of the judge on some fact about which he doubts or to ascertain damages which himself cannot ascertain.[3]

It is a settled principle that the opinion of the court must in some degree concur with that of the jury in order to give the conscience of the chancellor the satisfaction he requires. 2 *Eq. ca. ab.*[4]

This rule is founded on sound reason and policy. The trial by jury, which under its present modification we so justly prize, would become dangerous and might possibly destroy itself, if the superintendance and reasonable control of judges were entirely removed. Juries might sometimes be led by the most unlimited prejudices into such extravagant excesses as would render it doubtful, whether the institution should be considered as a blessing or a curse. The wisdom of the law therefore to preserve all the excellence of a trial by twelve honest and impartial men, without the ills which would otherwise attend it, has subjected their verdict to the opinion of Judges selected for that purpose. This controlling power tempers the excesses and checks the mistakes which juries may sometimes commit.

It is as necessary that this controlling power should exist over issues proceeding from a court of Chancery, as over those originating in a court of law. Was it not to exist, it would be as proper to try the fact in the usual manner, in which an inquest of office is taken, as in a court of law.[5] It would seem to be treating the law judges indecently to send a fact to their bar for trial, to oblige them to set during the trial, and yet to leave nothing to their opinion.

So long as the verdict of a jury on an issue directed out of Chancery may be as contrary to evidence, as the verdict of a jury on an issue made up in a court of law, the opinion of the judge who sits on the trial must be as important; and ought to be as operative in the one case as in the other. In this case the demurrer does not derogate from the importance of the opinion certified by the judges at law, because it does not contain the testimony offered on the part of the appellant.[6]

Unquestionably then the opinion of the court, if so expressed as to be decisive against the verdict, ought to procure a new trial:

The words of the certificate are: "Ordered, that it be certified to the High Court of Chancery, as the opinion of the judges of this court, that the weight of testimony on the trial of this issue was on the part of the defendant, and therefore that the verdict was not satisfactory to the court."

No form is prescribed to be used by the judges of law who certify their opinion to the Chancellor. It is only necessary that their opinion should be plainly and intelligibly expressed.

Had this been a case finally determinable at law, the judges if entirely dissatisfied with the verdict could have granted a new trial. Not having the power to grant a new trial, they can only certify their opinion to that court which possesses the power, and if their opinion is to have any weight, the judge to whom it is certified ought to act upon it, as they would have acted, had the power of granting a new trial been in them. It can scarcely be doubted but that the judges who gave the certificate in this case would have granted a new trial, had it been in their power; and if so, the chancellor ought not to have been satisfied with the verdict.

It was also contended that the testimony did not support the issue, and that the letter contained no slander, but rather the reverse as it evidenced the conviction Mr. Ross felt of the goodness of the title, and might be a necessary caution to his agent, not to be deterred from purchasing, by any report he might hear on that subject.

It was also contended that the demurrer ought to have been decided at common law.[7]

Printed, Daniel Call, *Reports of Cases Argued and Adjudged in the Court of Appeals of Virginia*, III (Richmond, 1805), 569–71. This was one of the 1790 cases reported by JM that Call appended to his third volume (see Case No. 33, editorial note).

1. The report states that Jerman Baker and JM argued the cause for the appellant and that John Taylor represented the appellee. The appeal was argued on 4 and 5 Dec. 1790. JM recorded a fee under date of 2 Dec. (Va. Ct. Ap. Ord. Bk. II, 42; *PJM*, II, 406).

Baker had been Ross's attorney when the case was before the High Court of Chancery and drafted his bill in chancery (Ross v. Pynes, Tucker-Coleman Papers, ViW).

2. Ross, as plaintiff in equity, sought to have the law judgment enjoined on the ground of surprise or accident—in this instance, the unforeseen absence of his chief witness. When the case was at the King William court, so Pynes stated in his answer, Ross's attorney John Warden repeatedly moved for continuances, thereby delaying the trial. Finally, at the July 1783 court Warden agreed that the trial should take place at the October court. At that time Warden again moved for a continuance on account of the absence of his witness. The motion was denied, Warden having no proof that the witness was summoned or that he was sick. The trial proceeded with only Pynes's witnesses present. The answer further stated that Ross appealed the county court judgment to the General Court, which affirmed the judgment in Apr. 1785 (Pynes's answer, Ross v. Pynes, Tucker-Coleman Papers, ViW).

3. When facts in a chancery suit were disputed, the chancellor, rather than rely on written depositions, usually directed an issue to be tried by jury in a court of law. In Virginia such "issues out of chancery" were routinely sent to the district courts for trial, with the verdicts to be certified to the chancery court (Tucker, *Blackstone's Commentaries*, III, 452 and n. 30; Hening, *Statutes*, XII, 465).

4. The citation is apparently 2 Eq. Ca. Abr. 736–37, 22 Eng. Rep. 624–26, a collection of cases under the heading, "In What Cases a New Trial Will Be Granted on an Issue Directed Out of Chancery."

5. An inquest of office was an inquiry by an officer—sheriff, coroner, escheator, etc.—concerning any matter entitling the Crown (or state) to possession of real or personal property. In Virginia the jury in an inquest of escheat consisted of an indeterminate number of "fit persons." In 1794 the law was changed to make the jury consist of sixteen freeholders (Tucker, *Blackstone's Commentaries*, III, 258 and n. 5; Hening, *Statutes*, XII, 158–59; Shepherd, *Statutes*, I, 296).

6. At the second trial, held at the King and Queen District Court, Ross demurred to Pynes's evidence, admitting the truth of the facts alleged but denying their legal sufficiency. The purpose of the demurrer was to take the question out of the cognizance of the jury and leave it to the court to decide. Giving no judgment on the demurrer, the court did find the evidence in favor of Ross and the verdict consequently unsatisfactory (see editorial note and n. 6). JM and Baker contended that the demurrer, though admitting the truth of Pynes's testimony, did not state the evidence on behalf of Ross and therefore should not diminish the force of the opinion certified by the district court.

7. John Taylor for the appellee Pynes argued against granting a new trial, two juries having agreed on a verdict. The only question to be decided, he said, was the amount of damages to be assessed, for which there was no exact standard. Perfect agreement between court and juries in such cases was impossible; if a court was to grant new trials until it was completely satisfied, juries would become "totally useless."

The Court of Appeals, speaking through Pendleton on 8 Dec., agreed with Taylor and upheld the decree of the High Court of Chancery. The evidence showed that Pynes had suffered "a real injury," for which "compensation ought to be made." The court, however, denied Taylor's contention that

Chancellor Wythe should have ordered Ross to pay £1,000, the amount of the second verdict, instead of restoring the damages to £500, the amount of the first verdict. "The increase of damages in the second verdict," said Pendleton, "might be produced by sudden passion, which in this case it was proper for the Chancellor to moderate, and to take that sum which two juries had affirmed" (3 Call 571–73).

37. Claiborne's Executor v. Hill

1793

Editorial Note

This case began in the High Court of Chancery in 1790 as *Hill* v. *Claiborne*. Marshall represented Edward Hill of King and Queen County in both the original suit and the appeal. Herbert Claiborne, who resided in neighboring King William County across the Mattaponi River, had struggled since the close of the war to extricate himself from financial embarrassments. In November 1784 Hill, one of Claiborne's creditors, had levied an execution against certain slaves and personal property—corn, cattle, and tobacco—found on Claiborne's plantation. He was unable to proceed in his remedy, however, because title to this property actually belonged to Augustine Claiborne, father of Herbert and a resident of Sussex County in the Southside. To give effect to the execution, Hill brought a bill in chancery to set aside Herbert Claiborne's prior conveyance of the property to his father.[1]

As stated in the answer to the bill, Herbert Claiborne had conveyed all of his sixty slaves and personal property (including household articles and furniture, thirty-six cattle, forty sheep, and one hundred hogs) by way of mortgage in February 1783 to secure a debt of three thousand pounds owed to his father. This debt arose from a transaction of June 1780 by which Augustine Claiborne turned over to his son his share of the profits of a business partnership with Carter Braxton. The answer recited other conveyances made by Herbert Claiborne in settlement of debts owed not only to his father but also to other creditors. In May 1784 Augustine Claiborne purchased outright the property that had been mortgaged to him, the sale price being credited to Herbert Claiborne's account with his father. The bill of sale, however, was not recorded until after Hill had levied his execution. The High Court of Chancery decreed in June 1792 that the mortgage of February 1783 was fraudulent and void as to the creditors of Herbert Claiborne and that Hill's judgment should be satisfied out of the assets of the estate of Augustine Claiborne. John Claiborne, executor of Augustine Claiborne, immediately appealed the decree.[2]

The father-son relationship, the timing of the mortgage, the dubious consideration for which it was given, the total disposition of the property, and above all the son's keeping physical possession of the slaves, cattle, and other property were circumstances suggesting, said Marshall, a fraudulent attempt to defeat the just claims of Hill and other creditors of Herbert Claiborne. To protect themselves against secret and collusive transfers of property (an age-old means of fraud practiced by debtors) creditors and purchasers had the benefit of two statutes enacted during the reign of Elizabeth I, the principles of which were first formally incorporated into the Virginia code in 1785. Unless made "upon good consideration, and *bona fide*," conveyances of landed and personal estate were deemed to be fraudulent against creditors and purchasers.[3] In Virginia creditors were further protected by laws requiring conveyances of personal as well as real property to be recorded in a county court and registered in the General Court.[4]

Herbert Claiborne's mortgage raised the important question of the applicability of English precedent to Virginia conditions. In England courts of equity were vigilant in detecting and suppressing fraud, holding with Lord Mansfield that the statutes of Elizabeth should be liberally construed for this purpose.[5] This was particularly true in regard to transfers of personal property; because there was no law in England directing such conveyances to be recorded, purchasers and creditors might easily be defrauded by means of prior secret trusts. The courts accordingly were quick to seize upon any sign of fraud to set aside conveyances. One clear mark, or badge, of fraud in a sale or mortgage of personal estate ("chattel mortgage," as a mortgage of personalty later came to be called) was where the former proprietor (the mortgagor) kept possession of the property. Possession of personal property, unlike the possession of land, was the highest indication of ownership. If one continued to have the use and disposal of goods and chattels that had been conveyed to another, that person thereby gained a false credit and the door was open for deceiving those who dealt with him.

While English authority seemed to point to Claiborne's mortgage as a fraudulent conveyance, counsel for the appellant in this case contended that these precedents did not apply to Virginia. In Virginia, so the argument ran, the recording laws served the same purpose as did the English courts of equity in preventing fraud. There was no need for Virginia courts to adopt the same broad construction of the statute against fraudulent conveyances. As long as the deed had been duly recorded, enabling creditors to discover the actual owner of personal property, the mere fact of a mortgagor's remaining in possession should not in itself constitute fraud. The principle of *caveat emptor* ("let the buyer beware") therefore properly applied to cases of this type in Virginia, though not in England where there was no way to guard against secret transfers of personal property.[6]

In stating the case for his client, Marshall was not content simply to invoke the English cases. Instead he preferred to ground his argument on a strict interpretation of Virginia's recording act of 1748. Claiborne's mortgage was invalid, he insisted, because it had not been recorded in the proper county court (King William). That he chose to make this his principal point suggests that Marshall doubted whether English precedent in this instance would influence the Virginia Court of Appeals in his favor.

1. On the Hill and Claiborne families, see Bagby, *King and Queen County*, 343–44; Harris, *Old New Kent County*, I, 431–33; II, 582–84, 594–96. JM recorded fees in Mar. 1790, when the suit began in the High Court of Chancery, and in Sept. 1792, after the chancery decree was appealed to the Court of Appeals (*PJM*, II, 386, 446). Herbert Claiborne was party to an earlier case of JM's in the Court of Appeals (Case No. 32).

2. 1 Wash. 177–79; Va. Ct. Ap. Ord. Bk. II, 226–27.

3. 13 Eliz. c. 5; 27 Eliz. c. 4; Hening, *Statutes*, XII, 160–62.

4. Hening, *Statutes*, IV, 397–99; V, 408–9.

5. Bacon, *Abridgment* (1st Am. ed.), III, 309–10 (citing Cadogan v. Kennett, 2 Cowp. 434, 98 Eng. Rep. 1172 [K.B., 1776]).

6. 1 Wash. 180, 184.

Argument
24 April 1793

MARSHALL for the appellee.[1] Whether the reason assigned, why the English cases, do not apply in this country be a substantial one, or not, will depend upon the just construction of the act of 1748, which is certainly very obscurely expressed.

The first clause of that law declares, that no lands, tenements, or hereditaments, shall alter, pass, or change, whereby any estate of freehold shall be made to take effect, unless the same be recorded in the General Court, or court of that county, where the land shall lie, within a certain time.[2]—Now, this clause cannot possibly apply to *slaves*, because the deed is to be recorded in the *county where the land lies*. The fourth clause declares, that *all* deeds of trust, or mortgage, must be recorded *according to the directions of this act*.[3] But the directory part of that act, as to the *place* of registration, is applicable to *land* only, for the reason before given.—But, if *slaves* are meant by the law, then by analogy to land, this deed, ought to have been recorded in King William County Court, because, the slaves were *in that county*, at the time the deed was made, and the execution served upon them. So that, either a mortgage of slaves is not comprehended within the law, or if it be, then, this deed has been registered in an improper county.[4]

Mr. Marshall. I contend that if the law apply to a mortgage of slaves, the deed in question, was not recorded in the proper County.

It is also an important question, whether the mortgagor of personal property, can retain the possession of it. The English cases lay it down, that a security upon personal property, is not properly a mortgage, but a pledge, or deposit, and remains in the pawnee's possession. What influence, the custom of this country (which is otherwise,) may have upon this point, I will not pretend to determine.[5] But, if all these points be against me, I rely with confidence, upon the many badges of fraud which attend this case.

In the first place, consider the *connection* between the parties; a mortgage by a son, to the father.—*The time*;—just previous to the affairs of Herbert Clayborn becoming desperate, and whilst his creditors were pressing him. A conveyance too, of *everything* he possessed, down to a knife case, with a sweeping clause, that nothing might be omitted. It is remarkable too, that only that species of property is conveyed, which might be resorted to by his creditors: for his real estate (not encumbered) was considerable, and is not conveyed.—If the transaction were *bona fide*, would he deprive himself of all the comforts of life, and the means of deriving profit from his lands? or would he not rather have retained a part of his personal, and in its room, substituted some of his real estate. All the cases agree, that a total disposition of a man's estate, or the remaining in possession, are certain badges of fraud[6]—there is also something remarkable in the consideration stated—to wit, that the father, and Braxton, in 1777, had formed a commercial connection—the father's capital was £6000.—In 1782, it is decided to have been a losing business; and yet, in 1780, the father sells the profits of this trade, to the son, for £3000 sterling, which is the consideration of the mortgage. But again: in 1784, the son makes an absolute conveyance to the father, for £1788: 18, after which, it must be agreed, that the son's retaining the possession is so strong an evidence of a secret trust, as not to be fairly accounted for. The property continues in his possession, when the execution is served, he receives the crops, disposes of them, converts the cattle, hogs, &c. to his own use, and in short, exercises the most compleat ownership over the whole.[7]

Marshall. There is but one possible way of construing the act of assembly, so as to make all its parts consist together, and at the same time, effect the purpose, for which deeds ought to be registered. The first section of the law directs, that deeds of land shall be recorded in the General Court, or Court of the County, in which the land lies.—The 4th section directs, that all mortgages, shall be recorded according to the directions of that act.—The 9th and 10th sections declare, that for the purpose of giving notice to purchasers of land, slaves, &c. of prior incumbrances, memorials of all deeds of lands, slaves, &c. shall be registered, by the clerk of the General Court; and the clerks of the different County Courts, are also directed to furnish the clerk of the General Court, with memorials of all deeds, recorded in their respective courts, which are also to be registered in the General Court. If then, the deed be of *lands and slaves*, it ought to be recorded in the General Court, or court of the county *where the land lies*—if of *slaves* only, then in the General Court: In this way only, will there be compleat notoriety of all deeds—if it may be recorded in the county where the mortgagee lives, a purchaser must first know, who is the mortgagee, before he can know to what County Court to apply. If it may be recorded in any county, then, if the clerk should fail to send forward the memorial to the General Court, the registration will afford no notice whatever.[8]

Mr. MARSHALL.—That act relates to *positive* gifts, the act of 1748, to *mortgages*—that, to conveyances *without* consideration.—This, to conveyances with consideration.—The deeds spoken of in that law, may be proved by two witnesses. Those mentioned in this law must be proved by three.—That is passed ten years after, and has no reference to this: there can therefore be no analogy between them.[9]

1. The appeal was heard on 24 Apr. 1793 (Va. Ct. Ap. Ord. Bk. II, 221). William DuVal spoke first for the appellant, denying the applicability of English cases, particularly Twyne's Case. In this 1601 case one Pierce, in debt to Twyne and another creditor, was sued by the latter. Pending the suit, Pierce secretly conveyed all his personal property to Twyne in satisfaction of his debt to Twyne, but at the same time continued in possession of the property. The court held that this was a fraudulent gift and sale. DuVal contended that Twyne's Case and others were "for many reasons too high toned, to apply in this Country." English courts, he said, were influenced by bankruptcy laws, which forbade one creditor from being preferred to another. Moreover, conveyances of personal estate in England did not have to be recorded, as was required by law in Virginia. Hence the danger of fraud was much greater there, and the courts consequently more inclined to set aside conveyances as fraudulent (3 Co. Rep. 80b, 76 Eng. Rep. 809 [Star Chamber, 1601]; 1 Wash. 179–80).

2. "An Act for settling the Titles and Bounds of Lands . . ." (Hening, *Statutes*, V, 408).

3. Ibid., 409–10. The recording requirements were spelled out more

clearly in a law of 1734, on which that of 1748 was based. It provided for the recording to be in the General Court or county "where the lands, or other things, lie, or where the parties live." Evidently this earlier law was not available to counsel and judges as an aid in construing the later one (ibid., IV, 398).

4. At this point Judge Lyons requested JM to read the tenth section of the recording act, which required a memorial of all bargains, sales, mortgages, etc. of real and personal property to be registered in the General Court. The memorial was to include, among other things, the number and names of the slaves and description of personal estate sold or mortgaged (1 Wash. 180; Hening, *Statutes*, V, 411–12).

5. A pledge or pawn was a deposit of personal property with the pawnbroker (pawnee) as security for a debt. In a mortgage of real estate possession usually remained with the mortgagor. In a mortgage of personal property the general rule followed by the English courts was that this property should be delivered to the mortgagee in the same manner as a pawn was deposited with the pawnbroker. Although he gave no specific citation, JM may have had in mind the discussion in the second chapter of John Joseph Powell's *A Treatise upon the Law of Mortgages* (3d ed.; 2 vols.; London, 1791), I, 17–27. Powell noted that the visible possession of land did not necessarily indicate ownership, which could easily be discovered because deeds for real property had to be recorded. The case was different with personal property, however, for possession was the strongest indication of ownership. A mortgagor's continued possession of personal property was therefore regarded as prima facie fraudulent against creditors. This rule was set forth in the case of Ryall v. Rowles, 1 Ves. Sen. 348, 27 Eng. Rep. 1074 (Ch., 1749), cited by Powell. In Virginia, unlike England, mortgages of personal property had to be recorded (as required by the 1748 law), and the question was whether the English rule should apply in these circumstances.

6. JM's discussion of the "badges of fraud," a term used in the law of fraudulent conveyances, echoed a passage in Bacon's *Abridgment*. If, said Bacon, a person continued in possession of goods after selling them, "this is an undoubted badge of a fraudulent conveyance, because the possession is the only *indicium* of the property of a chattel, which is a thing unfixed and transitory; so there are other marks and characters of fraud, as a general conveyance of them all without any exception, for it is hardly to be presumed, that a man will strip himself entirely of all his personal property, not excepting his bedding and wearing apparel, unless there were some secret correspondence and good understanding settled between him and the vendee, for a private occupancy of all or some part of the goods for his support." Bacon cited Twyne's Case in the margin (*Abridgment* [1st Am. ed.], III, 311–12).

7. John Warden, also representing the appellee Hill, spoke next. He urged the applicability of Twyne's Case, and referring to the cases discussed in Powell's *Treatise upon Mortgages*, he contended that mortgages of personal property in which possession remained with the mortgagor were fraudulent, "unless the *transaction itself*, necessarily accounts for, and justifies it" (1 Wash. 181-82).

8. President Pendleton here asked JM to read the 1758 act for preventing

the fraudulent gift of slaves, "observing, that this question might perhaps be determined by analogy to that." This law required a gift of slaves to be made by a will proved and recorded or by a deed in writing, proved by two witnesses or acknowledged by the donor and recorded in the General Court or court of county where one of the parties lived within eight months after the date of the deed (1 Wash. 182; Hening, *Statutes*, VII, 237–39).

9. Alexander Campbell for the appellant then made the concluding argument. He maintained that the mortgage deed was valid under the 1748 law because the memorial registered in the General Court provided sufficient notice. Since in Virginia mortgages of personal property had to be recorded and thus had full notoriety, the mortgagor's remaining in possession, said Campbell, was not an evidence of fraud (1 Wash. 183–84).

On 29 Apr. the Court of Appeals affirmed the decree of the High Court of Chancery, though in so doing departed from the English rule concerning mortgages of personal property. Chancellor Wythe had decreed the mortgage deed of Feb. 1783 to be fraudulent by reason of Herbert Claiborne's retaining possession of the property. President Pendleton (speaking for the Court of Appeals) was of the opinion that such possession was not evidence of fraud if the deed was made for a valuable and bona fide consideration and was duly recorded. At the same time, however, he held that the subsequent absolute sale of the mortgaged property by Herbert Claiborne to his father operated as a release of the mortgage and that the son's continuing possession after the sale—the deed for which was not recorded until five months after Hill levied his execution on this property—was fraudulent and void as to Hill (1 Wash. 184–85; Va. Ct. Ap. Ord. Bk. II, 226–27).

In effect, the chancery decree was upheld, though Pendleton made the case turn upon the sale rather than the mortgage. Since he delivered only a bare decree without elaboration, it is uncertain whether Pendleton based his ruling on the recent English case of Edwards v. Harben, 2 T.R. 587, 100 Eng. Rep. 315 (K.B., 1788). In that case an absolute sale of goods and chattels without immediate delivery of possession was held to be fraudulent with respect to creditors.

38. Watson & Hartshorne v. Alexander

1794
Editorial Note

Contracts made between 1777 and 1781, when paper money passed as a legal tender, provided a copious source of litigation in post-Revolutionary Virginia. To finance the War of Independence both Congress and the individual states resorted to voluminous emissions of paper currency. Expedients to keep paper on a par with specie proved unsuccessful; over the course of the war this currency steadily depreciated, precipitously so during the last year, when it became worthless. In Virginia the rapid depreciation of paper money prompted the General Assembly in November 1781 to adopt "an act directing the mode of adjusting and settling the payment of certain debts and contracts, and for other purposes." This law declared that paper money should no longer pass current and provided that all subsisting debts and contracts entered into in this currency between 1 January 1777 and 1 January 1782 should be reduced to their actual specie value according to a scale of depreciation. It set the ratio of paper to specie for each month of paper's circulation, beginning at 1.5 in January 1777 and ending at 1,000 in December 1781. The law also allowed the courts to give "such judgment as . . . shall appear just and equitable" where a settlement according to the scale would seem unfair.[1]

The purpose of the depreciation law was to prevent disputes over paper money debts and contracts. "The legislature," said Judge Roane, "have established this scale as a just rule, whereby to settle paper money contracts in specie. It was no doubt made after due deliberation, and upon good information. It has been generally acquiesced in by the people of this Commonwealth, and has prevented much litigation."[2] Although the law furnished a fixed and known standard to settle such contracts without the intervention of courts, not surprisingly there were numerous applications for an equitable departure from the scale as provided in the fifth section of the act. During the period of John Marshall's practice the Court of Appeals interpreted the 1781 depreciation law in sixteen reported cases. Marshall can be identified as counsel in eleven of these, including this one and *Walden's Executor* v. *Payne* (see Case Number 3, Document IV).[3]

In most of these cases the court had to decide whether the circumstances justified a departure from the legal scale of depreciation. The law furnished a "good *general rule* for scaling paper money contracts," said Judge Pendleton in a 1795 case, "but it was certainly not just in all cases."[4] For example, he had previously declared that the scale for 1777 and 1778 did not correspond with the prevailing opinion as to depreciation and that the scale as a whole did not provide "a proper rule for fixing the price of *imported* goods, which was influenced by the expence and risque of importation, as well as by the depreciation of paper money."[5] The court was careful not to open the door too wide, however, preferring to adhere to the legal scale unless compelling circumstances called for an equitable adjustment. To overrule the scale, said Pendleton, the circumstances had to be "such as arise in the contract sued on, shewing the parties, at that time contracted on the idea of no *depreciation*, or one different from the legal scale."[6]

Watson & Hartshorne v. *Alexander* dealt with the application of the scale of depreciation to a contract for rent executed while paper money passed current. Marshall represented William Thornton Alexander, son of John Alexander and Lucy Thornton Alexander of King George County.[7] John Alexander had devised to his son a tract of land in and adjacent to Alexandria, directing his executors to lease the land if conducive to the interest of the son. The executors accordingly in 1779 executed a deed conveying the lots that had been laid out from the tract to Alexandria merchants Josiah Watson and William Hartshorne. The deed reserved an annual rent of £78.10 "*current money of Virginia*," payable to William Thornton Alexander and his heirs. Alexander subsequently brought an action of covenant in the District Court at Dumfries for nine years unpaid rent. In May 1792 the district court gave judgment for Alexander, awarding damages without scaling the rent.[8]

1. Hening, *Statutes*, X, 471–74.
2. White v. Atkinson, 2 Wash. 99 (1795).
3. The other JM cases were Hill and Braxton v. Southerland's Executors, 1 Wash. 128 (1792); Wilson and M'Rae v. Keeling, 1 Wash. 194 (1793); Sallee v. Yates, 1 Wash. 226 (1793); Granberry's Executor v. Granberry, 1 Wash. 246 (1793); White v. Atkinson, 2 Wash. 94 (1795); Walker's Executor v. Walke, 2 Wash. 195 (1796); Pryor v. Adams, 1 Call 382 (1798); Taliaferro v. Minor, 1 Call 525 (1799); Taliaferro v. Minor, 2 Call 190 (1799).
4. White v. Atkinson, 2 Wash. 104.
5. Hill and Braxton v. Southerland's Executor, 1 Wash. 134 (1792).
6. Bogle, Somerville & Co. v. Vowles, 1 Call 245 (1798).
7. On the Alexander family, see *WMQ*, 1st. ser., X (1901), 182–83.
8. *WMQ*, 2d. ser., I (1921), 59, 60; II (1922), 291, 293; III (1923), 207; 1 Wash. 340–41.

Argument

5 November 1794

Marshall on the same side.[1] In the exposition of a statute, we should attend to the mischief meant to be prevented; and the remedy should be made commensurate with it: it should never be extended beyond the mischief, unless the expressions made use of, are so strong, as to render such a construction absolutely necessary. The difference which has been stated between *temporary* and *perpetual* contracts is a striking one.[2] In the former, the parties calculated the value of paper money at the day of making the contract, as well as the probable value of it, on the day of payment. If it continued to depreciate more rapidly than was expected, the debtor gained; otherwise he lost. The legislature put an end to the delusion; and rendered a performance of the contract impossible, by taking out of circulation that medium, upon which both parties calculated; and of course, it became necessary to provide a remedy to the evil, which the situation of this country had rendered inevitable. But in contracts, which, from their nature were calculated to continue long beyond the time when depreciated paper money could exist, or could furnish a standard by which to estimate the value of property, the parties would naturally look beyond that time for a standard, by which to estimate the present value of property, and would therefore make specie that standard. In the first case then, there existed a mischief, and the law is satisfied, by applying the remedy to that case, in the latter, no such mischief could happen, and therefore there was no necessity to provide a remedy. It is a strained, rather than a necessary construction to extend the law to such a case.

Second point. It is contended, that the benefit of the 5th clause must be confined to debtors.[3] The words of a law must be express and clear beyond doubt, which can warrant a construction so manifestly at variance with the fundamental principles of justice. On the contrary, the words are so general, that nothing could justify an exception, but to prevent the gross partiality, which the construction on the other side tends to produce. It is said, that the two cases, which are specially provided for, point to the benefit of the *debtors* only.[4] I do not think that the first case is intended to benefit the debtors, since the creditor who would, without this provision, have been obliged to accept of the identical money tendered and refused, is to receive in lieu thereof, an equitable payment. Tender and refusal are technical words, and will be construed to mean a *legal* tender, and not a mere *offer to pay*.[5] But I rely upon the latter part of the 5th clause, to prove, that creditors were as much the objects of justice with the legislature as the debtors. Suppose the clause in question had been left out of the law, then I think it clear, that a judgment rendered within the period during which the scale operates, (being undeniably a debt) would also have been scaled. But the court, by this clause, are to fix at what depreciation the damages are to be paid, having regard to *the original injury or contract*, which by referring to a period antecedent to the judgment, must operate against the debtor. If then, in the latter branch of the clause, creditors were intended to be benefited, upon what principle can it be said, that they were intended to be excluded in the former part of it. Again; in the former part of the clause, (let it be, that the two specified cases are in favor of debtors only,) what can the words which follow mean? Namely, "in *either case* it shall be lawful for the court to award such judgment as to them shall appear just and equitable." I might with more propriety contend, that the general part of the section, viz: *other circumstances* &c. relate exclusively to *creditors*, if the former part related to debtors.

As to the propriety of admitting parol testimony, it is to be remarked, that in the latter branch of the 5th clause, this sort of testimony is clearly to be heard and decided upon by the court, without bringing it before them by special pleading, and why is it to be excluded in the former part of the clause?[6] But it is contended, that by our construction, there would be no general rule at all. In ordinary cases, men may settle their differences by referring to the scale, without the necessity of a suit, and this *extraordinary* remedy is provided only for *extraordinary* cases.

As to the objection, that all the evidence which was laid before the District Court, should appear before this, it is to be observed that the bill of exceptions renders it unnecessary;[7] for it admits as does also the judgment of the court, that there were circumstances proved to the court sufficient to except this case from the general rule, and the only objection relied upon, is the impropriety of the court's hearing and deciding upon such testimony; so that, if we be right in contending that the court below were authorised to hear parol evidence, there is an end of this question. But if it should be determined, that the evidence ought to have been spread upon the record by the plaintiff, the court will then send back the cause for that purpose; since in cases like this, (as in appeals from decisions respecting mills, wills and roads,) the practice as to this subject remains yet unsettled.[8]

Printed, Bushrod Washington, *Reports of Cases Argued and Determined in the Court of Appeals of Virginia*, I (Richmond, 1798), 347–49.

1. The case first came before the Court of Appeals on 26 Oct. 1793; it was continued on 2 Nov. and again on 11 Apr. 1794. A second hearing took place on 5 Nov. 1794. Charles Lee led off for the appellants Watson and

Hartshorne, followed by Bushrod Washington for the appellee Alexander. JM spoke next for the appellee (Va. Ct. Ap. Ord. Bk. II, 246, 248, 261; III, 23; 1 Wash. 341–47).

2. Washington distinguished between temporary contracts, "which *might* be complied with whilst paper circulated," and continuing, or permanent, contracts (such as the one in question), "which, from their nature were to extend far beyond the possible existence of depreciated paper currency and which could never be fulfilled" while paper money circulated. The legislature, Washington contended, did not intend the scale to apply to continuing contracts (1 Wash. 344–45).

The second section of the act of 1781 enacted that "all debts and contracts entered into or made in the current money of this state or of the United States, excepting at all times contracts entered into for gold and silver coin, tobacco, or any other specific property," between 1 Jan. 1777 and 1 Jan. 1782, "now remaining due and unfulfilled, or which may become due at any future day or days, for the payment of any sum or sums of money, shall be liquidated, settled and adjusted agreeable to a scale of depreciation . . . that is to say, by reducing the amount of all such debts and contracts to the true value in specie at the days or times the same were incurred or entered into." The scale set forth in the fourth section of the act ranged from 1.5 paper to 1 specie in Jan. 1777 to 1,000 for 1 in Dec. 1781 (Hening, *Statutes*, X, 471, 472–73).

3. After considering Lee's first point, that the case fell within the operation of the scale established by the second section of the 1781 act, JM moved to the second point, that the fifth section of the act "was intended to reach the case of *debtors* only, and not that of *creditors*" (1 Wash. 343).

The text of the fifth section reads: "That where a suit shall be brought for the recovery of a debt, and it shall appear that the value thereof hath been tendered and refused; or where it shall appear that the non-payment thereof is owing to the creditor; or where other circumstances arise which, in the opinion of the court before whom the cause is brought to issue, would render a determination agreeable to the above table unjust; in either case it shall and may be lawful for the court to award such judgment as to them shall appear just and equitable. And where any verdict hath been given for damages between . . . [1 Jan. 1777 and 1 Jan. 1782], and the judgment remains unsatisfied, it shall be lawful for the several courts within this commonwealth, in a summary way, by motion to them made, either before any execution issues, or at the return day of such execution, to fix, settle, and direct at what depreciation the said damages shall be discharged, having regard to the original injury or contract on which the damages are founded, and any other proof or circumstances that the nature of the case will admit" (Hening, *Statutes*, X, 473–74).

4. Lee argued that the two specified instances in the fifth section—where payment was tendered and refused and where nonpayment was owing to the creditor—were "clearly intended for the benefit of the" debtor (1 Wash. 343).

5. In making a legal tender, the debtor had to produce the money at the time of his offer to pay (see Case No. 3, Doc. IV, n. 14).

6. At the district court the jury found a verdict for Alexander and assessed damages, subject to the court's opinion whether the rents in question should be scaled according to the depreciation act. After this verdict the court examined witnesses and then gave judgment for the damages in specie. Lee objected to this irregular procedure, contending that if such parol testimony was admissible to alter a written agreement, it should have been heard and decided upon during the trial or brought before the court by regular pleading (1 Wash. 340–41, 343–44).

7. The case came up on appeal by a bill of exceptions to the court's examination of witnesses. The actual evidence heard by the court below was not spread on the record; therefore, said Lee, the Court of Appeals had no means of deciding whether the lower court's opinion was right or wrong (1 Wash. 341, 344).

8. After a reply by Lee, the court requested arguments on the question of Alexander's title to the property. Lee and Washington then argued the point, and on 12 Nov. the court rendered judgment. Speaking for the court, President Pendleton, after dismissing the objections to the title, held that the contract in question was liable to be scaled according to the second section of the 1781 depreciation act. "The act is general," he said, "and not limited as to portions of time, nor can the court draw a line between a contract for payment at the end of two days or of twenty years or more." At the same time, however, he rejected the appellants' contention that the equitable relief stipulated in the fifth section was intended exclusively for the benefit of debtors: "Such partiality cannot fairly be imputed to the legislature, and it would require strong words to induce such a construction. In this law there is not the slightest ground for it." While agreeing that the District Court at Dumfries had full power to inquire into the circumstances of this contract and to admit parol testimony for this purpose, Pendleton objected to the method pursued by that court (see n. 6). The proper mode, he said, was either by a special verdict stating all the facts and circumstances, leaving it to the court to decide, or by a hearing of the evidence at the trial, with an instruction to the jury on the matter of scaling. The Court of Appeals therefore ordered the cause to be remanded to the district court for a new trial (Va. Ct. Ap. Ord. Bk. III, 32; 1 Wash. 349–57 [quotations at 352, 353]).

On 12 May 1795 the cause was reinstated on the docket for a new trial at the District Court at Dumfries. The outcome of this trial, if held, is not known (Prince William County District Court Order Book, 1794–98, 86–87 [microfilm], Vi).

39. Pickett v. Dowdall

1795

Editorial Note

This was one of three cases argued at the October 1795 term of the Court of Appeals concerning disputed titles to land in the Northern Neck. None of them touched on the larger controversy between the commonwealth and the Fairfax family over the title to this extensive territory then under litigation in both the state and federal courts. These suits do, however, illuminate the distinctive land system that operated in the Northern Neck during the colonial period up to the death of Thomas, sixth Lord Fairfax, in 1781.[1] Until that time grants for lands in the region were issued in the name of the proprietor from his land office located near Winchester. The rules and regulations for obtaining land were not part of the land laws of the colony but were drawn up and published separately by the proprietor.

Lord Fairfax's chief source of income from the proprietary was the collection of quitrents on tracts that he had granted in fee simple. These grants were made from the "waste and unappropriated" lands and produced no revenue until they were settled and patented. (The proprietor also made long-term leases of the "manor lands," which he reserved exclusively to his use.) One who wished to acquire land in fee simple first made an entry for the desired tract and obtained a warrant from the proprietary land office to survey the land. After the survey was returned and the office fees and "composition" (about thirteen shillings per hundred acres) were paid, the applicant received a patent. Once the grant had been made, the proprietor retained the right to collect annual quitrents on the property (at the rate of one shilling sterling for every fifty acres). If the landowner was in default of paying his quitrents for two years or longer, the proprietor could reenter the land and grant it to someone else.[2]

The dispute between James Dowdall and the brothers Martin Pickett and William Pickett began in the High Court of Chancery. Dowdall sued for the conveyance of two tracts of land in Fauquier County held by the Picketts, who were leading citizens of the county and frequent officeholders. They were represented by Marshall, a family friend who also served as counsel for their younger brother George Pickett.[3] Dowdall claimed a prior right to the land by virtue of a warrant issued to one James Crap in 1741, on which a survey was made and returned the same year. Crap died in 1773 without having paid the office fees and composition required to secure a patent. His son later assigned his interest in the land to Dowdall, who obtained a grant from the state land office in 1788. Although his patent issued from the state land office, to which the Northern Neck land records and papers had been transferred as a result of legislation enacted in 1785, Dowdall did not base his claim on the commonwealth's supposed title to the Northern Neck but rather on his being the assignee of a right dating from 1741.[4]

The land claimed by Dowdall had previously been parceled out to the Picketts by two patents issued in 1780: one to Martin Pickett based on a warrant and survey executed in 1762, the other to William Pickett based on a warrant and survey executed in 1779.[5] In March 1794 the High Court of Chancery decreed in favor of Dowdall. Chancellor Wythe stated "that the grant to the plaintiff of the land to which he is entitled ought to have relation to the time of the warrant [1741], by authority of which the said land was surveyed, so as to be prior in effect, to the title of the defendants." The Picketts sought to overturn this decree in the Court of Appeals on the grounds that Crap had abandoned and forfeited his interest in the land.[6]

1. The other cases are Johnson v. Buffington, 2 Wash. 116 (1795); Curry v. Burns, 2 Wash. 121 (1795). JM did not participate in either case. For the dispute between Virginia and the Fairfax family over title to the Northern Neck, see Case No. 11, editorial note. For other JM cases relating to the Northern Neck, see Hite v. Fairfax (*PJM*, I, 150–64); Case No. 4.

2. Groome, *Fauquier During the Proprietorship*, 56–57, 73–75.

3. See Case Nos. 32, 40. Martin Pickett's daughter Lucy married Charles Marshall, JM's younger brother. On the Pickett family, see *Fauquier Historical Society Bulletin*, 1st ser., no. 2 (1922), 207–9.

4. Dowdall's grant was for 586 acres (Northern Neck Grants, 1780–88, 545, Vi). Mr. Conley Edwards of the Archives Division of the Virginia State Library kindly furnished the editors with copies of documents from the Northern Neck land papers pertaining to this case. For the 1785 act, see Hening, *Statutes*, XII, 111.

5. These were adjoining tracts, one consisting of 243 acres, the other 420 acres (Northern Neck Grants, 1757–81, 375–76, 376–77, Vi; Northern Neck Surveys, Fauquier County, Box 11, Vi).

6. 2 Wash. 106–7.

Argument
24 October 1795

MARSHALL for the appellants.[1] The rule of *lord Fairfax's* office was, that those who did not within six months perfect their titles to lands for which entries had been made, could not afterwards demand a grant unless the same was consented to by the *Proprietor*. They were considered as having abandoned their right, and the estate revested in the *Proprietor*, who might grant the land to any other person. This rule is proved to have subsisted so early as the year 1734, of which the people in that District were constantly notified by advertisements inserted in the gazettes, and publicly posted up in the different counties. This rule being entered in the front of one of the entry books in the *Proprietor's* office, those who applied there to take up unappropriated lands, must be presumed to have had notice of it.[2] The existence of the rule is further established by the depositions of many witnesses, and is further strengthened by a consideration of *lord Fairfax's* situation. Possessed of a very extensive territory, the value of which depended entirely upon its being parcelled out amongst those who as a retribution therefor were to pay him certain quitrents, his revenue, as well as the means of supporting his office, depended upon the receipt of his fees, and of the stipulated rents, neither of which could be demanded, *until after a grant had been made*. It would have been highly unreasonable, that after a warrant had issued, the person owning it, should suffer it to lie dormant for many years, without going on to acquire the legal estate, and yet keeping off other applicants. I contend therefore, that *Crap*, by the rules of the office forfeited all right to the land, and that the *Proprietor*, might legally make any other appropriation of it. But independently of this point, I consider that the right of *Crap* was lost by abandonment, and rely for evidence of his intention to abandon, not only upon his declarations, as proved in the cause, but upon the unreasonable length of time which elapsed between the issuing of the warrant to him, and that to the appellants, during which period he seems to have shewn no disposition to obtain a grant.[3]

I should insist if it were necessary that the appellants were purchasers without notice; for though it is proved that they had heard that *Crap* had taken up land, yet it does not appear that they knew it to be the land in dispute.

But I do not wish to rely upon this, because I contend first, that the right of *Crap* was completely lost by forfeiture, and secondly, if not so lost, yet a Court of Equity will never set up this dormant right in favor of a man, who has been guilty of such inexcusable neglect, and who has lain by and permitted the appellants to take up and enjoy the land.[4]

MARSHALL in reply. It is not proved, (I conceive) that an application was made by the appellee for the papers before the transfer from *Crap* to *Dowdall*, and therefore, the argument of abandonment in *Crap* is not repelled.

It is true, that the grant relates back to the warrant, in cases unattended by circumstances which would render the relation improper; as if the sale be conditional, or relinquished, and a grant is made in the mean time to another, this relation to destroy the intermediate right could never be admitted.

As to the rule, it was entered in a book kept in the *Proprietor's* office, which was open to the inspection of all persons applying there to take up land. It is traced back to the year 1734 long before the date of *Crap's* warrant, and therefore, it was not as Mr. *Campbell* supposes, an arbitrary rule, made by the *Proprietor* for the purpose of forfeiting rights acquired under prior agreements with himself. But I ask, was not the rule a reasonable one? If dormant rights were permitted at any time to be revived, and to relate back to the warrant, no person could with safety have ventured to take up lands within that district, which would not only have been injurious to the *Proprietor*, but would have produced a great public mischief. If a grant had been made to *Crap*, he would have forfeited the land by non payment of the quitrents for three years.[5] Can he then be in a better situation by having violated his engagements; or ought he thus to gain a benefit to himself, and to impose an injury upon another by his own default? If the forfeiture were out of the question, yet I would rely upon these considerations as sufficient to deprive *Dowdall* of the equity he asks for, upon the supposition of an implied contract.[6] It is said, the rule appears by the evidence to be very uncertain. This is not the case. The rule itself, as taken literally from the book in which it was entered, is an exhibit in the cause. The advertisements of *lord Fairfax* were not intended to establish a rule. He had a right to avail himself of the forfeiture without giving the parties an opportunity of preventing it. These advertisements were intended as an indulgence to those, who had not complied with the rules of office, by granting them a further time to come in and avoid the consequences of the forfeiture which had incurred. But they did not alter, or do away the rule.

The act of 1786 might be objected to, upon the ground, that the legislature could not grant away the property of *lord Fairfax* any more than it could that of any other individual. But it is unnecessary to stir that question.[7] It is evident, that that law does not mean to authorise the register to issue a patent for lands, which had before *been granted by the Proprietor*.[8]

MARSHALL. As to the forfeiture not being recited in the grant to the appellants, I am inclined to think that this was never done, but where *prior grants* had been made and forfeited, as for non-payment of quitrents, not seating and the like; and it was done in those cases, because, if the forfeiture were not recited, the former grant might prevail over the latter.[9] But this was not done I believe where the forfeiture accrued in consequence of a non-compliance with the rules of office *in the earlier stages towards a title*.

But if an actual forfeiture had not taken place, yet I contend that the conduct of *Crap* and of *Dowdall* has deprived them of all claim upon the equity of this court. This is not a contest between *lord Fairfax* and *Crap*, but between two purchasers under *lord Fairfax*. How is it, that a prior mortgagee standing by and permitting another to throw away his money upon the same security, without disclosing his mortgage, shall be postponed? The principle of that case applies to the present.[10] For *Crap*, having notice (as is to be presumed) of the rule, and that many others might apply for a warrant to survey the same land, without a possibility of knowing what former appropriations had been made of it, he takes no step to perfect his title and to remove this difficulty out of the way of other applicants. *Lord Fairfax* could not have compelled those to receive grants who had obtained warrants, but the party might have abandoned the property if he pleased, and his refusing to abide by the rules of the office, was all he could do to evince his intended dereliction.[11]

Printed, Bushrod Washington, *Reports of Cases Argued and Determined in the Court of Appeals of Virginia*, II (Richmond, 1799), 107–8, 110–12.

1. The appeal was argued on 24 Oct. 1795, JM speaking first (Va. Ct. Ap. Ord. Bk. III, 76).

2. According to the statement of facts, the rule in question was inserted in front of one of the entry books, beginning in 1734. It stipulated that entries were not demandable after six months and that warrants were not to continue in force longer than six months unless renewed or consented to by the proprietor or his agent (2 Wash. 107).

3. There was "strong proof in the record of abandonment of the land in question both by old *Crap* and his son after his death, on account of the indifferent quality of the land, and the expence of obtaining a grant" (2 Wash. 107).

4. Alexander Campbell spoke next on behalf of the appellee Dowdall. He reiterated Chancellor Wythe's ruling that the grant to Dowdall had relation back to the time of the issuing of the warrant to Crap in 1741. To the objection that Crap, under whom Dowdall claimed, had forfeited his title, Camp-

bell contended that the rules of the proprietor's office were vague and arbitrary and further that the proprietor as a private individual had no authority to make rules concerning forfeiture "not sanctioned by the common or statute laws of the land." He relied on a 1786 act that allowed those who had made entries for Northern Neck lands before 17 Oct. 1785 to survey the land and return the surveys by 1 Oct. 1788 and those who had returned surveys for such lands before 17 Oct. 1785 to apply for grants up to 1 Oct. 1788.

Campbell also made these points: that the loss of papers prevented Dowdall from issuing a caveat against the Picketts; that the grant to the Picketts did not recite the forfeiture, as was the custom; and that the abandonment by Crap, if admitted, did not give any right to the Picketts (2 Wash. 109–10). For the 1786 act, see Hening, *Statutes*, XII, 238–39.

5. Northern Neck grants stipulated that nonpayment of quitrents for two years would result in forfeiture of the land. In grants issuing from the Crown the period was three years (Harrison, *Va. Land Grants*, 131; Hening, *Statutes*, IV, 41).

6. Judge Roane made the same point in his opinion in Curry v. Burns, also decided at this term: "I put it upon the ground of an implied contract between the *Proprietor* and the individual applying for his lands, that the legal fees should not only be paid, but that a title should be obtained within a reasonable time" (2 Wash. 125).

7. At that very moment there were cases pending in both the state and federal courts in which the title to the Northern Neck territory was directly at issue (see Case No. 11, editorial note).

8. Pendleton here interjected his agreement with JM: "It is surely unnecessary to labour this point, as it is too plain to be argued. The act of 1786, is not to be construed to extend to cases, where a *grant had been previously made by lord Fairfax*" (2 Wash. 111). See n. 4 for the 1786 act.

9. Pendleton confirmed this point in his opinion: "As to the custom of reciting in subsequent grants the prior forfeiture, I suppose it was similar to that which prevailed in the crown office, and there, it was never done, but in cases where there had been *a prior grant*" (2 Wash. 114).

10. The general rule was that if there were several mortgages of the same estate, the first mortgagee was to be preferred to the second, and so on. This rule was to "be understood with this restriction, that the first mortgagee be not guilty of any fraud or artifice, by concealing his mortgage, or otherwise, to induce another person to give credit to, or lend his money on, such subsequent security; for, if he be, the subsequent incumbrancer will gain a priority thereby" (Powell, *Treatise upon Mortgages* [Dublin ed.], 181, 183–84; Bacon, *Abridgment* [1st. Am. ed.], V, 39, 46–47).

11. On 26 Oct. the court unanimously reversed the decree of the High Court of Chancery, ruling that the Picketts had the superior title in equity. All three sitting judges, William Fleming, Paul Carrington, and Pendleton, gave opinions. Fleming maintained that Lord Fairfax had a right to establish reasonable rules for parceling out his land and that the regulation in question (requiring those who had made entries to perfect their titles within six months) was reasonable. Carrington considered the "case to be so extremely

clear, that it cannot be made more so by argument." Pendleton rejected the argument that Dowdall's title should relate back to the date (1741) of Crap's warrant: "There are such things as relations in law, but they are legal fictions, invented for the purposes of justice, and not to work an injury to innocent third persons, who in the mean time have fairly and legally acquired a title to the subject of controversy." He also dismissed the objection to the proprietor's rules as arbitrary, uncertain, and secret. Crap, he said, had clearly forfeited and abandoned his claim. Dowdall, by reviving this dormant claim, was to be considered merely a "volunteer," having an inferior claim in equity to one who had obtained an interest in the land for valuable consideration (Va. Ct. Ap. Ord. Bk. III, 77; 2 Wash. 112–15).

40. Pickett v. Morris
1796
Editorial Note

As in *Barrett* v. *Floyd* (Case Number 34), Marshall here represented a party contesting the jurisdiction of the High Court of Chancery in a dispute that had originally been tried at law in a county court. *Pickett* v. *Morris* began as a routine action of debt on a bond brought by Richmond merchant George Pickett against Richard Morris in the Henrico County Court.[1] Morris in 1785 had purchased an interest in Kentucky land from one Littlepage and in partial payment executed a bond in Littlepage's favor. A year later Littlepage assigned this bond to John Stockdell, also a Richmond merchant. Ultimately the bond came into Pickett's hands by assignment from Stockdell. Pickett sued Morris for full payment of the bond. The latter did not contest his bond obligation but sought to reduce his liability by asserting a bond debt, subsequently reduced to judgment, that Stockdell owed him. Morris, in short, claimed the right to set off Stockdell's debt to him against the debt he, Morris, owed to Stockdell's assignee, Pickett.

Resolution of this dispute would establish who would have to collect from Stockdell. If Pickett could enforce Morris's bond free from any set-off, Morris would have to pay Pickett the full bond amount and then try to collect his judgment against Stockdell. If, on the other hand, Morris could use Stockdell's debt as a set-off, Morris would owe Pickett only the difference (a small sum) and would assign his judgment against Stockdell to Pickett to collect. The mere existence of the suit suggests that Stockdell was insolvent and that Pickett was trying to avoid suffering the loss occasioned by the insolvency.

By statute a plaintiff bringing suit on an assigned bond was to allow all discounts that the defendant could prove either against himself or against the first obligee.[2] At the Henrico trial Morris's counsel moved the court to instruct the jury that Stockdell's bond was a proper discount against his client's obligation to Pickett, or to reserve the question for its decision by means of a special verdict. Whether because of outright refusal or of neglect, the county court refused to do either, referring the issues of both law and fact to the jury, which returned a verdict for Pickett. Following established procedure, the attorney for Morris tendered a bill of exceptions objecting to the court's refusal to declare the law regarding discounts. The judges refused to sign it, however, thereby preventing it from being spread on the record for consideration by an appellate court. A motion for a new trial, though not overruled, was withdrawn, evidently because

Pickett agreed to stay execution for a month while Morris applied to the High Court of Chancery for an injunction. Chancellor Wythe recognized Morris's right of discount, and his decree of 13 March 1795 enjoined all but a fraction—the difference between Morris's and Stockdell's bonds—of the amount of the Henrico judgment. Pickett then appealed to the Court of Appeals to reverse this decree.

In presenting Pickett's case Marshall only feebly contested Morris's right to discount. As it happened, this point was settled at the same term in *Norton* v. *Rose*. The court declared that the assignee of a bond took it subject to all the equity of the debtor against the assignor, even though he gave valuable consideration for the bond without notice of the equity.[3] Marshall attempted to show that Morris had waived his right to discount and could not reassert it, but he reserved his strongest argument for the jurisdictional question—clearly a delicate issue, for the court requested a reargument.

His strategy was simple but shrewd, designed to appeal to the sensitivities of judges struggling to maintain the proper division between law and equity. The case, said Marshall, had received a full hearing at law, with a verdict after due deliberation by a jury. The judgment of the county court, even if wrong in law, could not be re-examined by a court of equity; errors at law could only be corrected by an appellate tribunal. The heart of his case was that the High Court of Chancery's decree decided the same points previously determined in a court of law, implying that such interference undermined the precious right of trial by jury. Marshall, to be sure, had to gloss over the arbitrary and capricious conduct of the county court, a point that was not overlooked by opposing counsel and the judges of the Court of Appeals. Ultimately, the county court's extraordinary behavior, notably its refusal to rule on the point of law when requested, was decisive in the appellate court's eyes in bringing this case within the traditional grounds of equitable relief.

1. JM represented Pickett, also his client in an earlier case in the Court of Appeals (Case No. 32). Morris was a Louisa County planter, who had served in the House of Delegates in 1788 (Hutchinson, *Madison Papers*, I, 248 n. 2).

2. See Argument, n. 3.

3. 2 Wash. 233. See Argument, n. 14.

Argument

31 October–1 November 1796

MARSHALL for the appellant.[1] The first question which I shall consider is, whether the appellant[2] could at law, have set up his judgment against *Stockdell*, as a discount against the appellant. 2dly, Whether he can resort to a court of equity for the relief sought for by this bill.

1st, The assignee of a bond, by the law of this state, is bound to allow all just discounts against *himself*, or against the *obligee* before notice of the assignment. The discount offered by the appellee, is a judgment obtained against a *mesne assignee*, which I contend is not a case provided for by the act of Assembly.[3] *Morris's* bond, coming by assignment into the hands of *Stockdell*, could not be considered as being *ipso facto* discharged, in consequence of the latter being the debtor to the former to an equal amount. The reciprocal possession of each others bonds, did not amount to a *payment* of both, or of either. The one may be *discounted* against the other, unless the conduct of the parties hath prevented it.

This is the difference between *actual payment*, and off-setting mutual demands; in the first, the bond, is discharged by the silent operation of law; in the latter, both debts subsist, until *they are opposed* to each other; for the parties may *wave* the discount if they please.

In this case, *Morris*, evinced his determination not to discount, expressly, as well as impliedly. He refused it *expressly*, when *Stockdell* applied to him for that purpose; and impliedly, by bringing suit against *Stockdell* upon his bond, in which, if the discount had been offered, he must have been nonsuited.[4] And *Stockdell*, by assigning *Morris's* bond to *Picket*, evinced a similar disposition in himself not to discount.

After this, will it be contended, that *Morris* can reclaim his right of discounting, and that too, against a *bona fide* assignee?[5] But suppose *Morris*, was not deprived of this right by his own conduct, let us consider.

2dly, Whether he can be relieved in this court.

Every point in this cause, has once been before a court of competent jurisdiction, and without a possible objection to the fairness of the trial, the jury have decided in favor of the appellant. If the County Court gave an erroneous opinion upon the points submitted to them, or if they erred in refusing to give any opinion at all, the power of correction belonged exclusively to an *appellate court*. But a court of equity has no jurisdiction in such a case. It cannot correct legal errors in an inferior court, or rehear and rejudge the judgment of a court of law. If *Morris* was aggrieved by the judgment of the County Court, he might have excepted and appealed. If the justices refused to sanction the bill of exceptions by their signature, the law marks out a plain redress for the injured party.[6] But instead of pursuing those steps, the appellee voluntarily abandons them, and now seeks relief in a court of equity, *upon the very points*, which had been fully discussed, and fairly decided upon in a court of law. If he can hope to succeed, it must not be by asserting *the law* to be in his favor, for that has been determined against him by the proper tribunal, and therefore, the law is with his antagonist, until that decision be reversed.[7] He must then rely altogether upon his claim to *superior equity*.

Let the pretensions of the two parties upon this ground be compared. *Picket*, is a fair purchaser, for a valuable and full consideration, without notice of any objection upon the part of *Morris*.[8] On the other hand, *Morris*, had by his own conduct, completely discharged the bond in question from the danger of being discounted, against the debt due from *Stockdell*, to him. He refused the discount, as one of the depositions proves, for the unfair purpose of discharging his own bond in warrants, at a reduced price, and consequently for less than the real amount.[9] He institutes suit against *Stockdell*, as an additional evidence of his having disclaimed the discount, after which, his bond is assigned. Can he now talk of equity, who by his own conduct has been the cause of the very loss, he is unwilling to bear himself, and now seeks to throw upon *Picket*? If he had done at that time, what he now insists upon, the bond in question would long since have been cancelled, and deprived of its ability to deceive the world.[10]

Perhaps an attempt may be made to excuse this conduct of *Morris*, on account of the equity against his bond, which is faintly relied upon in the bill. If this had been any thing more than a pretence, *Morris*, instead of waving the discount by bringing suit upon *Stockdell's* bond, would have instituted a suit in equity to be relieved against the payment of his bond, by which means, third persons would have been warned not to purchase it.[11] But the decree of the Chancellor, by directing the difference between the two bonds to be paid by *Morris*, necessarily disallows his claim of equity on account of the *Kentucky* lands.[12]

I say nothing about the bill of exceptions, because not being signed, it contains no facts which this court ought to regard.[13]

MARSHALL in reply. Whether the equity attached to a bond follows it into the hands of the assignee or not, is a question I mean not to argue, because, I consider it to be unimportant in this cause.[14] If

Littlepage himself had been plaintiff, he could not have been opposed by this equitable objection. The only evidence of this equity is, the answer of *Littlepage*, a bill filed in *Kentucky* concerning this land, and a paper signed by *Johnson*, who contests the right of *Morris* to a fulfillment of *Littlepage's contract*. But none of these papers can be considered as evidence of the fact.

If then *Morris* had in reality no equity against this bond, his refusal to discount, was an absolute waver of his right. It is said that there is no time limited, within which the election to discount, or to wave it, is to be made, and that he might use it at the trial. I do not contend that he was bound to make it sooner, but if he expressly refuse before the trial to make it, and in consequence of his doing so, his bond is assigned away to a fair purchaser, he is bound by it, and cannot afterwards reclaim his right to discount. The reason assigned by *Morris* for his refusal was not real, but a mere subterfuge, used for the purpose of enabling him to purchase up his own bond for less than its value, and therefore it cannot qualify that, which I term an *express waver.*[15]

I do not say, that the bringing suit upon *Stockdell's* bond was of itself a waver, or that the judgment could not be made an offset; but it is *evidence* of his mind upon the subject, that the discount was not to take place; for if it had, *Morris* must have been nonsuited, as the bond due from him to *Stockdell*, amounted to a greater sum than what was due to him.[16]

I have contended, that by the literal words of the act, the defendant cannot set up a discount against an intermediate assignee; to which it is answered, that if the law be thus strictly interpreted, a bond can be assigned but once. I cannot clearly comprehend the justness of this conclusion, for it is plain from the words of the law, that any person or persons having the legal title may assign, which must mean, more than one assignment.[17]

If payments be made, or if property be sold to an intermediate assignee, this would be an *actual discharge* of so much of the bond, and might be given in evidence without the aid of the proviso; but this is very different from a *discount*, which could not be made were it not for this law.[18]

If *Morris* could not have set up the discount at law, there is an end of the cause. But if he could, he cannot now resort to a court of equity to get the benefit of it. The whole case has once been tried and decided upon before a competent jurisdiction. I contend, that the same question cannot be re-examined and rejudged in any but an appellate court. I am now speaking of the *discount* alone. The case of *Ambler* and *Wyld*, does not sustain the jurisdiction of the court of chancery as now contended for.[19] In that case, material testimony was not permitted to go to the jury, and of course, the *whole case* was not before them, nor decided upon by them. This court declared, that if the whole evidence had been laid before the jury, the decision would have been otherwise. In this case, nothing was kept back; the question which we are litigating here, is the very same which was contested and decided by the jury with the very same evidence which is exhibited to this court.

It is said, that the counsel and jury were entangled with a question which was unimportant, and by that means they were seduced from the true point in the cause. This is mere conjecture, and is not warranted by any part of the record. But if it were, I do not agree, that the mismanagement of counsel, or the misconceptions of the jury will give jurisdiction to a court of equity, over a subject which has been fully examined and decided upon by a jury.[20]

It is said, that the court of chancery had an original jurisdiction as to discounts which is not ousted by the statute.[21] This is admitted, and it then follows, that the courts of law and equity have concurrent jurisdiction upon that subject.

It will I presume be admitted, that those courts have also concurrent jurisdiction in matters of account; but because this is the case, will it be contended, that if a suit be brought at law upon an account, and a decision be there had, the very same subject may be reexamined in a court of equity? As well might a court of law rejudge a case decided upon in equity, under the plea of concurrent jurisdiction.

As to all the other pretences for giving jurisdiction to the court of chancery, they are mere conclusions of the counsel, without being warranted by the record; such are the supposed blunders of the counsel in discussing the equity, instead of the law of the case; in their being dazzled by *Picket's* offer of waiting a month, and being thereby put off from their first intention of moving for a new trial.[22]

It is contended, that *Picket* had notice of *Morris's* discount. This is not proved; but if it were, and if he also knew that *Morris* had *rejected the discount*, he certainly would not have been bound to admit it. Neither is there any evidence, that *Picket* had it in his power to save himself; or that there was any thing like usury in the transaction.[23] These, are points not stated in the bill, and therefore could not be noticed by the court, even if they were proved by the evidence.

As to Morris's judgment, it could not be even implied notice to *Picket*, who was not privy to, or bound by it.[24] But there is the strongest reason to believe, that the judgment was obtained after the assignment; for if it had been otherwise, it is highly probable, that *Stockdell* would have offered *Morris's* bond as an offset.[25]

MARSHALL. The principle which I have endeavored to maintain is this; that when the *whole question* has been completely before the jury, accompanied by no circumstance which could prevent a full and fair decision of the case, by that body, there is no remedy but in an appellate court. If the party apply for relief to a court of equity, he must rely upon other ground than legal errors in the decision complained of. Let all the cases which have been cited be examined, and it will be found in each of them, that the *whole* case was not decided upon by the jury. In 2 *Morg. Ess.* 291, the jury did not decide upon the discounts. 3 *Morg. Ess.* is no ways applicable.[26]

In the case of *Kent* and *Bridgeman*, there was an equity which was not determined at law; there was a fraud practised and proved, but still the party could not recover at law, without a copy of the judgment; of course, the subject of the fraud was not tried at all, and the jury were directed to find for the plaintiff, because the judgment was not produced. This is precisely within the rule I have stated.[27]

It is then contended, that if it were intended to object to the jurisdiction, it should have been done by plea. This is founded I suppose upon the act of 1787, which declares, "that after answer filed, and no plea in abatement to the jurisdiction of the court, no exception for want of jurisdiction shall ever afterwards be made &c."[28]

The construction of this law must necessarily be restrained to cases, where *the bill shews a right in the plaintiff to recover*. For where the plaintiff has no right at all, and if he be barred by a judgment at law, it is not necessary, nor would it be proper to plead to the jurisdiction. Such a plea admits the right of the plaintiff, but denies the power of the court to decide upon it. Thus, if a suit in chancery be brought upon a bond; the plaintiff having a right to recover, the defendant must apprise him in an early stage of the cause, that he means to object to the jurisdiction of the court. But if by the plaintiff's own shewing, or otherwise, it appears that the bond has been paid off, or that he had brought a suit at law upon it, and a verdict and judgment had passed against him; would a court of equity be bound to decree in his favor, because there existed an objection to its jurisdiction, which had not been taken advantage of by plea?

It is said, that the defendant should have pleaded the judgment in bar. But this is not necessary, where the same matter is stated in the answer, and is also relied upon in bar; or if (as in the present case[)], the plaintiff himself states the judgment in his bill. In *Ambler* and *Wyld*, the whole case was confessedly not before the jury; for the court would not permit them to hear all the testimony which was offered.[29]

In the case cited from *Finch. Ch. Cas.* 472, the court had no right to decide at all for want of jurisdiction, so that in fact, there was no judgment.[30]

In 2 *Vern.* 146, there was a secret equity, of which the defendant could not avail himself at law; for the court was not at liberty to enquire into the legal error, whilst the question was depending in a superior court.[31] In the case now before the court, there is no equity unmixt with law, since the discount might have been made at law. In the case last cited, the mistake was not triable at law, and of course, it was not enquired into nor decided upon by the jury. The case of *Bosanket* and *Dashwood*, *Talb.* 90, was a suit to be relieved against an usurious contract.[32]

If the jury mistook the law as to the discount, it does not from thence follow that a court of equity can interfere; for if so, every error of the common law courts may be re-examined and rejudged in this court. In the case of *Cockran* and *Street*, this court did not set aside the verdict because it was wrong, but because a part of the jury had been imposed upon by the others.[33]

As to the power which it is said *Picket* had to save himself, there is no proof of it.

I am at a loss to comprehend the distinction which is taken between cases of a merely legal nature, and such as are mixed with equity. I admit that in the latter case, the two courts have concurrent jurisdiction, but if the whole subject be decided in the court of law, equity can no more re-examine it, than the courts of law in a similar case could re-examine a decree of the court of chancery.

I admit, that a suit may be brought either at law or in chancery, where a bond is lost. But if it be decided in either court, the other cannot interfere.[34]

Printed, Bushrod Washington, *Reports of Cases Argued and Determined in the Court of Appeals of Virginia*, II (Richmond, 1799), 257–59, 264–66, 270–71.

1. The case was argued on 31 Oct. and 1 Nov. 1796. JM spoke first on behalf of the appellant Pickett (Va. Ct. Ap. Ord. Bk. III, 143, 144).

2. Should read "appellee" (Morris); this error was corrected in the second edition (Philadelphia, 1823) of Washington's reports.

3. Virginia first enacted legislation making bonds assignable in 1705, reenacting it with minor changes in 1730, 1748, and 1786. The transactions of this case were governed by the 1748 law, which provided that in suits on assigned bonds "the plaintiff shall allow all discounts that the defendant can prove, either against the plaintiff himself, or against the first obligee, before notice of such assignment was given to the defendant" (Hening, *Statutes*, VI, 87; ibid., III, 378; IV, 275; XII, 359).

JM presented a strict reading of the statute, which would have excluded discounts against "mesne," or intermediate, assignees. Morris had no set-offs against either the plaintiff Pickett or the "first obligee," Littlepage, the person in whose favor Morris originally executed his bond for the Kentucky land. Morris wanted to use Stockdell's debt to him, on which he had obtained a judgment, as a discount. Stockdell, however, was an intermediate assignee, having been assigned Morris's bond by Littlepage and having in turn assigned it to Pickett.

4. Stockdell, to whom Littlepage had assigned Morris's bond, was himself indebted by bond to Morris. He proposed to discount the two bonds, but Morris refused. The latter then sued Stockdell on his bond and recovered judgment (2 Wash. 255). If he had offered to discount, Morris would not have been able to maintain his action against Stockdell because, as JM pointed out in his second argument, the amount he owed by bond to Stockdell was greater than what Stockdell owed him.

5. JM slipped in a questionable assumption about his client's status as a bona fide purchaser of the bond, that is, one who took it for good value and without any notice of any discounts against it. One witness deposed that he thought he had given notice of Morris's equity to Pickett before the assignment. John Wickham, one of the attorneys representing Morris, also stressed the evasiveness of Pickett's answer to the chancery bill in not stating exactly how much he had paid for the bond (2 Wash. 256–57, 261–62).

6. The statement of facts does not mention the bill of exceptions tendered by Morris's counsel at the county court trial, though Judge Lyons referred to it in his opinion, noting that the judges refused to sign it. Upon the county court's refusal to sign the bill of exceptions, Morris could have petitioned a higher court to issue a writ of mandamus commanding the justices to seal the bill. Lyons was not persuaded that this was a suitable remedy, however, for Morris might have had to suffer execution "on an unjust and inequitable verdict" while pursuing a mandamus (2 Wash. 275).

7. JM defined "the law" as what the county court had held. Although courts ultimately determine what the law is, a lower court's opinion may be contrary to law and accordingly reversed by a higher court of law. Had the Henrico court instructed the jury to ignore Morris's claim of set-off on the grounds that the law did not recognize his right of set-off under the circumstances, an appellate court could have reversed the county court's understanding of the law and allowed the set-off. This is what, in effect, the chancery court had done, exercising a function that JM maintained properly belonged to an appellate court.

8. See n. 5.

9. The deposition alluded to is not summarized in the statement of facts, and none of the other attorneys or judges mentioned it. The "warrants" were probably those issued by the state auditor for a variety of purposes. They were receivable in taxes as specie and thus formed a circulating medium.

10. Stockdell evidently was insolvent. The suit between Pickett and Morris ultimately boiled down to which of the two would have to assume the loss occasioned by Stockdell's inability to pay.

11. According to the statement of facts Morris refused to discount with Stockdell because of pending litigation against him in Kentucky. Morris's bond to Littlepage (subsequently assigned to Stockdell) was for the payment of his choice of two distinct tracts of Kentucky land. Morris was later sued by

one Johnson, who claimed an undivided moiety of the two tracts. If Johnson succeeded, then Morris, who had contracted to purchase a separate tract of his choice, would have an equitable claim against discharging his own bond. With his bond liability in doubt, Morris, so his counsel contended, had a legitimate reason for refusing Stockdell's offer to cancel their bonds (2 Wash. 255, 259).

12. Chancellor Wythe dissolved Morris's injunction as to the amount by which his bond exceeded that of Stockdell; that is, he allowed Morris's claim of discount. This meant that the chancellor had concluded that Morris's bond liability was good. JM argued that the decree, by ignoring Morris's claim of equity against honoring his bond, buttressed his own contention that this equitable claim was a sham. Of course, by the time of the chancery suit, the Kentucky litigation may have been completed and Morris's bond liability established. If so, then Morris's refusal to discount with Stockdell could have been legitimate at the time, though subsequent events showed that his bond debt was enforceable.

13. See n. 6. Wickham spoke next on behalf of Morris, followed by Edmund Randolph on the same side (2 Wash. 259–64).

14. Wickham cited Norton v. Rose, 2 Wash. 233 (also decided at the Oct. 1796 term of the Court of Appeals), as having settled the point that the assignee of a bond takes it subject to the equity of the obligor against the original obligee. The court was at pains in this case to distinguish between bonds and bills of exchange and between assignability and negotiability. Bills of exchange, it was observed, passed as currency for commercial purposes and the equity originally attaching to them did not follow them into the hands of successive holders. Although bonds were assignable, the statute declaring them so was not intended to give them circulation like bills, but merely to allow the assignee to sue in his own name. The assignee thus took a bond at his own risk with respect to possible discounts against it. In Virginia promissory notes were assignable on the same terms as bonds, though in England they had an unqualified negotiability like bills of exchange. See the opinions of Roane, Carrington, and Lyons (2 Wash. 248–55).

15. Wickham maintained that there was no time limit established by law for asserting a discount and that therefore Morris had a right to do so at the time payment was demanded, that is, when Pickett sued him. He also denied JM's contention that Morris's refusal to discount with Stockdell amounted to an express waiver of his right.

16. Morris's suit against Stockdell, said Wickham, was not an implied waiver of his right to discount, but was instituted for the purpose of reducing the debt to a judgment, thus giving it a higher priority in law (see n. 4).

17. Wickham contended for a liberal construction of the 1748 law, in which the right to assign and the obligee's ability to assert discounts were commensurate with each other. JM conceded that the law authorized multiple assignments, but according to his interpretation the right of set-off would not extend beyond the first assignment.

18. JM's construction of the law would lead to injustice, said Wickham. If, for example, an obligor of a bond sold property or made payments to the assignee, he certainly would not lose these credits if the bond was subse-

quently assigned. JM, in response, distinguished a discount, which was created by statute, from a discharge, which automatically flowed from payment.

19. Wickham cited Ambler v. Wyld, decided by the Court of Appeals in 1794, to show that the court had upheld equity jurisdiction to relieve against errors at law. In that case the Henrico County Court refused to admit certain evidence without good reason. The General Court affirmed the judgment on appeal, but Wyld subsequently filed a bill in chancery in the York County Court. From there it went to the High Court of Chancery and then to the Court of Appeals. JM represented Jacquelin Ambler (his father-in-law) when the case was heard in the General Court in 1789, but whether he participated in the later phases of this litigation is not known (2 Wash. 36; *PJM*, II, 26–27).

20. Both Wickham and Randolph noted that Morris's counsel and the jury at the county court were misled into an irrelevant discussion of Morris's equity against his bond and Pickett's notice of it. Consequently, the trial strayed from the single point of law in the case, namely, Morris's right to discount the bond due from Stockdell. Embroilment in the wrong issue, they urged, amounted to mistake or accident, against which equity courts historically had jurisdiction to give relief.

21. Before the statute allowing discounts, parties had to apply to chancery to set them off. According to Randolph chancery retained jurisdiction in matters of discount even though the statute now permitted discounts to be raised in law actions.

22. Pickett agreed to stay execution of his judgment for a month while Morris applied for an injunction in the chancery court. This offer, said Randolph, diverted Morris's counsel from renewing his motion for a new trial at law.

23. Wickham implied that Pickett had paid Stockdell less than full consideration for Morris's bond. If therefore Stockdell became liable for the nominal sum (in case Morris did not pay), the transaction would be usurious, for Pickett would be repaid a sum that exceeded the legal rate of interest (5 percent).

24. Wickham observed that Morris had obtained his judgment against Stockdell in the town (Richmond) where Pickett resided, which should be considered presumptive notice as to the discount.

25. Here the court requested a reargument of the issue of jurisdiction. On behalf of the appellee Morris, William DuVal, Wickham, and Randolph each argued in favor of equity intervention in the county court judgment. They cited a number of English cases and precedents in the Virginia Court of Appeals (2 Wash. 266–70). JM then spoke in reply

26. John Morgan, *Essays upon I. The Law of Evidence. II. New Trials. III. Special Verdicts. IV. Trials at Bar. and V. Repleaders* (3 vols.; London, 1789), II, 291; III, 91. DuVal for the appellee cited Morgan's compilation of cases on new trials to show that equity will interfere if the jury is misdirected and that after many new trials have been granted at law a chancery court will grant another for the furtherance of justice (2 Wash. 266).

27. Kent v. Bridgman, Prec. Ch. 233, 24 Eng. Rep. 113 (Ch., 1704), which Randolph cited as establishing the principle that where there was concurrent

jurisdiction an equity court could entertain a matter examinable and previously determined by a court of law. In this case the plaintiff in equity, a sheriff's bailiff, in execution of a judgment, had levied against goods in possession of the defendant's father. The son (defendant in equity) then brought trover against the bailiff, claiming the goods were his, not his father's, the landlord having seized them for rent and sold them to him. The court determined that this sale was fraudulent because the father retained possession of the goods. The jury, however, returned a verdict for the son because the bailiff had not proved a copy of the judgment upon which he levied execution against the father. The bailiff then applied for and obtained from the equity court a perpetual injunction against the law judgment.

28. Wickham raised this point. JM cited the "act to amend the act, intituled An act for establishing a high court of chancery" (Hening, *Statutes*, XII, 464, 465).

29. See n. 19.

30. Vaulx v. Shelley, Rep. t. Finch 472, 23 Eng. Rep. 255 (Ch., 1680), concerned a judgment by the court of Berwick, in which the judge disobeyed process issuing from Westminster. Wickham cited it to show that in England equity courts granted relief against judgments of inferior courts on account of improper conduct. In Virginia, he said, there was even more reason for equity courts to intervene in cases decided by the county courts: "The want of legal knowledge in those courts, and the loose manner in which business is generally conducted there, will frequently produce improper and unjust decisions of cases, which in many instances could only be remedied in a court of equity" (2 Wash. 268).

31. Robinson v. Bell, 2 Vern. 146, 23 Eng. Rep. 701 (Ch., 1690). In this case an executor sought relief against a judgment in debt upon the plea that he had fully administered the assets. The bill stated that there were several debts still outstanding of a higher nature than the defendant's and that the plaintiff had instructed his attorney to enter a special plea of fully administered. The attorney, however, pleaded generally. A verdict was returned against the executor upon his own letter confessing a mortgage made to the testator for £300, which the judge took as evidence that the executor had so much in his hands. The executor proved in equity that this mortgage was worthless and that there were two prior mortgages on the same estate. The equity court thereupon granted an injunction.

32. The report cites the wrong page number. The correct citation is Bosanquett v. Dashwood, Cas. t. Talbot 38, 25 Eng. Rep. 648 (Ch., 1734). This is the first mention of the case; it was evidently cited earlier by counsel for the appellee, but the reporter omitted it. Equity courts frequently assumed jurisdiction in usury cases. Virginia's statute against usury permitted a borrower to exhibit a bill in chancery against a lender, compelling him to disclose upon oath the amount really lent (Hening, *Statutes*, XII, 338).

33. In Cochran v. Street, 1 Wash. 79, cited by Wickham, the Court of Appeals in 1792 upheld a county court decree (on the equity side) ordering a new trial. The decree was based on evidence that four of the jurors in the trial at law agreed to a verdict under the erroneous impression that a majority must prevail. The High Court of Chancery reversed this decree on

appeal, but its decree was in turn reversed by the Court of Appeals. JM was familiar with the case, having represented the appellant Cochran. He argued in favor of equitable intervention in that case. For the report of the case in the High Court of Chancery, see Wythe 133.

34. JM here was responding to points made by Randolph. Arguments were completed on 1 Nov. The Court of Appeals had the case under consideration until 11 Nov., when it unanimously affirmed the decree of the High Court of Chancery. The three sitting judges—Roane, Carrington, and Lyons (President Pendleton left on 21 Oct. and was absent the remainder of the term)—all delivered opinions. While conceding that courts of law and equity should be confined to their proper spheres, the judges were persuaded that the evidence of improper conduct by the Henrico County Court, which in turn resulted in jury error, was sufficient in this instance to sustain chancery's assumption of jurisdiction (Va. Ct. Ap. Ord. Bk. III, 149; 2 Wash. 272–76).

On 24 Mar. 1797, JM gave a receipt to Richard Morris for money received on behalf of George Pickett in settlement of this decree (*PJM*, III, 69).

41. Hopkins v. Blane

1798

Editorial Note

As President Pendleton observed in the course of deciding a 1791 case, trade between Great Britain and Virginia was largely conducted by factorage.[1] A British merchant doing business in Virginia customarily employed an agent or factor there to act on his behalf. The relations between the merchant and his factor and between them and third persons were governed by the law of principal and agent. Cases in this area of the law concerned either the agent's liability to his principal or, as in the one presented here, the principal's liability for the acts of his agent. The general rule in cases of the latter type was that an act done by an agent within the scope of his authority was binding upon the principal. Adjudications turned on the nature and extent of the agent's powers and whether he exceeded them.

In Virginia British factors were frequently authorized to draw bills of exchange upon their principals, a practice that arose, said Pendleton, from the necessity of advancing cash to the planters. The money for this purpose was raised by selling the bills.[2] The question to be decided in *Hopkins* v. *Blane* was whether a London merchant was liable for certain bills of exchange drawn on him by his agent and sold to a Virginia tradesman. Richmond merchant John Hopkins brought this case in the High Court of Chancery in May 1793.[3] The defendant was probably the Thomas Blane who had come to America in 1777 as a representative of two Glasgow mercantile firms. He returned to England in July 1785 and set up as a merchant in London.[4]

In the fall of 1789 Blane sought to take advantage of the scarcity of grain in France, Great Britain, and the West Indies. He corresponded with several Alexandria merchants, including William Hunter, Jr.,[5] and requested their assistance in obtaining cargoes of wheat, flour, and corn for several small ships he was about to dispatch to Virginia. They were to oversee the shipment of these staples to market as quickly as possible. Although grain was the grand object, Blane also mentioned an increased demand for shipping and enumerated other articles including tobacco that could be shipped as freight. The London merchant accordingly empowered Hunter and his other correspondents to purchase grain and draw bills of exchange on him. Within these broad instructions the agents were given full latitude to act on Blane's behalf and to negotiate bills of exchange on the best terms they could. Hunter's first drafts on Blane were dated 22 February 1790 and given to Hopkins for a quantity of tobacco. Hopkins later sent the bills to Blane, who protested payment of most of them. In 1793 Hopkins filed suit to recover the amount of the protested bills of exchange; two years later the High Court of Chancery dismissed his petition, and he appealed the decree to the Court of Appeals.[6]

In addition to *Hopkins* v. *Blane* two other cases arising out of Hunter's agency for Blane eventually came before the Court of Appeals: *Blane* v. *Proudfit* and *Blane* v. *Smith*, which were decided together in 1802. Marshall was also counsel in the former case when it began in the High Court of Chancery in 1791.[7] All three of Blane's cases had in common an attempt by the lawyers opposing the London merchant to bring the suits within the authority of *Hooe & Harrison* v. *Oxley & Hancock*, then the leading case in Virginia concerning principal and agent. In that case, decided by the Court of Appeals in 1791, a London merchant firm was held bound to pay the bills of its agent even though he did not follow the letter of his instructions.[8] As attorney for Hopkins, Marshall somehow had to persuade the court that the circumstances of his case were essentially the same as those of *Hooe*. This was a difficult assignment, for it appeared that Hunter had misused his agency to carry on strictly private business with Hopkins.

1. Hooe & Harrison v. Oxley & Hancock, 1 Wash. 24.

2. 1 Wash. 24.

3. John Hopkins (ca. 1757–1827) was a Richmond merchant and longtime commissioner of the continental loan office (Walter Lee Hopkins, *Hopkins of Virginia and Related Families* [Richmond, 1931], 211–14).

4. Thomas Blane before the Revolution had been a partner in the Glasgow firms of James Ballentine & Co. and John Ballentine & Co. When he went to America in 1777, he remained behind British lines until after the peace. From 1783 to 1785 he was in Virginia, residing in Westmoreland County, attempting unsuccessfully to collect the debts owed to his companies (*Va. Gazette* [Purdie and Dixon], 23 Sept. 1773; memorials of Thomas Blane, 24 Apr., 1 May 1786, Auditor's Office 13/107, 15–18, P.R.O.). For Blane's mercantile activities in the 1780s and 1790s, see his correspondence with Yorktown merchant James MacLeod in the suit papers of Blane v. MacLeod's Administrator, U.S. Cir. Ct., Va., Ended Cases (Unrestored), 1799. JM represented Blane in two cases in the federal circuit court in the 1790s, Blane v. Archer and Blane v. Hobday, U.S. Cir. Ct., Va., Ended Cases (Restored), 1795 (see *PJM*, II, 472).

5. William Hunter, Jr. (1731–1792), a native of Scotland, was mayor of Alexandria at this time (Mary G. Powell, *The History of Old Alexandria, Virginia* . . . [Richmond, 1928], 309–10, 361).

6. 1 Call 361–64; Va. Ct. Ap. Ord. Bk. III, 266.
7. 3 Call 207; *PJM*, II, 411.
8. 1 Wash. 19–26 (also discussed in the annotation to Argument).

Argument
24–25 October 1798

MARSHALL for the appellant.[1] That Hopkins made advances for the bills, and that he took the bills upon the authority of Blane's letter is clearly collectable from the circumstances of the case.[2] The question therefore is, whether Blane upon that authority is bound to pay the bills?

The mode of negociating the bills was left by Blane to the discretion of his agent; and the instructions were, to negociate them in the best manner in his power. Of course, the agent was not limited by his instructions; and therefore whether he appropriated them rightly or not, the bill holder could not be affected by it, since he had no controul over him; and consequently was not responsible for his conduct.

It does not matter whether the bills were negociated for tobacco or money, because the agent might as well have misapplied money as tobacco: and yet it was essential to his agency, that he should be able to change them into one, or the other. For it might not suit the merchant or planter here to take bills for his grain; and therefore the agent would be obliged to give them something which they would take; and this, he had no other means of raising, but by the bills. Either therefore he must have sold the bills for money, or if that could not be done for tobacco; which he might change into money, in order to make grain purchases with.[3]

The principles of this case have been already decided by this Court in *Hooe* vs. *Oxley*, 1 *Wash.* 19. But the case at bar is not so strong as that; for upon examining the record, in that case, it will be found that the authority of Ponsonby was much more limited there, than that of Hunter was here. In other respects the cases perfectly resemble each other in principle. For the bills there were drawn for other objects, than the principals intended, as well as here.[4]

The powers given in the letter were ample enough, to authorize Hunter to purchase tobacco itself and ship it to Blane. For it enumerates tobacco amongst the articles of commerce; and begs that dispatch may be used at all events, in any of the enumerated ways; as nothing could compensate the injury of delay. By which it may be fairly argued, that the purchase of tobacco was authorized.[5]

MARSHALL in reply. The authority of *Hooe* vs *Oxley*, as applied to this case, remains unimpeached. For although Blane did not receive value for his bills in this case; no more did Oxley and Hancock for theirs, in that.

Whether the principal receives value or not is unimportant; provided the agent has power to draw. The plaintiff clearly took the bills on the credit of Blane. It is, at first sight, presumable that the payee sees the authority, before he takes the bill; to omit it would be such a gross act of indiscretion, as few men would be guilty of. The conclusion therefore is, that the plaintiff saw the power, and having seen it, he was not bound to enquire further, whether the principal actually received value for the bills or not?

But whether the plaintiff saw the power or not he was bound by it; because he ought to have seen it: and if he did not, it was a folly; which would not avail him. For by contracting under it, he, in judgment of law, undertook to know it, and therefore was bound by its contents. But if he is bound by it, he should, on the other hand, have all the benefits of it.

In *Hooe* vs *Oxley* it was not proved that all the letters were shewn to the sellers; but Ponsonby held them; and therefore it was decided, that Hooe and Harrison might avail themselves of them, because they would have been bound by them.

The intimacy between the plaintiff and Hunter forms no objection; it would equally have held in *Hooe* vs *Oxley*: But it was considered as unimportant.

If the plaintiff has trusted Hunter only, he would have taken his note or bond; but omitting to do so, he must be held to have relied on Blane. Who, having trusted an improper man, should bear the loss when the trust has been abused; and not an innocent man; who, through him, confided in Blane.

The plaintiffs letters do not shew, that the bills were paid for, in tobacco, more than money. For he was only remonstrating with Hunter, whether he would suffer the bills to be sacrificed? but this did not destroy Blane's obligation, to pay the bills, which were properly issued.[6]

The bills were not taken as a pledge; for the plaintiff took them as a payment and had an immediate right to sell them.[7]

The argument, that Hunter was an agent for a particular purpose only, proves nothing. For if he was a particular agent, it was to draw bills within a certain limited time; and he has done it, within that time. He was not circumscribed by Blane, as to the mode of negotiating the bills; and therefore the payee was not bound to make enquiry, relative thereto.

As to the argument founded on the exception to the general principles laid down by the Court, with regard to agency, in *Hooe* vs *Oxley*;[8] the answer is, that there is nothing to bring the case within it. That exception means a fraudulent combination between the bill holder and the agent, to defraud the principal; as for instance to get payment of an old debt, or for some other corrupt purpose; but it was not intended to apply to the case of a fair bargain, for an article as current as money; and capable of being turned into it, at any moment. Such a transaction instead of being collusive, was actually putting funds into the hands of the agent, to enable him to exercise his functions.

But all the principles contended for, on the other side, were overruled in that case of *Hooe* vs *Oxley*; which is stronger than this, for another reason, beside that, which I mentioned before; namely, that here there was an express authority given the agent; which the Court thought could only be implied there.

In that case Ponsonby had no right to substitute himself for the planters; yet, the Court held the principals bound, by the substitution.

That Hunter was a merchant makes no difference; or if any it is against Blane. Because if Ponsonby was not a general merchant, it was more manifest that he acted as agent; and therefore the bill holder was the more bound to exact a stricter conformity to his agency, and to take care that he did not exceed his powers in the transaction.

The plaintiff's not sending the bills immediately does not alter the case; because no loss is proved to have been sustained in consequence of it; and, being amongst the first that were drawn, they could have created neither caution nor suspicion in Blane. Who would have concluded that they were drawn for the purposes of the agency. Besides it was held in this Court, in the case of *Stott* vs *Alexander* 1 *Wash.* 331, that eighteen months was a reasonable time, for negociating bills of exchange drawn here.[9]

Both agent and principal were liable, if the plaintiff chose to consider them so; and he might pursue them one after the other, if he thought proper.

In short, upon principle, as well as upon the authority of *Hooe* vs *Oxley* (which in all its parts comes compleatly up to the present case,) I contend that the decree is erroneous, and ought to be reversed.[10]

Printed, Daniel Call, *Reports of Cases Argued and Adjudged in the Court of Appeals of Virginia*, I (Richmond, 1801), 367–68, 371–73.

1. Arguments were heard on 24 and 25 Oct. 1798. JM spoke first (Va. Ct. Ap. Ord. Bk. III, 259).

2. Blane's letter of 23 Nov. 1789 authorized William Hunter to purchase grain and to draw bills of exchange on Blane for that purpose. Hopkins claimed in his chancery petition that Hunter showed him this letter and that on the credit of the letter he purchased bills to the amount of £400 sterling on 22 Feb. 1790. All but £50 of these bills were returned protested. Hopkins sued to have Blane declared liable for the protested bills (1 Call 361–62).

3. A witness who resided with Hunter at the time deposed that Hunter's bills on Blane were not sold to Hopkins for cash but were drawn for the payment of tobacco supplied by Hopkins to Hunter. The latter did not ship this tobacco to Blane, but to other merchants for an advance made by them to Hunter (1 Call 366).

4. As agent for the British merchant firm of Oxley & Hancock, Richard Ponsonby was authorized to draw bills of exchange for procuring consignments of tobacco from Virginia planters. He was instructed to draw bills only for this purpose, but in one instance he had been unable to obtain a cargo on consignment and instead purchased tobacco on his own account for shipment to Oxley & Hancock. His bills drawn on this shipment were protested, and a suit was instituted to recover the money. Chancellor Wythe dismissed the plaintiff's bill in chancery but was overruled by the Court of Appeals, which held that the London merchants were liable for the amount of the protested bills (Hooe & Harrison v. Oxley & Hancock, 1 Wash. 19–26 [1791]).

5. John Wickham for the appellee Blane followed JM. He contended that his client never received any value for the bills; that he was ignorant of the contract between Hopkins and Hunter; and that circumstances indicated the bills were not drawn on the credit of Blane's letter. Besides arguing that the dealings between Hunter and Hopkins were strictly private, Wickham further urged that Hunter's agency was limited to the specific object of purchasing grain and that he "had no authority to meddle with any thing else, whilst grain could be got." He distinguished Hooe v. Oxley by observing that Ponsonby acted solely as an agent, while Hunter was regarded as a general merchant and would not be presumed (in drawing a bill) to be an agent unless the circumstances warranted it. Edmund Randolph also spoke on Blane's behalf (1 Call 368–71 [quotation at 369]).

6. JM referred to Hopkins's letters to Hunter in the spring of 1790 stating his inability to sell the bills of exchange except at a low rate of exchange (1 Call 365–66).

7. Both Wickham and Randolph suggested the possibility that Hunter pawned the bills of exchange as a security for payment of the tobacco—in which case, they objected, the agent clearly exceeded his authority (1 Call 369, 370–71).

8. In the earlier case Pendleton, after enumerating the general principles of agency, said, "These, I hold to be clear principles of law. They exclude however, the idea of collusion between the bill holder and the agent, to abuse

the powers confided by the principal. Such a circumstance would defeat the bill holder in his attempt to charge the principal." Wickham argued that if Hopkins had seen Blane's letter to Hunter, he knew of the limits imposed upon the agent; the law would accordingly infer a collusion between them that would defeat Hopkins's attempt to recover from Blane (1 Wash. 24; 1 Call 370).

9. Randolph said that the delay in sending the bills to London showed that Hopkins did not think Blane liable and had probably tried to get payment from Hunter. The bills were dated 22 Feb. 1790, presented on 31 Aug., and protested on 2 Nov. 1790 (1 Call 371, 377, 379). In Stott & Donaldson v. Alexander & Co., 1 Wash. 331 (1794), the Court of Appeals held that notice of a protest given within eighteen months of the date of the bill was sufficient under Virginia's statute concerning protested foreign bills of exchange.

10. The court on 3 Nov. unanimously affirmed the High Court of Chancery's decree dismissing Hopkins's bill. In delivering the opinion of the court Pendleton, apparently wishing to diminish the force of Hooe v. Oxley as a precedent, was at pains to distinguish that case from the one at hand. Hunter, he said, departed from the letter and spirit of his powers in drawing bills on Blane for tobacco rather than for grain; Ponsonby, in the earlier case, merely employed an irregular mode of carrying out his instructions. Moreover, while Ponsonby undoubtedly acted in his capacity as an agent, the evidence indicated that Hunter and Hopkins dealt with each other on a private basis without reference to Blane. Pendleton also gave considerable weight to Hopkins's delay in transmitting the bills of exchange to Blane and then allowing two and a half years to pass after they were protested to bring suit. These circumstances, he said, showed that Hopkins took the bills upon Hunter's credit, that he looked to Hunter for payment, and that he resorted to Blane only after "Hunter's insolvency would otherwise occasion a loss of the money" (Va. Ct. Ap. Ord. Bk. III, 266; 1 Call 373–79 [quotation at 377]).

In the other cases arising out of Hunter's agency for the London firm, Blane v. Proudfit and Blane v. Smith (decided in 1802), counsel also relied upon Hooe v. Oxley to establish Blane's liability—again without success. "That case," said Judge Lyons, "carried the principle far enough, and we are not disposed to push it any further" (3 Call 214).

42. Pleasants v. Pleasants

1799

Editorial Note

This case marked the culmination of the efforts of Robert Pleasants, a leading Quaker opponent of slavery, to free the slaves conditionally manumitted by his father, John Pleasants.[1] In his last will the elder Pleasants, who died in 1771, desired that if allowed by the "laws of the land," all his slaves "now born or hereafter to be born, whilst their mothers are in the service of me or my heirs," should be set free at the age of thirty. At the time John Pleasants executed his will, Virginia law prohibited private manumission; he accordingly devised his slaves to his descendants on condition that if Virginia subsequently enacted a law allowing manumission, the legatees would free each slave so bequeathed when the slave turned thirty. John Pleasants devised a portion of his slaves to another son, Jonathan, who died in 1776, bequeathing the slaves on the same condition contained in his father's will. Robert Pleasants acted as executor of the wills of John and Jonathan Pleasants in bringing suit against the numerous legatees.[2]

In May 1782 the General Assembly passed an act authorizing private manumission by will or deed, precipitating the litigation over Pleasants's will.[3] Following the enactment of this legislation, Robert Pleasants applied to the legatees but met resistance, particularly from Charles Logan, husband of John Pleasants's daughter Mary, who had received nearly a hundred slaves under the two wills.[4] His next recourse was to petition the Virginia legislature. This mode of proceeding had resulted in two special acts in 1787 confirming the wills of Joseph Mayo and Charles Moorman, who like John Pleasants had provided for manumission of their slaves in case the law should permit it.[5] The Pleasants will was much more complicated, however, and the assembly rejected the executor's petitions for special legislation, submitted in 1790 and 1791, as "involving private rights, and depending on the legal construction of several clauses in the . . . wills, and on other circumstances not proper for the consideration of the Legislative, but of the Judiciary authority."[6] Pleasants probably brought suit shortly thereafter in the High Court of Chancery.

If Robert Pleasants succeeded in court, more than four hundred slaves stood to gain their freedom. Chancellor George Wythe, who heard the suit in the chancery court, and Judges Spencer Roane, Paul Carrington, and Edmund Pendleton, who sat on the appeal, fully understood that the dispute they were called upon to settle transcended the realm of the merely legal to embrace higher questions of morality and social policy. They were confronted with a difficult dilemma that seemingly forced them to choose between enforcing the laws of property and confirming the rights of human liberty. The case no doubt aroused great interest beyond the courtroom, for it was heard and decided at a time when reaction against the liberal manumission policy of the 1782 statute had already begun to set in among Virginians.[7]

The views expressed by the judges in this case betrayed no hint of such reaction, however. Indeed, the decree of the High Court of Chancery, pronounced 12 September 1798, reflected Wythe's deeply held antislavery convictions. In his typically quaint, highly formal, and sometimes impenetrable language, Wythe declared that not only those slaves aged thirty and above were entitled to immediate freedom but also those under thirty who had been born after the statute of 1782, whom he regarded as being free at birth. He went even further and ordered an account of profits, to be awarded to any slaves who had been wrongfully held in bondage—an unprecedented action by a Virginia judge in a suit for freedom.[8]

This radical decree did not withstand scrutiny by the Court of Appeals, though Wythe did have an ally (except on the matter of profits) in Spencer Roane. Roane also believed those children who had been born after the enactment of the manumission law were free at birth. The policy of encouraging emancipation, he said, "must always be dear to every friend of liberty and the human race," and he rejoiced "to be an humble organ of the law in decreeing liberty."[9] Carrington and Pendleton, who constituted the majority of the appellate court in this case, held that all the slaves affected by the will had to remain in slavery until they reached thirty, though children born of mothers over thirty after passage of the statute were declared free at birth. The resulting decree of the Court of Appeals thus severely restricted the scope of that pronounced by Chancellor Wythe.[10]

In upholding the manumission clauses of John Pleasants's will, the court considered and ultimately dismissed legal objections raised by counsel for the legatees. The most troublesome of these was that the will tended to create a "perpetuity," a condition attached to a grant or devise of property restraining its alienation forever or for a period beyond that allowed by law. The law, said Blackstone, "abhors" a perpetuity, for by this means "estates are made incapable of answering those ends, of social commerce, and providing for the sudden contingencies of private life, for which property was at first established." Hence arose the canon of property law known as the "rule against perpetuities," which held that the vesting of an estate could not be postponed beyond a reasonable period, defined as a life or lives in being plus twenty-one years. For example, if a man devised lands to such unborn son of his married daughter as first reached twenty-one, this "executory devise" was good: The estate would vest, if at all, within the lifetime of the daughter and the subsequent minority of her son.[11]

As applied to the will of John Pleasants, the rule presented a perplexing problem. Counsel for the appellants argued that the devise was void on its face because the contingency—the passing of a manumission law—was too remote. It unfairly restrained the heirs of Pleasants from freely disposing of their property. The will, said John Wickham, was "in effect, but a devise of the slaves in absolute property, with a condition, that the devisee shall not alien"—which was repugnant to the very nature of property rights.[12] Even though the act did pass during the lifetime of the slaves, the executory devise was still bad because in regard to children born after the death of Pleasants it would not take place within the time stipulated by the rule.

But in Pleasants's will the slaves themselves were also legatees. Their "estate" of freedom was to vest when they reached the age of thirty. The dual place occupied by the slaves in the will—both as property inherited by Pleasants's descendants and as heirs themselves of a legacy from him—reflected their ambiguous status in life. Were they property or persons? The real question in this case, as considered by the judges, was whether the rule against perpetuities was applicable to a bequest of liberty. The court decided that it was not, or at least that it should not be so rigidly applied as to defeat the intentions of John Pleasants. As Carrington remarked, "In the devise of chattels, property only, is concerned; but liberty is devised in this case. Both sacred rights indeed; but the rule of limitation not necessarily the same with regard to them."[13]

Marshall, along with John Warden, represented Robert Pleasants on behalf of the slaves. In his argument he seems to have deliberately eschewed the rhetoric of liberty in order to make the case on strict legal grounds. This was a sensible approach to take, for if he could show that the devise had some legal basis, there was even stronger reason to confirm it in this extraordinary case.

1. On Robert Pleasants, whom JM represented in a British debt suit, see Case No. 14. The editors are indebted to James H. Kettner of the University of California, Berkeley, for his copious notes on the Pleasants family and on the litigation concerning the will of John Pleasants. His information alerted them to many of the sources cited in the notes below.

2. The relevant clauses of the wills are quoted in the report (2 Call 319–22). The full texts are printed in [Clayton Torrence et al., eds.], *The Edward Pleasants Valentine Papers*, II (Richmond, [1927]), 1116–28, 1130–33.

3. Hening, *Statutes*, XI, 39–40.

4. Robert Pleasants to Samuel Pleasants, 15 Feb. 1781, Robert Pleasants Letterbook, 1771–81, ViW; Robert Pleasants to Jacob Shoemaker et al., 12 May 1788, Robert Pleasants Letterbook, 1754–97, MdAA.

5. Hening, *Statutes*, XII, 611–13, 613–16.

6. *JHDV*, Oct. 1790, 39, 58–60, 107; Oct. 1791, 44, 45, 63.

7. Winthrop D. Jordan, *White Over Black: American Attitudes Toward the Negro, 1550–1812* (Chapel Hill, 1968), 574–78.

8. *Virginia: In the High Court of Chancery, March 16, 1798* . . . ([Richmond, 1800?]; Evans #38963), 2–3. This imprint contains the chancery decree of 12 Sept. 1798, the appellate court's decree of 6 May 1799 (mistakenly dated in Call's report as given at the Apr. term, 1800), the reports of commissioners on the status of the slaves, and the final chancery decrees of 24 Sept. 1799 and 19 Mar. 1800.

9. 2 Call 340, 344.

10. See Argument, n. 11.

11. Baker, *English Legal History*, 152 n., 159; Blackstone, *Commentaries*, II, 173–74.

12. 2 Call 325.

13. 2 Call 347.

Argument

5–6 November 1798

Marshall on the same side.[1] As to the point of jurisdiction, there can be no question, but that the ordinary principles, founded on the general doctrines of trusts apply;[2] and the rather, perhaps, because, being a suit for freedom, the forms of proceeding will not be so strictly adhered to, as in other cases. This was decided in the case of *Coleman* vs *Dick & Pat*, cited by Mr. Wickham.[3] But it was clearly a trust; and therefore upon that ground, the Court of Chancery properly sustained its jurisdiction. Besides the difficulty of deciding the nature of the case, as whether freedom was actually given, so as that there might be a common law remedy? Or, whether it was not rather in the nature of a contract to be enforced in equity upon the happening of the events? Whether the property was in the heir or administrator? and which of them should perform the act? All these circumstances rendered the resort to the Court of Chancery proper.[4]

As to the question upon the right to freedom, The right of the testator clearly passed by the will. That was irrevocable; although the slaves would not have enjoyed their freedom, had the officers of government chosen to exert their powers, and sold them as the act directed.[5] But as the act of 1748 was repealed, without this being done, on the part of the officers of government, if they had the power in this case, the right of the *paupers* to their liberty continues.[6]

The question then is, whether the condition shall be performed?

If not, it must be, either, because it is against law, or because it is an attempt to create a *perpetuity*.

As to the first there is nothing *malum in se*, in it; and therefore, it is not void upon any principle of morality: Neither is it void, upon the ground of the statutory prohibition. Before the act of 1748, every person, who pleased might have emancipated his slave;[7] and that statute does not say, that the testator may not give his slave liberty, when the law shall permit. The old rule of devises to a child in *ventre sa mere* is, in principle, not unlike this case. For, according to that rule, an executory devise to such a child by words *de praesenti* was void; but it was otherwise, where the devise was future.[8] So here an immediate emancipation was liable to be defeated by the statute, but a future one, like this, was not.

The great question therefore is, as to the *perpetuity*; Now a perpetuity is a condition which may run forever, or to an unreasonable time. But this does not. For the will relates to several subjects; and therefore may be construed severally.

For instance as to those born, the devise is to be confined to a life in being; and for this purpose it may be taken distributively: So as to make the contingency with regard to them, fall within a life in being, or a reasonable period afterwards. Thus where a mother was born at the death of the testator, the most remote limitation would be a life in being, and thirty years afterwards. Which is a period not denied by any book. For the authorities are all *affirmatively*, that it may depend on a life in being and twenty one years afterwards; and not *negatively*, that it shall not depend on a longer time than a life, in being, and twenty one years afterwards. Therefore, as to the mothers born at the testators death, the bequest is good, upon the soundest principles of law.

The mothers born after the testators death may perhaps form a class of different cases; but that very circumstance shews, that the account directed by the Court was proper.[9]

The act of 1782 operated a clear repeal of that of 1748; and therefore the only impediment, which could be supposed to exist, is removed.

If justice requires it, the Court may compel the Administrators to emancipate; and the legatees, by taking the legacy, bound themselves to perform the trust. Of course they may be compelled to a specific performance of it. For if the testator was himself in that situation, he would be decreed to perform; and in principle, there is no difference.

With respect to the argument of inconvenience, from Logans having contracted debts,[10] if that were the case, the plain answer would be, that the creditors having trusted a contingent estate, must be subject to the contingency.[11]

Printed, Daniel Call, *Reports of Cases Argued and Adjudged in the Court of Appeals of Virginia*, II (Richmond, 1802), 330–32.

1. Arguments were heard on 5 and 6 Nov. 1798 (Va. Ct. Ap. Ord. Bk. III, 270–71). John Wickham led off for the appellants, followed by Edmund Randolph on the same side. John Warden spoke next for the appellee, Robert Pleasants. JM followed Warden on the same side.

2. Wickham contended that the slaves could have asserted their claim to freedom at common law and should not have resorted to chancery. JM, like Warden before him, countered that this was a case of a trust, a traditional area of equity jurisdiction. The legatees, so the argument ran, held the slaves in trust until the statute of 1782 enabled them to emancipate the slaves. The suit in equity was to secure the performance of this trust (2 Call 324, 329).

3. Coleman v. Dick and Pat, 1 Wash. 233 (1793), was a suit for freedom by two slaves claiming descent from a free Indian woman on the mother's side. JM was familiar with the case, having represented the slaves, as was Wickham, who had represented Coleman. In form, freedom suits were personal tort actions, usually trespass for assault and battery and false imprisonment. Wickham in the earlier case had objected that two or more persons could not join as plaintiffs in personal torts. Pendleton agreed that the point was well founded as applied to common tort cases, but said that freedom suits were fictitious actions, analogous to actions of ejectment, in which many parties could unite to try a joint right to land (1 Wash. 239). In the case at hand Wickham cited Coleman v. Dick and Pat to show that several slaves could join in an action at law and that therefore the circumstance of multiple plaintiffs should not give jurisdiction to chancery (2 Call 324).

In Virginia, suits for freedom by slaves, usually claiming Indian ancestry, had been brought during the colonial period and continued to occur with increasing frequency during the latter decades of the eighteenth century. Those that were reported have been collected, along with other cases relating to slaves between 1624 and 1873, in Helen T. Catterall, ed., *Judicial Cases concerning American Slavery and the Negro*, I (1926; New York, 1968 reprint), 53–268. See also the discussion in Duncan J. MacLeod, *Slavery, Race, and the American Revolution* (Cambridge, 1974), 109–18. JM was counsel in at least two other reported freedom suits brought in trespass for assault and battery and false imprisonment. He represented the slave in Hannah v. Davis in the General Court in 1787 and the master in Shelton v. Barbour in the Court of Appeals in 1795 (*PJM*, I, 218–21; 2 Wash. 64–65).

4. In his original bill in equity, Robert Pleasants stated his difficulty in deciding how to bring this case before the courts. The slaves could not sue at common law, he maintained, because they could be manumitted only accord-

ing to the terms of the 1782 statute. That statute required the person emancipating slaves, or his executor where the emancipation was by will, to deliver a copy of the instrument of emancipation to the slaves. In this instance Pleasants was trying to recover the slaves, either as heir or as executor, in order to carry out the terms of his father's will. If the slaves actually possessed a copy of the instrument of emancipation and were still kept in bondage, then the proper remedy was an action at law in trespass for assault and battery and false imprisonment. Pleasants noted further that the slaves claimed their freedom as a legacy, an equitable claim to be enforced in a court of equity (2 Call 322; Hening, *Statutes*, XI, 39).

5. The 1748 statute declared that no slave should be set free "except for some meritorious services, to be adjudged and allowed by the governor, and council." Any slave otherwise set free could be taken up by parish churchwardens and sold as a slave at public auction (Hening, *Statutes*, VI, 112). JM construed this act to mean that a testator, having the right to dispose of his property as he saw fit, could emancipate his slaves, though it was lawful for government officials to take up and sell slaves so freed.

6. Wickham contended that the 1748 law, which was in force at the time Pleasants made his will, prohibited emancipation, even a conditional one, and therefore the condition attached to his bequest of slaves was void as contrary to that act. The devise was unlawful at its creation and could not be made good by subsequent events (the 1782 law). He further maintained that the act of 1782 did not repeal that of 1748 but merely allowed certain specified emancipations as an exception to the general principle of the earlier law prohibiting manumission. The case of Pleasants's slaves, not falling strictly within the 1782 law, was thus governed by the 1748 law (2 Call 324–27).

7. In fact the law of 1748 reenacted a law of 1723 prohibiting manumission (Hening, *Statutes*, IV, 132).

8. Legal opinion at the time was divided over the question of whether a devise to an infant *in ventre sa mere* ("in his mother's womb") was good. There was no doubt that a devise to an infant "when he shall be born" was good (Bacon, *Abridgment* [1st Am. ed.], IV, 246).

9. Here JM chose not to attack the validity of the rule against perpetuities with regard to a bequest of liberty, but to argue that the rule construed positively on behalf of the slaves did not postpone the devise beyond a reasonable time. Chancellor Wythe took a different approach to the problem. He concluded that the rule against perpetuities, "if applicable to any cases, in which human liberty is challenged," was no objection to those slaves existing at the time of Pleasants's death or to those born after of mothers in being at his death. He reasoned that the bequest took effect upon the enactment of the statute in 1782 rather than when the slaves actually reached the age of thirty. In this way even those slaves born after the testator's death of mothers then existing fell within the legal limit of lives in being plus twenty-one years (*In the High Court of Chancery, March 16, 1798*, 2–3).

Judge Roane of the Court of Appeals was of the same opinion, holding that freedom became vested "in interest" in all the slaves at the time of the statute and vested "in possession" in those then thirty or who might become thirty. What, then, of those whose mothers were born after the death of John

Pleasants, who as JM suppposed might "form a class of different cases?" All the children of this description were born after the statute of 1782. Wythe and Roane, who was overruled on this point by the other sitting judges of the appellate court (see n. 11), declared them entitled to freedom at birth. The condition of the mothers of such children, said Roane, was that of indentured servants—free persons held to service for a term of years. The testator, even if his intention was that children of such mothers should be held in slavery until age thirty, could not restrain their right to freedom; his power had to yield to the principle that children of free mothers were born free. These children, then, were free "by birth and not by emancipation" (2 Call 338–39, 345).

10. Mary Pleasants, widow of Charles Logan and daughter of John Pleasants, received four slaves by her father's will and other slaves by the will of Jonathan Pleasants. In her answer to the bill in chancery she stated that her husband died indebted. Wickham argued that "upon principles of convenience" the emancipation should not take place. Suppose, he asked, Logan had contracted debts between the time of Pleasants's death and the enactment of the manumission law, should creditors lose their debts for presuming that no such law would pass? The Court of Appeals did not decide this question but remanded it to the High Court of Chancery (2 Call 320, 321–22, 328, 357).

11. Randolph for the appellants replied to JM, concluding the arguments of counsel. He repeated points made by Wickham: that chancery had no jurisdiction, that the statute of 1748 prohibited the manumission, and that the devise violated the rule against perpetuities (2 Call 332–33).

The Court of Appeals took time to consider this important case, postponing a decision until the next term. On 6 May 1799 a divided court issued a decree partly upholding and partly reversing that of the High Court of Chancery (Va. Ct. Ap. Ord. Bk. III, 313–15). The three sitting judges, Spencer Roane, Paul Carrington, and Edmund Pendleton, delivered opinions. They sustained the jurisdiction of the High Court of Chancery and agreed with Chancellor Wythe on the principal point, that the manumission devised in John Pleasants's will was good. The appellate court, however, drastically revised the chancery decree as to when the largest category of slaves was to enjoy freedom. Although Roane, like Wythe, insisted that all those born after the statute of 1782 were free at birth (see n. 9), he was overruled by his brethren, who held that only those born of mothers aged thirty and above were free at birth (not a large number). They decreed that the children born after the statute of mothers under thirty (and their increase) must serve until they reached that age. Thus, the difference between the chancery decree and the appellate decree had enormous consequences: Of approximately 230 slaves decreed not to be free until they reached age thirty by the Court of Appeals, more than 150 would have been set free immediately under Chancellor Wythe's decree. By the appellate decision, the youngest of these, born in Aug. 1799, was to remain in slavery until Aug. 1829.

The judges were unanimous in reversing that part of Wythe's decree awarding profits to the slaves for the time they were illegally held in bondage. "Among a thousand cases of palpable violations of freedom," said

Roane, "no jury has been found to award, and no court has yet sanctioned a recovery of the profits of labour, during the time of detention" (2 Call 343). The High Court of Chancery received the remanded case on 5 June, and after reports by commissioners ascertaining the ages and conditions of the slaves, the court issued final decrees conforming to the appellate court's decree on 24 Sept. 1799 and 19 Mar. 1800 (*In the High Court of Chancery, March 16, 1798*, 4–18).

43. Fleming v. Willis

1799

Editorial Note

The union of the Champes and the Carters, two prominent landowning families of King George County, precipitated the dispute giving rise to this case, which was not decided until nearly forty years after the event. On 17 April 1762 John Champe of Lamb's Creek and Charles Carter of Cleve (a son of Robert "King" Carter) signed an agreement in anticipation of the marriage of their children, John Champe, Jr., and Ann Carter: Charles Carter would pay one thousand pounds to John Champe, Jr., and John Champe the father would convey to his son in fee simple that part of his land "lying above the eastern branch of the old mill run, called Lamb's creek tract, and the land bought of [Jeremiah] Bronaugh *thereunto adjoining*." Carter at first refused to sign the settlement deed because it varied from his oral understanding with Champe that the lands to be conveyed to his prospective son-in-law included all those purchased from Bronaugh. He was concerned that the expression "thereunto adjoining" in the written instrument might exclude a tract known as The Farm, which was separated from the Lamb's Creek tract by a short distance. When Carter raised this objection at the time of signing the instrument, Champe assured him there was no need to alter the deed and that he meant all of Bronaugh's lands. Carter then asked a witness to the signing to take notice of this oral assurance.[1]

John Champe died soon after without deeding the property in question. By his will he devised his real estate entailed to William, his eldest son and heir, and to John, Jr. The latter thus had only an estate tail in the lands described in the marriage settlement. He continued to hold this property, including The Farm, until his death in 1774. John Champe, Jr., devised his estate to his wife Ann for life, with a remaining interest in tail in The Farm to his nephew John Taliaferro. His widow subsequently married Lewis Willis. The Willises and Taliaferro applied to William Champe for a deed in accordance with the oral understanding between Charles Carter and John Champe the father in 1762, but Champe refused, claiming that the words of the written settlement excluded The Farm. At his death in 1784 William left The Farm to his nieces Caroline, Jane, Lucy, and Mary Fleming, daughters of Judge William Fleming.[2] The Willises, after also applying unsuccessfully to Fleming (as guardian), brought suit in the High Court of Chancery for specific performance of the marriage settlement, seeking a conveyance of the disputed real estate. Chancellor Wythe issued a decree in their favor on 13 May 1794. Fleming appealed to the Court of Appeals, absenting himself when the case was heard.[3]

The legal question before the chancery and appellate courts concerned the admissibility of parol testimony, that is, any evidence other than the words of a written deed, to explain the meaning of that deed. Should the court allow such proof to establish the true intentions of Charles Carter and John Champe in executing the marriage agreement of 1762? The general rule was that parol evidence could not alter or contradict a written deed, will, or contract, though courts of equity frequently intervened to relax the rule in cases involving uncertainty, ambiguity, fraud, mistake, and accident.[4] As counsel for the Flemings, Marshall cited numerous English cases to construct a high legal wall that would admit parol evidence only under the narrowest of circumstances and never to contradict a written deed. Unfortunately for his clients this legal wall had already been breached by the Virginia Court of Appeals in the 1791 case of *Ross* v. *Norvell*, in which Pendleton set forth his own flexible rule: "The general principles of this case prove, that parole evidence, when there is a deed, is not to be admitted in *all cases*, nor refused *in all*, every case must depend on its own circumstances."[5] Unable to block the admission of parol testimony in *Fleming* v. *Willis*, Marshall could contend only that this evidence was insufficient to establish the claim of the Willises, but here he was on weaker ground than he was in his principal argument.

1. 2 Call 5–6, 10. For an extensive genealogy of the Champe family, see William Buckner McGroarty, "Champe of Lamb's Creek," *VMHB*, XLIV (1936), 269–82. For an abstract of the marriage settlement, see ibid., XXXVIII (1930), 365.

2. 2 Call 6–7. The wills of John Champe the elder and of his son William are printed in full in *VMHB*, XLIV (1936), 274–76, 280–81; abstracts of both appear ibid., XXXVIII (1930), 364–65. Lewis Willis was a cousin of George Washington's and served as an officer in the Virginia Continental Line during the Revolution (Maud Potter, *The Willises of Virginia* [Mars Hill, N.C., 1964], 76, 83, 91).

3. Va. Ct. Ap. Ord. Bk. III, 352, 353, 354–55.

4. Bacon, *Abridgment* (1st. Am. ed.), II, 652–59; Thomas Peake, *A Compendium of the Law of Evidence* (London, 1801), 74–80.

5. 1 Wash. 17; see also Argument, n. 11.

Argument

30–31 October 1799

MARSHALL for the Appellants.[1] Two questions occur in this cause; 1. Whether parol evidence is admissible at all? 2. Whether, if admissible, the evidence produced is sufficient to maintain the relief sought by the bill?

1. The cases on the first point are numerous. In some it is laid down as a clear principle that parol evidence can in no case be received to contradict a deed; and that it can only be received to rebut an equity. In others again it is admitted, that where there has been fraud, or a clear mistake, or a secret trust, there parol evidence may also be received to shew it. But in all it has been received with great caution; and none of them has gone so far as the present. *Cheney's* case in 5. *Co.* 68, and *Althan's* case 8, *Co.* 155, are the oldest cases upon the subject, and fully prove the rule.[2] But amongst the modern cases 1. *Wils.* 34. is express. For there was no attempt in that case to contradict the deed, and yet parol evidence was rejected.[3] The case of *Meres* vs *Ansel* in 3. *Wils.* 275 is precisely apposite and needs no comment.[4] That of *Brown* vs *Selwyn Cas: Temp. Talb.* 240, is very much to my purpose.[5] For although that was the case of a will, the circumstances were much stronger than in our case; and yet the parol evidence was not permitted. The general doctrine is confirmed in 1. *Bro.* 84;[6] and upon a full review of all the cases I conclude, the rule to be fixed, that parol evidence shall not be received to contradict or vary the terms of a deed; unless it be in some of the instances which I have before mentioned. For example, in the case of a latent mortgage not inserted in the deed; but that case turns upon the fraud: So in the case of a secret trust, because that affects the conscience of the trustee; or lastly, in cases of oppression imposition or mistake; which are circumstances necessarily to be shewn by parol evidence, or the relief could not be afforded.[7] But no case can be produced, which goes the length of deciding, that property not conveyed by the terms of the deed, can be comprehended therein by the aid of parol evidence, unless some of the ingredients, just mentioned, existed in the cause.

2. But if the testimony were admissible, that offered is nevertheless not competent to establish the claim of the plaintiffs. That of Jones is only that he drew the articles according to Champe's instructions; which so far from supporting, the bill goes to defeat it; because it affords a presumption that the articles correspond with the views of the parties.[8] The testimony of Robertson leaves the matter doubtful, and according to one way of considering his words, the declarations

of Champe are consistent with the deed. The reference to the articles seems rather to confine his meaning to the lands therein expressed.[9] At most his testimony is uncertain; and therefore can never be a proper foundation for overturning a fixed rule of law. For if evidence, liable to conjectures and doubt, be introduced into questions, relative to the construction of written instruments, then all the dangers of parol evidence, which the law has so anxiously endeavored to guard against, will be encreased.[10]

MARSHALL in reply. I admitted the principle in *Ross* vs *Norvell*; which only establishes the case of a latent mortgage; and the circumstances there were extremely flagrant.[11] But that case proves nothing, in the present controversy; because here it is said that other property, than has actually passed, was meant to be conveyed by these articles; and parol evidence is offered in support of it. But the cases which I cited, prove that it cannot be done. That in *Wils*,[12] was an attempt to prove that other property was included in the grant; but the attempt did not succeed. It is said that the circumstances here are important; because the lands were all conveyed to old Champe, by one conveyance: and therefore that they were meant to be comprehended by the articles. But, although they were all included in one conveyance, still they were different tracts; for they were at a considerable distance asunder. It was asked, if the parties did not mean to include them all in the articles, why did William suffer John to occupy them? and I, in my turn, ask, why if they did consider them as included did William undertake to devise them? These circumstances prove nothing. At most they only shew that at one time he misapprehended the articles, and at another, that he had informed himself, upon them. I repeat again, that if parol evidence is admitted at all, it should be clear, distinct and pointed; but here the testimony offered is equivocal and uncertain. It may be reconciled with the articles. For if old Champe meant to include the whole why did he particularize them by the words, *the lands purchased of Bronaugh in the settlement*?[13] It would have been enough if he said, the lands bought of Bronaugh; and it was not necessary to have added the other words. That addition seems to tie up the meaning; and confines it to the articles expressly.[14]

Printed, Daniel Call, *Reports of Cases Argued and Adjudged in the Court of Appeals of Virginia*, II (Richmond, 1802), 10–12, 13–14.

1. The appeal was argued on 30 and 31 Oct. 1799 (Va. Ct. Ap. Ord. Bk. III, 352, 353).

2. The Lord Cheyney's Case, 5 Co. Rep. 68, 77 Eng. Rep. 158 (Court of Wards, 1591), disallowed parol evidence as proof that the restraint on a

remainderman not to alienate lands was also intended to apply to the heir. The court maintained, however, that parol proof was admissible to explain a latent ambiguity in a will, as in the case of a devise to son "John" where the testator had two sons of that name.

Edward Altham's Case, 8 Co. Rep. 150, 77 Eng. Rep. 701 (C.P., 1610), held that a deed set forth in pleading could not be contradicted by an averment of matter separate from the deed itself.

3. Finney v. Finney, 1 Wils. K.B. 34, 95 Eng. Rep. 477 (K.B., 1743), rejected parol evidence that a husband had given a bond in lieu of his wife's dower, the bond itself not stating that it was for this purpose.

4. Meres v. Ansel, 3 Wils. K.B. 275, 95 Eng. Rep. 1053 (K.B., 1771). The parties made a written agreement to exchange the use of land and the hay growing on it for the use of a copper mine. The defendant took hay from a piece of land not specified in the agreement, claiming that it was orally understood to be included. The court rejected parol testimony to this effect and ruled that such evidence could not be admitted to annul or substantially vary a written instrument.

5. Brown v. Selwin, Cas. t. Talbot 240, 25 Eng. Rep. 756 (Ch., 1734). The testator devised the residue of his estate to his two executors, one of whom was indebted by bond to the testator. The court decreed that the bond debt was not released but was to be divided between the two executors, despite parol testimony that the testator intended to release it and had given instructions for that purpose to the attorney who drew the will. The court refused to admit this evidence, and its decree was sustained on appeal to the House of Lords in 1735.

6. Maybank v. Brooks, 1 Bro. C.C. 84, 28 Eng. Rep. 1000 (Ch., 1780). The court decreed that a legacy to a person dead during the lifetime of the testator had lapsed, although the words of the will were to "M. his executors, administrators, and assigns." It disallowed parol testimony that the testator knew at the time of making his will that the legatee was dead.

7. JM's classifications are similar to those recited by Pendleton in his opinion in Ross v. Norvell, 1 Wash. 15–16, which was a case of a latent mortgage: "To say that it [parol proof] shall be admitted in no case, would be to overturn all the decisions in which relief has been granted against deeds, upon the ground of fraud, mistake, oppression or imposition; or that they were made upon a secret trust between the parties." (The opinion was then available in the first volume of Washington's reports.)

8. Jones deposed that he drew the instrument according to Champe's written instructions; that Carter read it over and noted his concern that its description of the lands did not include The Farm; and that he (Jones) told Carter that he drafted the agreement according to Champe's memorandum and any doubts about the description should be clarified by Champe. The deposition is summarized in the report (2 Call 8–9).

9. John Robinson (both JM and opposing attorney Edmund Randolph referred to him as "Robertson"), who witnessed the signing of the agreement, deposed that Carter "objected to some words; which he said did not fully mention the lands promised. That the said John Champe the elder answered, that there was no occasion for an alteration; for his meaning was to

give his son his manor plantation and all his lands above Poplar swamp, and also the lands he bought of Jeremiah Bronaugh, mentioned in the marriage settlement" (2 Call 9).

10. Randolph then spoke on behalf of the appellees, Lewis Willis and his wife Ann (2 Call 12–13).

11. Randolph contended that Ross v. Norvell established the principle that the circumstances of each case were to determine whether parol evidence should be admissible or not. JM recorded a fee in this case while it was before the High Court of Chancery and presumably argued the appeal as well, though no attorneys' arguments were reported. He apparently represented Norvell and thus contended for the admissibility of parol evidence to show that a deed of sale for slaves was actually intended to operate as a mortgage (1 Wash. 14–15 [1791]; *PJM*, II, 379).

12. See n. 4.

13. JM referred to the words of Champe quoted in Robinson's deposition. JM's meaning would have been clearer if "mentioned" had been inserted after "Bronaugh" (see n. 9).

14. The Court of Appeals affirmed the decree of the High Court of Chancery on 4 Nov. Pendleton disposed of JM's first point by declaring that the court was "permitted by reason and authority (notwithstanding the agreement was reduced to writing,) to hear parol proof, of what was the real intention of the parties; the governing principle of the decree." He then interpreted the evidence presented in this case to show that the elder Champe clearly intended his son John to have the tract known as The Farm (Va. Ct. Ap. Ord. Bk. III, 354–55; 2 Call 14–15).

Appendix

John Marshall's Reported Cases, 1786–1800

This list represents all of Marshall's cases for which there is a printed or manuscript report. Case titles are in alphabetical order by year and are separated by court. Cases from printed reports are listed only by the year of the decision, and no attempt has been made to determine the exact date of the arguments. In printed reports that omit arguments or that do not identify Marshall as counsel, his participation has been determined from other sources, principally his account book. Cases reported in manuscript are listed according to the date (year, day, and month, or year and month) of Marshall's argument. Manuscript reports are taken from St. George Tucker's Casebook and from notes in his loose papers (Tucker-Coleman Papers, ViW). Reports of Marshall's cases from the Casebook have all been printed in previous volumes of *The Papers of John Marshall* under their appropriate dates. Those from the loose papers (here designated "Tucker MS") are presented in this volume for the first time. The citations to the printed chancery reports of George Wythe are from the 1852 edition, which includes cases Wythe published in 1795 and seven additional cases published as pamphlets between 1796 and 1799. Cases in this list that appear also in this volume are indicated by the case number within parentheses. The abbreviations "exr.," "admr.," and "admx." stand for executor, administrator, and administratrix.

1786

General Court
- Ashton v. West, Tucker Casebook, 13 October
- Gilbert v. Taylor, Tucker Casebook, April
- Robertson's Will, Tucker Casebook, October
- Sandford v. Conn, Tucker Casebook, 25 October

High Court of Chancery
- Dudley v. Crump, Tucker Casebook, 16 November

Court of Appeals
- Hite v. Fairfax, 4 Call 42 (*PJM*, I, 153–64)

1787

General Court
Bailey v. Morris's Admr., Tucker Casebook, 13 April
Bates v. Fuquay, Tucker Casebook, 13 April
Braxton v. Beall, Tucker Casebook, April
Brickhouse v. Brickhouse, Tucker Casebook, 2 October
Byrd v. Holcombe, Tucker Casebook, 15 October
Chrisman v. Trents, Tucker Casebook, 9 April
Dandridge's Exr. v. Allen, Tucker Casebook, 7 April
Duncan & Co. v. Dameron & Co., Tucker Casebook, 6 October
Fallen v. Green, Tucker Casebook, 9 April
Hannah v. Davis, Tucker Casebook, 20 April
Jacobs v. Nottingham, Tucker Casebook, 8 October
Muir & Wiatt v. Key, Tucker Casebook, 18 April
Court of Appeals
Pickett v. Claiborne, 4 Call 99 (Case No. 32)

1788

General Court
Bruce v. Chapman, Tucker MS, 24 October (Case No. 27)
Calvert v. Shropshire, Tucker MS, 8 October (Case No. 23)
Cassels v. Scott, Tucker MS, 7 October (Case No. 20)
DuVal v. Reynolds, Tucker MS, 11 October (Case No. 25)
Franks v. Ladds, Tucker MS, 24 October (Case No. 28)
Green v. Montgomery, Tucker MS, 7 October (Case No. 22)
Kirman Holmes & Co. v. Duncan, Tucker Casebook, 26 April
Pollard v. Schofield, Tucker MS, 7 October (Case No. 19)
Shackleford v. Thornton, Tucker MS, 7 October (Case No. 21)
Thorpe v. Thorpe's Legatees, Tucker MS, 9 October (Case No. 24)
White v. Letcher, Tucker MS, 17 October (Case No. 26)
High Court of Chancery
Farrar v. Jackson, Wythe 1
Court of Appeals
Grymes v. Pendleton, 4 Call 130
Hare v. Gay, 4 Call 151

1789

General Court
Adams v. Pickett and Currie, Tucker MS, 23 June (Case No. 29)
Conway v. Harrison, Tucker Casebook, 16 June
Gouldman v. Tayloe's Exrs., Tucker MS, 23 June (Case No. 30)
John Marshall's Case, Tucker Casebook, 10 June
Wild v. Ambler, Tucker Casebook, 22 June
High Court of Chancery
Overstreet v. Randolph's Exrs., Wythe 47

1790

High Court of Chancery
Hearne v. Roane's Exrs., Wythe 90
Hill v. Southerland's Exr., Braxton v. Southerland's Exr., Wythe 73
Court of Appeals
Barrett v. Floyd, 3 Call 531 (Case No. 34)
Beall v. Cockburn, 4 Call 162
Beall v. Edmundson, 3 Call 514 (Case No. 35)
Bracken v. College of William and Mary, 3 Call 573 (*PJM*, II, 72–81)
Crump's Exrs. v. Dudley, 3 Call 506 (Case No. 33)
Eppes v. Tucker, 4 Call 346
Groves v. Graves, 1 Wash. 1
Hughes v. Clayton, 3 Call 554
Johnston v. Macon, 1 Wash. 4; 4 Call 367
Johnston v. Meriwether, 3 Call 523
Ross v. Pynes, 3 Call 568 (Case No. 36)
Syme v. Johnston, 3 Call 558

1791

General Court
Mercer v. Beall, Tucker MS, 21 June (Case No. 31)
High Court of Chancery
Beverley v. Hipkins's Exr., Wythe 121
Cobs v. Mosby, Wythe 137
Cochran v. Street, Wythe 133
Dandridge's Exrs. v. Lyon, Wythe 123
Jones v. White, Wythe 111
Woodson v. Woodson, Wythe 129

Court of Appeals
Calvert v. Bowdoin, 4 Call 217
Claiborne's Exr. v. Winslow, 1 Wash. 31; 4 Call 308
Dade v. Alexander, 1 Wash. 30
Downman v. Downman's Exrs., 1 Wash. 26
Hambleton v. Wells, 4 Call 213
Hamilton v. Maze, 4 Call 196
Hudson v. Johnson, 1 Wash. 10
Mayo v. Carrington, 1 Wash. 45; 4 Call 472
Roane's Exrs. v. Hern, 1 Wash. 47
Ross v. Norvell, 1 Wash. 14
Shelton's Exrs. v. Shelton, 1 Wash. 53
Wilcox v. Calloway, 1 Wash. 38

1792

High Court of Chancery
Shermer v. Shermer's Exrs., Wythe 159 (Case No. 5)
Williams and Tomlinson v. Jacob, Wythe 145
Yates v. Salle, Wythe 163
Court of Appeals
Butler v. Parks, 1 Wash. 76
Cochran v. Street, 1 Wash. 79
Hill & Braxton v. Southerland's Exrs., 1 Wash. 128
Hoomes v. Kuhn, 4 Call 274
Hunter's Exrs. and Herndon's Exrs. v. Spotswood, 1 Wash. 145
Kennon v. McRoberts, 1 Wash. 96
Nelson v. Nelson, 1 Wash. 136
Ross v. Gill, 1 Wash. 87
Ross v. Poythress, 1 Wash. 120
Scott's Exrs. v. Call, 1 Wash. 115
Smith v. Mickie's Exr., 1 Wash. 135
Tabb v. Gregory, 4 Call 225
Taylor v. Dundass, 1 Wash. 92
Thompson v. Davenport, 1 Wash. 125
Thornton v. Smith, 1 Wash. 81
White v. Jones, 1 Wash. 116; 4 Call 253
Wood v. Davis, 1 Wash. 69

1793

General Court
- Anonymous Case, Tucker Casebook, 21 June
- Commissioners of Monongalia v. Warman, Tucker Casebook, 13 June
- Commonwealth v. Tyler, Tucker Casebook, 17 June
- Prentis & Co. v. Braxton & Co., Tucker Casebook, 17 June

High Court of Chancery
- Aylett v. Aylett's Exrs., Wythe 219
- Cary v. Buxton, Wythe 183
- Hooe v. Kelsick; Beckwith v. Hooe; and Beckwith v. Alexander, Wythe 190
- Hylton v. Hunter's Exrs., Wythe 195

Court of Appeals
- Anderson v. Bernard, 1 Wash. 186
- Baird & Briggs v. Blaigrove's Exr., 1 Wash. 170
- Bannister's Exrs. v. Shore, 1 Wash. 173
- Brown's Admx. v. Garland, 1 Wash. 221
- Claiborne's Exr. v. Hill, 1 Wash. 177 (Case No. 37)
- Coleman v. Dick & Pat, 1 Wash. 233
- Commonwealth v. Cunningham & Co., 4 Call 331
- Eustace v. Eustace's Exr., 1 Wash. 188
- Granberry's Exr. v. Granberry, 1 Wash. 246
- Hawkins's Exrs. v. Berkley, 1 Wash. 204
- Hooe & Harrison v. Mason, 1 Wash. 207
- Johnson v. Bourn, 1 Wash. 187
- Jones v. Williams & Tomlinson, 1 Wash. 230
- Kennedy v. Baylor, 1 Wash. 162
- McAlister v. McAlister, 1 Wash. 193
- Payne's Exr. v. Fleet's Exr., 1 Wash. 196
- Reynolds v. Waller's heir and Admr., 1 Wash. 164
- Sallee v. Yates, 1 Wash. 226
- Stevens v. Thornton's Admr., 1 Wash. 155
- Thweat and Hinton v. Finch, 1 Wash. 217
- Westfall v. Singleton, 1 Wash. 227
- White v. Johnson, 1 Wash. 159
- Wilson and McRae v. Keeling, 1 Wash. 194

U.S. Circuit Court
- Ware v. Hylton, Iredell MS (Case No. 13)

1794

High Court of Chancery

Hamilton v. Flemyng's Exr., Wythe 295
Harrison v. Allen, Wythe 291

Court of Appeals

Applebury v. Anthony's Exrs., 1 Wash. 287
Aylett's Exrs. v. Aylett, 1 Wash. 300
Brown's Exrs. v. Putney, 1 Wash. 302
Burnley v. Lambert, 1 Wash. 308
Carr v. Gooch, 1 Wash. 260
Cole v. Clayborn, 1 Wash. 262
Cooke v. Beale's Exrs., 1 Wash. 313
Dandridge v. Harris, 1 Wash. 326
Daniel's Exr. v. Cooke, 1 Wash. 306
Hewlett v. Chamberlayne, 1 Wash. 367
Leftwitch v. Stovall, 1 Wash. 303
Loudon's Exr. v. Hite, 1 Wash. 365
Nicholas v. Fletcher, 1 Wash. 330
Pendleton v. Vandevier, 1 Wash. 381
Ross v. Gill, 4 Call 250
Roy v. Garnett, 2 Wash. 9
Shermer v. Shermer's Exrs., 1 Wash. 266 (Case No. 5)
Smallwood v. Mercer & Hansborough, 1 Wash. 290
Smith & Moreton v. Wallace, 1 Wash. 254
Taylor's Admx. v. Peyton's Admx., 1 Wash. 252
Walden's Exr. v. Payne, 2 Wash. 1 (Case No. 3)
Ward v. Webber, 1 Wash. 274
Watson & Hartshorne v. Alexander, 1 Wash. 340 (Case No. 38)
Wroe v. Washington, 1 Wash. 357

1795

Court of Appeals

Bernard v. Brewer, 2 Wash. 76
Braxton v. Willing, Morris & Co., 1 Wash. 380; 4 Call 288
Brock v. Philips, 2 Wash. 68
Brown v. Brown's Admx., 2 Wash. 151
Brydie v. Langham, 2 Wash. 72
Claiborne v. Parrish, 2 Wash. 146
Currie v. Donald, 2 Wash. 58
Ferguson v. Moore, 2 Wash. 54
Foushee v. Lea, 4 Call 279

Harvey v. Borden, 2 Wash. 156
Jordan v. Neilson, 2 Wash. 164
Lee v. Turberville, 2 Wash. 162
McRae v. Woods, 2 Wash. 80
Newell v. Commonwealth, 2 Wash. 88
Payne's Exr. v. Sampson, 2 Wash. 155
Pickett v. Dowdall, 2 Wash. 106 (Case No. 39)
Shelton v. Barbour, 2 Wash. 64
Turberville v. Self, 2 Wash. 71; 4 Call 580
Turner v. Moffett, 2 Wash. 70
White v. Atkinson, 2 Wash. 94

1796

General Court
Commonwealth v. Hamilton, Tucker Casebook, 17 November
Court of Appeals
Booth's Exrs. v. Armstrong, 2 Wash. 301
Davenport v. Mason, 2 Wash. 200
Pearpoint v. Henry, 2 Wash. 192
Pickett v. Morris, 2 Wash. 255 (Case No. 40)
Ruffin v. Harwood's Exrs., 2 Wash. 184
Stephens v. White, 2 Wash. 203
Walker's Exrs. v. Walke, 2 Wash. 195
Winston's Exr. v. Francisco, 2 Wash. 187
Young v. Skipwith, 2 Wash. 300
U.S. Supreme Court
Ware v. Hylton, 3 Dall. 199 (Case No. 13)

1797

Court of Appeals
Cutchin v. Wilkinson, 1 Call 3
Guthrie's Lessee v. Guthrie, 1 Call 7

1798

Court of Appeals
Auditor of Public Accounts v. Graham, 1 Call 475
Cabell v. Hardwick, 1 Call 345
Graves v. Webb, 1 Call 443

Harrison v. Harrison, 1 Call 419
Hooe v. Marquess, 4 Call 416
Hopkins v. Blane, 1 Call 361 (Case No. 41)
Jones v. Jones, 1 Call 458
Proudfit v. Murray, 1 Call 394
Pryor v. Adams, 1 Call 382
Shaw v. Clements, 1 Call 429

1799

Court of Appeals
Anderson v. Anderson, 2 Call 198
Beverley v. Fogg, 1 Call 484
Chapman v. Chapman, 4 Call 430
Cooke v. Simms, 2 Call 39
Eckhols v. Graham, 1 Call 492
Eppes v. Demoville, 2 Call 22
Fleming v. Willis, 2 Call 5 (Case No. 43)
Garlington v. Clutton, 1 Call 520
Hackett v. Alcock, 1 Call 533
Lawrason v. Davenport, 2 Call 95
Lee v. Love & Co., 1 Call 497
Macon v. Crump, 1 Call 575
Noel v. Sale, 1 Call 495
Pleasants v. Pleasants, 2 Call 319 (Case No. 42)
Price v. Campbell, 2 Call 110
Ritchie & Co. v. Lyne, 1 Call 489
Rose v. Shore, 1 Call 540
Rowe v. Smith, 1 Call 487
Smith v. Dyer, 1 Call 562
Taliaferro v. Minor, 1 Call 524
Taliaferro v. Minor, 2 Call 190
Wayles's Exrs. v. Randolph, 2 Call 125 (Case No. 7)
Wilson v. Rucker, 1 Call 500

1800

Court of Appeals
Mayo v. Bentley, 4 Call 528

INDEX

In addition to persons and subjects, this index includes the titles of all cases mentioned in the documents and in the accompanying annotation. Identifications occur at or near the first mention of a person. If a person has been identified in an earlier volume, the volume number and page reference follow the name in parentheses. Where persons or subjects appear prominently in a particular case, the reference is to the case number (without title) rather than to page numbers. For example, the entry for Cornelius McHaney, plaintiff in McHaney v. George (Case Number 2), reads: "McHaney, Cornelius. See No. 2." Entries for cases presented in this volume include the case number in parentheses after the title: "Shermer v. Shermer's Executors (No. 5)" (followed by the inclusive page numbers of the case and other references). In preparing this index, the editors used the CINDEX program designed by David R. Chesnutt of the University of South Carolina, who generously shared his technical expertise. They also gratefully acknowledge the special aid provided by Pete Hoyle of the Computer Center at the College of William and Mary.